CRIMINAL JUSTICE ORGANIZATIONS

ADMINISTRATION AND MANAGEMENT

Third Edition

STAN STOJKOVIC
University of Wisconsin, Milwaukee

DAVID KALINICH
Florida Atlantic University

JOHN KLOFAS
Rochester Institute of Technology

THOMSON
——— ✦ ———™
WADSWORTH

Australia • Canada • Mexico • Singapore • Spain
United Kingdom • United States

THOMSON
WADSWORTH

Publisher, Criminal Justice: Sabra Horne
Acquisitions Editor: Shelley Murphy
Assistant Editor: Dawn Mesa
Editorial Assistant: Paul Massicotte
Technology Project Manager: Susan DeVanna
Marketing Manager: Dory Schaeffer
Marketing Assistant: Neena Chandra
Advertising Project Manager: Stacey
  Purviance
Project Manager, Editorial Production:
  Matt Ballantyne

Print/Media Buyer: Rebecca Cross
Permissions Editor: Joohee Lee
Production Service: Matrix Productions
Copy Editor: Ann Whetstone
Proofreader: Amy Haywood Dorr
Cover Designer: Annabelle Ison,
  Ison Design
Cover Printer: Phoenix Color Corp.
Compositor: G&S Typesetters, Inc.
Printer: Maple-Vail Book Manufacturing
  Group

Printed in the United States of America
1   2   3   4   5   6   7   06   05   04   03   02

For more information about our products, contact us at:
Thomson Learning Academic Resource Center
1-800-423-0563
For permission to use material from this text, contact us by:
Phone: 1-800-730-2214
Fax: 1-800-730-2215
Web: http://www.thomsonrights.com

Wadsworth/Thomson Learning
10 Davis Drive
Belmont, CA 94002-3098
USA

Asia
Thomson Learning
5 Shenton Way #01-01
UIC Building
Singapore 068808

Australia
Nelson Thomson Learning
102 Dodds Street
South Melbourne, Victoria 3205
Australia

Canada
Nelson Thomson Learning
1120 Birchmount Road
Toronto, Ontario M1K 5G4
Canada

Europe/Middle East/Africa
Thomson Learning
High Holborn House
50/51 Bedford Row
London WC1R 4LR
United Kingdom

Latin America
Thomson Learning
Seneca, 53
Colonia Polanco
11560 Mexico D.F.
Mexico

Spain
Paraninfo Thomson Learning
Calle/Magallanes, 25
28015 Madrid, Spain

ISBN 0-534-58410-1

TO OUR FAMILIES:

ILIJA STOJKOVIC, MILAN STOJKOVIC,

CAROLYN KALINICH AND

MARY BETH KLOFAS

CONTENTS

Criminal justice administration and management has come a long way since the President's Commission in 1967 called for a closer look at the administration of criminal justice organizations. Concerns about effective management practices are still central to criminal justice professionals as well as to the academic researchers who must evaluate and question their methods. During the three decades since the President's Commission, observers have seen the following become more prevalent in the criminal justice system: greater involvement of the courts in the administration of criminal justice agencies, increased politicalization of criminal justice administration, and a potential threat to criminal justice administrators from the private sector through the mechanism of privatization. In short, many in our society are questioning the administration and management of criminal justice organizations, and these institutions are undergoing some profound changes. As we enter into the 21st century, other challenges are facing criminal justice administrators. The third edition of this book is being written at a time when a new sense of focus and direction exists in the nation and among criminal justice administrators. Terrorism has struck home, and the criminal justice system is being asked to provide greater security to the country and its citizens. In addition, the face of crime is also changing, with more use of the internet and electronic means to commit crime. These new challenges are daunting for the criminal justice system and its administrators.

As in the first two editions of the book, we provide an analysis of criminal justice administration by critically examining the research literature and applying it to this new world of the 21st century. Our primary concern is to provide students with a conceptual and theoretical basis upon which to consider criminal justice administration and management. To this end, we have included the most recent and relevant literature across topics. In addition, we have continued our focus on empirical research and its importance to the subject matter. This combination of theory and research literature allows students to appreciate the importance of these topics to criminal justice administration as well as to visualize its complexities.

New to this Edition

Courses on criminal justice administration have multiplied considerably since the publication of the first edition of this book. In addition, more criminal justice organizations are investing in training and education as a way to help their employees address the obstacles they face in their day-to-day tasks. While not neglecting our commitment to colleagues in the academic world, we wrote both the second and third editions with the working criminal justice professional in mind. In the second edition of the book, we added three new chapters: one chapter on structure and criminal justice organizations, one chapter on employee supervision and evaluation, and a final chapter on research and criminal justice organizations. The chapters on structure (Chapter 2) and on research (Chapter 15) have been updated and the chapter on personnel supervision and evaluation (Chapter 8) has been rewritten with a focus on more practical methods of evaluating criminal justice personnel.

We have retained "Work Perspectives" sections written by current and former criminal justice professionals and administrators. We have added three new Work Perspective sections in Chapters 5, 7, and 8. As with the second edition, the purpose of these Work Perspective sections is to highlight issue(s) raised in the chapter as expressed through the experiential lenses of working administrators in the criminal justice field. These Work Perspectives represent the ruminations of people who are or were criminal justice administrators. They add a practical flavor to the chapters and, we think, improve the quality of the book.

Central Themes

As in the first two editions, we focus on three central themes in this edition: criminal justice; the system as a whole; and theory, research, and practice. Prior to the publication of the first edition, no texts on criminal justice administration emphasized the contributions of the growing number of scholars who were trained and educated in criminal justice. We have continued to integrate general notions of management and administration into this edition with the growing body of literature on criminal justice management and administration produced by criminal justice scholars.

Because there has been a research explosion in the field of criminal justice over the past thirty years, we now know more about the operations of criminal justice organizations than ever before. The disciplines of sociology, political science, psychology, and criminology have complemented research done in criminal justice to produce some valuable insights into the workings of the criminal justice system. We have integrated and applied these findings into this edition. Most important, we have relied heavily on what criminal justice practitioners have produced in the professional literature to guide us into a more comprehensive understanding of criminal justice administration and how it functions. We feel the positive contributions of both criminal justice researchers and criminal justice professionals require more review and acceptance. More than ever before, their collaborative efforts will direct the future of the criminal justice system into the next century.

Our second focus is on the systemic nature of criminal justice administration. By this we mean that our coverage of the subject matter includes how the various component parts of the criminal justice system—police, prosecution, courts, and corrections—work together. As noted in the first two editions, we see value in examining these component parts separately, yet we also see value in viewing the "big picture" to appreciate how the components interrelate. Our teaching experience and research literature alike underscore the importance of understanding the perspective of each component of the criminal justice system. Through an exhaustive review of the research literature across all sectors, we hope to broaden students' perspective on criminal justice administration.

Our final focus is on the integration of theory research, and practice in understanding criminal justice administration. The chapters move through the various topics applying theories, testing them, reviewing research findings, and discussing practical relevance and consequences. The noted social psychologist Kurt Lewin once said, "There is nothing so practical as a good theory." We believe in this aphorism and think it has relevance for an examination of criminal justice administration and management. We know that many students tend to be "practice-oriented" in their views, whereas instructors are often exclusively theoretical in their presentations. This edition plans to offer some middle ground in which theory and practice work together to produce an overview of criminal justice administration—all of its complexities as well as its simplicities. We hope to enhance the thought processes of students through theory research, and practice. To this end, we seek to produce students who will understand the central tenet upon which effective criminal justice administration is based: effective thinking. Good thinkers are good administrators. Our aim is to introduce students to good thinking skills through an integrative approach that appreciates theory, recognizes research, and identifies relevant practices among criminal justice administrators.

Organization of This Edition

The organization of this book follows the same format as the first two editions. Part One examines the nature of criminal justice organizations. Chapter 1 explores basic concepts associated with criminal justice administration and management and offers an examination of the complexity of criminal justice organizations and administration. Chapter 2 presents a description of the structure of criminal justice organizations. Chapter 3 examines the role of the environment in criminal justice organizations. Part Two deals with the individual in criminal justice organizations and includes chapters on communication, motivation, job design, personnel supervision and evaluation (a revised chapter), and leadership. Part Three focuses on group processes in criminal justice, including occupational socialization, power, and organizational conflict. Part Four, which looks at processes in criminal justice organizations, includes four chapters that explore decision making, organizational effectiveness, change and innovation, and research in criminal justice organizations.

In addition to the revised chapters, this edition also continues to provide *introductory quotations* at the beginning of each chapter to introduce some important points raised in the chapter. These quotations are statements made by criminal justice administrators or researchers who have evaluated a particular issue or concept explored in the chapter. At the end of each chapter, this edition also includes *case studies* written from the perspective of either a real or imagined practitioner in the criminal justice system. We have included two new case studies in Chapters 5 and 11. These case studies flesh out some point, issue, or concept presented in the chapter. The case studies are supplemented by *case study questions* designed to tease out significant issues found in the case studies.

The chapters finish with *discussion questions* and a *For Further Reading* section. The former enable students to think further about issues presented in the chapter, while the latter provides other readings that expand on points raised in the chapter. Students are encouraged to go beyond the introductory views offered in the chapters and expand their horizons through these relevant readings.

Each chapter contains a *Work Perspective* section written by a current or former criminal justice administrator. These sections are meant to bring the chapter alive with the viewpoints of those who work or have worked in the criminal justice system as administrators. The Work Perspectives have been provided by a wide range of people: police chiefs, the Executive Director of a treatment facility for female offenders, a former parole chairman, a prison warden, and a former president of a national criminal justice association and jail administrator, to mention a few. We hope these Work Perspectives enrich the text and provide the student a reality perspective that shows integration of theory, research, and practice.

As in the first two editions, citations are found in the body of the chapters and full References are found in a separate section at the end of the book. A perusal of the References section can be useful to students who seek to further expand their knowledge base, since many of these references are the most recent and relevant to criminal justice administration. We encourage all readers of the book to review these sources.

As with the second edition, an Instructor's Manual with test bank is also available and written by Professors Paul Katsampes and Hal Nees from Metropolitan State University, Denver, Colorado. Microsoft® PowerPoint® slides have also been created by Professors Katsampes and Nees and are available as an instructor download from Wadsworth's Criminal Justice Resource Center web site. Both students and instructors can access the Criminal Justice Resource Center web site by going to <http://cj.wadsworth.com>. This site provides additional information regarding this book as well as other texts in the criminal justice field.

Our primary purpose in this edition is the same as in the first two editions: we seek to offer a comprehensive and thorough discussion of criminal justice administration through the presentation of theory, the examination of research findings, and the application of ideas to the practices of criminal justice organizations. We hope this integrated approach provides students with a sound foundation to examine and question criminal justice administration from a number of diverse viewpoints. Such a reflective process can only enhance a thorough examination of how criminal justice administration functions in our society Through this process as well, questions about efficiency, effectiveness, efficacy, and equity within the criminal justice system can begin to be addressed.

Acknowledgments

This third edition of the book has received the assistance of a number of people. First and foremost, we appreciated the support and encouragement provided by Shelley Murphy. Her patience in dealing with us is noteworthy. Very few people can put up with the rationalizations of three authors simultaneously and still show support; we appreciate her efforts more than she may know.

We benefited greatly from the expert opinions of our reviewers: Michael Reisig, Michigan State University; David Olson, Loyola University, Chicago; George Eichenberg, Wayne State College; David Jones, University of Wisconsin, Oshkosh; Robert Wadman, Weber State Univesity.

The book has benefited from the work of others who are unknown to the authors. We would also like to thank all those criminal justice professionals, both past and present, who provided the Work Perspective sections at short notice; we appreciate their hard work. Finally, we would like to thank our families who supported us with their encouragement: Ilija Stojkovic, Milan Stojkovic, Carolyn Kalinich, and Mary Beth Klofas.

Stan Stojkovic
David Kalinich
John Klofas

THE NATURE OF CRIMINAL JUSTICE ORGANIZATIONS

The study of criminal justice organizations and management emerged during the 1970s as a vital part of the criminal justice curriculum. As part of the great social agenda of the day, concern with crime was fueled both by presidential commission reports and by federal funding. Scholars and managers began to examine criminal justice within the framework of traditional organizational studies, and criminal justice organizations were identified as a loosely connected system ranging from the police to courts and corrections. Theory and research on organizations have continued to include criminal justice organizations and to identify their common and unique features. Research during the 1980s and 1990s confirmed the basic notion that criminal justice agencies can be studied as organizations. Part One of this book explores two areas: First, these chapters examine where criminal justice organizations fit within the broad body of organizational theory, and second, they provide a general foundation for the discussion of specific topics in the chapters that follow.

1

CHAPTER 1

BASIC CONCEPTS FOR UNDERSTANDING CRIMINAL JUSTICE ORGANIZATIONS

The symbolic frame [of organizations] . . . abandons the assumptions of rationality. . . . It treats organizations as tribes, theater or carnivals. In this view, organizations are cultures that are propelled more by rituals, ceremonies, stories, heroes, and myths than by rules, politics, and managerial authority. Organization is theater: various actors play out the drama inside the organization, while outside audiences form impressions based on what they see occurring on stage.

    (Bolman & Deal, 1997)

Dear Wardens:

    Attached is a copy of our response to the officious and intrusive conduct of the mastership. We have tried to be tolerant and meet the demands of the court and its Master but reached a point where the security and safety of our units have been endangered. We have therefore felt it necessary to resort to the courts and ask for dissolution of the mastership.

    (Letter from Texas Prison Director W. J. Estelle to his wardens regarding his response to the court-appointed special master in the case of Ruiz v. Estelle, *from Martin & Ekland-Olson, 1987:199)*

Public problems are interconnected, they cross organizational and jurisdictional boundaries, and they are interorganizational. No single agency, organization, jurisdiction, or sector has enough authority, influence, or resources to dictate visionary solutions. Thus, contemporary strategies for organizational leadership are less effective in addressing public problems in an interconnected world. Public leadership faces a different set of challenges.

    (Luke, 1998)

Organizations are an integral part of our lives. We are immersed early in schools and scouting, churches and athletic teams. We continue in colleges and universities, military service, employment, and our organized social life. This membership in organizations continues throughout our lives, and, in the end, our obituaries will include a chronicle of our organizational attachments.

    Among the many organizations that touch our lives are those of the criminal justice system. Many Americans will be only indirectly involved in these organizations. They may find themselves fighting a traffic ticket in court or touring the local jail while serving on a grand jury. Other Americans will find themselves in the criminal justice system when they are processed as offenders. Still others will be employees of criminal justice organizations. This book is about the management and administration of those organizations, and the goal of this chapter is to lay a basic foundation from which to study them.

    Our ties to organizations differ, as do the size, structure, and purpose of those organizations. The analysis of those differences forms a large part of the research and theory on organizations from which this book draws. Our approach to this material is eclectic. We do not intend either to introduce a new organizational theory as it applies to criminal justice or to reflect any single theoretical perspective in this book. Instead, our goal is to provide an overview of organizational theory and research as it applies to criminal justice.

We cannot proceed, however, without devoting special attention to some key theoretical concepts and ideas. In this chapter we define and describe those widely accepted concepts that we believe are necessary as a foundation for the study of criminal justice administration and management.

What Is an Organization?

This may seem like a straightforward question. We all know when we are in an organization, and criminal justice organizations are no exception. The police officer, probation officer, and prison officer are certainly aware of their organizational attachments. But identifying organizations is not the same as defining them, and an adequate definition of organization continues to be the subject of debate among scholars (see Hall, 1982:28).

Definitions of the term *organization* hinge on three important issues: structure, purpose, and activity. The issue of structure was raised by Weber (1947), who first distinguished the corporate group from other forms of social organization. For Weber, the corporate group is marked by limited admission to the group and by a structure that usually involves a leader and a staff. Weber's ideas invite us to think of organizations as bureaucracies—that is, as entities requiring a particular formal structure. In Weber's bureaucratic model, that structure included a rigid hierarchy of offices, a clear division of labor, and formal rules that govern action. Many organizations, however, do not possess a bureaucratic structure. For example, Clynch and Neubauer (1981) point out that trial courts can be viewed as organizations but lack the attributes of bureaucracies. Trial courts are relatively autonomous units not closely tied to a larger structure. Their formal rules are often ignored, as demonstrated by the fact that the presumed adversarial nature of the courtroom has often been revealed to be much more cooperative than the rules would suggest.

Barnard dealt with the issue of structure in a way much more consistent with Clynch and Neubauer's view of the courts. His basic definition of an organization is "a system of consciously coordinated activities or forces of two or more persons" (Barnard, 1938:73). Such a definition suggests boundaries but allows for a variety of organizational structures and makes it clear that courts, public defenders' offices, and other key components of the criminal justice system may be profitably studied as organizations.

Barnard's definition leaves the second issue, that of purpose, open. But other theorists have viewed the pursuit of goals as fundamental to organizations. Etzioni, for example, describes organizations as "social units deliberately constructed and reconstructed to seek specific goals" (1964:3). The question of goals, however, is complicated. Although it seems clear that the police, courts, and corrections agencies all have goals, the waters quickly get murky when we try to spell out these goals. The police prevent and solve crimes, but they also maintain due process, reduce community conflicts, and seek to provide a good working environment for officers. Courts may pursue justice but temper that goal with mercy. They may also have retribution, deterrence, humaneness, or equity as goals. Among the goals of corrections organizations are punishment, rehabilitation, maintenance of order, and, perhaps, avoiding publicity. Even profit-making corporations must balance short- and long-run profit goals, quality and quantity concerns, and pollution or environmental interests. Thus, organizations have many goals, and their goals often conflict. It is important to avoid the oversimplified view of organizations as pursuing a single goal or even a most important goal.

The third issue is whether organizations themselves act or are simply collections of individuals who act. We will deal with this question in detail in several of the following chapters. At this time, however, we acknowledge that our view in this book is that organizations do act. In this view, leadership in organizations is more than simply the leadership of individuals. Likewise, socialization in organizations involves not just attitudes and values held by individuals but also an organizational ethos. Decision making, too, is shaped by influences beyond those of individual decision makers.

The three issues discussed here shape the view of organizations that underlies this book. According to that view, organizations require some boundary and structure but are not limited to rigidly bureaucratic forms. Organizations pursue goals, but those goals are complex, multiple, and often conflicting. And, finally, organizations act in that their influence extends beyond that of individual members. For this analysis, then, we may define an *organization* as a collective that has some identifiable boundary and internal structure and that engages in activities related to some complex set of goals.

An organization is a fascinating beast. It develops cultures that guide the behaviors of its members as well as of the organization itself. Organizations are rich in politics: bargaining, negotiating, and intimidation by their members in search of resources, power, status, and influence. Members attempt to meet their psychological, ego, and emotional needs within an organization's range of opportunities for challenges and activities. A latent goal of an organization is survival, which usually translates into competition for resources and constant expansion. Organizations are complex and beyond complete understanding; surprising, because outcomes of decisions are hard to predict; deceptive, because they camouflage surprises; and ambiguous, because events are disjointed, complex, and beyond coordination (Bolman & Deal, 1997).

Our focus in this book is on those complex, surprising, deceptive, and ambiguous organizations related to criminal justice. Perspectives on criminal justice organizations are particularly unique compared with other public sector organizations that carry the authority of government because criminal justice agencies and their members alone may apply legitimate coercive force to control citizens.

What Is Management?

This, too, seems to be a straightforward question. Like organizations, however, management seems easier to identify than to define. The names of managers can be found high on the organizational chart. Their offices may give them away, as may their salaries. But the function of management is not as clear in criminal justice as in many other types of organizations.

Management has been defined as the "process by which the elements of a group are integrated, coordinated, and/or utilized so as to effectively and efficiently achieve organizational objectives" (Carlisle, 1976). In this definition, management is a process in the sense that it is ongoing; it does not constitute an end in and of itself. Instead, management is directed at the attainment of organizational goals. We have little trouble with this view as long as the complexity of those goals is appreciated.

This definition, however, ignores the notion of office. It does not say whether management is a function of a specific office or is spread throughout an organization. Usually we associate management with a particular office or point on the organizational chart. In this book, however, we prefer to view management as a function that may not be the sole responsibility of any one office. Although we recognize that wardens, chiefs of police, and others are managers, we also believe that even frontline police and corrections officers exercise some management responsibility. We have two reasons for holding this view. First, frontline staff supervise others. Whether police are directing citizens at the scene of a crime or corrections officers are controlling the routine of inmates, frontline staff manage people. In this sense, they are neither fish nor fowl. Their positions are at the bottom of the organizational hierarchy while their work requires that they manage many people in difficult situations.

Lipsky (1980) discusses a second reason for viewing the management function as not limited to particular offices. He argues that frontline staff in street-level bureaucracies, which include most of those working in criminal justice, determine organizational policy. They do so because the nature of their work requires that they exercise a great deal of discretion, and the collective use of that discretion reveals organizational policy. In these organizations, then, it may be productive at times to consider the hierarchy as inverted. Frontline staff may exercise considerable power in influencing the direction of the organization.

Management of organizations, thus, is not the sole province of executives. It is best thought of only as the process by which organizational members are directed toward organizational goals. This view of management suggests that many workers in criminal justice influence the direction of their organizations and that the study of management is consequently important to anyone interested in criminal justice.

As Hall warns, "Discussions of definitions can be quite deadly." Still, some appreciation of the complexity of the terms *organization* and *management* is necessary for understanding this book (1982:35). Organizational theory also provides a number of other concepts that are central to understanding administration and management in criminal justice. We discuss them in the following sections.

What Is Leadership?

Leadership "refers to a process that helps direct and mobilize people and their ideas . . ." (Kotter, 1990). Leadership is tribal in nature (Dupree, 1989) and focuses on an organization's symbols, rituals, and culture. By contrast, managers create, maintain, protect, and perpetuate systems. They focus on planning and budgeting, setting short-term goals and developing procedures to reach the goals. Moreover, managers concern themselves with developing organizational structures, implementing controls, and problem solving. In that context, management sciences create and perpetuate the mythology of achieving rationality in organizations based upon goals, rules and regulations, and control. Leaders establish direction by developing a vision of the future, align people through shared values and vision, and motivate and inspire people to move them toward the shared vision (Kotter, 1990). Leaders challenge existing processes and systems, focus on the future of the tribe, and immerse themselves in the culture of their organization. They challenge basic assumptions, values, and beliefs, and they identify and alter organizational principles to create the basis for structural or programmatic change. Leaders manipulate and evoke symbols to create change and practice the art of statespersonship. Planning documents usually gather dust in organizations that lack leadership.

Leaders are primarily concerned with motivating organizational members and enabling them to act by creating a shared vision: "A realistic, attractive, credible future for your organization" (Nanus, 1992 : 8). Kotter suggests leaders motivate by "the articulation of a vision that stresses the values of the audience being addressed . . . involving people in deciding how to achieve that vision . . . enlisting the enthusiastic support of their efforts at achieving that vision . . . and the public recognition and rewarding of all their successes" (1990:63). Stojkovic and Farkas (2003) view correctional leadership as fundamentally linked to the creation and perpetuation of a specific set of values that underlie an organizational culture. Others, like Schein (1997), argue that effective leadership within organizations cannot be understood without reference to the manipulation, management, and, in some cases, the destruction of organizational culture.

The impact of leadership on organizations is crucial to their long-term capacity to function effectively and meet anticipated changing environmental demands. This is the area in which leadership in criminal justice is often lacking. Prison and jail overcrowding along with the increasing number of geriatric, mentally ill, and other problematic inmates were issues all foreseen by most practicing professionals. However, it took court intervention combined with crisis-level manifestation of the problems before they were actively addressed. The vision was apparent, but leadership to act and move the organization to prepare for obvious future environmental demands did not exist. Conversely, law enforcement leadership did foresee a needed change in police services so that, to some extent, a move from traditional to community policing has taken place.

The criminal justice system has a well-established history of creating a cadre of managers whose experience and subsequent socialization has trained them to work heroically to protect their existing systems and culture from intrusion, outsiders, and environmental forces. Criminal justice managers have assumed and struggled to behave as if they were working in a closed system. Leadership, however, requires an explicit understanding that they work in a dynamic world and within an open system, anticipate the changing environment, and prepare for future demands. Moreover, the criminal justice environment is becoming more complex, with other agencies and functions being important to criminal justice organizations. In the words of Jeffrey Luke (1998), the public world, in which criminal justice managers and leaders function, is becoming increasingly interconnected, and effective leadership can no longer be connected only to one organization. The 21st-century criminal justice leader confronts issues of mental illness, school truancy, and substance abuse on a daily basis. Being interconnected with other social service and private agencies becomes essential to effective leadership across the components of the criminal justice system (see Chapter 7 for a further discussion of this issue).

Open-System Theory

In the past, many students of organizations have focused exclusively on what took place inside the organizations they studied. Perhaps the great model of that approach is found in the work of Frederick Taylor (1919, 1947). As we will see in later chapters, one of Taylor's chief concerns was with increasing the efficiency of work through job design. Such an orientation ignored many variables outside the workplace that could influence the efficiency of labor. As we will discuss in detail, it was not until the advent of the human relations school that managers began to consider extraorganizational influences.

Taylor's orientation reflects a *closed-system* view, in which organizations are regarded as self-contained and unresponsive to their environments. For a closed-system organization, the factors in the environment are unchanging constants. Such an approach to analyzing organizations has some appeal in the sense that it reassures us that relevant variables are clear, easily understood, and controllable. The model has its origins in *systems theory,* the view found in biology, mechanics, and other fields that assumes that complex entities are composed of interrelated parts. Thus, as closed systems, organizations are composed of elements that are all related to one another. In this view, communication follows the lines of hierarchy; power and authority are a function of office; and change is slow and directed by management.

Although this approach to analyzing organizations may be adequate in some circumstances, it is now seen as too simplistic for most studies. In criminal justice, for example, a closed-system analysis would suggest that the causes of a prison riot could be found only in administrative practices and procedures, types of inmates, and other such internal variables. Clearly, however, the 1971 riot in New York's Attica prison cannot be explained without reference to the political climate of the time. Likewise, the prison riots of the middle and late 1980s cannot be understood without reference to conservative criminal justice policies and the resulting overcrowding in prisons.

Eisenstein, Flemming, and Nardulli (1988) revealed the limitations of closed-system views of criminal justice organizations in their study of trial courts. Critical of the view that the courts can be understood as simply applying the law, these authors concluded that the great differences they found in nine criminal courts could not be understood by focusing on only the legal aspects of the courts. They suggest that the metaphor of the courts as communities is productive. This view recognizes differences in the extent of prosecution–police interaction, political relationships of judges, and approaches to plea bargaining, among other factors. These differences originate in the community context and the environment of the courts, and they influence both the process and product of the legal system.

Problems of Campus Law Enforcement

A campus law enforcement agency, unlike a municipal or county agency, is often considered a means to an end, not an end unto itself. The primary reason to incorporate or establish municipalities is to provide government services, of which law enforcement is one of the most important. The primary reason to establish a college or university is to provide an education, not government services. The campus equivalent of such services exists only to support the primary goal, education. Where there is a conflict between the primary goal of the institution and the secondary goals of its law enforcement organization, the enforcement goal frequently ends up subordinated to the educational goal.

It might be thought that no conflict exists between the goals of running a college or university and of enforcing the law. This is not always the case. Conflicts between the values of academic culture and the self-interest of the institution may present serious ethical and legal dilemmas for campus law enforcement. Campus officers may be ordered not to enforce certain laws, make arrests, or report certain statistics, if such actions would conflict with other, more important institutional goals—the most prominent example being the failure to arrest or prosecute student athletes who commit serious crimes.

Many members of a college community perceive their campus as being selectively immune, at the discretion of the faculty, from the laws that govern society as a whole. Obedience to the law is believed to be less important than the intellectual pursuits in which the campus is engaged. If the law interferes with such pursuits, then the law must be disregarded in favor of the greater good to be gained by continuing these pursuits free of constraining regulation.

In addition, the values of academic culture make the campus officer's job more difficult. Academic culture by its nature tends to be liberal, permissive, theoretical, decentralized, and democratic and has no particular sense of urgency about coming to a decision about anything. This perspective contrasts with the nature of police work, which tends to be conservative, nonpermissive, pragmatic, paramilitary, and authoritarian and which involves highly time-critical decision making. In addition, the civil disturbances of the 1960s left an unfavorable attitude towards law enforcement with many senior academics.

As a result of these attitudes, many campus officers may be faced with Nuremberg-type decisions in which they are ordered by campus authority to violate their sworn legal and statutory responsibilities. Such pressures are not unique to campus law enforcement; political pressures can have the same effects on noncampus law enforcement. (The author wishes it known that his institution does not impose such pressures upon his department, nor, to the best of his knowledge, has it ever done so.)

In a county or municipality, the law enforcement function is often the largest and most visible component of the organization in personnel and budget as well as importance. In one Midwestern city, for example, roughly 25 percent of city employees work for the police department, whereas only about 1 percent of the employees of an adjoining university work for the campus police. Many campuses place their police under the same chain of command as the custodial and maintenance departments, in contrast to most municipalities, where the police chief answers directly to the mayor or chief executive. Consequently, campus police often encounter uncertainty about their legitimacy as law enforcement officers as well as negative perceptions from the campus community, the larger community, and other law enforcement agencies. Widespread misconceptions about their authority, besides affecting officer morale, may lead to unnecessary conflict.

The physical environment of the typical campus is often different from that of the typical municipal department. Instead of streets and houses, campus police patrol parking lots and large buildings. Their duties are also often different from stereotypical police duties and include a high degree of non-law enforcement or service activities. Most campus police departments can be classified as either of Wilson's famous watchman or service styles. Campus crime rates are almost always lower than those of the nation as a whole or of the surrounding community, especially if it is an urban campus.

However, as one study of campus crime put it, "The nation's campuses, while not entirely crime free, are, on the whole, remarkably free of violent or irrational crime." A campus law enforcement chief has said: "Crime is primarily committed by people who have no job, no education, and no hope. Everyone on this campus has at least one of these, probably two, and is working on the third." This low level of criminal activity may be frustrating to the young and enthusiastically proactive police officer who wishes to experience all the law enforcement experience has to offer, although older, less proactive, officers may find it a relief.

Counterbalancing the low crime rate is the fact that the campus population is primarily, if not exclusively, drawn from the ranks of those most likely to commit crimes due to their age (18–22 years). Community policing is more difficult in the campus environment because of the youth and transient nature of most of the campus population. Unlike other communities, many members of the campus community have no significant emotional, financial, or time-related investment in their community.

Besides having a population composed largely of those in the age group most likely to commit crimes, the average campus has a population of those most likely to become the victim of crimes, which is one and the same as the crime-prone population. Their youthful sense of immortality and their desire to experiment and experience all that life has to offer, combined with a rather imperfect awareness of some of the uglier aspects of human behavior, all make college students vulnerable to being crime victims. In addition, their tendency to view all adult authority figures and their admonitions in much the same way as they view their parents and their admonitions can make crime prevention a difficult task. The constant turnover of the student population means that crime prevention efforts must be constant as well.

OFFICER JAMES HEINZ
University Police
University of Wisconsin-Milwaukee

The community analogy suggests the usefulness of an *open-system* view of the courts. In this framework for analysis, organizations are viewed as constantly interacting with their environments. In business, for example, profitability fluctuates with the availability of raw materials, consumer interests, and even taxes, tariffs, and the value of the dollar relative to foreign currency. In criminal justice, isolated heinous offenses have led to major changes in legislation and policing practices. Public conservatism has led to tougher sentences, which in turn have caused prison and jail crowding and increased prisoner violence. The influence of the environment, however, need not be so dramatic. State laws permitting unionization of public employees have had tremendous effects in criminal justice. Even changes in local economies have affected the number and qualifications of applicants for police and corrections jobs.

In their social–psychological analysis, Katz and Kahn (1978) describe organizations as open systems characterized by inputs from the environment, throughput (the process of changing those inputs), and outputs (the product or service of an organization). They point out that this simple model offers some advantages over closed-system analyses. First, it highlights the importance of studying organization–environment relations. Second, because the organization cannot be equally open to everything in the environment, it highlights the need to study the selection process. For example, how are job descriptions determined? What makes some constraints on decisions more important than others? How are criteria for measuring effectiveness determined? Finally, the open-system approach indicates we should also study how organizations affect their environments. It permits us to see that organizations are not necessarily passive. For example, high-profile crime-control efforts that reassure the public may lead to increased police budgets. In some states, corrections officials have used the threat of releasing prisoners to obtain support for prison construction. Community treatment programs have been closed because they have negatively affected their environments through high recidivism rates or notorious offenses by their clients.

Complex Goals

We first discussed the question of organizational goals in our effort to define the term *organization*. The point is important enough, however, to risk redundancy here. The organizations of the criminal justice system have multiple and conflicting goals. We will deal here with the consequences of this complexity.

The implications of having multiple and conflicting goals were first spelled out in a classic work by Simon (1964). To be successful, organizations must endeavor to meet all their goals. For example, profit-making firms must meet production goals, quality goals, environmental protection goals, and many others. Simon pointed out, however, that the pursuit of all these goals impinges on the degree of goal attainment. Borrowing from the field of mathematics, Simon used the notion of a *Pareto Optimal Solution,* from which everyone benefits (though not equally), to show that organizations inevitably seek satisfactory levels of attainment of several goals simultaneously rather than attempting to maximize attainment of every goal.

Goals thus not only provide direction but also serve as constraints or limits (Wilson, 1989). For example, a manufacturing firm has both production and sales goals.

For the sales force, production goals limit the quantity of items they can sell; and for production workers, sales goals may set limits on the quantity of items they can produce. In criminal justice, the police may strive to control crime, but due process goals constrain their effectiveness. Likewise, prosecutors may seek justice through rigorous prosecutions, but they are limited by the goal of not having crowded dockets. Plea bargaining may represent the Pareto Optimal Solution to these multiple and conflicting goals in the prosecutor's office.

Although complex and conflicting goals may serve as constraints, they need not be viewed in negative terms. For example, the limitations that due process requirements put on police powers are fundamental to our freedoms. Wright (1981) argues that goal conflict is, in fact, desirable and that a unified criminal justice system with consensus about goals would be undesirable. Goal conflict, according to Wright, limits the expression of diverse viewpoints and provides for the mediation of interests so that no single perspective dominates. Goal conflict may also promote efficiency in offender processing by enhancing the adaptability of the system. Studies of effectiveness in criminal justice, of corruption and subcultures in criminal justice organizations, and of how these organizations change or fail to change all require an understanding of multiple and conflicting goals.

Complex Environment

As with the other topics in this chapter, we will return to organizational environments throughout the book. Chapter 3 deals with the topic in detail. In this section we briefly examine the impact of the environment on criminal justice organizations.

Some researchers have attempted to specify how environments impinge on different types of organizations. For example, Lipsky (1980) argues that the conflicting goals of human services organizations are the result of unresolved disagreements in society at large. The police, too, will always be subject to criticism as they pursue both crime control and due process because the public cannot agree on what goal or what balance of goals is appropriate.

Walmsley and Zald (1973) agree with Lipsky that public organizations absorb conflict from their environment. They also describe other effects of the environment on public organizations. They argue that because the productivity of public organizations such as the police or prisons is difficult to measure, the structure of those organizations is more closely tied to public beliefs about what the organizations should do than to what goes on in those organizations. For example, the public view is that prisons should attempt to rehabilitate offenders. Prisons, therefore, maintain elaborate treatment divisions despite the fact that the staff members of those divisions are engaged primarily in security functions such as classification and discipline. Likewise, Duffee (1986:65) points out that the modern police department continues to be organized along paramilitary lines that were instituted when police were first organized to put down labor unrest and protect the wealthy. The structure of the courts, too, more closely reflects beliefs about what they should do than about what they actually do. Their rigid structure is a reflection of faith in the adversarial process, but it is widely acknowledged that the courts function in a much more collegial than adversarial way.

Walmsley and Zald (1973) also point out that not only is organizational structure affected by the environment, but so is the way in which these public organizations are evaluated. First, clients are not the legitimizers of these organizations, so service delivery may not be rewarded. For example, prisoners are not viewed as legitimate evaluators of their prisons. Second, because the marketplace does not determine the value of public organizations, they are generally evaluated on the importance of their mission rather than on the results they achieve. The enforcement of laws and dispensing of justice are seen as important missions. Police and courts, therefore, are valued despite difficulties in measuring productivity. But the value placed on these organizations may diminish if public views change, even though the organizations' effectiveness does not change. With the movement away from the treatment model, for example, probation agencies were devalued until they took on the more valued roles of intensive custodial supervision, pretrial release evaluation, and home detention. Now, at the beginning of the 21st century we are seeing a reinvention of treatment as a desirable goal for correctional organizations.

As this brief discussion indicates, in public organizations like those of the criminal justice system, environmental influences are highly complex. In Chapter 3 we examine those influences in depth.

Complex Internal Constituencies

Our discussion of basic concepts for this book must include one additional subject. One way to look at organizations is to consider them as arenas in which struggles for power occur (Hall, 1982:300). Perhaps the most obvious examples are workers' struggles for increased wages and better working conditions. Although the external environment of organizations is complex, then, internal constituencies are also relevant to organizational form and function.

Criminal justice literature is only beginning to acknowledge the potency of these internal groups. As noted, clients often are not the legitimizers of criminal justice organizations. They cannot, however, be regarded as wholly insignificant. The prisoners' rights movement clearly illustrates the point that even inmates can dramatically influence prisons. Although these changes have also involved powerful external groups, inmates obviously exercise some power, not only through their individual lawsuits but also well beyond court mandates. As a result of litigation, prisons have become more bureaucratized, prison staff have become more demoralized, and a strong movement to establish prison standards has begun (Jacobs, 1983b:86).

Internal constituencies are not limited to clients. They may include groups of employees who come to pursue a distinct set of interests. Departmental legal counsel and budget managers, for example, set requirements that constrain organizations. Likewise, groups such as court stenographers and secretaries have special goals. In fact, the most significant internal constituency in many criminal justice organizations today may be the workforce. Through traditional grievance mechanisms and now through collective bargaining, labor is having an increasingly significant effect. The public employee unionization movement of the 1960s paved the way for organized labor in corrections and more recently in policing. Unionization has dramatically changed the role of management and has influenced everything from job and shift assignments to occupational safety. In some prisons, guards and prisoners have even united to call for better and safer institutions (Jacobs, 1978). Additionally, in some states, correctional officers have strengthened their positions through the political process and have become astute and skilled in representing their interests before legislatures and governors (Stojkovic and Farkas, 2003).

Summary

This chapter provides a brief foundation for the discussions in the rest of the book. We have covered concepts that we regard as central to understanding criminal justice administration and management. It is important to bear in mind that these concepts are not presented here as indisputable facts but as analytical tools. For example, criminal justice organizations may be studied as open or closed systems. But it is not the organizations that are open or closed, only our analyses. For the purposes of this discussion we find important benefits in viewing criminal justice organizations as open systems interacting with and responsive to their environment, an environment that has become increasingly complex and interconnected with other public agencies.

Likewise, we prefer a rather general definition of the concept of organization. For this analysis, organizations are not limited to groups with specific structural arrangements or groups that pursue limited and clearly defined sets of goals. Similarly, we regard managing and leading as general processes or functions that, to some extent, are performed by a variety of organizational members and not hierarchically bound.

Apart from these basic definitions, we have identified three concepts that seem particularly germane to criminal justice organizations. First, those organizations pursue many and often conflicting goals. Second, the organizations operate in a complex environment that exercises considerable influence. And, third, internal constituencies in these organizations are becoming increasingly powerful.

This is, no doubt, a difficult chapter, full of rich theoretical concepts that we have just begun to discuss. Students with a penchant for theory will wish to investigate the suggested readings and to follow up on the citations in the chapter. Students without such a penchant may feel relieved that the chapter is over. It does, however, cover topics to which we will return time and time again, and we believe it provides a needed background. That background will first come into use in Chapter 2, where we explore the organizational structure of criminal justice in detail.

Case Study

Who's Running This Organization Anyway?
Jail Structure, Goals, and Environment

The Marion County Jail serves as the detention facility for the county, the City of Indianapolis, and the cities of Beech Grove, Lawrence, Southport, and Speedway, Indiana—a total population of approximately 800,000. The four-story jail, completed in 1965, had an official capacity of 776. Built with security and control as the primary concerns, it was, according to one observer, obsolete before it opened.

Just a few years after the jail opened, it was the subject of a lawsuit that was not fully settled until a new . . . wing was completed. . . . Briefly, the events and charges are as follows: In September 1972, a suit was filed by the Legal Services Organization (LSO) on behalf of pretrial detainees at the Marion County Jail. Named as defendants in the suit were the sheriff of the county, the jail commander, the commissioner of the State of Indiana Department of Corrections, the mayor of Indianapolis, and specific members of the Board of County Commissioners. The complaint, brought under Section 1983 of the Civil Rights Act (42 U.S.C. 1983), alleged violations of the pretrial detainees' rights under the First, Fourth, Fifth, Sixth, Eighth, Ninth, Thirteenth, and Fourteenth Amendments to the U.S. Constitution. At issue were overcrowding; [poor] physical and sanitary conditions; failure to classify prisoners for housing assignments; inadequate medical and dental care; and lack of recreation, contact visits, and access to telephone and mail services.

Because of crowding, detainees were sometimes required to sleep on the floor in the shower rooms. Although mattresses were provided, mattress covers often were not. Jail-issue clothing consisted of dresses for females and trousers for males. The prisoners wore the underwear they had on when admitted. Although they could purchase more underwear, as well as towels and pillows, or receive them from a visitor, indigent prisoners often had to do without. No provision was made to launder clothing or towels. Though these could be washed in cell-block basins, it was against regulations to hang them up to dry.

All detainees could purchase postage and writing materials. They were allowed to mail only one letter containing no more than one piece of paper per day. Jail officials read all correspondence to and from family and friends. Telephone calls were not permitted except by special arrangement. There was no recreation program or exercise area. Playing cards could be purchased, and there was a meager library. Detainees could exercise only in the open area of the cell block. No televisions or radios were available. There was no regular dental program, no provision for medical examinations, no law library. Visits were "closed": the detainee visited from inside the cell block looking through a small plexiglass window and talking through a metal grating. Only two visitors were allowed per week. Children were never permitted.

In 1975, a consent decree and partial judgment corrected many of the physical and sanitary problems. New jail rules were formulated and submitted to the court. These covered the sanitizing of mattresses, issuance of jail clothing and provisions for laundering them, improvements in medical and dental care, counseling services, and more liberal correspondence rules. However, many of these were "paper" changes only.

A 1976 court order required attention to all areas left unresolved by the consent decree. The judge ordered that clothing be issued and laundered weekly and that a bed above floor level be provided for each detainee along with sheets, pillow, blanket, and mattress cover. He ordered that telephone calls be permitted "in reasonable number and for a reasonable length of time without censorship" and that correspondence opportunities be greatly expanded. Contact visiting was ordered, with the visitation schedule to be equal to that provided by the state for the convicted. Reasonable facilities for both indoor and outdoor recreation were also ordered. The court recognized that many deficiencies resulted from lack of funds but ordered that appropriations be made in order to correct them.

The defendants' official response was the appointment of a steering committee, with representatives of the mayor, the county commissioners, and the sheriff as members, to select consultants who would propose solutions. The contract to the consultants was let by the Department of Metropolitan Development, an arm of city government attached to the mayor's office. The consultants' report was submitted fourteen months later in June 1977. In January and February 1978, the mayor's office and the sheriff's office submitted memoranda based on the report to the court advocating certain of the compliance options that particularly addressed the problem of overcrowding. These memoranda were followed by the plaintiffs' memorandum in opposition to some of the proposed solutions.

In August 1978, interrogatories to the sheriff were propounded by attorneys for the plaintiffs and were answered in the required thirty days by the sheriff. There were eighty-seven questions, and it was clear from the responses that no major concerted effort had been made to implement the judgment of the court. Neither the 1977 nor the 1978 sheriff's budgets had allocated funds for compliance, nor had the sheriff requested special funds. Whatever improvements had been made had come from the jail's normal operating budget. The 1979 budget request included $12 million for an addition to the jail, but it was denied by the county commissioners.

In 1979, seven years after the suit was initiated, the jail commander sent letters to jail officials throughout the country seeking advice and assistance in achieving compliance. During this year also, the sheriff's department assumed command of the city lockup. All prisoners were then booked at the lockup, and transient prisoners (held for up to three days) were not transferred to the jail. This had the immediate effect of reducing the population. But on December 28, lawyers for the plaintiffs filed three motions: an order to show cause why defendants should not be held in contempt of court and assessed fines and damages of over $300,000; a motion to appoint a special master to oversee compliance with the order issued three years earlier; and a motion to restrain further incarceration of detainees at the Marion County Jail.

These motions produced immediate action. By January 14, 1980, an Ad Hoc Jail Committee had been appointed. It included criminal court judges, city–county councilmen, representatives of the mayor's office, the sheriff's office, the prosecutor's office, and the auditor's office, and the Greater Indianapolis Progress Committee (GIPC), a privately funded citizens group advisory to the mayor.

In the court's stipulation and order of May 1980, the GIPC was appointed jail commission, and two [additional] commissioners were named. The court held in abeyance the show-cause order and the motion to restrain incarceration but ordered further progress toward compliance within six months and recreation, televisions, radios, and private attorney–client conference booths by July 1, 1980. Threatened with a contempt-of-court citation, the defendants began to engage seriously in compliance attempts. A new classification system went into effect in March 1980; in July, both contact visits and outdoor exercise were begun; by August, private attorney–client cubicles were in use; and by the end of the summer, there was a television set for each cell block.

The Ad Hoc Jail Committee met regularly throughout the year and ordered an update of the 1977 consultants' study, which was submitted in December. In December, the City–County Council passed a resolution to undertake a survey of jail renovations and additions. The federal court judge cooperated . . . by accepting improvements and postponing action on the 1979 motions.

In April 1981, expansion of the jail and a necessary bond issue were approved by the City–County Council. Architects' drawings were approved in June 1982, construction bids were accepted in the fall, and contracts signed in December. Construction began in April 1983. This new addition would bring the jail into full compliance in all areas requiring additional space and structural change.

By March 1983, compromises had been made on the larger issues: outdoor recreation was available once per week rather than daily; holding cages had been converted for contact visitation by setting up folding chairs on each side of the bars; cubicles were made available for attorney–client conferences; telephones had been installed in each cell block with sixteen to twenty-four hours of access per day (collect calls only); and a law library was in operation. Compliance was lax in other areas: mattresses were not hygienically treated on a regular basis; clean clothing was not regularly issued; the promised counselors were interns from a nearby university's school of social work; and often there were not quite enough blankets, pillows, or towels for every inmate.

From "Jails and Judicial Review" by N. E. Schafer. In D. Kalinich & J. Klofas (Eds.), *Sneaking Inmates Down the Alley,* 1986. Courtesy of Charles C. Thomas, Publishers, Springfield, Illinois.

Case Study Questions

1. From the discussion of conditions in the jail, what would you say its goals were? How did those goals change over the course of the suit?

2. How would you describe the role of internal and external constituencies in the saga of this jail case?

3. How would you describe the role of management in the course of this legal action? How effective was it at directing the organization, and what constraints was it under?

For Discussion

1. Using the concepts discussed in this chapter, describe your local probation department. What is its structure? What management functions are performed and by whom? What people and organizations outside the agency exert an influence on it? How does that influence show in organizational structure or process?

2. Discuss the goals of a victim–witness program. In what ways are they complex or conflicting? In what ways do some goals serve as constraints? Now consider those goals in the context of where in the organization the program is located. Will they differ if the program is attached to the prosecutor's office or if it is an independent unit?

3. Using both a closed-system and an open-system analytical framework, describe your local jail. How might these frameworks lead to different views of the jail's effectiveness or of the causes of jail violence? Describe how jails are affected by their environment and how they may influence that environment.

4. Sheriffs' departments usually carry out a variety of tasks, including enforcing laws in rural areas, serving summonses, maintaining courthouse security, and managing the jail. In light of this range of tasks, what internal and external constituencies are powerful? How is the importance of those constituencies affected by the fact that county sheriffs are elected officials?

For Further Reading

Duffee, D. *Correctional Management: Change and Control in Correctional Organizations.* Prospect Heights, IL: Waveland, 1986.

Eisenstein, J., Flemming, R., & Nardulli, P. *The Contours of Justice: Communities and Their Courts.* Boston: Little, Brown, 1988.

Fyfe, J., Greene, J., Walsh, W., Wilson, O., & McLaren, R. *Police Administration,* 5th ed. New York: McGraw-Hill, 1997.

Katz, D., and Kahn, R. L. *The Social Psychology of Organizations,* 2nd ed. New York: John Wiley, 1978. (Especially Chapters 1–3).

Langworthy, R. *The Structure of Police Organizations.* New York: Praeger, 1986.

Luke, Jeffrey S. *Catalytic Leadership: Strategies for an Interconnected World.* San Francisco: Jossey-Bass, 1998.

CHAPTER

2

STRUCTURE OF CRIMINAL JUSTICE ORGANIZATIONS

Overview of Organizational Structure

Dimensions of Organizational Structure

Mission, Policies, and Procedures

Policies and Procedures in Organizations

Work Perspective: A Day at Work

Informal Structures in Organizations

Organizational Frames

Summary

Case Study: Decentralizing Decision Making in a Correctional System

For Discussion

For Further Reading

Organization as a way of coordination requires the establishment of a system of authority whereby the central purpose or objective of the enterprise is translated into reality through the combined efforts of many specialists, each working in his own field at a particular time and place. It is clear from long experience in human affairs that such a structure requires not only many men at work in many places at selected times, but also a single directing executive authority. The problem of the organization thus becomes the problem of building up between the executive at the center and the sub-division of work on the periphery an effective network of communications and control. It is the function of this organization to enable the director to coordinate and energize all of the sub-divisions so that the major objective may be achieved efficiently.

(*Gulick, 1937*)

The hierarchy of positions, with graduation of honors and privileges, which is the universal accompaniment of all complex organizations, is essential to the adjustment of non-material incentives to induce the services of the most able individuals or the most valuable potential contributors to organization, and it is likewise necessary to the maintenance of pride of organization, community sense, etc., which are important general incentives to all classes of contributors.

(*Barnard, 1938*)

Overview of Organizational Structure

Organizations, as we explained in Chapter 1, have a purpose, a structure, and activities. Organizations are also comprised of a formal structure and an informal structure, a phenomenon that was recognized by Chester Barnard in the 1930s: "Formal organizations arise out of and are necessary to informal organizations; but when they come into operation, they create and require informal organizations" (1938: 120). This book examines the forces that impact criminal justice organizations and nurture the informal side of those organizations. It is important, therefore, to review the formal structure of organizations here to set the stage for the following chapters. This chapter closely examines the basic structures and dimensions of organizations and describes the logic of various structural configurations that can be implemented by agencies. In addition, the chapter reviews the basic concepts of organizational *mission, policies, procedures,* and *practices* and briefly introduces the informal side of organizations. Throughout the chapter, we apply the concepts of organizational structure to criminal justice agencies.

The structure of an organization provides a framework within which its members carry out their prescribed activities that, collectively, will cause the organization to achieve its purpose. The framework is composed of the organization's mission, policies and procedures, and a hierarchy of authority to direct members in the pursuit of its purpose. The formal structure creates formal roles and relationships, divides labor and allocates responsibility, and promotes rules and a hierarchy of authority to co-ordinate activities (Bolman and Deal, 1997).

Criminal justice organizations vary greatly in their size and structure. The vast majority of these agencies in the United States are relatively small and serve subur-ban and rural communities. For example, most jails in the United States are relatively small, housing fewer than 50 to 300 inmates. At the other extreme, about 6 percent of the nation's jails house almost half of jail inmates (NIJ, 1995). The largest jails are New York City's Riker's Island, Chicago's Cook County Jail, Los Angeles County's multiple complexes, and Houston's Harris County Jail (NIJ, 1995). Adult correctional systems obviously vary greatly in size. The Federal Bureau of Prisons manages a prison system that extends across the country. Within systems, institutions vary dramatically in size. In Michigan, for example, the prison system is comprised of one prison, constructed in the 1880s, which houses more than 6,000 inmates, along with institutions with popu-lation capacities of 500 or less and a number of camps that hold fewer than 100 inmates.

Law enforcement agencies across the nation also vary dramatically in size and scope of mission. For example, the Bureau of Alcohol, Tobacco, and Firearms, the U.S. Customs Service, and the U.S. Secret Service fall under the jurisdiction of the De-partment of the Treasury. The U.S. Department of Justice has authority over the Fed-eral Bureau of Investigation, U.S. Drug Enforcement Administration, the U.S. Marshals Service, and the Immigration and Naturalization Service. The Department of the In-terior, whose mission is to protect the nation's natural resources, has authority over the Fish and Wildlife Service, National Park Service, and the U.S. Park Police. Most law enforcement agencies, however, fall within state and local jurisdictions. "Big city" police departments are, by the nature of their jurisdictions, comparatively large. For example, the New York City police department has more than 44,000 employees, with the majority, more than 36,000, sworn law enforcement officers. At the other extreme are 13,000 municipal police departments and 3,000 sheriff's departments. Many small agencies have just one full-time sworn police officer or are composed solely of part-time officers (Schmalleger,1999).

Given the diversity in size and scope of criminal justice agencies across the coun-try, it is not possible to describe an organizational structure generic to all or even most organizations. A few key dimensions, however, are common to almost all or-ganizations, regardless of size or structure. This chapter will provide a general de-scription of those organizational dimensions and show how they operate in criminal justice agencies. The discussion will begin with a general description of two distinct models of organizations: the *closed-system* model, most commonly referred to as bu-reaucratic, mechanistic, formal, or hierarchical, and the *open-system* model, alter-nately referred to as organistic, professional, or informal.

Henry (1975) provides a sound sketch and comparison of both these models. Bureaucracies—the closed-system model—are predicated upon stable environmen-tal conditions that create routine demands for services. In this type of organization, therefore, tasks tend to be specialized and divided among the labor force—that is, each member has a narrow range of duties that contributes to the agency's overall mis-sion. Means or process are emphasized over outcomes. It is assumed that if all work-ers perform their tasks correctly, the final product will result naturally. Every job is spelled out clearly in a formal job description that also dictates and limits the amount

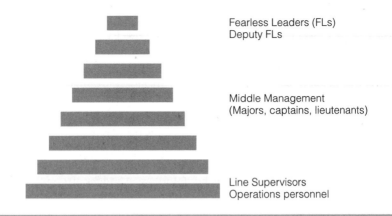

Fearless Leaders (FLs)
Deputy FLs

Middle Management
(Majors, captains, lieutenants)

Line Supervisors
Operations personnel

FIGURE 2-1   Organizational Hierarchy

of authority and responsibility each individual has. Bureaucracies tend to be *hierarchical*, with a chain of command delegating authority and responsibility from the central authority downward (see Figure 2-1). Communications, power authority relationships, and loyalty are expected to flow vertically between superiors and subordinates. Bosses legitimately give orders, and subordinates obey. However, power is constrained by the organization's reliance on written rules and regulations that delimit authority and responsibility.

Knowledge and expertise is assumed to exist at the top of bureaucratic organizations. Therefore, planning, conflict resolution, and decision making in general are primarily a function of top-level supervisors. Promotion of personnel to higher levels of authority and responsibility within bureaucratic organizations is based upon their years of service and an assessment, usually subjective, about their capabilities. It is assumed that knowledge and expertise accumulate with longevity of career service.

Large metropolitan law enforcement agencies—often referred to metaphorically as "big city policing"—and state and federal correctional and law enforcement agencies are examples of criminal justice agencies structured along bureaucratic lines. It is common for large agencies, while adhering to bureaucratic structure, to decentralize their operations by creating field offices or, in the case of large metropolitan police agencies, command districts. Interestingly, law enforcement and corrections agencies are often categorized as paramilitary organizations because a rigid chain of command exists; subordinates are trained to "follow orders"; and members are uniformed, armed, and authorized to apply coercive force in carrying out their duties.

Bureaucratic systems emphasize means rather than results. In evaluating individuals or agency effectiveness and in supervising personnel, supervisors focus upon the expected activities and routines of agency personnel (the means of production) rather than what they produce. For example, correctional officers are expected to make rounds on a predetermined time schedule; doing this, it is assumed, will ensure supervision and control of inmates. In fact, some jails require corrections officers to punch cards at time clocks located at the end of each cell block to ensure they patrol the cell blocks at designated times. Similarly, law enforcement officers assigned to traffic control may be judged on the number of violation tickets they give out during a particular time period. Police agencies commonly check starting and ending mileage on patrol cars to ensure that patrol officers are patrolling their assigned sections. This emphasis explains why the criminal judicial system is often accused of delivering "assembly line justice" as prosecutors plea bargain cases so that courts can eliminate or keep up with backlogs, without considering the effects or results of these processes or practices. A systematic method of measuring the effects of random patrols or plea bargaining on agency goals and objectives is rarely pursued.

The hierarchical structure of a bureaucracy forces official communication to occur vertically. Commands and policy directives emanate from the top and are sent downward through the chain of command; information and reports on the activities of subordinates or problems within the organization are sent upward to appropriate levels. Since it is assumed that expertise and knowledge reside at the top of a bureaucratic agency, major policy and operational decisions tend to be made at this level. In the hierarchical structure, it follows logically that clear superior–subordinate relationships exist among personnel. A management style is, therefore, directed toward command and obedience. Loyalty toward the organization and supervisors is generally expected from subordinates.

Professional or *organistic* agencies—open systems—are the extreme opposite of bureaucracies. Such organizations are ideally suited to function within unstable environments that demand outcomes requiring nonroutine tasks. In this type of organization, tasks are not specialized and any member of the agency may have the expertise or knowledge to take on a variety of tasks. Tasks may also be assumed by groups or teams sharing expertise. Since tasks are not specialized and responsibility is not constrained by written procedures, rules, and regulations, ends are emphasized over means. Decision making—conflict resolution, planning, policy development, and the like—is mostly a result of structured and informal interaction between personnel rather than a prerogative reserved for executive or top managers. Decision making can emanate from groups or any individual because knowledge and expertise are assumed to be possessed by all personnel, at least within each individual's specific task area.

In open systems, interactions tend to be horizontal rather than vertical, through a chain of command, as prescribed for a bureaucratic agency. Leadership relationships tend be peer oriented rather than superior–subordinate. Advice and coaching, therefore, replace commands. Thinking about organizations as open systems leads to understanding the importance of the environmental demands and an agency's willingness and ability to be responsive to community needs. Organistic agencies within the criminal judicial system include small prosecuting attorneys' offices, law enforcement departments, and jails commanding less than ten professional personnel. Research or planning departments within agencies will also likely organize as organistic systems, taking on an informal organizational structure.

It is unlikely that any one agency is purely bureaucratic or organistic; both structures are advantageous for different tasks or missions. This is apparent in large bureaucratic agencies that develop organistic units within their structures to meet demands and perform tasks not suited to a mechanistic approach. Here the traditional conflict between prison treatment and custody staff provides a common example. A great deal has been written about this phenomenon. Generally, the conflict is viewed as a philosophical or operational conflict. What also must be considered is that custody personnel work under a bureaucratic or paramilitaristic system of management, whereas treatment staff—psychologists, social workers, and counselors—have a great deal more discretion because they work in an organistic or professional subsystem of the prison. The differing degrees of autonomy and discretion among the groups also creates conflict, especially as it relates to enforcement of inmate rules and regulations.

Conversely, professional organizations, such as universities, also have chain of command, job descriptions for staff, and many other acquirements of a bureaucratic agency. A close look will show that even the academic side of universities tends to form as organistic from the bottom up and bureaucratic from the top down. Moreover, small agencies such as small-town law enforcement agencies or jails in smaller jurisdictions will function along the lines of an organistic agency. Lines of authority tend to be weak, and decision making often evolves from consensus building. However, some degree of authoritative command exists even in small agencies. Team policing is likewise an attempt to remove a unit of law enforcement officers from the restrictions of the agency's hierarchy and structure to allow officers the freedom to work as a professional problem solving unit (Shanahan, 1985).

Courts are generally depicted as organistic systems. Defense attorneys, prosecuting attorneys, and judges work together as semiautonomous agents guided by formal procedural rules, a code of ethics, and informal rules of conduct (Neubauer, 1983). This is an easy conclusion to draw if we understand courts from the perspective of the courtroom: the judge, prosecutor, and defense attorney engage in an adversarial relationship controlled by judges and serviced by lawyers. More often, proceedings take place outside the court in a negotiative process. All participants are highly paid, well-educated, trained professionals, and bureaucratic organization is not immediately visible. However, the criminal judicial process also includes courtroom personnel, including the bailiff and court stenographer; the clerk of courts office, which is the records and information management arm of the court; the prosecutor's office; and the adult probation department. In larger jurisdictions, the clerk of courts, prosecutor's office, and probation department begin to develop a hierarchy, attempting to specialize tasks, make rules and regulations, and create other bureaucratic mechanisms in an attempt to control and regulate the flow of work. In fact, large courts will add a court administrator to their system to coordinate and regulate the flow of work across all units of the court system.

Dimensions of Organizational Structure

In the first section, we provided the reader with a general description of bureaucratic and organistic structures. In this section, we will examine the elements of structure and the logic of their development in more detail. Organizations have in common a number of structural dimensions that determine the extent to which a bureaucratic or organistic structure develops. These dimensions are task specialization, formalization, span of control, centralization versus decentralization, complexity, and the allocation of personnel in line versus staff positions (Baron & Greenberg, 1990).

Task specialization is the process of dividing the work process into a number of smaller tasks. It can be high or nonexistent, depending upon an agency's size and the divisibility of the work process. High levels of task specialization suggest that each person or subunit performs a very narrow range of activities, as in an auto plant assembly line. Low task specialization implies that employees or subunits perform a wide range of tasks. Criminal justice agencies feature both high and low task specialization. Corrections officers may be given specialized assignments that include supervising intake and receiving, recreational facilities, or the infamous "yard." Each assignment requires a unique and specialized array of knowledge and expertise. Yet each assignment also requires both knowledge of the overall prison operations and a rather wide range of human relations and communications skills to carry out the task.

Police agencies also divide tasks by related function. For example, a large law enforcement agency has units to deal with homicide, burglary, drugs, gangs, traffic, and a multitude of other tasks. Each officer, however, will be expected to respond to a broad array of situations during the course of his or her duty. Small criminal justice agencies do not have enough personnel or a sufficiently complex workload to be concerned with high, often excessive, specialization. It is not uncommon for one or two individuals to be responsible for everything from booking prisoners to responding to service calls.

Formalization consists of the establishment of rules and regulations, usually written, that govern the work activities of an agency's personnel. Rules and regulations are often considered or identified as policy and procedures. An agency with a high degree of formalization will have rules governing almost every aspect of the work process, and the expected work behaviors of the organization's members will be spelled out in great detail. High levels of formalization reduce uncertainty and clearly define authority, responsibility, and decision-making procedures in most situations. Prisons typically have pages of written rules and regulations. Prison personnel face written regulations on issues ranging from employee parking to the amount of force that can be used on inmates. In spite of claims of professionalism, law enforcement personnel also often face a high degree of formalization. A case in point is the midsize law enforcement agency claiming to be professional and progressive that was in the habit of disciplining officers for being out of their cars without wearing their caps. The judicial process is also governed by a number of written rules and procedures. Colleges and law schools offer classes in criminal procedures that describe in detail the rules and regulations that govern the criminal side of courts.

Agencies with low levels of formalization rely on the expertise of staff rather than rules and regulations to direct work activities. Subordinates are allowed a great deal of latitude and authority in decision making. Typically, more "professional" organizations, in which tasks demand a high level of expertise from subordinates, require low levels of formalization. The prosecutor's office, while bound by legal procedures in formal court hearings, rarely has written rules on selecting cases, charging, and plea bargaining. Instead, judgments are guided by prosecutors' experience and expertise in analyzing individual cases.

The *span of control*—the number of subordinates reporting to a supervisor—is another significant dimension of organizational structure. (The number of individuals reporting to one supervisor is often referred to as the *scaler principal*.) A wide span of control implies that a large number of subordinates report to one supervisor. Conversely, a narrow span of control suggests that a small number of subordinates report to one supervisor. Deciding if the span of control should be wide or narrow depends upon the size of the organization, the task at hand, and the skills of subordinates. For example, a shift sergeant may have ten to twenty street patrol officers under his or her supervision, constituting a wide span of control. This may be appropriate if patrol officers know what is expected of them, have the skills to carry out their tasks, and need little supervision or coaching. In the same law enforcement agency, the shift lieutenant may supervise only five sergeants, who in turn are supervising twenty patrol officers. This narrow span of control may exist in part as an artificial artifact of the way the agency has set up five districts, each with twenty patrol officers. If, in this example, the complement of sergeants was doubled to improve supervision over patrol officers, the span of control under the sergeants would have been narrowed while the span of control under the lieutenant would have been widened.

Organizations described as having *tall hierarchies* contain a relatively high number of supervision levels. A tall hierarchy is generally found in organizations that utilize a narrow span of control, which is employed to provide intense supervision over subordinates. This suggests a work situation in which staff lacks competence to carry out the work without supervision or requires a great deal of coordination imposed from above. Organizations with *flat hierarchies* have few levels of command and typically exhibit wide spans of control at most levels. Figure 2-2 contrasts a tall organization with a narrow span of control with a flat organization with a wide span of control.

Decision making in organizations may be centralized or decentralized. Decision making is *centralized* to the extent decisions on personnel actions, planning, formulation of policies and procedures, adjudication of conflict, and other significant issues are made by managers at the top of the hierarchy. Decision making is *decentralized* if decisions on significant issues occur with routine frequency throughout an agency or by staff at the grassroots level. The extent to which decision making is centralized or decentralized depends upon the organization's basic values and management philosophy as well as on rationally constructed decision-making processes. Observers of bureaucracies view centralized decision making as a natural state resulting from a basic organizational belief that top managers have the expertise and systemwide vision to make the most effective decisions (Baron & Greenberg, 1990). A warden of a correctional institution, for example, is usually a career civil servant who has been promoted based upon professional merit, skill, and time employed, all characteristics typical of top-level public administrators. The warden is viewed as having greater decision-making skills than subordinates as a consequence of coming up through the ranks and serving at a variety of posts along his or her career.

However, the warden in his or her wisdom may decentralize the decision-making process for a number of reasons. First, the warden may believe that participation in decisions creates commitment in subordinates. Also, taking into account the limited knowledge a top manager may have about all components of the agency individually or synergistically, the warden may believe that the work or goals of each component are complex and dynamic and will, therefore, institute a decentralized decision-making process. Federal law enforcement agencies such as the Federal Bureau of Investigation have a common set of policies and procedures and recruit, train, and assign personnel

A Day at Work

Thirty years ago, when I was an officer, line staff had a great deal of discretion but little or no training. Today, it is just the opposite. Lots and lots of training, but little discretion remains. My training consisted of two nights working in the yard with a veteran officer and two nights in segregation with another officer. On my fifth night they put me in charge of half of the institution's dormitories with 300 prisoners. Needless to say, not much got done that night.

By contrast, today's correctional officer in Michigan must complete 450 hours of intense training at the Corrections Training Academy. Forty-hour weeks of classroom instruction regarding prisoner behaviors, psychology, and corrections policy is augmented by rigorous physical training and hands-on learning in gun squad practice, handcuff application, shakedown procedures, and self-defense. But that training is reserved for those who are actually hired. Prior to employment, candidates for the corrections officer position must demonstrate their fitness by completing fifteen (15) semester hours of college credit through five specific courses. The term corrections officer has replaced prison guard, and the goal is to create a professional corrections officer or, at least, to professionalize the occupation.

I believe it is much more difficult to be a corrections officer in today's prison environment. Officers are required to wear many hats and to function differently with each hat. For example, an officer may be involved with his or her housing unit team developing a strategy to deal with a problem prisoner. During the team discussions, the officer is encouraged to be resourceful and innovative. Ten minutes later, when the emergency siren blows, for practice or for real, the same officer is marching in close formation with a shotgun as part of a gun squad. Gone is individual resourcefulness and innovation, replaced by strict discipline under a paramilitary command structure.

When I started, we didn't have written rules and regulations. With little committed to writing, there was an informal "code" or conduct for both prisoner and staff that was not taken lightly by either group. A sense of justice existed that indicated how far prisoners and staff could go. In those days, prisoners would help break in new officers because they understood the authority that went with the officer title and prisoners wanted new officers to rule with a judicious hand. Nowadays, less discretion and authority for the officer, more often than not, means less respect from the prisoner.

Thus, today's operation is more formalized, with policy, procedure, and rules guiding just about everything from the amount of time permitted between prisoner meal lines to what prisoner stores are authorized to sell. While some benefits accrue from a more consistent operation, especially given the court's scrutiny, the environment has also become more sterile in relationships between prisoners and staff. As the bureaucracy becomes larger and larger, it tends to become bounded by more rules and policies, both as a perceived necessity to regulate the large organization in a predictable fashion and as a means to exert control over the far flung realm.

Replacing generally accepted rules of conduct and behavior by consensus in smaller organizations are thick volumes of policies created to protect the bureaucracy. In fact, today's correctional officer must possess a monumental memory to remember the 200 departmental policies currently in the books accompanied by more than 200 local operating procedures (which explain exactly how to implement policy). Augmenting policies and procedures are post orders, which explain how to do each job, but they are often three inches thick and contain applicable policies and procedures. Finally, log books are placed everywhere to document everything during the whole process of corrections management.

In the old days, experienced officers taught the rookies, or "fish officers," those skills necessary to get along in the institution, the general perception being street smart is better than book smart when you work inside the penitentiary. This did not mean that book-smart skills were not required. It did mean that employees needed to acquire some of the street-smart sense that their clients brought into the institution.

Unfortunately, rapid expansion of the prison system has virtually depleted the cadre of experienced officers and first-level supervisors whose unofficial job it was to educate the new officers. Prior to the 1970s, it was not unreasonable for a new officer to spend three to five years on the night shift before seniority permitted a move to days or afternoons. Today we have expanded so rapidly that employees are being elevated to the post of prison captain after five years. A cadre of experienced corrections officers that can manage prisoners and train new officers has virtually ceased to exist.

Without experienced staff, discretion and authority by necessity are withdrawn from the lower levels and moved to higher levels where experience has gathered. At the least, administrators tend to have longevity in correctional employment, which is often translated into experience. Rapid expansion in Michigan is driving decision making ever higher. The decisions may be driven to central office staff, regional administrators, and/or deputy directors to reach the necessary experience level.

As remote administrators become overwhelmed with more and more decisions, another layer of managers can easily be added to the bureaucratic hierarchy to deal with the perceived problem area. New middle managers must justify their existence by obtaining information for reports and analysis from the employees immediately below them in the organization. Ultimately, the line staff must provide the answers, often at the cost of real work.

In the 1980s, a study was conducted on correctional officer stress. Not surprisingly, the two greatest stressors were: (1) prisoners and (2) administration. Where experienced staff thirty years ago told the rookies, "We will teach you what you need to know," tomorrow's experienced officers may well tell rookies, "We will teach you how to deal with, and get around, the administration (bureaucracy) so you can do your job." The danger is that they're already doing it!

JOHN ANDREWS, DEPUTY WARDEN
Alger Maximum Correctional Facility
Michigan Department of Corrections

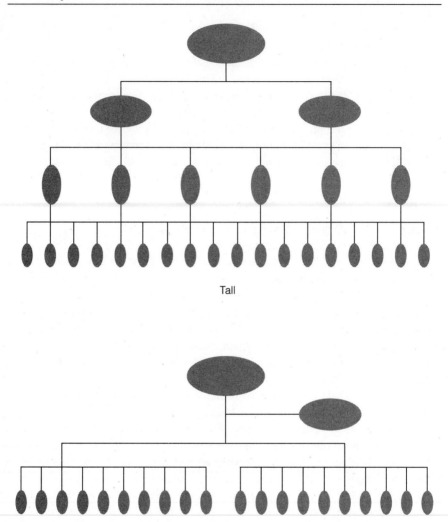

Tall

Flat

FIGURE 2-2 Tall and Flat Hierarchical

to field offices from its central office. Decision making on aspects of case management, however, are decentralized to the field offices.

Organizations are considered simple or complex depending on the number of levels in the chain of command—*vertical complexity*—or the number of existing divisions or subunits across the organization—*horizontal complexity*. Large organizations with a number of functions are both vertically and horizontally complex. A big city police department usually has a tall hierarchy with a number of layers between the chief and line staff. The department is horizontally complex if tasks are divided or specialized and task sets are assigned to individual units. A large police department, for example, has a homicide investigation unit, a burglary unit, and traffic control coupled with parking enforcement, drug enforcement, lock-up, and a number of units too numerous to mention here. Conversely, small police departments may have a chief and a number of officers and thus almost no hierarchy. Also, all their officers perform a wide range of tasks and perform traffic safety, drug enforcement, crime prevention, and investigative and other functions during the course of a shift. Thus, small police departments tend to be simple organizations, vertically and horizontally.

Organizations of any size have both line and staff personnel. *Line personnel* are those individuals directly responsible for production or the delivery of services. *Staff personnel* are support staff that assist and/or serve line personnel in their performance. Line personnel can be found in the chain of command of an organization's hierarchy. Staff personnel have slots in the hierarchy but do not have command authority over staff personnel. Large agencies have proportionally more staff personnel than smaller, less complex agencies. The California Correctional Peace Officers Association (CCPOA), a union that serves California correctional officers, employs a number of lawyers on its payroll as staff personnel to provide legal support. The president, vice president, and regional representatives of CCPOA, by contrast, are line personnel. Other examples of staff personnel in organizations are accountants, secretaries, mechanics, and trainers, to name a few. Moreover, large prisons may hire psychologists (staff personnel) to help correctional officers (line personnel) deal with stress-related problems. A final note: The term *staff* is used interchangeably and can cause confusion. Often *staff* is used to denote agency personnel such as the jail staff. *Staff personnel* refers more precisely to organizational support personnel.

Mission, Policies, and Procedures

The ideal bureaucracy has a written mission that is logically implemented by policies and procedures. The mission, policies, and procedures will be contained in a neatly bound policy and procedure manual. All personnel understand and accept the agency's mission and have a general knowledge of policies as well as a working knowledge of policies and procedures that apply to their specific duties. Ideally, all personnel will carry out their tasks in accordance with their job description and applicable policies and procedures.

A mission is a statement or description of an organization's common purpose; continuing purpose for existing responsibility to its clients or constituents; and, at least by implication, its ideology, values, and operating principles. Walton (1986) reviews Ford Motor Company's adoption of its "Total Quality Management" philosophy. The process, which began with a reexamination of the organization's goals that evolved into a mission statement, took three years to complete. The mission statement emphasized the need to continually improve products to meet customers' needs. Only through meeting these needs, it was reasoned, could the company prosper. The mission statement was followed by a statement of organizational values proclaiming that people are the source of the company's strength, that the company would ultimately be judged by the quality of its products, and that profits would be the ultimate measure of how efficiently customers were provided with quality products. Ford's statement was strengthened by a set of guiding principles paraphrased as follows (see Walton, 1986:136):

Quality comes first.

Customers are the focus of everything we do.

Continuous improvement is essential to everything we do.

Employment/involvement is our way of life.

Dealers and suppliers are our partners.

Integrity is never compromised.

Criminal justice agencies typically have written mission statements. A state department of corrections mission, for example, might read:

> The mission of the Department is to incarcerate convicted felons safely; to keep inmates secure, safe from physical and psychological harm or deterioration; and to provide inmates with opportunities for a successful crime-free reentry into society while providing a safe, secure, and stress-free work environment for staff.

Ideally, the mission can provide organizational members and constituents a clear understanding of an agency's purpose, goals, and objectives. The mission for the hypothetical corrections agency just given, for example, suggests a number of agency goals, including positive treatment and relationships of staff and inmates. In addition, the mission can direct or mold the activities of organizational members according to the organization's stated preference for specific guiding principles or values. Moreover, an agency's mission statement can serve as an anchor, or direction, for all organizational activities and can keep an organization from drifting away from its original purpose. Keep in mind, however, that formal statements of organizational mission, values, and guiding principles can be written only to gather dust. Successfully implementing an organizational philosophy throughout an agency means that policies, procedures, practices, and routines supported by individual values, beliefs, and behaviors based upon the organization's mission statement must permeate the organization.

Not all organizations have written or clearly articulated missions, but all organizations have a mission. This paradox can be understood by considering the creation of an agency's mission. Private groups that form may charter their own mission by consensus of the members. For example, a group may come together with the purpose of housing street people, feeding the community's poor, or forming planned activities for local teenagers. Private enterprises may organize to earn a profit, but their mission will be to provide goods or services to consumers efficiently and effectively. In other words, the mission is based upon providing a needed service or commodity. Therefore, the core of the mission—the organization's purpose—is found in meeting the needs of groups or individuals usually external to the organization (a number of organizations, such as college fraternities or sororities, exist to meet their needs exclusively). Political scientists posit that governmental agencies, and government itself, evolve to meet social needs that presumably cannot be met effectively by the private sector (Schattschnieder, 1969). In the *ideal* state, then, the purpose or mission of a public bureaucracy or a criminal justice agency is determined by the services required by society.

The mission of public bureaucracies emanate, in part, from legislation that mandates their existence and general purpose. Moreover, much of a criminal justice agency's ideology and value structure is imposed upon it by external environmental forces. Constituents served want agencies to manifest a preferred ethos or to hold a particular ideology as well as to more narrowly define their purpose. Decisions rendered by both state and federal courts have also constrained and directed criminal justice agency missions, hence the statement in our example of a local jail's mission—protect the constitutional rights of inmates." A key role of top administrators in public agencies is to render the general or broad mandates their agencies have received from legislation and pressures from other external sources into more narrow operational mission statements for their agencies.

Agencies, especially large bureaucracies, are not, however, helpless in the face of demands placed upon them. Rourke (1976) argues that agencies have a great deal of power with legislators and the legislative process. In effect, bureaucracies have sufficient power to influence legislation and direct their legislative mandates. Agencies are also becoming more proficient in civil litigation and protecting themselves from judicial intervention. For example, the Los Angeles County Jail System successfully litigated in the U.S. Supreme Court to overturn a federal district court order to reinstate contact visitation for inmates (see *Block v. Rutherford,* 104 S.Ct. 3227, 1984). The court ruled that implementing contact visitations was a penological, not a constitutional, matter. A general concern of public administration theorists is the reluctance or inability of public bureaucracies to be responsive to the public (Denhardt, 1984). In other words, in a less than ideal world agencies may establish their missions with limited sensitivity to public needs or demands.

Most members of an organization have a view or understanding of their organization's purpose and values. However, members' understanding may not necessarily be congruent with their agency's mission statement. This is true for a number of reasons, most of which will unfold throughout this text. The pivotal point here is that the collective values, attitudes, expectations, and behaviors of an organization's members—the true culture of an organization—also impact the organization's mission. The culture may impact directly and formally on the mission and be reflected in the written presentation of the mission. Or, as suggested earlier, the culture may create a *de facto* mission that may differ substantially from the *de jure,* or official, mission of the organization. As a result, the purpose, structure, and activities of the organization may differ from those officially prescribed or planned.

The extent to which the actual organizational purpose, structure, and activities differ from official purpose, structure, and activities is a function of several factors. Most significant to this chapter is the ability of the organization to promulgate and implement policies and procedures that are congruent with its official mission.

Policies and Procedures in Organizations

The link between an organization's stated mission and the activities of its members lies in the promulgation and implementation of policies and procedures. Organizations tend to specialize tasks and create a number of subunits. Each unit of activity is directed by policies and procedures. A policy is a clear statement that defines what action is to be taken and why. A well-written policy provides a statement of purpose, action, and a rationale for the purpose. Here is an example of a policy about inmate visitation in a typical jail:

INMATE VISITATION POLICY

The Pine Mountain County Jail will provide inmates with every reasonable opportunity to visit with family members, lawyers, social workers, clergy, and other pertinent professionals. Visitation will be limited by safety and security needs and court schedules. Inmates will not be denied visitation with legal counsel except in extreme circumstances.

RATIONALE

Visitation supports inmate morale and may alleviate much of the stress involved in being separated from families. Also, most of the inmates will be released back into the community. Visitation and contact with families and professionals will help prepare them for their release. Inmates with good morale and low stress will be more manageable and more likely to conform to inmate rules and regulations and behave in a civil manner while incarcerated. It is especially important to provide inmates who conform to jail rules ample opportunity for family visits at the jail.

Table 2-1 shows the number of components of a jail system that must be directed by policies.

Procedures are step-by-step descriptions of the activities agency members need to follow to achieve the objective or goal put forward by policy. Agency policies should be directed by an agency's mission and procedures directed by its policies. Policies also direct and define authority as well as subdivide the agency's work into specialized areas from which specialized tasks can be derived. The following is an example of procedures directing activities to carry out the preceding policy example:

INMATE VISITATION PROCEDURES

1. Family visitation hours are Monday through Friday 8:00 A.M. to 8:00 P.M., and Saturday and Sunday 9:00 A.M. to 7:00 P.M. Inmates will have three visits per week for 20 minutes.

2. Visitation with legal counsel, probation and parole officers, registered clergy, social service workers, and medical personnel is authorized 24 hours a day, unless extreme security and safety problems will occur concurrent with the visit (see Policy and Procedures #176-5 on managing violent inmates). The time of the visit will be determined by the visiting agent but will be reasonable in length.

3. Minimum security inmates only may have contact visits. Inmates will be pat-searched before and after contact visits. Inmates may be strip-searched after contact visit if the supervising officer has reason to believe the inmate may be attempting to smuggle contraband into the jail (see Policy and Procedures #282-7 on inmate searches).

4. Inmates with a history of violence or hostility between them, such as members of opposing gangs, may not be in the visitation area at the same time.

This list of procedures can be expanded to cover every aspect of visitation, including rotation of inmates to visits, rights of officers to deny visits, and reasons to remove visitors or otherwise conclude visits.

TABLE 2-1

Jail Operations

1. Physical Conditions—plumbing, lighting, bedding, and so on
2. Visitation—friends, relatives, attorneys, and so on
3. Correspondence—in and out flow; letters, packages, and so on
4. Telephone Calls
5. Exercise
6. Law Library
7. Street Clothes for Court Appearance
8. Religious Services—church and individual
9. Disciplinary Proceedings
10. Use of Incorrigible Cells
11. Inmate Guide—rules of behavior, lockup policies, and so on
12. Classification Procedures
13. Intake Screening
14. Special Problems
    a. handicapped
    b. suicide threats/risks
    c. medically ill—epileptic, diabetic, and so on
    d. mentally ill/mentally impaired
    e. alcohol/drug problem
15. Medical Care—dispensing medication, doctor/dental care, and so on
16. Use of Force—both deadly and nondeadly
17. Application of Leg and Hand Irons
18. Feeding—times, quantities, diet, special diets, and so on
19. Showers/Cleanliness—personal and area
20. Detoxification Cell and Practices
21. Jail/Lockup Personnel Standards—numbers, where essential, and so on
22. Pre-employment Issues—records/background checks, criteria for employment, EEO issues, and so on
23. Preservice Training
24. In-service Training
25. Employee Evaluation
26. Employee Disciplinary Matters

We can see how procedures become operational rules and regulations and further organize task specialization. The more specialized and formalized an organization becomes, the more written procedures will be promulgated to direct the activities of its personnel. In the ideal bureaucracy, the actual practices of an agency's members— the routinized activities of the agency staff—will conform to agency policy and procedures. In the ideal bureaucracy, all staff will achieve a comprehensive understanding of policies and procedures through some form of training or education. Also, the chain of command theoretically provides levels of management and supervision to direct the activities of subordinates toward conformity with agency rules and regulations. Training, education, and supervision in the ideal organization also serve to socialize staff to conform to the official or approved organizational culture (see Chapter 9 on occupational socialization).

A common state of affairs among organizations, however, is that mission, policies, and procedures evolve and accumulate in an unsystematic manner. New policies are created to deal with problems as they arise, and old policies and procedures are rarely reviewed, changed, or eliminated. Under these conditions, a legitimate or useful set of written policies and procedures may not exist. Moreover, policy and procedure manuals may gather dust, and the activities of agency members are based instead upon how "it's always been done"—or on well-established organizational routines. Dominant values and guiding principles of agency members will be based upon unwritten but well-known organizational traditions as well as the values and beliefs imported by individual staff.

Another consideration is the scope and detailed nature of policies and procedures. This consideration is a function of the overall structure of an organization as well as its management philosophy. As discussed, agencies may form as bureaucracies or as professional or open systems. Large criminal justice agencies such as big city police departments, county sheriff systems in large counties, and state and federal correctional and law enforcement agencies tend to take on bureaucratic structures. These agencies develop comprehensive and detailed policy and procedure manuals and provide intensive training to increase the likelihood that staff activities will conform to desired agency rules and regulations.

For criminal justice agencies in general, written policies and procedures and the expectation of staff conformity to them have taken on added significance in the last two decades. Civil suits against criminal justice agencies, especially corrections and law enforcement agencies, have become a rather common occurrence. Individuals who believe they have been harmed as a result of being involved with criminal justice agencies as suspects, offenders, inmates, victims of crime, or employees readily sue agencies to redress their perceived damages. Civil litigation almost always begins with a review of agency written policies and procedures. The first test is whether agency policies and procedures conform to applicable statutory and administrative law and general constitutional requirements. The second test asks if policies and procedures prescribe "sound" practice for the staff based upon current standards for the field. Given the first two tests, the third general test asks to what extent staff is conforming to prescribed policies and procedures. Also, to the extent staff does not follow policies and procedures, it asks to what extent failure to follow policies and procedures is a function of faulty training and/or supervision. Other questions and issues impact civil suits. The significant point here is the importance for criminal justice agencies of developing a mission statement as well as policies and procedures in a deliberate, planned manner. Moreover, agencies need to be reasonably certain that official policies and procedures will usually be followed by staff, especially in high-risk activities.

Informal Structures in Organizations

So far we have discussed the formal or official side of organizations—that is, the purpose, structure, and activities of an organization desired by top management and as it usually appears on paper. An informal side also develops in almost all organizations. By *informal structure,* we are referring to goals, activities, or structures that are not officially acknowledged. An organization's informal structure differs to a greater or lesser extent from its formal structure depending upon the ability of top administrators to control the behaviors of staff and/or the extent to which staff buys into the organization's mission, policies and procedures, and desired culture, if one is articulated. As a complicating factor, the informal structure is also a product or manifestation of an organization's actual culture. We will describe here a number of informal organizational phenomena.

Almost all agencies have a formal communications system. In hierarchical systems, official communications flow upward and downward through the chain of command (blame, of course, always flows downward). Communicating through the chain of command, however, can be inefficient and ineffective, as we will see in Chapter 4. Also, the original source of messages is readily identifiable. As a result, every organization has a robust and often intractable communication network often referred to as the rumor mill or grapevine. Information, usually not verified but often credible, moves with speed vertically, laterally, and across working units. It can easily be argued that subjective evaluation of the performance or worth of a criminal justice practitioner begins and ends with information distributed through the informal communications network.

Almost all organizations develop informal work groups in which individuals work as loosely knit teams on an *ad hoc* or ongoing basis. The work groups may be comprised of members of different components of an agency and different levels of its hierarchy. Informal work groups may be productive if they are working toward organizational goals and following sanctioned organizational means. Informal groups can also be considered productive even in the case where groups circumvent the organization's sanctioned means while pursuing organizational goals. Van Zelst (1952) and Long (1984) point out that productivity can increase with the development of informal work groups. Court systems function based upon informal work groups rather than formally structured work systems (Neubauer, 1983). Informal work groups, however, can become completely aberrant and utilize the legitimacy and resources of the organization to pursue group goals and ignore legitimate means. An extreme example of this phenomenon is displayed in the well-known book and movie *Serpico*, describing a group of New York City police officers who became corrupt, pocketing money from the drug trade for themselves and only minimally pursuing organizational goals.

Informal leadership also emerges in organizations. Informal leaders are organizational members who do not have formal authority vested in them by rank or supervisory status but who have developed sufficient power to routinely influence other members. Informal leaders are typically individuals who are perceived as having a great deal of knowledge and expertise about the organization and its business and typically have above-average communication skills (see Chapter 7 on leadership and Chapter 10 on power). Moreover, as informal work groups form, informal leaders evolve to provide groups with direction and structure. Even among prisoners, a group subjected to intense formal structure and discipline, informal groups and leaders emerge to meet their particular needs. Research on prisons has described the emergence of informal leaders among prisoners who contribute to the order maintenance goal of correctional institutions (see Stojkovic & Lovell, 1997).

The emergence and perpetuation of informal structures within organizations are explained to a great extent by the process of socialization within organizations.

Individuals are socialized into the culture of an organization by formal, or sanctioned, and informal means (see Chapter 9 on occupational socialization). The development of a culture within an organization dictates to a great extent the values, attitudes, and behaviors of its members. Through the mechanisms of recruiting, training, and supervision provided by their formal structure, organizations attempt to impose a set of attitudes, values, and behaviors on their members. However, a degree of leakage of power exists in most organizations, especially large systems. As a result, the culture of an organization is based to some degree on the values and preferences of its members. Hence, the organization's formal structure provides the framework for the emergence and establishment of its informal structure.

Organizational Frames

Bolman and Deal (1997) state that organizations are composed of a structural frame, a human resource frame, a political frame, and a symbolic frame. Conceptualizing organizations with four frames allows analysis to become more discrete than does considering only formal and informal structures. Each frame describes significant attributes of organizations and encompasses considerations that apply to both formal and informal structures of organizations. The authors suggest that understanding the four frames provides paths to understanding and locating root sources of organizational problems, guides planners and change agents, and is significant to management and leadership. The substantive issues and concepts that fall within each frame are discussed throughout this book. The structural frame has been discussed throughout this chapter and will not be discussed further here.

The *human resource frame*, "based on the ideas of organizational psychologists, starts with the fundamental premise that organizations are inhabited by individuals who have needs, feelings and prejudices. . . . From a human resource perspective, the key to effectiveness is to tailor organizations to people" (Bolman & Deal, 1997:14). Most theories of motivation are based within this frame. Organizations typically develop programs and awards to meet their members' need for recognition. Promotions based upon merit are a prime example. Also, police or corrections "officer of the month" awards are common tools for providing recognition. Criminal justice bureaucracies that are paramilitary in structure are often criticized for lacking the ability to motivate staff and for suppressing motivation by overmanagement or practicing excessively authoritarian supervision. Recognition for successful work is often lacking, and routinized feedback to staff from the hierarchy takes place through formal evaluation procedures that often become hurdles rather than sources of legitimate recognition.

Correctional and law enforcement agencies typically screen applicants to weed out individuals who will not fit into the organization. Rigorous preservice training programs are also required that serve to screen out individuals who presumably will not be able to cope with the problems prevalent in the work. The concept of *job design* considers changing the fit between jobs and people. Also, restructuring tasks allows staff to fulfill their need for challenges and responsibility. Restructuring a police agency from the traditional to community policing mode drastically alters the role of officers. Problems may occur when traditionally oriented police who have accommodated their needs within the old mode are asked to take on different roles, responsibilities, and activities.

Human resource issues also focus on the interpersonal dynamics that underpin staff relations, formation of cliques, networks, and subcultures. Concern for interpersonal relations always comes to light in the informal socialization process of criminal justice practitioners. Training and supervision are often weak attempts by the formal structure to socialize its members with its values. The inability of organizations to impact the interpersonal relations of its staff, however, allows staff to create their subcultures. This has been a particular problem with rapid recruitment of minorities and women into the male-dominated criminal justice work world. Criminal justice agencies are almost always at a loss in dealing with the interpersonal relations between traditional staff and newly recruited personnel from different races and genders. Administrators typically fall back on tools available to them in the formal structure and promulgate rule and policies against gender and ethnic harassment. Rather than relying on a human resource approach to deal with this crucial issue, administrators typically fall back on formal structure tools and promulgate rules that ban profane language and sexually oriented humor. This approach shows their inability to form partnerships with the informal structure to deal with problems. Police agencies that want to improve relationships with citizens or enter into community policing must consider the added dimension of increasing the frequency and quality of interpersonal relationships with the general public.

The *political frame* "views organizations as arenas in which different interest groups compete for scarce resources. . . . Problems arise because power is concentrated in the wrong places or because it is so badly dispersed that nothing gets done" (Bolman & Deal, 1997 : 14). Politics here consists of the application of influence and power, and it abounds in both the formal and informal structures of agencies. A clear example of the redistribution of power is the growing membership in corrections and law enforcement officer unions. The power of these groups is used primarily to extract material benefits from their employers. Unions are also concerned with working conditions and often impact policy decisions to meet that goal. They may go outside the organization, directly to the public and to political bodies to obtain legislation favorable to their membership or to impact funding or its allocation within the agency. Internally, groups and cliques form on a semipermanent or temporary basis and can influence the outcomes of programs or policies. Informal leaders with no formal authority but with political clout commonly emerge among the rank and file of criminal justice agencies. A number of studies examine the process by which corrections officers gain political power in their institutions (Jacobs, 1977; Johnson, 2002; Welch, 1996). Law enforcement officers have reportedly resisted organizational change, and successful change has depended upon the organization's leaders' ability to directly influence the informal structure and garner sufficient power to affect the planned changes (Skolnick & Bayley, 1986). Inmates take on political power within institutions by virtue of the cliques, gangs, and social systems they form, and often corrections officers must utilize the power of the inmates to manage their institutions (Kalinich & Stojkovic, 1985). Administrators who rely solely on the tools of the formal structure to control political power will ultimately be rendered ineffective. During the bombardment of civil and constitutional rights for inmates, for example, corrections officers passively resisted the change and retreated to the walls of the institutions.

The *symbolic frame* "treats organizations as tribes, theater, or carnivals. . . . Organizations are cultures that are propelled more by rituals, ceremonies, stories, heroes and myths than by rules or managerial authority. . . . Problems arise when actors play out their parts badly, when symbols lose their meaning and rituals lose their potency" (Bolman & Deal, 1997:14). One could argue that the criminal justice system is designed to put on major dramatic performances for the public. Uniforms and artifacts of authority are worn by judges, police, and corrections officers to display the role and power of the actors in the criminal justice theater. This display of righteous authority and power is intended to frighten thieves and cutthroats and reassure the citizenry that they are safe from the criminal element, protected by the system's players. The notion of deterrence requires a rather dramatic announcement of the punishment received by the wrongdoers. Manning (1997) suggests that drama touches every aspect of police work and the public theater serves to give a picture of an ordered and controlled system, while the back stage drama serves to protect the clandestine nature of police work. Crank and Langworthy (1992) and Kalinich, Lorinskas, and Banas (1985) further argue that myth and symbols are instinctively invoked by criminal justice organizations to protect their agencies' boundaries from instrusion by powerful constituents. The drama paradigm would suggest capital punishment may be favored by those that require a high level of drama be evoked by the system. Race and gender stereotyping along with scathing labeling of offenders may serve to keep everyone working from the same theatrical script or, from an organizational paradigm, providing role/task clarification.

The number and popularity of cops-and-robbers television programs is indicative of the drama expected from the criminal justice work world. This drama is also often represented by folklore, war stories that represent the players' beliefs either about their tasks/roles or the roles in which they would like to be cast. The "war" on crime and on drugs is an example of evoking symbols that cast the tasks/roles of actors as dramatic, heroic, dangerous, and important. The extent to which the public gives law enforcement officers greater status than corrections officers may lie in the visibility of police drama. Prison drama, in contrast, is hidden behind prison walls though the prison walls alone may evoke a symbol sufficient to appease the audience.

Danger and terror are distinct possibilities for criminal justice players, but a great deal of their drama consists of mundane and often boring activities, for which exciting folklore and drama cannot be easily produced. And the actors often resent being reminded of the mundane and boring aspects of their work for fear their heroic image will become tarnished. The vision of correctional reformers for a system focusing on treatment and reintegration of criminal offenders was destroyed in the early 1970s, when rehabilitation as a symbolic statement representing the role of correctional institutions lost its effectiveness. Ironically, both political liberals and conservatives opposed rehabilitation because the symbol and its accompanying rhetoric dramatized a profoundly disparate set of evils for each group (Travis, Latessa, & Vito, 1985).

The formal structure builds the stage and organizes the theater. Managers may see that the scripts are played out correctly in the informal structure. Leaders attempt to alter the script. But the question remains: Who writes the script?

Summary

The discussion of informal structures and organizational culture impinges on theories of organizational behavior. A vast body of literature studies and theorizes about organizations from a behavioral perspective—that is, how organizations actually work as contrasted with how they are supposed to work. This chapter reviewed elements of the formal structure of organizations and touched briefly on the emergence of informal structures. As Barnard (1938) points out, the formal and informal states of organizations exist simultaneously as a natural state; the informal structure is the oil that keeps the organizational machine running smoothly. Barnard suggests that the administrator's role is to form a working partnership between the formal and informal structures of an agency, a wise piece of advice to administrators that is often lost. Downs (1967), for example, describes a cycle common to bureaucracies in which administrators, fearing erosion of control, add mechanisms and resources to the agency in order to strengthen control. Agency members soon find ways and means to circumvent the new set of control mechanisms; and administrators respond with more control efforts, using more agency resources. This practice is antithetical to the principle of forming a partnership between the informal and formal structures of an organization.

Criminal justice agencies typically work diligently at controlling the informal structure of their organizations through formal socialization of members and enforcement of official policies and procedures. Beyond such common and accepted approaches, special offices to investigate critical deviations from mandated practices are often created. An internal investigation bureau per se is appropriate for this purpose. If the zeal of administrators to impose control is strong, however, a breach between the formal and informal sides of an organization will likely be created and will be manifested in passive behavior from personnel, who will delegate minor problems and situations upward. Moreover, an informal "code of silence" among line personnel will be invoked within the informal organizational structure.

Historically, management and leadership literature has, by implication, addressed Barnard's administrative prescription to build a partnership between the formal and informal structures of organizations. Simply stated, all approaches that posit the participation of personnel in decision making are means to a working partnership between the two structures of an organization. The importance of participative management and leadership is discussed throughout this text; meaningful participation is the essence of motivation. Forming this partnership by involving subordinates in decision making at every level softens the notion of subordination of personnel and stimulates their sense of ownership and empowerment.

Case Study

Decentralizing Decision Making in a Correctional System

Because its jail population had been steadily increasing and had reached a population of almost 2,000 inmates, Pine Mountain County was in the process of building a new jail. The old jail had been annexed twice and held a rated population of 900 inmates, and a decision was made to build a "new generation" jail.

Bonnie Smith, slated to be the jail administrator, had worked in corrections for more than fifteen years as a social worker and social work supervisor. Her intense work and dedication in planning the new jail as well as her corrections background earned her the appointment, although many suspected gender was the key determinant. The old jail had been run along traditional bureaucratic lines in which everyone was used to a chain of command, taking orders and avoiding responsibility. For Bonnie, who believed in the New Generation jail philosophy—which gave corrections officers both the responsibility and the authority for managing the inmates in their units—change presented a number of exciting obstacles. Her enthusiasm was fueled by the challenges ahead. With a fairly clear notion of the reactions staff would have toward the new management philosophy, she was prepared.

Bonnie called a staff meeting of key personnel, including command staff, union representatives, medical staff, and social service personnel, in which she presented the mission of the new jail and the management philosophy. The overriding mission of the jail, she explained, would be to ensure that inmates were not harmed physically, medically, or psychologically as a result of their jail experience. The medical and social service staff nodded in agreement, whereas the corrections staff exhibited strained facial responses. To carry out the mission, Bonnie added, inmates would have to be controlled; to do so, the corrections officer would be considered the cornerstone of the operation. At this, the corrections staff looked surprised and the professional staff bemused. "The CO," she explained, "will be given the tools and discretion to run his or her unit." A lieutenant from the command staff replied: "These officers must follow policies and procedures. They can't have any discretion. We tell them how to handle inmates."

"Not any more," Bonnie said. "COs are going to be fully trained, and so will everyone else in this jail. Shift sergeants and other command staff will act as coaches, advisors, and communicators. They'll back up the COs' decisions as long as those decisions are legitimate."

A sergeant asked: "You mean COs are going to be able to decide when inmates will be punished?"

"Yes, within limits, and also when they will be rewarded. As long as they stay within their limits, no one will countermand their decisions." Looking at the social service staff, she added: "If an officer locks down an inmate for a day or takes away visitation or phone privileges, you folks will not interfere in that decision."

Up to now, the social service staff had always had almost complete prerogative in dealing with inmates. An experienced social worker who was also a friend of Bonnie's asked: "But, if in my opinion, a change of the inmate's status is important to his or her treatment, I will be allowed to change the CO's decision, correct?"

Bonnie was prepared for his question. "In a word, John—no. You can discuss the case with the officer and with his or her sergeant. But the general rule is that the CO will have the final say."

"What about a medical problem?" a nurse asked.

"You will have authority in emergencies," Bonnie explained. "But the fact is, COs are on the front line, and they will be the ones to spot emergencies, both medical and psychological. They will be summoning both the medical and social service staff for support. Let me say it again: The CO is the cornerstone of the jail. Everything we do is intended to support and serve the CO staff. We work for them."

"That's nuts!" cried a shift lieutenant. "These bozos don't know a medical problem from their you know what. If we didn't stay on top of them, this jail would be in a shambles."

Bonnie was prepared for this bit of enthusiastic criticism. "If you look at the assaults, attempted escapes, suicides, and documented rapes over the years, if you listen to the noise level, look at the broken-down and filthy condition of this jail, I would say this jail is a shambles. COs follow procedures, but inmates do whatever they want. That's coming to an end. We are going to run this jail, not the inmates. And it will be done by giving the COs professional status. They will be given the tools, training, discretion, and support from all of us to do their job."

A seasoned sergeant, grinning, verified Bonnie's description of the jail. "You're right about the jail, Bonnie. I don't know if your system will work. But all we do is keep inmates from escaping. They do whatever else they want to. The only COs that do have some control routinely violate jail policies. And by the way, the rest of the COs couldn't tell a jail policy from their you know what."

The union representative applauded. "God bless you, Bonnie. I hope you can pull it off. If you provide training and status to the COs, you'll have my support."

Ellen from the social work staff joined the dissenters. "And you have just degraded my status and the status of all of the social service staff. We supported you for this appointment. That was a big mistake. We all have degrees, and most of us have master's degrees in social work. Now you're telling us the COs will have more to say about inmates than we will. This is an outrage. I'm sending my résumé out tomorrow."

"Good luck," Bonnie thought to herself. The fun was just beginning.

Case Study Questions

1. To what extent is Bonnie forming a partnership between the new formal structure and the informal structure that will emerge? Explain.

2. Eventually, a great deal of participation in decisions will exist at every level of the organization. Is Bonnie being participative at the meeting? Why do you think she took the posture we have described?

3. Will the new jail have an extensive, moderate, or loose formal structure? Explain.

For Discussion

1. Discuss the strengths and weaknesses of an organization structured with a tall hierarchy. Discuss the strengths and weaknesses of a flat chain of command. Can a large police agency move from a tall to flat hierarchy without losing command control? Discuss.

2. What steps should an administrator take to build a partnership between an agency's formal and informal structures? How can this be accomplished without legitimizing informal cliques that are corrupt or counterproductive?

For Further Reading

Baron, A., & Greenberg, J. *Behavior in Organizations: Understanding and Managing the Human Side of Work*. Boston: Allyn and Bacon, 1990.

Crank, J. and R. Langworthy, "An Institutional Perspective of Policing." *Journal of Criminal Law and Criminal Justice*, 1992, 83:338–363.

Denhardt, R. B. *Theories of Public Organizations*. Belmont, CA: Wadsworth, 1984.

Gains, L., Southerland, M., & Angell, J. *Police Administration*. New York: McGraw-Hill, 1991.

Houston, J. *Correctional Management: Functions, Skills, and Systems*. 2nd ed. Chicago: Nelson-Hall, 1999.

Jacobs, J. B. *Stateville: The Penitentiary in Mass Society*. Chicago: University of Chicago Press, 1977.

Johnson, R. *Hard Time: Understanding and Reforming the Prison*. 3rd ed. Belmont, CA: Wadsworth, 2002.

Manning, P. *Police Work, The Social Organization of Policing*. Chicago: Waveland, 1997.

Schmalleger, F., *Criminal Justice Today*. New Jersey: Prentice Hall, 1999.

U.S. Department of Justice, "The Jails Hold Record 490,442 Inmates." *Press Release*, May 1, 1995.

Welch, M. *Corrections: A Critical Approach*. New York: McGraw-Hill, 1996.

CHAPTER

3

THE CRIMINAL
JUSTICE SYSTEM
IN ITS ENVIRONMENT

Defining the Environment of the Criminal Justice System

The Political Environment

Task Environment Elements Specific to the Criminal Justice System

Environmental States

Organizational Response to the Environment

Managing Environmental Forces

Implications for Administrators

Summary

Case Study: Time to Dig Out

For Discussion

For Further Reading

The theoretical and philosophical treatises and the structural analysis which advocate a monolithic criminal justice system seem to have conveniently ignored the sociopolitical environment in which the system exists. Such an oversight may by helpful in gaining public attention to one's ideas but is most unfortunate from a practical and pragmatic standpoint. The essence of a system as complex as criminal justice simply cannot be understood from the perspective which considers it an isolated system. Nor can any proposal for significant planned change of the system claim any validity without considering the effects and constraints of the environment on that system.

(Wright, 1981)

Our Korean colleague turned to several of his fellows and proceeded to summarize a year of education with consummate oriental terseness. He said, "Crime affects criminal justice; criminal justice does not affect crime."

(Duffee, 1980)

In the early 1980s four corrections officers who were undergraduate students at the time offered, based upon the observations of firsthand experience, their outlook for corrections. Over coffee conversation, they predicted that in the next decade imprisonment rates would soar, followed by problems of overcrowding, then by a prison-building binge. They also offered that the size, number, and sophistication of youth gangs from the inner city areas would increase and the number of mentally ill inmates would increase at rates greater than the general inmate population, and facilities would be constructed or dedicated to managing mentally ill inmates. They all saw a huge investment for medical treatment of inmates in the future and suggested that the AIDS virus would become rather common among prisoners and a psychological problem for both inmates and staff. It was obvious to the officers that the rapid expansion of prisons would result in a large group of relatively young inexperienced officers and administrators. They all predicted the corrections system would respond to the problems they predicted only after their impacts became so blatant that politicians and policy makers would be forced to take action.

However heuristic, these predictions were extremely accurate. The uncanny ability of these young professionals to see the future came from their intuitive ability to "scan the environment." In other words, they understood that environmental forces and conditions external to the department of corrections had a powerful impact on its course. They also had the insight (or external sight) to understand how environmental conditions, events, forces, and circumstances would alter their department's purpose, structure, and activities. From their observations, they understood the criminal justice system is an open system and ultimately governed by environmental forces (Perrow, 1986).

In this chapter we discuss the interdependence of the criminal justice system and its environment. Our focus is on the constraints environmental forces place on the system. As we will see, these forces affect the mission of the system and its individual agencies as well as its objectives, policies, procedures, and day-to-day practices.

In addition, we discuss how environmental forces allocate resources and personnel to the criminal justice system. Finally, we argue that environmental forces can be stable or complex and unpredictable; they often push the criminal justice system in contradictory directions. Environmental forces, however, will be the final determinants of the effectiveness and efficiency of that system. In short, we describe here how environmental forces impose conflicting demands on members of criminal justice agencies and how those agencies attempt to survive in this complex environment.

Defining the Environment of the Criminal Justice System

In a loose sense, we may define an organization's environment as any external phenomenon, event, group, individual, or system. This sweeping definition can be broken down into finite dimensions to make the concept of the interdependence of an organization and its environment understandable. The environment of an advanced society is at least composed of technological, legal, political, economic, demographic, ecological, and cultural forces (Hall, 1982). Each of these plays a role in creating, maintaining, changing, or purging organizations. As environmental conditions change, demands for goods and services, legal and resource limitations, and support for and opposition to the programs of both public and private organizations may also change. To adapt to new demands, constraints, and pressures, new bureaus or businesses may be created, and existing agencies alter their missions or policies. Agencies, public or private, that fail to meet changing demands, expectations, or constraints may suffer severe loss of resources or public support before they catch on. Those agencies that fail to catch on may become extinct.

It is easy to understand how technological changes affect our lives as well as our organizations. Our ability to mass produce electricity has improved our lives in general and made organizations increasingly productive. Yet the blessing has cursed us with acid rain and other pollution that may damage us severely in the not-too-distant future. To deal with the negative effects of pollution, the government, through new or existing agencies, has attempted to regulate the utility companies in response to public demands (political forces) for clean air and a safe environment. Every similar effort by government to regulate organizations or individuals will, in some manner, necessitate the use of agencies of the criminal justice system. We discuss here each of the environmental forces and, through the use of examples, examine the effect of each on the criminal justice system. Figure 3-1 displays the environmental conditions as forces that affect the criminal justice system.

Technology

Technology has had many direct and indirect effects on the criminal justice system. The introduction of the automobile into our society is an excellent example. The automobile allowed police agencies to increase the efficiency of patrols. Yet autos became a major social control problem for the criminal justice system to deal with. The automobile expanded the range of operations for thieves. The high price of autos and auto parts make them valuable items to steal and resell to "chop shops" and other outlets.

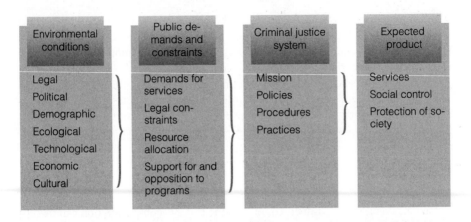

FIGURE 3-1   How Environmental Conditions Affect the Criminal Justice System

Automobiles also create a public safety problem. For example, in 1995 approximately 45,000 people died in highway accidents and other traffic-related incidents. Currently, great efforts and resource expenditures are allocated to prevent motorists from driving under the influence of alcohol.

In a reverse example, the current resurrection of neighborhood policing has eliminated the use of police cars for patrol. Patrol is done on foot or with mountain bikes, a recent technological change. The communications revolution allows instant communication of information. For example, the Law Enforcement Information System (LEIN) allows officers to obtain information on suspects and warrants from computers; video cameras are often mounted on the dashboards of patrol cars to record arrests. However, the infamous Rodney King beating at the hands of the Los Angeles police was taped by a citizen and received widespread television coverage that likely contributed to subsequent civil protests and riots. Most of the nation had the opportunity to watch Judge Lance Ito in the O. J. Simpson trial obtain case law on his laptop computer. Theoretically, this instant access to information should have sped up the proceedings, but it may also hold judges to higher standards, cause them to suffer an information overload, and serve to slow the process down or create confusion. Computer technology also impacts the corrections system with the development of electronic tethers that can be strapped to offenders to bolster probation surveillance. Higher-risk offenders who would ordinarily be incarcerated can now be safely monitored under community supervision programs. Theoretically, this use of electronic monitoring can reduce prison and jail populations and increase the use of community corrections. Concurrently, agencies must create technology-based systems and train practitioners to utilize the innovations.

However, the computer information age has created an opportunity for an array of innovative high-tech crimes. Grau (1999), for example, describes the ability of "computer hackers" to destroy linked systems out of malice and to penetrate online banking, finance, and investment systems to steal money without guns. He also provides some description of incription systems that can be useful in protecting legitimate computerized networks and communication systems. Yet incription systems can also be utilized by sophisticated criminals to protect their communication systems from intrusion by law enforcement agencies. New laws, policies, procedures, and practices must be created to deal with computer-based theft from electronic banking systems. Criminal investigators must have expertise in tracking crimes created on the World Wide Web or Internet. Police patrol patterns now must consider protecting bank customers who use automated banking machines. The extensive list of technological changes that will impact the system could be extended here. But the point is clear: technology impacts the inner workings of the criminal justice system and changes the demands it must face.

Law

Legislation and court decisions provide the basic rules and authority for the criminal justice system. The mandate for all public agencies lies in state and federal statutes. As discussed in Chapter 2, an agency's mission is directed by its legislated mandate. Criminal justice agencies are also bound by laws that direct their activities. Procedures for arrest, pretrial detention, bail bond, and adjudication procedures are often laid out, in part, by statute. In short, the criminal justice system is framed with legislation. The legal definition of crime is, of course, statutory. Criminal sentences and procedures for sentencing are directed by legislation. California recently created the "three strikes and you're out" legislation, which mandates a life sentence for conviction of a third felony within a category of crimes. Thought to prevent crime, "three strikes," will have a profound impact on jail and prison populations and create a growing number of geriatric prisoners needing extensive and expensive medical care. Offenders facing "three strikes" sentencing will have no incentive to plea-bargain for a reduced charge and will invariably seek jury trials. This pattern will create backlogs for criminal courts, increase workloads for the prosecutor's office, and impact the population capacity of local jails.

Case law—actual court cases that review activities of criminal justice practitioners—impacts powerfully on criminal justice agencies. Case law can be a review of criminal court cases by state and/or federal appellate or supreme courts; it can also emanate from civil litigation filed against criminal justice agencies. Typically, case law reviewing criminal cases stemming from the U.S. Supreme Court are the most salient and have national impact. For example, *Tennessee v. Garner* (1985) restricts the ability of a police officer to shoot a fleeing felon. *Furman v. Georgia* (1972) in effect ended capital punishment in the United States for over a decade. Civil litigation has also had a powerful impact on the criminal justice system. Successful litigation against agencies may impose monetary and/or injunctive relief against the agency (defendant) in favor of the individual or group bringing suit against the agency (plaintiff). Monetary relief provides the plaintiff with a sum of money, paid by the defendant agency, to rectify the harm done to the individual bringing the suit. Monetary relief can serve to compensate for the actual damages received by the plaintiff or punitive damages against the agency to punish the agency for its actions. Significant monetary awards against an agency typically cause the agency to change its practices. Injunctive relief is, in effect, a court order requiring the agency to make changes in its practices. Moreover, courts have often taken control of agencies through injunctive relief and appointed a court monitor who administers the agency *de facto* until the required changes have been met. Agencies also enter into a negotiated consent decree, an agreement with the court to make changes in the future, as a response to civil litigation.

Civil litigation can be filed with state or federal courts; state court litigation is based upon simple common law tort action. Typically, states provide criminal justice practitioners with immunity for simple negligence because it is expected they will make mistakes—acts of negligence—in their complex environment. Thus, a plaintiff would have to show that agency agents acted with gross negligence, wanton or deliberate indifference, or in a criminal manner that caused damages to the plaintiff.

Cases that most dramatically impact criminal justice agencies are federal cases filed under United States Code (U.S.C.) 1983, enacted in 1871. The essence of the act is to prevent governmental agencies from circumventing "under the color of law . . ." the constitutional rights of citizens: "Every person who, under the color of any statute, ordinance, regulation . . . subjects . . . any citizen of the United States or other persons under the jurisdiction thereof . . . shall be liable to the party injured." Suits filed under U.S.C. 1983 are referred to generically as federal civil rights suits and have implications for agencies in all states. The major body of law referred to as "corrections law" that provided limited constitutional rights to prisoners and dramatically changed the operations of corrections has its base in case law emanating from civil litigation (Baro, 1988), often based upon USC 1983, the Civil Rights Act of 1871.

The Civil Rights Act created by Congress in 1964 has also had an impact on the criminal justice system. The requirement of equal opportunity has changed the personnel composition of criminal justice agencies so that they include more minorities than they did before. Women are now police and corrections officers, positions that were traditionally male. Agencies have to recruit from minority groups to meet affirmative action guidelines; consideration has to be given to assimilating minorities into the predominantly white male system. Policies and procedures protecting minorities from racial and sexual harassment have to be developed within criminal justice agencies. In some prison systems, preservice training now includes courses for female corrections officers to help them cope with the unique problems they face in male prisons. Changes in the legal sector of the environment have thus created a new set of constraints to which the criminal justice system must adapt.

Case law also has had an impact on the court system itself. The evolution of suits in the criminal justice system has created a snowball effect; suits ranging from gender and race discrimination by employees and potential employees to tort and civil rights actions by inmates are now common and have dramatically increased the workload of the courts. In effect, case law has changed past practices and rules of the court to allow more access to address grievances.

Economic Conditions

Clearly, the resources available to public bureaucracies limit the numbers and scope of these organizations. In a highly productive society, a great many resources are available, but many organizations are required to produce and distribute goods and services and to regulate the production and distribution system. These organizations compete for resources, however plentiful. In our society, business cycles cause production and employment rates to fluctuate, and the resources allocated to public agencies fluctuate along with business cycles. Even though it derives its funds from government rather than the marketplace, the criminal justice system is affected by the business cycle because it competes with private and public organizations and with other regulatory agencies for existing resources. For example, during times of high unemployment, criminal justice agencies have a large labor pool to pick from and have the opportunity to be highly selective in recruiting personnel. During periods of prosperity, criminal justice agencies have little difficulty in obtaining resources but cannot be highly selective in personnel recruiting because members of the labor force have so many career choices.

Economic conditions may influence the criminal justice system in other ways. To the extent that unemployment rates affect crime rates and jail and prison populations, economic conditions affect the workload of criminal justice agencies. The research on unemployment rates and crime rates is conflicting (Thompson, Svirdoff, & McElroy, 1981). However, Belknap (1989) suggests that income inequality may be a better indicator of crime rate than poverty or unemployment. The differences in criminal participation among young black and white males may reflect, in part, differences in labor market conditions. Also, the increasing rate of incarceration of African Americans may be linked to labor market conditions (Meyers & Simms, 1989). Research also suggests that homicide rates may be linked to economic discrimination against social groups (Meisner, 1989) and that larceny and other property crimes may be the result of a society's growth in material wealth (Shichor, 1990). Moreover, the literature indicates that prison populations and sentencing rates increase as unemployment increases, and vice versa (Yeager, 1979). In spite of the lack of certainty in this area of research, it serves as a good example of how environmental conditions beyond the control of the criminal justice system can affect it. Workhouses were built in London during the fifteenth century to incarcerate large numbers of unemployed and vagrant citizens (Barnes & Teeters, 1959). In this historical instance, a corrections system was created in response to the economic conditions.

Demographic Factors

Factors such as the age, sex, race, ethnicity, and number of people in a community all have an impact on organizations. For example, the majority of criminal activity is carried out by individuals under the age of twenty-five (Reid, 1982). A community with a high proportion of individuals under the age of twenty-five will probably have a relatively high crime rate. Large cities tend to have higher per capita crime rates than smaller communities, and cities with more citizens of lower rather than higher economic status also have higher per capita crime rates (Sutherland & Cressey, 1978). A sudden influx or exodus of people creates a new set of demographic characteristics within the community that, in turn, can alter crime patterns. For example, an increase in the population of a state generally indicates that the state will soon be building additional prisons (Benton & Silberstein, 1983). The flight of the working-class and middle-class population to the suburbs has left inner cities with the poor and minorities, creating a new clientele for urban police departments. The flight to the suburbs has also significantly eroded the tax base for major cities (Grubb, 1982; Danziger & Weinstein, 1976; Frey, 1979) and has limited resources for their criminal justice systems at a time when they have to deal with a problematic population.

Migration and immigration patterns obviously impact demographics. Historically, industrial expansion in the cities created mass migration from rural farm communities as well as encouraging immigration from foreign nations (Faris, 1948). Groups of individuals from different cultures, often with limited skills but great will, converge in industrial cities seeking work. A dramatic increase in the population of a city will automatically increase its crime rate and press the system for additional services; and agencies will be required to deal with cultures that often differ profoundly from the dominant, established culture. The moral code conflict of merging cultures will itself manifest a variety of unfamiliar behaviors, some of which will be offensive and considered criminal by the dominant culture and, in effect, create more crime (Sellin, 1934).

Cultural Conditions

Culture can be defined briefly as the collective norms, values, symbols, behaviors, and expectations of a society's members. Ultimately, a society's political and economic system reflects its culture. Thus, laws are codified social norms. Moreover, the roles attributed to a society's organizations are based in its culture. In other words, the missions, constraints, images, symbols, and validity of organizations are rooted in a society's cultural makeup. Society's dictates are imposed on bureaucracies through its political–legal system, which is linked to its cultural and social fabric. This is especially true for the criminal justice system, which is expected to carry out its duty of providing safety for the public in a manner the public approves of.

American culture, however, is heterogeneous and dynamic, and the demands on and expectations of its institutions often conflict. During the racial riots of the 1960s and the anti-Vietnam War riots of the early 1970s, for example, many citizens were outraged by the conduct of the police; charges of racism and brutality were common. However, other individuals approved of the police's conduct; demands for "law and order" and the use of coercive force to end rioting and looting dominated the rhetoric of many groups. In general, liberals viewed the social control problems as a result of poverty, racism, and a justice system biased against the lower class. Conservatives, however, viewed the civil disobedience, rioting, and looting simply as lawless conduct and advocated the increased use of coercive force to deal with it (Rosch, 1985).

These conflicting views of crime and civil disorder are an excellent example of the lack of consistency in norms and values among the members of our society. Our cultural mix can create homogeneous or heterogeneous demands (Hall, 1987), depending on the issues at hand as well as our collective or individual perceptions of the issues. When demands are heterogeneous, government and organizations must work to appease or mitigate conflicting interests or must ignore one set of interests in favor of others. A striking historical example of our conflicting norms can be seen in the attempt to eliminate the consumption of alcohol through federal legislation. The Eighteenth Amendment (the Volstead Act), passed in 1919 and repealed in 1933 (the

Twenty-First Amendment), created the nation's infamous period of prohibition. Basically, a coalition of politically powerful moral and religious groups created the amendment, which was intended to make the nation righteous by preventing a large number of Americans from consuming alcohol. The law forbidding the consumption of alcoholic beverages for recreational purposes was to be implemented by the criminal justice system at the federal, state, and local levels. However, alcoholic beverages were nonetheless consumed by "good citizens" from all walks of life. Beer and gin were often homemade, but bootleggers and members of organized crime supplied most of the beverages to the consuming public.

Because the values and preferences of large numbers of Americans seemingly were ignored by the Prohibition lobby, the criminal justice system was, in effect, mandated to enforce a law that a great number of people would not follow. While the amendment ignored the wishes of "drinking" citizens, local criminal justice systems ignored the amendment; stories from the "Roaring Twenties" recount the corruption of local law enforcement officials who allowed speakeasies to market beer and liquor openly. Hence the power the "moral minority" had over others was mitigated in favor of the "drinking minority" by the practices of local criminal justice systems.

In many respects, our present attempts to control the consumption of recreational drugs, such as marijuana, heroin, and cocaine, resemble our efforts at prohibiting the use of alcohol (Warren, 1971). Again, a large enough minority of American citizens forms a lucrative market that attracts suppliers of illegal recreational drugs. Traditional organized crime has its share of the illegal market, and new criminal cartels have been formed to supply illegal drugs to consumers. Despite the war on drugs, increased sentences for the sale and use of drugs, and intensified enforcement efforts, we seem unable to prevent the marketing of a product demanded by a substantial number of citizens. However, a belief exists in today's political climate that harsh sentencing for the sale or use of drugs will in the end coerce those individuals with a market preference for illegal drugs to cease their consumption. The clash of values, preferences, and behaviors between the dominant culture and subculture continues to be acted out with ever-increasing coercive efforts against drug users. The outcome of the cultural conflict contributes to the constantly growing rate of incarceration, the need for more prisons, and pressure for more resources for the criminal justice system.

Ecological Conditions

Ecological factors are components of the environment such as climate, geographical location, size of a community, and its economic base—industrial, service, agrarian. Ecological factors make a major contribution to the total environment of an organization and subsequently affect its mission and constraints. A small city in the midst of a farm area is profoundly different from a small city with an industrial base, and both are profoundly different from a large industrial community. Small agricultural communities tend to have homogeneous cultures and a history of relative stability. The criminal justice system in small communities typically does not receive mixed signals from community members. An immediate link between criminal justice agencies and community members exists because citizens typically have access to political leaders and criminal justice officials and probably associate with them consistently on a social basis. From an operational point of view, most community members are probably well known to the local police, and many problems are handled informally based on local preference rather than on formal procedures.

As communities change from agrarian to industrial, migration patterns bring in new citizens who may have values different from those of the long-time residents, thus creating a heterogeneous environment for the criminal justice system. In addition, crime patterns may change, and an increased number of social control problems may require formal rather than informal processing. Large urban industrial communities offer an even more complex environment for criminal justice agencies to work within. Values of community members and their demands for services from governmental and criminal justice agencies may vary greatly. Social control problems are handled with formality. Criminal justice bureaucracies become large, and their members may not be easily accessible to citizens. Therefore, direct input from community members into criminal justice agencies may be limited.

Geographical conditions also have an impact on both the services demanded in a community and the resources available. In northern cities, winter climates create traffic hazards. Western areas have forest fires and droughts. Coastal areas or lakes and streams present safety hazards. Areas that attract tourists have distinctive social-control problems; Las Vegas, for example, attracts more than its share of drifters and criminals as well as legitimate tourists looking for excitement. Little imagination is needed to consider how the problems the Las Vegas criminal justice system faces compare with those of stable industrial or rural communities.

Political Conditions

Political conditions can affect an organization directly through pressures from constituents and clients and indirectly through governmental action. The governmental response to political conditions can be passed on to organizations and agencies in a number of ways. To focus on public agencies, governments can alter agency budgets, change mandates, alter the composition of top administrative personnel—something that often happens after an election—or write legislation that changes the purpose or power base of a bureaucracy. Court decisions that affect the operations or mission of an agency are made in the existing political climate and are not exempt from political forces. As we saw earlier in the chapter, a body of case law has evolved as individual rights have become a deep political concern.

Political pressure by interest groups can be placed directly on criminal justice agencies rather than through the governmental structure. For example, Mothers Against Drunk Driving (MADD) has been successful in causing police agencies to be concerned with the safety hazards created by drunk drivers. The MADD group has been able to focus national attention on the highway safety problem created by drunk drivers, which has, in turn, pressured courts to impose stiffer penalties and police to increase the frequency of arrest of those driving under the influence of drugs or alcohol. The National Association for the Advancement of Colored People (NAACP) is a well-organized political force that has historically placed direct pressure on police agencies for fair treatment of African Americans and for equal opportunity employment within criminal justice agencies. In addition, the American Friends Service

Committee (1971) has a history of attempting to bring humane reform to our prison system. Finally, pleas from the public at large often ask for tougher criminal sentencing. Judges, as elected officials, are vulnerable to such pressures.

Because demands placed on the political–legal system and ultimately on the criminal justice system often conflict, criminal justice agencies have difficulty establishing priorities. Justice may, therefore, be applied inconsistently within a particular criminal justice system and differently from system to system. As a result, some dissatisfaction with the performance of the criminal justice system will always be present among certain members, groups, or forces in its environment.

Much of what has been discussed in this section on political conditions within the environment is based on cultural considerations. Cultural views and values become political when we try to operationalize them or make them part of the official domain of government. A society utilizes its political–legal system to perpetuate its most basic values. In addition, the political–legal system becomes a conduit between the forces of the environment and governmental agencies by rendering the conflicting demands and needs of the environment into manageable mandates for governmental agencies. Thus, criminal justice agencies are linked directly to and must be most responsive to the political environment they function within.

Moreover, implicit up to now is the fact that environmental conditions merge and interact within the political environment and create or manifest a political climate. We have already seen how environmental conditions create demands and constraints on government, which, in turn, places demands, constraints, and expectations on public bureaucracies. Often the policies, activities, or subsequent outcomes of government or its agencies impact environmental conditions, creating a new set of problems and demands. For example, the fear of crime and war on drugs often fueled by political leaders has led to a prison-building and incarceration binge, which in turn has expanded the number of corrections officers across the country. The fear of personal liability resulting from chronic litigation, as well as concern for wages and working conditions, has advanced collective bargaining for corrections officers. Corrections officers' unions in several states have expanded; they are well funded and sophisticated in influencing both the formal and informal political systems. In short, the unions have the political strength to lobby openly for legislation, support legislators and governors, contribute large sums of money to political candidates, and fund public relations activities to vest their interest directly and indirectly into the political process. Prison guards, who once lacked professional and often personal status, have now become politically powerful, a predictable outcome not foreseen by policy makers or political leaders, but resulting from environmental conditions funneled through the political environment.

The Political Environment

The political environment of the criminal justice system can be thought of as a complex decision-making apparatus containing both formal and informal overlapping subsystems (Fairchild & Webb, 1985). The *formal political system* includes legislative bodies at the federal, state, and local levels. These bodies pass legislation that determines and limits the operation of the criminal justice system; they also allocate to criminal justice agencies resources that can have a substantial impact on operations. Legislative bodies, in theory, pass on demands from the general public to public service agencies. They are also subjected to the potential influence of pressure groups, whose goal is to influence the policies or operations of the criminal justice system (Fairchild, 1981; Stolz, 1985).

The court system, while a component of the criminal justice system, is also a part of the formal political system. The court system, especially the federal system, regulates the operations of criminal justice agencies. Regulation imposed by the courts is, in theory, based on statutory and case law and constitutional law, much of which is constantly being redefined by new court decisions or case law. In making sure the criminal justice system operates within the law, the courts are theoretically blind to demands of the general public or changes in cultural and other environmental factors. A significant body of research, however, suggests that judges, whether elected or appointed, make decisions congruent with the values they bring to the office. Their decision making often reflects the regional or political values they have acquired more than a strict interpretation of the law (Cole, 1988; Frazier & Block, 1982; Kolonski & Mendelsohn, 1970).

The *informal political system* comprises those sources of pressures and demands that are placed directly on the criminal justice system. These pressures support or oppose existing programs or practices or demand new programs or services. In other words, individuals, groups, or organizations may bypass the formal political system and focus directly on a criminal justice agency—or attack the formal political structure and agency simultaneously—to bring about a desired effect. In the previous section on political environmental factors, examples were given of change imposed on the criminal justice system by direct pressure from such groups.

Informal pressure can also be placed on the criminal justice system by legislative bodies. Short of writing new laws, legislatures may voice support for, or opposition to, agency programs or practices. In short, governmental bodies may interfere with the routine operations of an agency as well as define the agency's official goal or mission (Guyot, 1985). Most state legislatures have both house and senate committees on corrections, police, courts, or the criminal justice system. Such committees may show intense interest in a criminal justice agency program or operation and may voice an opinion on appropriate agency philosophy, policies, or procedures. Such an opinion itself may create a response from the agency without official legislation. In Michigan, for example, the state senate Committee on Criminal Justice argued for the development of a military camp for young inmates. The state department of corrections, initially opposed to the boot camp, eventually established one to house 150 inmates—compared with 20,000 in the state prison system—presumably to appease the committee.

The formal and informal political systems faced by the criminal justice agencies are not mutually exclusive. The example just given shows how members of the formal political system exert informal influence. We can also return to MADD to see other ways in which the two systems mix or overlap. MADD can consistently pressure police agencies to increase the frequency with which they arrest drunk drivers and can pressure judges to give out tough sentences while lobbying legislators to toughen legislation against drunk drivers and provide increased resources to improve anti-drunk driving efforts.

Agencies may respond directly to pressure from the public or from a particular constituency and plan to affect an operational or programmatic change. They may first, however, approach the formal system for support by asking legislative bodies for additional funding (Cordner & Hudzik, 1983) or statutory support for their plan. In this manner, the formal political system is pressured by the agency to respond to demands from the informal political system. The move to community policing, or the foot patrol program, is a rich and interesting example of the political interactions, initiated by the police, among the community, the police, and city hall.

In Flint, Michigan, an industrial town that had unemployment rates of up to 23 percent in the 1980s, the crime rate rose rapidly, and community members demanded increased police service. City funds were unavailable because of the economic problems, but the Mott Foundation, a local organization created to assure the quality of life in Flint, funded the establishment of a foot patrol experiment. Funds from Mott were used to pay foot patrol police officers' salaries for a three-year period. The program was evaluated periodically through direct interviews with residents in the foot patrol neighborhoods. Although the foot patrol program did not seem to affect crime rates, it provided residents with increased perceptions of safety, and they favored the availability of foot patrol officers (Trojanowicz, 1983). When the Mott Foundation grant ran out, the community voted overwhelmingly for a tax increase to continue the program as a permanent part of the police force.

The foot patrol program was not overly popular, however, with many police administrators or members of the city government. Although they were pleased with the tax increase, members of both groups continued to struggle to have the monies allocated lumped into the total police department budget rather than earmarked for foot patrol operations. When administrators also observed that the foot patrol officers were gaining, or had the capacity to gain, credibility and political influence among the constituents in the neighborhoods they served, they became concerned with the possible loss of bureaucratic control over foot patrol officers (Trojanowicz, Steele, & Trojanowicz, 1986). These officers were, in effect, now capable of being significant figures in the informal political system themselves through the influence and credibility they built within the community.

Clearly, the political environment varies greatly in influence, structure, and form. In small rural communities, for example, criminal justice actors may be subjected to constant community input because they are part of the local social system. Citizens may be able to get something done by attending city council meetings, banging on the police chief's desk, or seeking out the judge at the local restaurant. In large urban communities, criminal justice agencies are shielded from such direct input from community members. Citizen complaints are handled through formal channels with much red tape. Influence is gained only through concerted interest group effort, which must usually include pressure through the formal political system and pressure on the criminal justice system itself (Olsen, 1973). State and federal agencies, especially corrections systems, are large, bureaucratic, and distant from the general public. They are, therefore, protected from the informal political system. To the extent they are vulnerable to political influence, it is likely to be from the formal political system.

Public agencies take their general mandates from the political system and are constrained by the legal and budgetary control of the formal political system. However, they are subject to other pressures, demands, and constraints from clientele and constituencies served, competing and cooperating agencies, and other specific elements of their task environment. In the following section we attempt to identify these groups.

Task Environment Elements Specific to the Criminal Justice System

The task environment of an agency can be defined generally as the forces in the environment that are related directly to the goal-setting and goal-directed activities of the criminal justice system (Steers, 1977). The task environment is composed of a number of groups, agencies, and organizations that fall roughly into six categories: beneficiaries, funders, providers of nonfiscal resources, providers of complementary services, competitors, and legitimizers (Lauffer, 1984). *Funders* include governmental bodies that allocate scarce resources to public agencies. Planned activities, programs, goals, agency problems, and future challenges will be reviewed by funders before allocating budget requests. *Competitors* are other public agencies competing for limited resources. With the move to privatization, firms such as Corrections Corporation of America are competing for tax dollars to provide correctional services (May & Gray, 1996). The public at large can be considered *beneficiaries*. However, particular groups often demand specific service from the system. Merchants want business districts to be safe and orderly for customers, and Mothers Against Drunk Driving was successful in requiring stricter enforcement and sentencing of drunk drivers.

Employees are major benificiaries. Police and corrections officer unions are common. In addition to bargaining for wages, they often play a role in policy development and attempt to force bureaus to alter their practices toward employees (Swanson, Territo, & Taylor, 1988). New personnel bring their own values and beliefs into an organization; to the extent their values vary from existing values, they may affect goals, practices, and decision making within the system (Eisenstein, 1973). It was hoped, for example, that upgrading the educational levels of police officers—that is, making a baccalaureate degree common—would make officers nonracist and able to relate well to members of the communities they served (National Advisory Commission on Criminal Justice Standards and Goals, 1973b). Affirmative action has also had an impact on particular aspects of criminal justice agencies. Hiring women police and corrections officers has caused agencies to alter physical requirements for recruitment, including physical fitness testing for entry (Booth & Harwick, 1984). More important, perhaps, the mixing of genders has forced agencies to provide methods to assimilate female personnel and accord them professional status (Price, 1974). Agencies must now provide procedures to protect each gender from sexual harassment from the other, especially when one has a position of authority over the other.

Criminal offenders can easily—if not ironically—be considered nonfiscal resource providers. The type and number of offenders clearly have an impact on the operations of criminal justice agencies. The emergence of street gangs causes police agencies to alter policies, procedures, and resources. Antigang units are often formed to respond to the gangs as a crime threat or in response to public fears (Center for Assessment of the Juvenile Justice System, 1982). The increased arrest of gang members affects the corrections system, especially large jails and prisons, because gangs tend to coalesce in correctional institutions and attempt to rule them (Irwin, 1980; Jacobs, 1983a). Increasing the number of arrests—as a result of increased crime, public pressure on police, luck, or skill—will affect operations throughout the criminal justice system. The populations of local jails and lockups will increase, court dockets and caseloads of prosecuting attorneys will expand, and, perhaps, plea bargaining will favor defendants more than usual as a result of high caseloads. Finally, prison populations may increase.

Changes in the quality and type of criminal activity may affect the operational goals and procedures of agencies. In our example of street gangs, allocating additional law enforcement resources to that problem will take resources away from other activities. Response time to burglaries or accidents may increase and traffic control may be reduced, as resources are taken away from these areas to deal with street gangs. Prison administrators may become more concerned with maintaining order than with treatment or rehabilitation in institutions populated by street gang members.

A striking example of the vulnerability of the system to specific elements in its environment can be seen in the interactions between state mental health systems and the criminal justice system, especially jails and prisons. Both systems are ultimately involved in social control. Historically, mentally ill citizens were confined in state mental institutions; in effect, they were controlled through incarceration. During the late 1960s and early 1970s, mental health professionals and legislators moved away from confining mentally ill people for long periods of time and instituted a program of community mental health, keeping mentally ill citizens out of institutions unless they posed a substantial danger to themselves or others. This change came about in part in response to the recognition of abuses and arbitrary decision making within mental institutions. In addition, mental health professionals reasoned, individuals suffering from mental problems could be cured only in the community, where they must ultimately live and survive. State mental hospitals were thus emptied during the 1970s, and since then, strict legal constraints have kept mental hospital admissions at a low level.

Moving to a community base, however, has created problems for criminal justice agencies, especially jails and prisons. Mentally ill citizens who behave in criminal or antisocial ways now have to be controlled and cared for by the criminal justice system instead of by the state mental health systems (Guy, Platt, & Zwerling, 1985). As a consequence, a growing number of jail and prison inmates across the nation are mentally ill (Steadman, Monahan, Duffee, Hartstone, & Robbins, 1984). In analyzing the data from the U.S. Bureau of Justice Statistics in the Survey of Jail Inmates, researchers found that approximately 16 percent of inmates incarcerated in our nation's jails in 1983 reported symptoms of mental illness or prior institutionalization in a mental hospital. In addition, current standards of care for inmates imposed on jails and prisons by the courts require that they be provided with adequate psychiatric and medical assistance (Embert, 1986). In effect, the role of the local jail and prison has been modified by changes within the mental health system. Policies, procedures, and behaviors of jail and correctional institution employees must also be changed to perform the new task imposed by its environment.

Components of the system and individual agencies become providers of complementary services, and they are all interdependent. Changes in the practices or priorities of one component or agency will have an effect on the other agencies. Moreover, human service agencies often become complementary providers of services because they often have problems and cases common with the criminal justice system. Dealing with child abuse cases is a clear example of substantive interactions between the criminal justice and social welfare agencies.

Legitimization, finally, derives directly from legislation, pre-entry training, and educational requirements. Practices, performance, and personal standards can be dictated by legislation and implemented in part by mandated training and education. Most states have established standards and curricula for police training academies. The academies almost always are required to accept only applicants who meet personal, physical, and mental and emotional standards. Federal agencies and many state correctional agencies require extensive training before a trainee works in the system. The key officers of the courts, judges and lawyers, have graduated from law school and, by virtue of their expertise and knowledge, are trained to practice. Legitimization can be derived indirectly from professional organizations as well as unions. Professional organizations such as the American Correctional Association, American Jail Association, and state and local bar associations attempt to set standards for their profession. It can be argued that the popularity of criminal justice programs at colleges and universities across the country has allowed higher education to provide legitimacy for the criminal justice system in much the way law schools legitimize the legal profession.

We could continue at great length, giving examples of how specific factors within an organization's task environment can impact an agency and cause it to alter its mission, policies, or procedures and practices. The important point is a general analysis of the dynamics of an organization's environment can provide an understanding of the general nature of environmental forces. Understanding environmental forces is pivotal to administrators in understanding the expected role of his or her agency. In the next section, we add another dimension to our understanding of the systems environment by exploring the types of environment that exist within an organization.

Environmental States

The specific environment of an organization can range from simple to complex and from static to dynamic. A *simple environment* is one in which the external forces that affect the organization, or with which the organization must interact, are few in number and are relatively homogeneous. Conversely, an organization that deals with a number of heterogeneous external factors exists within a relatively *complex environment* (Duncan, 1972). Each *environmental state* will affect the behavior of an organization differently. Police agencies that work in small communities with stable populations and little demographic change face a limited number of problems, most of which are recurring and predictable. The small-town cop probably knows many of the citizens personally, knows who the troublemakers are and where trouble spots are, can predict the behaviors and expectations of the political leaders, and is in a position to influence aspects of his or her environment. If such a Sleepy Hollow begins to change demographically, economically, or culturally, the environment becomes increasingly complex. If, for example, a relatively large firm moves into Sleepy Hollow, the population will increase, additional housing will be built, individuals with different ethnic backgrounds may settle there, traffic patterns will change, and crime and interpersonal conflict may increase. The police agency may need to expand, be concerned with the behavior of the new community members (at least initially), and cope with altered traffic patterns, more taverns, and tavern patrons. The environment for the small-town cops thus moves from placid and simple to complex and diverse. They will no longer personally know all the people they will be dealing with and, as a result, will become increasingly formal in their interactions with citizens. If a new firm creates hazardous waste, think of the new expertise and enforcement obligations the officers of Sleepy Hollow will need to acquire.

There are profound differences between big city and rural policing because of their complex versus simple task environments. The most complex environment for criminal justice agencies exists within a densely populated industrial county in which a number of cities of varying sizes have police agencies, courts with misdemeanor jurisdiction, and lockups, all of which link to the county or circuit courts of felony jurisdiction and the county sheriff (road patrol and county jail). The members of the criminal justice system must deal with a number of jurisdictions, agencies within and across jurisdictions, and heterogeneous political and cultural systems. We would expect criminal justice practitioners in such large or densely populated jurisdictions to behave in impersonal and highly bureaucratic ways. In addition, criminal justice practitioners in large jurisdictions have little opportunity for personal contact with influential community members and political figures. Such contact is left to criminal justice administrators, who interact with the political–legal system, interpreting public opinions and demands into criminal justice policy.

An organization's environment may be static or dynamic as well as simple or complex. A *static environment* is one that remains constant or stable over time; it is predictable. The Sleepy Hollow police department worked in a static environment before the hypothetical economic and demographic changes took place. As demands on an agency become diverse and unpredictable, the environment takes on a dynamic nature. A *dynamic environment* is one that is subject to unpredictable change (Duncan, 1972; Steers, 1977). A single task environment can also have both simple and dynamic components. Much of the criminal justice practitioner's work is routine, repetitive, and predictable; yet some facets are unpredictable. In many respects, the ultimate art of the criminal justice practitioner or administrator is to predict or anticipate as many contingencies as possible, thereby simplifying some aspects of a complex, dynamic environment. For example, police agencies attempt to predict crime patterns, traffic patterns, and gang behavior. Parole boards attempt to predict the postrelease behavior of inmates. Inasmuch as certain demands placed on the criminal justice system are routine or can be made predictable, one portion of its agencies' environment can be considered stable. However, criminal justice agencies are often confronted with surprises and new demands from their environment. The influx of mentally ill inmates into the jails and prisons may, in retrospect, have been predictable, but it was not predicted, at least in an operational sense. The smooth flow of cases through a prosecutor's office and the court may be disrupted by a heinous crime that gains a great deal of notoriety. The prosecutor and staff may be forced to spend a great deal of time and energy on the case to satisfy public expectations for successful prosecution.

Urban police work can often be highly complex and unpredictable. An excellent example occurred in New York City in 1967, when a citywide power outage occurred because of a problem in a utility company generator. In the chaos that followed, looters pillaged retail stores, breaking windows and removing merchandise. In mobilizing and dealing with this unexpected contingency, the police increased arrests, which, in turn, put pressure on lockups, bail and bond systems, prosecutors' staffs, courts, probation departments, and county correctional facilities. An important implication here is that the criminal justice system typically bears the responsibility for dealing with unique and unforeseen situations that impact the social infrastructure.

Organizational Response to the Environment

The more dynamic and complex an organizational environment is, the greater the uncertainty associated with it. And the more an organization perceives uncertainty in the cues and demands from its environment, the more difficulty it will have in making effective decisions.

Environmental Uncertainty

The perception of uncertainty in the environment is the result of three conditions: a lack of information about environmental factors important to decision making; an inability to estimate how probabilities will affect a decision until it is implemented; and a lack of information about the cost associated with an incorrect decision (Duncan, 1972). Table 3-1 provides a good general description of how environmental states affect certainty or uncertainty. What is pivotal, as we will see later in this chapter, is an organization's ability to respond appropriately to its environment. A public agency that fails to maintain successful relationships with its environment will fail to be responsive to demands, will not appropriate adequate resources and support for its activities (Sharkansky, 1972; Rourke, 1986; Wildavsky, 1974), and will be unable to adapt to significant environmental change (Scott, 1987).

Decoupled Organizations

To add to the issue of uncertainty, large organizations tend to become *decoupled*—that is, face multiple environments and interact with each environment at different organizational levels. To complicate matters further, an environment may have two *subenvironments* an agency may have to respond to: the political–legal and service–delivery subenvironments. We can understand this concept by looking outward from organizations as they interact with the environment. Large organizations tend to break into overlapping subgroups, the dominant coalition and the work processors. The *dominant coalition* is the small group of employees who oversee the organization and dictate policy decisions; the *work processors* are the bulk of the organization's members, who are directly involved with its primary clientele (Nokes, 1960).

TABLE 3-1

Characteristics of Various Environmental States

	CELL 1: *Low Perceived Uncertainty*	CELL 2: *Moderately Low Perceived Uncertainty*
STATIC	1. Small number of factors and components in the environment 2. Factors and components are somewhat similar to one another 3. Factors and components remain basically the same and are not changing	1. Large number of factors and components in the environment 2. Factors and components are not similar to one another 3. Factors and components remain basically the same

	CELL 3: *Moderately High Perceived Uncertainty*	CELL 4: *High Perceived Uncertainty*
DYNAMIC	1. Small number of factors and components in the environment 2. Factors and components are somewhat similar to one another 3. Factors and components of the environment are in continual process of change	1. Large number of factors and components in the environment 2. Factors and components are not similar to one another 3. Factors and components of environment are in a continual process of change

Source: Reprinted from "The Characteristics of Organizational Environments and Perceived Environmental Uncertainty," by R. B. Duncan. Published in *Administrative Science Quarterly* 17 (1972), by permission of *Adminstrative Science Quarterly.*

Each subgroup of the organization faces different demands and pressures from different sources. Members of the dominant coalition interact with the political–legal system, administrators of related organizations, organized support and opposition groups, and the news media; they typically become the focal point of public pressure. These policy-level administrators must deal with political and public opinions that reflect the often conflicting views of the organization's multiple constituency. In responding to the variety of pressures from the political environment, the dominant coalition must be concerned with their agency's myths, image, and posture. The work processors, in contrast, deal directly with agency clientele and deliver services to them (Meyer & Rowan, 1978; Nokes, 1960). In large systems, work processors become "street-level bureaucrats" who negotiate rules for the allocation of scarce agency resources with clients (Lipsky, 1980). Figure 3-2 shows a decoupled organization interacting with its subenvironments.

Decoupled organizations face a unique set of problems. To begin with, the cues, pressures, and constraints that the dominant coalition faces may be profoundly different from those faced by members of the work process group. For example, elites may demand that wife abusers be arrested more frequently—or policy makers may

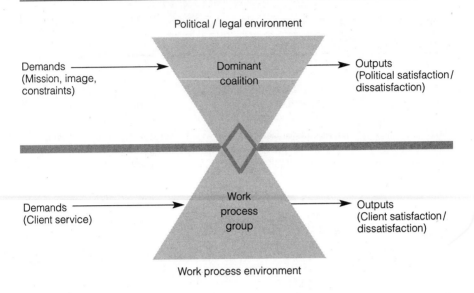

Political / legal environment

Demands ——————————▶ Dominant ——————————▶ Outputs
(Mission, image,   coalition   (Political satisfaction/
constraints)   dissatisfaction)

Demands ——————————▶ Work ——————————▶ Outputs
(Client service)   process   (Client satisfaction/
                                    group   dissatisfaction)

Work process environment

FIGURE 3-2   A Decoupled Organization

perceive that such demands will be forthcoming—and policy will be directed toward increased arrests of wife abusers. However, street police officers may be reluctant to do so because past experience with their clientele has convinced them that arresting wife abusers may not be an effective way to deal with the problem (Galliher, 1985). Or administrators may feel they must wage wars on drugs or gambling, while law enforcement officers may understand that certain forms of drug use or gambling are approved behaviors within their community and may actively avoid controlling those types of crime on their beats (Wilson, 1968).

Corrections systems provide especially fruitful examples of decoupled organizations. Corrections reform has been the concern of concerted political elites since 1870, when the National Congress of Penitentiary and Reformatory Discipline met in Cincinnati. This group called for sweeping reforms and implementation of standards for the maintenance and management of inmates. Since then, other meetings of establishment elites (Quinney, 1974) have been convened with this goal, and lasting groups, such as the American Correctional Association, have been formed and have prescribed standards for corrections. Courts have intervened and provided inmates with constitutional rights and have examined prison and jail conditions under a constitutional microscope. Even though it is reflected in the written policies and procedures of most corrections systems, however, this collective effort for change has primarily functioned to maintain and legitimize the corrections system by updating the language and symbols that explain the system to the public (Kalinich & Banas, 1984).

As demands from the political–legal environment are absorbed and iterated back through language and symbolism by the dominant coalition, within the bowels of the system the work processors—corrections officers and other staff—work pragmatically with the raw material—the inmates—to keep the system in some semblance of order. Day-to-day work is typically based on a series of informal rules negotiated between corrections staff and inmates (Kalinich & Stojkovic, 1985) and may have nothing to do with the prescriptions and standards promulgated by interested elites, pressure groups, or the courts.

The process of decentralizing, or federalizing, large bureaucracies is typically done so that work processors have enough flexibility to deal with their local clientele or to respond to the demands of their local constituents. Decentralization is, in effect, a recognition that local environmental dimensions may differ at various levels of the organization and that the organization may face more than one environment. Police agencies in large metropolitan areas are often broken into a number of districts that are governed by district commanders, who work with some degree of autonomy from the central bureaucracy. Parole agencies are typically governed loosely by a central office and broken into geographical districts, with each district expected to function with some degree of autonomy. However, the different environments faced by an agency can create friction between central office staff and field staff even in formally decentralized bureaucracies (McCleary, 1978; also see Pfeffer, 1978, and Selznik, 1949).

McCleary's (1978) interesting organizational study of a parole system describes the impact of different operational philosophies held by the dominant coalition—the central office—and the work processors—parole officers and district supervisors—on fundamentals of parole supervision in a state agency. The central office, for example, attempting to update the system, felt that it was inappropriate for a modern, professional parole system to have its officers carry guns. Parole officers argued, however, that dangers existed within their work environment that made carrying a gun a necessity. The central office, nonetheless, officially decreed that officers would no longer be allowed to carry guns in the field. Parole officers, however, continued to carry guns, and their supervisors supported them by not enforcing the central office ban on firearms. In effect, the central office attempted to alter the image of the agency to be congruent with external expectations for professionalism and for effecting rehabilitation among its clients. However, the parole officers responded to their perceived environmental constraints.

It might be argued that the differences of views in this situation were based primarily on the personal values of the community members. However, many of our job-related values and norms come from our immediate work group, which is affected by the environment it is immersed within (Hall, 1987; Steers, 1977). Basically, each group was responding to what it perceived to be the realities or expectations of its own environment. However, their perceptions of environmental demands were filtered by their work-group norms, past practices, and personal agendas (McCleary, 1978). But organizations are not helpless entities that ritualistically respond to environmental forces. Rather, organizations have generally policed their boundaries well and exert some degree of control over the flow of environmental inputs into their systems. In the following section, we discuss the common methods agencies use to manage environmental forces.

The Impact of Environmental Forces on Private Security

One area in the field of criminal justice that has experienced a great deal of growth is the field of private security—both proprietary (in-house) and contracted security services. Many of these changes in the security industry are attributed to environmental influences.

Many clients report that a driving force for improving a security department, contracting with a security agency, or increasing security services is the perceived or actual reduction of services provided by the traditional agents of social control—the police. Some examples include: apartment complexes that demand more services to prevent vandalism, improve the quality of life, and reduce property-related crimes; the booming sales and installation of alarm and surveillance systems; neighborhoods and organizations that have contracted with private security for uniformed or visible security foot and vehicular patrols; undercover and other surveillance activities requested by organizations to control drug use and sales, arson, destruction of property, and workplace violence; and other activities that impinge upon the organization's reputation and bottom-line profits.

Coupled with the increase in the demand for security services is the recognition by some organizations of the need to change the perception and functions of security in their organization. This is readily apparent in proprietary-based security organizations. In Grand Rapids, Michigan, one of the local hospitals recognized that the local police services did not meet the needs of the hospital. The police were slow or failed to respond to calls, while overall crime (and fear of crime) increased on the hospital campus. As a consequence, the hospital's security staff have now been certified as peace officers. These security personnel, while on duty, possess full arrest powers for misdemeanors and felonies on the hospital's property.

Besides changes in the external environment, the internal environment of some organizations has led to changes in the organizational structure and practices of security. At another hospital in Grand Rapids, Michigan, employees were not satisfied with the quality and professionalism of the existing contract security firm. When examined in the context of the cost of security services, management soon decided that changes were necessary. This resulted in the shift to a proprietary-based security organization driven by the needs of the customer—the staff of the hospital, patients, and visitors. Through the proper design and implementation of this security department, costs have remained stable; the number of security personnel has increased; the quality of and commitment to professionalism by the staff has increased; the hospital is directly in charge of hiring; security officer salaries have increased (because there are no large administrative fees associated with contract security services); and customer satisfaction surveys have indicated improvements in the delivery of security-related services.

As the security industry matures, however, environmental forces will continue to challenge and change its structure and operations, particularly in the context of the labor market. Some regions are experiencing a very tight labor market, that is, a low unemployment rate. Coupled with traditional low wages in contract security, this presents a challenge for the security administrator—a small labor pool, underqualified individuals, and a high turnover rate as these individuals gain those requisite job skills and move into better-paying positions in the labor market. This recurrent problem of undereducated and inexperienced officers often leads to a debate over the degree of professionalism the security industry upholds.

Environmental constraints in the context of limited funds and knowledge have also been a driving force for change. One of the current trends in security is private–public security networks. These security networks "pool" the expertise of the private industry and police, resulting in the exchange and sharing of information, resources, and expertise to make the delivery of local law enforcement and security more efficient and effective. One example is the Lakeshore Security Network, located in western Michigan. Through monthly meetings between local industries (some of which are *Fortune* 500) and the law enforcement community, communication barriers and the animosities that may have existed between the "professional" police and private security have been reduced. Proactive crime control measures and order maintenance activities have also improved.

Another environmental challenge facing the security industry is licensing and control. Many states are currently wrestling with this issue as the debate arises as to who is responsible for monitoring the activities of private security. Should this be a state organization or a private agency operating under state statute or control, or should the security industry go unregulated and rely upon the free market system to eliminate those companies that do not provide quality services to their clients? No firm decisions have been made regarding this issue.

Of further interest is the question of whether private security is truly a "private" function or does it include "public" duties? While not true of all private security organzations, in some organizations this differentiation has becom clouded. Shopping malls, many covering large tracts of land, are patrolled by private security forces; cities that have a large number of government buildings, office and industrial parks, and apartment complexes may also have large security forces. When taken in the context of total numbers of personnel, security-related positions often far exceed the number of sworn public police officers in a municipality. Paradoxically, some individuals propose that these and other environmental changes have made private security the "unofficial" police, reducing the presence of traditional police to smaller areas of the city. This perception has also resulted in a shift in law enforcement practices. Now the police have taken over their traditional role as the crime fighter responding to "serious" calls for service. Private police, on the other hand, now serve as the order-maintenance segment of the public police.

The challenges facing the security manager, either proprietary or contract, as well as the security industry as a whole are often complex. There is one common denominator in all of them: environment. For this industry to survive and change, it must understand its internal and external task environments. No longer can individuals base decisions only on the needs of their organization or their subjective opinions; the environment will have a large impact on their success and their future.

BRIAN R. JOHNSON
Assistant Professor and Security Consultant
Grand Valley State Universiy
Allendale, Michigan

Managing Environmental Forces

Almost all organizations are vulnerable to environmental forces, although to varying degrees (Jacobs, 1974). Organizations are open systems dependent upon, and constrained by, environmental systems for mandates, authority, and resources, and they must produce goods or services for their clients. In effect, organizations must enter into exchange relations across their boundaries with other systems (Scott, 1987). This is an important consideration, because the ability of an organization to develop favorable exchange relations with its environment is ultimately related to its effectiveness (Osborn & Hunt, 1974). Organizations, however, often do not maintain such relations and instead attempt to behave as rational, or closed, systems. They expend efforts at setting and policing their boundaries in an effort to protect their core from external environmental influences (Thompson, 1967). Organizations are, therefore, subjected to the task of managing and coping with their environments. Managing environments requires exerting control over environmental forces or creating mechanisms to buffer the agency from inputs. Production organizations stockpile raw materials, accumulate cash reserves, and control their markets with advertising and other strategies, all in an attempt to make them less dependent on their environments (Blau, 1955). As public bureaucracies, criminal justice agencies get their inputs (mandates, resources, support and opposition for programs) from the political–legal and cultural systems. Like other public agencies, they can protect their boundaries by invoking their bureaucratic power in both the formal and informal political system or by conforming or appearing to conform to environmental demands or expectations through symbols and rhetoric.

Influencing Input

It is tempting to think of public bureaucracies, especially criminal justice agencies, as apolitical or above politics in the performance of their duties. An earlier version of this rationalistic view of public organizations posited that the political structure created policy and that public administrators carried out policy (Henry, 1975). However, bureaus have the power to influence policy inputs from the political system (Long, 1949). Legislators who control budgets and create social policy depend on agencies to carry out their programs. In addition, agencies have expertise that lawmakers depend on in creating policy changes (Rourke, 1976). Agency administrators are typically called on to provide information and to advise or state their position to legislative bodies that are proposing legislation that would restrict or broaden the scope of an agency's duties or powers. Legislative committees routinely call on directors of corrections, chiefs of police, and jail administrators to define problems and solutions, or to respond to questions and issues put to them by the public. Police, courts, and correctional agencies also forward budgets and programs annually to their governing political bodies and argue their positions based on their unique understanding and expertise. The budgeting process is an opportunity for criminal justice administrators to propose programs and legislation that would alter the scope of their organizations' duties as well as expand their resources (Cordner & Hudzik, 1983).

Those criminal justice administrators who understand the political process and are capable of acting as "statespersons" (Downs, 1967; Rourke, 1976) for their agencies can have extraordinary influence and power over political inputs. The Federal Bureau of Investigation under the directorship of J. Edgar Hoover is a testimony to the ability of a criminal justice agency to protect its boundaries through its influence over the formal political process (Powers, 1987). Chiefs of police or corrections administrators who either reject the political aspects of their role or are simply inept at functioning within the political process typically fail to protect their agencies from political inputs.

Bureaus may also influence the open political system by gathering support from public groups. A number of groups exist outside the criminal justice system that attempt to constrain, support, or direct the system. Such groups include the American Correctional Association, National Sheriffs' Association, American Friends Service Committee, Fraternal Order of Police, American Bar Association, American Civil Liberties Union, and to some extent for corrections, the American Medical Association (Fairchild, 1981; Stolz, 1985). While their means may differ—the American Civil Liberties Union brings issues to the public through law suits and public decrees and the American Correctional Association promulgates standards for corrections operations—the views of such groups can have an effect on the formal political and legal system (Stolz, 1985; Melone, 1985). However, criminal justice administrators may use these groups for support in the open political system because the membership of many of these organizations is made up primarily of criminal justice practitioners and administrators.

The news media act as a conduit between agencies and the environment. A media message can create support for or opposition to an agency or its programs and can also be a vehicle for a bureau to influence key sources in its environment. It is common for agencies at the federal level to exploit the news media to influence their immediate environment as well as the public. Information can be leaked, for example, to test for responses or to bring pressure to bear on other subcomponents or hierarchical levels of a bureau (Halperin, 1978). Using the media's influence to protect agency boundaries is a robust technique that criminal justice agencies do not exploit, even though the opportunity seems eminently available; public interest in "cops and robbers" appears insatiable. Criminal justice agencies have made clumsy ventures at public relations and public influence by using the media, especially with police community relations (Radelet, 1986) ad campaigns encouraging citizens to take steps to prevent crime. The exception to this rule is again the Federal Bureau of Investigation, which has done an outstanding job of developing contacts with the media and presenting an impeccable image of itself. Also, most elected sheriffs, being political by nature, have typically had a good sense of how to deal with the media.

However, police and corrections agencies have typically received negative press coverage, both because of the sensationalism of the enterprise and perhaps in part because of the lack of motivation local or state civil servants may have compared with a politically oriented administrator such as an elected sheriff or federal bureaucrat. Our heuristic view is that media information about the criminal justice system has been generally negative and has brought occasional hostile pressures to bear on criminal justice agencies rather than presenting their practices in a favorable light to the public and the political-legal system (Radelet, 1986).

Using Symbols

An organization can also protect its boundaries by using symbols, slogans, and pithy rhetoric to express its philosophy, policies, and means of operations in abbreviated form. The limited understanding of bureaus by most outside their boundaries, along with the sloppiness of human thinking, causes excessive reliance on symbolism, making it a powerful communication tool. The symbols, slogans, or rhetoric evoked by an organization become a code representing agency philosophy and lending meaning to entrenched policy:

> To the extent that antagonistic constituencies view them [symbols] as legitimate, or at least acceptable, [symbols] promote consensus. . . . By communicating easily consumable statements . . . they link society as a whole with its institutions by identifying generalizable values. . . . They insulate organizations from conflicting contradictory pressures and help prevent dysfunction. (Kalinich, Lorinskas, & Banas, 1985:431)

The process of evoking symbols is a significant aspect of the criminal justice system because the system is shaped by innumerable symbols and myths (Atkins & Pogrebin, 1981). Organizations consequently spend a significant part of their resources on such window dressing (Wilensky, 1967). Symbols can be seen, for example, in sweeping goal statements that are nonoperational and encompass the needs or demands of a broad constituency. Agencies use these general symbolic statements to give them the appearance of conforming to the demands of clients, constituents, and other forces in the environment. When environmental pressures demand changes in an agency's philosophies, scope of duties, activities, and the like, the agency will search for the least profound change (Downs, 1967) and do so by first manipulating its symbols (Kalinich, Lorinskas, & Banas, 1985). In other words, bureaus manipulate their symbols to ward off pressures for substantive change. The art of manipulating symbols thus becomes a technique to protect the bureau's boundaries.

Examples of the use of symbols in the face of environmental pressures are abundant (Lovell & Stojkovic, 1987). As times changed, the posture of penology has moved from a philosophy of discipline to corrections and rehabilitation. Guards became corrections officers; convicts turned into prisoners, then inmates, and finally clients. In many places, corrections officers wear blazers rather than uniforms and badges. Police no longer fight crime; they "serve and protect" or act as agents for crime prevention. Reform bodies such as the National Advisory Commission on Criminal Justice Standards and Goals (1973a) may have actually inhibited change because they gave the system the appearance of having changed simply by revising and updating the language through which the system is conceptualized (Kalinich & Banas, 1984).

It can similarly be argued that police–community programs were symbolic responses to protect police agencies from political inputs. Traditionally, police projected the image of crime fighters. When the racial riots of the late 1960s brought hostile pressure on police agencies from minority and liberal groups, the police responded with the temporary measure of creating, with limited resources, police–community units aimed at promoting shallow public relations. Police agencies avoided expending substantial resources on these programs to avoid structural changes (Kalinich, Lorinskas, & Banas, 1985).

Responding to Client Demand

Agency boundaries, especially those of decoupled agencies, are also permeable at the operational level. A very good example of this effect is found within prisons. The administrators of corrections systems—the director of corrections, wardens, and deputy wardens—promulgate policies, procedures, and rules for corrections officers and inmates to follow in the institution's day-to-day operations. However, bureaucracies experience a great deal of leakage of authority between the hierarchy and the line staff (Downs, 1967)—in this case, the corrections officers. In an effort to keep order in the cell blocks, corrections officers conform to many of the demands of the inmates, their clients, rather than to the formal organizational rules. In effect, an informal system of governance that circumvents many of the formal policies, procedures, and institutional rules is created based to a great extent on inmates' values, needs, and norms (Kalinich & Stojkovic, 1985).

In the police world, line police officers are granted a great deal of discretion to deal with the day-to-day problems they face within the communities they serve. Officers have choices in how and on whom they will enforce the law or implement policy and procedures. In the "watchman" style of policing (Wilson, 1968), the officer is extremely sensitive to community norms and ignores law and agency policy in favor of local norms and behaviors. For example, if gambling is an accepted form of behavior at or in the community, the officer will not enforce antigambling statutes in deference to community members. In both these instances, the norms of the client influence and alter the formal rules of the agency. In the jargon of organizational theory, the agency's boundaries have been penetrated by the norms of the clientele and the agency has become debureaucratized (Kaufman, 1969; Scott, 1987).

We have already seen several examples of boundaries permeated by nonorganizational norms in this chapter; the failure of local law enforcement officials to enforce the Eighteenth Amendment and the politicization of foot patrol programs are dramatic examples. It can be argued that eliminating the foot patrol officer in Chicago in favor of putting police in patrol cars was Taylorism in action (Fischer & Sirianni, 1984); separating police officers from their community constituents was an effective way to seal off the police organization from its immediate environment and to exert control over the rank and file. Organizations can attempt to protect their boundaries from infringement at the operational level by attempting to control the norms and behaviors of their members. This control can be accomplished by indoctrinating its members in organizational norms, clarifying organizational behavioral expectations through declarations of crisp policies, and enforcing organizational rules and regulations.

Control over agency members limits their responsiveness to demands from external sources and keeps the organization from becoming debureaucratized. Organizations, however, have less than complete control over their members. In fact, criminal justice practitioners exercise a great deal of discretion and power and routinely make ad hoc decisions in the course of their work (Atkins & Pogrebin, 1981). Making judgment calls on a case-by-case basis—the application of discretion—defines criminal justice practitioners as professionals. In addition, it is difficult for agencies to control subordinates' behavior, especially where (as is the case with most criminal justice agencies) the structure of the agency requires that line staff perform their duties without continuous observation by supervisory personnel. Hence, the operational boundaries of criminal justice agencies, especially decoupled ones, are highly permeable.

Decreasing Vulnerability to Pressure

Organizations vary in their vulnerability to environmental pressures (Jacobs, 1974). Large, well-established organizations with sufficient resources to police their boundaries, influence their environments, and function within predictable work environments are the most impermeable agencies. Conversely, those that are dependent on their environments, have limited resources, and function within turbulent environments are forced to adapt to environmental conditions and demands or fail (Hall, 1987; Scott, 1987). Organizations that do not modify their structures will also fail to manage environmental demands (Hannan & Freeman, 1984), whereas agencies that have inherent flexibility can readily adapt to changes in the environment (Duffee, 1985).

Criminal justice agencies are, for the most part, well established and can be thought of as rather large systems within the immediate community each serves. Goffman (1961) described prisons and mental institutions as "total institutions," suggesting that they were almost closed systems. Historically, these institutions were highly protected from intrusion from environmental forces. Prisons were protected from the legal system by federal courts, the legal system itself, and the "hands-off" doctrine, which kept prisons exempt from civil litigation. Because the hands-off doctrine eroded, prisons are now vulnerable to civil litigation. In urban settings and at the state and federal levels, the boundary between the criminal justice system and the general community at the policy level may be difficult to penetrate, but the boundary between the system and the community may be porous at the operational level, suggesting that large criminal justice systems tend to be decoupled. They face heterogeneous constituencies and a wide range of problems and function within a turbulent and somewhat unpredictable environment. In small communities, the social exchange between community members and members of the criminal justice system may effectively minimize boundaries except in symbolic ways, and policies and practices may be heavily based on local values and demands. Criminal justice agencies in these communities usually have homogeneous constituencies and a relatively narrow scope of problems, and they function within a stable and predictable environment. Administrators need not expend great efforts protecting the agency's boundary.

Implications for Administrators

We have described environmental pressures at length and have discussed the notion of organizational boundaries, which protect organizations from unwanted pressures. We have also provided a general description of the methods that bureaus typically use to control environmental pressures and avoid becoming debureaucratized. In this regard, we have discussed the administrator's role as defending the agency against environmental intrusions. We have not explicitly discussed the related, yet opposing, role of an administrator: to make the agency responsive to the community or its constituencies. Parsons (1960) argued that organizations can be viewed as having three distinct parts: technical, managerial, and institutional. Organizations possess a core technology that is accommodated by management. Organizations exist, however, by virture of their contributions to the greater social system. The need for the organization's contribution legitimizes the organization's right to exist and command resources. The role of management, therefore, is to mitigate the uncertainty imposed by the agency's institutional role and increase the certainty needed by the agency's technical core. In other words, management attempts to keep the internal workings of an agency "rational" by buffering the agency from environmental forces, smoothing input–output relations between the agency and its clients, and/or adapting to anticipated changes in environmental demands (Thompson, 1967). An organization must, on one hand, survive and maintain some sense of internal stability and protect its established routines in order to deliver services successfully (Nelson & Winter, 1982). On the other hand, it must provide services by means that are congruent with community preferences. Although organizational members may make decisions about what constitutes appropriate services, environmental constituents ultimately judge the value of an organization's outputs. In other words, an agency that develops favorable relations with its environment will likely be perceived as a responsive, productive, and contributing organization.

Administrators bear these responsibilities for an agency's relationships with its environment. Their presentation of the organization as possessing crucial expertise and dedicated members and their dynamic leadership will have an influence. Agencies that present themselves as "rational" and goal-directed will typically enjoy highter status with legislative bodies and be able to compete favorably for resources (Greene, Bynum, & Cordner, 1986). To the extent that demands and pressures from the environment vary, administrators may need to make structural, functional, or symbolic changes within the agency. Administrators who resist change may find themselves out of work or find the formal political-legal system bringing change to the agency.

A reactive posture can be taken, and administrators may respond to altered demands and constraints as they fall on their desks. However, administrators cannot respond to all inputs if environmental demands are contradictory or capricious: They must consider the agency's forms, resources, expertise, and scope of authority, as well as turf issues and relationships with cooperating and competing agencies and clientele, before meeting new demands. Responding in a knee-jerk fashion to all demands may create chaos within an agency rather than responsiveness.

Ideally, administrators should predict environmental changes and enter into planned change; prepare for future demands; and prepare the members of the organization to be responsive to changes in environmental demands (Weiner & Johnson, 1981). Our previous discussion of the impact that emptying mental institutions has had on the corrections system is an example of a change that could have been predicted and planned for. However, planned change is easier to write about than to implement. Many changes are easy to predict only after they have taken place. And although an organization may be able to readily predict future demands on the system, support from the organization's members or the formal or informal political systems may not be sufficient to provide it with enough momentum to reallocate resources, change philosophies or policies, or remove the impediments to change.

During the late 1970s and early 1980s, for example, many public and political figures predicted that the prisons would become overcrowded and argued for facility construction. In fact, a bond issue to build more prisons was put on the ballot in Michigan in 1981. Despite support from the state attorney general, the bond issue failed. Seven years later, overcrowding was a reality rather than a predicted possibility, and prisons were being built at a rapid rate. The uncontrolled influx of offenders from the environment overpowered the environmental forces that resisted the construction of new facilities. Change in this case was reactive rather than managed through planning and was created by environmental conditions beyond the control of the corrections system.

We will not provide a crisp set of ready-made procedures that a criminal justice agency administrator can apply in dealing with environmental pressures. (These issues will be examined in some detail in Chapter 14, which discusses change and planned change.) However, we can offer some general prescriptions. Most importantly, administrators of criminal justice agencies should avoid believing they work in a closed, or rational, system. Enforcing laws, being encumbered by written policies and procedures, working within a classic chain of command, and wearing uniforms and badges can contribute to the myth that criminal justice stands aloof from environmental pressures and its boundaries are sacred. But administrators interact with agency environments whether or not they accept that reality, and they must be prepared to protect the agency from capricious or disabling inputs while staying responsive to legitimate demands. They must be able to interpret legitimate environmental demands to their organization's members and attempt to adapt to these demands in a systematic way. Ultimately, criminal justice organizations receive their mandates, authority, and resources as inputs from the environment. Judgments on the performance and effectiveness of criminal justice agencies and practitioners will ultimately be made by the broad and conflicting range of constituencies they serve.

Summary

Throughout this chapter we have examined the interdependence of the criminal justice system and its environment. In effect, all organizations function in the general environmental conditions that exist within a society. Further, all public organizations are integral to society's formal and informal political environment. Finally, criminal justice organizations function within a specific environment that includes clients, related agencies, and other systems that make immediate demands. Environments may be static (stable and predictable) or dynamic (turbulent and unpredictable). Regardless, the organization, and specifically its administrators, must be in tune with changing environmental conditions. Administrators have a duty to be responsive to legitimate demands and changing constraints while protecting the organization from capricious, inappropriate demands. Ultimately, an agency will be evaluated on its ability to negotiate its interdependence with its environment.

The ability of a criminal justice agency to negotiate with environmental forces depends on the ability of the agency and its members to communicate effectively with external groups. Chapter 4 examines the problems of communication in criminal justice organizations. In that chapter, the obstacles that agencies encounter in building and maintaining effective communications with exogenous individuals, groups, and organizations are discussed at length. The discussion of communication is, in many ways, an extension of the discussion of environmental forces and provides further insights into the problems criminal justice agencies may have in interacting with the environment.

Case Study

Time to Dig Out

A confluence of forces and past decisions had placed the state's governor and his party's legislators in a difficult position. Major changes had to be made to the state's correctional facilities. The cost of the rapid prison construction of the last decade had sneaked up on the policy makers and become a central issue. Before the prison-building binge, the department of corrections required only 1.7 percent of the total state budget. This sum increased to 15 percent, and was projected to rise substantially in the future. During the same period, the state's industrial base was changing from industry and production to services. Thus, the state's budget base was eroding concurrent with the dramatic increase in dollars allocated to prison expansion. A further budgetary consequence was that other state services were suffering from both the increased funding for corrections and the reduction in the state's tax revenues. Supporters of higher education argued that state universities were underfunded, causing increases in tuition at such a rate that a college education was too costly for working-class families, who would, nonetheless, pay taxes funding higher education. In addition, funds for social welfare, mental health services, and state police were being limited. More important, perhaps, funds for parks, campgrounds, and road and highway construction were rationed, threatening the state's vibrant tourist business and a significant part of the state's tax base.

Recognizing this set of contingencies, the governor had declared at the beginning of his second term that there would be no further prison construction. Two new prisons were then opened to meet the ever-increasing influx of inmates. And, citizens from an economically depressed region of the state were lobbying hard for a prison to be built in their area. Exacerbating the problem, the citizens voted overwhelmingly for a proposal sponsored by the governor to shift K–12 school funding from property taxes by increasing sales taxes by 2 percent. Those funds would be disbursed by the state back to school districts. Supporters of K–12 education were still not satisfied with the level of funding, and property owners were opposing attempts by local government to increase property taxes. Read the taxpayers' lips: "No more taxes!"

The message was clear: *Carte blanche* funding for corrections was over. Moreover, legislators were finding it desirable to reduce funding for corrections in the not-to-distant future. However, they also sensed that the political climate was still frenziedly anti-crime in the aftermath of drive-by shootings and other highly visible events, even though the state's crime rate was not increasing and had cycled downward with the reduction of the size of the 15- to 25-year-old population. Some legislators were even discussing passing a version of California's "three strikes" criminal sentencing; others were attempting to outlaw radios, televisions, and other recreational opportunities in prisons in a move to "get tough on crime."

The governor's response was to propose a "truth in sentencing" bill that would eliminate parole. This was sold as a get-tough-on-crime measure. Those close to the legislative process, however, saw "truth in sentencing" as an opportunity to review, change, and control criminal sentencing to reduce the inmate population without reducing public safety. Recently, a conservative legislator announced an interest in changing legislation guiding criminal sentencing in the state. He is seeking input from the usual sources—judges, prosecuting attorneys, and law enforcement and corrections officials. In addition, he intends to consult with criminal justice professors at universities across the state. No doubt, new legislation will appear in the next few years and sentencing policies will be altered. How they will be altered, and how they will affect cost, public safety, the state's budget, and the political climate remains to be seen.

Case Study Questions

1. Identify the groups, organizations, and political constituents likely to support a reduction in funding for the state's department of corrections. Which of those groups would also publicly support changes in criminal sentencing that would reduce the prison population? Identify the stakeholder groups or individuals who benefit from funding the department of corrections or prison construction.

2. Identify the threats and opportunities to each component of the criminal justice system implicit in need to reverse expenditures for corrections to help "dig our way out" of the state's fiscal problems.

3. What changes can the department of corrections anticipate in the near future? Spell out the best- and worst-case scenarios, keeping in mind the fact that whenever the subject of sentencing criminals is open for discussion and change, most legislators and a number of interest groups will throw their plans into the decision-making hopper. How can the department of corrections affect the outcome?

For Discussion

1. In what way do environmental factors contribute to the conflicting goals and priorities of the criminal justice system? How does the bureaucratic structure of criminal justice agencies mitigate some of the conflicting demands and expectations the system faces?

2. Correctional agencies need to protect their boundaries yet be responsive to public sentiment, political inputs, and the needs of their clients. What guidelines would you give to corrections administrators to help them keep a balance between responsiveness and protecting their agency's boundaries?

3. What mechanisms or techniques can a police agency develop to make it sensitive to changing environmental circumstances? Is this more an issue of organizational philosophy than of technique? Explain.

4. How does the status of a criminal justice agency help it enter into favorable negotiations and exchange relations with its environment? Or should the question be: Does the agency's ability to enter into favorable negotiations and exchange relations with its environment affect its status?

For Further Reading

Cole, G. (Ed.). *Criminal Justice: Law and Politics,* 8th ed. Pacific Grove, CA: Brooks/Cole, 2002.

Fairchild, S., & Webb, V. (Eds.). *The Politics of Crime and Justice.* Beverly Hills, CA.: Sage, 1985.

Grau, J., "Technology and Criminal Justice." In *Vision for Change,* edited by R. Muraskint & A. Brooks, pp. 231–247. New York: Prentice Hall, 1999.

Mays, L. and Gray, T. (Eds.). *Privatization and the Provision of Correctional Services.* Cincinnati, OH: Anderson, 1996.

Olsen, M. *The Logic of Collective Action: Public Goods and the Theory of Groups.* Cambridge, MA: Harvard University Press, 1973.

Parsons, T. *Structure and Process in Modern Society.* New York: The Free Press of Glencoe, 1960.

Rourke, F. *Bureaucracy, Politics, and Public Policy.* Boston: Little, Brown, 1976.

Thompson, J. *Organizations in Action.* New York: McGraw Hill, 1967.

PART TWO

★ ★ ★

INDIVIDUALS IN
CRIMINAL JUSTICE
ORGANIZATIONS

Managers manage people. In the smallest organization or the largest, managers must be concerned with how individuals react to the organization and how managers can influence those reactions. In criminal justice organizations these concerns often take on added significance. Here the work may range from the monotony of lengthy stakeouts or duty in the prison tower to the intense pressures generated by a robbery in progress or a prison riot. It may range from dealing with common misdemeanors to making decisions about the life and death of offenders or members of the public. The work is often stressful, frequently chaotic, and always marked by competing demands and goals. In Part Two we look closely at the role of the individual in criminal justice organizations. Our focus will be on how individuals are affected by their organizations and how managers can influence that process.

CHAPTER

4

PROBLEMS OF
COMMUNICATION

The weaknesses of a hierarchical communication system is that each link has a finite capacity for handling information. As an organization's subtasks increase in uncertainty, more expectations must be referred upward in the hierarchy. As more expectations are referred upward, the hierarchy becomes overloaded. Serious delays develop between the upward transmission of information about new situations and a response to that information downward. In this situation, the organization must supplement rules and hierarchy.

(Galbraith, 1973)

The brief snippets of information conveyed in police calls were not, in and of themselves, sufficient bases for police action. Police encoded and decoded messages consistent with their own vision of the nature of the problem. They applied their own routine solution to what they defined as the problematics of the calls. Generally little affected the nature of police response, since virtually all calls viewed as valid produced the dispatch of officers in cars. . . . Communication to the police and processing thereof was deemed important only in regard to its roles in producing various paper presentations of police work. . . . By close tracking of the flow of messages within the police organization in two nations, it becomes clear that noninformational matters shaped communications processing dramatically.

(Manning, 1992)

It took us four years to win the Second World War, but it took us more than five years to build a car that could compete with the Japanese.

(A pithy metaphor by Ross Perot that quickly communicated his opinion of the state of American industry)

The literature on organizational theory and communication alike refers to communication as the glue that holds organizations together. Karl Weik (1979) describes the organizational process as a method to resolve ambiguities through the collective processing of information. The typical organization—private firm, federal regulatory agency, police, court system, or corrections agency—is structured in some logical way. But whether or not the organization functions logically, in a coordinated manner, and achieves its goals depends greatly on the quality of its communication—its ability to process information. Hence all members of an organization are given "permission," if not training, to communicate along certain pathways and within certain limits to facilitate coordination among members and among components of the organization.

Most, if not all, organizational members understand the importance of communications. Poor communication, however, is often blamed for problems that occur within an organization. For example, when subordinates disobey directives and are difficult to control, it is often convenient for managers to assume communication is faulty rather than examine more fundamental issues, such as the applicability of directives or the willingness of subordinates to follow orders.

The pivotal question here is what we mean by poor communication or, for that matter, communication itself. Communication impacts and is scripted by an organization's environmental forces, formal structure, human interactions between its members and clients, and organizational politics and by the theater, rich with symbols and self-expression, in which organizational members play out their roles (Bolman & Deal, 1997). In complex organizations, poor communication in the theater of human dialogue carries implications far beyond a poorly worded memo or a broken fax machine—although both phenomena also contribute to poor communications. Identifying an organizational breakdown as a function of faulty communication is often a convenient solvent for problems but is typically only the tip of the proverbial iceberg. To understand communication in organizations—processing information through symbols and metaphors—it is important to understand the formal and informal pathways and hurdles through and over which information is determined to flow.

The basic element of communication is a *dyad:* two individuals transmitting symbols back and forth or, more simply, two people communicating. Dyads may range from intimate to professional to *ad hoc* (Trenholm & Jensen, 1992). To understand the complexity of communication within organizations, we can think of an infinite number of interchangeable dyads attempting to process information using an infinite number of symbols through a number of charted and uncharted pathways and over a number of identifiable and invisible hurdles.

This chapter is an attempt to briefly identify and discuss the complex strands of communication in the criminal justice system. We begin with a description of the basic dyad and briefly discuss the hurdles and pathways faced by actors playing a role in the criminal justice system. We also apply the basic theories of communication to individual practitioners in the criminal justice system, considering the unique and varied interactions they routinely perform. We conclude with prescriptions for criminal justice administrators, advising our readers not to view communication as a phenomenon separable from an organization's formal and informal structures and its culture. Communication dyads dance in a complex and changing community.

Basic Theory of Communication

Interpersonal communication begins with a basic dyad—one individual sending a message to another. Communication between two people can be thought of as a sequential process with Person A encoding a message and then transmitting it through some medium, after which the message is received by Person B and decoded. If a message sent from Person A fails to get to Person B, no communication has taken place.

Process

Encoding is the first step in the communication process. The sender feels the need to convey a message to another individual or individuals and encodes the meaning of the message into symbols. Words are the most familiar symbolic form to us, although communication with nonverbal symbols—Morse code, flag signals, codes used by police dispatchers to briefly describe situations or orders—is also common. But the sender's

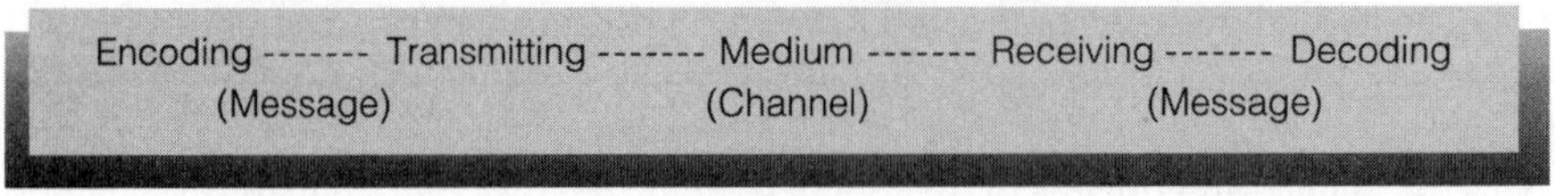

Encoding ------- Transmitting ------- Medium ------- Receiving ------- Decoding
(Message)   (Channel)   (Message)

FIGURE 4-1   The Basic Communication Process

thoughts and meaning must be encoded into some verbal or nonverbal symbolic form before the message can be transmitted. The next step in the process is to transmit the message through a medium the sender selects. The intended receiver of the message must then receive the message and decode it—that is, the receiver interprets the symbols conveyed in the message and gives them meaning. If the communication flows both ways, the receiver responds to the message with communication back to the sender, who now becomes the receiver. Figure 4-1 shows this basic interaction.

Barriers to Communication

Although this process seems straightforward and reliable, we all know from personal experience that simple messages between two individuals are often not communicated effectively. The communication process is frequently unreliable, if not convoluted, for a number of reasons. Senders may not formulate their meaning properly in symbols that can be transmitted to the receiver; stated simply, one must say what one intended to say. Assuming the sender has encoded and transmitted the message to the receiver with some accuracy, a series of communication barriers may intervene to block the communication or alter the meaning of the message. These include:

1. Preconceived ideas
2. Denial of contrary information
3. Use of personalized meanings
4. Lack of motivation or interest
5. Noncredibility of the source
6. Lack of communication skills
7. Poor organizational climate
8. Use of complex channels

Let's examine each of these communication barriers in more detail to understand how they can impede or distort messages.

Preconceived ideas.   "People hear what they want to hear" best describes this phenomenon. If we have a preconceived idea about the information transmitted to us, we tend to receive and understand the message as that idea. Because, for example, conflict and mistrust between inmates and corrections officers is often based upon the stereotypical views each group holds toward the other (Kagehiro & Werner, 1981), it is not uncommon for corrections officers to encode their views inaccurately.

Denial of contrary information.   Messages that conflict with information we have already accepted as valid are often denied or rejected. For example, after assessing the message, we may reject information about the stock market based on prior information. This is a prudent or rational communication decision. However, the message may conflict with our personal beliefs or values, in which case we reject it or deny its validity without any deliberation or thought. This process, known as cognitive dissonance in the psychology literature, is the kind of denial of information that creates a communication barrier. Offenders who are addicted to drugs or alcohol often deny feedback from their counselors about their addiction. They may reply, "I use drugs because I like it, not because I need it," or "I can take it or leave it." Denial is also a common problem faced in rehabilitating offenders. Social skills training, of which communication is a significant part, is considered therapeutic for young adult and juvenile offenders. Henderson & Hollin (1983) suggest improvement of such skills, including communication skills, will improve offenders' ability to overcome denial and adjust to their environments.

Use of personalized meanings.   The words chosen by the sender may have a different meaning for the message receiver. Professional jargon or legal terminology may have little, no, or a different meaning to those outside the profession or legal system. Words and sentences that convey images of pleasure for one party may convey contrary images for another. A young person may refer to an experience with enthusiasm and say it was "really bad," meaning it was very good. Guilt is based on fact in the criminal justice system, but in psychiatry it depends on the state of one's conscience.

Lack of motivation or interest.   Motivation in communicating and interest in the message must exist for both the sender and receiver, at least to some reasonable extent, if a message is to be communicated effectively. Memo writing in organizations is a standard method of communication. However, if memoranda become excessive, personnel may lose interest in spending time reading them. If such a situation exists, a motivated communicator may supplement memos with a fresh or unique medium to get the attention of receivers.

Noncredibility of the source.   The sender of a message may not be believable for a number of reasons. Individuals who have given out inaccurate information in the past lack credibility, while individuals who have a history of providing reliable information are considered highly credible senders of messages and get the attention of prospective receivers. Individuals with relatively greater status in an organization have more credibility than those with little or no status.

Lack of communication skills.   Poor communication skills can be attributed to an individual's lack of proper training, educational level, experience, and cognitive capacity as well as personality traits. Practitioners in the field of criminal justice must master the art of receiving, collecting, recording, and disseminating information. This can be accomplished through formal education, academy training, and experience throughout the practitioner's career. A "streetwise" education is also important for developing a full range of communication skills. It is necessary to understand street language and even be fluent in it to achieve maximum delivery of services to clients and the public.

Poor organizational climate.   An organization that promotes openness and trust among its members encourages active communication. Typically, organizations that decentralize decision making, include subordinates in higher order policy decisions, and foster risk taking in their members will have a favorable communication climate. Highly formal organizations may discourage all but formal and approved communications among their members. This insistence on formality often promotes an active, informal grapevine, which often creates a suitable climate for gossip.

Use of complex channels.   The more gates that communication must pass through, the more likely it is that the message will pass slowly and be altered. The highly complex channels of communication, endemic to large, complex organizations, make communicating inefficient and ineffective. Such organizations tend to create red tape and usually become rigid because important information cannot be transmitted readily from clients or to policy makers.

Communication gap.   These barriers to communication can create a communication gap: the difference between the message the sender intended to communicate and what the receiver understands the message to be. The existence of a communication gap between individuals in an organization becomes an organizational problem that impedes effective management and operations.

Communication in Organizations

As the discussion of barriers to communication illustrates, simple messages between individuals can be inadvertently filtered or even lost. Moreover, when the individual is a sender or receiver within an organization, additional factors—organizational climate and complexity of communication channels—can make the communication process even more difficult. Both the formal organizational structure—the chain of command and hierarchy—and the informal social system within the organization affect the organizational climate and the complexity of communication channels.

Chain of Command

Scholars concerned with organizational behavior have pointed out that the innate weakness of the communication process in a large bureaucracy can lead to a weakening of administrative power or to leakage of authority (Downs, 1967). This conclusion is somewhat ironic because the traditional chain of command provides a clear set of communication paths for its members. An agency's policies and procedures, as well as traditionally accepted practices, direct members' official communications rather explicitly. Directives from top management are usually sent down through the chain of command, and subordinates are routinely required to report to superiors.

However, each level of a chain of command through which messages must pass can filter and alter information. Each level in a typical agency's hierarchy thus becomes a gate that imposes control over the communication flow.

Messages can be filtered intentionally or unintentionally. Subordinates can intentionally avoid putting forward information that will make them look inept; similarly, supervisors can avoid communicating directives to subordinates that they feel will create problems in productivity or lower their status. Messages may be filtered unintentionally as they pass through the chain of command because of the personal barriers to communication—preconceived ideas, use of personalized meanings, or lack of motivation or interest. Memos sent upward or downward through the chain of command may stack up on the desk of a middle manager. Thus, individual efforts at affecting official communication through formal channels can be a challenge rather than a matter of routine.

Kreps (1990) summarizes the process, advantages, and problems of the hierarchical flow of information. *Downward communication* allows executives a clear path to send information downward. It gives organizational members job-related information, job performance review, and indoctrination in recognizing and implementing organizational goals. *Upward communication* provides managers with their primary source of feedback, allows lower-level staff to share information with managers, and can encourage employee participation. Both types of communication, however, have their drawbacks. Downward communication tends to be overused; it is often unclear and can communicate superiors' lack of regard for subordinates. Superiors also tend to distribute contrary and conflicting messages to line personnel. Upward communication by subordinates can also be problematic. It may be risky for subordinates to be truthful with superiors because bosses may not be receptive to criticism. Upward channels of communication are also typically not sufficient to carry messages from all subordinates up the funnel of the hierarchy.

Horizontal communication among organizational members at the same level can facilitate task coordination, provide a means of sharing information, provide a formal channel of communication for problem solving, and facilitate mutual support for staff involved. Horizontal communication can also isolate groups from the hierarchy with excessive reliance on horizontal communication.

Informal Communication

Because it is cumbersome, the flow of information through formal channels gives rise to the grapevine, or *informal communication,* since formal channels fail to provide an agency's members with sufficient information to satisfy their curiosity or needs. Informal channels are not encumbered by formal organizational rules and hurdles, but information is typically altered as it passes through the gatekeepers of the informal system. Organizational members privy to accurate information can derive power and informal leadership status. They can use the information for barter and to influence other organizational members. McCleary (1968) showed that the Hawaiian prison system lost control to younger inmates—reform school graduates—when older inmates who ran the institution lost their power after being denied access to information from the warden's office. The following sections in this chapter will discuss networking, information exchange, and Likerts' "linking pin theory of organizational effectiveness," all of which rely on informal channels of communication.

Organizational Rules for Communication

Every organization has a set of rules for communication, which may be spelled out clearly in written policies and procedures. *Exclusionary rules* in criminal trials dictate the admission of evidence into court proceedings and prohibit the communication of evidence that has been obtained in ways that are considered illegal—a coerced confession, for example. In effect, this purposeful communication barrier sometimes creates a difference between "real" facts and "legal" facts—facts that can be presented in a court. Chapper (1983) suggests the efficiency of the civil appeals process could be increased by changing the rules and requiring oral rather than written arguments in specific cases. Because the present format of instructions inadvertently restricts most juries by limiting their decision alternatives, Craig (1983) argues that juries can be more flexible in their findings if the instructions from the judge are altered so that juries have more discretion. Katzev and Wishart (1985) discuss methods of judicial instruction to jurors to avoid false testimony of eyewitnesses.

In hierarchical organizations, subordinates are typically required to give particular information to their supervisors, and supervisors are expected to provide direct instruction and guidance to their subordinates. Routine reports that discuss production status, arrest rates, and violation of the rules by inmates are often required. Often, rules are unwritten but traditional. For example, it is usually unacceptable for a supervisor to chastise a subordinate who is not directly under that supervisor. Standard courtesies, such as calling a superior by title, also fall into this category (Cushman & Whiting, 1972).

In addition to well-established and explicit communication procedures and protocols, rules may be subtle and based on the organization's social system. "Informal rules that exist within the organization, e.g., rules governing when to meet face-to-face rather than send a memo, or which topics are appropriate and which are not" are far more common than formal rules (Farace, Monge, & Russell, 1977:134). Communication rules can be *content rules,* which govern standard word usage or consensus on the name of a concept, or *procedural rules,* which deal with the actual ways that interactions take place.

New members of an organization typically learn communication rules through trial and error or informal training (Farace, Monge, & Russell, 1977). Failure to understand or conform to these rules impedes successful communication. In a complex system such as the criminal justice system, which comprises many interacting agencies and diverse work environments, members face a complicated and diverse set of communication rules.

Informal Communication Networks

Every organization has its formal or official structure as well as its informal work groups. Each has its channels of communication, which to some extent overlap. The communication between individuals within and between the official and informal subsystems can be viewed as a communication network. A simple definition of a communication network is "those interconnected individuals who are linked by patterned flows to any given individual" (Hellriegel, Slocum, & Woodman, 1986). If these communication networks have been developed purposefully by management, they are considered formal networks. Whether formal or informal, a communication network can be a production network, an innovation network (where messages about new ideas and concepts are shared), or a maintenance network (through which members learn about social roles and power relationships and links between work groups) (Book et al., 1980). Likert (1961), in his classic study of medical organizations, found that organizations with individuals who communicated across subgroups and thereby linked them together were highly productive.

Individuals may also be part of *kinship networks* within organizations. These social groups are formed more for personal than for professional motives and may not have much to do with the goals of their agency. Such networks, called "Old Boy" groups, may comprise old college friends or people with the same political views or other significant personal similarities (Book et al., 1980). Police and corrections officers often meet socially at a local tavern after their shifts. At these meetings, a great deal of discussion about work-related problems—shoptalk—goes on and strengthens the bonds of the group. Entry into a kinship network is typically restricted, and it is difficult for an outsider to be a communicator within this type of network.

In a connected group of organizations like the criminal justice system, the basis for a kinship network can be the uniqueness of one's task role or the prescribed role of the agency itself. Each component of the criminal justice system has different roles: Police fight crime, courts protect the rights of the accused and distribute justice, and corrections controls and treats offenders. Those differing roles create commonalities for members of each agency. But within each agency the role is further subdivided. Police, for example, do road patrol, walk beats, investigate crimes, and administer the agency. Officers who work in the streets have a great deal in common with each other and much less in common with administrators. Thus, kinship networks form within the criminal justice system as a natural consequence of its differing structures and junctions in addition to those factors that typically help develop networks in the workplace.

Nonverbal Communication

Communication theorists consider nonverbal communication an extremely powerful part of the communication process for an organization and its individuals. Nonverbal codes are older, more trusted forms of communication; they are more emotionally powerful, express more universal meaning, and are continuous and natural. They express meaning in and of themselves, modify verbal messages, and regulate the flow of interaction (Trenholm & Jensen, 1992). Police investigators commonly interpret nonverbal communications when they interview and interrogate suspects (Waltman, 1983). However, verbal communication has been studied by scholars at far greater length than nonverbal communication, and as a result, our discussion of nonverbal communication will be brief.

Nonverbal symbols may stand on their own but are usually integrated with verbal messages. Organizations may intentionally use nonverbal symbols to represent them. Capital punishment is a strikingly clear example of a stand-alone, nonverbal message sent to would-be perpetrators of certain crimes about the potential consequences; in effect, criminal deterrence is premised on the symbolic message evoked through punishment of the criminal offender. On a lower level, police officers wear distinct uniforms and carry guns to make an authoritative statement. Judges wear black robes and sit at an elevated bench to set them apart and above everyone else involved in the process. The nonverbal behaviors of administrators may send messages that describe the agency, messages that may be congruent or incongruent with the organization's written or stated purposes or philosophy. For example, criminal justice administrators who give the appearance of being corrupt or inept may reduce the credibility of their agencies' stated purposes. Internally, bosses who advocate participative management but pay no attention to feedback from subordinates send a nonverbal message that is incongruent with their stated message.

Individuals convey nonverbal messages through facial expressions, hand gestures, and other physical language. Messages may also be conveyed through dress, hair style, tone of voice, or actions (Book et al., 1980). Reading nonverbal messages is an important part of interviews, interrogations, and even polygraph exams (Inbau, Reid, & Buckley, 1986). Again, using nonverbal messages that are congruent with verbal messages or the substance of the intended message is important for clear communication. Conversely, the recipient of nonverbal symbols needs to understand the sender's nonverbal repertoire to decode a message accurately. Limited understanding of nonverbal codes can thus pose an additional communication barrier.

Information and Communication

The terms *communication* and *information* are often interchangeable. However, they are distinguishable concepts if we think of communication as the process of passing on information. In other words, information is the substance that we attempt to share through symbols in communication. Communication becomes, then, the exchange of symbols that represent the information. Borrowing freely from Farace, Monge, and Russell (1977), we will briefly look at the relationship between information and communication, considering such factors as communication load; absolute versus distributed information; and environmental, motivational, and instructional information.

Communication Load. *Load* is the rate and complexity of communication inputs to an individual. Rate is the number of pieces of information that are received and resolved per time period. Complexity is the number of judgments that must be made or factors that must be taken into account while communicating. *Overload* occurs when the flow of messages exceeds an individual's or system's capacity to process them.

There are three major determinants of load for an individual or system. First is the environment; a stable and predictable environment provides a less complex set of messages than does an unstable environment. In addition, the extent to which a person or system depends on elements in the environment affects the input of messages. Second, the capacity of the individual or system to assimilate messages plays a key role in determining overload. Third, the individual's or system's desire for information affects information load. Computer technology can greatly increase the criminal justice system's capability to collect and store information, thereby expanding the communication load at the input end. However, because the ability to process and utilize the information is a function of organizational intellect, not of computer technology, an information overload may be created.

These three determinants of communication load affect the management of information and communication within an organization. Criminal justice agencies, structured along traditional bureaucratic lines, provide stable working environments even though a great deal of uncertainty exists within those environments. At the same time, limited resources and old habits help keep criminal justice agencies from being able to process information efficiently.

Absolute Versus Distributed Information.   *Absolute information* is an idea or piece of knowledge expressed in recognized symbolic terms. *Distributed information* is an idea or piece of knowledge that is dispersed throughout a system. In other words, "what is known in an organization and who knows it are obviously very important in determining the overall function of an organization" (Farace, Monge, & Russell, 1977 : 27). In criminal justice organizations, information is often tucked nicely into a policy and procedures manual—when such a manual exists—where no one ever sees it. The rationale for training is, in part, to assure the distribution of absolute information.

Forms of information.   We can say that information, or communication, takes on three forms that are important for the well-being of an organization or its members. First, information can be environmental—that is, it describes the environment that surrounds the organization or its members; recipients of the communication are getting information that describes actions, events, constraints, or processes in the world in which the individuals exist. Corrections officers, for example, are instructed that inmates must be given due process before being punished for an infraction of a prison rule.

Second, motivational communications provide information about organizational or personal goals or values. Corrections officers may dislike the fact that inmates must have a hearing before they can be punished for violating a prison rule. Therefore, officers must be told that they will be held accountable for punishing inmates without giving them the benefit of a hearing. Or they may be sold the idea that giving inmates a hearing will increase the system's credibility with inmates and make their job easier.

Third, instructional information, or communication, tells individuals how to proceed or what course of action to take to reach a goal. Continuing with our example, corrections officers must receive instructions about how the hearing will proceed and what their role is in it. Simply stated, individuals in an organization must be provided with information about the environment, expectations, and how to perform their role in it. Cogent communication on these three topics is, therefore, the most basic step of policy and program implementation and the basis of training in organizations.

Communication Roles for Criminal Justice Practitioners

In this section we briefly discuss communication networks in the criminal justice system. To expand our earlier definition of a network, we refer to a group of individuals who are connected over some time period by purposeful communication that is common to all members. A network is dynamic rather than static because members may enter or leave the network system.

We can apply this concept most readily by examples. Corrections officers in a large prison may be part of four or five networks simultaneously. They are part of the formal network—the chain of command—by decree. Also, as the literature has established, experienced officers build working relationships with pro-order inmate leaders. Because of this high turnover rate, however, those corrections officers who remain for any length of time probably have formed their Old Boy network that includes both officers and inmates. Officers may also be active union members, thus making up a part of that network. An officer respected by the administrative staff may further be a member of the organization's dominant coalition. These networks are not mutually exclusive but overlap. Where these subsets of networks merge, another network is created with membership from all subsets.

We do not wish to imply that corrections officers are the only focal point of networking in a corrections system. Middle managers may network with those above and below them in the agency's hierarchy. Top managers may network with community members or political figures. Figure 4-2 diagrams the interlocking of the networks just described. The street police officer may be the focal point of an even more diverse subset of networks; Figure 4-3 explores the possible links. Prosecuting attorneys may be the focus of the network shown in Figure 4-4. To meet the demands of managing a modern jail, administrators may attempt to build a network that includes jail personnel, local courts, probation departments, police agencies, and community social service agencies as well as key members of the community. Figure 4-5 depicts such a network.

We could continue to design hypothetical networks within and across criminal justice agencies, as well as networks that link members of criminal justice systems to exogenous political forces, community members, and public and private agencies. The number of potential official, kinship, and informal networks is virtually endless. The important point is that both formal and informal communication networks must focus ultimately on results and productivity for efficient operations. However, rather than nurturing productive informal networks, bureaucracies expend resources to thwart their development in an effort to protect hierarchical authority. Such quasi-military efforts are naive and counterproductive. Concepts like team policing, for example, are implicitly based on networking, but agencies put little effort into the development of informal networks with such a focus.

Communication Barriers

More pronounced communication barriers exist in the criminal justice system than in other systems because historically criminal justice has been organized so that its agencies check and balance each other. In theory, police arrest offenders whom they

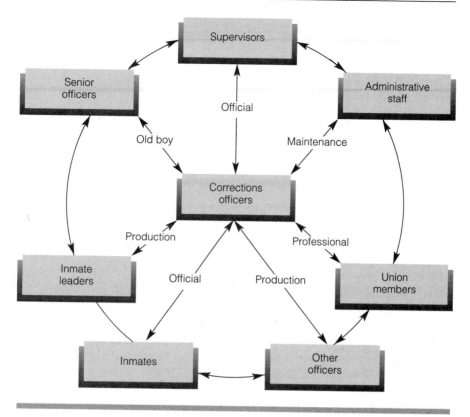

FIGURE 4-2   Multiple Networks for Prison Corrections Officers

view as probably guilty, whereas the court system assumes the offender innocent until proven guilty. Although plea bargaining makes this proposition questionable, conflicts in roles and priorities do exist between police and court personnel. The conflict becomes even more pronounced in the interactions among police, prosecutors, and defense attorneys. The murky role of corrections, including the probation systems of local courts, is often viewed negatively by police, prosecuting attorneys, and even local judges as providing services for convicted offenders.

Communication among criminal justice agencies, in short, is carried out by individuals with different views on how criminal offenders should be treated and processed as well as on the role and purpose of the criminal justice system. Thus, communication networks that include individuals from different agencies must begin by overcoming preconceived ideas about the treatment of offenders and different perceptions of the role of the criminal justice system in general.

We can see how other communication barriers can become exaggerated because of basic differences in perceptions. For example, if a parole officer suggests to a police officer that many offenders mend their ways, the police officer may be inclined to deny this information and respond that criminals just get more skilled at crime and therefore don't get caught.

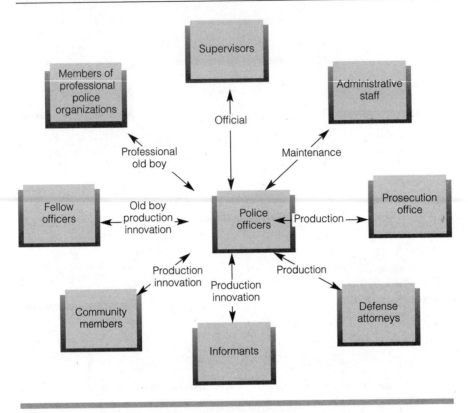

FIGURE 4-3 Multiple Networks for Line Police Officers

The personalized meaning of words and phrases varies from agency to agency. Police have official codes and abbreviations, courts and lawyers rely heavily on legal language, and corrections has its own professional jargon relating to the sentencing and processing of offenders. Criminal justice practitioners from any agency should learn the unique languages of other agencies and know how to use it in the proper context for good communication to take place.

At the official level, the motivation for and interest in communicating certain information from one criminal justice agency to another may vary greatly. Police provide evidence on a case to the prosecutor, and after conviction both agencies pass that information on to the corrections system. But they are often reluctant to pass information on to other criminal justice agencies. The police are not open with defense attorneys about a case; defense attorneys by oath do not provide information about a criminal defendant that will harm the defendant; corrections agencies are often reluctant to open their files to police agencies, fearing police will use the information to the detriment of a corrections client. In addition, police agencies with similar functions in the same jurisdiction may not be willing to share information because they view themselves as competitors. Thus, agencies are motivated to conceal information because

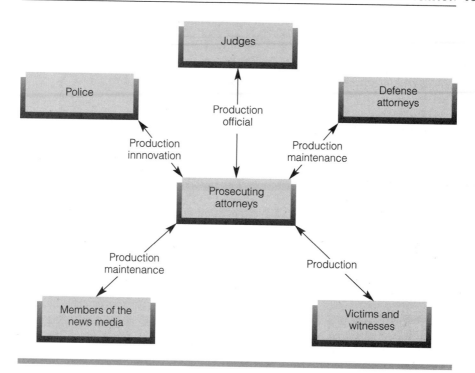

FIGURE 4-4 Multiple Networks for Prosecuting Attorneys

of their conflicting perceptions of the function of the criminal justice system. As we will see later, however, information is often readily exchanged among agencies and individual practitioners as networks based on an exchange model are developed; this model provides inducements to trade information that ordinarily might be withheld.

It is easy to understand how the conflicting roles of criminal justice agencies and the differing perceptions of their practitioners can create an organizational climate that is not conducive to ongoing and open communication. Clearly, the credibility of a communicator from another agency or even one's own agency can be suspect. Another mitigating factor is the complexity of formal communication channels in the criminal justice system. Large criminal justice organizations and their component agencies have many hierarchical levels, many specialized subunits, and much isolation of members from one another. Channels of communication in such an organization will be much more complex than those in a smaller criminal justice organization.

Besides communicating with others in the criminal justice system, practitioners may come into contact with victims, suspected or convicted offenders, witnesses, members of public interest groups, news media representatives, employees of public social service agencies and private security companies, and even elected officials. These individuals have differing values, nonverbal codes, subgroup languages with personalized meanings, motivations for and degrees of interest in entering into communication, and communication rules and styles. Barriers to communication will be

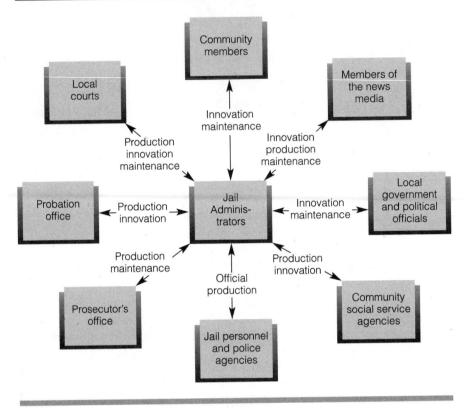

FIGURE 4-5 Multiple Networks for Local and County Jail Administrators

different for each set of individuals the criminal justice practitioner must deal with, and these barriers can confound the communication process with harsh regularity.

Developing Informal Communication Networks

We have suggested that communication networks can be important for efficient and effective operations in criminal justice agencies and the criminal justice system. Unofficial or informal networks within and among agencies evolve in the search for efficient methods to achieve the goals of the system—at least as perceived by the network members. These networks are often based on one of two principles: exchange theory or linking pins.

Exchange

The basis of *exchange theory* is relatively simple: Worker A assists Worker B, and B pays for the assistance by helping A in some way. This shared assistance may be in the form of effort or labor, but typically it is information or help in cutting bureaucratic red tape. The exchange is based on bargaining among practitioners in the criminal justice system over time and is a product of the social system in which it functions (Marsden, 1981). Exchanges may be random or *ad hoc*. It is common, however, for exchange systems to be somewhat stable and to include a cadre of participants who link up with peripheral members when appropriate.

It is sometimes difficult for outsiders to understand that such a system exists in bureaucratic organizations. It would seem that if everyone performed duties as prescribed, there would be no need to trade effort for effort. However, there are several reasons for such a system. First, large bureaucratic systems tend to pass on work and information slowly, requiring a relatively high number of transactions. By forming exchange networks that circumvent the formal structure, workers can economize on effort, time, and resources by cutting down the number of transactions (Williamson, 1981). In effect, through exchange systems the work of the organization can be done with relative efficiency.

Second, the rules that govern practitioners' work efforts and territories are not rigid, and an individual worker may shift resources, efforts, and priorities for some external motivation or reward. In an exchange network, the reward may be an implied promise of extra effort from the recipient in the near future. For example, a police officer may forward information to a parole officer on the conduct of parolees if the parole officer will reciprocate. The information may be exchanged by phone or over lunch rather than through formal communication links.

Third, the exchange of information helps both parties perform their legitimate functions and contributes to the attainment of the overriding goals of the criminal justice system. The system exists for the mutual good of its participants. If participants are seeking legitimate agency goals, it will serve the goals of the criminal justice system. "Continued exchange relationships generate a sense of trust between the system's participants, which in turn promotes a cooperative attitude that is strengthened by the organization's reward structure" (Cole, 1983:112). The glue that links exchange systems together is communication. Thus, exchange systems become communication networks that enhance the productivity of their members. Because the members' motivation for and interest in communicating are based on self-interest, they are able to overcome the usual communication barriers.

However, exchange networks and informal communication systems aren't always created to enhance an organization's efficiency. The traditional agency grapevine may carry false or inaccurate information. Networks may be created to facilitate personal rather than organizational goals. In addition, well-intentioned workers may pursue their own interpretations of their agencies' goals in their exchange networks, interpretations that may often be different from those of the system's policy makers, who presumably are attuned to public demands through the political system. And although information may flow freely within a network, members may intentionally or unintentionally withhold crucial information. As we discussed in Chapter 3, most large public service agencies are decoupled, with policy makers and workers responding to demands from separate environments. Exchange mechanisms may further decouple the administrative arm of an organization from the work-processing sector.

Administrative Communication in Police Agencies

"What we have here is a failure to communicate." The resounding truth of those words from the Paul Newman film *Cool Hand Luke* has been the bane of police administrators everywhere. Police departments have not been alone in struggling with the dubious issues involved in communications. Private industry and government alike have fallen victim to misinterpreted directives, policies, and memos, often resulting in litigation.

Administrators have often underestimated the extraneous forces that shape the thinking of management personnel and patrol officers alike. Informal influences carry more weight in determining the direction of a rule, policy, or directive than a chief may be willing to acknowledge. In more recent times, police chiefs have taken these factors into consideration during policy development, and many agencies now coordinate their efforts through *ad hoc* committees consisting of multiple levels of personnel. Representatives from the ranks of patrol officers and sergeants are invited with greater frequency to policy development meetings, assuring greater chances for policy success.

Communications in a police agency carry significant weight beyond their intended objective. Whether communications are verbal or written, if they originate from the administration they are, in fact, directives and, therefore, orders. It is not unusual for a supervisor to assess the work of a patrol officer and question what it is she or he is doing. When challenged by a supervisor, the officer zealously professes to following a recently invoked order or policy. Clearly, some officers follow an order for the benefit of the order and not for its intended result.

The fundamental mistake made by the police chief or supervisor in presenting formal communications to officers is the failure to recognize the informal influences affecting the officer's interpretation of the communication. This mistake is repeated in almost every communication, whether it is a rule, policy, directive, or memo. The officer recognizes formal communication but interprets the communication based on informal factors as well as subjective beliefs based on those prejudices most influential to the officer.

Considering the impetus behind the order, a police chief should not be amazed at the confusion created by a written order. Most orders, whether they are rule, policy, or directive, are a direct consequence of outside influences. These informal influences include politicians, courts, prosecutors, activist groups, and community associations. Each group has its own expectation of the results, which often exceed police resources as well as legal considerations.

Almost invariably, the police chief writes a forceful directive in favor of a particular result, and the chief typically treats that result as being clear and beyond dispute. Police chiefs rarely acknowledge serious factual and legal uncertainties in their directives. In addition, their failure to concede at least the legitimacy of competing arguments and concerns creates hostility within the ranks of those officers expected to carry out the order. The result oriented directive is doomed to failure.

The administrative team, consisting of captains and lieutenants, can expect the same evaluations depending upon their position. Upper-level management and mid-level management personnel expected to carry out the order are in the most critical position in the communication process. While they are directly or indirectly involved in the decisions communicated from the office of the chief, they may not hold the same conviction the chief holds. The chief who invites supervisors to assist in policy formation often finds personal opinions and even disagreement invisible during policy formation, but in the absence of the chief, particularly during presentation to the officers, these initial supporters publicly denounce the policy. Those administrators unwilling to decry the policy divorce themselves from the policy by denouncing its author.

Recognizing this possibility, police chiefs approach communications from a stylistic standpoint. Policies and directives become unnecessarily lengthy and redundant and are poorly written. Comunications begin to detail facts in an effort to demonstrate clarity, but in fact the directive diminishes officer discretion. These types of communications generally recognize mid-level supervision weakness as this exaggerated memo is moved through multiple shifts and supervisors alike.

What does the chief really expect in communicating the needs of the department to his personnel? Minimally, it is expected that a change of course will occur, even if it is incrementally accomplished. Compliance is desired, but it is tempered with patience as police officers buy into the order through time-tested practice. The chief hopes that no egregious breach of law or acts of stupidity result from the officer's application of the order. Finally, most police administrators recognize that an officer's agreement is unnecessary to carry an order, but a commonsense uniform application is paramount to the success of the order. Can anything more concise be expected?

Communication in its most simple form can be the most contentious issue facing police departments. Moving communications from the office of the chief to the patrol division is like carrying water in a sieve; the issue is strained beyond recognition in many cases.

GARY MIKULEC, POLICE CHIEF
Whitefish Bay Police Department
Whitefish Bay, Wisconsin

The Linking Pin

Likert (1961) found that productivity in industry was highest in companies that were coordinated by a hierarchy of interlocking groups rather than by a traditional chain of command and its directed policies and procedures. The interlocking groups are bound together by *linking pins,* persons who serve as members of two or more groups or are part of the social system of two or more groups. Linking pins are individuals who make a concerted effort to have credibility and influence in their own units as well as in other units that affect the efficient operation of their units. The linking pin acts as an informal coordinator, making *ad hoc* efforts to smooth the work flow between units. We can surmise that the person acting as the linking pin could overcome the barriers of communication between units and probably establish an exchange system between units.

Implications for Criminal Justice Managers

It is clear that effective and efficient communication is crucial for an organization to function. However, communication in all organizations will be less than perfect. This is especially true of criminal justice organizations, which face multiple and conflicting constituents and a complex and changing environment. The challenge of improving organizational communication must be understood as an ongoing and difficult process. Communication is always a bit broke and always needs fixing. Several general areas that criminal justice administrators need to emphasize to improve communications for their organizations are discussed here.

Communication with the Environment

Understanding the role of communication to the external environment requires a unique perspective. The criminal justice system has inherited the perceived responsibility of providing society with a sense of personal and psychological safety. Society expects crimes to be solved and criminal offenders to be successfully prosecuted and justly punished. Theoretically, prosecuting and punishing offenders will, by example, deter others from criminal activity. This assumption is premised upon the notion that the punishment of criminal offenders is communicated to the public (Kohfeld, 1983). However, no systematic efforts exist to communicate clearly to citizens the factual relationship between an offender's crime and his or her punishment. This situation is made more problematic because the punishment of juvenile offenders is generally kept from public knowledge by expungement of juvenile records (SEARCH Group, Inc., 1982). Communicating the outcomes of the criminal justice system is left to the media and politicians, who communicate and reinterpret the system's activities to the public, often in a pejorative light, to enhance their own popularity. Administrators need to develop routinized methods of providing useful information to the public and the political system; they must learn to cultivate, not shun, media relations.

Dealing with the public through the news media to produce favorable police–community relations may be fraught with deep and fundamental problems. For example, Selke and Bartoszek (1984) found through surveying criminal justice and journalism students that a great deal of suspicion and distrust exists between the two groups even before they enter the field. Hence, both sender and receiver in the police–media dyad have preconceived notions about the information communicated, and the communicator typically lacks credibility. Building a relationship with the media is a formidable challenge fraught with potential problems, but it must be a major goal of an agency administrator.

In the last decade, forms of systematic communication to the public have been attempted. A major attempt to communicate the problem of crime and encourage citizens to take personal action to protect themselves was a Sears-sponsored public relations program titled "Take a Bite Out of Crime." The campaign utilized the media and provided public service ads that encouraged citizens to take standard precautions to protect themselves from crime. Follow-up studies by the Center for the Study of Mass Communications Research (1982) and by O'Keefe and Mendelsohn (1984) showed that community members had seen or heard the crime prevention ads and were motivated to take some anticrime steps in their communities.

Efforts at developing team and foot patrol policing rely heavily on the interaction and exchange of information between police and community members (Trojanowicz & Banas, 1985). Attempts have been made to improve the contacts between police and community members by improving procedures for citizens' complaints against police (Brown, 1983). Scott (1981) suggests that police services and community relations were dramatically improved for a metropolitan police department as a result of a referral system developed by the department to refer citizens who contact police for social service assistance to appropriate agencies. Improved referral systems among metropolitan police departments, the community members who contact the police, and other public service agencies can improve police services and community relations (Scott, 1981). Tullar and Glauser (1985) and Missonellie and D'Angelo (1984) also recommend improved use of technology to strengthen police communications with the public.

While technology, referral methods, and so on can be added to systems to improve communication, often a fundamental practice or structure of a police agency can hamper police–community interactions. Capowich (1998), for example, tracked the communication between community members and local police in a community policing program. He discovered that many of the special police programs aimed at solving community problems were flawed because they were formulated by top administrators based upon information received via traditional communication channels such as dispatch reports and reports through the chain of command. Both traditional organizational procedures tended to reframe the information to fit the traditional organizational paradigm, hence limiting the chance for community members and community police officers to identify and solve local problems.

Relations between corrections and the public can sometimes lead to conflict. In an effort to improve the information flow between corrections and the media, the National Jail Coalition (1984) produced a short manual briefing reporters on complex jail issues. Tully, Winter, Wilson, and Scanlon (1982) present recommendations to assist corrections departments with community relations. In the case of a corrections department that is attempting to build a facility in a resistant community, they recommended that speakers from corrections trying to sell these programs know how to communicate with the public and have credibility with them. They should not simply be administrators or public relations people drafted for this purpose.

Victims, who should be considered beneficiaries in the larger task environment, are often left out of the criminal process, yet they are immediate stakeholders who will evaluate the process and the system. Hagan (1983) suggests that victims need to be made active participants in their cases by being kept abreast of progress and having procedures explained to them. After extensive interviews with six hundred victims, Hagan found that those who were kept advised of the progress of their cases and who understood the criminal justice process as it applied to their cases were typically satisfied with the outcomes. Conversely, those who were not given information were typically unhappy about the outcomes of their cases.

Administrators, therefore, need to build bridges and communications links to funders, legitimizers, beneficiaries, and other components of their agency's task environment rather than simply allowing communication to occur in an *ad hoc* or as-needed manner.

Intraorganizational Communications

Intraorganizational relationships and communication within the criminal justice system are, by design, ineffective. The components of the criminal justice system were historically designed to oppose each other to assure the rights of the criminal defendant. Thus, members of different components have differing roles, duties, and perceptions about the purpose and mission of the system. As we have seen, members of different agencies thus have their own preconceived notions about the world and possess their own unique rhetoric. The conflicting roles of criminal justice agencies often cause the day-to-day interaction and communication between practitioners to be adversarial rather than cooperative in nature and intent. Hence practitioners are often denied permission to communicate cooperatively and with certain of their colleagues. Nonetheless, administrators and individual practitioners can develop programs and initiatives to improve communication across agencies.

When Ryan (1981) examined conflict levels between police and probation officers, for example, he showed that the quality and quantity of contacts between police and probation officers had an impact on their level of conflict. For officers with a great deal of work-related and personal contact, conflict was extremely low. Such contacts may minimize inaccurate stereotypes and communication barriers between the two groups. Finally, Pindur and Lipiec (1982) found that a system that required continual and immediate contact between arresting police officers and members of the prosecuting attorney's staff improved the relationship between the two agencies.

Communication can be improved within each agency by improving the climate. Nuchia (1983) suggests that law enforcement officers should exercise their own "First Amendment right" to be critical of their departments. Archambeault and Wierman (1983) recommend that police bureaucracies move away from the traditional chain of command to the so-called *Theory Z* approach, which encourages teamwork rather than adversarial and competitive relationships among agency staff. Similarly, Melancon (1984) argues that police agencies should institute quality circles, which are similar in concept to Theory Z and facilitate the participation of line staff in management.

Dickinson (1984) argues that prisons should radically change communication policies toward inmates and allow them much more contact with the outside world than they now have. Concerning inmate rehabilitation, Jacks (1984) recommends an eclectic approach for interacting with inmates called *Positive Therapeutic Intervention.* The approach simply requires that corrections staff be trained to be good listeners and pay constant attention to inmates when they discuss their problems. In a similar vein, Cole, Hanson, and Silbert (1982) suggest that the implementation of inmate mediation within a prison system precludes full-blown formal litigation, saves time and resources, and achieves amicable solutions.

All forms of participatory management tend to increase the frequency and quality of communication among organization members. Although such improved communication is the foundation of most modern management or human relations approaches to management, the process and theories of communication are rarely an explicit part of criminal justice research. Only three of the articles cited focused directly on communication, and communication is underrepresented in the research on organizations in general (O'Reilly & Pondy, 1979). Much more attention, it seems, should be given to the glue that holds organizations together.

General Considerations

It is easy to conclude that efficiency in organizations is linked to good communications. If individuals within and among organizations communicate poorly, they will find it difficult to coordinate their work and link their tasks. If directives and orders are communicated ineffectively, programs, plans, and changes in routine tasks are hard to implement. Managers and practitioners would agree on this conclusion, at least in principle, and so does current research (Snyder & Morris, 1984). Therefore, managers and practitioners in criminal justice agencies should actively seek to improve communication channels and individual communication skills. Typically, the task of improving communication is ignored or is relegated to occasional training seminars that do not teach that art in the context of the organization. This situation is unfortunate because a great deal has been written on improving individual communication skills, and training programs to develop effective communication skills are abundant.

Assisting organizational members to improve their skills through ongoing training could significantly decrease communication barriers. But most criminal justice practitioners, left without such training, instead pick up the values, priorities, and jargon of their agency in short order as they are socialized into their work groups. Since they are rarely given any direct or formal training about the values, priorities, and jargon of those outside their organization, however, communication is often stymied. To the extent that formal training in communication is provided to criminal justice practitioners, it focuses on law, agency rules and protocol, chain of command, and other formal aspects of communication. Report writing may be offered to new recruits, but comprehensive training in interpersonal communications is not a common part of training agendas. Some criminal justice agencies, however, do offer training in communications for their professionals. The Michigan Department of Corrections, for example, provides extensive human relations training for their corrections officers, who are taught how to recognize and deal with communication barriers between staff and inmates and about the psychological games some inmates play. They then learn effective communications skills to overcome these barriers and problems. Taking this approach, other agencies could teach their members the values, priorities, and language sets of groups they routinely deal with as part of their training programs.

Not all communication problems in criminal justice agencies are simply interpersonal. Communication among members of different components of the system is often limited because of conflicting goals. To the extent that members perceive interagency relationships as more conflicting than negotiative, interagency communication will be limited, formal, and closed rather than informal and open. Agencies can improve interagency communication simply by making clear to their members which issues involve legitimate goal conflict and which allow for negotiation and cooperation. This procedure would give agency members permission to interact and communicate with some openness in many areas.

In addition, in those criminal justice agencies that are large enough to organize bureaucratically—with formal hierarchies, chains of command, rules and regulations, and guiding tasks—formal communication is channeled vertically, limiting the extent to which members can communicate laterally or among subcomponents. Small agencies that attempt to organize in a quasi-military manner probably also insist on vertical channels of communication. Such attempts limit the range of communication for the organization's participants. We have seen, however, that members break out of such restrictions by forming networks and entering into exchange systems with information as the commodity of trade. It would seem wise, therefore, for agencies to promote or openly sustain innovation or production networks as well as beneficial exchange arrangements. In other words, large organizations should seek to promote and control lateral communication within and between agencies by establishing formal lateral links and promoting informal socialization between pertinent members.

The development of new technology using computers to store and process communications has increased markedly during the last decade. A great deal of emphasis is being placed upon training criminal justice practitioners in computer skills (Ricker, 1996; Van Buren, 1996; Leiberg, 1996; James, 1996), such as in developing the communication skills of police dispatch and emergency services, areas that are in obvious need of technical upgrading. As communication systems become more efficient and can connect individuals and agencies to information from across the globe, information management will become extremely important. Anecdotal information suggests that the sudden leap in the ease of communicating through e-mail, interactive TV conferencing, and cellular phones has created an information overload, jamming the communication networks and intruding on unwilling recipients. Managers will have to revamp communication channels and prioritize information before the informal structure takes steps to slow down the information flow. The ease of access to information will also make the technical side of confidentiality a new task for managers.

Administrators will be forced to deal internally with many of these problems by restructuring or streamlining communication channels and provide training to agency members. As information becomes more readily available to the public, agencies will need to improve their ability to communicate within the paradigms and symbol structure of individuals and groups external to the system. The quote from

Manning (1992) that begins this chapter tells us that communication is shaped by "noninformational" matters. Encoding and decoding of information are filtered, as we have seen throughout this chapter, by the perceptions, values, beliefs, and biases of individuals and groups. In other words, the forces that constitute noninformational matters are a product of a group's organizational culture. Information processing, therefore, can be viewed as interpretation through an individual's or group's paradigm, a set of well-established rules for analyzing and understanding information.

Administrators understand the need to provide training to upgrade staff skills to match current technological advancements. However, most administrators are probably unfamiliar with the concept of communication paradigms that constrains the flow of information. This is especially true of administrators who become bureaucratized and allow "noninformational" matters to shape communications. As a result, administrators and loyal, dedicated and well-indoctrinated practitioners work hard at imposing their paradigm for communication on the rest of the world. This is an important consideration for administrators who wish to develop or improve agency relations with citizens, legislators, media, or other groups. It is also a significant obstacle within agencies as work groups at different levels of the hierarchy or with differing functions will develop unique frameworks for encoding and decoding information bases upon significant "noninformational" matters within each group. To improve communications among external constituents and internal subgroups, administrators need to develop an understanding of the cultural forces that shape communication paradigms.

To improve agency communications, administrators should think of developing skills and technical training for staff as a lower-order need rather than as a solution for communication problems. Administrators need to develop an understanding among organizational members of the impact that "noninformational" matters have on the processing of information as well as on the routines developed by traditional practices and those that structure the agencies' communication paradigm. To do so requires that communication paradigms be pulled up from the subconscious of organizations and made explicit, understandable, and tractable. If agency administrators find it desirable to expand the agency's boundaries into the territory of external groups or agencies, the communication paradigm of indigenous members of the new territory needs to be understood before communication in any depth can take place. Merely training staff in communication skills and upgrading computer skills will not in itself ensure effective communications.

Summary

The administration and management of the criminal justice system are authoritarian in nature. In such an authoritarian, bureaucratic system, information is viewed as flowing downward. It is often assumed that poor communication is simply a subordinate's error in not getting the message rather than an ongoing problem that needs constant attention. The assumption ultimately underlying the bureaucratic mentality is that if everyone knows and follows agency policies and procedures, the work will get done; if policies and procedures are not followed, it is because members do not read directives or because they read them and ignore them. For the classic bureaucrat or authoritarian administrator, this mistaken assumption constitutes the basis of all major communications problems. A breakdown in communication is typically interpreted by administrators as an authority gap or leakage of control. The solution to the problem, they believe, is to tighten controls and to reestablish authority at the top (Downs, 1967).

Hence, an important step toward improving communication in criminal justice agencies and within the criminal justice system is for policy makers, administrators, and managers to start moving away from boss-centered management toward subordinate-centered management. This prescription is certainly not new. The literature on criminal justice management is rich with discussions of the value of participatory management, Theory Z, management by objectives, and similar concepts. Proposals such as team policing, foot patrol, and therapeutic community corrections environments have active and open communication as fundamental elements. These concepts are discussed and written about with much greater zeal than they are utilized, however. Authoritarian values persist within criminal justice organizations.

Chapter 5 will apply theories of motivation to the criminal justice system, revealing the importance of effective communication in motivating agency personnel. We will see that effective communication between administrators and subordinates becomes the vehicle by which subordinates can participate in the mission of their organization.

Case Study

Reframing Noninformational Matters

From day 1, the newly elected governor of the State of Utopia knew the underlying problem in her state was the shrinking revenues in the state budget. She knew that increasing taxes in any form would be unpopular. In fact, she had pledged to improve state services within the existing tax structure. In viewing the budget, she noted that the budget for corrections had grown from 1.7 percent of the state's budget to 16 percent in a decade. Here is the culprit, she thought. If she could cut that allocation substantially during her first term, she could redistribute those funds, keep her pledge, and certainly get reelected. She fully understood that getting tough on crime was still a popular political gimmick, but she also recalled the lesson she had learned from her criminology professor years before: the certainty of punishment was a far stronger deterrent than the severity. She had an ambitious idea: if she could develop and implement a plan to streamline and coordinate the components of the criminal justice system and improve coordination of efforts across political jurisdictions, she could wage a war on crime that would focus primarily on crime prevention and apprehension of offenders. With such efforts, which allowed her to posture as a "tough-on-crime" governor, she could then safely begin to reduce criminal sentences, reinstate a parole system, return good time credits to inmates, and expand the use of community corrections. If successful, the plan might actually reduce crime rates, she hoped, and would certainly reduce the number of inmates incarcerated—which in turn would drastically reduce expenditures for corrections. To begin the study and development of her plan, she planned to put together a task force.

Case Study Questions

1. Other than her immediate advisors or cabinet members, who should the governor seek for advice on the plan?

2. Who should be appointed to her task force?

3. What language and metaphors should she use in her presentation to the individuals she would ask to serve on the task force? Should it be different for individuals representing different groups? If it is different for each potential appointee, will the members have in their minds different perceptions of her idea when they meet? Does it matter? Can her request be worded differently to each potential member without creating confusion?

4. How should the governor announce her plan to the public? How should she word her briefing to the media? Develop rhetoric and metaphors for her to use in developing her briefing to the media. Think about the tough questions she will get. Keeping in mind that the announcement comes before any concrete plans have been established—and even before the task force has met—develop answers to those questions.

5. What barriers to communications will exist between the task force members you have selected in response to question 2 above? How can those barriers be overcome?

6. Assuming that the task force creates a plan, how can the principles of this plan be best communicated to the operational staff that will have to implement it—local administrators, prosecutors, law enforcement officers? What general barriers to communications will exist among the task force members and levels of policy makers, administrators, middle managers, down to the operational staff?

For Discussion

1. How do the different work environments of police, courts, and corrections inculcate in personnel ideas that will become barriers to cross-agency communications?

2. The professionalism of police officers can create immense barriers to communication between police officers and members of the general public. Do you agree or disagree with this statement? Think of the different ways a professional can be defined as well as the traditional structure and hierarchy of police agencies.

3. What, in your opinion, are the major barriers to communication among components of the criminal justice system? What steps can be taken to eliminate the barriers you have identified?

4. How does organizational decoupling affect interorganizational communications? How does decoupling facilitate communications between practitioners and the client and interest groups being served?

5. Can a criminal justice organization develop a linking pin position in its formal organization? Or does a linking pin naturally evolve into that role? Discuss how

a criminal justice agency can develop linking pins. Where should they be placed in your hypothetical agency? How will you select and recruit them?

For Further Reading

Book, C., Albrecht, T., Atkin, C., Bettinghaus, E., Donohue, W., Farace, R., Greenberg, B., Helper, H., Milkovich, M., Miller, G., Ralph, D., & Smith, T. *Human Communication: Principles, Context, and Skills.* New York: St. Martin's Press, 1980.

Capowich, G. *Police Communication Systems and Boundary Spanning: An Exploratory Case Study of Information Distortion.* Paper presented at the Academy of Criminal Justice Sciences, 1998.

Farace, R., Monge, P., & Russell, H. *Communicating and Organizing.* New York: Random House, 1977.

Inbau, F., Reid, J., & Buckley, J. *Criminal Interrogation and Confessions.* Baltimore: Williams & Wilkins, 1986.

Kreps, G. *Organizational Communication.* 2nd ed. New York: Longman, 1990.

Likert, R. *New Patterns of Management.* New York: McGraw-Hill, 1961.

CHAPTER

5

MOTIVATION OF
PERSONNEL

Motivation Defined

Understanding Organizational Theory and Motivation
from a Historical Point of View

Theories of Motivation

Work Perspective: Some Thoughts on Motivation

Prescriptions for Criminal Justice Management

Summary

Case Study: Motivating the Police Officer

For Discussion

For Further Reading

Even though [corrections] officers can now bid on the institutional assignments they perform, it is not the specific duties that are involved in a particular job that seem to be the officer's primary concern. The motivations for working on a particular job assignment are, for the most part, a reflection of individual attempts to relate meaningfully to their work environments, rather than attempts to find positions from which they will be able to make meaningful contributions to the correctional task.

(Lombardo, 1981:45)

Since the pay raise my people get is tied to the ratings I give them, there is a strong incentive to inflate ratings at times to maximize their pay increases to help keep them happy and motivated, especially in lean years when the merit ceiling is low. . . . Conversely, you can also send a very strong message to a nonperformer that low ratings will hit him in the wallet. . . . There is no doubt that a lot of us manipulate ratings at times to deal with the money issue.

(Longenecker, Gioia, & Sims, 1987:185)

Incentives to officers to improve the quality of their performance are limited in the police field. Salaries are fixed. Few opportunities exist for promotion, and they are often strongly influenced by factors beyond the control of the administrator. . . . Against this rather bleak background, problem-oriented policing creates the opportunity for many intrinsic rewards. An officer can derive satisfaction from dealing with and solving problems. In addition to a personal sense of accomplishment, the officer will receive positive feedback from his or her department and from members of the community who benefit from the officer's actions.

(Goldstein, 1990)

In truth, there is no such thing as a motivator. You can't just apply the right treatment and "get" employee motivation, as if you were doing some chemistry experiment. People who are highly motivated are self-motivated period. They have a strong will to achieve, to succeed, to learn, to perform. External factors are insignificant in comparison with internal motivation to succeed. Impose external threats or incentives in too heavy handed a manner, and these self-motivated people will lose their strong commitment and become as careless as the rest.

(Hiam, 1999)

From these four quotes, we can begin to see that the process of employee motivation is often puzzling and difficult to understand. Different people need different incentives. Moreover, differing job tasks may require an array of motivational techniques to get an employee to accomplish them. In some instances, the provision of increased monetary rewards may be satisfactory for getting employees motivated; in other instances, employees may require attention to their personal needs and increased emphasis on their input in producing a product or service. The first quote demonstrates that some corrections officers expect meaningful structuring of their tasks, including the ability to be autonomous or to contribute to the well-being of prisoners. Research has demonstrated that proper motivation of criminal justice employees reaches far beyond purely monetary incentives; criminal justice administration must, therefore, develop and advance other methods of motivating personnel.

The purpose of this chapter is to examine the subject of motivation and how it applies to the criminal justice process and its personnel. We review the major theories of motivation developed in the field of organizational behavior and, more important, apply these theories to the various components of the criminal justice system. Because of the dearth of material in this area specifically focused on criminal justice personnel, it is necessary to review the major findings from other fields and attempt to apply these results to criminal justice. In short, our goal is to answer the following questions: What are the major theories of motivation? Which theories of motivation are able to explain the behavior of criminal justice personnel? How can we restructure existing criminal justice bureaucracies to motivate employees to work efficiently and effectively?

Before we attempt to answer these questions, however, it is important that we provide a definition of motivation.

Motivation Defined

Motivation can be looked at in two ways. First, we can view motivation as a psychological concept, examining the state of mind of the individual and why he or she exhibits a certain type of behavior. American culture values the work ethic, and much of this attitude can be traced to personal values transmitted to children in their formative years. Learned values, therefore, play a critical role in whether a person is motivated to perform various tasks. (Later in this chapter we will discuss, from both a human and an organizational point of view, those factors that lead or cause a person to act in a certain fashion.) The psychological definition of motivation depends on how the individual perceives the world and on the "psychological contract" between the individual and the work environment (Schein, 1970). In terms of criminal justice, we could ask, for example, what factors motivate people to become police officers or, more important, what factors in the police environment motivate individuals to do their jobs? Even more telling would be an examination of those structures in the police organization that simultaneously promote the fulfillment of individual needs and motivate people to do their jobs.

Second, we can view motivation from an organizational point of view, exploring the kinds of managerial behavior that induce employees to act in a way consistent with the expectations and demands of the organization. This organizational way of examining motivation enables us to explore those motivational strategies that promote the best interests of both the individual and the organization. In seeking a sense of congruence between the employee and the organization, management has the responsibility of providing mechanisms that enable employees to be highly motivated to do the work expected of them. In criminal justice agencies, we could ask, for example, how the administrator of a police organization or a correctional institution motivates employees or what the best strategies for motivating rank-and-file police officers or corrections officers are.

In the remainder of this chapter, we attempt to provide answers to these questions. Because there has not been much research on motivation in the criminal justice system, we focus on those theories of motivation that address issues fundamental to criminal justice. In addition, we provide some prescriptions for criminal justice systems based on our understanding of motivation. First, let's briefly examine the historical development of the theories of motivation. From there, we will examine specific theories.

Understanding Organizational Theory and Motivation from a Historical Point of View

Theories of motivation evolved over the last century concurrent with the industrial revolution, the expanded role of government, and the growth of large institutions. If we examine the influence of *classical* writers within organizational theory in the early part of the 20th century, such as Frederick Taylor, Henri Fayol, and Mary Parker Follett, to mention a few, we see that their ideas on management have significance for understanding motivation and *how* employees are motivated in the work setting. These classical writers believed in the importance of a centralized system of management and the coordination of management activity directed toward the most efficient ways of performing work. Additionally, they viewed the proper role of management and administration as the creation of clear lines of authority, a well-defined chain-of-command, and rules and regulations to guide and assist workers in the performance of their duties.

For classically oriented writers, motivation was first and foremost a product of the efforts of managers to create clearly defined work rules and supervision strategies that reinforced what the job entailed and how the work was to be best accomplished. From the workers' perspective, they were to be self-motivated, but more importantly, the responsibility for developing and maintaining a motivating environment among workers was in the hands of supervisors who directed, led, and watched over employees such that maximum performance was enhanced and work was accomplished in a timely and efficient manner. We see that for many criminal justice organizations the ideas of the classical writers have had a profound influence on their structures and their views on motivation. We discussed these ideas in Chapter 2, and they will come up again in later chapters.

In contrast, later writers on organizational theory, known as proponents of the *human relations school,* were concerned about how employees fit into organizations beyond simply being workers. Writers such as Chester Barnard (1930s) and Peter Drucker (1950s), and even the more contemporary writers such as Demming (1980) and Schein (1997), viewed motivation as much more an interactive process between workers and supervisors. For supporters of the human relations school, motivation was tied to *how* their supervisors treated employees and how organizational relations between managers and employees were cultivated to achieve organizational goals. In short, organizations are cooperative ventures. In the words of Barnard (1938), all organizations must be viewed as "moral entities" that require the give-and-take of concerns expressed by both administrators and employees. Under a human relations model, motivation is best understood as a *process* where both managers and employees work together to create a motivating environment. The motivation of employees rests with both the employer and the employee. Research conducted in the 1950s and 1960s sought to understand the relationship between the *behavior* of managers and leaders and subordinates that produces a motivating environment. It also has relevance to understanding leadership and job design in organizations.

The *behavioral school* of management emphasizes the importance of manager and leader behavior to motivation and other critical administrative actions. By focusing on the behaviors of leaders and managers, it is hoped that proper ways of interacting and supervising employees will lead to more motivated employees. In fact, the entire field of *organizational development* has its roots in the human relations school and the behavioral research findings of the 1950s and 1960s. Organizational development in the 21st century is more focused on the integration of ideas on motivation, leadership, and job design into one area that centers on developing motivating environments, building organizational leaders, and designing the best possible ways to organize large numbers of persons to accomplish specific organizational goals. It is impossible to think about motivation without thinking about other important concerns among administrators, for example, leadership and job design.

As you examine the theories of motivation defined below, do not lose sight of the importance of the history of ideas on motivation and how they are linked to broader theories of organization that have evolved during the 20th century and still influence our comprehension of how people are motivated in organizations. These ideas, in addition, have clear implications for how criminal justice administrators, managers, and leaders work toward inspiring and motivating their employees.

Theories of Motivation

A number of theories have been developed to explain motivation. We will highlight here those approaches most relevant to the criminal justice system and grounded in empirical literature. Six such theories can be identified:

1. Need theory
2. Theory X and Theory Y
3. Achievement-power theory
4. Expectancy theory
5. Equity theory
6. Theory Z

Need Theory

The most recognized theory of motivation comes from the work of Abraham Maslow (1943), who argued that we can examine motivation as one result of various physical and psychological needs. The central theme of *need theory* is that all people have needs, both physical and psychological, which affect their behavioral patterns. Maslow argued that human beings have five basic needs.

Physiological needs, such as food and water, assure the basic survival of the individual, which must be assured before any other needs can be fulfilled. After physical needs comes the need for safety and security. Human beings must feel safe in their environments and free from any threat of attack by aggressors; they also need to live in a secure and certain environment in which they can act as social beings. Belonging needs are reflected in the desire to be loved and to belong to a group. In addition, people need to have and show affection toward other human beings. Both needs may be expressed either in joining groups or by receiving support from one's family, friends, and relatives. Besides being loved, other needs of individuals center around self-esteem, self-image, and how one is viewed by peers. Individuals seek prestige and recognition from their loved ones and their fellow workers. Self-confidence is intricately tied to this perception of self-worth.

Self-actualization needs, finally, center on one's potential to grow and to do one's best in endeavors. According to Maslow, these needs are different for every individual, which is why it is difficult to develop a motivational strategy that is able to meet the self-actualization needs of all employees. Figure 5-1 displays Maslow's hierarchy, divided into higher-order needs and primary needs. Higher-order needs are belonging, esteem, and self-actualization; primary needs are physiological as well as safety and security. What does the research evidence show about need theory? Tosi, Rizzo, and Carroll (1986:221) conclude that there is empirical support for need theory and, in particular, Maslow's conceptualization of need theory. They believe research has demonstrated that when lower-level needs are not met, concern for higher-level needs decreases; that when an individual need is satisfied, it becomes less important, except in the case of self-actualization; and, finally, that there is a difference in need orientation among occupational groups. Rank-and-file workers, for example, consider lower-level needs to be more important in work situations than do managers. Managers perceive higher-level needs to be more important than lower-level needs.

In addition, some research indicates that age is a critical factor in need orientation. Criminal justice research in particular suggests that older police officers and those with higher levels of education perceive control of their environments and some autonomy as critical to job satisfaction. Moreover, older police officers seek self-actualization through the completion of tasks (Griffin, Dunbar, & McGill, 1978:77–85). Providing these officers with control of their jobs through structural changes in the police department may be a way to retain and satisfy them.

Support for need theory has also been documented in the field of corrections. For example, research suggests that many corrections officers leave their positions because of the organization's inability to meet their needs for improved working conditions. Intrinsic working conditions, such as degree of autonomy, perceived variety of tasks, amount of authority, and learning opportunities, are all critical to turnover (Jurik & Winn, 1987:19–21).

Managerial behavior, therefore, requires attention to the various levels or stages of development of workers and how to motivate them to meet higher-level needs as they travel up the need hierarchy. This seems to be a dilemma for current managers of organizations, including criminal justice, because how these needs are not only identified but also met within an organization becomes somewhat problematical (Witham, 1980). Police organizations, for example, are composed of such a wide variety of personalities that it would be difficult to identify motivational strategies for

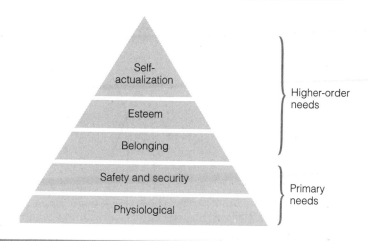

FIGURE 5-1 The Need Hierarchy (From *Motivation and Personality* by Abraham H. Marlow. Copyright © 1954, 1987 by Harper & Row, Publishers, Inc. Reprinted by permission of the publisher.)

all the differing levels. Ideus (1978) addresses this issue in institutional corrections, suggesting that the importance of motivational theory lies in its ability not only to identify these needs but, more important, to match employee's individual needs with the demands of the job. Ideally, efficiency and effectiveness would be enhanced if corrections organizations were able to match individuals to clearly identifiable tasks.

Bennett (1981) goes further by suggesting that the structuring of the police role makes it difficult for some needs to be met. Specifically, he suggests that many lower-order needs, such as physiological ones, cannot be adequately met because of the long hours and waiting associated with the job. Of greater significance, however, is the police organization's inability to deal with the self-esteem needs of officers. Bennett argues that within many police departments leaders do not promote a sense of belonging among officers. This lack of belonging usually manifests itself in conformist behavior, which inhibits an open atmosphere of trust and recognition. Because recognition is infrequent, many officers become cynical. Although Roberg (1979) has identified this problem in relation to police management, little has been done to prescribe for police managers, or for that matter other criminal justice managers, how they are to function given the needs of their employees.

Obviously, the motivational process is complex, and it is often difficult to discern which of the many variables are the most critical. Yet it does become apparent from research conducted in criminal justice organizations that the fulfillment of needs is crucial to motivating employees. Cordner (1978) suggests that many public service employees, particularly police officers, generally have their lower-level needs met by the organization. It follows, as a result, that the organization must focus on higher-order needs, in particular, the need to be recognized, to participate in decision making, and to be given responsibility. At present, fulfilling these needs is not a possibility in many public service organizations; and criminal justice agencies are no different.

What criminal justice managers can do is recognize those needs that require attention so that job tasks can be completed. For a police officer, for example, patrolling the same area day after day may not be the most self-actualizing activity, yet it is a job that must be done. Providing attention to basic needs, such as ensuring the officer's safety, may be enough for this task. In similar ways, other needs of police officers must be understood in light of organizational tasks. It may also be that many tasks associated with the police role, at least at the line level, cannot fulfill the higher needs of the rank-and-file police officer. For middle managers, finally, the issue of higher needs is more critical than for line officers. Presently, administrators in criminal justice organizations have not addressed this type of issue.

Theory X and Theory Y

The second theory of motivation consists of two parts—Theory X and Theory Y—and is based on the work of Douglas McGregor. In his seminal article "The Human Side of Enterprise" (1978), McGregor describes these two approaches to human behavior and management, which are based on a number of assumptions about human behavior. Theory X is derived from three fundamental beliefs that McGregor (1978:13) considers collectively as the conventional views of management.

1. Management is responsible for organizing the elements of productive enterprise —money, materials, equipment, people—for economic ends.

2. Management directs the efforts of personnel, motivates them, controls their actions, and modifies their behavior to fit the needs of the organization.

3. Without active intervention by management, people would ignore—even resist—organizational needs. They must, therefore, be persuaded, rewarded, punished, controlled; their activities must be directed. This is management's task. We often sum this process up by saying that management consists of getting things done through other people.

Theory X is also based on a number of ancillary beliefs about individuals in organizations: they are lazy, lack ambition, are predominantly self-centered, are resistant to change, and on the whole are not too bright. This approach to management works to the detriment of meeting the higher needs of employees. As McGregor (1978:16) states:

> The carrot-and-stick theory does not work well at all once man has reached an adequate subsistence level and is motivated primarily by higher needs. Management cannot provide a man with self-respect or with the respect of his fellows or with the satisfaction of needs for self-fulfillment. It can create such conditions that he is encouraged and enabled to seek such satisfactions for himself, or it can thwart him by failing to create those conditions.

As a result of the inadequacy of this approach for meeting higher human needs, of which McGregor believes ego needs, social needs, and self-fulfillment needs to be the most important, he proposes an alternative view of management—Theory Y, which views the human condition in an optimistic way. Theory Y is based on the following assumptions (McGregor, 1978:16–17):

1. Management is responsible for organizing the elements of productive enterprise —money, materials, equipment, people—for economic ends.

2. People are not ignorant of or resistant to organizational needs. They have become so as a result of their experience in organizations.

3. Motivation, potential for development, capacity for assuming responsibility, and readiness to direct behavior toward organizational goals are present in people. Management does not put them there. It is a responsibility of management to make it possible for people to recognize and develop these attributes themselves.

4. The essential task of management is to arrange organizational conditions and methods of operation so that people can achieve their own goals by directing their own efforts toward organizational objectives.

As can be seen, this approach to management is based on assumptions about humans and their functioning in large organizations that are different from the assumptions of Theory X. It suggests, fundamentally, that management has a crucial role to play in motivating employees. More important, this approach to motivation suggests that there is a definite relationship between job satisfaction among employees and management style. This management approach has been supported by many in the police field, such as Roberg (1979), who argue that Theory Y is more conducive than Theory X in helping police deal with the demands of competing groups in today's society. Furthermore, they argue that a system of supportive management is the most effective because it provides a satisfying work environment for the individual officer (Cordner, 1978). This conclusion seems to be equally applicable to prosecution, courts, and criminal corrections. But additional research on motivation and criminal justice operations needs to be conducted. Although Theory X has been the norm in traditional criminal justice organizations, Theory Y deserves increased attention both by those interested in explaining motivation in these systems and by those who seek advice on how to motivate criminal justice employees.

Moreover, we do have some insight into the motivation process among administrators. For example, Downs (1967) suggests that the motives of employees are not always consistent with those of administrators. His model of motivation in public organizations is tied to aspects of both Theory X and Theory Y. According to Downs (1967:84–85), public administrators, such as those in the criminal justice system, have two types of motivations that are manifested in a number of goals. First, power, money, income, prestige, convenience, and security are all manifestations of self-interest (Theory X), the motivating factor for many public administrators. Second, public administrators may, however, be motivated by altruism (Theory Y), where the goals of loyalty, pride, desire to serve the public interest, and commitment to a specific program of action take precedence over self-interest goals.

Achievement-Power Theory

The *achievement theory* of motivation was originally developed by Donald McClelland (1965). In addition, attention is now being paid to the power motive. It seems appropriate to discuss these two motives (achievement and power) together. We begin by examining achievement. Individuals can be led toward specific behaviors because these behaviors produce feelings of achievement.

McClelland (1965:322) suggests that people with high achievement values do the following:

Developing a Motivating Work Environment

Working with offenders, particularly women offenders, is a difficult job even on the best of days. In order to maintain a working staff team that is cohesive and stable, great care and attention must be devoted to the work environment. An effective work team directly relates to the quality of the treatment provided to our women clients. If the team suffers, the clients suffer as well in not getting the best treatment possible.

In working with women offenders in a residential setting, we are attempting to facilitate change. Changes does not occur for most women in an environment that is not "safe," that is, an environment they perceive as punitive, unstructured, not driven by their best interests, and certainly one that they do not perceive as helpful.

In parallel fashion, if we are to provide such an environment, our staff must perceive it as "safe," that is, an environment they perceive as supportive, clear, driven by their and the client's best interests, and one that they see as helpful to both staff and clients. Social service agencies that hold a double standard for staff and clients are a stage for professional burnout. That double standard is "provide good care for clients but work overtime constantly, do not get sick, be careful about those vacations, and don't expect much in return."

Providing a healthy work environment is high priority stuff in maintaining an excellent treatment program over time. A women's facility hires mostly women employees to work with its clients. Women have different ways of relating than men in traditionally male work environments. Women need inclusion and comfortable relationships, flexibility on the job, trust in other team members, particularly management, and a feeling of being valued.

Female staff need to feel "a part of" the total running of the agency and to know how and where they fit in the agency. Good and consistent communication is a large part of this. All need to have clear information about clients and between staff. They need consistent communication about clients and inclusion from the management team as to the status of the agency. Staff meetings that are inclusive of all staff are important in this process. Once a month staff meetings are held with all clients as well, so that we can see ourselves as one whole. A sense of community is critical for both staff and clients.

Women tend to define themselves in terms of relationships. Our identity lies in our relationships. It is critical that work relationships be comfortable in order to maintain positive energy in the workplace. This involves trust, and trust requires attention and commitment on the part of all staff. Employee "fit" with the agency becomes critical. When interviewing potential employees, it is essential that they understand how important the issue of trust is and that it requires effort for all involved. Each staff person must be able to tolerate a certain amount of the anxiety that comes from dealing with interpersonal issues. All workplaces have gossip mills and conflicts, but in a healthy residential treatment center it is imperative that staff issues be dealt with smoothly and efficiently. There also needs to be a mechanism whereby staff can air their concerns about how their team members are dealing with a very challenging client population and an atmosphere that will be supportive and not punitive. This develops trust. When the energy that is generated by trust is absent, the workplace becomes "contaminated," and both staff and clients will suffer. Clients will play the parts of children in a dysfunctional family and begin to act out in any number of ways.

Flexibility is especially essential in working with women staff. Women do not primarily find their identity in work but in their relationships, including their relationship to their work. Employers need to see women as having priorities outside of work that at times requires attention. For example, sick children need their mothers with them. There are emergency calls from school that require staff to leave work, and ill family members may require attention. Some staff may require flexibility around school attendance that will benefit the job as well. The ability to adjust to the day-to-day needs of staff is necessary at times in order to maintain a supportive work environment.

This flexibility also helps build trust in management. Some staff are fearful that traditional management will not validate their needs as women but will remain rigid and place them in a traditional male-oriented "top down" position. Women do not operate well in a hierarchical environment, but they respond well to a workplace where they are assigned roles and a feeling that all jobs are important and essential to a working team. It is up to management to be accessible, responsive, and sensitive to staff concerns. So the management team must hear complaints in a non-defensive manner and accommodate reasonable requests.

Helping staff feel valued is the ongoing responsibility of every team member, and the tone is set by management. Praise must be constant, heartfelt, and encouraged by everyone. Staff need to be well compensated for their work with a difficult population and not be expected to work overtime. Management must set the tone for excellent self-care and require it in all staff, encouraging time off for vacations as well as for health reasons when appropriate. Innovative thinking in providing an extra boost for the spirits is always welcome. In fact, time is spent in weekly staff meetings to attend to our spiritual aspect. By doing all of this, we acknowledge that our staff and our workplace is more than the job itself but also the people who work in those jobs.

CONSTANCE SHAVER
Executive Director
Horizons, Inc.
Milwaukee, Wisconsin

1. Seek to achieve success through their own efforts and not have their success attributed to other factors.

2. Work on projects that are challenging but not impossible.

3. Receive identifiable and recurring feedback about their work and avoid situations where their level of achievement is in question.

This last proposition was tested by Stoller (1977) in his analysis of the effect of feedback on police performance. He examined the relationship between feedback and increased police productivity as measured by issued citations. Increased performance was achieved by forty-eight of the fifty-four officers who received the feedback. This seems to be a recurring theme in much police research: consistent feedback from upper-level managers can promote increased productivity among line officers (Roberg, 1979:114). Other research done on police has indicated that many officers need to increase their level of responsibility and participation in decision making. Hernandez (1982) found in the Mesa, Arizona, police department that a "professional model" of policing, which involved participation in problem solving and decision making, increased the officers' level of commitment to the department and their level of motivation.

The second motive associated with this theoretical position is the power motive. A growing body of literature attempts to document the role that power plays in organizations, particularly in decision-making processes (see Salancik & Pfeffer, 1977; Porter, Allen, & Angle, 1981; & Pfeffer, 1981). Our goal, however, is to examine power as an aspect of motivation. The power motive can be defined as a person's need to have some type of influence over another's behavior, and this can be expressed in two ways. First, it may be in the form of personalized power, as manifested through an adversarial relationship. Person-to-person competition is emphasized, and domination is a by-product. People are viewed simplistically as winners and losers, with the main goal being the achievement of power over others. Second, socialized power is impersonal and is expressed through a concern for others; it is employed by individuals who are sensitive to the fact that someone's gain means another person's loss. This type of power orientation is humanistic and is employed by those in leadership roles in social organizations (Tosi, Rizzo, & Carroll, 1986:228).

This presentation of the achievement-power theory of motivation enables us to see how the factors of achievement and power are instrumental in the motivation of individuals. Surely we can say that individuals are motivated by the quest for either achievement or power or both. Little research supports either of these positions completely, but we do know, for example, that achievement, as defined by promotion, is important in the police field. Gaines, Tubergen, and Paiva (1984) concluded that promotion is extremely important in meeting the needs of police officers. In particular, they found that for some officers higher needs were more important than lower needs and that promotion was, in part, related to the satisfaction of those needs. In effect, the officers' desire to achieve, in this case through promotion, was crucial to their levels of motivation.

With respect to the power motive and criminal justice personnel, research has been done primarily within correctional institutions. Stojkovic (1984) documents the types of socialized power within inmate social systems and how they affect the operation of a prison. Socialized power among corrections officers was also explored by Hepburn (1985) and by Stojkovic (1987). Specific bases of socialized power were employed by both inmates and officers to complete their respective job assignments and tasks. For example, corrections officers considered the use of legitimate power—reasonable instructions and rules—a useful tool in motivating prisoners to do what is expected of them. Additionally, the use of coercive power or force was not rated highly by corrections staff as a way of gaining compliance among prisoners. Power as a motivational tool has also been documented by research on corrections administrators (Stojkovic, 1986).

Understanding the social bases of power within the prison is crucial not only for motivational reasons but also for exploring the organization itself. Chapter 10 examines the concept of power in the context of criminal justice organizations.

Expectancy Theory

Expectancy theory, based on the belief that if a certain amount of effort is put forth, a calculated outcome will result, is a rational approach to motivation. This theory posits that police work, for example, relies on an expectation among police officers that their efforts will produce a reduction in crime. The individual officer's motivation to perform depends, in part, on reduced crime rates. From an idealistic perspective, rational activity on the part of the police officer should reduce crime and increase the officer's satisfaction.

Figure 5-2 depicts some key concepts in expectancy theory. We summarize these concepts here (Tosi, Rizzo, & Carroll, 1986:240). A basic concept is that performance equals motivation times ability. Performance is a function of the individual's ability to complete the task along with the motivation to do the task. More important, if either motivation or ability is not present, then there will be no performance. Motivation and ability are related in a multiplicative fashion.

An *expectancy* is the likelihood that an event or outcome will occur. Expectancies take two forms. First are *effort–performance expectancies,* in which the person believes that a specific level of effort will result in a particular performance. The police officer, for example, may believe that a connection exists between the level of patrol activity and the crime rate in the precinct. In short, there is a correlation between the amount of work done and the end result, which in this example is the amount of crime in a specific area. Second are *performance–outcome expectancies,* in which the person has an "expectation about the relationship between a particular level of performance and attaining certain outcomes" (Tosi, Rizzo, & Carroll, 1986:243). In this form of expectancy, the police officer may believe that a relationship exists between activity and a positive evaluation from superiors that is ultimately expressed in some type of reward, such as a promotion. However, the relationship between police activity and crime rates is somewhat problematical. If, for example, there is a low probability that police activity will lead to an actual reduction in crime, then it is difficult to see how one can reward individual police officers to produce the desired performance, that is,

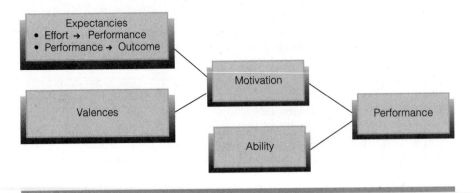

FIGURE 5-2   Some Key Concepts in Expectancy Theory (from *Managing Organizational Behavoir,* by H. L. Tosi, J. R. Rizzo and S. J. Carroll. Copyright© 1986 by Pitman Publishing Company. Reprinted by permission of Harper & Row, Publishers, Inc.)

reduced crime. In addition, if it is unlikely that the officer will gain any reward from the activity, he or she will not be motivated to do the activity. As a result, we would expect that the motivational levels of individual officers would be low because there is a low probability that their work activity produces the desired performance. Therefore, the individual officer may not choose crime reduction as an outcome. More important, the officer may desire other outcomes more, typically those that are attainable and rewarded consistently by the police organization.

Valences are the level of satisfaction or dissatisfaction produced by various outcomes. In brief, they are the individual's estimate of the advantages or disadvantages of a particular outcome. In the police example, if the effort required to produce a reduction in crime among officers does not lead to a satisfactory level of reward from the organization, this activity has a low positive valence; it is not worth the effort to pursue the activity knowing the low level of reward attached to the effort.

These principles taken together are represented in Figure 5-3. We can see from this figure how the various expectancies operate to produce the outcomes or payoffs.

Tosi, Rizzo, and Carroll (1986:243–244) discuss how expectancy theory can be expanded to include other factors that affect the motivational level of employees. They argue that motivation is a function of expectancies and valences. Ability is a function of performance potential and organizational factors. Performance results from motivation and ability and leads to both intrinsic and extrinsic rewards. The level of performance affects the effort–performance expectancies. The rewards received for performance affect performance-outcome expectancies in later periods, and rewards also affect satisfaction. Figure 5-4 depicts this expanded expectancy model.

Interpreting and applying this model to police officer motivation, we can say that first the individual motivational levels of police officers are a function of what they expect and what valence they assign to their various activities. Second, the ability of an officer to do the job is a function of the officer's performance potential or the range of skills used in the achievement of objectives (Tosi, Rizzo, & Carroll, 1986:244). These skills may be limited by structural factors such as job descriptions, policies,

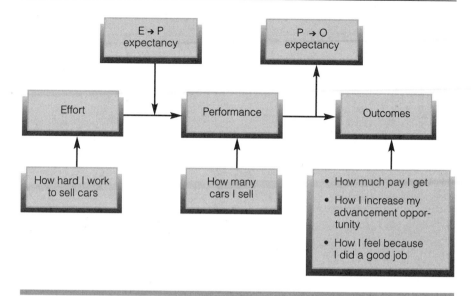

FIGURE 5-3   Effort-Performance and Performance-Outcome Expectancies

and technology. Arresting all known criminals, for example, would be impossible because of the limited resources of police organizations and the policies of the organization toward full enforcement of the law (Goldstein, 1984).

Third, when police activity leads toward some performance and that performance
is a function of motivation and ability, then we would expect that a reward would follow. If an increase in arrest activity leads to an increase in pay or a promotion, then the
officer receives an extrinsic reward for the performance. Additionally, if arresting individuals provides the community with a safe environment and gives the officer a good
feeling about doing the job, the officer receives an intrinsic reward; this reward is typically self-administered by the individual. Many have suggested that a clearly identified
reward structure within police departments is what is needed to properly motivate
officers (for example, Gaines, Tubergen, & Paiva, 1984:265–275). However, others
have argued quite persuasively that these rewards are far and few between and are limited by the structure of many police departments. Conser (1979:286) contends that
motivation is difficult in police organizations because the opportunities for advancement and promotion are limited. He recommends a number of mechanisms that would
raise the motivational levels of officers, including merit pay packages, extra vacation
leaves, and extra pay for education. Nevertheless, some research suggests that extrinsic rewards, such as increased pay and promotion, are only a small part to the motivation of police officers. Intrinsic rewards, such as achievement (Baker, 1976), are just as
valuable. More important, it seems clear that proper motivation of specific officers requires a multitude of management strategies. Figuring out the most appropriate strategy within a certain context and with the right officer is the responsibility of managers.

Fourth, when an officer perceives that a level of performance will consistently
produce a similar positive outcome from the organization, such as a reward, this

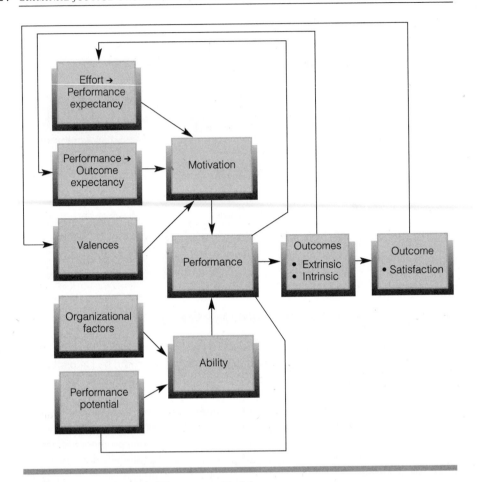

FIGURE 5-4 An Expanded Expectancy Model

perception will affect future expectancies; this process is nothing but learning by the officer and reinforcement by the organization through the reward structure. As the police officer learns that ticket writing, for example, is positively rewarded by the organization, the officer will continue to perform the activity until rewards are discontinued by the organization. In effect, the performance expectancy is a function of reinforcement and feedback by the organization (Stoller, 1977:57).

Finally, if the police officer is consistently rewarded, both extrinsically and intrinsically, then we can say that he or she has a high level of satisfaction with the organization. Conversely, if the police officer is not receiving rewards, then we can expect that dissatisfaction is high and will continue to stay at this level until modifications are made. Criminal justice managers need to be aware of and sensitive to the level of dissatisfaction if organizational objectives are to be met (Witham, 1980: 10–11). In fact, it may be accurate to discuss organizational deviance within criminal justice bureaucracies as a function of dissatisfaction among employees (see Manning & Redlinger, 1977).

Equity Theory

Equity theory holds that an individual's motivation level is affected by her or his perception of fairness in the workplace and that individual motivation must be understood in relation to how other employees are treated by management and the organization. Fundamentally, equity theory stresses the importance of fairness in the organization and how employees perceive its application in the workforce. In addition, equity theory rests on two fundamental assumptions: Individuals evaluate their interpersonal relationships as they would any other commodity; and second, individuals develop expectations about their evaluation in the organization equivalent to the amount of individual contribution they make. As such, an examination of both inputs and outputs is critical to understanding and applying equity theory.

Inputs are those items brought into the organization by the individual. Common examples of input include age, seniority, training, and education, to mention a few. *Outputs* are the visible products of individual effort. Examples of outputs are promotion, salary or pay, recognition, and benefits. All inputs and outputs are not weighted the same. For some police officers, for example, the value of experience "on the street" is weighted much more heavily than educational attainment. As an organizational input, these same officers would view the outcome of pay to be determined more by experiential level than by educational level. For them, the weighting of work experience would be higher and deserving of greater reward. For other officers, the reverse may be true. It is the differential level of attachment to various inputs and outputs that makes equity theory problematical.

Every individual in the organization determines the relative weights of inputs and outputs. It is the ratio of a person's outcomes to inputs relative to the ratio of ouputs to inputs of others that determines the level of perceived equity. Inequity occurs when the individual perceives the ratio of outcomes to inputs to be unequal. The potential negative consequences of this perceived inequity concern both managers and administrators of organizations.

For criminal justice organizations, the perception of inequity is fostered by a number of factors beyond the control of administrators. The rigid structure of public contracts, for example, limits the ability of criminal justice organizations to deal effectively with perceived inequities. In addition, it is difficult for employees to feel motivated if they perceive a disjuncture between their work performance and their pay in relation to the work performance and pay of similarly situated employees. As such, it is reasonable that some research has identified this perception of inequity as causing a loss of morale and motivation among public sector employees (Schay, 1988). For criminal justice managers, this perception of inequity can have negative effects on the motivation of employees.

What can be done? Research has suggested two strategies. First, criminal justice administrators can do everything in their power to see that employees are treated equitably. One of the advantages of a union contract is that it equalizes, for the most part, everyone in the organization, yet it still can produce inequity among those who feel they are performing better than most other employees but receive no greater financial payoff for their efforts. Despite this situation, criminal justice administrators can do a great deal to ensure equitable treatment of employees, including having clearly articulated policies and procedures and applying them to all employees in a fair and consistent manner. Criminal justice adminstrators can best reduce perceptions of inequity if employees perceive equal application of the rules and regulations, even in organizations where remuneration is perceived to be low for work performed.

Second, emphases on other aspects of the job outside of pay can be brought to employees' attention. Within criminal justice organizations, employees perform a number of duties that go beyond pay considerations. As noted in the quote in the beginning of the chapter, pay scales as a primary motivation device for police officers, for example, are a poor incentive. Pay incentives typically do not exist in most criminal justice organizations. Instead, we can stress to subordinates that the problem-oriented focus of their work provides them with much autonomy, which can be motivating. Such freedom allows greater individual expression and input on how tasks can be performed. Similar observations can be made about the work of probation and parole agents as well as those who work in correctional institutions (see Chapter 6 on job design). Such considerations can be expressed to employees by administrators and managers through job design efforts, training, and employee evaluation and supervision approaches. Such efforts can mitigate the adverse effects of perceived pay inequities among employees within criminal justice organizations.

Theory Z

Earlier in the chapter we discussed the differences between Theory X and Theory Y. Here we present an extension of Theory Y known as *Theory Z,* which suggests that management must come to grips with the fact that organizations, either private or public, can no longer exist in a social vacuum. They not only function within a larger context but also are expected to effectively deal with the needs, desires, and problems of their employees in creative and diverse ways. Proper management and administration of contemporary organizations must consider the needs of the employee and, more important, how those needs can be met within the context of both the organization and society as a whole. For this reason, Theory Z is viewed as a holistic approach to management and administration. In the area of employee motivation, Theory Z recommends broad changes and reforms.

Before we discuss these changes and how they would affect criminal justice administration, we need to examine the basic tenets of Theory Z. Of its many proponents, Ouchi (1981) is probably the most notable. He suggests, along with others, that Theory Z is based on three beliefs:

1. Management is concerned with production, a position expressed in Theory X.

2. Management is concerned with the well-being of workers as productive employees. This position is similar to a basic assumption of Theory Y.

3. Finally—and this belief distinguishes Theory Z from Theories X and Y—the organization cannot be viewed independently of the larger social, economic, and political conditions in society. More important, the work setting must be understood in conjunction with other institutions in society, such as family and school.

What distinguishes Theory Z from both Theory X and Theory Y is that it attempts to integrate the concerns of both of these theories while simultaneously reaching beyond the organizational structure into the very fabric of society. Because it holds that organizations cannot be isolated from other social forces, Theory Z offers a synthesis of the previous theories and a macro-orientation on employee motivation. It suggests that motivation is not only organizationally determined but also influenced by broad and powerful influences in society.

A number of benefits accrue from applying Theory Z to the administration of criminal justice agencies. Though Theory Z has had limited application in public organizations, including criminal justice, there has nevertheless been support for such an application. Archambeault and Wierman (1983), for example, argue for the application of Theory Z to policing, suggesting several changes that have to occur in the management of police organizations for police administrators to become more responsive than they now are to their employees and their communities.

First, there must be shared decision making in police organizations, with individual officers having increased input on matters that affect them, although management would still be the final authority on key administrative issues. Although this approach is intuitively appealing, it would not be honest to suggest that such an arrangement would be easily accepted by older and more experienced officers. The traditional structure of police organizations would have to be drastically changed for Theory Z to succeed. As Archambeault and Wierman (1983:427) suggest, top administrative officials in police organizations would have to make a serious commitment to such a radical approach before it could be implemented. Without such a commitment, Theory Z would have a low probability of succeeding.

Second, supporters of Theory Z propose a team approach to policing, with emphasis on the collective responsibility of officers. The idea here would be to get police away from the traditional notion of individual responsibility and individual work. Theory Z envisions officers working together toward the attainment of collectively defined goals, even though final responsibility would still lie with police administrators.

Third, police officers would have a clearly identified career path, with attendant rewards and promotional opportunities laid out in advance. This idea has some disadvantages because it seems to assume infinite reward opportunities and promotional paths. Although this may sometimes be the case, on the whole promotional opportunities are often few and far between in many criminal justice organizations. What if the rewards and career opportunities are just not available? What is to be done with the police officer, for example, who has become "cross-trained" in a number of specializations yet is never able to get a promotion? As fiscal constraints increase, it is not clear how Theory Z would resolve these thorny issues. This is not to suggest that nothing can be done, but at a minimum proponents of Theory Z are going to have to offer concrete answers to some of these practical concerns.

Fourth, Archambeault and Wierman (1983:427) suggest that the police organization must be more "holistic" in its dealings with police officers by appreciating the fact that officers exist in society. They have needs beyond the work setting, which include but are not limited to, for example, educational, personal, and family needs. Although it would be unrealistic to expect criminal justice organizations in this country to provide for all of the needs of their employees, as is done in Japan, it is reasonable for administrators in criminal justice to be sensitive to the needs of workers, and, in return, for employees to make a personal and professional commitment to the organization. The result of this arrangement is loyalty to the goals of the organization by subordinates and a smoothly run organization.

Similar ideas have been put forward by Houston (1999) in his examination of the relevance of Theory Z to the field of corrections. Quoting management expert Tom Peters (1987), Houston suggests that Theory Z has application to corrections in two specific areas. It is important first, to involve everyone in everything, and second, to use self-managing teams in task completion. Integrating these ideas into a motivation plan will enhance employees' sense of commitment to the organization and increase their performance. Although such an approach is desirable in criminal justice, we must again question its feasibility. It is not clear how administrators would be able to provide a structure that deals with the many needs of subordinates. Clearly, criminal justice managers and administrators need to be attuned to their workers, but what are the most effective approaches for attaining that objective? It is likely that Theory Z may require more than can be realistically expected from those who administer our criminal justice systems.

This is not to suggest, however, that there is no room for the application of Theory Z to criminal justice management. Its most positive aspect is the belief that there is a relationship between organizational structure and the motivation of employees. In this chapter we have contended that employee motivation cannot be understood independently of organizational structure. Theory Z posits that management has a responsibility to structure a work environment that promotes the highest level of employee motivation. If Theory Z enables managers and administrators to rethink their roles in shaping and influencing their subordinates, then it has begun a movement of real value to the administration of criminal justice systems. Presently, it needs to be critically examined. No theory is flawless; only through future critical evaluation will we see the benefits of the application of Theory Z to criminal justice.

Prescriptions for Criminal Justice Management

Clearly, the motivation process is complex. Moreover, the application of existing theoretical models to the various criminal justice systems is problematic because no single theory of motivation can explain the many factors that affect the motivation of criminal justice personnel. Nevertheless, we can provide some suggestions to criminal justice managers about the approaches and programs most suited to their employees. One key element links all the differing theoretical positions on employee motivation: The needs, perspectives, and viewpoints of employees are instrumental not only to their individual growth but also to organizational effectiveness. More directly, it would be accurate to conclude that effective criminal justice management recognizes that the motivation of employees requires the growth and maturity of those employees through proactive and flexible management strategies. Without such flexible approaches to motivation, employee development is stymied and organizational effectiveness is reduced. Lynch (1986:53) states:

> The present challenge to police managers is to provide a work climate in which every employee has the opportunity to mature, both as an individual and as a member of the department. However, the police manager must believe that individuals can be essentially

self-directed and creative in their work environments if they are motivated by the management.

While recognizing that the management of criminal justice systems is different from the management of private companies or other public institutions, we still believe that a number of programs can be taken from these other sectors and applied effectively to criminal justice processes. We review and interpret two of these programs here: quality circles and management by objectives. An examination of other useful programs related to job design is provided in Chapter 6. Students are encouraged to review these programs here, because they are equally applicable to the motivation process. We conclude the chapter by examining a basic model of motivation derived from a review of the research.

Quality Circle Programs

Quality circle programs are based on two fundamental assumptions. First, interactions among employees should provide for the maximum growth of the individual. Quality circles are meant to enhance workers' abilities to improve themselves, both personally and professionally. Second, by providing conditions for the growth of employees, the organization will become increasingly effective. In short, it is in the organization's best interests to promote the well-being of workers. Operating on these two assumptions, *quality circles* are defined as small groups of employees, typically nonmanagement personnel from the same work unit, who meet regularly to identify, analyze, and recommend solutions to problems relating to the work unit (Hatry & Greiner, 1984: 1). Additionally, management must support these groups of subordinates.

Within the police subsystem of the criminal justice process, researchers have strongly recommended this approach. After conducting probably the most exhaustive study to date of the implementation of quality circles and other participatory management programs in policing, Hatry and Greiner (1984) conclude that the use of quality circle programs greatly enhances the potential for producing small-scale service improvements and improving work unit morale among officers. These improvements are crucial, in our opinion, to the motivation of police officers.

Moreover, this approach to improving the motivational levels of police officers is also applicable to other workers in the criminal justice process, such as corrections officers, counselors, and court personnel. Although many of the prescriptions currently being made concern the improvement of police, the application of these quality circle programs to the other components of the criminal justice system is sorely needed. Brief, Munro, and Aldag (1976) describe the applicability of such approaches, particularly job enlargement programs, to correctional institutions. And although Saari (1982) is cautious on accepting management practices that he defines as fads, he does see the value of providing more information about management programs to those who run and manage our court systems.

Although the research literature has been generally supportive of quality circle programs, it would be naive to suggest that they can be applied to all situations in criminal justice. Understanding the motivation process requires an analysis of organizational tasks. It may be inappropriate to suggest, for example, that quality circle programs be adopted by corrections administrators faced with increased militancy among both prisoners and staff. Even though it may not be a panacea for all motivation problems, we do suggest, however, that the quality circle be considered as a possible alternative to increase the motivation levels of criminal justice employees.

Management by Objectives (MBO)

Probably no other innovation within management circles since the 1950s has had as much influence on organizations as management by objectives (MBO). *Management by objectives* can be defined as a process whereby individual managers and employees identify goals and work toward their completion and evaluation within a specific time period. Much research evaluates the effectiveness of MBO programs within organizations (Carroll & Tosi, 1973). And, in addition, this program has been widely adopted in the various components of the criminal justice system (Angell, 1971; Sherman, 1975; More, 1977; Archambeault & Archambeault, 1982). However, the efficacy of the model for the various components of the criminal justice system remains unproven. Some believe its application to criminal justice can make the system effective, and can help improve the level of motivation among criminal justice employees. Others, however, do not consider MBO to be universally applicable in criminal justice. A review of some of the research on this topic is required.

Beginning with research that supports the application of MBO to criminal justice operations, the police field has the greatest number of advocates for this view. Angell (1971) was the first to suggest that the implementation of MBO in policing would be of great benefit. In particular, Angell sees the democratization of police organizations as a step toward improving the delivery of services. Opponents, such as Sherman (1975), suggest that this democratic model, as conceived by Angell, would be deleterious to police organizations because it grants decision-making authority to teams of police and diminishes the power of middle managers in the traditional police hierarchy. In fact, Sherman argues persuasively that his own research on team policing indicates that middle management will resist the efforts of higher-echelon personnel to democratize police organizations. Essentially, he believes that any planned change within police departments must include all members of the department. Anything short of total involvement will be viewed by the rank and file as just another one of the "boss's pet projects" (Sherman, 1975:377).

More recent research, however, supports the application of MBO to police departments and suggests that it is critical to effective management. Hatry and Greiner (1984) employed multiple research methods to assess the effectiveness of MBO programs in a number of police departments. In addition, they evaluated motivational programs in more than seventeen police departments and reviewed materials provided by an additional thirty police departments. From this evaluation, they concluded that "MBO systems have considerable potential for motivating management employees to improve service outcomes and service delivery efficiency" (1984:130). More important, they suggest that much can be done to improve the operation of MBO systems in police departments if proper attention is given to them by administrators.

Archambeault and Archambeault (1982:92–93) suggest that for MBO to work in correctional institutions a number of conditions have to exist. First, as others have stated, administrative personnel have to be committed to the MBO program. A lack of commitment only breeds contempt for and disapproval of the program in lower-level employees. Second, administrative staff must be able to receive criticism and suggestions from employees. Otherwise, management will not be attuned to the workings of the organization. Third, any MBO program must take into consideration the organization's power structure. It is often difficult for managers to share power with subordinates; it has been a recurring problem in many MBO programs that administrators deny that power to make decisions must be shared with all workers. But the empowerment of employees and the subsequent enrichment of their jobs are implicit in the MBO approach. Fourth, workers as well as management must believe that the MBO process is worth pursuing. In many organizations, lack of commitment has led to the demise of MBO programs.

An Integrated Model of Motivation

It is possible to generate some conclusions on an integrated model of motivation that may be useful to criminal justice employees (California Department of Corrections, 1994b). This model would be based on key elements of the theories and literature discussed above. The model has six basic elements:

1. Emphasis on personal motives and values. An effective motivation plan must take into consideration the motives and values of employees. Criminal justice workers have motives and values that stress public service as well as personal interests; they want to be in a profession that is both appreciated and remunerated fairly and appropriately. Often criminal justice administrators are indifferent to or unaware of just how important the motives and values of employees are. Those in leadership positions must offer a set of motives and values as guidance for subordinates. By having an articulated mission statement, for example, the important motives and values of the organization become known and employees are able to see how they fit into the larger picture of the organization. This strategy will be examined more thoroughly in Chapter 8.

2. Use of incentives and rewards. Employees need incentives to meet expectations and appropriate rewards for jobs well done. A major challenge for criminal justice administrators is the creation of formal and informal approaches to recognize and reward employees. The types of rewards can be varied. Monetary rewards are often difficult to provide, but other types of rewards, such as informal praise when a job is handled well and employee recognition programs, can be given.

3. Reinforcement. Administrators must develop feedback mechanisms so that workers understand that their performance is appropriate on assigned tasks. More often than not, the immediate supervisor provides no or little feedback to subordinates. This creates much anxiety and uncertainty among employees, causing their motivation to wane.

4. Specific and clear goals. All theories of motivation highlight the importance of goals or expected outcomes to the motivation process. This is probably the most difficult and problematical area in motivating criminal justice employees. As public agencies, criminal justice organizations are expected to address multiple, and sometimes conflicting, goals; consequently, specifying goals and prioritizing them can be very difficult. This difficulty, more than any other, poses problems for administrators. Goal

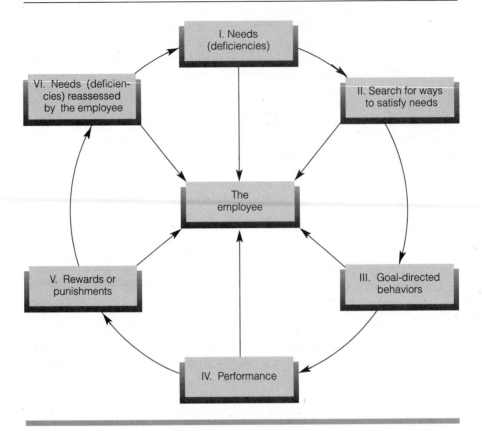

FIGURE 5-5 The Basic Motivation Process (From P. Hellriegel, J. W. Slocum Jr., and R. W. Wooaman, *Organizational Behavior,* 5th ed. Copyright © 1989 by West Publishing Company. Reprinted by permission.)

clarity and goal consensus may not be possible in criminal justice organizations and, as a consequence, developing effective motivation plans will be difficult (see Chapter 1).

5. Sufficient personal and material resources. The organization must have a sufficient number of resources, both human and financial, to create a proper motivating environment for employees. Examples of such resources include support and training programs for employees, outlets for employees that allow socialization and the development of informal groups, and material support, such as adequate supplies and equipment for tasks to be accomplished and goals attained.

6. Interpersonal and group processes that support members' goals. In criminal justice organizations, this means the development of work groups that identify with employees' individual interests as well as group concerns. Criminal justice organizations can create work environments where individuals would work together in accomplishing group goals, exercising greater flexibility in work assignments and job responsibility, and selecting group leaders. Group processes would work toward the accomplishment of tasks yet be sensitive to member needs. Individual employee needs are considered as part of the process of an effective group.

Taken together, these ideas can make criminal justice organizations more aware of the motivation needs of employees. Figure 5-5 highlights them in a model of the motivational process. The diagram shows the importance of employee needs, goal-directed behavior, performance, rewards and punishments, and reassessment of needs within the motivational process. Criminal justice administrators need to devote particular attention to these issues in developing and maintaining a motivational environment for employees. The goal is to create a motivational environment in which maximum effort can be exhibited by employees. Further research will have to test these ideas to demonstrate their relevance to employee motivation in specific situations as well as criminal justice administration in general.

Summary

The purpose of this chapter was to expose the student to a definition of motivation and provide some historical foundation for the exploration of theories of motivation. We found that a number of theories of motivation were applicable to criminal justice, yet no one model was able to explain the diverse and complex motivation processes of all criminal justice personnel. One recurring theme did run through many of the theories, however: management needs to recognize that subordinates have needs, abilities, and opinions that are crucial to the effectiveness of the organization. Whether the subject was policing, courts, or corrections, this requirement still applied.

In addition, we reviewed two models for improving the motivation level of criminal justice employees: quality circle programs and MBO. We proposed that criminal justice management and administration can be improved through the proper use of these models. Furthermore, our recommendation of these programs was based on the empirical literature. Clearly, additional research needs to be done on these programs and their applicability to criminal justice operations. Finally, we proposed an integrated model of motivation that represents a synthesis of the theories and research presented in the chapter. Future research will have to test these ideas to demonstrate their usefulness to criminal justice administrators.

An understanding of the motivation process cannot be divorced from other relevant aspects of an organization. Subsequent chapters, starting with Chapter 6 on job design, address important issues that also affect the motivation of criminal justice workers. Leadership, power, and socialization all have an impact on the motivation of police officers, court personnel, and corrections workers.

Case Study

Motivation and Control:
The Police Supervisor's Dilemma

Captain Frebe had spent a number of years watching some of his fellow officers find ways to avoid responsibility, ignore agency policies, and do just enough to get by. As a member of the command staff, his memory of slackers was still fresh, and he was receiving complaints and rumors that a number of his officers were still effective at being deadwood. He also knew from his experience that most officers were intent on doing their job well, but the productive officers were often demoralized by the fact the few deadwood officers usually got away with doing just enough to get by. Captain Frebe reasoned that a duty he owed to the productive officers was to make the slackers accountable for their lack of activity. He set out, therefore, to develop a highly structured system of accountability and a tighter system of supervisory authority.

Under his new system of supervisory accountability, Captain Frebe instructed his sergeants to exhibit a more invasive strategy of supervising rank and file officers. This meant sergeants would spend more time on the street supervising officers, to hold them more accountable to rules and regulations. Sergeants were required to write up brief reports summarizing their evaluations of police performance. More frequent performance evaluations were required, and internal investigations to expose inappropriate behavior by officers were increased. Quota systems for parking and traffic tickets were also invoked. In addition, officers were required to submit daily activity reports that included odometer reading to measure mileage against activity reports. Finally, incident reports were thoroughly scrutinized and randomly verified for content and accuracy. In Captain Frebe's mind, this was the best way to address the slackers and deadwood in the department.

Six months after implementing the new supervisory routines, the following outcomes were noticed by the higher-ups in the department: greater accountability was evidenced, with clearer indications of work being performed. For the administrative brass, such initial findings were encouraging. Nevertheless, more ominous outcomes were also found. Sergeants were asking for more transfers from Captain Frebe's district, absenteeism was rampant, internal investigations were at an all-time high, morale among the troops was abysmal, and the district was viewed by many veteran cops as the place where Captain "hard balls" Frebe ran a tight but sinking ship.

Captain Frebe was encouraged by the initial findings of increased performance under his new system of supervisory accountability, but the negative effects of this new system on the morale of officers dismayed him. Did the officers really respect him, and what about the "good cops" who were motivated to conform to the new accountability system? Was his concern for greater accountability too extreme and detrimental to motivating officers to perform their best? Did he have to achieve a balance between control and officer accountability on the one hand and, on the other, a loosening of the reins to motivate officers?

Frustrated by the effect of his new program, Captain Frebe ask his old friend Sergeant Hamilton why his system was backfiring. Hamilton replied, "When the hell do we have time to do police work?"

Case Study Questions

1. Is there a relationship between the amount of control desired in a police organization and the ability of police officials to create a motivating environment among rank-and-file officers? If so, how is balance arrived at between these two apparently opposite concerns in police organizations?

2. How could have Captain Frebe instituted the mechanisms for officer accountability without alienating officers? What role do officers have in creating a motivating environment within police organizations?

3. Is it true that you really cannot motivate persons in organizations? If this statement is true, then is there any role for administrators and managers in the motivation of their employees? Are there unique concerns that face police supervisors that make motivation of employees difficult? If so, what are they, and how would you address them?

For Discussion

1. It is often said that criminal justice employees are unmotivated. Comment on this assertion and discuss possible ways in which the motivational levels of criminal justice workers can be raised. In addition, examine what you believe to be the role of criminal justice managers in the motivation of subordinates.

2. Discuss a particular theory of motivation and apply it to one of the components of the criminal justice system. Cite both advantages and disadvantages of the approach in motivating subordinates.

3. Invite a police chief to class to discuss specific strategies he or she employs to motivate officers. Examine these strategies and identify their positive and negative aspects. Finally, discuss approaches you think will improve the motivation of police officers.

4. Examine quality circle programs and MBO models in criminal justice organizations. What are both the prospects for and problems with these types of programs in criminal justice? Go to the library and review the recent literature on the effectiveness of these programs in both private and public organizations. Discuss with the class how you think these types of programs would benefit the various organizations of criminal justice.

For Further Reading

Herzberg, F., Mausner, B., and Snyderman, B. B. *The Motivation to Work.* New York: Wiley, 1959.

Hiam, A. *Motivating & Rewarding Employees: New and Better Ways to Inspire Your People.* Holbrook: Adams Media Corp., 1999.

Likert, R. *New Patterns of Management.* New York: McGraw-Hill, 1961.

Maslow, A. *Motivation and Personality.* 2nd ed. New York: Harper & Row, 1970.

McClelland, D.C. *Assessing Human Motivation.* Morristown, NJ: General Learning Press, 1971.

Rainey, H.G. *Understanding and Managing Public Organizations.* 2nd ed. San Francisco: Jossey-Bass, 1997.

CHAPTER

6

JOB DESIGN

To me, when I was a kid, the policeman was the epitome—not of perfection—was good and evil in combination, but in control. He came from an element in the neighborhood, and he knew what was going on. To me a policeman is your community officer. He is your Officer Friendly; he is your clergyman; he is your counselor. . . . Now all we are is a guy who sits in a squad car and waits for a call to come over the radio. We have lost complete contact with the people. They get the assumption that we're gonna be called to the scene for one purpose—to become violent to make an arrest. No way I can see that. I am the community officer. They have taken me away from the people I'm dedicated to serving—and I don't like it.
    (Officer Vincent Maher, quoted in Terkel, 1974:188)

[For the corrections officer assigned to the tower, the job is a] residue of the dark ages. He requires 20/20 vision, the IQ of an imbecile, a high threshold for boredom, and a basement position in Maslow's hierarchy.
    (Toch, 1978:20)

Top administrators can no longer—if they ever could—bring about major changes in operating philosophy through fiat. And serious limits exist on what can be achieved simply by reassigning personnel, changing the organizational structure, recruiting new personnel, and conducting training programs. Problem-oriented policing, with its strong commitment to engaging rank-and-file officers more fully in the operation of the police agency, greatly increases the likelihood that rank-and-file officers will support needed change, because they are an essential part of it.
    (Goldstein, 1990)

Design is people leading companies who are thoroughly pissed off at the absence of great design in any nook and cranny of their company (or anyone else's).
    (Peters, 1994)

We are at work for much of our lives. This is true whether the duration of our careers or the amount of time we spend on the job every day is measured. For many of us, work is not only a place where tasks are accomplished but also an experience that adds to the value and meaning of our lives. Although we have many work-related personal goals, our jobs also fulfill organizational goals. Our efforts may contribute to the control of crime, the processing of offenders, or the treatment of those convicted.

    In this chapter we examine the interplay of these personal and organizational goals. We focus on how the structure of work can satisfy or fail to satisfy these goals. After reviewing some of the criteria for a "good job," we consider the technological aspects of job design and the influence of Frederick Taylor in industry and in the human services. We also examine some of the undesirable consequences of poorly designed work. The chapter then turns to advancements made in theoretical approaches to job design and finally to examples of job design and redesign in criminal justice.

What Is Job Design?

In criminal justice, the design of jobs is often taken for granted: police officers police, corrections officers guard, probation officers manage their caseloads, and judges deliberate. It is often assumed that these tasks govern the design of work. Both theory and research in industrial settings, however, question such assumptions. The term *job design* has been used to describe the "deliberate, purposeful planning of the job including all of its structural and social aspects and their effect on the employee" (Hellriegel, Slocum, & Woodman, 1995).

There are many approaches to job design and many lists of criteria for a good job. Although efficiency was once the chief concern, a wide variety of other goals has been recognized. One popular list of "psychological job requirements" includes the following factors (Emmery & Emmery, 1974:147):

1. *Adequate elbowroom.* Workers need a sense that they are their own bosses and that (except in unusual circumstances) they will not have a boss breathing down their necks. But they don't want so much elbowroom that they don't know what to do next.

2. *Chances to learn on the job and go on learning.* Such learning is possible only when people are able to set goals that are reasonable challenges for them and to know results in time for them to correct their behavior.

3. *An optimal level of variety.* Workers need to be able to vary the work—so as to avoid boredom and fatigue and to gain the best advantage from settling into a satisfying rhythm of work.

4. *Help and respect from work mates.* We need to avoid conditions where it is in no one's interest to lift a finger to help another, where people are pitted against each other so that one person's gain is another's loss, and where the individual's capabilities or inabilities are denied.

5. *A sense that one's work meaningfully contributes to social welfare.* Workers do not want a job that could be done as well by a trained monkey or an industrial robot machine. They also do not want to feel that society would probably be better served by not having the job done, or at least not having it done so shoddily.

6. *A desirable future.* Workers do not want dead-end jobs; they want ones that continue to allow personal growth.

These qualities of a good job reflect a common concern in the literature and can be traced to the warnings of Karl Marx, who said:

> What do we mean by the alienation of labor? First, that the work he performs is extraneous to the worker—that is, it is not personal to him, is not part of his nature; therefore he does not fulfill himself in work but actually denies himself; feels miserable rather than content, cannot freely develop his physical and mental power but instead becomes physically exhausted and mentally debased. (Cited in Josephson and Josephson, 1975:871.)

These concerns were echoed in a 1973 federal government task force report entitled *Work in America.* The conclusion of the report begins with the words of the existentialist philosopher Albert Camus: "Without work all life goes rotten. But when work is soulless, life stifles and dies" (Special Task Force to the Secretary of Health, Education and Welfare, 1973:186).

Engineering and Efficiency in Job Design

The task force report was most critical of jobs characterized by "dull, repetitive, seemingly meaningless tasks" and traced these impoverished jobs to the "anachronism of Taylorism" (1973:xv). Throughout most of the last century, technological criteria or concern with the efficient completion of tasks dictated the design of most industrial jobs. Frederick Winslow Taylor and his associates are properly credited as the major influence behind this trend. Increasing the efficiency of labor through the fragmentation of work, the use of time and motion studies, and the motivation of workers with pay incentives was the main component of Taylor's *Scientific Management* (1947). From the marriage of task and technology emerged such innovations as the "science of bricklaying," worked out in detail by Frank Gilbreth.

> He developed the exact position which each of the feet of the bricklayer should occupy in relation to the wall, the mortar box, and the pile of bricks, and so made it unnecessary for him to take a step or two toward the pile of bricks and back again each time a brick is laid. . . . Through all of this minute study of the motions of the bricklayer in laying bricks under standard conditions, Mr. Gilbreth has reduced his movements from eighteen motions per brick to five, and even in one case to as low as two motions per brick. . . .With union bricklayers in laying a factory wall . . . he averaged, after his selected workmen had become skillful in his new methods, 350 bricks per man-hour; whereas the average speed of doing this work with the old methods, in this part of the country, was 120 bricks per man-hour. (Taylor, 1947:81)

Taylor's influence on the design of jobs cannot be fully appreciated without examining his underlying assumptions. Throughout his works Taylor presents unflattering views of human nature. In his often-cited description of a highly trained pig-iron handler, Taylor refers to him as being "as stupid and phlegmatic as an ox" (1947:62). In Taylor's view, most people are unmotivated by work itself but are motivated by leisure and increases in pay. Close supervision by college-educated, highly trained managers and financial incentives in the form of increased wages for increased production will counteract the natural tendency toward laziness.

Taylorism in the Human Services

Scientific Management formed the foundation of industrial engineering and technology and has remained a principal influence in the engineer's design of job content in industrial settings. Taylor, however, was careful to distinguish the "mechanisms" of Scientific Management, which may have limited applicability outside the machine shop, from the "essence" of Scientific Management, which would have much wider utility:

> Scientific Management is not an efficiency device. . . . not a new system of figuring costs; it is not a new scheme for paying men; it is not a time study; it is not a motion study. . . .

These devices are useful adjuncts to Scientific Management. . . . In its essence, Scientific Management involves a complete mental revolution on the part of working man. (Taylor, 1919:68–69)

In the human services, the essence of Taylorism has been a potent influence, but the mechanisms have not been ignored. Time and motion study has been used to determine the best location of instruments for dentistry, the need for mechanized hospital beds, and even the advantages of rhythmic movements for surgeons. Beyond these studies, however, Taylor's concern with increasing efficiency through the fragmentation of work and close supervision has found wide application in the "people work" industries. Unlike managers in production industries, however, managers in the human services can rarely define their workers' roles in terms of the requirements of an assembly line or machine. In a review of policing, public welfare, and other street-level bureaucracies, Lipsky (1980:14) notes that most human services work is characterized by considerably more discretion and variety than are jobs in a factory. These differences, however, have not insulated human services work from tight bureaucratic control. For example, Karger (1981) notes the similarities between the alienating features of industrial and human services work:

The routinization of public welfare is complemented by increased specialization and the creation of continually narrower job descriptions. . . . Accountability is achieved through daily logs, regular breaks, and performance objectives. The assumption is that workers are selling their labors rather than their skills. . . . Even in private welfare we see "numbered contact hours"—a designation referring to quantity rather than quality. . . . The workplace in a large public bureaucracy—with its large rooms filled with long rows of cubicles—appears more like a bureaucratic assembly line than a private environment in which to discuss personal matters. The client is objectified as a problem that must be processed as the line grows longer. (See Hagedorn (1995) for a further discussion of these issues.)

Taylorism in Criminal Justice

In the field of criminal justice, policing has been described as a "Taylorized occupation" (Harring, 1982; Fyfe, Greene, Walsh, Wilson, & McLaren, 1997). Concern with productivity has led administrators to fragment the role of the police officer. Automobile-based patrolling and the use of nonsworn personnel for traffic control, bus monitoring, and other tasks have taken away from regular line officers the "Florence Nightingale" duties that Harring argues provided a broad, humane role for the police. He concludes that the Taylorization of police institutions is important to study because it can undermine the notion that the police are immune from the dehumanizing experiences of other workers.

This trend toward decreased discretion and increased control has been referred to as the deprofessionalization syndrome (Stone & Stoker, 1979; Sharp, 1982). The irony behind the syndrome is that as management has increased its professionalization through increased accountability and bureaucratization of work life, the status of frontline personnel has diminished. As Hahn notes: "The professionalization of police departments, therefore, acts to undermine the professional stature of individual police officers by limiting their personal discretion in handling the problems of 'clients' in the community" (1974:23).

Similar concerns about deprofessionalization are seen in the areas of probation and parole. Because probation officers generally come under the jurisdiction of the courts, Lawrence (1984) argues that they have traditionally been uncertain of their professional status. He reports that many probation officers see themselves more as judicial servants caught in the civil service malaise than as professionals. The revolution in technology in the field of community supervision may further erode the autonomy and discretion of frontline workers (Rosecrance, 1999a). The introduction of standardized classification instruments is an example. The instruments frequently use information about an offender's criminal history and other background variables to establish a numerical score reflecting the appropriate security level. These devices not only restrict the judgment of probation and parole officers in assessing their cases but also dictate the amount of time they can spend on cases regarded as requiring maximum, medium, or minimum supervision.

The development of electronic monitoring systems for offenders also appears to be altering the jobs of probation and parole agents. Such devices track the offender's location through an electronic device generally strapped to the ankle. A review of these and other changes in the processing of information in probation and parole offices suggests that they are likely to have a major impact on the nature of probation and parole jobs. The devices will accentuate the clearly defined law enforcement role of probation and parole officers and diminish the discretionary aspects of their work, which are generally associated with their treatment function (Moran & Lindner, 1985; Clear, 1995).

In corrections, jobs have frequently been described by highly circumscribed responsibilities. Civil service job descriptions in New York state list the corrections officer's duties this way:

> Correctional officers supervise the movement and activities of inmates; make periodic rounds of assigned areas; conduct searches for contraband; and maintain order within the facility. They advise inmates on the rules and regulations governing the operation of the facility and assist in solving problems.

The President's Commission on Law Enforcement and the Administration of Justice, (1967) described corrections officers as the "employees who man the walls, supervise living units, escort inmates to and from work, and supervise all group movement around an institution." These responsibilities were clearly distinguished from the professional role of other corrections staff. Such descriptions reify the corrections officer's job by ignoring the discretionary human relations aspects of the role.

Parallels between criminal justice and industrial work can be overemphasized, however. As Toch and Grant suggest, "no matter how badly off human service workers are, their fate is less circumscribed than that of the men and women who serve machines and are constrained by their technology" (1982:85). Lipsky (1980) makes a similar point when he remarks that police, judges, and probation officers continue to exercise considerable discretion because of the way their jobs are designed.

Jails of the Future and Enriched Job Design

American jails, like most other penal institutions at the state and federal levels, have traditionally followed a paramilitary model where much of the decision making is reserved for middle and top management. At the beginning of the 21st century, however, criminal justice historians can look back at the introduction of the direct supervision model pioneered by the Federal Bureau of Prisons in the mid-1970s and its beginning at the local level in 1981 in Contra Costa, California.

By 1995, the National Institute of Corrections identified 146 direct supervision jails, 16 jails that had converted to direct supervision, and 52 jails that had a combination of both traditional and direct supervision. The rated capacity of the total beds located in direct supervision pods and dorms total 94,170—a phenomenal growth in twenty years by any correctional measurement. This is only a small number of the 3,000-plus jails in the United States, but it totals nearly one-fifth of the 518,492 inmates held under jail supervision on June 28, 1996. The growth of direct supervision jails continues unabated and their popularity remains high, as attested by the annual symposium on direct supervision management held every year since 1986 at the annual training conference of the American Jail Association.

The officer in a direct supervision pod for his shift has the responsibility for the management and supervision of the inmates living there. Inmates' programs held in the pod—whether they be formal education, counseling, substance abuse treatment, or vocational training—allow the officer to make a contribution over and above his supervisory and security duties. This presumes, of course, that the officer is educated and trained up to a certain standard—that all line correctional staff are thoroughly educated in the use of new technology, especially computers, and that the specialists who deliver the services are willing to share their knowledge with the officer. Experience has shown that both officers and specialists benefit from these interactions.

When the Pima County direct supervision jail in Tucson, Arizona, began its drug treatment program, one of the strategies for breaking down the barriers was cross training of both the officers and the specialist staff so that each side received an education about the importance of what both the officers and treatment counselors did. Some of the problems addressed were contraband in the institution, confidentiality issues, fear of not being treated as professionals, use of ex-addicts as counselors, and the like. The honest discussion that followed helped resolve many of the problems anticipated by staff on both sides. It provided officers with a deeper understanding of substance abuse treatment and the implications of progress and failure. The next logical step in such an approach is officer involvement in the program itself, which requires a commitment from top management.

Those familiar with jails realize that more than 25 million people a year go in and out of the American jail system. That is more than the combined population of the states of Ohio and Illinois. Annually there are almost thirty times as many admissions to local jails as there are new court commitments to state and federal prisons. Roughly 60 to 80 percent of those booked into the jail get released within the first seventy-two hours. Many of these people have substance abuse problems, mental disorders, educational deficiencies, unemployment problems, family difficulties, and so on.

Well-trained jail booking officers who gather all this information when the individuals are booked into the jail could function beyond this stage and actually provide direction to those in need of help. A knowledgeable officer could put such persons in touch with a home health clinic, personnel employment specialists, education and vocational training centers, and a community mental health agency. These officers would need to have actual knowledge of the various agencies in the community and what they could offer. Such booking staff could profit by visits and specialized training courses offered to them by other community agencies.

The unexpected dividend to the jail is being regarded by these community agencies from another perspective than the traditional view of the jail as the dumping ground for criminals and social misfits. Short-term discharge planning can plant seeds for more fruitful collaboration once such a regime is initiated.

KEN KERLE
Managing Editor
American Jail Association

Responses to Job Characteristics

Much of the recent interest in job design has grown out of concerns raised in studies of worker satisfaction. Although more than 85 percent of American workers report general satisfaction with their jobs, detailed inquiry has revealed sharply declining levels of satisfaction with specific aspects of the work environment (see Hackman & Oldham, 1987). Discontent among hourly and clerical workers has risen to the highest level since those measurements began to be made in the 1950s. Other research has identified young workers as the most dissatisfied and the most likely to be concerned with job design issues (Sheppard & Herrick, 1972). The discontent of workers was dramatically illustrated in the early 1970s at a strike in a Lordstown, Ohio, automobile plant. Workers there did not protest low wages but instead voiced opposition to routine and boring labor. A Lordstown employee described the frustration workers felt: "You have to . . . break the boredom to get immediate feedback from the job because the only gratification you get is a paycheck once a week, and that's too long without any kind of gratification from the job" (quoted in Kreman, 1973:17).

Criminal justice research lacks the longitudinal data necessary to indicate changes in levels of job satisfaction. Still, the literature is suggestive about employees' expectations of their work. A study of police officer satisfaction, for example, paralleled findings in industrial settings when it revealed that many officers described themselves as generally satisfied with the tangible benefits of their jobs but concerned about such issues as opportunities for advancement and opportunities to improve their skills. Only about half the officers reported that they would recommend police work to a friend, and many reported that their enthusiasm for the job had diminished over time (Buzawa, 1984; Bayley, 1994; Alpert & Dunham, 1997).

Patterns of job satisfaction appear to be similar for police and corrections officers. Attitudinal changes appear to occur following training. During the initial years on the job, satisfaction decreases and cynicism increases (Niederhoffer, 1969; Van Maanan, 1973). Researchers have also described an inverted, U-shaped curve in which negative attitudes are highest in the middle of careers and lowest among officers with the least as well as the most seniority (Poole & Regoli, 1980; Toch & Klofas, 1982). Education levels have also been found to be negatively correlated with job satisfaction among police officers. Evidence indicates that a disproportionate number of the more educated police officers voluntarily leave their jobs before retirement (Buzawa, 1984; Carter, Sapp, & Stephens, 1989). It has been suggested that this turnover results from the frustration of working in a rigid setting. One study, however, suggests that this turnover may be the result of increased job opportunities (Buzawa, 1984).

In human services occupations, reactions to work also include stress and burnout. Both of these concepts refer to physical and psychological reactions to the work environment. After reviewing the available literature, Whitehead and Lindquist (1986) argue that chronic, intense stress may lead to burnout, which has been defined as "a syndrome of emotional exhaustion and cynicism" (Maslach & Jackson, 1981).

Although much of the literature on burnout in the human services has focused on issues surrounding client contact (see Maslach, 1976), some researchers have examined organizational causes. Cherniss (1980) suggests that burnout may arise from boredom, excessive demands, and such job design problems as role conflict, role ambiguity, and lack of participation in decision making. In criminal justice research, organizational factors have been identified as the major causes of stress and burnout. In studies of corrections officers in New Jersey, Pennsylvania, Illinois, and Washington, Cheek and Miller (1982, 1983) found that "administrative sources" were the primary reasons for stress on the job. Administrative sources included lack of communication from management, lack of clear guidelines, and lax or inconsistent administrative practices (Stojkovic, 1997). The researchers argue in favor of a redesign of the corrections officer's job.

Whitehead and Lindquist (1986) came to similar conclusions from their multivariate analysis of burnout among corrections officers. Using a standardized instrument developed by Maslach and Jackson (1981), these authors found that inmate contact was not only a cause of burnout, but also that such contact was positively associated with feelings of accomplishment. However, administrative policies and procedures were identified as sources of stress. This finding was also replicated with a sample of federal corrections officers (Lasky, Gordon, & Srebalus, 1986). Whitehead and Lindquist suggest that these findings may support the view that managerial control efforts conflict with officers' desires for autonomy and discretion. In another study by Stohr, Lovrich, Menke, and Zupan (1994), the authors found that correctional officers in jail settings were much more satisfied in work environments that stressed employee concerns and more involvement in the day-to-day operations of their facilities rather than simply bald, custodial control of prisoners. Moreover, Britton (1997) suggests that there are differences among correctional officers concerning their perceptions of their work environment along racial and gender lines and that the work environment does affect, in part, the perceptions of correctional officers.

Whitehead (1985) also studied burnout among probation and parole officers. Using the *Maslach Inventory* (Maslach & Jackson, 1981) with a sample of nearly 1,500 probation and parole officers in four states, he found that respondents scored higher than other human services workers on most of the burnout dimensions. In considering causes, Whitehead argues that his data do not support theories that link burnout to emotionally charged contact with clients. Instead, burnout among probation and parole agents was tied to the officers' need for efficacy and a sense of providing competent service to clients. These findings support theoretical perspectives that view job design factors as important sources of burnout. (See Alpert & Dunham, 1997, as well as Fyfe, Greene, Walsh, Wilson, & McLaren, 1997 for a discussion of these issues in relation to police organizations.)

Job Design Theory

Ten years after Taylor first published a description of Scientific Management in 1911, the Hawthorne studies at the Western Electric Company in Chicago began to demonstrate the importance of non-technological considerations in job design. In these studies, researchers under the direction of Elton Mayo tested the effects of experimentally induced conditions on worker fatigue and monotony. Set up as standard engineering experiments, the research focused on independent variables that were physical or technological in nature. Researchers found, however, that productivity increased regardless of increased or decreased illumination and regardless of the timing of work breaks or the length of the working day. The researchers soon abandoned concern with the technological variables and focused on social and psychological explanations (Roethlisberger & Dickson, 1939).

Although workers performed dull, repetitive tasks that required little skill and afforded little status, productivity and job satisfaction increased under the attention of the investigators. One explanation for the increases became known as the *Hawthorne effect,* which suggested that the novelty of having research conducted and the increased attention from management could lead to temporary increases in productivity. To explain persistent increases, the researchers focused on the informal interpersonal relationships of the workers. From these findings developed the human relations school of management, which became associated with the work of Mayo (1946), and Roethlisberger and Dickson (1939).

The human relations school replaced Taylor's portrait of the workers as motivated by money and leisure with a view of workers as motivated also by social attachments. (For a critical examination of the human relations school, see Perrow, 1986.) Contemporary job redesign theories have built on these models and have also incorporated increasingly complex theories of motivation. Much of modern job design theory can be traced to the motivational sequence proposed by Maslow (1943) and applied to management by McGregor (1978) (see Chapter 5) and to the empirically based theories of Herzberg (1966). Although some have argued for the redesign of jobs as a response to changes in society, most contemporary theories have been described as "classical theories of job redesign" with a foundation in the works of Maslow and Herzberg (Kelly, 1982:37).

Job enrichment can be traced to the work of Herzberg, beginning in the 1950s. *Motivation–hygiene theory* was developed by Herzberg from critical incident research in which he asked workers to describe the high and low points in their work lives. The research uncovered two sets of factors involved in motivation at the workplace (Herzberg, Mausner, & Snyderman, 1959; Herzberg, 1966). *Hygiene factors* are external to the work being performed. These include pay, supervision, physical conditions at the work site, and interpersonal relations. Contentment with these factors, however, does not motivate workers; it simply prevents dissatisfaction. Herzberg labeled a second set of factors *motivators*. These factors, intrinsic to the work itself, include responsibility, recognition, and opportunities for achievement and growth. (One study replicated Herzberg's finding regarding hygiene factors and motivators with a sample of corrections officers [Hayslip, 1982].) Job enrichment models, which Herzberg calls "orthodox job enrichment," build on motivation–hygiene theory by assuming that workers will be motivated only after hygiene needs are met and sources of intrinsic satisfaction are built into jobs. Job design, according to this theory, is concerned not simply with improved efficiency but with motivating employees by meeting their higher-order needs.

Some research (Hackman & Oldham, 1987), however, has not supported the original dichotomy between hygiene factors and motivators and suggests that the findings may be an artifact of the particular interview techniques used by Herzberg. The substantive issue flowing from this criticism concerns the relationship between

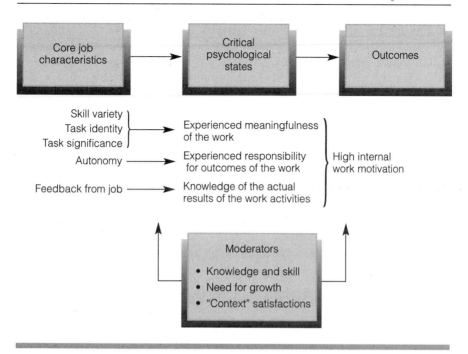

FIGURE 6-1   Job Enrichment Model (From J. Hackman and R. Oldham, *Work Redesign.* Reading, MA: Addison-Wesley © 1980 p. 83. Adapted by permission.)

satisfaction with extrinsic factors and motivation. For instance, some theories argue that motivated employees need not be satisfied with the contexts of work (Morse, 1973). A related criticism of motivation–hygiene theory is that it pays too little attention to differences in workers' responses to jobs. Workers may attach different interpretations to job situations, and they may respond differently to jobs with varying levels of enrichment (Hackman & Oldham, 1987:57). Some workers may thrive in enriched jobs, while others may respond with confusion, resentment, and inability to cope with the new demands.

Enrichment theory and research have expanded to accommodate criticisms of the motivation–hygiene theory, and other theoretical orientations have been incorporated into job design efforts. One popular approach to job enrichment has been developed by Hackman and Oldham (1987). This model has the virtues of being empirically based and attentive to individual differences. For Hackman and Oldham, job redesign involves increasing certain core job dimensions that influence the psychological states of workers, which in turn affect personal and work outcomes. This sequence can be moderated, however, by certain variables: an individual's level of knowledge and skill, need for accomplishment and growth, and satisfaction with pay and working conditions. The complete model is shown in Figure 6-1. This theoretical perspective recognizes the importance of matching individual workers with their jobs. Under the model, job enrichment is inappropriate and is likely to have negative consequences if workers have a low need for growth and jobs are relatively high on the core dimensions. However, when jobs are low on the core dimensions and workers are satisfied, have appropriate knowledge, and possess high needs for accomplishment and development, the potential for job enrichment is great.

As part of their theory, Hackman and Oldham (1987) describe the job characteristics they regard as most significant for employee motivation. These characteristics can also be combined into a single measure of the motivating potential of a particular job. These are the core job dimensions:

1. *Skill variety*—the degree to which jobs require a variety of different activities, skills, and talents

2. *Task identity*—the degree to which a job requires the completion of a whole task rather than bits or pieces of a project

3. *Task significance*—the extent to which a job has a meaningful impact on others; the importance of the job

4. *Autonomy*—the degree of freedom, independence, and discretion provided by a job

5. *Feedback*—the extent to which workers get direct and clear information about the effectiveness of their performance

Job design efforts have frequently incorporated a process known as job analysis, or the study of work assignments with the goal of specifying the precise skills and training needed for the work. Most often, job analysis is limited to the technical dimensions of jobs and is used to produce job descriptions (Ghorpade & Atchison, 1980) or to identify appropriate levels of compensation.

Hackman and Oldham's model takes a broader view than job analysis of the kinds of information needed in job redesign efforts. The authors have developed an instrument, called the *Job Diagnostic Survey,* that allows managers to measure all the variables in the theory and to assess both jobs and workers with regard to the need as well as the potential for job enrichment. The *Job Diagnostic Survey* provides measures of the core job dimensions as well as measures of the worker-related variables. Considerable research has been done with the instrument, and Hackman and Oldham have published averages for all the variables for nine separate job families. The *Job Diagnostic Survey* has also been used to study criminal justice occupations. Brief, Munro, and Aldag (1976) used the instrument as the foundation of a data-based argument for redesign of some corrections officer tasks. The researchers found that the most satisfied corrections officers were those whose jobs had the highest variety, task identity, feedback, and autonomy. They also found, as the theory predicts, that these relationships tended to be moderated by individual needs for growth.

Similar ideas are expressed by Houston (1999) and Wright (1994). Houston suggests that effective correctional employees require opportunities to grow and develop in their jobs. Increasing the variety of work, as well as the employee's scope of influence in decision making, provides correctional employees avenues to experiment in their jobs. Through such experimentation, employees learn to adapt to their problems, and the organization learns new ways of approaching challenging situations. Wright reinforces this view by stating that correctional employees are the essence of prison organizations. Greater recognition of their experiences and ideas can only work toward the attainment of organizational objectives. Moreover, the correctional employee views himself or herself as an integral part of the organization. Goldstein (1990) offers similar views in his examination of the influence of traditional police organizations and their stifling structures on police officers' development and growth. In his view, police organizations require more decentralization and greater autonomy for police officers to enable them to respond to the varied needs of the community. This would require an examination of the tasks that are central to the police role and the method(s) of structuring that would be the most appropriate to respond to them. Job redesign issues are, therefore, critical for effective criminal justice administration.

Job Redesign Programs

Since IBM first began to experiment with job redesign in 1943, programs have been implemented in numerous work settings. In reviewing much of the literature on these programs, Kelly (1982) suggests that three approaches to work redesign have emerged. In mass production industries, often characterized by fragmented jobs on assembly lines, job redesign efforts have sought to reduce or eliminate assembly lines. In continuous process industries, such as chemical production, jobs have been enriched through the creation of autonomous work groups. In service industries, Kelly argues that enrichment has occurred principally through the combination of work roles from different parts of the job hierarchy. Other authors have distinguished job enlargement, which involves the addition of tasks to job descriptions, from job enrichment. Still others have characterized programs as involving additions along the horizontal dimension, as in job enlargement, and strengthening the vertical dimension, as in job enrichment.

Many redesign programs have included combinations of strategies. In a well-known redesign of assembly-line tasks, AB Volvo of Sweden incorporated a variety of approaches (Gyllenhammer, 1975). In one auto assembly plant, managers turned to job enlargement by adding variety to workers' tasks. Some 1,600 workers rotated their jobs, often making several changes a day. In another plant, Volvo rotated assembly-line jobs within teams of twelve to fifteen members. Workers themselves decided how to rotate jobs within the groups and also met regularly with management to discuss how the work could be improved. In the production of trucks and buses, which was considered slower and more complex than the auto assembly line, Volvo formed smaller work groups with increased autonomy. Within these groups some workers performed specialized assignments, while others opted to alternate tasks. In their new plants, Volvo eliminated assembly lines and replaced them with work teams, each operating out of separate sections of the shop floor and responsible for completed parts of the final product.

In another well-known redesign project, managers at Texas Instruments sought to enrich the jobs of building janitors and matrons. The program began with training in managerial techniques, including those derived from McGregor's (1978) Theory X and Theory Y (see Chapter 5). Early program recruits later hired additional staff and chaired regular meetings, which included training in management concepts as well as discussions of work-related problems. Teams of workers became responsible for redesigning the maintenance tasks as well as for quality control. The results of the program included improved cleanliness at reduced costs, reductions in worker turnover, and other improvements, including the following worker-originated innovations (Toch & Grant, 1982:78):

1. Teams eliminated cleaning carts, installed supply cabinets, and took responsibility for their own inventories.
2. Work groups divided and controlled their own work, including scheduling the closing down of washrooms to minimize unpredictability for other employees.
3. Matrons, unhappy with a disinfectant that had corrosive effects and caused dermatitis, negotiated with a vendor who developed a new chemical to their specifications. Cleaning time was cut in half when the new chemical was packaged in spray form.
4. Janitors and matrons took responsibility for inspections of facilities.
5. The workers also became concerned with preventive maintenance.

Texas Instruments also embarked on an ingenious campaign to educate and involve the users. For example, matrons spoke to new hires as part of the company's employee-orientation sessions to explain their cleanliness goals and to solicit cooperation. In another approach, matrons and janitors photographed areas that were particularly untidy or dirty. These photos were circulated on production lines in an attempt to elicit cooperation from factory, laboratory, and office employees.

The Texas Instruments program is cited for disconfirming the assumption that the higher reaches of the Maslowian hierarchy have been reserved for skilled workers. As Toch and Grant (1982:79) point out, "if toilet bowls can acquire motivating potential, any job is more enrichable than we first suspect." Other redesign efforts have been accomplished and documented by researchers in a number of different occupational settings (Kopelman, 1985; Lawler, 1986).

Job Redesign in Criminal Justice and Other Human Services

Although few job redesign efforts in human services have incorporated the specific types of data called for by Hackman and Oldham, considerable research supports the efficacy of such efforts. Sarrata and Jeppensen (1977), for example, found that the job design features that Hackman and Oldham identified as producing satisfaction in blue-collar workers functioned the same way for child-care workers.

Research has also shown that human services workers often value the most enriched aspects of their work or even take steps to enrich their own jobs. In a classic job design study of psychiatric aides, Simpson and Simpson (1959) found that the attendants reported intrinsically rewarding tasks involving patient care as their main reasons for staying on the job. The same aides reported originally being attracted to the job for extrinsic reasons, including job security and pay. In a study of corrections officers, Toch (1978:19) found that 20 percent of officers were independently experimenting with nontraditional enriched roles, which included "the officer as dispenser of mental health services, as a person who resonates to adjustment problems of inmates in crisis." Lombardo (1981) and Johnson (2002) also identified diversity in the way corrections officers perform their tasks.

Apart from the efforts of individual innovators, numerous formal programs have also involved the redesign of work in the human services. In mental health settings, aides' jobs have been enriched through the addition of treatment responsibilities (Ellsworth & Ellsworth, 1970). In criminal justice, the jobs of frontline workers have been redesigned through a variety of approaches including job enlargement, vertical loading (job enrichment), and the creation of autonomous work groups.

One of the earliest documented job redesign efforts in corrections occurred under Howard Gill, superintendent of the Norfolk Prison Colony in Norfolk, Massachusetts, between 1931 and 1934 (Doering, 1940). Under Gill's grand scheme for creating as normal a community setting as possible, a new kind of prison guard was required. While the officers who patrolled the perimeter and stood watch in the towers played the traditional role, inside the colony house officers performed additional tasks that included casework and counseling as well as facilitating inmate self-government within the housing units.

Lindquist and Whitehead (1986) report on a more recent experiment in job enlargement involving corrections officers. In the Alabama Supervised Intensive Restitution (SIR) program, corrections officers supervised inmates in the community as a solution to the problem of prison overcrowding. The officers managed caseloads of approximately thirty-five and acted much the same as probation and parole officers. The SIR officers experienced a greater sense of personal accomplishment and higher levels of job satisfaction than a sample of regular corrections officers and a sample of probation and parole officers.

Several efforts have also been made to enrich criminal justice jobs. Rather than add tasks to the job description, these programs generally increase responsibilities of frontline staff, a process known as *vertical loading*. One example is Carter and Wilkins's (1976:211) caseload distribution program in probation and parole. In the Work Unit Parole Program begun in California in 1965 and later introduced in Wisconsin, cases are assigned a weight based on the amount and type of supervision needed, and caseloads are determined by equal distribution of weighted cases. This program has allowed staff to spend time in the treatment and custodial supervision of cases, where the need is greatest (Dickey, 1988, 1996).

A different approach to the vertical loading of jobs is seen in the work of Toch and Grant (1982). They added responsibilities often reserved for management to the tasks of both police and corrections officers by involving frontline staff in examining and resolving significant work-related problems. Although Herzberg (1978:40) argues that such participation is not part of the work itself and is, therefore, a hygiene factor rather than a motivator, Toch and Grant argue that participation is a necessary part of job enrichment in the human services because of the wide discretion human services workers have. As they point out, "enriching a guard's or police officer's job means expanding the prison's or police department's human services involvement, a task that cannot be accomplished by edict" (1982:133). Similarly, Skolnick and Fyfe

(1993) argue that police violence against citizens can be tied to the military structure of police organizations, where officers are discouraged, not encouraged, in providing input on how to perform their jobs. Skolnick and Fyfe suggest that greater police officer and citizen involvement in the definition of what the police role entails may reduce the likelihood of future violent confrontations between police and citizens. Furthermore, Fyfe (1994) argues that good police officers can be recruited to identify the characteristics of good policing. This valuable information can be used in the selection, training, and evaluation of police performance.

In a program with the Oakland, California, police department, Toch and Grant used groups of officers with records of violent confrontations with citizens to study and resolve problems of police violence. The groups collected and analyzed data (tape recordings of confrontations) and devised innovations, including peer-review panels, specialized training, and mediation units to deal with family crises and landlord-tenant disputes. In a project with New York State corrections officers, group participants were selected on the basis of their interest in job enrichment as determined by a questionnaire. The groups at four separate prisons analyzed the corrections officer's job and suggested alterations. The project resulted in blueprints for training, increased involvement of officers in treatment and classification, and mechanisms for increasing communication with management.

In a replication of the Toch and Grant method, Klofas, Smith, and Meister (1986) used groups of jail officers to plan the operation of a new jail in Peoria, Illinois. In a program lasting two years, frontline officers wrote policies and procedures for the facility. Included in the products of their planning were innovations in classification and programming and a revision of the shift pattern and job assignments. Job satisfaction increased over the course of the program, particularly in perceived support from supervisors and opportunities to contribute new ideas.

Perhaps the best-known restructuring of the traditional police role is offered in Angell's (1971) model of team policing, which parallels autonomous work groups in industry. Linking police morale problems to the practices of classical management, Angell provides an alternative to the traditional police hierarchy. The core of his democratic model of policing involves teams of police generalists who provide services to designated neighborhoods. Teams are composed of officers of equal rank who are assigned to relatively small geographical areas for extended periods, which gives them a chance to become familiar with the culturally homogeneous neighborhoods and to work closely with residents (Trojanowicz & Bucqueroux, 1990). The team initiates all investigations and may call in specialists if they are needed. Evaluations of team policing have highlighted its potential but have also called attention to forces within the organization that are resistant to change (Sherman, Milton, & Kelly, 1973; Mastrofski, 1991). In a review of innovations in policing in six American cities, Skolnick and Bayley (1986) also elaborate the benefits of team policing. They argue that while the old professionalism leaned toward "legalistic" styles of policing, the new professionalism is marked by a service-oriented style. They illustrate their arguments with a review of changes in several cities: "Detroit's ministations exclusively organize community crime prevention; and Santa Ana's substations function as community . . . meeting areas as well as locales for disseminating crime prevention information" (1986:214). The programs thus benefit the community as well as the participating officers.

In their discussion of a Houston program that integrates patrol, investigation, and intelligence collection, Skolnick and Bayley (1986:95) highlight another advantage of decentralization:

> To be successful, this kind of teamwork among patrol officers and specialists requires a radical change in the traditional management style. Decisions must be made from the bottom up rather than the top down. The supervisor's job is not to produce conformity with a preordained plan but to help develop a plan out of the insights of the many people doing the work on the street. . . . Not only will policing become more purposeful this way, but, it is hoped, officers will develop greater enthusiasm for their work. No longer are they spear carriers in someone else's drama, they become responsible directors in their own right.

Revitalization of community policing is also being advocated by members of the Executive Session on Policing, which is associated with Harvard University's Kennedy School of Government (Kelling, 1988). Sometimes referred to as "problem-oriented" policing, the approach calls for police to work closely with citizens in identifying and solving problems before crimes occur. Officers and citizens resolve problems such as broken windows, local bullies, and other disruptions that make neighborhoods look and feel unsafe (Iannone, 1994; Bayley, 1994). As its supporters note, "The resourcefulness of police officers . . . can at last be put to the service of the department" (Sparrow, 1999).

Programs creating autonomous work groups have also been initiated in correctional institutions. Under the Unit Management system, pioneered in the Federal Bureau of Prisons, an alternative to the traditional prison hierarchy is established (Levinson & Gerard, 1973). Large institutions are divided into architecturally distinct housing units, which typically have from fifty to one hundred inmates. Inmates can be assigned to the units based on similar treatment or security needs. A group of corrections officers and counseling staff has ongoing contact with a small group of inmates in their unit. Frequently headed by a corrections officer, the teams are responsible for all decision making in the unit. Although the distinction between custodial and treatment staff remains, officers and counselors share some duties. The roles of the team members are thus changed in both the horizontal and vertical dimensions.

Both Houston (1999) and Wright (1994) argue that Unit Management is the wave of the future in corrections. Through decentralization and more employee autonomy, correctional personnel are given the opportunity to "own" their work environments. Wright (1994) shows through a process of sharing power, the functional capabilities of the unit and the prison are enhanced. Similar ideas are forwarded by those interested in the "direct supervision" model of jail management (Zupan, 1991). Research has shown how such a management philosophy and job redesign effort has revolutionized the way in which correctional workers view their work and the organization. Stohr, Lovrich, Menke, and Zupan (1994) report how workers in direct supervision jails are much more satisfied in their work when compared to the attitudes of correctional workers in more traditional jail settings. The authors attribute these positive attitude changes to the new philosophy of employee empowerment exhibited in a jail managed under the direct supervision philosophy. Additionally, Stojkovic and Farkas (2002) argue the importance of leadership in redesign efforts within prisons and how they can be used to alter the culture of a prison. Finally, we see a move toward more education and training requirements for correctional personnel that will demand a serious look at how employees are recruited, trained, and supervised. Camp and Camp (2000) report that correctional officers in the year 2000 had to complete, on average, a 9.9 month probationary period before becoming full-time correctional officers, 250 hours of introductory training, and 38 hours of in-service training. These increases in training and probationary periods make the 21st-century correctional officer better trained and equipped to handle the tasks of the job than his predecessor. Moreover, correctional officers will be demanding more of their managers and administrators on how they will be organized and supervised to address the tasks they will face, so job redesign issues will continue to be an important issue for prison administrators.

In probation and parole, the Community Resource Management Team (CRMT) has been developed as an alternative to the traditional caseload model (Clear & O'Leary, 1983:126). Based on the assumption that "no one person can possess all the skills to deal with the variety of human problems presented by probationers" (Dell' Appa, Adams, Jorgensen, & Sigurdson, cited in Clear & O'Leary, 1983:126), the model creates specialists in skill areas. Probation officers act as advocates concerned with the purchase of services or referrals in specific areas such as employment, counseling, legal assistance, and drug abuse. CRMT staff thus have "duty areas" or functional responsibilities rather than caseloads.

Clear and O'Leary (1983) describe a project that gave probation officers functional rather than caseload responsibilities. The project directors discovered that some officers naturally adopted functional approaches:

> One officer, regarded as especially skilled in intensive counseling activities, had in fact stopped seeing some of her caseload so that she could see a minority of cases more intensively. Other areas of officer interest and knowledge included drugs, the military, and language problems. One officer had developed a system of mail reporting for a large non-contact caseload. The problem facing the supervisor was to make the best use of these existing officer skills and interests in the supervision of clients. (Clear & O'Leary, 1983:127)

Probation officers in the large urban department involved in the change project altered the organizational structure to accommodate officer interests as well as the existing classification scheme. A two-person team became responsible for intake and initial case analysis. One of the intake officers also handled low-risk cases on a low-reporting basis. Medium-level cases were handled by a team divided by functional interests, and high-risk cases were handled in small caseloads by single officers with counseling interests. Clear and O'Leary, however, make the important observation that this model may not be appropriate for other agencies or even for some other big city agencies. They call for the direct involvement of staff and for flexibility in the redesign of probation officer tasks so that each organization can take advantage of its own resources. Dickey (1996) reports that in the state of Wisconsin, attempts are being made to restructure the probation officer role so that greater attention can be given to the law enforcement and supervision requirements of the job. Wisconsin, like other states, is interested in improving its supervision of offenders while in the community. Part of this focus includes concern over offender/staff ratios, as well as the appropriate usage of finite resources. Utilizing employees as scarce resources is a theme consistent with a belief that community protection can be enhanced through more effective ways of designing job tasks among probation officers. Job redesign efforts, as part of a larger refocusing strategy in corrections, provide a rationale for more investment in community corrections (Petersilia, 1996).

The idea of job redesign, however, is not limited to corrections. Police organizations have gone through some revolutionary changes over the last twenty years, and the issue of police organization has raised some serious questions concerning the ways in which departments are organized and personnel supervised (Whisenand & Ferguson, 1996). Police organizations of the 21st century are much larger and more diverse with respect to the number of minority personnel, the degree to which line officers have a college education, and a commitment to a community policing philosophy. According to the Law Enforcement Management and Administrative Statistics survey (LEMAS, 1999), as of June, 1996, there are 922, 200 sworn officers in the country, an increase of 9 percent since 1992, and an increase in minority representation from 14.5 percent to 21.5 percent in local police officers for the same years. With respect to educational requirements for officers, 14 percent of local police departments and 11 percent of sheriffs' departments had some type of college education requirement. One percent of agencies require a four-year degree. The increase in educational levels as an entry level requirement among police officers makes job design questions of extreme importance to police administrators. More educated officers demand different ways of organizing and administering police organizations.

Nothing, however, has had more of an impact on police organization than the move toward community policing. The LEMAS survey reveals that nine in ten local police departments serving a population of 25,000 or more had full-time sworn personnel regularly engaged in community policing activities. Among municipal police departments, 62 percent had a formally written community policing plan, 76 percent operated one or more community substations, 73 percent had full-time school resource officers, and an overwhelming majority of these police departments invested dollars and other resources into community policing training for both officers and citizens alike.

Fyfe, Greene, Walsh, Wilson, and McLaren (1997) suggest that many issues of both philosophy and practice must be considered when moving a police department from a traditional police organization structure with its top-down management philosophy to a community policing structure that emphasizes more decentralization and involvement by line police officers in the structuring of police duties and activities. Issues of job design become very important to police managers and administrators. Recruitment, selection, evaluation, and the retention of employees are significantly altered under a community policing approach. Fundamentally, line officers, supervisors, and administrators require more group cohesion to effectively operationalize the community policing philosophy. Most important, line officers require the support of frontline supervisors to make community policing strategies viable. Communication must be improved and increased across groups in the police organization. Officers have to feel their ideas have merit and will not be routinely dismissed. In the words of Fyfe and colleagues: "But line officers will not do so [increase communication] unless their cooperation is sought out and encouraged" (1997:272).

Job Design and the Community

Job design issues within criminal justice organizations cannot be adequately addressed without the inclusion of broader issues of the community and how they affect job design efforts. One of the most revolutionary recent social changes was the passage of the Americans with Disabilities Act (ADA) in 1990, which changed how the law views people with disabilities. Like other human service organizations, provisions of ADA have direct relevance for criminal justice organizations. Job design efforts in criminal justice have to consider the importance of ADA on how we alter or modify criminal justice organizations.

The U.S. Department of Justice (2000) in the document *Enforcing ADA: Looking Back on a Decade of Progress* notes the significant gains made within criminal justice organizations to be in compliance with ADA mandates. The monograph notes the advances but also points out the central concerns ADA places on criminal justice administrators. Most notable are the issues of access to the courts, the fair treatment of persons with disabilities in law enforcement, employment opportunities for persons with disabilities within criminal justice organizations, architectural issues and accessibility to criminal justice buildings, and access to health care and emergency services for those with disabilities.

With regard to design efforts in criminal justice organizations, the ADA has had a major role in directing criminal justice administrators. People with disabilities have the full force of the law in how these job design efforts are created and enforced by criminal justice organizations. The Department of Justice's study makes clear that criminal justice organizations can work with those with disabilities to make their work settings aware of the concerns they have and include the use of mediation to resolve issues and address ADA requirements.

Similarly, job design efforts must be cognizant of the demographic changes occurring within criminal justice organizations. With the increased diversity of criminal justice personnel, they will need to be aware of how this diversity will challenge traditional ways of designing criminal justice organizations. The most notable demographic change is the greater involvement of women within criminal justice agencies. More women within criminal justice organizations pose serious challenges for criminal justice administrators. Research literature has documented the difficulties women have faced in both police and correctional organizations (Pogrebin & Poole, 1997). The Bureau of Justice Assistance (2001) offers a self-assessment guide for recruiting and retaining women in law enforcement. Job design efforts within criminal justice organizations will have to be sensitive to the contributions that increased diversity brings to the workforce and diligently work toward incorporating changes that recognize diversity as a value to the overall functioning of the organization.

Summary

In this chapter we have attempted to integrate knowledge about task design from the fields of general management and criminal justice. Human services appear to lag behind industry in the design of jobs. Human services managers, however, including those in criminal justice, are showing increased concern with the nature of the tasks performed by frontline staff. Research on job satisfaction and burnout has contributed to this concern. At the same time, technological changes and increased bureaucratization in criminal justice threaten to limit frontline discretion and impoverish job tasks in much the same way that Scientific Management has had negative consequences in industry.

One response to the deprofessionalization syndrome is to carefully reconsider the design of jobs in criminal justice. Theory and research in industrial settings can guide these efforts. Design theories now incorporate concern for individual differences with measures of task-related variables. A substantial record of job redesign in industrial settings can guide the criminal justice manager, and a valuable body of research and practical experience is developing within the field of criminal justice itself. Existing efforts range from enlarging jobs by adding tasks to completely restructuring organizations in order to enhance jobs and increase effectiveness. Additionally, criminal justice organizations of the 21st century will become more diverse on a number of dimensions, and, therefore, job design efforts will need to be more sensitive to this diversity to increase the performance of individuals and organizations.

In the next chapter we focus on another topic in the discussion of the role of the individual within criminal justice organizations. Concerns with communication, motivation, and job design all rely heavily on leadership within organizations, the topic we tackle next.

Case Study

A Program of Job Redesign in Corrections

A year ago, a bitter strike rocked the department of corrections. For nearly three weeks the National Guard replaced striking corrections officers in prisons throughout the state. What was unusual about this job action was that it wasn't over money or fringe benefits, or even working conditions as we usually think of them. At the bottom of this strike was the feeling among the corrections officers that their contributions were not valued, that they had lost status over the years, and that administrators didn't care about them.

As is usual in a labor strike, there were no real winners. The kinds of things the officers wanted didn't fit neatly into the contract. Administrators also had no reason to smile. The strike had revealed how disaffected the corrections officers were and called into question the quality of management in the department. The inmates, too, lost. Not only was their regimen restricted by the strike, but when it was over, they faced a further embittered and frustrated guard force. An uneasy tension pervaded the state's prisons.

The administration and the union leadership knew things couldn't continue in the same way. Something had to be done to resolve the issues underlying the strike—issues that didn't fit neatly into collective bargaining agreements and issues that didn't go away just because the officers were back at work. After discussions with university faculty, administrators and union leaders settled on a model for addressing work-related problems that had been developed in the auto industry. There, Quality of Work Life programs were cosponsored by the United Auto Workers and auto manufacturers to address problems that were not covered in contracts. In the program, workers participated in assessing work-related problems and in developing solutions to those problems through collaborative efforts between the union and the company and between the workers and the managers.

An outside consultant was brought in to manage the program in the department of corrections. The program was to be data based and to involve groups of officers studying work-related problems and proposing solutions. The data for the program came from a survey of corrections officers that tapped levels and sources of dissatisfaction on the job as well as interest in enriching jobs. Job enrichment items focused on officers expanding the human services aspects of the work. The survey revealed the disaffection among officers in the department. The officers felt buffeted by policies developed in the central office without their input. They felt their ideas were ignored and administrators cared little about them. Many officers also felt their jobs provided few opportunities to pursue their interests and use their skills in dealing with inmates. They felt constrained by limited custodial roles.

Volunteer groups of corrections officers at the maximum security prisons, under the direction of the consultant, reviewed the data from the survey, studied problems at their particular institutions, and proposed solutions. The groups produced formal proposals, which included an elaborate statement of the problem to be addressed, a description of the proposed program, and a budget for the program, as well as an analysis of the resources and obstacles affecting implementation. The problems ranged from conflicts with the central office to difficulties with particular types of inmates. The variety of problems reflected differences across as well as within the state's prisons. Here are some of the programs developed by the officers:

- A program for on-the-job training of new officers using experienced officers. The aim was to improve training as well as to utilize officers' experience. The proposal detailed procedures for training new recruits in assignments throughout the facility and for evaluating the training efforts.

- A program to provide special training in counseling for officers with high inmate contact. The program included continuing in-service training, liaison arrangements with social service staff, and a record-keeping process for handling inmate problems.

- A program to provide frontline officers with opportunities to evaluate and comment on noncontractual policies that affect their jobs. The proposal spelled out the logistics for providing written feedback from line officers to prison wardens and central office on the problems created by or the advantages of new policies and procedures.

- A program of peer support for officers having problems connected with work. The proposal established training procedures for peer counselors, who would be available to assist officers with work-related problems such as abuse of sick time, unusual conflicts with inmates, or emotional problems.

- A program to involve officers in the classification of inmates and the assignment of inmates to jobs. The program built on officers' knowledge of facility resources and needs and provided for frequent exchanges of information between officers and civilian classification and placement staff.

The programs developed were tailored to the needs of the institutions where the volunteer groups of planners worked. They did, however, have some things in common. The programs recognized a variety of work-related problems experienced by officers; they provided input by officers into the management of the prisons; and they created opportunities for officers to expand their roles.

Case Study Questions

1. Consider the causes of the corrections officers' strike. In what ways do these issues seem related to job design? How do officer proposals address these design issues?

2. What theoretical approach or approaches underlie the job redesign project?

3. What roles do you think management and organized labor and frontline workers can play in work redesign? Do you think collaborative efforts can be successful in the long run?

For Discussion

1. The argument has been made that Scientific Management has been influential in criminal justice and that, as managers have become more advanced professionally, frontline criminal justice jobs have become more impoverished. Is the de-professionalization syndrome an inevitable consequence of improvements in the technology of criminal justice? How would you suggest that jobs, such as those in probation and parole, be designed to provide opportunities for enrichment while still utilizing risk-assessment instruments, electronic monitors, and other technological advances?

2. Consider a specific job within the criminal justice system. What characteristics of that job are sources of motivation and what characteristics may lead to dissatisfaction or burnout? How would you redesign the job to emphasize the first set of characteristics and deemphasize the others? Do you think others would agree, or are there important individual differences to take into account?

3. Examine the job characteristics model of Hackman and Oldham. How well does that model account for motivation in criminal justice workers? Describe the core job characteristics of a particular job. How do they relate to important psychological states? What specific kinds of knowledge and skill, needs for growth, and satisfactions with pay and working conditions can influence the outcomes of your particular job? There is some disagreement about the importance of participation in the redesign and enrichment of human services jobs. Do you feel that such participation by frontline staff is desirable? What level of participation do you support? What benefits and problems might be associated with worker participation in job design in criminal justice?

For Further Reading

Bayley, D. *Police for the Future.* New York: Free Press, 1994.

Cherniss, C. *Staff Burnout: Job Stress in the Human Services.* Beverly Hills, CA: Sage, 1980.

Fyfe, J., Greene, J., Walsh, W., Wilson, O., and McLaren, R. *Police Administration,* 5th ed. New York: McGraw-Hill, 1997.

Hackman, J. R., and Oldham, G. R. *Work Redesign.* Reading, MA: Addison-Wesley, 1987.

Houston, J. *Correctional Management: Functions, Skills, and Systems,* 2nd ed. Chicago: Nelson-Hall, 1999.

Skolnick, J. H., and Bayley, D. H. *The New Blue Line: Police Innovation in Six American Cities.* New York: Free Press, 1986.

Toch, H., and Grant, J. D. *Reforming Human Services: Change Through Participation.* Beverly Hills, CA: Sage, 1982.

Wright, K. *Effective Prison Leadership.* Binghamton, NY: William Neil, 1994.

CHAPTER

7

LEADERSHIP

The preparation of future leaders is the most pressing need of the Department of Corrections into the next century. The Leadership Institute has the responsibility of producing future leaders who will face significant challenges on how prisons and parole agencies will operate. The development of leaders is the most important and significant commitment I can make to the department of corrections. My success in achieving this goal will be my legacy to the department of corrections.

(*Director James Gomez, speaking to the first class of graduates of the Leadership Institute of the California Department of Corrections, February 1995*)

The bottom line for leaders is that if they do not become conscious of the cultures in which they are embedded, those cultures will manage them. Cultural understanding is desirable for all of us, but it is essential to leaders if they are to lead.

(*Schein, 1997*)

The Sheriff is a politician; his job is to get the resources his organization needs and keep the political wolves away. The under-sheriff manages the police operations and the jail administrator runs the jail. The sheriff has to make sure they can do their jobs.

(*Anonymous Michigan Sheriff, 2000*)

One is tempted to say that the research on leadership has left us with the clear view that things are far more complicated and "contingent" than we initially believed and that, in fact, they are so complicated and contingent that it may not be worth our while to spin out more and more categories and qualifications. . . . At the extremes, we can be fairly confident in identifying good or bad leaders; but for most situations we will probably have little to say. We may learn a great deal about interpersonal relations but not much about organizations.

(*Perrow, 1986*)

When I am asked what leadership means to me, the first thing that comes to mind is getting the job done the way I think it should be done. That is why I always believed being an effective leader or warden in a prison really means convincing the public, the politicians, the inmates, and the correctional employees that my way of doing things is the best possible way of doing things. If I can convince people of that reality, then, I think, I am a good leader.

(*Warden of a maximum security prison in the Midwest, 1986*)

The contemporary criminal justice administrator is expected to be an effective leader, an expectation that fits with the general demand for competent leaders in all organizations, both public and private. Although a great deal of prescriptive material tells the criminal justice administrator how to lead an organization effectively, there is little empirical evidence on what effective leadership actually involves. More important, few of the existing theoretical models of leadership created in other disciplines have been applied. In this chapter, we provide a review of the relevant aspects of these models and apply our understanding of the leadership process to the requirements of the criminal justice system.

Our review, however, will not be prescriptive. Instead, we will offer an analytical framework rooted in empirical research and theoretical models of leadership. In this way, we hope not only to provide increased understanding of how the process of leadership works in criminal justice organizations, but also to suggest what our expectations of criminal justice leaders should and should not be.

To accomplish these objectives, we explore several areas. First, we define leadership and argue that because criminal justice administration is fundamentally politically driven, it is useful to understand leadership within the political arena. Second, the chapter reviews the major theories of leadership that have been developed in research on organizational behavior. Our discussion in this section integrates what we know about leadership research done in other organizations and how these findings apply to the criminal justice system. Our review in this section includes an analysis of behavioral and contingency theories of leadership, two theories that hold promise for explaining the leadership process in criminal justice organizations.

The chapter also explores criminal justice research that addresses the issue of leadership. Although much of this literature is overly prescriptive and does not reflect the realities of criminal justice organizations, we provide an overview of those few pieces of research that empirically test theoretical models of leadership and make some recommendations for future research. In addition, we present a model of leadership education actually in operation in a department of corrections. This model suggests future concerns that criminal justice administrators need to consider to be effective leaders. Finally, we conclude with a brief discussion on leadership and organizational culture and its relevance to criminal justice administration.

Leadership Defined

Four distinct, but not separate, ideas about administration guide our definitions of leadership. First, leadership is a process that effectively accomplishes organizational goals. Leadership cannot be conceptually separated from organizational effectiveness (Tosi, Rizzo, & Carroll, 1986) and the accomplishment of objectives.

Second, administrators can learn leadership skills. Even though the process of leadership is complex, we believe it can be learned and applied to the effective administration of criminal justice organizations. Much of criminal justice management literature assumes that effective leadership can be taught, and millions of dollars have been spent since the 1960s by criminal justice organizations, especially police, to develop training modules that help administrators accomplish organizational goals. Although there may be little or no value in knowing the "correct" style of leadership, the characteristics of good leaders as identified by empirical research can serve as the basis of suggestions and recommendations to criminal justice administrators. These leadership characteristics, however, are always subject to the tasks, functions, and objectives the organization expects to accomplish.

Third, leadership is a group process. To accomplish organizational objectives, leaders must influence a number of people, or to put it simply: No group, no leader. The process of leadership must thus be examined in light of the strategies leaders use to get people to achieve the tasks necessary for organizational existence and survival. Ostensibly, we may be talking about methods of compliance and power in organizations. Chapter 10 will examine these topics in criminal justice organizations. For now, however, we want to know the kinds of techniques that are used in the relationship between a leader and subordinates. Yukl (1981:12–17) suggests *eleven techniques* of influence, used singly or in combination, that affect the leadership process:

1. *Legitimate request.* A person complies with an agent's request because the person recognizes the agent's "right" as leader to make such a request.

2. *Instrumental compliance.* A person is induced to alter his or her behavior by an agent's implicit or explicit promise to ensure some tangible outcome desired by the person.

3. *Coercion.* A person is induced to comply by an agent's explicit or implicit threat to ensure adverse outcomes if the person fails to do so.

4. *Rational persuasion.* A person is convinced by an agent that the suggested behavior is the best way for the person to satisfy his or her needs or to attain his or her objectives.

5. *Rational faith.* An agent's suggestion is sufficient to evoke compliance by a person without the necessity for any explanation.

6. *Inspirational appeal.* A person is persuaded by an agent that there is a necessary link between the requested behavior and some value important enough to justify the behavior.

7. *Indoctrination.* A person acts because of induced internalization of strong values relevant to the desired behavior.

8. *Information distortion.* A person is unconsciously influenced by an agent's limiting, falsifying, or interpreting information in a way conducive to compliance.

9. *Situational engineering.* A person's attitudes and behavior are indirectly influenced by an agent's manipulation of relevant aspects of the physical and social situation.

10. *Personal identification.* A person imitates an agent's attitudes and behavior because the person admires or worships the agent.

11. *Decision identification.* An agent allows a person to participate in and have substantial influence over the making of a decision, thereby gaining the person's identification with the final choice.

Think of how administrators in criminal justice use any one or a combination of these techniques to influence their subordinates and lead their agencies. For example, the prison warden who rules his institution with an iron fist employs coercion as a method of leadership, while the police sergeant who suggests to the beat officer that cordial interactions with citizens are essential to effective police work is using persuasion. Effective leaders, however, are able to get subordinates to work toward the stated objectives of the organization regardless of method.

Techniques of leadership are not the same as styles of leadership. A *style of leadership* consists of all the techniques a leader uses to achieve organizational goals. The prison warden who employs coercion, information distortion, and indoctrination as techniques of influence with inmates and corrections officers is exhibiting an autocratic style of leadership. Later in the chapter we will explore other styles of leadership, some of which are more effective than others in criminal justice administration.

Fourth, leadership in public bureaucracies such as criminal justice agencies is inherently political and must be examined within the political arena. Leadership in organizations is often discussed with an internal focus. Little is said about the external nature of leadership, even though an external view is critical to a complete understanding of how public agencies are run. A common criticism of applying research findings on leadership in private organizations to public organizations has been its limited value, given the political contexts within which public organizations operate. In fact, some would say that the lack of research attention to the external and political nature of leadership makes many existing theories on leadership of little or no value to those who operate public bureaucracies. For criminal justice organizations, the importance of the political process cannot be overstated.

In many criminal justice organizations, formal leaders are elected officials who run for office. A prime example is the county sheriff. There are over 3,000 counties across the country, each with an elected sheriff. Being an elected official makes the sheriff accountable to the electorate, yet many decisions that affect a sheriff's department are outside the control of the sheriff. While accountable to the public, the sheriffs have to work within the constraints imposed by other elected officials, such as county supervisors and boards, who control their budgets. The sheriff may be an elected official, but others control the department budget to some degree. This places controls on how the sheriff can lead and to whom the position is responsible. In addition, the elected sheriff is different from police or correctional leaders who are appointed by a board or another elected official, such as a governor. The politics that define this type of arrangement are different from those an elected criminal justice official has to face. The political arena is potentially broader for the criminal justice leader who has to be sensitive to local concerns and also, if perhaps a head of a department of corrections appointed by a governor, has to be concerned about wider political concerns raised within the domain of state politics.

Existing theories of leadership are relevant to understanding the leadership process within the criminal justice system, but some consideration must be given to how criminal justice administrators, as public bureaucrats, lead their agencies. In other words, we need an examination of the leadership phenomenon as it operates within the political arena. For example, take the career of former FBI Director J. Edgar Hoover, who was said to have employed charismatic and legitimate forms of authority (techniques of influence) to lead the FBI. This characterization, however, does not describe the political relationships that made him an effective leader of a large public bureaucracy over a forty-year period. Leadership must thus be understood as a process that reaches well beyond the formal boundaries of the organization. As the quote by the warden at the beginning of the chapter suggests, leadership in criminal justice agencies involves convincing both subordinates and those outside in the political arena that a particular method (usually the leader's) is the best one for accomplishing organizational objectives.

Many leaders of criminal justice bureaucracies understand the political nature of their positions, but they must equally be aware of the vacillations in public interest in and concern about their agencies. Thus, leadership of a criminal justice agency requires flexibility, but, as Selznick (1957) reminds us, public agencies must also clearly define their mission, structure this mission into their hierarchy, maintain the values of the organization that give it its identity, and control conflicts among competing interests within the organization. In short, criminal justice administrators must operate their organizations in tune with the political realities of the external environment while simultaneously maintaining their own role identities. Because of the tension between changes in the external political environment and the administrators' desires to keep control of the organization, leadership is a crucial and critical process. Dealing with this tension makes criminal justice administration difficult today, especially since many observers have noted the increased politicization of criminal justice policy and practice. While the political process is integral to the development of criminal justice policies and external influences direct what policies will be developed, the degree to which politics plays a role in leader decision making has become more pronounced and, in some people's minds, detrimental to rational policy making at the executive level of criminal justice organizations (Gomez, 1995).

In sum, we can define leadership as invariably tied to the effectiveness of an organization; as learnable, contingent on the tasks, functions, and objectives of the organization; as carried out in a group setting; and, probably most important of all for criminal justice agencies, as focused on political and public concerns.

Theories of Leadership

Much of what we know about leadership comes from research taking one of three approaches: The first, and probably the oldest, assumes that a leader is born and not made. This approach, which tends to emphasize inherent personality traits, also assumes that leadership can be evaluated on the basis of these traits. Much research, however, questions whether personal characteristics of "leadership" actually exist or, more important, can be viewed separately from the situational context (Tosi, Rizzo, & Carroll, 1986:553; Bass, 1981). Thus, it is difficult to know whether the leader's overall personality or particular traits are critical to the leadership process. An authoritarian police sergeant may be successful in a situation that requires a clear, concise, and immediate response, such as a hostage situation, yet this style of leadership may be totally ineffective in a situation that requires deliberation and patience, such as police officer training. Because of a number of difficulties associated with this approach, it has been largely abandoned by those studying the leadership process. Kotter (1990), for example, suggests that trait approaches minimize the influences that are structurally part of the organization and serve to either enhance or inhibit effective leadership. Examples of practices and structures that promote leadership are the following: challenging assignments early in a career, visible leadership role models, and assignments that broaden individuals. Examples of practices or structures that inhibit leadership include a long series of narrow and tactical jobs, vertical career movement, rapid promotions, and measurement and rewards based on short-term results only.

Much contemporary research done on leadership now takes one of two other approaches. The *behavioral* approach, which emphasizes the behaviors of individual leaders, is the focus of much of the criminal justice research on leadership. As suggested by Tosi, Rizzo, and Carroll (1986:554–557), behavioral approaches fall into two distinct areas: the distribution of influence and the task and social behaviors of leaders. The *contingency* approach is relatively recent and tends to emphasize multiple variables, particularly situational variables that constrain leadership. These situational variables include characteristics of subordinates, organizational context, and style of leadership.

Our review of behavioral and contingency models in this chapter provides us with insight into theories of leadership from the perspective of organizational behavior. Our next goal is to see how and whether these theories fit the actual leadership process in criminal justice. We begin our review with an examination of the behavioral approaches.

Behavioral Models

Because of the many problems associated with the character trait approach to understanding leadership, researchers have increasingly focused on behaviors instead. This approach suggests that effective leadership depends on how leaders interact with their subordinates. More important, the behavioral approach accentuates how leaders get subordinates to accomplish organizational tasks, a process known as *initiating structures*. Using a behavioral approach, for example, we would be interested in knowing the ways in which the warden of a prison interacts with administrative staff, treatment specialists, and corrections officers so that the tasks essential to the prison's mission are completed.

The behavioral approach is also concerned with how employees are able to achieve personal goals within the organization at the same time that they accomplish its central tasks. In our example, we would be interested in what the prison warden does to accommodate or consider staff opinions, ideas, and feelings about the day-to-day workings of the prison. Do the corrections officers feel supported? Do treatment personnel feel they have a central role? Is there room for advancement in the prison's hierarchy?

These two concepts, consideration for subordinates and initiating structures, guide the behavioral approach to leadership. They evolved from two sets of leadership studies done in the 1940s, 1950s, and early 1960s: the Ohio State studies and the Michigan studies. In addition, a popular model of supervision was created at this time; it is known as the *managerial grid*. Originally devised by Blake and Mouton (1964), this grid was based on two dimensions of behavior—"concern for people" and "concern for production"—that are analogous to the concepts of consideration and initiating structure. Fundamentally, according to Blake and Mouton, the most effective manager is equally concerned with high levels of production among employees and their needs. The managerial grid has been extensively applied to criminal justice (see Duffee, 1986). Here, however, we will not focus on the grid itself but instead will present the original research from which it was derived.

The Ohio State studies, which began in the late 1940s, concluded that leadership could be examined on the two dimensions of consideration and initiating structure. *Consideration* is the leader's expression of concern for subordinates' feelings, ideas, and opinions about job-related matters. Considerate leaders are concerned about employees, develop trust between themselves and subordinates, and more often than not develop good communication as well. *Initiating structure* is the leader's direction of himself or herself and subordinates toward specific goals. The role of the leader is to make sure that an adequate structure is available for employees so that organizational objectives are accomplished. The Ohio State studies concluded that effective leadership is present in an organization when the levels of consideration and initiating structure are high among leaders.

As suggested by Hellriegel, Slocum, and Woodman (1995), however, the central limitation of the Ohio State studies was a failure to recognize the importance of specific situations in the leadership process. The police sergeant who heads a tactical unit, for example, does not need to be considerate of employees when faced with an emergency situation; rather, the sergeant needs to delineate roles and duties to patrol officers in the unit as quickly as possible. A high degree of initiating structure, in other words, is critical. The Ohio State studies thus seem applicable only to specific situations where both consideration and initiating structure are appropriate.

The Michigan studies, in contrast, sought to dichotomize the leadership process into two dimensions of supervisory behavior: production centered and employee centered. We know that not all supervisors have the same outlook toward their jobs, employees, and tasks required to meet the organization's objectives and goals. Some police sergeants, as immediate supervisors, are interested in high activity by their subordinates, whether that be ticket writing, arrests, or some other police performance measure. Other police sergeants are concerned with the perceptions of rank-and-file officers about their roles in the organization. These supervisors care about how officers fit into the organizational hierarchy and about their level of satisfaction with their work. According to the Michigan studies, the effective leader mostly attempts to be employee centered, a behavior that in turn engenders productive subordinates. It is questionable, however, whether the phenomenon of leadership can be understood as either employee centered or production centered.

The findings of both studies, in fact, have serious problems that limit their application to criminal justice organizations. First, it is not clear that either the Ohio State studies or the Michigan studies adequately assessed the concept of leadership. We are concerned here with the methodological problem of construct validity. Do these studies actually measure the notion of leadership? Distinctions must be made, for example, between leadership and power. Does the prison guard who befriends an inmate and is respected by the inmate exhibit some type of leadership or what is known as referent power? How do we know what factor is operating in this relationship? How can we separate the two processes both conceptually and practically? Because much of the behavioral research has not made distinctions between these concepts, as a result, it is not evident that leadership itself is being studied. The same point can be made about distinctions between leadership and authority. (For further discussion of the concepts of power and authority, see Chapter 10.)

A second related concern is that much of the leadership research within the behavioral framework is based on convenient but limited conceptualizations of the leadership process. By viewing leadership in a dichotomous fashion, we are creating for ourselves, as researchers, an easy method for exploring the process while limiting our overall understanding of it. Dichotomies are convenient, yet they do not always provide us with an explanation that is both testable and comprehensive. Take, for example, police sergeants. Can we understand their leadership behavior simply by stating that they are either employee-centered or production-oriented supervisors? Isn't it realistic to say that any sergeant could be both? For that matter, couldn't a sergeant exhibit other leadership behaviors besides merely these two?

More important, isn't a sergeant's leadership approach highly influenced by the tasks to be accomplished, along with the technology available? A task may require subordinates to follow a predetermined set of policies and procedures, as the only acceptable or the only tested way of accomplishing that task. The sergeant of a tactical unit, for example, may need a production-oriented style of leadership because of the nature of the work—many dangerous tasks and highly uncertain situations. Thus, to suggest that one approach to leadership is more applicable than the other in criminal justice organizations is simplistic and not sufficient to explain the intricacies of the leadership process in those organizations.

Third, our concern with external validity requires us to question the application of research findings done largely in private organizations to public organizations such as criminal justice. Is it possible for the police sergeant or the corrections manager to be employee centered in the same way that a bank manager is? In addition, what does employee centered mean in the context of the expected roles of both supervisor and subordinate in criminal justice organizations? How are the dimensions of leadership identified by this body of research affected by the tasks of the organization? In attempting to be employee centered, is the police sergeant constrained by the tasks required? In short, is leadership affected by the situation and the tasks of the supervisor and the subordinate?

With these three criticisms in mind, we must be cautious in applying the findings from either the Ohio State studies or the Michigan studies to the workings of middle-level managers or administrators in the criminal justice system. Instead, we can say that these behavioral studies were the first to address the concept of leadership in an accessible way, and much of the research in criminal justice leadership has been rooted in these studies. Although we are somewhat critical of this research, we believe that the application and testing of these theoretical models in criminal justice organizations have provided the incentive to view the leadership process in a comprehensive fashion. Recent leadership research has been directed toward understanding the situation in criminal justice organizations. This research is rooted in contingency theories of leadership, which we will discuss next.

Prison Leadership

Being a leader today is more complicated than ever before. As leaders in the 21st century, we are faced with the challenge of leadership in a world where changes occur so rapidly that long-term planning appears ineffective. The workplace is more chaotic today than ever before. Our workforce is experiencing rapid change, as employees have different expectations about work, their employer, and their lives. Prison leaders are all faced with greater demands from a growing number of external influences. We must be prepared to respond to the changing expectations of the public, the legislature, control agencies, and special interest groups.

These workplace challenges are the same for both private and public sector. The private sector is able to respond quickly. For the private sector, it is either respond to change or perish.

Government responds slowly to change. In the past, this may have been bothersome to employees and others; but in time, government did respond. In general, people understood; and for the most part, they accepted the slowness and the politics of government processes in response to problems and issues. This is no longer the case. Our employees and the public do not demonstrate the patience and understanding they once did.

As a warden, my greatest challenge is managing this radically changing work environment. This work environment includes baby boomers, generation X, the Net generation, people not born in this country, and people with distinct views about the work-place. There has never been a more diverse workforce with such vastly different ideas and personnel.

A warden must understand these leadership challenges and be prepared to change. The way one leads today may not fit the circumstances one faces tomorrow.

Wardens must also understand and accept the external forces that impact the running of a prison. In doing so, a warden must bring about changes by involving all stakeholders in the process. Today's stakeholder map is broader and more inclusive than ever. A warden must be committed to open and continuous communication, both outside and within the institution.

This style of leadership requires open dialogue with inmates, their families, attorney groups, politicians, and special interest groups. This style of leadership recognizes the need to view those individuals as customers and create a customer-friendly environment. To acheive this, you must have the commitment of prison staff. Your employees must recognize the need to respond to outside stakeholders.

Internally, a leader today must be more employee friendly, demonstrating a greater commitment to employee services. Today's workforce expects more and, at times, demands more from their employer. A warden must respond to the needs of his or her workforce in order to gain a commitment to the goals of the organization. A warden who fails to do this will be unsuccessful in today's environment.

Our workforce today is not as impressed with the chain of command as in years past. Today's workforce also has shorter organizational commitments. New employees do not enter our organization with the idea they will complete a career with the Department of Corrections. Staff with years of experience are no longer the norm. The involvement of people because of their expertise or because they will be impacted by the change is critical. This approach recognizes that rank does not always guarantee expertise in all aspects of running a modern day prison. A leader today has to find and develop talent and be committed to a teamwork approach to problem solving. Expertise will achieve a desired result. Including staff affected by the change will allow an organization to grow in knowledge and skill.

Leading change through teamwork accomplishes two goals. Teamwork allows you to bring a broader perspective and more ideas to problem solving. Teamwork also assists in keeping your workforce challenged and enthused in their job. By doing so, you will maximize your ability to retain staff because today's workforce requires challenges and expects personal growth. Involvement of staff also leads to greater commitment to organizational goals.

The success of a prison warden today depends on a warden's ability to respond quickly to the rapidly changing work environment. A warden must demonstrate a flexible leadership style. The leadership of the warden must give staff and others the belief that he or she is in charge of the prison, while at the same time reassuring staff and other stakeholders that you will listen and seek the knowledge and address the concerns of others.

This is not an easy task. In the large multi-mission prisons of California, a warden must have energy and give unselfishly of time. This is essential if a warden is to be successful in staying in touch with staff at all levels in a prison such as San Quentin, with its 1,400 staff and 6,000 inmates. For San Quentin is a multi-mission prison with three primary missions:

1. A reception center with an intake of 2,000 inmates per month
2. Housing the male condemned—a population of 570 inmates
3. Level II General Population

Any one of these missions could be a full-time job for a warden.

Being the warden of such a complex prison has been a wonderful experience. I have learned the value and necessity of teamwork. This difficult mission has required that I discover better ways to keep communication flowing. It is a job that has taught me the rewards of walking and talking. By staying open to the ideas of all stakeholders, I have experienced success in implementing change.

A successful warden will embrace the changing environment and be prepared to be flexible in his or her leadership style. This will bring out the best in staff and create an environment that is able to respond to the needs of the organzation. I work each day to achieve this leadership goal.

J. S. WOODFORD
Warden
CSP–San Quentin

Contingency Theories

Contingency theories of leadership differ from both trait and behavioral theories in emphasizing the situation or context. Examining situational variables is central to understanding leadership in organizations, according to contingency theorists. We can see how this approach is useful for studying leadership in criminal justice organizations. The lieutenant in a prison, for example, is constrained by situational factors in dealing with both corrections officers and prisoners. Prison officials cannot exercise total power; depending on the organizational structure of the prison, there are limits to what can be done to lead groups toward organizational objectives. The leadership style employed is, therefore, contingent on the situational aspects of the prison and the nature of the relationship between keeper and kept.

The two contingency theories we examine in this chapter, Fiedler's contingency model and the path-goal theory, both have distinctive elements that contribute to our understanding of leadership in criminal justice organizations. In addition, we can draw different implications from each model for the management and administration of criminal justice systems.

Fiedler's Contingency Model.   According to Fiedler (1967), the leadership process is constrained by three major situational dimensions. First, *leader–member relations* are the level of trust and the degree of likeability the leader enjoys with subordinate groups. According to Fiedler, how well a leader is able to guide immediate subordinates is contingent on the relationship he or she has with them. It is easy to see in police organizations, for example, that some supervisors are better liked by rank-and-file officers than other supervisors. The leader who is not liked or well received by subordinates is constrained by this situation and can be ineffective in guiding and influencing workers to accomplish organizational tasks.

Second, the *task structure* of the organization is, in Fiedler's (1967:53) words, "the degree to which the task is spelled out . . . or must be left nebulous and undefined." Routinized task structure has clearly defined procedures for accomplishing organizational objectives. The machine-based factory has clear directions for running the machine. It is easier to lead when the task structure is clearly defined and open to direct monitoring by the supervisor. The organization with an undefined task structure or uncertainty about achieving its objective presents problems. Most of the activities of criminal justice organizations have uncertain task structures, even though these agencies have relatively stable policies and procedures, simply because it is not all that certain that the tasks accomplish the goals professed. It is one thing to say, for example, that officers patrol the streets of the city (a task), another to say that this task accomplishes the goals of crime prevention and societal protection. This uncertainty about the relationship between task performance and goal accomplishment produces agencies that, more often than not, are unstructured and loosely coupled. As a result, effective leadership becomes problematical for both administrators and immediate supervisors.

Third, *position power* is the leader's ability to exercise power in the organization. Fiedler's test of position power is the ability to hire and fire subordinates. A leader with high position power is able to hire or fire at will. A leader with low position power has limited authority in this area. Here again, we can see how criminal justice administrators are constrained because of their limited authority to hire or dismiss someone. Because they are public agencies, many organizations of criminal justice are governed by civil service or independent commissions that regulate, monitor, and control all personnel decisions. Administrators cannot dismiss someone without going through an elaborate process of review, typically by an external group or agency. Moreover, immediate supervisors—for example, police sergeants—have no power to make such critical decisions. In fact, much of the position power in the immediate supervisory positions of criminal justice has been limited by legal decisions, an environmental constraint over which administrators have little control. Although it would be inaccurate to state that administrators and frontline supervisors have no position power at all, that power is limited and is relatively weak when compared with the position power of comparable groups in the private sector.

Given these situational dimensions—leader–member relations, task structure, and position power—we can match the proper leadership styles with the right situations to produce the most effective form of leadership. Leadership style can be determined by asking leaders to describe, either favorably or unfavorably, their least-preferred coworker. This is known as an *LPC score*. According to Fiedler, the leader who describes a least-preferred coworker in a favorable manner tends to be permissive and human relations oriented; the leader who describes a least-preferred coworker in unfavorable terms is concerned with task production and getting the job done. Moreover, Fiedler suggests that for the most part task-production leaders tend to be more effective in structured situations, whereas human relations–oriented leaders are more effective in situations that require a creative response from supervisors and subordinates.

In addition, a leader has *high situational control* when he or she has good leader–member relations, a high task structure, and high position power. *Low situational control* exists when the opposite conditions are present: poor leader–member relations, low task structure, and little or no position power. Finally, *moderate situational control* means the situational characteristics are mixed; some characteristics work to the advantage of the leader (for example, high leader–member relations), while others do not (poor position power) (Tosi, Rizzo, & Carroll, 1986:503–504).

By matching the degree of situational control with differing LPC orientations, says Fiedler, we can determine the most appropriate leadership approach. The low-LPC leader would be the most effective in situations where there is low situational control (poor leader–member relations, low task structure, and little or no position power). In this example, the low-LPC leader would be most effective in situations that required situational control and specific directions to employees; workers might believe that their own success in accomplishing the tasks of the organization was related to the guidance of the leader. The human relations–oriented leader (high LPC) will be the most successful where the group has structured tasks and a dislike for the leader. The human relations–oriented leader is effective in a situation where the group likes the leader and has an unstructured task to perform.

Within criminal justice organizations, we can see how leadership style can be effective depending on situational factors. The sergeant who directs a tactical unit in a police organization may be more effective by employing a task-oriented rather than human relations–oriented leadership style because many tactical unit tasks are structured, leader position power is relatively high (the sergeant often has direct input into who is in the unit and how they function), and strong identification with the leader is critical because of the nature of the tasks being performed. We would not expect the sergeant in this unit to ask for input from subordinates on how to run the unit because the sergeant has to issue orders and directives to achieve the goals of the unit.

The situational factors faced by a supervisor of corrections officers, however, may require a different type of leadership style. If the supervisor is well liked by officers, if tasks are only vaguely related to the goals of the organization, and if the supervisor has weak position power, it may be advantageous to be human relations oriented. In fact, in institutional corrections today, it has been said that the uncertainty about the relationship between tasks and organizational objectives on one hand and the weak position power of both supervisors and administrators on the other requires leaders to be more oriented toward human relations. In effect, corrections supervisors need to be open and flexible with subordinates if their organizational goals are to be accomplished. Yet task-oriented leaders can argue equally that if leader–member relations in correctional institutions are poor, tasks unstructured, and leader position power weak, an autocratic management style would be more effective.

Two basic criticisms can be leveled against the contingency model of leadership. First, Fiedler seems to treat LPC as a dichotomous and one-dimensional variable, implying that leaders are either totally task oriented or totally human relations oriented; the theory does not admit the possibility that leaders could be equally high on both dimensions. Our understanding of administrative behavior intuitively suggests that this kind of polarization is not the case and that managers do exhibit both styles of leadership depending on the situation.

Second, this theory implicitly assumes that task structure and leader–member relations cannot be modified or changed by the leader's style. Fiedler argues that it is easier to alter situations within the organization than the style of leadership exhibited by the leader. If leader–member relations are not good, for example, it may be more appropriate to spend time rearranging this situation than trying to change the leader's style. There may be much truth in this statement, yet there is no reason to believe that style of leadership cannot be modified as easily as situational dimensions. In fact, it can be reasonably argued that leadership style can affect some situational dimensions and change them for the good of the organization. Is it not possible, for example, for a leader to modify his or her style so that an unstructured task becomes more structured?

Two implications of this theory for criminal justice management can be drawn. First, if effective leadership is the goal in criminal justice organizations, then matching the right leader with specific tasks becomes critical; yet this luxury may not be possible. Given that many administrators and supervisors in criminal justice organizations are not chosen because of their ability to lead but rather because of their years of service, scores on tests, and loyalty to the organization (to mention only a few criteria), it is not clear how leaders can be matched to specific situations. Although private organizations may have the luxury of removing and replacing ineffective leaders, such is typically not the case in criminal justice organizations. Second, if Fiedler's ideas on leadership are to be applied to criminal justice agencies, then administrative officials and those in supervisory positions need training to become aware of their personality orientations and the organizational consequences of expressing these orientations. Although officials have been requesting it for many years, such training is still severely lacking (Geller, 1985).

We will return to a discussion of contingency theory later in the chapter when we apply some of its ideas to a broader notion of leadership and how contingent external factors affect criminal justice organizations.

Path-Goal Theory. While Fiedler's theory of leadership attempts to isolate situational characteristics and leader orientation to understand the leadership process, *path-goal theory* suggests that the interaction between leader behavior and the situational aspects of the organization is important (House & Mitchell, 1985). Additionally, this theory argues that leadership is linked to an expectancy theory of motivation (see Chapter 5), which posits that the leader's behavior directly influences the actions of employees if it is a source of satisfaction for them. Effective leadership, according to path-goal theory, is situational and does not depend on a single style or theory. Moreover, effective leadership is tied to the degree of direction and guidance the leader provides in the work situation. This guidance and direction can be tied to four styles of leadership that are independent yet can be exhibited by one leader in different situations.

Directive leadership emphasizes the leader's expectations and the tasks that subordinates perform. The leader instills into subordinates the importance of the organization's rules and regulations and their relationship to task performance. Under this style of leadership, the leader provides the necessary guidance to subordinates to motivate them to accomplish the tasks required by the organization. *Supportive leadership* stresses a concern for employees. This type of leader is friendly with employees and desires to be approachable. The leader's primary concern is both to accomplish the organizational tasks and meet workers' needs. *Participative leadership* emphasizes collaboration of the leader and subordinates. The leader employing this style attempts to involve subordinates in the organization's decision-making process and assures them of their importance in the organization. *Achievement-oriented leadership* is concerned with having subordinates produce results. Such a leader expects that workers will attempt to do their best and that if goals are set high enough and subordinates are properly motivated, they will achieve those goals. The leader confidently expects that employees will achieve the stated goals and tasks.

Two contingency factors shape subordinates' performance and level of satisfaction in this theory. According to House and Mitchell (1985:494), three *subordinate characteristics*—aspects of the worker, most of which are rooted in personality—determine which leadership style will be most effective. These are *locus of control*, in which internally focused individuals are receptive to a participative leadership style and externally controlled individuals are comfortable with a directive form of leadership; *authoritarianism*, in which individuals high in authoritarianism react positively to directive leadership and those low in authoritarianism are receptive to participative leadership; and *ability*, in which employees who are highly competent in their jobs do not need to be led or directed and benefit from a participative style of leadership, whereas those who are not so competent need directive leadership.

Environmental factors are characteristics of the work situation. According to path-goal theory, three environmental factors affect a subordinate's ability to perform the tasks required; these factors intervene between the subordinate and the leader. *Task* is the structure or level of uncertainty that enables the employee to accomplish the task or prevents the employee from accomplishing the task. The directive style of leadership may be appropriate when the subordinate does not understand how to do the task. Without proper leadership, the subordinate will never be able to clear the path necessary to accomplish the task; proper leadership style is critical here.

The *formal authority system* of the organization is a second critical factor in the environment. If, for example, the worker perceives the formal structure of the organization as a barrier to the accomplishment of goals and thereby to the rewards associated with the accomplishment of those goals, the leader must remove the barriers so that the worker can effectively meet the organization's stated objectives.

Finally, the *primary work group* is the third environmental factor that may prevent the worker from achieving organizational tasks and objectives, which in turn affects the number of rewards the worker will receive from the organization. The leader, therefore, makes sure that the task expected of the worker is clearly stated and defined, that goals of the organization are attainable and have rewards, and that there are no barriers to performance. Under optimal conditions, the leader provides the atmosphere where uncertainty about the relationship between task performance and organizational rewards is low. The leader thus clears a path through these environmental factors primarily by increasing the value of tasks and rewards, removing barriers to the accomplishment of organizational goals, and reducing uncertainty so that subordinates can achieve tasks.

Figure 7-1 diagrams path-goal theory. From this representation, we can see how specific leadership styles are effective given the contingent factors in the worker and the environment. Directive leadership is clearly the most effective (effectiveness being defined by the degree of satisfaction expressed by workers) in situations where the task is ambiguous and uncertain, but this leadership style produces lower levels of satisfaction among workers when the task is relatively clear and the workers are easily able to complete the task. Supportive leadership is best employed when the tasks being performed by subordinates are stressful, dissatisfying, and frustrating. Finally, participative leadership may be the most effective when the individual is highly involved in the task or when the task is relatively non-routine and somewhat ambiguous. In this situation, the leader provides the necessary platform for the subordinate to express concerns about how the task can be accomplished and rewards maximized. Once again, path-goal theory suggests that the primary role of the leader is to provide the paths by which subordinates' rewards can be maximized while simultaneously meeting the objectives of the organization.

Path-goal theory can make three contributions to criminal justice administration. First, criminal justice administrators need to spell out clearly the types of rewards that subordinates can receive if and when they follow specific paths designed and structured by the organization. If, for example, Officer Jones is told that she will receive a promotion or a positive evaluation from her supervisor if she accomplishes the tasks assigned, there must be a reward system in place that promotes and reinforces that behavior. All that path-goal theory suggests is that subordinates will follow and accomplish tasks defined and assigned by the organization if rewards are attached

Leader behavior	and	Contingency factors			Cause	Subordinate attitudes and behavior
1. Directive		1. Subordinate characteristics: Authoritarianism Locus of control Ability	Influence	Personal perceptions		1. Job satisfaction Job → Rewards
2. Supportive						2. Acceptance of leader Leader → Rewards
3. Achievement-oriented		2. Environmental factors: The task Formal authority system	Influence	Motivational stimuli Constraints Rewards		3. Motivational behavior Effort → Performance
4. Participative		Primary work group				Performance → Reward

FIGURE 7-1 Summary of Path-Goal Relationships (From R. J. House and T. R. Mitchell, "Path-Goal Theory of Leadership," in *Organizational Behavior and Management,* 4th ed., edited by H. L. Tosi and W. C. Hammer, p. 496. Cincinnati: Grid, 1985. Reprinted by permission of the authors.)

to the accomplishment of those tasks. If leadership cannot develop and promote such a structure, then leadership is at fault.

Such, in fact, may be the case in many criminal justice organizations. Take police organizations as an example: If the principles of path-goal theory were followed, administrators would have as a primary goal the removal of obstacles to officers so that they would follow the rules and regulations of the organization with the hope of being promoted someday. Often, police rules are written where full enforcement of the law is not possible. Limited resources, for example, make full enforcement problematic. On one hand, officers are told to enforce the rules for evaluation and promotion purposes, yet on the other hand they are not given adequate resources and support to complete their jobs. By applying various styles of leadership, contingent on the personal characteristics of subordinates and the environmental characteristics of the work situation, leaders would clear the path for subordinates to accomplish the goals of the organization while simultaneously meeting their own expectations and enhancing their rewards, such as a promotion.

Yet police organizations often cannot provide the rewards sought by police officers. Because supervisors have little control over reward distribution, the style of leadership they exhibit is somewhat meaningless. If, for example, a court orders a police department to hire and promote minority candidates over majority candidates because of past practices of discrimination in the department, the police supervisor may have limited control over who gets promoted and, more important, may have a difficult time convincing subordinates that there actually is a "clear" path to promotion or mobility in the organization. Additionally, the issue of clear policies and procedures in criminal justice organizations is problematic for other reasons.

Oftentimes the policies and procedures in criminal justice organizations are vague, ambiguous, and contradictory, lending themselves to much interpretation and working against the stated goals of the organization. Under such an arrangement policies and procedures will not paint a clear path toward goals to be realized. Moreover, ambiguous or contradictory policies and procedures may hinder goal achievement. What is likely under these circumstances is that informal leaders who effectively learn to circumvent the ambiguity of extant policies and procedures to ultimately achieve the goals of the organization ascend from the rank-and-file personnel. These leaders will, in effect, legitimize an informal process to achieve the goals of the organization, thereby leaving the formal leadership process out of the loop when it comes to individual behaviors and tasks that relate to organizational goals.

Use of force by correctional officers is a good example of ambiguity and vagueness in policies and procedures. All corrections departments have policies and procedures that define the appropriate use of force on prisoners, and all of them suggest use of force that is necessary to address a problem. Yet, it is difficult to know what is an appropriate use of force in the prison context. For correctional officers, the ambiguity and vagueness are addressed through informal leaders who develop *ad hoc* practices about what is an acceptable use of force in the prison. It will be difficult for correctional administrators to develop a clear path to the goal of using force appropriately in the correctional environment when informal leaders have defined it for correctional officers in a way that works for them. For example, during the 1970s correctional administrators were faced with lawsuits by inmates on a number of matters, including the use of force. Initially, a policy to guide the use of force within new litigation was not developed. As a result, many officers ignored situations—retreated to the walls—in order to avoid being civilly sued for improper or excessive use of force (Lombardo, 1996). More often than not, these informal practices work against the stated goals of the formal policies and procedures.

Second, path-goal theory suggests, correctly, that no one style of leadership is sufficient for all the situations faced by criminal justice administrators and supervisors. This point cannot be stated too often. In many instances, good administrators in criminal justice organizations have recognized that proper leadership requires a correct assessment of the situation. Additionally, it becomes clear that leadership is an ongoing and proactive process that demands constant evaluations of multiple situations. More important, leaders must constantly reevaluate the situations faced by subordinates and how paths can be cleared for the attainment of both organizational objectives and employee goals.

Third, path-goal theory requires that criminal justice administrators design paths and goals for criminal justice employees that are reasonable and attainable. Path-goal theory assumes active leadership on the part of supervisors. Criminal justice administrators who do not clarify paths for subordinates only create confusion for themselves and much alienation and disillusionment among employees. Such ineffective leadership places obstacles between supervisors and subordinates that may be difficult to overcome.

Leadership Research in Criminal Justice

As we have seen, little empirical testing of the theoretical models of leadership in criminal justice organizations has been attempted. What has been done, moreover, is still rooted in the 1950s research of the Ohio State and the Michigan studies. This situation may be caused either by slow application of current theoretical models of leadership to criminal justice organizations or the limited number of reliable instruments to test the new theoretical positions. However, some new research, particularly in the police field, does tell us about leadership in criminal justice agencies; from it we can draw implications for management.

Research by Kuykendall and Unsinger (1982) suggests that police managers have a preferred leadership orientation. Employing an instrument created by Hershey and Blanchard (1977), the researchers found that police managers are likely to use styles of leadership known as *selling* (high task and high relationship emphasis), *telling* (high task and low relationship emphasis), and *participating* (high relationship and low task emphasis), with very little concern for *delegating* (low relationship and low task emphasis). Of these styles of leadership, which are similar to those discussed previously, the most preferred style is selling. The researchers suggest that police managers are no less effective than managers in other organizational settings and that the selling, telling, and participating styles lead to organizational effectiveness.

Similar findings were generated by Swanson and Territo (1982) in their research involving 104 police supervisors in the Southeast in the late 1970s. Using the managerial grid, the researchers found that their sample of police supervisors showed high concern for both production and people and emphasized team management in their organizations. Employing other measures, the researchers also found that police supervisors used a style of communication that emphasized the open and candid expression of their feelings and knowledge to subordinates rather than a style of communication that emphasized feedback from subordinates to managers about their supervisory capabilities. This research suggested that police managers had an open communication style with subordinates and supported the idea that police managers were indeed democratic in their leadership styles. (At least, they professed to be.)

Later research, however, suggests that such a participative and democratic leadership style is not as ubiquitous in police organizations as previously indicated. Auten (1985), for example, found in his sample of police supervisors and operations personnel in state police agencies in Illinois that the dominant managerial model was the traditional paramilitary one, with one-way communication. In addition, these police supervisors and operations personnel strongly believed that they had no meaningful role in organizational decision making. The researchers suggest that there were communications breakdowns between the supervisory and operations personnel and the administrative heads of the agencies.

Not only is there limited consensus on what type of leadership styles predominate among police managers and administrators, but when police supervisors are asked to think about a leadership style as opposed to acting out a style in a specific situation, they tend to change their approaches to leadership (Kuykendall, 1985). Clearly, what a supervisor regards as an appropriate style of leadership may not be in agreement with what he or she actually does in a given situation. Current research, for example, on occupational stress, high turnover, absenteeism, and substance abuse in the police field suggests that the traditional paramilitary structure of police organizations, with its emphasis on an autocratic style of leadership, creates and perpetuates these problems. These problems may be traced to other factors in the police role, such as the danger associated with the job, yet it is important to examine how specific leadership styles contribute to many of these problems. Much leadership research in policing is lacking in this area.

In the field of corrections, much of what we know about leadership is rooted in highly prescriptive material, which limits our understanding of the process. However, many of the problems experienced in police organizations are experienced equally in correctional organizations; hierarchical structure, limited and often rigid communications systems, and centralized decision-making authority in correctional organizations produce many of these problems (Archambeault & Archambeault, 1982). Like police research, leadership research in corrections is not only limited but also offers little information that is useful to corrections administrators.

Given the current state of leadership research in both police organizations and correctional organizations, we recommend that the following issues be addressed by future researchers. First, we need additional research on how criminal justice administrators actually lead their organizations; from this data, prescriptions for policy can be made increasingly informed and useful to the criminal justice manager. Much existing research is out of date and tells us little about the increasing complexities of the leadership process.

Second, the contemporary models of leadership offered by organizational behavior theory need to be examined. Contingency approaches should be examined in relation to criminal justice organizations, along with refinement of instruments to test these theories in the criminal justice environment. The situational factors influencing the leadership process must be examined in the operations of criminal justice systems. Too often, research in criminal justice organizations has been set up to ascertain whether administrators are participative or autocratic in relation to their subordinates. It is possibly time to stop searching for the perfect criminal justice manager and to begin examining situational aspects of the work environment that constrain administrators in their leadership functions.

Third, to understand fully the leadership phenomenon in criminal justice organizations, we must use the new methodologies to look at the intricacies associated with the leadership process. Traditional survey methods in criminal justice organizations have yielded some valuable information, yet field methods would provide information about the actual leadership mechanisms used by criminal justice administrators. To understand the leadership process, it is helpful to watch and document what criminal justice leaders actually do and, more important, be able to distinguish effective criminal justice leaders from ineffective ones. In this way, prescriptions for administrators would be informed by data and useful in their day-to-day interactions with subordinates.

Finally, we need to discuss how much we can expect of our criminal justice managers in terms of leadership. It is common to blame the poor performance of subordinates on ineffective management or leadership; we often hear this complaint in criminal justice organizations. Yet it is shortsighted to suggest that all problems in criminal justice can be attributed to faulty leadership. Criminal justice administrators have limited or no control over some aspects of the work of their organizations. As a result, requesting a new leader "to set the organization back on path" is probably, in the words of Hall (1982:158), "little more than a cosmetic treatment." An uncertain and unstable political environment, for example, makes multiple demands on a police chief. Not being able to appease all groups all the time, the chief is constrained in decision making. On many occasions, because the chief has limited resources and multiple demands, all community expectations for police services cannot be met. Too often the chief is viewed as an ineffective leader when leadership has little to do with this problem. To be effective, a leader must provide some degree of control over the external environment. But we need to be realistic about how much a police administrator can control. Perhaps for this reason, many experts recommend that incoming police chiefs develop clear and stable relations with local political groups so that expectations can be spelled out on both sides (Murphy, 1985).

Similar concerns can be raised about leadership in the courts, prisons, and probation and parole organizations. Leaders of these departments have problems trying to understand the political process and how it affects their organizations. Many have concerns about how much of their organizations they really control, particularly in tight fiscal times when resources are stretched and competition among social service agencies for finite dollars is fierce. Like police administrators, court and correctional administrators are often expected to perform tasks that they neither agree with nor have the resources to successfully complete. A prime example of this difficulty is the "three strikes" initiative that swept the country during the early 1990s. For many departments of corrections' leaders and prison administrators, such a law was impossible to live with and had dire practical consequences for prison management. Yet its political appeal was so great that political leaders jumped on the bandwagon to pass laws that were difficult to implement and, in some cases, draconian in their effects (Irwin and Austin, 1995). Under such difficult circumstances, how are criminal justice administrators to respond? An answer to this question may lie in a model of leadership education to which we now turn.

Leadership Education: The California Department of Corrections Experience

In response to unprecedented growth in both employee and offender populations in the California Department of Corrections, the director responded by developing a Leadership Institute in joint collaboration with the California State University at Chico Center for Regional and Continuing Education. This initiative, designed to prepare future leaders within the department, viewed leadership as an educational process that could be taught to administrators. The primary emphasis was on education rather than training. Participants were asked to move beyond their formal structures, policies and procedures, and ways of doing business to question critically the direction and methods of operation within the department. Participants were selected based on their years of experience, commitment to productive change, and potential for promotion within the department. All participants were screened by the DOC director and charged with addressing a significant issue facing the Department of Corrections then and into the 21st century.

In the fall of 1994, the Leadership Institute convened for the first time. Unlike other leadership training programs, this effort was much more intensive and project oriented. Participants were required to attend week-long sessions over a six-month period, totaling six weeks of intensive study on leadership development and application within the Department of Corrections. Within each cohort, approximately twenty-five persons were assembled from varying management and administrative positions within the Department of Corrections. Attendees came from the prisons, medical services, procurement services, training and evaluation, and parole agencies, to mention a few. They were split up into four groups of six individuals and jointly developed an issue facing the department through a series of exercises given to them in the first two weeks. Upon completing the institute, the groups would present their issues, solutions, and findings to the director and top administrative staff at a graduation ceremony.

Through such an intensive process, the institute's organizers hoped that the key elements of leadership could be transmitted to individuals through a number of complex exercises and tasks. Many of the exercises required the use of computer-assisted technologies as well as library and external resources. Instructors were all university professors who had experience working within the field of corrections and were serving as consultants to the DOC. The institute recognized specific elements as essential for effective leadership for any criminal justice administrator. The experiences of the participants through the various exercises indicated that effective criminal justice leaders must possess the following attributes:

1. *Possess traits indicative of a proactive approach to leadership.* These traits include, but are not limited to, good communication skills, an honest and trustworthy approach to dealing with staff, an attitude of excellence, and a firm knowledge of the organization and the problems and issues it faces.

2. *Be aware of the importance of building professional relationships with employees.* Effective leaders recognize that listening to employee concerns is relevant to achieving organizational goals. Showing concern for employees as persons, rewarding excellence in performance, and conveying a friendly and approachable manner or presence are critical for effective leadership. Such behaviors show a concern for employees as members of a team working toward the attainment of specific organizational objectives.

3. *Balance the needs of employees with concern for production.* Effective leaders encourage cooperative decision making through shared ideas and shared power; they also encourage participation in decision making as well as allowing freedom for employees to grow and experiment with new methods to accomplish tasks. They recognize that failure is a part of a learning process for employees.

4. *Incorporate a sense of "vision" within the organization and serve as a transformer of culture when necessary.* The purpose behind the identification of vision is to specifically direct employees and their behaviors toward the central purpose(s) of the organization. Good leaders are able to identify challenges that the organization faces as well as specify appropriate alternatives when addressing current problems and those well into the future. Effective leaders understand that employee acceptance of the organization's vision means that there may need to be cultural change within the orga-

nization. The good leader is able to identify new symbols and values for the organization that employees will accept. These symbols and values may be new to the organization, and the leader recognizes that cultural change is a prerequisite for long-term change. The leader solicits support among employees and shows the value of such transformation toward the accomplishment of organizational objectives and goals.

5. *Recognize that an array of contingent strategies are required for effective leadership.* Recognizing the right tool for the job is a central task. Leaders understand that changes in the political environment, for example, may require changes in how the organization functions and completes its tasks. Leaders must identify effective mechanisms to predict these changes and make appropriate adjustments either to deflect them or to alter ways of doing business so that the changes are no longer problematical for the organization. Having a diverse set of strategies improves the chances that changes will not have an adverse impact on the organization. For example, effective and contingent strategies for dealing with the political environment may be invaluable to protecting the organization from a budget cut or a reduction in personnel.

These elements make up the core of effective leadership as identified by participants in the Leadership Institute. The list is by no means exhaustive, yet it does oblige us to think about what criminal justice leadership actually is and how important some issues—such as leadership traits, employee development, balancing the needs of employees with production concerns, incorporating a sense of vision to the organization, and using multiple and contingent strategies—are for effective leadership. A review of Chapters 5 and 6 shows how these issues are also relevant to employee motivation and job design.

Criminal Justice Leadership: A Brief Word on Organizational Culture

Individuals are either elected or appointed to lead criminal justice organizations. These leaders usually have come up through the ranks of the organization. They understand the importance of creating and setting the "tone" in the organization and, in the words of Schein (1997), influencing the culture of the organization. Criminal justice literature is replete with accounts of both the good and the bad in the cultures of criminal justice organizations.

Whether these accounts reflect corruption in police organizations (Fyfe & Skolnick, 1994) or the alleged violence and brutality of correctional work (Conover, 2000), concerns have been raised about how such cultures are created, sustained, and perpetuated in criminal justice organizations. For many the issue hinges on the role of leadership in influencing organizational culture. Many writers on criminal justice administration have noted the importance of leadership to organizational culture (Crank, 1997; Stojkovic & Farkas, 2003). This research suggests that effective leadership within criminal justice organizations must pay attention to how cultures are created, the mechanisms which transmit culture to new employees, the role of leaders in the transmission of culture, and how culture can be influenced by administrators. Future research in criminal justice leadership will have to address the importance of organizational culture and offer suggestions on how it can be created and nurtured to fulfill organizational goals.

Summary

This chapter began with an examination of criminal justice leadership in a political context. Our purpose was to suggest that the criminal justice administrator has to be politically astute. Additionally, however, only so much can be expected of the criminal justice administrator; the charge of ineffective leadership is often incorrect and unfair.

The chapter reviewed theories of leadership offered in the literature on organizational behavior. All the models can provide us with some information about leadership in the organizations of criminal justice. Clearly, leadership is a complex and often misunderstood process. Understanding styles of leadership, contingent factors that affect the leadership process, and paths that enable employees to accomplish both personal and professional goals is valuable in understanding criminal justice administration and offering prescriptions to managers in these organizations.

We have not fully applied or tested many of these theoretical insights in criminal justice, where much of the literature has been prescriptive and not data-informed. Moreover, most theoretical testing that has been done in criminal justice organizations has been limited and exclusively applied to police organizations. We called for additional research and suggested that contingency approaches be examined in the organizations of criminal justice. Only through critical research can we comprehend how the leadership process operates and, more important, offer valuable insights to those people who administer and manage our criminal justice organizations.

A review of the Leadership Institute offered by the California Department of Corrections showed that effective qualities of leaders can be identified and taught to criminal justice administrators. The program, however, must be evaluated to determine its effectiveness in transmitting the principles of leadership to the real world of criminal justice management and administration. Such future evaluations will help identify primary elements of criminal justice leadership and will also prove invaluable to criminal justice administrators in confronting the day-to-day challenges of being leaders of large public organizations.

A nascent view of criminal justice leadership centers on organizational culture. Criminal justice administrators play a significant role in developing, nurturing, and transmitting organizational culture within their organizations. The future of criminal justice leadership will depend, in part, on how effectively the issue of organizational culture is addressed by both researchers and criminal justice administrators.

Case Study

Supervising the Police Officer: The Leadership Factor

The Ragsdale Police Department had a long history of operating under the traditional paramilitary model, with a clear chain of command and discernible lines of authority. More often than not, police officers understood and legitimized this structure. The common council, however, demanded that the department alter its method of operation and become receptive to the demands of the community after a number of incidents involving police officers and members of the minority community. In one such incident, the police were accused of employing heavy-handed tactics with the patrons of a local bar owned by a prominent black politician. This incident, along with some minor altercations with other minority citizens, led the Fire and Police Commission to demand changes in the department. Under pressure, the conservative long-time police chief resigned.

In came an outsider from a large, urban department who had a progressive philosophy toward policing. In particular, he emphasized openness and flexibility in interacting with the public. The first thing newly hired Police Chief Erik Beckworth instituted was a democratic management style in the department. Officers were encouraged to question and discuss the policies of the department and to make suggestions. Initially, officers were somewhat hesitant about the new police chief. Why did he feel it necessary to change the old ways of doing things in the department? Many officers expressed the opinion that the chief was only playing into the hands of all the citizen groups. One of those officers was Michael Jeske.

Jeske was a veteran with more than twenty-five years in the department and a cynical attitude toward new policing ideas, "All this talk about opening up the department to the public is a bunch of baloney. What the hell do citizens know about policing, anyway?" Spouting his views at a local union meeting, Jeske received a lot of support from fellow officers. "And another thing," he shouted. "All this bullshit about how the department is going to be more open to the officers and listen to their input is dangerous. I have seen this in the past, and it never worked. It's like your honeymoon; after the first couple of weeks, it's all downhill." Knowing that the officers were somewhat hesitant to accept some of his progressive ideas, the chief decided to meet with the recognized leaders of the department, those who were respected by other officers and wielded much power among them.

Because the department had only five hundred officers, Chief Beckworth was able to identify the informal leaders among the officers through their sergeants. Chief Beckworth met with twenty officers whom his lieutenants and sergeants had identified as the leaders among the troops. Chief Beckworth began the meeting by saying, "My goal here is to get to know you guys better and to discuss any suggestions that you have about running this department."

Officer Jeske sat in the back of the room and listened intently as other officers asked superficial questions. "Is there any way we can get warmer jackets for the winter months?" Knowing that the meeting wasn't going anywhere and getting somewhat frustrated, Chief Beckworth decided to end it when Officer Jeske jumped in and shouted, "Pretty damn frustrating, isn't it?" Chief Beckworth looked toward the back of the room where Jeske was sitting and replied, "Yes it is, and what are you going to do to relieve my frustrations here?" Jeske quickly responded, "Now you know how the officers feel about the leadership in this department." Chief Beckworth, realizing that he had an opening with the men through this incident, jumped on it quickly. "What do you mean, and what can be done to improve the leadership in the department?"

Officer Jeske leaned back and looked at Chief Beckworth while the other officers sat in their chairs motionless. "The first thing you administrators have to realize is that we aren't dummies and can figure out when we're getting snowed. You say that your ideas are going to open up the department and make it more flexible. You say that you're going to listen to the men more than in the past. The one thing you did not ask before this all started was whether we were even interested in your ideas. You talk about having us participate in the organization, but you didn't even ask us if we wanted to. I think that a number of us officers believe that leadership in the department starts with the chief being honest with the troops from the beginning. You've got to remember that a lot of chiefs have come and gone in this department and almost all of us have experienced the changes. We know a good leader; it starts with honesty up front and concern for the officers' welfare. Right now we don't know if you're an honest chief or another political hack from City Hall."

Chief Beckworth was amazed by Officer Jeske's openness and promised to be honest with his officers. "I guess we're going to have to see your honesty and leadership in action. Then we'll make a decision about you," replied Jeske. Chief Beckworth could only hope that he would turn out to be the leader his officers expected. He left the informal meeting knowing that effective leadership was going to exist only if a commitment to it was shown by the administrators at the top of the organization—starting with himself.

Case Study Questions

1. Given the climate of the Ragsdale Police Department, what recommendations would you give Chief Beckworth about leadership?

2. How should Chief Beckworth approach Officer Jeske about his cynical attitude toward the department?

3. Can you suggest a career path model to Chief Beckworth that would improve the morale of officers in the Ragsdale Police Department?

For Discussion

1. Discuss the limitations of leadership in criminal justice organizations. Do the best individuals become criminal justice administrators or managers? If not, why not? In addition, are many of the problems associated or attributed to criminal justice leadership really leadership problems? Discuss prison overcrowding, for example. Can we expect a prison warden to effectively manage an overcrowded prison? Is overcrowding in prisons a corrections problem that administrators can address, or is it a societal problem? Explore this issue in terms of the role of leaders in trying to deal with this complex problem.

2. Explore the findings of the Ohio State studies and the Michigan studies as they apply to the agencies of criminal justice. Are their findings applicable or not? What about participation in leadership in criminal justice systems? Should criminal justice managers be concerned with the personal aspects of employees' lives? Will this concern necessarily translate into effective leadership and productive criminal justice employees? Why or why not?

3. Suggest a specific path-goal model a criminal justice manager could employ. Discuss the implications of your path-goal model for effective leadership in that organi-

zation of criminal justice. Finally, examine possible obstacles that would prevent subordinates from attaining goals under this approach to leadership.

4. Offer some concrete suggestions about leadership to a police chief, using one of the theories of leadership examined in this chapter as a model. Ask for feedback from the chief on the feasibility of your proposals and their effectiveness in a police organization.

5. Examine the ideas offered by the Leadership Institute of the California Department of Corrections. Would these ideas be effective in most criminal justice organizations, or just a few? Which few? Why is it important to have a "vision" in a criminal justice organization?

For Further Reading

Bass, B. M. (Ed.). *Stodgill's Handbook of Leadership*. New York: Free Press, 1981.

Fiedler, F. A. *A Theory of Leadership Effectiveness*. New York: McGraw-Hill, 1967.

Geller, W. A. (Ed.). *Police Leadership in America: Crisis and Opportunity*. Chicago: American Bar Association, 1985.

Kouzes, J., and Posner, B. *The Leadership Challenge: How to Keep Getting Extraordinary Things Done in Organizations*. San Francisco: Jossey-Bass, 1997.

Ouchi, W. *Theory Z: How American Business Can Meet the Japanese Challenge*. Reading, MA: Addison Wesley, 1981.

Schein, E. *Organizational Culture and Leadership*, 2nd ed. San Francisco, CA: Jossey-Bass, 1997.

Wright, K. A. *Effective Prison Leadership*. Binghamton, New York: William Neil, 1994.

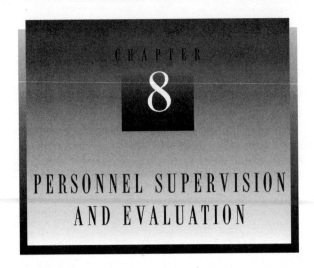

PERSONNEL SUPERVISION AND EVALUATION

The commitment of a department's supervisors is essential to the success of a performance evaluation system. Supervisors are the individuals directly responsible for the quality of the department's work. Line supervisors oversee the transformation of the department's goals, objectives, policy, and procedures into performance. The effectiveness and efficiency of this effort depends on the supervisor's ability to make accurate judgments about job performance and people.

(Fyfe, Greene, Walsh, Wilson, & McLaren, 1997)

Unit Management increases institutional and inmate control by vesting authority and decision-making powers with those staff most closely associated with inmates. Increased and repeated interactions build continuity into staff/inmate relations and provide for better communication and understanding. Information collected about inmates from interactions and observations becomes cumulative and thereby provides a much richer source of knowledge about inmate behavior.

(Wright, 1994)

Successful supervision comes only through conscientious effort. A considerable degree of dedication to the job is necessary, but no one should feel it necessary to become a workaholic. The person who gives everything to the job to the exclusion of all else is most likely using the job as an excuse to fill other needs. Rather, the effective correctional manager is a person who has reasonable liking for the work, who has a sincere interest in delivering quality services to inmates, and who can bring to the job the perspective of a private citizen who evaluates prison operations in terms of decency and humane treatment.

(Phillips & McConnell, 1996)

A problem facing administrators of direct supervision facilities concerns deficiencies in personnel systems. Since the success of direct supervision depends in large measure on the complex and sophisticated management skills of line-level corrections officers, personnel processes such as selection, training, compensation, and retention take on critical importance to the jail organization. Antiquated personnel systems developed to meet the staffing needs of the traditional jail are inappropriate in the New Generation facility, and may even be dangerously dysfunctional.

(Zupan, 1991)

The performance of anybody is the result of a combination of many forces—the person himself, the people that he works with, the job, the material that he works on, his equipment, his customers, his management, his supervision, environmental conditions (noise, confusion, poor food in the company's cafeteria). These forces will produce unbelievably large differences between people. Differences between people arise almost entirely from action of the system that they work in, not from the people themselves.

(Demming, 1986)

Previous chapters have examined the importance of motivation, job design, and leadership to criminal justice administration, issues that are central to the smooth functioning of criminal justice organizations. Another critical issue facing criminal justice administrators is personnel supervision and evaluation. This chapter will examine the topic of supervision and evaluation as it relates to individual performance. Appropriate models of employee supervision will be explored within the context of an organizational setting. The issue of organizational effectiveness will not be addressed in this chapter; Chapter 13 will tackle that thorny topic.

As an organizational issue, employee supervision and evaluation has gained heightened importance among criminal justice administrators. In fact, scholars have called into question the basic tenets of personnel supervision and evaluation that have dominated criminal justice organizations for many years (Goldstein, 1990). Most of these traditional efforts focused on "hard measures" of performance (for example, arrests for police organizations) with very little concern over how these measures in any way related to larger organizational and societal objectives and goals (Bayley, 1994).

Current attempts at restructuring police organizations, court systems, and correctional organizations have centered on questions of how employees will be supervised and evaluated as well as questions about the efficacy of newer methods to maintain control in these organizations (Skolnick & Bayley, 1986). Among criminal justice administrators, the question has become more direct and practical: How do I maintain control of employees so that their behaviors are consistent with organizational goals? A corollary question is: What specific changes need to be implemented to enhance the supervision and evaluation of employees? Answering these questions will be the focus of this chapter.

In addition, this chapter will examine contemporary methods and models of employee supervision and evaluation. The discussion presented will be guided by the goals and expectations we have for criminal justice organizations. Any examination of personnel supervision and evaluation must include an analysis of the goals we are seeking to achieve. As Chapter 1 stated, the goals of criminal justice are multiple, complex, and often contradictory. To talk about the supervision and evaluation of criminal justice employees, therefore, we must include a specific set of goal contexts that focus our understanding. We will begin the discussion with the idea of multiple goals, goal consensus, and criminal justice administration; move to an examination of structural aspects of criminal justice organizations; explore models of employee supervision and evaluation; and conclude with a commentary on the efficacy of these ideas as they relate to the administration and management of criminal justice organizations.

Criminal Justice Administration: The Search for Goal Consensus

It is a common and widely held belief that criminal justice organizations are expected to provide multiple services to the community. All components of the criminal justice system have multiple goals and functions. In some cases, these goals contradict one another, and it is difficult to discern the primary direction of the organization. Within police organizations, for example, we not only expect the police to provide community protection, but also to maintain community order and respond to multiple calls for service (Goldstein, 1990:11). These calls for service have very little to do with the traditional notion of being a "crime fighter." Research has shown how the police role is multidimensional and often involves conflict about the primacy of goals, particularly in view of the fact that the police are the only group in whom coercive force is accepted and legitimized by society.

Egon Bittner (1970) posed the central dilemma faced by police administrators in enforcing the law: How should nonnegotiable, coercive force be exercised in a society that stresses freedom, democracy, and peace? According to Bittner, this is typically accomplished through the development of myths, symbols, and various images that legitimize, and in some cases conceal, the very assumptions upon which police organizations function. Similar views have been offered by critics of the modern community policing ideal. To these critics, community policing represents another attempt to justify and legitimize the central function of police, which is to exercise coercive force (Klockars, 1991).

Others have also suggested that correctional organizations and the courts have operated under similar premises. Stojkovic and Lovell (1997) have argued that myths, symbols, and image maintenance cover fundamental ways in which correctional administrators make decisions. Many of these decisions support the idea that the primary purpose of prison is actually punitive control over large segments of the offender population, with very little concern about rehabilitation or change among prisoners. Given the growth in prison populations, it is uncertain how prisons can do more than simply warehouse offenders (Irwin & Austin, 1997). In some states, such as California, the prison populations have grown so quickly that it is unclear how correctional administrators will even be able to meet the basic needs of the prisoner population. Thus, in discussing prison goals, the only consensus to be reached is that there are too many inmates and too few resources to manage them. Lofty assertions about deterrence, selective incapacitation, rehabilitation, and societal protection may be far removed from the operational realities of prisons, which are trying to maintain prisoner control under conditions of severe resource shortages.

Such a view is also supported by recent research examining the work of probation and parole officers. To some, given the large number of offenders supervised by probation and parole agents, it is difficult to expect that anything beyond simple surveillance is the primary goal of these organizations. In fact, traditional practices such as presentence reports have come under fire by researchers, who claim that such reports are superfluous since most probationers are "typed" by the officer into specific categories based on offense and criminal history (Rosecrance, 1986). A particular emphasis is placed on the potential threat the probationer or parolee presents to the community.

Horror stories have highlighted the plight that many probation and parole agents face when one of their offenders is caught committing a heinous offense. In the case of Jeffrey Dahmer, the Milwaukee mass murderer, his probation officer was given a waiver on home visits because of the officer's huge caseload and the apparent fact that there was no evidence that Dahmer posed a threat to the community. The aftershock of the Dahmer affair has caused many probation and parole departments to tighten up their policies and procedures and to direct their efforts toward greater surveillance of offenders. The reality, however, is that because of limited resources and an unlimited demand for service, probation and parole organizations, like other social service agencies, will always operate under conditions of scarcity (Lipsky, 1980) and adapt to their situations as best they can.

Similarly, court systems face large numbers of cases with too few resources to process all defendants adequately. Critics of the court system point to the fact that many offenders plea-bargain and escape justice, while supporters argue that the mandate of due process requires full constitutional protections for all criminal defendants. Represented as the concerns for crime control and due process, the courts face the dilemma of how to control crime while remaining sensitive to the legal requirements of due process for those suspected of criminal activity.

Contrary to public opinion, most criminal court cases do not involve felonies. According to Walker (1994), the criminal courts for the most part process lower-level cases; the sheer volume of these cases is what overwhelms the system. Accordingly, the idea that the courts process cases in an assembly-line fashion makes sense. The real goal is the quick processing and efficient handling of cases. Research has shown that this is true and, in addition, that the process is the punishment (Feeley, 1979). Because many of the costs of going to court are too high for typical misdemeanant defendants, many will "cop" pleas to lower charges and accept a minimal penalty. To ask for rights, in many cases, would really cost for the defendant more money than the penalty of pleading guilty—though the consistency of this finding is questioned by some researchers (Schulhofer, 1985, cited in Walker, 1994:36). Thus, pleading guilty is in the best interests of most defendants.

It is the conflict between assembly-line justice on one hand and concerns of due process on the other hand that pose difficulties for the court administrator (Mays & Taggart, 1986). Like the other components of the criminal justice system, the courts have to function within the context of limited resources. It is simply impossible to guarantee that most defendants will receive due process when finite resources dictate to a large degree how due process concerns can be addressed.

Moreover, there are larger normative issues of goal consensus that overshadow the resource problem in criminal justice organizations. These concerns include how a criminal justice system should look, the degree of fragmentation among system components, and the role diversity plays in its operation. There has been a growing awareness that the criminal justice system as it has been portrayed over the past twenty-five years (President's Commission, 1967) is not reflective of most local systems of justice across this country. The documented variety and differences across the organizations of criminal justice within the states and the federal government start to raise a question of whether or not goal consensus is a reality or even a desirable state.

Wright (1981) has argued that the construction of a monolithic system of criminal justice tied together by the activities of its various components does not make sense either organizationally or politically. Attempting to construct a single "system" of criminal justice contradicts commonly held beliefs about the relationship between the people and their government. Fragmentation, or a lack of unification across the components of the criminal justice system, is often viewed negatively by proponents of a systems approach to criminal justice, yet such a view denies the importance of fragmentation to the democratic principles we cherish about diversity of viewpoints as expressed through the criminal justice system.

Without fragmentation and diversity across the criminal justice system, it would be difficult for those organizations to deal with their different and varied communities. In this sense, a lack of coordination and unification within the criminal justice system is desirable because diverse points of interest can be expressed and reflected in local systems of justice. To achieve goal consensus within a criminal justice system could be construed as undemocratic and dangerous. Additionally, searching for a singular goal may simply be pointless, given the multiple expectations of communities concerning the operations of their local systems of criminal justice.

Thus, many efforts to integrate local systems of criminal justice into one system are doomed to failure since all of these systems have to respond to local constituencies and environments. This is most true of federal initiatives that mandate specific policies and goals for state and local criminal justice systems. The passage of the Violent Crime Control and Law Enforcement Act of 1994, for example, was an attempt by the federal government to mandate the direction of crime policies in the states; however, critics argue that most crime is local in nature and that these communities should be allowed to dictate how their criminal justice systems will respond to it. Forcing some type of consensus onto the direction and purpose of local systems of criminal justice has always been problematic for legislatures and politicians. The results of such efforts have been questioned by many who have been critical of federal attempts to confront crime (Conley, 1994).

Criminal justice administrators have had many organizational difficulties trying to operationalize and implement plans that are ill conceived and poorly thought out. The effort to incarcerate large numbers of repeat felons, known as the "three strikes and you're out" initiative, has proven to be an organizational nightmare for criminal justice administrators. Nowhere is this more problematic than in the state of California, where estimates indicate that the state will be financially unable to meet the demand for bed space to accommodate the increasing number of offenders who will require incarceration under the new law.

Such practical problems make it difficult for criminal justice administrators to arrive at some consensus about what their organizations should accomplish. One cynical corrections official told this author that his view of correctional administration was that he was a successful administrator as long as his name didn't appear in the newspapers. His idea of goal consensus was predicated on surviving the everyday crises he faced. Goal consensus is virtually impossible given the multiple tasks criminal justice administrators are expected to achieve, the limited resources they have to work with, and the wide and varied expectations of their respective communities.

The central objective of criminal justice administrators is to determine the goals of their communities and the most efficient ways to meet those goals. For some communities, attaining specific goals may be less cumbersome than for others. In communities with large, diverse populations, arriving at goal consensus on what the local system of criminal justice should be accomplishing is no small task. Equally important are the methods or strategies employed by criminal justice personnel to achieve community goals. It is at the street level that the reality of criminal justice is presented to the community, and this is why the rank-and-file worker, whether that is a police officer on the beat or a correctional officer in a prison, is the most important part of the administration and management of criminal justice organizations. These "street-level bureaucrats" (Lipsky, 1980:5) are the essence of the criminal justice system, and how these employees are supervised and evaluated is one of the most pressing issues facing criminal justice administration in this century. Before we can turn to that issue, we need to comment on the importance of organizational structure to employee supervision.

Organizational Structure and Employee Evaluation and Supervision

Organizational structure influences employee evaluation and supervision. It is clear, for example, that the size of a criminal justice organization affects how employees are evaluated and supervised. Criminal justice organizations with a large number of employees are more complex, and employee evaluation and supervision methods are constrained and limited in comparison to smaller criminal justice agencies. No one would disagree that the mechanisms used to evaluate and supervise employees in the New York City police department, with over 39,000 police officers, need to be different from those evaluation and supervision strategies found in a police department of fifty officers.

Due to the variations found among criminal justice organizations on various dimensions, criminal justice administrators have to be creative in how they devise evaluation and supervision methods. Other issues besides size that can affect the evaluation and supervision approaches employed by criminal justice administrators are budget, differing goals, and the degree to which the organization is centralized or decentralized in its decision-making processes. We will offer some general guidelines on evaluation and supervision of criminal justice employees at the end of the chapter.

Models of Employee Supervision

Models of employee supervision have proliferated over the past few decades (Rainey, 1997). Public agencies seeking improvement in the quality of employee supervision have attempted to apply the principles and practices of private-sector management to the public sector (see Ouchi, 1981; Peters & Waterman, 1982). Some applications have been in the criminal justice system. We discussed the relevance and application of these contemporary ideas in the context of motivation (Chapter 5) and job design (Chapter 6) earlier. Our objective here is to show how these ideas translate into specific models of supervision. The reader is asked to place these models within the contexts described previously—namely, an organizational goal context and an organizational structural context.

The Traditional Model of Employee Supervision

The traditional model of employee supervision stresses centralized authority, clear-cut rules and regulations, well-developed policies and procedures, and discernable lines of authority operationalized through a chain of command—in short, high degrees of centralization, formalization, and complexity. Contemporary critics, however, question the effectiveness and appropriateness of this model of supervision to the changing societal expectations of the criminal justice system. We will have more to say on this line of criticism later. For now, it is useful to flesh out the key elements of the traditional model of employee supervision used in most criminal justice organizations.

The traditional model is made up of the following elements: a hierarchy that stresses an identifiable span of control, a precise unity of command, and a clear delegation of authority; rulification; and specialization of services and activities of employees (Gaines, Southerland, & Angell, 1991).

Span of control refers to the appropriate number of employees that can be managed by any one supervisor. What this magic number should be has been part of debates among scholars and practitioners alike. This concept can be applied to both employees and the people they supervise. For example, span of control is a central question in the delivery of services to probationers and parolees (McShane & Krause, 1993). Concerns over the maximum number of probationers who can be supervised by one agent have plagued community corrections officials for years (Clear & Cole, 1994). For police departments, span of control refers to the number of officers that can be reasonably monitored by a supervisor.

Unity of command refers to the placement of one person in charge of a situation and an employee. The importance of this concept to traditional supervision revolves around multiple and conflicting orders from supervisors. For control and supervision to be maximized, there has to be one supervisor, known by every employee. In this way, confusion about directives and commands is reduced and the employee is aware of to whom he or she must report. In the words of one correctional administrator, "There have to be one chief and a lot of Indians in prison."

Delegation of authority maintains the integrity of the organization by clearly defining tasks and responsibilities of employees as well as delegating power and authority to complete required tasks. For police organizations, this means providing employees clear direction on what their responsibilities are, the necessary skills to accomplish tasks, and the requisite authority to achieve objectives. Each employee understands his or her role in the accomplishment of tasks and where they fit into the larger goals of the organization.

Rulification emphasizes the importance of rules and regulations to the organization. Every policy, procedure, and directive must have some specific written referent. In this way, clarity of organizational tasks and purposes is maintained, as well as documentation concerning appropriate behaviors by employees. As a control mechanism, rules, policies, and procedures are the essential components of the organization. One cannot imagine a police or correctional organization existing and functioning without well-specified rules, policies, and procedures. Through rulification, the primary purposes of criminal justice organizations can be understood and transmitted to the public at large and "impermissible outcomes" monitored (Wilson, 1989:339). The rules define the scope and direction of criminal justice agencies.

Specialization involves the division of labor in criminal justice organization. Each employee knows his or her tasks and is held accountable to those tasks. Specialization enhances employee supervision because it is through exact job definition that employees can be evaluated, disciplined, promoted, and dismissed. In most cases, increases in specialization enable advances in employee supervision, since there is an increase in responsibility, yet increased specialization may also create administrative coordination problems (Gaines, Southerland, & Angell, 1991:101).

Through the concepts of span of control, unity of command, delegation of authority, rulification, and specialization, supervisors are presumed to enhance their supervisory capabilities. For decades, training within police departments and correctional organizations have stressed these important concepts for effective employee supervision. Current advocates, such as DiIulio (1987, 1991), argue that the role of effective management should not be downplayed. DiIulio believes that greater attention should be paid to improving the effectiveness of managers and administrators. While his ideas were originally presented within the context of prisons, it is clear that they have equal relevance and application to other criminal justice organizations, such as police departments. Recently, however, research has questioned the efficacy, effectiveness, and efficiency of such a model. Critics point out many practical difficulties with the traditional model of supervision.

One of the most ardent critics of the traditional model of police supervision has been Fyfe (1994:110–114). In his view, traditional ideas about police supervision and employee performance have been predicated on largely fictionalized accounts of the police role and inappropriate assessments of police work; they are, he says, more often than not based on perceptions of police supervisors with no input from the officers themselves. The traditional model of supervision stresses arrest statistics, for example, as one outcome measure of performance, yet there is no consideration of the relationship between arrest activity and the realization of organizational goals.

As such, Fyfe argues that it is not clear how the elements of the traditional model of police supervision actually enhance the supervisory process and, more important, how the model itself is related to the goals of police organizations. What gets produced instead is a fractured and misleading picture of police as primarily "crime fighters." Additionally, critics have argued that the traditional model produces authoritarian supervisors, precludes organizational innovation, stymies information flow, and reduces the motivational levels of officers (see Gaines, Southerland, & Angell, 1991:105–107).

More recently, Skolnick and Fyfe (1993:117–124) have argued that many police problems can be traced to the paramilitary style that pervades police organizations. If such criticisms are correct, the utility of the traditional model to the attainment of organizational goals must be questioned. Goldstein (1990:157) suggests that the reason the traditional model of employee supervision has lasted so long relates to the ease with which supervision can be routinized. Under the traditional approach, supervision is rather straightforward and predictable. Asking police supervisors— sergeants and lieutenants in particular—to supervise through innovation consistent with the changes and demands of the community is a more difficult task.

For example, community policing efforts, while expanding the role of rank-and-file officers through decentralization, create enormous challenges for the immediate supervisor. Supervisors now have to respond to the demands of the community in ways that often defy routinization. Furthermore, supervision defined as control becomes more difficult under arrangements that place individual officer autonomy as a higher organizational imperative. For these reasons, traditional police supervisors are highly suspicious and unaccepting of contemporary attempts to redefine the police role more consistently with community policing or problem-oriented police models. These models of police management accentuate the importance of attending to multiple expectations of the community and, as such, demand new ways of doing business in police organizations.

Similarly, correctional organizations are going through changes that are calling into question the relevancy and usefulness of the traditional model of employee supervision when faced with competing and multiple demands from the community (Johnson, 2002; Wright, 1994). Correctional institutions, parole agencies, and probation departments are all being asked to protect society from criminals; in addition, they are expected to do something productive with offenders so that criminal propensities are reduced. This, too, is no simple set of expectations. Nevertheless, such expectations are altering the context within which correctional agencies, as well as other criminal justice organizations, are functioning. Newer models of employee supervision have been proposed to augment the functioning capabilities of employees to meet these new challenges. One model in particular has shown promise for criminal justice organizations, and it is to this model we now turn our attention.

The Human Service Model of Employee Supervision

Unlike the traditional model of employee supervision, which emphasizes monitoring through tight organizational controls, the human service model views the supervision process within the context of both individual employee goals as well as larger organizational goals. The human service model attempts to integrate employee goals into organizational goals. This task is first addressed by examining what employees seek in their organizations (see Chapters 5 and 6) and the diversity of "operator" (Wilson, 1989:31–112) roles in criminal justice organizations.

What do employees want? They want a number of things, with surprising consistency—both to accomplish job tasks and to feel fulfilled within their roles. Toch (1978), as one of the first to comment on the traditional assumptions we hold about rank-and-file criminal justice workers, states:

> A correctional officer assigned to tower duty is a residue of the dark ages. He requires 20/20 vision, the IQ of an imbecile, a high threshold for boredom, and a basement position in Maslow's hierarchy.

Similar views have also been offered about police officers ("street cops") and their vitriolic attitudes toward administrators ("management cops") (Reuss-Ianni, 1984). The result of such a split is often hostility and a sense of separation between officer and manager. Such a split is directly related to the military-style organization found in most police departments (Fyfe, 1994:117).

Such a view highlights the tension that is created between rank-and-file employees and administrators when assumptions about employees are less than flattering and there is no appreciation of the diversity of their role and the job performed. The traditional model of police supervision does not recognize either the importance of this diversity or that organizational control—the single most important goal under the traditional model—is only one goal among many. It is this recognition of diversity in both personal and organizational goals that defines the human service model of employee supervision.

Within the context of a problem-oriented approach to police organization, Goldstein (1990:149) argues that the traditional model of supervision must be supplanted with a model of supervision that fosters a "relationship with management built on mutual trust and on agreement that an officer has the freedom to think and act within broad boundaries." Similarly, Johnson (2002) has shown how effective correctional officers are those who stretch the role of custody to include the delivery of goods and services to prisoners, even though there are very few inducements for such behavior. Why do some officers exhibit such behaviors? The answer to this question, offered by Johnson (2002:256), serves to define the basic assumption of the human service model of employee supervision:

> Why, then, do some [correctional] officers persist in activities that take time and effort, are neither recognized nor rewarded by others, and must be hidden or played down for fear of trouble with administrators, peers, treatment staff, or recalcitrant inmates? The reason . . . is simply this: *human service activities make the officer's job richer, more rewarding, and ultimately less stressful.*

A recognition of the true nature of the employee's role enables managers and administrators to grasp that supervision must include a rather expansive definition of employee tasks and activities. Less centralization, fewer and more clearly defined rules, and less bureaucracy are central tenets of the human service model of employee supervision. Unlike the traditional model of employee supervision that emphasizes tight controls and limited decision making among employees, this approach stresses the importance of decentralization of authority for greater decision-making capabilities among lower-level members, fewer rules to encumber the enlarged activities of employees, and a breaking down of the traditional hierarchy found in most police and correctional organizations.

Such views are consistent with popular ideas expressed by contemporary management experts such as Peters and Waterman (1982:150), who stress autonomy and entrepreneurship (less centralization); simultaneous loose-tight properties (less formalization); and simple form, lean staff (less complexity). Such approaches have proven to be invaluable to the corporate world and have equal relevance to criminal justice administration and management. All are consistent with the human service model of employee supervision. Both experts and reformers alike have called for the application of these ideas in transforming the supervision process within criminal justice organizations (see Christopher Commission Report, 1991: 242–244).

According to Goldstein (1990:157–172) a new supervision model in police organizations requires a decentralization of authority, a new dimension of supervision that capitalizes on the knowledge of frontline supervisors, such as sergeants and lieutenants, an alteration in the criteria for recognizing and evaluating performance among officers, a change in the recruitment and selection of new officers, a revitalized sense of purpose and direction in training, and the development of new sources of information and new knowledge on how to address crime-related problems within communities. In other words, this model must be able to integrate the knowledge and concerns of officers into a coherent and strategic plan to deal with community problems, such as crime.

Similarly, Wright (1994) offers identical prescriptions for correctional administrators and managers. He suggests that correctional institutions can be made more cohesive and work toward both organizational goals as well as developing people in the organization. Wright's ideas center around three fundamental concepts: employee ownership, delegation, and the sharing of power.

Employee ownership refers to gaining a greater voice in the creation of institutional policy. According to Wright, correctional employees who are able to express their concerns within the context of decision making are more productive employees and experience less stress. In his words, "People who 'own' their job and 'own' their organization feel strong, capable, and committed" (1994:48).

This ownership is structured within the concept of *delegation*. Delegation allows employees, within prescribed limits, the opportunities to make decisions that affect their ability to perform tasks. As such, delegation is not unstructured nor undirected participation by lower-level employees; it is the ability to maximize the knowledge and skills of employees in a directed fashion. In short, delegation exploits the experiences of the workers.

The *sharing of power* follows nicely from the concept of delegation. Sharing of power assumes that power is not a finite entity. Instead, power is viewed as "energy, potential, and competence" (Wright, 1994:51). Power is given to employees in such a way that they are able to enhance their performance levels and adjust to contingencies of the institutional environment. Under such a view, the correctional worker is viewed as an active contributor to the organization, not simply a reactive automaton to institutional policies and procedures.

Taken together, these three ideas generate a work philosophy that seeks to institutionalize greater authority in the hands of employees and respects their intelligence and creativity to a changing correctional environment. Such a philosophy has been the model for the Federal Bureau of Prisons since the mid-1960s and is known as *unit management*.

Unit management is an organizational design as well as an operating philosophy for the Federal Bureau of Prisons. Houston (1999) defines unit management as having the following components:

- A small number of inmates (50–120) who are permanently assigned together
- A multidisciplinary staff (unit manager, case manager(s), correctional counselor(s), full- or part-time psychologist, clerk typist, and correctional officers whose offices are located within or adjacent to the inmate housing unit and are permanently assigned to work with the inmates of that unit)
- A unit manager who has administrative authority and supervisory responsibility for the unit staff
- A unit staff that has administrative authority for all within-unit aspects of inmate living and programming
- Inmates who are assigned to the unit because of age, prior record, specific behavior typologies, need for a specific type of correctional program such as drug abuse counseling, or random assignment
- Unit staff who are scheduled by the unit manager to work in the unit evenings and weekends, on a rotating basis, in addition to the unit correctional officer

Policies and Procedures and Jail Operations

Managers of county jails are aware that they must have written policies and procedures on key aspects of jail operation. They know this is important from a liability risk management perspective, and as a way to direct employees in the performance of their duties. Some jail managers meet this obligation by getting copies of policies from other jails and using them as the basis for their own policies, hopefully tailoring the policies to their individual jail operations. Other managers start from ground-zero and develop their own policies. Either way works.

Two common problems occur. One is that too few managers make a proactive effort to secure "buy-in" for the written policies from line staff members or even from first-line supervisors. The second is that too few managers make an adequate effort to be sure that staff members know about and comply with written policies, which only happens when there is good staff training and ongoing supervision by first-line supervisors.

The first problem is too often a result of the "top down" management style. In such a system, often, minimal effort is made to involve line staff members or first-line supervisors in formulating policies and procedures. No substantive attempt is made up front to give staff members the idea that the policies are also "theirs" and to get them to support the policies. Yet experience has clearly shown that unless line staff members and supervisors support and "buy into" policies and procedures, they are less likely to follow them as carefully as they should. In some cases, they may even sabotage policies.

Certainly, policies are a management prerogative; managers have the right to formulate and implement policies. But managers also have the obligation to do what they can to ensure that employees are satisfied and will act as members of an overall team.

In a law enforcement or correctional agency, one of the best ways to secure staff support for policies is to plan proactively for staff involvement in the policy development and revision process. There are a number of ways to do this. One good method is to formulate committees composed of line staff members and first-line supervisors and to give them specific policy and procedure tasks. For example, a committee might have the responsibility for formulating procedures for specified security policy issues—key control, tool control, cell searches, inmate searches, and so on. It is not necessary to write a policy and procedure, just to come up with the specific information to be included on that issue. With that, it is easy enough for someone to write the policy. Or, a committee may be assigned to review a draft of a policy on one or several issues, to critique it, and to come up with any ideas for revision or improvement. It is always best to be very specific as to the tasks that are expected of committee members.

In the best case, jail managers have line staff and supervisors work on policies and do not even look at those policies until those employees have completed their work and submitted it to the managers. Then, the manager reviews the policies and makes final decisions, exercising the management prerogative to determine the final contents of the policy and procedures. In such a case, line staff and supervisors have had maximum input. They understand that management has empowered them, listened to them, but has the final say.

This "bottom up" management style is a good way of securing support for written policy directives.

The second problem—inadequate training and supervision—is also a result of the tacit assumption that just giving copies of written policies and procedures to employees will result in their knowing and following those policies and procedures. In too many agencies, employees are given a big policy manual and asked to sign a piece of paper that says that they have been given the policies, understand them, will follow them, and understand that they can be disciplined for failing to follow them. But that practice is poor for two reasons: (1) it does not relieve managers of the responsibility to train employees about policies, and (2) it gives employees the message that the main purpose of the written policies is to "nail" them when they "screw up."

Thus, training employees on the contents of written policies and procedures is critically important. This is particularly true of "critical task" policy issues—those that potentially affect safety and security and/or are clearly related to constitutional rights of inmates. Training need not be complicated or time-consuming, but it must happen. Training can occur in many ways: traditional classroom training; shorter, roll-call sessions; computer-based training; field-training; and so on. The outcome of training must be to ensure that employees have (1) sufficient cognitive knowledge of the contents of the policies and procedures, at least on key points and issues, and (2) proficiency in key psychomotor skills necessary to carry out, or implement, policies and procedures. Ideally, the training will include some sort of evaluation component, both of cognitive knowledge and psychomotor skills, so that managers know whether employees know how to do their jobs.

Supervision to ensure that policies and procedures are being complied with is the other critical element. In this regard, first-line supervisors, such as sergeants and lieutenants, are vitally important. First-line supervisors should be the people who are most familiar with an agency's written policies and procedures and committed to being sure that policies and procedures are adhered to. If supervisors do not know the policies very well, they cannot ensure compliance with the policies by line staff members. Therefore, supervisors probably ought to be the first persons trained in the content of policies, and then they probably ought to serve as the trainers (or some of the trainers) to line staff about policies.

It is management's responsibility to be sure that supervisors know about policies and are committed to making them work. This can be important in sheriffs' departments where sergeants or lieutenants come to the jail from patrol or another division and do not necessarily have a great deal of jail experience or orientation.

In short, it is not enough simply to *have* a policy manual that sits on a shelf and is brought down only when there is a crisis and someone asks questions about what the agency's policy is. There must be a proactive effort to be sure that policies are living, breathing documents that mean something and that people know about and act in accordance with.

MARTIN DRAPKIN

Training Officer

Bureau of Training and Standards

Wisconsin Department of Justice

Within the institution, the guiding principle is to have a flexible set of rules and regulations that allows staff the discretion and direction to complete tasks.

For advocates of unit management, the advantages far outweigh the disadvantages. Houston (1999:325) suggests the following advantages: a greater sense of cohesion and community between inmates and staff, an increase in the contacts between inmates and staff that leads to better communication and a positive work environment, a decentralizing of decisions within the correctional units that improves decision making, and greater program flexibility.

Such advantages must be weighed, however, within the context of competing disadvantages. Houston (1999:325-326) offers the following disadvantages to unit management. Unit management is costly and labor intensive; takes much time and resources to implement; and, most telling, threatens the organizational status quo. In particular, it challenges fundamental ways of doing business in the prison. Instead of the traditional hierarchical control found in most prisons, unit management increases the flexibility of subordinates and decentralizes authority at the operational level—in this case, within the housing unit where staff complete the day-to-day functions of the prison.

Wright (1994:54) offers the primary reason why correctional administrators have been slow to adopt unit management:

> Some top executives may feel uneasy about giving up control . . . They may wonder whether they can depend on line staff to make critical decisions. Yet, most prisons are too large for a few administrators to get to know all the inmates well. Unit Management provides for more efficient and informed decision-making because the individuals making the decisions spend the most time with inmates.

In this statement we see the fundamental difference between the traditional model and the human service model. The traditional model's primary concern is control of the employee, whereas the human service model stresses the completion of organizational tasks. As we suggested in Chapter 3, the environment of administrators is not the same as the work setting of subordinates. Each has differing goals and objectives.

The often tumultuous and uncertain political environment forces criminal justice administrators to stress accountability and control of employees. Employees' concerns, meanwhile, center around task completion. Often there is conflict between the organization's search for control and certainty and the desire to accomplish "soft" organizational objectives and goals. Wilson (1989:168–171) has documented how many public service agencies are what he called "coping organizations." Unlike product-based organizations, these types of organizations cannot observe their own outcomes and outputs. It is often difficult to identify what tasks are actually related to the accomplishment of specific goals in coping organizations.

Given this situation, it will be difficult, if not impossible, for administrators in coping organizations to give up power, decentralize their organizations, and empower employees. They fall back on what they can do well, and that usually means hierarchy and other traditional practices that, on the surface, provide greater control of employees as well as measures of output that have a control focus. Wilson (1989:171) states:

> In coping organizations . . . management will have a strong incentive to focus their efforts on the most easily measured (and thus most easily controlled) activities of their operators.

They cannot evaluate or often even see outcomes, and so only the brave manager will be inclined to give much freedom of action to subordinates.

Such a view questions the applicability of the human service model to criminal justice organizations. Wright (1994:43–47) discusses how correctional administrators often stress centralization of authority, clear rules, and uncertainty avoidance in their organizations. This means greater bureaucracy and tighter organizational control. Yet advocates of the human service model seek a loosening of the organizational reins by administrators. Is this really possible?

Is the Human Service Model Possible in Criminal Justice Organizations?

Commenting on the entire human relations movement in organizations, Charles Perrow (1986:94–95) cynically states the fundamental problem in trying to "humanize" organizations:

> The search for authenticity and spontaneity should be never-ending, and if it must occur in the guise of better productivity in organizations, let it. The trainees will return refreshed to a world of hierarchies, conflict, authority, stupidity, and brillance, but the hierarchies and the like probably will not fade away. Most organizations remain highly authoritarian systems; some even use T-groups to hide that essential fact.

For criminal justice administrators, citizens (the consumers of our products), and reformers, such organizational issues as decentralization, employee empowerment, and delegation are significant concerns today and into the future. Yet given the uncertain, conflicting, and multiple goals facing criminal justice organizations, it is not clear how such issues can become relevant to administrators.

Criminal justice administrators, as we have emphasized in this and other chapters, face many constraints and receive multiple expectations from their constituents, with finite resources. This forces goal ambiguity about their purpose and direction. Because of this, they adopt a structure and system of employee supervision that emphasizes what they can accomplish. More often than not, this means routinization, an overemphasis on employee control, and consistent policies and procedures. Such a structure reduces uncertainty and stabilizes all threats from the environment.

More important, humanistic attempts to reorganize the ways of doing business in criminal justice organizations require greater clarity of purposes (identifying the product), consensus on the purposes (agreement among competing interests about the product), and a well-defined technology or methodology to produce the product (how to make the product). Public service organizations, such as the criminal justice system, possess no such clarity about these issues. In fact, Wilson (1989:315–332) shows how agreement on these matters is neither possible nor desirable. Traditional bureaucracy, therefore, is the only possible outcome.

Wilson argues that issues of accountability, equity, fiscal integrity, and efficiency serve as possible obstacles to innovation in public organizations. While Wilson applies these concepts to an analysis of public organizations in general, we can apply them to employee supervision as well. *Accountability* centers on employee performance and issues of supervision and control. *Equity* focuses on fairness and treating similarly situated employees in the same way. *Fiscal integrity* means ensuring that public dollars are spent on those personnel and functions mandated to the organization. Finally, *efficiency* involves employing a sufficient number of employees, not too many nor too few, to accomplish the organization's tasks within the prescribed level of resources.

Taken together, these concerns, along with conflicting goals and missions, serve as constraints on how employees are to be supervised. Police organizations, for example, that attempt to reorganize under a community policing philosophy would find enormous difficulties in trying to decentralize their structures while still being sensitive to public accountability, equity among officers, fiscal concerns about the appropriateness of deploying staff in such a way, and efficiency concerns. Would the creation of ministations in police organizations be cost effective? Would they allow accountability to be monitored? What about issues of exercising discretion and monitoring of discretionary acts among officers by supervisors?

Similar questions could be raised about correctional organizations. One state department of corrections lost a major judgment in court on the payment of overtime to probation and parole officers. The department responded bureaucratically and tightened procedures so that overtime was no longer possible for agents, even though it knew that officers required greater time and flexibility to complete tasks, such as home visits of offenders. While attempting to decentralize their decision making for agents, correctional officers were more concerned about the public impression that the department was not being efficient and lacked fiscal integrity in their operations. These concerns overshadowed treatment and offender supervision issues. The net result was that services were cut back and the department became even more rigid. Additionally, the department created mechanisms to control the time and workings of agents to the point where many agents complained that there was no professionalism in the job.

Proponents of the humanistic model of employee supervision, consequently, need to address how concerns over accountability, equity, fiscal integrity, and efficiency would be handled outside the traditional structure of criminal justice organizations. To date, many supporters of the humanistic approach have not moved beyond an abstract discussion of how criminal justice organizations will presumably benefit from the adoption of their principles. What still has to be examined is how these ideals can become real within the context of multiple goals, interests, and constraints. This is a formidable challenge for those who administer the criminal justice system, yet not an impossible one. Responding to this challenge will be a primary initiative for criminal justice administrators in the new century.

Guidelines for Supervision and Evaluation

All guidelines for supervision and evaluation of employees require a roadmap on how to proceed. The supervision and evaluation of employees is no easy task, nor is there any single approach that can be given to criminal justice administrators to follow. Instead, there are key issues and concepts that can assist and guide criminal justice administrators. Yukl (2002) provides a list of guidelines to aid supervisors in the performance of their jobs. They include the following: defining job responsibilities, assigning work, and setting performance goals. Each of these areas has a number of sub-areas that define the supervision process.

Within the realm of defining job responsibilities, explaining the important job responsibilities, clarifying the person's scope of authority, explaining how the job relates to the mission of the unit, and most importantly, explaining important and relevant policies, rules, and requirements are essential.

When assigning work, the supervisor must clearly explain the assignment, explain the reasons for the assignment, clarify priorities and deadlines, and check for comprehension among employees. Similarly, setting performance goals means setting goals for relevant aspects of performance, setting goals that are clear and specific, setting goals that are challenging but realistic, and setting a target date for the attainment of each goal (Yukl, 2002:68).

Oettmeier and Wycoff (1998) offer a model for evaluating and supervising police officers within the context of community policing efforts. This model offers three levels upon which evaluation and supervision can be examined. At the first level, the evaluation and supervision efforts focus on individual performance and can include the following elements: traffic stops, arrests, and directed patrols toward specific crimes, to mention a few. At the second level, the evaluation and supervision parameters are focused at the team level within the organization. The efforts of the team are evaluated on how well specific aims are met and incidents addressed. For example, officers may be evaluated on how well they implement a driving-while-intoxicated squad and how many arrests are made. The focus of the evaluation is on team performance, not individual performance. The third level of evaluation examines the organization's internal activities or procedures to address certain problems. At this level of evaluation, the administration is introspectively examining the operations of the organization with a focus on improving a process or procedure. An example is the procedures employed in the disciplinary process. The focus of the evaluation is to move beyond the individual or a team of officers; instead, the purpose is to evaluate the processes and procedures used to realize organizational goals.

This model has been applied to both small and large cities, and research has documented the trials and tribulations associated with this new way of evaluating police performance. In Houston, Texas, for example, application of the model has proven to be challenging and rewarding. Oettmeier and Wycoff (1998: 377–391) report that Houston police officials learned new ways to improve their performance evaluation systems and supervision approaches. These researchers offer the following changes in police performance evaluation to assist police administrators: adopt new assumptions concerning performance evaluation, specifically how and when performance evaluations are conducted, define the purposes of evaluation, identify new performance criteria, measure the effects of officer performance, strengthen the verification of performance among officers, develop new instrumentation to evaluate officer performance, solicit officer feedback about the performance of frontline supervisors, such as sergeants, and, finally, revise rating scales.

The evaluation and supervision of employees will always be problematic. Developing guidelines and specific approaches to evaluation and supervision will always be questioned. Nevertheless, personnel supervision and evaluation are a major task for criminal justice administrators. How this is accomplished is, in part, the test of an administrator's skill level. The 21st-century criminal justice administrator will be pressed to provide more credible information and ways to assess employee performance. It will be one of the continuing challenges facing criminal justice administrators.

Summary

This chapter examined employee supervision and evaluation. We discussed how such a concept must be placed within the context of multiple and competing goals. Criminal justice organizations are expected to accomplish many things for many different people; arriving at consensus about the purposes and direction of these organizations is often problematic. Unlike product-based organizations, criminal justice organizations have many stated outcomes, yet it is not clear which outcome has primacy over another. Lack of consensus about purposes and outcomes forces criminal justice administrators to adopt structures that critics and reformers find antiquated and nonreceptive to the demands of changing communities.

Additionally, criminal justice managers face competing and rival concerns in developing models of employee supervision and evaluation. We proposed two models of employee supervision. The traditional model with its emphasis on formal structure and control through increased centralization, formalization, and complexity strives to maintain, as much as possible, direct supervision over employees, even though we questioned the efficacy of such an approach in the accomplishment of larger objectives in criminal justice organizations. This model of employee supervision has many critics.

In contrast, the humanistic model of employee supervision seeks to break down the traditional bureaucracy found in public service organizations. We examined how a humanistic model of employee supervision could be realized, given the constraints and limitations that face public organizations. The challenge facing criminal justice administrators will be how to remain attentive to the demands of employees while maintaining an organizational structure sensitive to conflicting interests, competing goals, and multiple constraints. We concluded the chapter with some guidelines on how employee evaluation and supervision can be conducted, recognizing that any strategy of employee evaluation and supervision must fit the needs and structure of the organization.

Part 3 will explore group issues facing criminal justice administrators, specifically the topics of power, occupational socialization, and conflict. Each of these areas has implications for those who manage and administer organizations of criminal justice.

Case Study

Broken Windows, Damaged Gutters, and Police Supervision

Officer Mike Strzykalski was a ten-year veteran of the police department of Merrysville, a city of 500,000 people. The department had more than 2,000 police officers and a reputation of "no-nonsense" policing, an attitude instilled by a former police chief who believed that the central purpose of the department was to "catch the bad guys and throw them in the can." Officer Strzykalski, known as "Big Mike," was an early supporter of this approach to policing and was respected by many of his peers. He knew that effective law enforcement meant identifying the bad element in the community and dealing with them directly and forcefully. More contemporary approaches to policing, such as community policing ideas and practices, were "bullshit" and coddling criminals, as far as he was concerned. For Officer Strzykalski, policing meant making arrests and showing numbers. He learned early on in his career that getting the numbers was everything, and he also knew that it looked favorable for him at promotion time if he could show that he was productive. Officer Strzykalski, however, was to see all this change with the hiring of a new chief from outside the department.

Chief Harold Furman, a progressive police professional, believed that the quality of policing was tied to how the department resolved community problems. He also knew that his ideas were foreign to this rather conservative community, yet he had the full support of the mayor in trying to bring the department into the 21st century. For Chief Furman, the little things were what mattered. He operationalized his philosophy of policing similar to the ideas of former New York City police commissioner William Bratton. Bratton had adopted an idea postulated by some Ivy League types that the erosion of quality of life in a community led toward urban decay and ultimately unchecked crime. Bratton boasted, both within police circles and among city politicians and the citizenry, that attending to community concerns had caused a significant decrease in crime during the early 1990s. For Bratton and Furman, effective policing meant dealing with the little things in the community, from assisting communities in cleaning up their neighborhoods to arresting individuals who were negligent in paying their tickets and municipal fines.

With these principles in mind, Chief Furman restructured the Merrysville police department with a greater emphasis on community policing principles. His most drastic change came in the structure and deployment of police resources, specifically patrol officers. He contracted with the local Boys and Girls Clubs to rent space for police ministations where officers were close to their respective communities. He required precinct captains to have weekly meetings with neighborhood watch groups about problems in their communities. He solicited business and landlord support for removing drug houses from the most crime-infested areas of the city, and he worked with other city officials to provide more direct services to the community, such as more flexible hours for the health department to screen inner-city children for diseases prior to the beginning of the school year. To this end, he even tried to get police officers to offer ride-alongs for underprivileged parents and their children to the health department. He fought with the police union about this issue and ultimately lost in court; nevertheless, he proposed radical changes in the way the department responded to crime.

For Officer Strzykalski and other veteran officers, these changes were too drastic and ineffectual. In Big Mike's mind, the most significant change in the department under Chief Furman was the way street officers were evaluated by the department. Under the old system, numbers of arrests, field interrogations, and tickets were the primary ways in which officers were evaluated. The old system of employee evaluation was individually based and culminated in six-month performance appraisals of each officer (evaluations that most officers knew were worthless, but they made the bosses happy). Under the new system, officers had to attend to things that most seasoned officers, including Officer Strzykalski, viewed as a waste of time.

Contacts with citizens were not only encouraged but were mandated, along with the nature of the contact; if a problem was presented to the officer, he or she had to offer a potential solution that was documented in a daily log. In addition, officers were required to keep tabs of "quality of life" measures on their beats. Noting such things as graffiti, gang activity, unkept public places, run-down apartments, and the number of absentee landlords, to mention a few, were critical activities for the police officer. The purpose of these efforts was to get a feel for the "pulse of the community and its problems," according to the official communication from the chief's office.

Officer Strzykalski hated these ideas and thought they removed the police from their real job: catching crooks. He could not see how these efforts were tied to "real" crime. Like other officers, he accepted the new mandate reluctantly; however, he chose to fight what he considered to be the most ill-conceived idea: to alter performance evaluations from being individually based to group-based. He and other officers— for the first time—were being evaluated as a team as to how well they improved the quality of life among residents within their respective districts. What Officer Strzykalski particularly disliked was not being able to see how his performance was going to be individually evaluated and separated from that of other officers and, more important, how these evaluations were going to be used in the promotion process.

At the same time Merrysville police supervisors, such as captains, lieutenants, and sergeants, were told to loosen up their commands and interact with officers, soliciting their support in the identification of crime spots and community problems. Supervisors were also told to seek advice from officers about the most effective ways to handle problems in their communities. The officers, in effect, were the experts. The supervisors served as support and liaison between the officers and higher-ups in the department as well as a conduit to various community groups. Initially, experienced officers such as Strzykalski were opposed to this new philosophy of policing, and some even tried to sabotage it by getting the union involved, arguing that the practices were in violation of the labor agreement between the city and the officers' union.

This form of objection and protest was short lived, and most officers made adjustments in their behaviors when they could see that this new philosophy was actually in their best interests and gave them a greater say in how they performed their jobs. After the initial period of confusion and distrust had settled, both supervisors and police officers started to see the philosophy work in action. For Officer Strzykalski, the turning point was gutters and broken windows.

On routine patrol, Officer Strzykalski had noticed that a number of garages in his district had their gutters removed and windows broken. He stopped by one resident who was repairing his garage window to ask how the window had gotten broken. He learned that there was a gang of "young hoodlums" who were vandalizing garages as an initiation rite into a more established gang. The citizen viewed his garage as a casualty of this gang rite. Officer Strzykalski asked if this was common and if he knew of any other citizens who had their garages vandalized in a similar fashion. The citizen responded that he knew of at least four other garages that had been vandalized in the last week.

Seeing this as an opportunity to impress his superiors, Officer Strzykalski was able to obtain the names and addresses of other citizens in the district who had their garages vandalized in the last three months. He collected over twenty names and addresses. With this information, he organized, with approval from his sergeant and lieutenant, times when he could meet with each victim and the group as a whole. The supervisory staff viewed Officer Strzykalski's efforts as innovative and consistent with the new mission of the department: crime reduction through community involvement. After three months, Officer Strzykalski had not only assisted the citizens in protecting their properties more effectively, but also had been able to gather intelligence information on gang activity and feed this information back to the gang squad to help in their efforts to suppress gang-related crimes.

After one year, Officer Strzykalski's work was singled out by the department as an example of effective community policing. Chief Furman commended him and other officers at a formal awards banquet. For Officer Strzykalski, the most important insight was that working with the community was not only a better form of policing, but one that was personally rewarding and satisfying. For three months straight, officers in his district were commended by the police administration and various community groups for their efforts to address community problems. A promotion followed shortly thereafter. As a sergeant, Strzykalski viewed his role as a facilitator for the rank-and-file officers. He felt this supervision style allowed him to empower officers to address the problems most significant to the community. Moreover, officers felt that they were more part of a solution rather than a problem, as well as a team committed to the improvement of their district.

Sergeant Strzykalski could only reminisce about the old days in the department: too many quotas, too much in-fighting, and very ineffective policing. He thought how the change in the department opened his eyes to doing something different, something he would not have ever dreamed of one year earlier. He reflected how change for him was predicated on broken windows and damaged gutters. He kept these recollections as a reminder of how policing, especially police supervision, was and what it had become. He dedicated himself to never returning to the ineffective ways of policing because, in his words, "they never really accomplished anything, either for the citizen or the cop."

Case Study Questions

1. What are some primary obstacles police reformers face when trying to implement a community policing philosophy within a police department? What issues of police supervision are the most important in making a switch from a traditional police organization to one structured by the principles of community policing?

2. Would many patrol officers embrace the model of supervision emphasized by community policing? Why or why not? What about frontline supervisors, such as sergeants? What difficulties would they have supervising officers under a community policing approach?

3. Is Officer/Sergeant Strzykalski too idealistic about police supervision in this case study? Why or why not? What can police supervisors do to address the fears of patrol officers about community policing ideas and practices?

For Discussion

1. Will goal consensus in criminal justice organizations ever be possible? What are the major obstacles and disadvantages to having goal consensus in criminal justice organizations? How is goal consensus undemocratic and inefficient for the criminal justice system?

2. This chapter discusses the importance of structure to the delivery of criminal justice services. Can police organizations or prisons, for example, be less formal and more decentralized in their structures? Why or why not? What goals of police organization are sacrificed, if any, through decentralization? What about decentralization and employee accountability?

3. What are some major problems with implementing the ideas of a human service model of employee supervision in criminal justice organizations? How would employees react to such a supervision style?

4. Given the nature of criminal justice organizations, is the traditional model of employee supervision the best possible choice? State the advantages and disadvantages. Do the critics of the model overstate their case?

For Further Reading

Bayley, D. H. *Police for the Future.* New York: Oxford University Press, 1994.

Bolman, L., and Deal, T. *Reframing Organizations: Artistry, Choice, and Leadership,* 2nd ed. San Francisco: Jossey-Bass, 1997.

Fyfe, J., Greene, J., Walsh, W., Wilson, O., and McLaren, R. *Police Administration,* 5th ed. New York: McGraw-Hill, 1997.

Oettmeier, T. N., and Wycoff, M. A. *Personnel Performance Evaluations in the Community Policing Context.* Washington, D.C.: U.S. Department of Justice, 1998.

Trojanowicz, R., and Bucqueroux, B. *Community Policing: A Contemporary Perspective.* Cincinnati, OH: Anderson, 1990.

Wilson, J. Q. *Bureaucracy: What Government Agencies Do and Why They Do It.* Glenview, IL: Basic Books, 1989.

★ ★ ★

GROUP
BEHAVIOR
IN CRIMINAL
JUSTICE
ORGANIZATIONS

An organization is more than a collection of individuals. Organizations are entities that influence the people within them in both formal and informal ways. The vertical and hierarchical interactions of individuals within the organization as well as contact with offenders or the general public all contribute to the culture and ethos of criminal justice organizations. In this field, theory and research have looked beyond the individual to group influences to explain such problems as conflict, corruption, and the abuse of power. In Part Three we examine the role of the group within criminal justice organizations: how groups shape the organizational process and how managers can influence that process.

CHAPTER

9

OCCUPATIONAL
SOCIALIZATION

Becoming a federal judge is like being thrown into the water and told to swim.
(A federal judge, quoted in Carp & Wheeler, 1972:3721)

When the recruits first come to the academy, each staff member is introduced to the recruits and allowed time to say a few words to them. When it is my turn, I tell them in no uncertain terms that I am there to train them and that they are there to do what they are told. When I am done with my speech, I make every one of them get out of their seats and do twenty push-ups. I don't care if they're in a suit or in a dress, they do the push-ups. I want them to know right off who the boss is.
(A police academy trainer, quoted in Charles, 1986:341)

And I walked in the first day and an officer threw a big bunch of keys down on the table and walked out. Didn't tell me nothing. But there was an inmate who broke me in. His daddy and my daddy used to work in the mines together. He broke me in, the inmate did.
(A corrections officer, quoted in Roszell, 1986)

Stanley Kubrick's film *Full Metal Jacket* vividly portrays the process of turning young recruits into marines, trained and willing to fight and die for their country. All organizations have processes (usually less rigorous than those used by the marines) for converting people into organizational members with appropriate attitudes and behaviors.

In this chapter we examine the process by which recruits in the occupations of criminal justice become seasoned. We examine socialization influences on judges, parole officers, and other criminal justice professionals from both a theoretical and practical perspective. We also consider difficulties in the socialization process that may contribute to such problems as stress or misconduct. In particular, we review the research on the socialization of police and corrections officers, focusing on recruitment as well as formal and informal training practices. Finally, we consider the ways in which managers influence the process of socialization in criminal justice organizations.

Occupational Socialization

Occupational socialization is the process by which a person acquires the values, attitudes, and behaviors of an ongoing occupational social system. It is a continuous process that includes both intentional influences, such as training, and unintentional influences, such as locker room or work group cultures. The attitudes, values, and behaviors acquired as a result of occupational socialization can include those regarded as appropriate and legitimate for the job as well as those that are illegitimate and even illegal. Thus, judges may learn appropriate sentence lengths for offenders, but judges convicted in the 1986–1988 Greylord investigations in Chicago argued that they also learned to accept bribes because of the shared view that they were underpaid compared with their lawyer peers. Similarly, police learn to implement the law of arrest, but even "good" cops learn to bend the rules on the job. When Officer Robert Leuci (whose story was told in the movie *Prince of the City*) was collecting evidence on police corruption in New York for the Knapp Commission in the early 1970s, he also testified to giving drugs to addicted informants in exchange for information, and some believe he committed many more serious crimes (Dershowitz, 1983).

Habitual behaviors of individuals in organizations, both good and bad, persist as long as the attitudes, beliefs, perceptions, habits, and expectations of organizational members remain constant. This consistency is particularly evident in criminal justice organizations, where the practices of police officers and prison staff, for example, often seem unchanging and even resistant to change efforts. One common assessment of legal efforts to change criminal justice organizations is that the courts seem more efficient at bringing about procedural than substantive change. Prison discipline hearings, for example, continue to be characterized as dispositional rather than adjudicatory despite case law requiring impartial, trial-like hearings. How can we account for the fact that almost all inmates are found guilty by prison disciplinary boards? Although inmate behavior is probably the most important determining factor, part of the explanation may also be found in the concept of organizational role. Katz and Kahn (1978) give the social-psychological concept of role a central place in their theory of organizations. For them, organizations are best understood as systems of roles. These roles link the individual to the organization and assure its continued stability.

Organizational Culture

The behaviors of individual members of an organization as well as the organization are a product of the organization's culture and also create its culture. An *organizational culture* can be briefly described as a set of assumptions, values, and beliefs shared by members of an organization. Moreover, the assumptions, values, and beliefs create language, symbols, and folklore and ultimately serve to direct the behaviors of the organizational members, especially in response to work-related problems. Edgar Schein (1997) summarizes common meanings of organizational culture, which include observed behavioral regularities, such as language, patterns of interactions, rituals, norms that evolve in working groups; dominant values espoused by an organization such as rehabilitation, crime prevention, the philosophy of the organization toward employees or clients; rules of the game for getting along in the organization's social system; and the feeling or climate created in an organization by the way employees are managed or interact. Arguing that these common meanings may reflect an organization's culture but are not the essence of the culture, Schein (1997:12) defines organizational culture as

> a pattern of basic assumptions—invented, discovered, or developed by a group as it learns to cope with its problems of external adaptation and internal integration—that has worked well enough to be considered valid and, therefore, to be taught to new members as the correct way to perceive, think, and feel in relation to those problems.

In other words, the process of socialization in an organization serves to impose the organization's patterns of basic assumptions upon its new members. Understanding an organization's culture and its socialization process, especially in a large or complex organization, is a difficult task. It is therefore instructive to begin by reviewing the basics of culture in the broadest sense. *Culture* is often defined as the complex whole of a society and includes knowledge, belief, art, laws, morals, customs, and other capabilities and routines acquired by the society's members (Tylor, 1958). This is a rather standard definition of culture—one, however, that does not provide an understanding of its essence. An alternate view describes culture (much like Schein does) as problem solving, a pattern of basic assumptions invented by a group as it learns to cope with problems of external adaptation and internal integration:

> Whenever people face recurring problems, cultural patterns evolve to provide a ready-made solution. This does not mean that it is the best or only solution, merely that the culture develops a set of standard patterns for dealing with common problems. . . . The more frequently a society relies upon its ready-made solutions, the more deeply entrenched the culture. (Brinkerhoff & White, 1991:58)

Societies develop language to solve the problem of communicating, and language thus becomes the framework for culture. Groups also have desirable goals, which are expressed as *values*. *Norms* evolve specifying what people should or shouldn't do. Also, *folkways* (standard ways of doing things), *mores* (strong views of right and wrong) and *laws* (codified mores enforced by the group) develop. Once a society or group has developed its culture—a set of ready-made answers or established patterns, language, beliefs, behaviors, to solve its problems—it attempts to perpetuate the culture.

The process of perpetuating conformity to the established culture, *social control*, provides a series of *sanctions*—rewards and punishments—for individual conformity or nonconformity to established behavioral patterns, language, values, mores, folkways, and laws. Most sanctions are informal because they are not codified and are applied in daily interactions between individuals. Social or informal sanctions can be more powerful than legal sanctions. *Formal sanctions* are abstract and stem from impersonal sources. *Informal sanctions,* such as peer pressure, however, can be personal and evoked by sources valued by an individual receiving sanctions. Rewards from supervisors, such as the "Corrections Officer of the Month" for meritorious performance, will not have the same influence upon officers in general as the immediate day-to-day and often subtle pressures from peers. In spite of attempts at social control, societies generally have *subcultures*, groups that have their own beliefs and norms while sharing the values of the dominant culture. *Countercultures*, groups whose shared values differ substantially from those of the dominant culture, typically exist within any large society.

Organizations can be considered microsocieties within which distinct cultures emerge. That is, the mixture of individuals who belong to any organization create—through their attempts to solve organizational and personal problems or achieve organizational or personal goals—sets of ready-made solutions, a shared language, values, folkways, and mores unique to the organization. The pivotal questions for an organization is how the culture is formed, what forces are critical in forming the culture, how the cultural arrangements impact the organizational goals, and how and to what extent administrators can influence the cultural arrangement of their agency.

The culture of an organization is first impacted by problems of external adaptation—problems imposed by demands, constraints, and pressures from its environment. If those problems are recurring ones, the organization will attempt to develop ready-made solutions to meet them. Organizations, however, face more problems than those explicitly identified as their mission. For example, all organizations also strive to acquire status and respectability, grow and garner resources, set and expand boundaries, control environmental forces, and, when the chips are down, survive. Police, for example, are dramatized as crime fighters, but the duties of law enforcement officers include crime prevention, traffic and parking regulation, and a host of other problems that the public faces and expects law enforcement agencies to solve. Courts attempt to process criminal offenders efficiently while seeing that rules of justice and fairness are followed. Corrections carry out the role of criminal punishment while meeting the basic physical and social needs of offenders.

The criminal justice system has been assigned aspects of social control that society feels it cannot solve directly. The criminal justice system attempts to meet three missions: crime control, justice, and provision of forms of social service (Sherman & Hawkins, 1981). Each component of the criminal justice system attempts to solve a different aspect of the overall problem-solving mandate, but also shares to a greater or lesser extent the burden of all three functions. Each component has developed its unique set of ready-made solutions and patterns of basic assumptions to cope with or solve its problems, along with its language, norms, mores, and the like. In other words, each component of the system has its own unique culture.

Likewise, each member of an organization also attempts to meet personal goals and needs (solve problems) within the framework of the organization. For example, each member shares, to a greater or lesser extent, an economic need and the needs to belong and be respected, to acquire status and power, and to be considered successful. While individuals can meet their needs directly through the formal structure of the organization by carrying out its objectives, they often fulfill these needs through the informal structure or social system that develops within the organization.

Large organizations have hierarchies and a range of component agencies. Each component agency and level of the hierarchy has a different set of problems to solve, which in turn requires the development of a set of ready-made solutions and assumptions. Therefore, each component or hierarchical level of an organization will be a subculture of the greater organizational culture. Because each component of a large organization faces different problems of external adaptation, the process of internal integration evolves under a different set of conditions. In Chapter 3, for example, it was argued that large organizations decouple because top administrators and work process functionaries work in different environments and face different sets of demands and constraints. In short, administrators and operational staff have different sets of problems to solve; each group, therefore, creates its own set of ready-made solutions and acceptable patterns, resulting in different subcultures of the organization.

There are many subcultures within the criminal justice system or its component agencies. Within correctional systems, some degree of conflict usually exists between the treatment and custody staffs. An important component of the conflict is the cultural difference that arises from the different set of problems each group has been assigned to solve. Detective work is usually viewed as having a higher-order status because detectives do not deal with typical street cop problems. Rather, the problems they solve are cerebral in nature—they investigate, interact directly and often with members of the prosecutor's staff, are assigned office space, and wear suits and ties to set them apart. Judges as well as prosecuting and defense attorneys work in a world almost foreign to most criminal justice practitioners. Sophisticated legal-based expertise and knowledge symbolized by the legalistic language sets this subculture apart from other criminal justice system subcultures. The administrative/management culture is identified by the constant search for numbers and statistics. Administrators must solve the problem of "accountability" to the public and political system, and numbers provide the solution. To the "street-level bureaucrat" (Lipsky, 1988)—the correctional officers, police officers, probation and parole officers who carry out the work—numbers may have little value and are viewed as "red tape."

The intentional filtering of communication upward and downward through the chain of command (discussed in Chapter 4) is an artifact of organizational culture. Middle managers screen and reinterpret directives coming to make them "fit" into the established routines developed to solve problems. Conversely, information in reports on activities sent upward are biased toward success to solve the individual practitioners' need to protect personal or unit status within the organization. This practice is a common artifact of most organizations, especially criminal justice agencies, where organizational members believe that rules must be violated to get the job done.

The cultural milieu of an organization is also impacted by the mix of cultures imported by its personnel. Relatively small organizations, such as small local jails, courts, or police departments, may hire staff from the local community with a homogeneous culture. In this case, it is likely that the agency's organizational culture will be similarly homogeneous and cultural conflict will be minimal. However, large agencies that recruit personnel from urban areas with heterogeneous cultures will absorb a mix of individuals from different ethnic groups, socioeconomic groups and a growing number of women, who may bring with them somewhat different values, mores, and established patterns of problem solving that create misunderstandings and conflict with the male-dominated system. The mix of cultures can also conflict with a traditional and well-established formal structure that is supported by and is congruent with the prevailing management culture. With the influx of women into the criminal justice system, management is held responsible via regulations evolving out of federal equal opportunity guidelines that address organizational hostilities toward women and minorities. The implications clearly make management responsible for controlling and impacting the culture of the organization to create an accommodating or non-hostile culture for women and minorities.

The major role of top-level administrators is to define the organization's mission and identify the problem or problems it has been mandated to solve. Moreover, lower-order problems must be assigned to levels of the hierarchy, line and staff functionaries, and subcomponents of the system. Management then requires that the problems and means to solve the problems be identified and spelled out with clarity and that the ready-made solutions or routines be followed. In other words, the task of management is to perpetuate their version of the organizational culture: the assumptions about the organization's role, the sub-roles of individual members, and how the roles are to be carried out. Role giving and taking includes the organization's philosophy, values, norms, laws, expected observable behaviors, and language. Managing the culture is, for most administrators, a hidden agenda (often from themselves as well) as they attempt to direct and control the organization by directing and controlling the behaviors of its members.

Administrators typically attempt to control the behavior of agency staff through the formal frame of their systems. Control efforts are based upon training, policies and procedures, supervisory structures, and formal sanctions that can be imposed to ensure conformity. Again, the example of integrating minorities and women into the organization clearly manifests the administrator's reliance on the formal structure to impact cultural variables. Policies, procedures, rules, and regulations are typically written to protect the interests of women and minority staff. The rules usually attempt to control, if not ban, behaviors, such as offensive language, that would make life in the agency difficult for women and minorities. One state department of corrections in the Midwest defines any statement, comment, or communication that can be construed to have sexual content as sexual harassment. Formal sanctions are also created to prevent organizational members from violating policies, rules, and regulations that are created to protect minority groups. Currently, the formal occupational socialization process includes hiring women and minorities and providing diversity training to sensitize staff to ethnic and gender differences to promote positive relationships across ethnic and gender lines.

Clearly, administrators do impact an organization's culture through formal frame mechanisms. However, the informal structure of an organization also impacts powerfully on its culture. First, staff may develop methods that differ from the formally prescribed methods to solve the problems assigned to them. The informal methods of achieving the agency's objectives may be viewed by staff as a better way to operate. The frontline police or corrections officer acting as a street-level bureaucrat (Lipsky, 1988) creates his or her own unwritten policies and procedures in response to the immediate problems he or she faces in the task environment. Corrections officers, for example, often ignore inmates who violate prison rules to maintain order, and police officers develop methods to circumvent rules of evidence to solve and favorably prosecute a criminal case. The informal methods adopted may also fit the staff's own skills, personal needs, value preferences, and need for behavioral expression.

While new staff members are indoctrinated into the formal culture through mechanisms provided by the organization, organizational members are also subjected to informal socialization and role giving by existing staff. Newly trained staff are commonly told to "forget everything they learned at the academy" because the real training takes place in the field. Rites of passage await the rookie or "new fish" employee. They serve to both test and sanction the newcomer to begin the informal socialization process.

Hence, an organization's culture results from pressures from the formal structure to solve organizational problems in ways prescribed by administrators and well-established patterns of problem solving developed by staff that differ from the formal prescriptions and also meet personal needs of the staff. For organizations with a long history, such as the agencies of the criminal justice system, the cultural pattern found in both the informal and formal structures is deeply entrenched. The pattern of problem solving and assumptions about the world in which the organization is immersed are not easily altered without perceived dramatic changes in the organization's environment.

Training in the California Department of Corrections

The California Department of Corrections (CDC) supports employee training; over $40 million is spent annually in delivering training to employees. The challenge of any training program, however, is to create a system that is both cost effective and responsive to the organization's management concerns for employee performance. Training should be fully integrated with the process of work. Ideally, the training experience would be indistinguishable from the work experience. Trainees would perform as they learn and would do so as needed by the organization. The "fit" between work and training would appear seamless.

The employee-training program within the CDC is authorized within the state's Government Codes and Penal Codes, in the California Code of Regulations, specific to the CDC, and in the administrative rules and policies of the CDC. The statutory mandates (codes) are well meaning. That is, the legislature and governor responded to constituent concerns on a perceived lack of training or understanding among the civil servants. As well intentioned as they are, the mandates frustrate the purpose of well-designed education and training because they are generally directive, not prescriptive. The mandates have no real accountability requirements, nor do they provide recognition of funding needs to ensure that the desired results are realistically achievable. The focus of training at the CDC has been on quantity, not quality. The measure of success is generally the number of hours spent in class. There is no consistent departmental quality control over the design, implementation, evaluation, and updating of training, nor is there a strategic plan to guide the overall training efforts.

There have been employee-created incidents within the prisons that have been investigated and reported in the media. These incidents have had a profound effect on the image of the CDC and the involvement of federal courts and agencies in the CDC's business, policies, and practices. These incidents also caused the state legislature to scrutinize the management of the prison system, the employee-training program, and the control exercised by the supervisors and managers who are ultimately held responsible for gross errors within the system. Individual employee performance is usually explainable to the employee. Multiple employee performance is usually attributable to the managers and supervisors of the procedures and systems.

The CDC administration is constantly aware of a myriad of problems and challenges within the following larger issues:

- Continued overcrowding
- No new prison construction projects
- Diminished inmate rights/privileges resulting from public demands through legislation
- Inexperienced staff in large numbers
- Increasing propensity for inmate violence from those with longer stays

Numerous studies of prison violence in other states have indicated the presence of most, if not all, of the above problems. Training cannot solve or prevent all problems, but it does play a critical role in preparing staff at all levels to manage successfully increasingly overcrowded and complex institutions.

The CDC's current training program is fragmented, lacks adequate personnel and technology, and is primarily focused on the delivery and administration of training as opposed to curriculum design. As a result, the majority of training is not standardized, generally is not competency based, often fails to take advantage of the most effective delivery options, and is predominantly aimed at custody staff to the exclusion of other classifications. Nor has the training function been able to support the CDC in the complex but critically needed area of organizational development (OD).

The lack of training resources within the department and the extent to which development and presentation of training is fragmented results in a number of adverse impacts. Among the most pressing adverse effects are:

- Lack of standardized core curriculum
- Impact often unclear (was anything really learned?)
- Classes that may not properly address the identified performance problem
- Training applied as a remedy to non-training problems
- Lack of coordination between functional area managers (confusion in the field and directions which may be at cross purposes)
- Continued inability of training to assist in OD activities
- Continued reactive rather than proactive training

The lack of standardized lesson plans and presentations results in inconsistencies in the handling of similar situations throughout CDC. Various employee and inmate grievances and lawsuits filed against the CDC have been based partially on lack of consistent staff training. The monetary cost to the CDC has been extremely high in the cases where staff has been found acting inappropriately.

The CDC does not conduct in-depth training needs analyses. Consequently, training does not necessarily address the identified performance problem or may be applied to non-training problems. What initially appears to be the problem often becomes something very different after detailed assessment. It is not uncommon to discover, for example, that the real problem lies within the organization's systems and procedures, not in the individual performer. In other words, people know how to do their jobs but are prevented from functioning effectively by some aspect of the organization's structure and/or policies.

Employee training costs money. The escalating costs of travel, per diem, expenses, and lost productivity due to absence from the work site are driving costs higher each year. Without an efficient and cost-effective way to deliver training, the CDC and its employees will be increasingly vulnerable to continued litigation, the potential for escalating violence, and support services which at times fall short of desired operational efficiencies.

ARMAND R. BURRUEL

Former Assistant Deputy Director, Office of Human Resources Development

MARY WILLIAMS

Former Assistant Chief, Training Services Branch

A deeply entrenched organizational culture and its powerful socialization process will cause behavior in organizations to remain remarkably stable despite frequent turnover of personnel. Katz and Kahn (1978) define role behavior as the recurring actions of an individual that are appropriately related to the repetitive activities of others so as to yield a predictable outcome. In addition, they view *role behavior* as a function of social setting, rather than the individual personalities of people in organizations. Role theorists, therefore, suggest that workers engage in both formal and informal learning processes to become aware of and committed to behavioral norms that are seen as appropriate for their job.

This socialization hypothesis, however, is not the only explanation for the shared sets of behaviors that appear to be associated with some occupations. Some researchers have suggested that occupational behaviors are a function of personality rather than socialization. That is, some occupations may attract certain types of people. Research on the working personality of the police has been influenced by this perspective. Some researchers have argued that the personality traits of individual police officers differ from those of the general public prior to their entering the police field (Rokeach, Miller, & Snyder, 1971). Police work has been said to attract recruits who are more authoritarian, more cynical, and more oriented toward excitement than the public at large. This explanation of police behavior is, however, currently out of favor. A number of studies have failed to find significant differences in the attitudes of police officer recruits and the general public, and the original research has been criticized for methodological shortcomings (see Bennett, 1984). Researchers continue to utilize the socialization model, which focuses on the nature of police work itself and the process by which novices are recruited from the general public and become experienced officers.

The Socialization Process

A study of judges illustrates the process of socialization within the federal judiciary. Through in-depth interviews with federal judges, Carp and Wheeler (1972) were able to describe the process by which a lawyer becomes an experienced trial judge. Legal training itself is a lengthy and intense socialization experience. Still, the authors found that novice judges were ill prepared for the problems they faced.

The problems encountered by new judges fell into three categories: legal, administrative, and psychological. The first of these problems arose because of the limited legal experiences of the judges. Most had come from firms dealing primarily with civil suits, and the most common problem of these judges was ignorance of criminal law. The second complaint was heavy caseloads and difficulty in preventing backlogs. Finally, the judges complained of the psychological stresses of loneliness, of maintaining judicial bearing on and off the bench, and of local pressures in decision making.

The research described a variety of formal and informal mechanisms for addressing these problems. The most conspicuous source of formal socialization is the New Judges' Seminars sponsored by the Federal Judicial Center in Washington, D.C. Although the purpose of these seminars is formal education through speakers and workshops, the judges noted that their primary benefit was informal discussions with other judges. Although less obvious, the most potent source of socialization for new judges was practicing judges in the same court as well as court staff. Carp and Wheeler highlight the distinctive local nature of judicial socialization and its resulting perpetuation of local and regional differences in the judiciary. Senior judges perpetuated local procedures and attitudes by providing their junior colleagues with legal information, administrative advice, and personal reassurances. Likewise, local attorneys with particular specialties often influenced novice judges with limited knowledge in these areas.

One judge described the net result of the socialization process as membership in a fraternal organization characterized by mutual respect and a feeling of brotherhood. (There were no female judges in the study.) The power of socialization, however, can be overstated. The fact that socialization is not perfect is illustrated in the case of Federal District Judge Harry Claiborne, who refused to resign his post and continued to collect a salary while imprisoned for income tax evasion. The Senate ultimately voted to impeach the judge as the only way to remove him from office.

Stages of Socialization

The case of judicial socialization calls our attention to several factors important in the transmission of organizational roles. In particular, socialization is a *process*. A model of socialization, therefore, must deal not only with the substantive dimension of the roles but also with change over time and the nature of the influences producing change. The literature on socialization generally divides the process of change into three distinct stages: anticipatory, formal, and informal.

The socialization process begins before an individual enters an occupation. In this stage of *anticipatory socialization,* those considering a particular field look forward to the demands and expectations of their future job. They begin to adopt attitudes and values they believe are consistent with the occupation, and they come to view themselves as members of a group. During this stage, individuals are influenced by two main reference groups. First, those tangential to the occupation, such as friends and family, may transmit their views of the job. For example, a lawyer seeking to join the judiciary may be influenced by family members' views of the job's status. Second, members of the occupation may directly transmit information about the job. Lawyers working with judges gain insight into what is perceived as appropriate or inappropriate behavior for a member of the judiciary. Along with these sources of influence, both the amount of time in the anticipatory stage and the accuracy of information received affect the adoption of organizational roles.

When a person joins a particular occupation, the second stage, *formal socialization,* usually occurs. This is generally a period of formalized training. For judges, the formalized training period is shorter and less powerful than that for many other occupations within criminal justice. The New Judges' Seminars are the primary means of formal socialization. In police work and corrections, the training academy immerses recruits into an occupational role. Aside from providing important information about doing a job, the formal training process serves a variety of other functions through exposure to experienced veterans. This reference group provides normative prescriptions for the attitudes and behaviors of the recruits. In doing so, it also creates feelings of belonging and acceptance. The New Judges' Seminars are valued not only for imparting technical knowledge but also for fostering relationships that provide membership in a group. Here the origins of the judicial fraternity can be found.

The third and ongoing stage is *informal socialization*. In this stage the relevant reference groups are peers, managers, and even clients to whom a worker is exposed on a daily basis. Here the routine of the job shapes the role of the criminal justice worker. For judges, daily associations with their staffs and with lawyers influence the uniquely local nature of their roles. For some police and corrections officers, the positive values gained at the academy may give way in the informal stage to cynicism, alienation, and even corruption.

A Model of Influences

Although the stages of socialization illustrate the process of change, a specific model is needed to explain the manner in which socializing influences affect the individual. A theoretical model of the process of taking organizational roles has been detailed by Katz and Kahn (1978). Their social-psychological model of *role taking* relies on four key concepts, as shown in Figure 9-1. *Role expectations* are the standards by which the behavior of an organizational member is judged. Supervisors, peers, clients, and even the general public may hold different and even conflicting expectations. The *sent role* is the communication of those expectations to the member. The *received role* is the person's perception and understanding of the sent role. Finally, *role behavior* is the person's response to the complex information received. According to this model, then, the behavior of an organizational member is the result of expectations communicated by significant others and filtered through his or her own psychological processes. The role-taking model thus calls our attention to key variables that may help explain role behavior.

The model also indicates that a person's behavior affects expectations through a feedback process—that is, conformity or lack of conformity to role expectations may influence the sent role over time. In her study of parole, Studt (1978) describes "escalation episodes," in which parolees dramatically altered the role of parole officers. Ordinarily, parole officers viewed their role as one of helping within a context of casual surveillance. This role was sustained by the lack of information about a parolee's misbehavior. When officers did receive information about even minor transgressions, however, they escalated their surveillance role.

In one example, an agent arranged for the release of a parolee who had been arrested for an unpaid traffic ticket. The agent set up a meeting with the parolee that afternoon, but the parolee was late. The common-law wife was at home with her new baby; she took this occasion to tell the agent she was considering leaving the parolee because he was sometimes physically rough with her. The rest of the afternoon was largely devoted to activities that ranged from searching the extensive case record for evidence of previous violence to investigating the possibility that the parolee's aged parents could provide housing for him temporarily, pending the results of further investigation. By the end of the afternoon, although the parolee had not yet been interviewed, the agent and the supervisor were outlining the case for revocation (Studt, 1978:80–81).

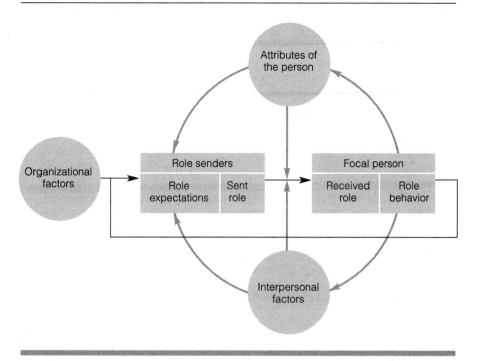

FIGURE 9-1 A Theoretical Model of Factors Involved in the Taking of Organizational Roles (From D. Katz and R. L. Kahn, *The Social Psychology of Organizations,* 2nd. ed. Copyright ©1978 by John Wiley & Sons, Inc. Reprinted by permission.)

Katz and Kahn also point out that the process of role taking does not occur in isolation and is shaped by several other factors in the model, including organizational, interpersonal, and individual factors. Studt points out, for example, that organizational concerns are a strong factor in the decision to revoke parole. The important question in this case was the extent to which the parolee's conduct could expose the organization to criticism. Other organizational factors that may affect role taking include organizational size and level of bureaucratization. Large, bureaucratized organizations, for example, may support impersonal attitudes among staff. Finally, evidence indicates that position in the organizational hierarchy influences role taking. Even when supervisors are recruited from the front lines, they may take on new roles widely different from those of their former colleagues. Some managerial orientations are a result of position rather than individual character, as illustrated in a study of corrections staff by Duffee and O'Leary (1980), in which frontline officers viewed their activity as centering on order maintenance and restraint, but supervisors were supportive of rehabilitation goals.

Another moderator of the role-taking process is interpersonal relationships. The relationship between parole officer and parolee, for example, appears to affect the parole agent's role. It takes time for a parolee to understand an officer's expectations. Once those expectations are understood, surveillance may be de-emphasized. Even a "good" relationship, however, can be disrupted by an incident that triggers an escalation episode.

Finally, roles are also influenced by individual differences in approach to the job. Studt found that some agents were "just doing the job," while others seemed most interested in catching offenders for rule violations. Some emphasized treating parolees with a modicum of respect; some emphasized predictability in their supervision relationships. The general model of role taking can still accommodate such individual orientations.

Problems in the Socialization Process

Evidence for the power of the role-taking model can be found all around us in the patterned behavior of organizational members. Still, there is abundant evidence that the process of role taking is not as straightforward as the model may imply. In criminal justice the most often-discussed problem is that of role conflict. In the model, *role conflict* is the occurrence of two or more role expectations in such a way that compliance with one makes compliance with another difficult or impossible. Conflicting expectations may come from two or more role senders or may emanate from a single role sender. These problems are endemic in all street-level bureaucracies and particularly in criminal justice. Lipsky (1980), for example, argues that one of the defining characteristics of all street-level bureaucracies is competing goals. This competition is expressed in the conflicting expectations of frontline workers. Police officers are charged with controlling crime as well as meeting due process constraints. Probation and parole officers must provide surveillance of their caseload to prevent crimes and assure compliance with rules, but they must also provide a supportive atmosphere and services to assist in adjustment to the community. In addition to conflicts over substantive goals, all human service workers are sent conflicting messages about the process of their work. Although the importance of providing custodial or helping services is stressed, these services are to be provided to large caseloads of clients. Probation and parole officers may supervise an average of seventy clients. Demands on time thus accentuate conflicts in the role.

Perhaps the literature on institutional corrections best illustrates the problem of role conflict. In his study of a Rhode Island maximum security prison, Carroll (1974:52) described the basis for role conflict:

> Prior to 1956, the officers were "guards" and their role was precisely defined. The sole functions of the guard were to maintain security and internal order. . . . Today the official title of the custodial staff is "correctional officer," a title that both incorporates and symbolizes the conflicting and ambiguous definitions of their current role. As the term "officer" connotes, the custodians remain organized in a military hierarchy, the function of which is to ensure security and order. But the adjective correctional connotes an additional expectation of equal priority—that of changing offenders.

In his study of corrections officers at Auburn, New York penitentiary, Lombardo (1981) found a similar sort of role conflict. Although the security role of officers required a high degree of social distance from inmates, the informal counseling roles adopted by some officers demanded low social distance. About a third of the officers studied found conflict between these roles. One officer provided the following illustration of the conflict:

> There's been times I could have done something for a guy, but I couldn't because of the rules. In one situation where they'd gassed a whole section, the guys [inmates] were vicious. They [other officers and supervisors] wouldn't help them. I opened the windows and turned on the water. One guy was vomiting. I called the medical authorities. The guy wanted air, and I wanted to give him a cup of milk. The medical personnel says no. So there was nothing I could do (Lombardo, 1981:138).

Research into the effects of role conflict indicates that it results in low job satisfaction and poor performance. Role conflict has been found to be a principal cause of stress among corrections officers. It has also been suggested that the conflict "immobilizes" officers and makes them ineffective in both their roles. Other research suggests that conflict over roles causes staff to emphasize their most clearly defined tasks. In their study of Illinois prison guards, Jacobs and Retsky (1975:27) found that "guards are most likely to fall back on their security and maintenance role because it is the only role on which they can be objectively evaluated." Related to role conflict is the problem of role ambiguity. *Role ambiguity* means uncertainty about what the occupant of a particular office is supposed to do—that is, the sent message is unclear. This problem often manifests itself in lack of clear performance criteria, a common complaint among police and corrections staff and a major source of stress on the job (Terry, 1983:162). Wilson (1968), for example, notes that the police have been given tasks that cannot all be performed to the satisfaction of society. Police are destined to be viewed as either ineffective or overly repressive. In their maintenance function, for example, differing expectations about what constitutes a just resolution of a dispute between two parties often leave police officers with great discretion and little direction.

In his classic essay *The Society of Captives,* Gresham Sykes (1958) describes the ambiguity in the role of the corrections officer. He points out that the goals of punishment and rehabilitation provide little direction. Questions of what is appropriate punishment remain unanswered, and the technology for changing offenders' behavior is uncertain. The corrections officer is, therefore, left with an uncertain mandate. The officer must gain compliance from inmates and maintain control within the prison. This mandate is accomplished through accommodations, which Sykes describes as the corruption of the guard's authority. Officers allow inmates to violate some minor rules to gain cooperation "when it counts." Others also note that the corrections officers who are regarded as good by their superiors are the ones who get the best compliance without having to resort to formal disciplinary procedures. General performance prescriptions provide little concrete advice for officers. As with role conflict, officers may seek additional direction. After a survey of maximum security guards, Poole and Regoli (1980) concluded that *role stress,* defined as perceived uncertainty about job expectations, was positively associated with custodial orientation—that is, those officers experiencing role ambiguity were most likely to define their job in narrow custodial terms.

Lee and Visano (1981) discuss a special case of role-related problems in criminal justice. These authors focus on the concept of *official deviance,* which they define as "actions taken by officials which violate the law and/or the formal rules of the organization but which are clearly oriented toward the needs and goals of the organization, as perceived by the official, and thus fulfill certain informal rules of the organization" (1981:216). Thus, official deviance does not benefit the individual, as corruption may, but is aimed at furthering the perceived goals of the organization. In most cases, role incumbents regard official deviance as expected and thus as part of their job. This was the case when Lieutenant Colonel Oliver North and Admiral John Poindexter testified in the Iran Contra hearings that, believing they were acting in the best interests of the country, they originally misled Congress to avoid disclosing they had provided weapons to the Nicaraguan Contras without congressional approval.

Criminal justice provides numerous examples of official deviance. Blumberg's (1967) study illustrates official deviance among public defenders. Defense lawyers and particularly public defenders are expected to maintain ongoing relationships with judges and prosecutors. Relationships with most clients are transitory. As a result, defense attorneys often pressure clients to plead guilty in order to process cases efficiently. They may even conspire with other courtroom actors to increase punishments for seemingly guilty clients who insist on going to trial.

The pressures supporting official deviance were also revealed in investigations of the security service of the Royal Canadian Mounted Police (RCMP). Members of the RCMP are formally bound through law and the rules of the RCMP organization to uphold the laws of Canada. But they are informally instructed that they must engage in such "dirty tricks" as illegal break-ins and wire tapping, kidnapping, theft of documents, faking of documents, and even arson. Superior officers of the RCMP have admitted to a federal inquiry on RCMP wrongdoing that members of the security services who refused to engage in dirty tricks because they were illegal would be punished by transfers, denial of promotions, and so forth. At the same time, Mounties were warned that if they were caught, the RCMP would deny any knowledge of their activities and leave them to defend themselves as best they could (Lee & Visano, 1981:218). The cases of public defenders and Mounties clearly show differences in the severity of official deviance, but both reflect responses to conflicting demands in criminal justice. Neither example can be explained by viewing individual actors as bad apples; instead, all are responding to expectations.

The bad-apple theory has also been rejected as a useful explanation for corruption, which does result in personal gain. In fact, in its investigation of police corruption in New York, the Knapp Commission (1972:114) went so far as to note that the elimination of bad apples was a "proven obstacle to meaningful reform." The explanation of corruption as the product of a few aberrant individuals ignores organizational structures and operational codes that establish norms and expectations that permit corruption to grow and spread through organizations. As the Knapp Commission noted, "even those who themselves engage in no corrupt activities are involved in corruption in the sense that they take no steps to prevent what they know or suspect to be going on" (1972:114).

No aspect of criminal justice is immune to corruption. Investigations into corruption in the Cook County, Illinois courts between 1986 and 1988 resulted in nearly sixty federal indictments for case fixing and payoffs. Probation officers have been known to exact sexual favors from clients who sought to avoid revocation; corrections officers have been prosecuted for smuggling drugs into prisons and even for aiding in prison escapes. Most of the research on corruption, however, has focused on the police.

Studies of police corruption have investigated behavior ranging from accepting an occasional free meal to participating in burglary rings. Much of the research has examined the sources of support for corrupt practices. Sherman (1974), for example, argues that a rookie police officer's work group exercises considerable influence. The likelihood of new officers' accepting bribes is related to the extent to which such practices already occur in the work group. In fact, failure to indulge in corrupt practices may not be sanctioned by an officer's peers. Sherman reports that officers who rejected peers' invitations to receive payoffs to overlook illegal gambling often transferred to different jobs. Rejection of solidarity left officers isolated from their peers.

Aside from the influence of peers, there may also be supervisory support for corrupt practices. In 1967, the President's Commission on Law Enforcement and the Administration of Justice pointed to administrators as having a direct influence on the ethical standards of frontline officers. Police executives can contribute much to a department's tolerance of or intolerance for corruption and the establishment of departmental norms for behavior through their influence on organizational roles. Corrupt police officers, however, do not view themselves as corrupt, and the sent role is viewed as one of non-deviance. Thus, corruption is shared with other officers who provide open support for each other (Reiss, 1971:171), and such support is accomplished through the legitimization of corruption. Wilson (1968) points out that police justify some types of corruption by pointing to declining moral standards in the general community. They note the hypocrisy in the desire to have police officers who will not take bribes when even prominent citizens may wish to bribe them. Skolnick (1966) also explains that police officers legitimize some corrupt practices by distinguishing between practices that will or will not harm the public. In the study, graft associated with bookmaking was regarded as acceptable in a West Coast police department, but bribes associated with drugs were not.

Others have also indicated that the same role-sending process that supports corruption also sets its limits. Thus officers may differentiate between clean graft (acceptable) and dirty graft (unacceptable) (see Sherman, 1974) or may distinguish between accepting a bribe and extorting money from someone. Extreme forms of corruption appear to be rare and require an explanation that looks at factors beyond the occupational socialization model.

We have discussed both the stages in which socialization occurs and the specifics of the process itself. In the following sections we examine the content of socialization, which varies according to different occupations. We look at socialization among the police and among corrections officers, areas where there is sufficient research to describe occupational socialization. These generalizations, however, are not meant to downplay the significance of the moderators of role taking, which we discussed previously.

Socialization and the Police

The suggestion that large numbers of recruits are attracted to police work because they have authoritarian and violence-seeking personalities has not been supported by the research. Instead, novice police officers seem drawn to the task by a variety of motives. One early study found that nearly a third of recruits were "always interested in being a policeman"; others were attracted by prestige, working with people, and the variety in the work (Reiss, 1967). For these officers anticipatory socialization was a powerful influence. These interests, however, have not generally been confirmed in other studies. Although most recruits may possess an accurate impression of police work prior to selection, the nature of the job is not necessarily what draws them. Motivations are complicated, but the stability of civil service employment and economic benefits attract a significant number of officers (Niederhoffer, 1969; Harris, 1973). Female officers, however, are likely to be attracted to the job by the "interesting" nature of the work (Ermer, 1978).

Regardless of motivation, anticipatory socialization leads a police officer candidate to certain expectations about the job. Veteran officers also have expectations of the candidates. In a study of the Fort Wayne, Indiana police, Charles (1986) discovered that in the past officers in the department were given a list of potential police candidates and asked to vote on whether an applicant should be accepted or rejected. Now objective and subjective exams define whether a candidate is "good police material," but that assessment still depends heavily on the candidate's image of police work as gained through anticipatory socialization. "Good police material," in general, "portrays an individual who is pro-police, highly motivated to become a police officer, willing to remain in the department for at least twenty years, accepting of an authoritarian atmosphere, and interested in fighting crime" (Charles, 1986:37).

Anticipatory socialization determines the ease with which the recruit fits into the social systems found in the formal and informal stages of socialization. The formal socialization process is perhaps more elaborate in policing than in any other occupation within criminal justice. Academy training can last sixteen weeks, with candidates living together and spending only weekends at home. Life at the academy is characterized by "absolute obedience to departmental rules, rigorous physical training, dull lectures devoted to various technical aspects of the occupation, and a ritualistic concern for detail" (Van Maanen, 1985). Although the curriculum includes subjects from report writing to hand-to-hand combat, the lessons of the academy go far beyond the technical information imparted by instructors. Bennett (1984) summarizes four main functions of academy training for the police. First, it provides prescriptions for attitudes, values, and behaviors. Second, it provides opportunities for recruits to evaluate their own behavior and performance against the behavior and performance of their peers. Third, the academy reference group provides a sense of belonging, acceptance, and being rewarded by the group. And, fourth, the reference group acts as a controlling influence by withholding acceptance in the face of inappropriate attitudes or behavior.

The basis for identification with the police reference group was examined in a study of a training academy. Harris (1973) found that three structural factors strengthened the ties between individual recruits and the police peer group. First, police work is depersonalizing. Officers are stereotyped by administrators and by the public, and their views are oversimplified. They find themselves stripped of individuality. Behavior that was previously accepted is no longer permitted. Drinking in public may bring criticism from the public and from police officials. Similarly, the officer's newly acquired authority often molds interactions with the public. The police officer finds that his or her social identity is equated with the occupation. In or out of uniform, a cop is a cop. Thus isolated from the community, the recruit turns to peers for support. In fact, a study of resignations from a police academy found that recruits were most likely to resign when they felt police solidarity did not adequately compensate for social isolation (Fielding & Fielding, 1987).

A second factor in police solidarity can be found in the drive toward police professionalism. Harris argues that this drive is in some ways an effort to cover feelings of isolation, fear, and disappointment with the hostile reaction of the public. Professionalism assumes that only other police are qualified to judge police behavior, and thus there is support for secrecy, distance from the public, and close bonds to one's peers. A third source of solidarity is the ambiguous nature of police work. The unpredictable routine and lack of appreciation from politicians, the press, and other groups breed defensiveness and contribute further to the ingrown nature of police groups. The informal and continuing stage of socialization involves learning to cope successfully in the real world. In policing, this initiation into reality is done through field training officers (FTOs), who supervise the novice officers on the street. Experienced veterans, including the FTOs, often provide an insightful summary of the academy experience for the new officer. One mentor cautioned a new officer:

> I hope the academy didn't get to you. It's something we all have to go through. A bunch of bullshit as far as I can tell. . . . Since you got through it all right, you get to find out what it's like out here. You'll find out mighty fast that it ain't nothing like they tell you at the academy (quoted in Van Maanen, 1985:20).

The rookie's evaluation of the academy is thus confirmed, and the new officer continues to learn that peers are the people who can and must be trusted. The FTO or other experienced officers provide continuous coaching of the novice. Westley (1970:157–158) vividly describes it:

> Eight hours a day, six days a week . . . they talked with their partners. Long hours between action have to be filled; and the older men, hungry for an audience, use them to advantage. Here the experienced man finds an opportunity to talk about himself as a policeman, about his hardships and happiness. Here is someone to whom he is an expert. . . . Thus, amidst an increased barrage of warnings as to silence, the recruit is initiated into the experience of the man, the history of the department, the miseries of police work, the advantages of police work, and the gripes and boasting of a long series of men. . . . This is the training and the initiation.

A critical moment in that training and initiation is what Van Maanen has identified as the enforcement encounter. The first enforcement-related contact of an officer's probationary period demonstrates the hostility between police and the public. Continued encounters make for a reality shock, which highlights the discrepancy between "idealistic expectations and sordid reality" (Niederhoffer, 1969:52).

Perhaps the most extreme description of informal socialization of the police is presented in Westley's (1970) study of a Midwestern police department. The officers Westley studied formed a distinct subculture marked by clear norms of conduct. These norms included secrecy—a strong prohibition against discussing police business with outsiders—and the use of violence. Many of the officers supported the use of violence in the form of roughing up suspects simply when disrespect to the police was shown or to obtain information. The roots of this morality, this subculture ethos, lay in the perception of hostility from the public. In response to public criticism, police solidarity grew and officers protected their comrades even to the extent of excusing beatings and graft.

Such extreme cases are unlikely today, and the adoption of subculture values is clearly moderated by individual variables. At the minimum, however, police officers seem to resolve their conflict with the public and with police administration by relying on advice to "lie low, hang loose, and don't expect too much" (Van Maanen, 1985:212).

Socialization in Corrections

Although the reasons for taking up any occupation are complex and varied, the attraction for corrections officers seems less complicated than that for the police. In a study of new corrections officers in Canada, Willett (1977) described the motivations of recruit officers as "prosaic." Lombardo's (1981) study of New York guards came to a similar conclusion. Most of the new recruits were attracted to the job mainly by the promise of regular pay and job security. Many officers come to corrections from periods of unemployment or insecure jobs. For these officers, the nature of the work is not the attraction; in fact, recruits do not know much of the nature of corrections work prior to entry into the field. Anticipatory socialization for corrections officers is thus marked by incomplete and inaccurate information. Potential recruits acquire their images of prison from the popular media long before they decide to become guards. Stereotypes from James Cagney movies and television portrayals of prison violence mingle to create the impression that the job of corrections officer is one of watching (at a distance) over a mélange of dangerous subhumans. As one recruit put it, "I thought a prison guard was like a turnkey, and inmates were fierce monsters standing around looking at you" (quoted in Willett, 1977:430). Even recruits who have friends and relatives working in the prison may have little accurate information about the job. One officer in Lombardo's (1981:23) study noted:

> I had some help having a cousin down there. He got me a copy of some old rule books and some other things. Even these didn't give a full understanding of what you're getting into. Again, just ideas from the movies. Guards, not pushing inmates but still the bad guys. But I knew some guards and knew they weren't like that. I was willing to take a chance.

Just as the rookie police officer may be jolted on first contact with a hostile public, the rookie corrections officer experiences a significant reality shock on first contact with inmates. New officers learn that they will be in close contact with inmates, and the stereotype of the dangerous convict dissolves. Officers begin to see inmates as a diverse group, many of whom are "no different from the run of guys on the street" (quoted in Willett, 1977:433). As anticipatory socialization dissolves under the weight of real experience, the informal and formal processes begin.

Corrections officers often attend the training academy only after weeks or even months of on-the-job training at an institution. This schedule is the result more of necessity than design. Officers are usually available and needed in the institutions well before a training academy class is scheduled. This arrangement does, however, expose the recruits to the reality of prison work, and many officers quit shortly after this exposure. In Jacobs and Grear's (1977) study of officers who were fired or quit at Stateville Prison in Illinois, 41 percent of resignations and 60 percent of terminations occurred during the first six months on the job. Such high rates of turnover so soon after initiation are indicative of the power of the socialization process. Officers who are not responsive to it leave.

The informal socialization process for new guards is often marked by mistrust and often hostility from their experienced peers (Conover, 2000). At the same time that recruits are learning that inmates are human like anyone else, their preconceptions of other officers as "pretty good guys" dissolve. This change in perceptions usually relates to strong prohibitions against normalizing relationships with inmates. Although the rookies are taught to be firm but fair, only formal contact with inmates is expected. In fact, the informal socialization process in some institutions has been described as going so far as to support and even demand unnecessary violence against inmates (Marquart, 1986b). Older officers seem particularly concerned that recruits maintain considerable social distance from inmates. The irony is, however, that such distance is difficult to maintain in light of the constant contact between officers and inmates and is generally not maintained by the older officers.

The field training officer (FTO) programs common among the police are generally not as formally organized in corrections. Although there is some effort to pair rookies with experienced officers on job assignments, these efforts often break down because of staff shortages. Not infrequently, new officers find themselves alone on job assignments, surrounded by inmates, and poorly supervised. In such cases, rookies often turn to inmates for help in carrying out assignments. Lombardo (1981) points out how inmates provide some of the most significant training for officers. They even offer instruction on procedures such as searches and shakedowns. One officer noted:

> An inmate broke me in. Inmates trained officers. Really! He told me to stand back and he showed me how and where to frisk. He hit the table to sound it out. Rap the bars to see if they were solid. (quoted in Lombardo, 1981:321)

As the informal socialization process for corrections officers begins, then, conflicting role expectations are sent to the rookie. Veterans and supervisors emphasize the guard's formal role, while at least some inmates send expectations of reasonableness, dependence, and friendship. The officers thus see themselves caught in the middle. Such confusion is often accentuated by the formal training process. Whatever the curriculum, the corrections academy is often viewed much as the police academy is, and experienced guards counsel recruits to "listen carefully, give it back at the exams, then forget it and do as we do. Treat the course as a good holiday from the real work" (quoted in Willett, 1977:433).

The first corrections academy opened in 1859 with the goal of training guards who would have a good influence over inmates (Sellin, 1934). It was not, however, until the 1960s, with financial incentives from the Law Enforcement Assistance Administration (LEAA) and the urging of the Joint Commission on Correctional Manpower and Training (1969), that academy training gained wide support. That support has continued from the Commission on Accreditation for Corrections, which has established minimum training requirements. The length of academy training fluctuates from as few as four to as many as sixteen weeks.

The curriculum generally includes technical information, such as firearms training and emergency procedures, and a smattering of behavioral sciences. As with the police, however, the informal lessons of the academy are also significant. Corrections academies often employ the same model of regimentation as the police in an effort to create unity and professionalism among the recruits. Without the anticipatory socialization characteristic of the police and with constant manpower shortages, however, corrections academies often have difficulty enforcing regimentation. In Lombardo's (1981) study, the academy's failure to dismiss rule violators increased recruits' cynicism. The novice officers' expectation that the academy experience is of little relevance to the actual work may also be confirmed. Officer cadets often complain that subjects are too academic, and even instructors are sometimes seen as teaching one thing while believing another (Willett, 1977:438).

Frequently the impression of the academy as irrelevant is reinforced once a new officer is back in the institution (Liebentritt, 1974). The informal socialization process then continues throughout an officer's career. Studies suggest that this process involves changes in officers' attitudes over time. New officers tend to be relatively naive, with low levels of cynicism and generally positive attitudes. The oldest officers show a similar disposition, perhaps accepting their fate. In the group between these two, however, negative attitudes are high.

Although the concept of a subculture has been useful in studies of the police, its appropriateness in describing corrections officers is debatable. Evidence indicates that officers share some basic concerns about security and appropriate social distance from inmates (Crouch & Marquart, 1980), but studies indicate too that corrections officers vary considerably in their attitudes toward inmates. Lombardo (1985) also notes that the processes needed for the formation of a subculture are not present among corrections officers: corrections officers are not attracted to the field by some shared sense of mission; they generally do not work together; they do not share in the decision-making process; and there is limited communication among them. Relations among officers are often characterized by suspicion rather than solidarity.

Rather than describing corrections officers as a subculture, some authors have used the concept of *pluralistic ignorance*. Under conditions of pluralistic ignorance, individuals falsely believe that their own opinions are not widely shared. Thus Klofas and Toch (1982) found that corrections officers reported themselves as being less punitive and less custodially oriented than their peers. Some officers were effective opinion leaders and convinced the majority that their view was widely shared. In reality, the officers greatly exaggerated the punitiveness of those peers and only a small group of officers could accurately be described as primarily custodially oriented. The subculture was a myth.

Socialization and Community Expectations

Anticipatory socialization sets the context for many employees in the criminal justice system. Their perceptions and expectations about the job are strong influences throughout their careers. Yet another influence centers on public expectations of people in the criminal justice system. These public expectations affect how criminal justice personnel perceive support from the community. Surveys and research on public perceptions and attitudes toward the criminal justice system and its employees are numerous (see the U.S. Bureau, 2000b). Most paint a flattering picture of criminal justice professionals.

Perceptions and attitudes toward the police are the most common. Research on public confidence in the police is the most positive: close to 90 percent of people surveyed in one national opinion poll have a great deal/quite a lot and some confidence in the police. Almost two-thirds (62 percent) in the same national survey believe the police can either do a great deal or quite a lot in protecting them from violent crime. Similar findings are found with respect to the public's perception of the Supreme Court, with over 80 percent of those surveyed expressing confidence in the court. While the Supreme Court's activities are not representative of the duties performed by other lower courts, there is still wide consensus that these courts perform their functions in a satisfactory way.

Where public confidence may be questionable is in the area of corrections, specifically in the ability of correctional officials to rehabilitate criminals and protect prisoners and correctional staff from harm in prisons. Nevertheless, the socialization of police officers, court personnel, and correctional officers is affected to a great degree by how the public views them as being capable and competent in the performance of their jobs. The only profession related to the criminal justice system where public attitudes are fairly low is that of lawyers. The legal profession receives uniformly low scores from the public on the dimensions of honesty and ethical standards (Sourcebook, 2000:114). For criminal justice administrators, these findings are encouraging and puzzling.

While, on the one hand, public confidence is high for many criminal justice organizations, there is, on the other hand, a perception among criminal justice professionals that they are viewed negatively by the public. Addressing this apparent contrast is where many criminal justice administrators focus their efforts. For the new recruit in policing or corrections, knowledge that the public is behind you in your efforts is critical and affects job performance and commitment to a career in the criminal justice field. The socialization process through formalized training, for example, is directly influenced by how the public supports criminal justice organizations with resources for training and education required to perform the duties of the profession.

This is most evidenced in the increases in training and education requirements for both police and corrections professionals. Unlike the legal profession where a four-year college degree is required as well as three years of law school, many police and correctional organizations have until recently had minimum education and training requirements for new employees. Yet, the trends in both the police field and corrections profession are for major increases in both entry-level requirements and in-service requirements. Camp and Camp (2000), for example, report steady increases in both pre-service and in-service training requirements for entry level correctional officer positions since 1990. In some states, due to budgetary constraints, these requirements have slipped, but across the country there has been a general increase in both educational and training requirements for entry-level positions in police and correctional agencies.

With higher levels of education and training for criminal justice personnel, there is a concomitant increase in both the public's expectations concerning job performance and the expectations of personnel who demand more from their organizations on many work dimensions: recruitment, promotion, and discipline, to mention a few. For criminal justice administrators in these organizations, the expectations influence the ways in which they structure the work environment, how they supervise employees, and how they manage and deliver services to the public.

Strategies for Socialization

The process of socialization is not immutable. By deliberate design or by their failure to design, managers continuously influence the socialization process. In this section we examine the ways in which managers affect the process of socialization in criminal justice. As discussed, the socialization process begins with the anticipation of occupational roles. A manager's impact at this stage is generally limited and indirect. At best, managers can support what they regard as desirable images of the occupation. When the television show *Miami Vice* portrayed corrections officers as sadistic and corrupt in one episode, for example, the American Correctional Association sought and received an apology with the hope of deterring any such portrayals in the future. Police community relations programs provide a similar function. When police officers escort McGruff, the crime dog, on tours of elementary schools and shopping malls, they are spreading an image of police professionalism.

A direct influence on socialization occurs during recruitment and selection. The determination of job titles and qualifications is the first step in this process. Some communities, for example, use the title of *police agent* rather than *police officer* to convey a sense of professionalism. The change in title from *prison guard* to *corrections officer* was also meant to connote a different role for frontline prison staff. Likewise, *campus security* carries a different set of expectations than *campus police,* and *state trooper* conveys its own images. (See *Work Perspective* in Chapter 1.)

Job qualifications also directly influence socialization. Experience, education, and even fitness requirements determine the paths that candidates must take. In 1969, the Joint Commission on Correctional Manpower and Training noted that age requirements affected organizational roles by creating a generation gap between workers and clients in criminal justice. At the time, the gap was regarded as detrimental. Presidential commissions have long been concerned with educational requirements (National Advisory Commission on Criminal Justice Standards and Goals, 1973a, 1973b). In the 1960s and 1970s, the Law Enforcement Education Program provided funds for the education of criminal justice employees. A college education, now required for most social service positions, is regarded as beneficial for almost all entry-level positions in criminal justice (Waldron, 1984).

An obvious influence on organizational roles is exerted in the selection process itself. During this process a variety of criteria, often intuitive, sometimes systematic, is used to weed out candidates. A common approach was described by Willett (1977) in his study of Canadian corrections officers. The selection procedures involved informal and un-standardized interviews. The interviewers possessed no particular skill and were given no particular instructions but focused on maturity and intelligence, ability to supervise, ability to organize, and ability to communicate. In policing, hiring practices are often elaborate and include required civil service tests, physical fitness evaluations, character investigations, and even polygraph examinations in addition to oral interviews.

Efforts to introduce psychological assessments into the selection process are still more sophisticated but not necessarily more successful at discriminating between good and bad employees. Standardized tests, such as the *Minnesota Multiphasic Personality Inventory* and the *Cattell 16PF,* have been used, but a review of the research determined that, for corrections officers, the empirical studies are not of sufficient quantity or quality to warrant conclusions (Wahler & Gendreau, 1985). Research, however, continues. Psychological screening has become common in policing (Territo, Swanson, & Chamelin, 1985) and is beginning to be utilized in corrections. New York State requires psychological screening of all corrections officer candidates (Morgenbesser, 1984). These tests are used in the hope of identifying highly unusual psychological profiles rather than making subtle distinctions between candidates.

A different approach is found in behavioral-skills assessments as a basis for selection. These assessments are based on job analyses and focus on the ability to perform specific tasks or the potential to acquire necessary skills through training. Some criminal justice organizations are developing assessment centers that use simulations of on-the-job performance (see Byham & Thornton, 1982).

The formal stages of training provide significant opportunities to influence socialization. Here the process as well as the training content influences role taking. Van Maanen (1982) describes some variables or strategies in the training process that influence socialization. Managers should be aware of the ways in which manipulation of these variables can affect socialization.

The *degree of formalization* is the extent to which training is segregated from the ongoing context of work. In criminal justice, the police academy represents a highly formalized process, while most probation officers undergo a much less formalized process of on-the-job training. Formalization has several important consequences. The more formalized it is, the more the training will stress adoption of appropriate attitudes and beliefs and the more new employees will be stigmatized in the organization, usually by segregation in a rookie class. At the same time, formalized training is often technical in nature and its relevance for day-to-day work is likely to be questioned by both rookie and experienced employee, regardless of content.

Collective socialization strategies involve the training of new members as a group. Individual strategies involve an apprenticeship approach to socialization. Collective strategies inevitably create feelings of comradeship and peer support as trainees feel they are in the same boat. Among the police, for example, collective strategies may be useful because officers often must depend on each other in the field. The cost, however, may be that these strategies create distance from supervisors and enhance subcultural supports. *Individual socialization* strategies depend on the affective bonds between individuals and breed dependence on mentors or on established ways of doing things. The new probation officer who shares a mentor's caseload may get individualized attention but be slow to gain autonomy. In probation, where close supervision of frontline staff is difficult, this dependence in the training phase may be desirable.

In *sequential socialization,* a trainee passes through discrete stages on the way to becoming a fully accepted member of an organization. Police, for example, go through a sequence of academy training, field training, and a probationary period, while corrections officers frequently begin with on-the-job training prior to entry into the academy. When training is divided into these relatively separate steps, coordination of those stages becomes important. Lack of coordination may mean that material is contradictory or that trainees can disregard material learned in one stage, as is often the case in the transition from training academy to on-the-job training. This lack of continuity can lead to cynicism among the recruits.

Serial socialization relies on experienced veterans to groom newcomers in organizations. Criminal justice organizations frequently rely on serial practices. Experienced police officers, for example, often get academy instructor assignments and FTO jobs. Similarly, novice judges turn to experienced judges for advice. Such practices ensure that organizations will change only slowly. Established attitudes and practices are passed on, and new ideas gain little support. Such stability may not always be beneficial, however, and disjunctive practices may be useful in introducing change. University faculty, for example, may be called on to discuss police-community relations or offer training in new procedures for classifying probationers.

Investiture strategies make membership in organizations easy by accepting the recruit's credentials as the major entrance requirements. Education and the practice of law grant entry to the judiciary and form the foundation for a professional identity. However, *divestiture strategies* strip away certain characteristics before entry is allowed. Academy training requires regulation haircuts, special uniforms for the novitiate, and separation from friends and family. Although perhaps mild compared with the experience of a Marine recruit, this experience is designed for similar reasons, to dismantle the identity of the newcomer and replace it with an appropriate organizational identity. This process binds the rookie to the organization and promotes a strong sense of fellowship among those who have traveled the same path.

Socialization is more prevalent during the early, rather than later, stages of a career (Schein, 1971), and thus recruits are more susceptible than experienced workers. Nonetheless, managers must be aware of the socializing influences that continue to confront staff. Personnel practices such as shift assignments or bidding procedures for job assignments may influence socialization. For example, Klofas and Toch (1982) found that anti-inmate attitudes among young corrections officers received support when the rookies were clustered on the 3 to 11 P.M. shift. The officers lacked the seniority to bid on assignments that would have integrated them with their experienced peers on desirable shifts. Assignment to vice divisions or repeat-offender programs may expose employees to additional subcultural influences. Technological changes may also influence socialization. Continued training may alter expectations or relationships between employees and clients. And the dynamic of the new generation of correctional architecture, with its emphasis on direct supervision of inmates, may alter assumptions about inmates (Menke, Zupan, & Lovrich, 1986). Although socialization influences may be most prominent at the beginning of careers in criminal justice, those influences should not be neglected at any time.

Summary

In this chapter we have provided an overview of organizational culture and its complexity to provide a framework for the discussion of the socialization process that molds criminal justice practitioners. Further, we examined the process by which the novice employee in a criminal justice organization is transformed into a seasoned veteran. The process includes a variety of influences, beginning before an employment application is filed and continuing throughout a career. Role expectations are sent from organization outsiders and insiders. The individual filters those expectations to produce attitudes and behavior regarded as appropriate for a member of the occupation. The consistency of these attitudes and behaviors in all individual employees provides stability for the organization.

In search of stability, criminal justice organizations have designed elaborate processes to affect the attitudes and behaviors of their members. From image-building programs to apprenticeship and academy training, criminal justice workers are molded by their organizations. Each step transmits not only technical knowledge but also the ethos of the organization. The product, however, is not an organizational automaton. The roles sent to workers are complex, varied, and often conflicting. Such demands may foster a range of undesirable outcomes, from cynicism to stress and from official deviance to corruption.

Understanding occupational socialization is thus fundamental to management in criminal justice. Here we have closely considered the processes for both police and corrections officers. These processes reveal the influences, both positive and negative, on criminal justice staff. Through planning, management can gain some control over these influences and consciously affect the occupational-socialization process.

In Chapter 10 we consider another topic central to the management of criminal justice organizations. The mandate of these organizations includes the authority to deprive individuals of their liberty and even their life. This reality makes the analysis of power in criminal justice organizations uniquely important.

Case Study

Reflections on a Career

I struggled through all of the crap in law school to join the noblest of professions, I thought. I had a belief in the system of justice, that through the adversarial process, the truth would be discovered and justice would be served. I knew about plea bargaining, but I was totally naive about the legal system and how the "old boys" ran things. I passed the bar exam and joined a decent law firm. I was intent on being a defense attorney. The state had a skilled staff of prosecuting attorneys and the power of skilled detectives to work with to get convictions. To have a balanced adversarial process, skilled and dedicated defense attorneys were important. Then I got my first case.

The court appointed my firm to represent an individual who had earned a solid criminal record and was indigent. My boss was happy to assign the case to me—to prime the pump, as he put it. Negotiate the best plea you can for your client, was his advice. The defendant had served time and did not seem troubled by the possibility of returning to prison. However, he maintained his innocence and was opposed to accepting a plea. I discussed the case with the prosecutor assigned to it and asked to look over the file. I was treated well, but clearly as a beginner. As I perused the file, I noted and commented on several discrepancies in the case. The tone of our conversation changed, and the prosecutor became somewhat miffed about my analysis. I patiently pressed my point of view. However, the chief prosecutor, who was in earshot of our conversation, intervened. She made it strikingly clear that this was a plea-bargain case. She firmly explained that my client had committed a string of burglaries over the years, that this offense fit his pattern, that everyone knew it was his job, and that we didn't need to expend time and money agonizing over discrepancies in the case. She further explained that I was assigned the case as a personal favor to allow me to get some experience with the system and make a few easy bucks. By this time, she was in my face lecturing me about waking up and forgetting all of the crap I had learned in high school civics or law school. This put me over the edge. I asked for my copy of the file and told her and her assistant that I would see them in court.

To make a long story short, I took the case to a jury trial and obtained a not guilty verdict. Along the way, I embarrassed the investigating detective, who was not well prepared for the obvious plea-bargain case; angered the judge, who, as I later found out, thought my client was guilty as sin; and completely alienated the chief prosecutor and her assistant who tried the case. My boss attempted to mend the few fences I broke and asked me to apologize and be gracious with the people I had beat up in the process. I was stunned and outraged. The jury found my client not guilty; therefore, in my mind, that was the truth. The adversarial process should prevail over egos or convenience, I thought. I stood my idealistic ground and refused to apologize to anyone. A month after the acquittal, my client committed another burglary, was appointed another attorney, although he requested I represent him, pleaded guilty to a lesser offense, and was sentenced to prison. Two months later, I was asked to resign from my law firm and advised to practice on my own.

Well, I still do criminal defense work, and the thieves and convicts love me. But they usually can't pay their fees. I have to pay the rent and my bills, so I developed a pretty good divorce practice. But the real truth is that most of my domestic relations clients can't afford to go to court and have their case reviewed through the adversarial process. So we bargain and settle.

Case Study Questions

1. Describe the occupational socialization process illuminated in the case study.

2. What major weaknesses appear to exist in the stages of socialization?

3. What appear to be the real rules of the game, and how does the legal system benefit from these rules?

For Discussion ===

1. Describe the content of the role of a probation officer. What are the norms and values associated with this work? Include those that can be regarded as legitimate as well as those regarded as not legitimate. What are the sources of these norms and values? How do education, training, and the work experience influence them?

2. How can you distinguish between corruption and official deviance in policing? What socialization processes support each of these? Design an in-service training program whose chief goal is to combat the organizational processes you describe.

3. If you were selecting volunteers to work in a maximum-security prison, what attitudes and values would you find desirable and why? What attitudes and values would you like to see transmitted in the formal socialization process and in the informal stage of socialization?

4. Your job is to develop a program for training corrections officers for a special internal affairs unit. They will investigate problems of contraband and violence in prison while working as regular officers. Whom would you recruit, and how would you structure the process of training? What would the content of training be? What problems with the socialization process do you anticipate?

=== For Further Reading ===

Charles, M. T. *Policing the Streets.* Springfield, IL: Charles C. Thomas, 1986.

Conover, T. *Newjack: Guarding Sing Sing.* New York: Random House, 2000.

Katz, D., and Kahn, R. L. *The Social Psychology of Organizations,* 2nd ed. New York: Wiley, 1978.

Lombardo, L. X. *Guards Imprisoned: Correctional Officers at Work.* New York: Elsevier, 1981.

Schein, E. H., *Organizational Culture and Leadership,* 2nd ed. San Francisco: Jossey-Bass, 1997.

Terry, W. C. (Ed.). *Policing Society.* New York: Wiley, 1985.

CHAPTER
10

POWER AND POLITICAL BEHAVIOR

The sentencing power is so far unregulated that even matters of a relatively technical, seemingly "legal" nature are left for the individual judge, and thus for whimsical handling, at least in the sense that no two judges need be the same. . . . The point is, I hope, sufficiently made that our sentencing judgments splay wildly as results of unpredictable and numerous variables embodied in the numerous and variegated inhabitants of our trial benches.

(Frankel, 1973:25)

The nature of the work supervised, including the technology involved, the nature of the enforcement pattern, the spatial context in which it is carried out, the occupational cultural norms of the subordinates, the type of group structure involved, environmental constraints affecting the definition of the crime, the constraints of the definition of legitimate intrusion as defined by subordinates, the nature of the citizens in contact and their specific roles, the uniqueness of discretion involved in their work, and the task demands and superior expectations demanded, all interact to constrain and define the position of the [police] sergeant in each specific organizational context vis-à-vis other, alternate, organizational control mechanisms.

(Tifft, 1978:104)

Those who got it in with them officers got connections. They got drugs with them coming into the place. . . . Everybody need some satisfaction, so you go to the man. In here, it's the white boys. They got the drugs and power cause they give what you want. . . . Nobody has real power in here except them people with stuff [marijuana]. If you be running it, well you got what you want and what others want. . . . That makes you king, so you try to get some. . . . If you got connections on the outside, you can get it in and make money. Them officers and visitors bringing it in. . . . and that's what is done.

(Inmates quoted in Stojkovic, 1984:520)

Everything in corrections is politics. Today, unlike the past, everything we do has to be approved by the Governor or his staff. I am not saying that politics didn't influence the department in the past, but today everything we do is political. It is a matter of degree. It is too political today. This is bad because no one is willing to tell the truth out of fear of being fired or reprimanded. We know that locking up all these offenders does nothing to reduce crime, but it sure looks good for the Governor. He plays politics with the department and we suffer.

(Anonymous correctional administrator, California Department of Corrections, 1996)

These statements vividly demonstrate that the concept of power is expressed in different forms in the various arenas of the criminal justice system. The sentencing judge, the police sergeant, the prisoner, or the corrections administrator—all rely on power to gain compliance from others and are affected in turn by power relationships. A police supervisor may wish to exercise control over the beat cop, or a prisoner may desire to control another prisoner. Expressions of power are ubiquitous in criminal justice organizations, and who has the power and how they acquire it are further variables. Moreover, power and politics are inseparable in the criminal justice system. To the chagrin of some criminal justice employees, often that power seems to be used inappropriately and to the detriment of their organization. The consequences of such perceptions can be injurious to the organization, something we will examine later in the chapter. Suffice it to say that expressions of power—and the consequences of these expressions—are ubiquitous in criminal justice organizations.

Police organizations, for example, employ different types of power to gain compliance from officers. The types of power used depend on the tasks and functions of the particular unit. Supervisors in the vice unit do not use the same types of power as those in the detective unit because each unit has its own duties and responsibilities. In correctional systems, the types of power used by supervisory personnel are often constrained by a number of factors inherent in the prison structure. As an example, we know that pure coercive power rarely works in prison, in part because inmates significantly outnumber staff. As a result, corrections administrators and officers use other types of power to gain compliance from prisoners.

Our purpose in this chapter is to review the literature on power and apply this material to criminal justice organizations. As some scholars suggest, the investigation of power in organizations is not new. Few studies, however, have examined the complexity of the issue (House, 1984) and many researchers have suggested that measurement of a quantity like power is extremely difficult (Podsakoff & Schriesheim, 1985). More important, we have few studies of the exercise of power in criminal justice organizations. Nevertheless, in this chapter we will seek to identify the types of power and authority employed in criminal justice bureaucracies by examining the major research available. We will also discuss the consequences of power relations in organizations, emphasizing the political nature of power in organizations and the strategies criminal justice officials can employ to maintain their power positions. We begin, however, with a definition of power and distinguish this concept from authority.

Power Defined

Power is one of the most difficult concepts to define, as witness the multiple definitions found in the literature on organizations. Hinings, Pugh, Hickson, and Turner (1967), for example, believe that power is analogous to bureaucracy. Some authors have viewed power in only one dimension—that is, as purely coercion (Bierstedt, 1950; Blau, 1964). Dahl defines power in this way: "A has the power over B to the extent that he can get B to do something B would not otherwise do" (1957).

Although this somewhat simple definition has been accepted by many interested in power in organizations, others have seen power as being much more complex and have defined it more broadly. They look at power at the organizational level and include the role of social systems in organizations (Emerson, 1962; Dubin, 1963; Crozier, 1964; Lawrence & Lorsch, 1967)—that is, the interactions of people and units.

If we view organizational power as a product of exchange relationships in organizations, we can see how the interdependent nature of organizational tasks creates power for some people.

Perrow (1970) has demonstrated that sales departments within industrial firms are much more powerful than other units within the organization. He argues that specific units within an organization are able to exhibit what is known as "interdepartmental power" and that any investigation of power must be able to discern those units, which are critical to the operation of the organization. If some sectors of an organization are more powerful than others, what within these units makes them powerful and central to the organization? One possible answer is that these units are effective in dealing with uncertainties in the organization's task environment. In effect, they are able to absorb the uncertainty created by an often turbulent and unstable environment (March & Simon, 1958).

Criminal justice organizations, however, often do not operate in unstable environments, and they are not influenced greatly by market concerns. They generally operate in consistent and predictable ways. Power acquisition, therefore, among subunits in these organizations is typically not based on how well they can deal with uncertainties in their task environments. What is important to criminal justice organizations is that they accomplish their tasks in an efficient manner while simultaneously meeting the demands of the public.

Thus, some have suggested that it is not the interaction with the environment that is important to understanding organizational power. More critical is how units operate to accomplish tasks that are crucial to the organization's survival. Hicksen, Hinings, Lee, Schenck, and Pennings (1973) have demonstrated that organizational units that cannot be replaced in an organization (substitutability), that have a pervasive and immediate relationship to the workflow of the organization (centrality), and that deal with contingencies effectively are usually powerful in organizations.

This assertion is borne out by much evidence gathered in institutional corrections and in police organizations. Early research by Sykes (1958) demonstrated how the help of inmates is required to run prisons. In the words of Sykes, there is a "defect of total power" in our correctional institutions among custodial staff. Because inmates are crucial or central to the operation of the prison, are not likely to be replaced by other workers, and can deal relatively well with the various contingencies of prison life, it is easy to see how they would have power within the institution. This observation is equally applicable to police officers. Research has documented how certain police positions are more powerful than others and that the types of power used by police are constrained by the task required and the police hierarchy (Tifft, 1978:104).

Sergeants in tactical units, for example, have high reward and coercive power available to them. They make the determinations, in most cases, of who will come and go into the unit. Moreover, many sergeants have high expert power. Their knowledge of the activities of the unit makes them hard to replace and critical to the police organization.

Before we continue, however, we need to summarize the key aspects of power in organizations. First, power denotes that "a person or group of persons or organization of persons determines, i.e., . . . affects, what another person or group or organization will do" (Tannenbaum, 1962:236). Second, power exists among the units of an organization as well as at the interpersonal level. Much of the research has emphasized the interpersonal aspects with little regard for the organizational level, thus obscuring the importance of departmental power in the organizational setting. Third, power in an organization depends on how subunits deal with uncertainty and on whether they meet the criteria of substitutability and centrality. A hypothesis in the literature is that units that meet these criteria are able not only to influence the direction of the organization but also to solidify themselves in power positions (Michels, 1949).

Finally, we must differentiate between power and authority. Many have considered these terms interchangeable, yet, as Pfeffer (1981) suggests, doing so is not helpful to an understanding of the process of power acquisition in organizations. He posits, therefore, that the two can be best understood by examining the extent to which employees "legitimize" their use. He further argues that the use of authority seems legitimate to those being supervised or controlled in an organization. Power, however, especially purely coercive power, is not a form of compliance that sustains organizational life. Power that is legitimized over time becomes characterized as authority. This view of power and authority has many ramifications for organizations. Ultimately, organizations seek the expression of authority rather than power. Pfeffer (1981 : 4) states:

> By transforming power into authority, the exercise of influence is transformed in a subtle but important way. In social institutions, the exercise of power typically has costs. Enforcing one's way over others requires the expenditure of resources, the making of commitments, and a level of effort that can be undertaken only when the issues at hand are relatively important. On the other hand, the exercise of authority, power that has become legitimated, is expected and desired in the social context. Thus, the exercise of authority, far from diminishing through use, may actually serve to enhance the amount of authority subsequently possessed.

For our purposes here, we want to know the types of power and authority employed in criminal justice organizations. In addition, it is equally important to match types of power and authority with tasks. Police, for example, may require specific types of authority or power or both to perform their jobs. The same is true for corrections. As a result, the issue becomes identifying those types of power or authority that enhance the ability of a component of criminal justice to successfully complete its objectives. Some types of power and some types of authority are more suitable than others.

Types of Power and Authority

Any discussion of the types of authority must begin with the work of Weber (1947). From his earliest writings, Weber distinguished authority and power, with authority denoting compliance to particular directives essential for achieving a common or shared goal. Power is based on coercion, not compliance, and is used in organizations that emphasize strict obedience, for example, slave-labor camps and some prisons. Weber delineated three types of authority: traditional, charismatic, and legal. *Traditional authority* is authority that is vested in the position a person holds and that has a long tradition in a culture or organization. This type of authority can be found in countries with traditional monarchies. Within organizations, one can say that old and well-tested methods of operation are part of the organization's tradition or, equally important, may reflect the interests of those who run the organization in maintaining the status quo. As Hall (1987) suggests, traditional authority is expressed in the saying, "The old man wants it that way."

The second type of authority is *charismatic authority*. This type is founded in the personal attributes or actions (or both) of a particular individual in an organization. President John F. Kennedy, for example, wielded tremendous amounts of charismatic authority, largely because many people found attractive qualities in him. An example in the criminal justice field is the veteran police officer. Many officers who have spent a long time on the streets adopt a "police personality" that they are able to turn into charismatic authority. The flamboyant police officer described in many novels expresses this type of authority.

Finally, there is *legal authority*. This type of authority is based on an appeal to the formal rules and regulations of an organization. In addition, legal authority is rooted in the hierarchy of the organization. It is predicated on the belief that subordinates are expected to follow the orders and commands of those above them in the formal chain of command. Much of the authority exercised within criminal justice agencies is of this type. Corrections officers are organized in a chain of command, and officers assume that those above them in the institutional hierarchy have the right to impose rules and regulations. We will see how this type of authority breaks down under the strain of day-to-day activity in later chapters of this book.

Although Weber's ideas about authority have been widely adopted by those who seek to explain compliance mechanisms in organizations, his concept of power has not found as much acceptance. Current research has fostered an increased awareness of power in organizational settings, but most of this research has focused on power at the interpersonal rather than organizational level and, in addition, is open to criticism on the grounds of validity and reliability. This is equally the case for research done on power distribution in the criminal justice system. These problems aside, we can still identify bases of power found in organizations—and discuss them in light of what we know about criminal justice administration.

According to French and Raven (1968), there are five bases of power in all organizations. These bases (or types) of power are used to gain the compliance of subordinates. We will see that some are akin to the types of authority described by Weber. Others, however, match the traditional definition of power given previously in this chapter. The five types of power are reward, coercive, legitimate, referent, and expert. Although these bases of power were originally meant to explain the behavior of subordinates and supervisors at the interpersonal level, they may also be used to analyze power at the organizational level (Hall, 1987:135). Moreover, these types of power are meant to be explored as interactions and relationships among individuals in organizations. In short, there is no power unless it is expressed by one person and received by another. The person who expresses the power is called the *power holder,* and the receiver is called the *power recipient.*

Reward power is based on the power recipient's perception that the power holder can grant some type of reward or remuneration for compliance with orders or commands. An example of this type of power is the piecework system found in many factories. Workers do what the supervisor tells them to in order to get paid. Without the reward by the supervisor or the company the supervisor represents, workers will not perform as ordered. It is the reward, in the form of a salary or hourly rate, that makes workers comply with the supervisor's directives.

Coercive power is based on the power recipient's perception that failure to follow orders will bring the threat of punishment or punishment itself. This type of power has been associated with traditional prison structures, where it is widely believed that an inmate who does not comply with the wishes of corrections officers will be punished. This is not always the case, however, and the belief in coercive power as the primary compliance mechanism in prison organizations remains somewhat problematical given the nature of institutionalization today and the other forms of power available to corrections officers.

Legitimate power is exercised when a power holder is able to influence a power recipient to do something based on the power recipient's internalized belief. This type of power is most closely aligned to Weber's concept of authority. The internalized norm can be traced to many sources: cultural values, social structure, or a designated and legitimized informal leader. French and Raven suggest that an individual in an organization may follow the directives of a superior because the superior's power is legitimized by another, informal leader in the organization. Police officers may follow the commands of the shift sergeant not totally because of the traditional authority the commander has but because an informal leader, such as a veteran police officer who is viewed as their legitimate representative, follows those commands. In this way, legitimate power can be expressed not only by those in the organization's chain of command but also by those in its informal sector. Problems arise when orders and commands made by those in the formal sector of the organization (police sergeants, for example) are not consistent with the expectations and demands of leaders exhibiting legitimate power at the informal level who are respected by rank-and-file workers (police officers). Such problems are a direct consequence of power relations in organizations, which we address in another section of the chapter.

Power based on the identification of the power holder with the power recipient is known as *referent power*. This fourth type of power is predicated on the power recipient's attraction to the power holder. French and Raven state: "In our terms, this would mean that the greater the attraction, the greater the identification and consequently the greater the referent power" (1968:265). This type of power can be seen in correctional institutions. In many instances, inmates view officers in a positive light and may even attempt to emulate a favored officer's attitudes and beliefs.

An important difference between referent power and reward and coercive power is the mediation of rewards and punishments. In both reward and coercive power, the power holder is able to control rewards and sanctions. Referent power depends on the power recipient's identification with the power holder, regardless of the consequences of the relationship, positive or negative. An individual, for example, may have an opinion on a subject but will go along with the group because of a desire to be like other members of the group. The group in this case is exhibiting a strong form of referent power over the individual.

The literature on police socialization is replete with examples of individual officers who, because of intense peer pressure, go along with the demands of their group even though this behavior violates police rules and regulations. Research on this topic has suggested that to understand the power of the group we must understand the socialization process of police officers and how it reflects the expectations of society (Manning & Van Maanen, 1978; Stoddard, 1983). Chapter 9 discusses occupational socialization within criminal justice organizations.

The final power base offered by French and Raven is expert power. *Expert power* is based on the power recipient's belief that the power holder has a high level of expertise in a given area. Based on the power recipient's "cognitive structure," expert power fosters the dependence of the power recipient on the power holder, although this dependence may lessen over time. In the social system of the U.S. courts, for example, both defense and prosecuting attorneys undeniably exercise tremendous amounts of expert power over their clients, who rely on their attorneys' special knowledge and comply with their wishes.

Besides the French and Raven typology, other forms of power identified in the research literature are applicable to criminal justice administration. Bacharach and Lawler (1980) discuss information as an important source of power in organizations. Individuals or groups may have power because of their ability to control information flow in the organization. Most important is the ability to control information essential for maintaining operations (Pfeffer, 1977a). This power can be distinguished from expert power because it is derived from position in the organization rather than knowledge. For example, inmates who understand the legal system exhibit expert power, whereas inmate clerks have access to information (such as knowing whose cell will be searched by corrections officers) that allows them to manipulate the prison structure to their advantage.

A final type of power is based on the ability to acquire and provide needed organizational resources. Research has shown how certain subunits in organizations become powerful because of their ability to acquire critical resources (Salancik & Pfeffer, 1977:3–21). Another work by Pfeffer and Salancik (1974) has suggested that subunit power is contingent largely on the ability of the subunit or department to gain outside grant and contract funds. This ability enables the subunit to have more prestige than the other subunits and to gain a lasting position of power in the organization (Lodaht & Gordon, 1973).

Consequences of Power Relations

Research on the effects of varying types of power in organizations is plentiful (see Hall, 1987:136–139). Using the French and Raven typology, Warren (1968) has shown that on the dimensions of *behavioral conformity* (conformity without internalization of norms) and *attitudinal conformity* (conformity and internalization of norms) schoolteachers showed high levels of attitudinal conformity when they were subject to expert, legitimate, and referent power, but displayed behavioral conformity when they were subjected to reward and coercive power. It is important to recognize that differing kinds of power exist in organizations and that behavioral output changes noticeably when different types of power are employed.

This interpretation is further supported by Lord (1977), who analyzed the relationship between types of social power and leadership functions. Lord concludes that legitimate power is highly related to the leadership functions of developing orientation (providing direction to employees), communicating, and coordinating, whereas coercive power is most highly related to facilitating evaluations, proposing solutions, and total functional behavior. He maintains that various types of power have differential impacts on the organization and its members.

In a study of power in hospitals, Julian (1966) concludes that, depending on the type of hospital, different types of power are utilized. Voluntary hospitals, for example, rely on a legitimate power system with talks and explanations provided to patients. In contrast, veterans' hospitals employed methods of coercion in gaining compliance. By using sedation and restriction of activity, workers were able to get compliance and at the same time fulfill their primary organizational goal: control of patients. An implication from this research is that differing organizations use diverse types of power to accomplish their organizational goals, and the type and amount of power used are variable and contextual.

The same is true of criminal justice organizations. Tifft (1978:90), in his analysis of control systems and social bases of power in police organizations, attempted to examine the "structural conditions" that affect the location of power. In addition, he was interested in exploring how these conditions affect the exercise of power, how they can be altered to increase organizational control, and what the consequences of these structures are on the people within the organization. He concludes (1978:104) that there are structural factors within police organizations that contain the bases of power available to police sergeants. He further suggests that differing policies would have to be implemented within different police units for the effective exercise of police sergeant power. Detective units, for example, would be best suited if sergeants had previous experience in the unit, since expert power or knowledge is critical to the sergeant role. Knowledge of the methods and operations of burglars and robbers provides the sergeant with requisite information that is respected and valued by subordinate detectives. Because expert power is so critical to the sergeant's role in a detective unit, it would be prudent for police administrators to place people in the unit who have had some experience as detectives. In this way, organizational control is enhanced. The consequence of such a policy would be greater effectiveness and efficiency within the unit.

Tifft further states that the various functional units of a police force allow differing types of power to be developed. He mentions that a patrol sergeant has coercive and legitimate power because of that unit's specific tasks, whereas a tactical unit exhibits high levels of referent, legitimate, and expert power because of its own unique structural design and activities. Traffic sergeants are not able to develop referent and expert bases of power because of the nature of the unit's tasks, the rapid rotation of officers out of the unit, and the minimal types of expertise required to conduct routine traffic investigations. Thus, we would expect that legitimate, reward, and coercive power are the primary tools of compliance available to the traffic sergeant. In addition, as Tifft (1978:100) states, even coercive and reward power may be circumscribed by the ideology, intraorganizational conflicts, and size of the unit.

Stojkovic (1984, 1986) reports similar findings on the expression of power in correctional institutions. He found five types of social power among prisoners: coercive, referent, legitimate, provision of resources, and expert. Coercive power was employed by prisoners in the inmate social system to gain "respect"; referent power was the mechanism of compliance used by various religious groups; legitimate power rested with those inmates who were older and had longer periods of confinement; provision-of-resource power was exhibited by those inmates who could distribute contraband materials, often illegal narcotics; and expert power was found among those prisoners who were knowledgeable about the legal system and could provide legal assistance to other prisoners.

Stojkovic concluded that the social bases of power are much more circumscribed for corrections administrators than for inmates. He found only three types of power among corrections administrators: coercive, reward, and access to information. These bases of power were easily eroded, however, and had limited effectiveness in gaining the compliance of inmates and corrections officers. Prisoners, for example, perceived access-to-information power as the result of active "snitch" recruiting on the part of corrections officials and thus pernicious and destructive to the institutional environment. This finding obviously raises questions about which types of power are more conducive to organizational stability.

Both Stojkovic (1987) and Hepburn (1985) report interesting findings on the power of corrections officers. Hepburn (1985) found that because of significant changes in the administration of prisons and the demographics of prisoners, corrections officers are required to do their jobs much differently today than in the past. Interestingly enough, he does not depict prison guards as solely concerned with punishing or coercing prisoners. He found that both legitimate and expert power were used by corrections officers; that referent and reward bases of power were weak; and that although it was not as prevalent as other types of power, coercive power was used by some guards.

These findings contrast with those of Stojkovic (1987:6–25) in his analysis of power among corrections officers. Although Hepburn (1985) found reward power to be weak among the officers he surveyed, Stojkovic found the reliance on reward power to be strong among corrections officers in his study. This finding is consistent with previous research that suggested that "accommodative relationships" are at the core of the relationship between corrections officers and prisoners (Sykes, 1958:40–62; Sykes & Messinger, 1960). In addition, although Hepburn found that many corrections officers he studied relied on coercive power less than other forms of power, later research suggests that, at least in some parts of the country, this method of gaining compliance among prisoners is still strong (Marquart, 1986b). Future research will have to be conducted to assess accurately the bases of power among corrections officers.

In summary, we have seen that the social bases of power vary from organization to organization and that certain structural characteristics affect the types of power within an organization. The important question becomes: Under what conditions and with what tasks are specific types of power more appropriate than others? We have found that depending on the police unit and function, different types of power are required. Within the institutional corrections system, we have seen how the bases of power differ from group to group. For criminal justice administration, then, the key issue is recognizing the correct type of power for the situation while being aware of the structural constraints of the organization. Obviously, certain types of power are not going to be useful within many criminal justice organizations. Gaining compliance in correctional institutions through purely coercive methods, for example, is doomed to failure because of the nature of the institutional groups. In fact, this type of response was attempted and failed miserably in many correctional institutions (Jacobs, 1977).

This same argument can be applied to the police field. Employing coercive methods of compliance among rank-and-file officers, usually through strict rules and regulations, is no longer satisfactory because many officers are averse to such strategies. In fact, many have called for a loosening of the police organizational structure to make it receptive not only to the changing nature of the police officer but also, and more important, to the role of the police in society. External groups and demands from these groups have also had a tremendous impact on the operating methods of police departments.

In essence, some traditional methods of compliance in criminal justice agencies may not be perceived as legitimate by many criminal justice employees and the general public. Since legitimacy is crucial to effective criminal justice administration, several important management questions remain: What types of power are perceived as legitimate by those who perform criminal justice functions? If improper types of power are employed by criminal justice administrators, what are the end results? These questions lead us to the topic of the next section of this chapter, the connection between the legitimacy of power and political behavior in criminal justice organizations.

The Legitimacy of Power and Political Behavior

According to Tosi, Rizzo, and Carroll (1986:527), "when legitimate authority fails, political behavior arises." *Political behavior* may be defined as any action by a criminal justice worker that promotes individual goals over organizational goals. In their opinion, political behavior exists in organizations when there is (1) a lack of consensus among members about goals, (2) disagreement over the means to achieve goals, or (3) anxiety about resource allocation. Because each of these problems exists within many criminal justice agencies, political behavior among criminal justice employees is inevitable. Let us examine these three problems within correctional institutions, beginning with the lack of goal consensus among corrections staff.

Research in correctional institutions since the 1950s has indicated that disagreement over goals among corrections staff has created not only political behavior but also ineffective operations. This disagreement essentially concerns treatment versus punishment. Is it the purpose of correctional institutions primarily to punish offenders, to rehabilitate them, or both? This debate has not only created conflict about the purpose of imprisonment but, in addition, has raised the issue of whether such conflicting goals can realistically be met within the prison setting. Current research has clearly indicated the variability of attitudes among corrections employees about the real purpose of imprisonment (Klofas & Toch, 1982). This research has also questioned whether there is any public consensus about the primary purpose of our correctional institutions. Lack of agreement, both internally and externally, has created a situation conducive to political behavior. Without the legitimacy engendered by agreement on goals among corrections workers and acceptance of these goals by the public, prescriptive recommendations about the appropriate types of power to be employed in these organizations are of little or no value. The only value in suggesting specific types of power within criminal justice organizations is if they are able to create legitimacy and acceptance among those who work in these organizations.

A similar issue arises in discussing the proper means to achieve the goals agreed on. For years, for example, police organizations have debated the issue of what types of patrolling are the most appropriate, efficient, and effective in achieving the generally accepted goals of crime prevention and societal protection. Whether the debate is over foot patrol versus motorized patrol or one-person cars versus two-person cars, the lack of agreement among police administrators, the general public, and officers on the beat about the appropriate means to achieve these goals has created a climate in which political behavior flourishes. Once again, prescribing proper methods of obtaining compliance within criminal justice organizations becomes pointless when legitimacy is absent. Moreover, in recent times, there have been questions about the appropriate measures to accomplish the goals of crime reduction and community safety.

Both supporters of police and ardent critics have debated what the most effective organizational structure is for police departments. Supporters have suggested that reinforcing the paramilitary structure within police organizations and providing greater resources for aggressive patrol strategies are the most effective ways to guarantee crime reduction and community safety (Bratton, 1996). Others, however, question the long-term utility of such an approach and seek reorganization of police departments to be more consistent with decentralized organizational structures (Goldstein, 1990; Trojanowicz & Bucqueroux, 1990; Fyfe, 1994). These critics suggest that more community-oriented and problem-oriented approaches would be more effective in the reduction of crime and the enhancement of community safety. The debate between these two schools of thought on police structure has caused much opportunity for political behavior to flourish within police departments. In addition, it has produced a situation in many departments where differences among officers, supervisors, and administrators are split along various dimensions, including but not limited to race, educational level, experience level, and gender.

Finally, administrators of criminal justice agencies rely on political behavior when they are not certain about their future budgets. Because criminal justice agencies rely on the public budgeting process and must compete with other social service agencies for funds, it is inevitable that political behavior results. Political behavior, in this instance, may not be bad in and of itself, because it can be useful in acquiring resources for the organization. In fact, political behavior is a very necessary skill for an effective criminal justice administrator to possess. In this case, appropriate political behavior may be viewed as legitimate by not only employees but also by others in the political arena. When the expression of political power is viewed as illegitimate by employees, the public, and significant political figures in the community, it can have a deleterious effect on the organization.

Our purpose in this section is not to speak pejoratively about political behavior in criminal justice organizations, especially as it relates to budgeting. Our purpose is rather to propose some bases of power conducive to the development of legitimate authority in criminal justice organizations that prevent the perpetuation of political behaviors that do not contribute to the effective and efficient operation of these agencies. We begin with an examination of the political processes of criminal justice organizations.

Politics and American Corrections

Partisan politics always has been, is now, and probably always will be inextricably intertwined with corrections in America. This is true in all sectors of the correctional enterprise: local, state, and federal; institutional and community based; juvenile and adult; and public and private.

Its shortcomings and vulnerabilities notwithstanding, the political character of American corrections increases the likelihood that the values and preferences of the citizenry will be reflected in: (1) the prioritization corrections receives compared to other public interests (for example, law enforcement, education, transportation, health care) and (2) the nature, extent, and management of correctional programs. The primary clients of our correctional programs are not our inmates, probationers, or parolees, but rather the taxpaying populace who pay for the programs and depend upon them for their personal safety and peace of mind. The astute correctional administrator does not confront politicians as opponents, but rather approaches them as potential allies in defining and implementing correctional programs that are in the public's best interests.

Here are four suggestions for the correctional executive who strives to work collaboratively with his jurisdiction's political establishment:

1. Be a leader. Whether or not they say it in so many words, and whether or not they even realize it, politicians across the land are looking to the corrections profession for answers to crowding, cost containment, and other pressing issues that plague it. Correctional executives need to be ready to respond. They need to be leaders, not just managers.

2. Bring them in. Politicians cannot understand correctional problems by simply reading flip charts, computer printouts, annual reports, and newspaper accounts. They must experience corrections. These visitors should be walked through cells, dayrooms, booking and receiving areas, classrooms, kitchen and laundry facilities, medical facilities, and recreation areas. They should be fed an inmate meal and encouraged to talk with both prisoners and officers. They will be more knowledgeable and sensitive participants in attempts to resolve correctional problems because they have gone beyond detached media coverage and agency reporting to sensually "experience" corrections first hand.

3. Determine what is in it for them. Politicians will be more likely to get involved and be supportive if they perceive that they will benefit by their involvement. Too often, corrections officials couch their request for support in terms of their own benefits (for example, better staff/inmate ratios, more spacious facilities for inmate programs) instead of the benefits to be realized by the legislators or county commissioners to whom their requests are directed (for example, reduced liability exposure, reduced capital expenditures, reduced life-cycle operating costs, increased public safety). Those benefits should be clearly defined and brought to politicians' attention.

4. Demeanor is important. A vague, imprecise, and rambling delivery during a presentation to a legislative body is likely to turn legislators off. A specific, precise, well-organized, and relatively brief presentation is more likely to spark their interest or at least not alienate them.

Politics is an unavoidable and desirable ingredient of American corrections. Prudent correctional leaders do not fight the political system, but rather work within it to their, and hopefully the public's, advantage.

RICHARD G. KIEKBUSCH

Associate Professor of Criminology

University of Texas–Permian Basin

Past President, American Jail Association

Dalton (1959) suggests that the diffusion of types of power in organizations produces a concomitant rise of powerful cliques or coalitions. These cliques defend their members in response to various threats to organizational autonomy. Pfeffer (1981:36) points out that such cliques and coalitions are highly political, relying on various strategies to advance their own purposes and causes over those of other coalitions in the organization. This political nature of coalitions and their power configurations are relevant to decision-making processes in organizations (March, 1962; Kaufman, 1964; Allison, 1969; Pandarus, 1973). More important, these political behaviors erode employees' sense of legitimacy and may lead to a number of dysfunctional behaviors in the organization.

Such results are nowhere more apparent than in the agencies of criminal justice. Prisons, for example, have been fragmented along interest-group lines for many years, both internally and externally (Stastny & Tyrnauer, 1982). Because inmates, corrections officers, and administrators have been traditionally alienated from one another, prisons have been ineffective in accomplishing many of their goals. This observation is consistent with our previous observation that lack of consensus among groups in an organization reduces legitimacy and engenders political behavior. Only by obtaining consensus can the issues of means to achieve goals and resource allocation be resolved.

Many similar observations can be made in police systems. Much research has been done since the 1960s on management models for effective police supervision; volumes of research have discussed how police supervisors should manage their subordinates. Yet much basic disagreement remains about what police should be doing and what methods are the most effective for the accomplishment of their goals. We can speculate that because of a lack of consensus on goals, disagreement over what means should be applied to achieve those goals that are agreed upon, and uncertainty over resource allocation, police organizations are prime places for political behavior to occur. In fact, much of the research on police socialization is, in effect, research on the political actions or behaviors of police officers, for example, police corruption.

Similarly, organizational behavioral research has demonstrated how competition for scarce resources among both employees and departments within organizations inevitably leads toward political behavior, but it also suggests that where great uncertainty exists about decision-making procedures and performance measures among employees, there is a high probability that political behavior will flourish (Beeman & Sharkey, 1987). Again, criminal justice organizations tend to have both of these characteristics. These organizations are, therefore, fertile ground for political behavior.

Is political behavior only a function of situational or structural characteristics of criminal justice organizations? Hellriegel, Slocum, and Woodman (1995) suggest that certain personality traits make some people more prone to exercising political behaviors in organizations. These four personality traits are the need for power, Machiavellianism, locus of control, and risk-seeking propensity. The *need for power* is a common trait among both effective and noneffective leaders. Depending upon what the leader desires, this may or may not be an effective trait. Leaders who seek simply to dominate others through expressions of power will create climates where political behavior is more likely than those leaders who seek power to move employees toward some identifiable and acceptable levels of performance.

Machiavellianism is predicated on the ideas of manipulation and deceit. Administrators who exhibit this trait view political behavior as a prerequisite to effective leadership. Such a trait accentuates manipulation of employees for specific ends and, in the long run, perpetuates greater division among employees and between employees and administrators.

Locus of control refers to an individual's ability to control his or her fate within an organization. Persons with a high *internal locus* believe they are able to control and influence other people and their surroundings. Political behavior is simply an expression of that high internal locus, willfully expressed.

Similarly, individuals with a high propensity for *risk taking* are much more likely to engage in political behavior than those individuals with a low risk-taking propensity. These persons view risk taking as a necessity within a politically charged organization. They enjoy taking the risks and acting out the political behavior that is a necessary element of taking risks. Risk taking is highly correlated with desired states or goals among risk takers.

These four personality traits, again, are not necessarily bad, yet more often than not they can produce deleterious political behavior. Such traits must be assessed as effective or ineffective dependent upon what the person exercising them is seeking. In criminal justice administrators, political behaviors can be evaluated on the basis of whether or not they are directed toward the long-term interests of the organization or the narrow interests of the supervisor, manager, or administrator. If the latter is the predominant perception among employees, then they will view their superior's political behavior in a negative light. If, however, the political behavior is understood as unifying employees toward legitimate objectives and goals of the organization, then employees will interpret the political behavior as positive for the organization. The leader's personality traits and concomitant political behaviors must be understood within this context. In some cases, being able to control those personality traits that lead toward adverse political behaviors is a true test of a criminal justice administrator. In other cases, the proper exercising of these traits is useful and desirable within criminal justice organizations and is viewed as legitimate by criminal justice employees.

Effective Types of Power

The critical question becomes: What types of power are criminal justice employees most likely to consider legitimate? Borrowing from the work of Tosi, Rizzo, and Carroll (1986:540–542), we can identify the psychological effects of specific types of power on individuals, as represented in Figure 10-1. In this model, the five bases of power correspond to the French and Raven (1968) typology, examined previously in the chapter. (Charismatic power is analogous to French and Raven's referent power.) There are three possible effects of these types of power: (1) the exercise of legitimate, charismatic, and expert power leads to employee acceptance; (2) reward and coercive power may lead to acceptance if the power is used for some legitimate purpose; or (3) reward and coercive power may lead to two dysfunctional effects—learned helplessness and resistance—if the power is used for illegitimate purposes. For example,

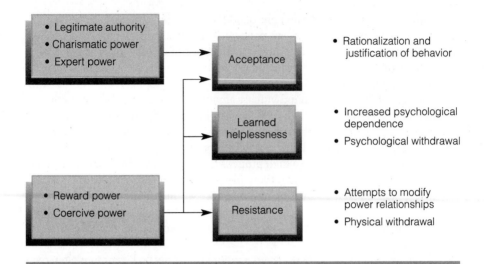

FIGURE 10-1   The Psychological Effects of the Use of Power in Organizations (From H. L. Tosi, J. R. Rizzo, and S. J. Carroll, *Managing Organizational Behavior.* Copyright © 1986 by Pitman Publishing Company. Reprinted by permission of Harper & Row Publishers, Inc.)

when a police sergeant employs coercive power to motivate an officer, the officer perceives this use of power as having a legitimate purpose and therefore accepts it.

This model also stresses ancillary effects of power exercised in organizations, all of which are relevant to criminal justice administration. Although legitimate, charismatic, and expert bases of power lead to acceptance from employees, this acceptance leads to the rationalization and justification of the behavior. In short, the power recipient legitimizes, understands, and accepts the directives of the supervisor. When learned helplessness and resistance are the effects, there is increased psychological dependence, psychological withdrawal, attempts to modify power relationships, and possible physical withdrawal from the organization. These effects may be manifested through appeals to reason by the power recipient to the power holder, minimal compliance, sabotage, development of a counterforce, and departure from the organization. All are common reactions to power expression in criminal justice organizations, and their frequency may decrease the efficiency and effectiveness of these organizations.

Many researchers have suggested that prisons are prime breeding grounds not only for the political behavior mentioned previously but also for the dysfunctional behaviors associated with coercive and reward types of power. It is all too common in the literature on prisons to see that both inmates and corrections staff, suffering from learned helplessness, ultimately withdraw from the institution in either a psychological or a physical sense. In fact, stress among corrections employees and prisoners is a central concern among prison administrators. Many of these characteristics may be, in part, reactions to the exercise of coercive power by supervisors in these organizations. More directly, much of what we know about social systems in prisons can be tied to the illegitimacy of current types of power exercised by both corrections administrators and officers. The inmate social system may represent a counterforce to the power of those in command of the organization.

These effects of the use of power are seen equally in police organizations. Much current research has explored the problems associated with the traditional police structure. We are arguing here that the types of power traditionally associated with that structure are, in part, the cause of resistance, most notably the development of a police counterforce and of departures from the organization. The research literature has documented the development of subcultures in police organizations that may oppose the formal structure or may be mechanisms for adapting to the formal structure and its methods of gaining compliance among officers. In addition, the high turnover in many police departments can be tied to the types of power exercised by supervisors.

However, if legitimate, charismatic, and expert bases of power lead to acceptance among employees, as shown in Figure 10-1, then it would seem logical to attempt to employ these uses of power in our criminal justice organizations. A body of research supports this position. Etzioni (1961) suggests that organizations enjoy a high level of commitment from members if they are involved in the organization, which they cannot be if coercive and reward power are used. Current research reports similar findings. The amount of control exhibited by employees in their organization is directly related to compliance to organizational rules and regulations (Houghland, Shepard, & Wood, 1979; Houghland & Wood, 1980; Styskal, 1980). In effect, as the organization is legitimized by subordinates, it gains compliance from them.

Much can be said about the value of instilling a sense of legitimacy in criminal justice employees. As we have seen, political behavior tends to surface in organizations where legitimacy is not present. Such seems to be the case in many criminal justice organizations; to suggest otherwise would be naive. The future of criminal justice administration hinges to a great degree on how legitimacy will be gained from both subordinates and the general public. The use of other methods of compliance in these organizations is just one avenue that deserves attention by those who administer our agencies of social control. The traditional types of power employed in these agencies no longer promote effective administration. Other bases of power would seem to be conducive to criminal justice management. We can only speculate about what these other bases would be. It is easy to say that legitimate, expert, and referent bases of power need to be developed, yet this statement assumes that we have goal congruity, methods to achieve goals, and certainty about budget allocations in these organizations. Attention must be given to these problems if effective compliance structures in criminal justice organizations are to be created. We can then develop bases of power that are consistent with our objectives and, more important, are perceived as legitimate by the lay public and by those who perform the day-to-day tasks in criminal justice agencies.

Moreover, we must concern ourselves with the role that political behaviors play in criminal justice administration. As one of our chapter opening quotes indicates, some criminal justice employees and administrators believe that "everything is politics." This cynical view exists at two levels within criminal justice organizations. At the first level, it is understood as part of a larger political process that dictates and directs how criminal justice organizations will function. For many criminal justice administrators, political behavior means playing politics with legislators, public interest groups, governor's staff, unions, and other interested parties. This type of activity comes with the territory of being a criminal justice administrator, yet as we proceed into the 21st century, many criminal justice administrators express the concern that politics and political interests have too much influence on the daily operations of their organizations. Such a view of politics suggests that it is too invasive and pervasive in criminal justice organizations and negatively affects the ability of administrators and managers to do their jobs effectively. (See Lehr & O'Neill, 2001 for a fascinating account of how "bad politics" influenced the FBI in its dealing with Boston organized crime figures.) This is a legitimate concern among criminal justice administrators, yet it is not clear how this situation can be altered.

Given the public nature of criminal justice organizations, political influences will always shape how these entities perform their duties. At this level, the criminal justice administrator will have to develop and hone his or her political skills in such a way that protection of organizational turf is possible while simultaneously attending to their concerns. This means becoming more politically astute and active in the determination of their fates. Too often criminal justice administrators have shown passive attention to political detail. Such a strategy will no longer attend to either the needs of the organization or the concerns of individual employees. As a consequence, playing politics may not be a bad thing for criminal justice administrators at this level. In fact, it is a necessity.

At a second level, however, political behavior within criminal justice organizations may be detrimental to long-term stability and functioning if that behavior is too removed from the concerns of employees who perform the routine tasks of the organization. Herein lies a fundamental disjuncture between the interests of employees (typically centered on accomplishing tasks) and administrators (centered on political concerns of their bosses or significant others). At the administrator level, employees view playing politics as a dirty process. A common sentiment among employees is that their interests are often sacrificed for larger political interests. At this level the expression of power is most felt by criminal justice workers. Not only must administrators display effective uses of power that are legitimized by subordinates, but these expressions of power must also be understood as having a political dimension. Effective criminal justice administration means being sensitive not only to the political demands of external interests, but showing concern for the constraints and difficulties experienced by subordinates. The exercising of differing forms of power are clear examples of where priorities lie for criminal justice administrators.

Not to recognize the importance of the way expressions of power fall along these two dimensions is a critical error commonly made by those who administer criminal justice organizations. Criminal justice administrators, supervisors, and managers must stay aware of this two-dimensional perspective on power. Only through such awareness will they fully appreciate the effective use of power.

Summary

This chapter described types of authority and power in organizations and how they produce specific consequences for organizational members. The discussion suggested that the types of power found in many criminal justice organizations produce effects that are, in the long run, dysfunctional. We further suggested that certain types of power may be more useful than others to administrators of criminal justice organizations. These types of power were legitimate, expert, and referent. But they can be effective as compliance mechanisms only when other key issues of goal consensus, means to achieve goals, and resource allocation are addressed.

We suggested that a proper compliance structure may not yet exist for many agencies of criminal justice. Given the nature of their tasks and the expectations of society, criminal justice management must decide on proper compliance structures for their organizations. Finally, criminal justice administrators must grasp the two-dimensional nature of power expression within their organizations. Without a proper consideration of this issue, criminal justice agencies will remain in conflict. Conflict in organizations is the topic of the following chapter, which concludes our examination of group behavior in criminal justice organizations.

Case Study

The Corrections Officer's Dilemma: Who Has the Power in the Joint?

Nantucket Prison, built well before the beginning of the 19th century, was the end-of-the-line prison in a state correctional system that was overcrowded and under-funded. Besides housing some 200 inmates above its rated capacity, the prison was run by gangs with such authority that corrections officers often feared for their lives and did not have any ideas on how to interact with them effectively. This situation changed when veteran Robert Stones was transferred from the state's small camp system to the prison. Stones had been in corrections for almost twenty years and understood how to deal with inmates or, in his words, "deal with the inmate mentality." He was viewed by Warden Jimmy Johnson as someone who could train the corrections officers to deal effectively with inmates.

The corrections officers were hesitant and somewhat uncertain about what Stones could teach them that they did not already know. Stones emphasized that his real value to the institution would be training the new officers. Warden Johnson agreed that Stones should work with the young corps of officers who were receptive to his ideas of dealing with inmates. The first corrections officer assigned to work with Stones was a new recruit named James Bowers. Bowers had a background in community-based corrections and knew about how former inmates, those on parole, reacted to authority. Because much of what he knew was community oriented, Stones wondered whether Bowers understood what prison life was about, even though he had been to prison transporting parolees who had their paroles revoked. Knowing that what Bowers learned he would tell the other officers, Stones was methodical in his training.

"The first thing you have to remember, Bowers, is that prisoners run the joint," said Stones. "Even more important is the fact that inmates could take over a prison any time they wanted, and that is why you have to understand where the powerful inmates are coming from." Somewhat bewildered by Stones's statement, Bowers asked, "If inmates run the prison, what the hell kind of role do corrections officers have in this process? What are we, just babysitters for these guys?" With a smile, Stones responded, "Well, to a degree, and with some inmates we are nothing but babysitters.

But you have to recognize that inmates do have a say about their incarceration. Forget the idea that we have total power here. Most of what we do is compromising. You got to compromise." Bowers did not know how to respond, but he remembered Stones's suggestions and thought them over.

Three months later, he had his first chance to use them. It was an ordinary day in cellblock C when Officer Bowers noticed three inmates cornered in the maintenance room. His initial response was to go over and break up the inmates. Seeing what Bowers was going to do, Stones stopped him and suggested that he make sure other inmates in the cellblock were ready for lunch. Later in the day Bowers asked Stones why he prevented him from breaking up the inmates. Stones responded, "Those three inmates were making a deal for some marijuana, and the white guy was the dealer. He has a lot of power in here, and I respect him and his position." He added, "He distributes the dope, and I let him, while at the same time he controls the disruptive inmates in the block. We have our little deals that keep this place running. Now I want you to know that it's not a lot of dope, just enough to keep the prisoners happy."

Bowers could not believe what he had heard. He responded angrily, "How can you let such things go on in the prison? We have to have greater control." With a grin on his face, Stones replied, "We have control because of what I do. It gets back to what I said earlier—that you have to respect the fact that some inmates have power in this prison and that pushing dope is one type of activity that gives them power."

Bowers responded that he thought this type of dealing with inmates was dangerous in the long run because it caused fights and violence among prisoners. But Stones reaffirmed that his dealing with powerful inmates who distributed marijuana was essential to the stability of the prison. He added that control problems with inmates in the past were related to the inability of officers to recognize the power that prisoners have in the prison and that power can be expressed in a number of ways, including the selling of dope.

"Now I don't want you to get the wrong idea," said Stones. "I don't think that we should let these guys do whatever they want in here, but there has to be a recognition by the officers that dope peddling gives some guys a lot of power and that it has been in prison for a long time and will continue to be around. The fact is that we can't get rid of all of it; we can only hope to control it. The same is true of those religious leaders in here. Do you think those Muslim leaders get what they want from these other inmates and officers? You bet they do, and it's all because they are respected by a lot of the inmates. To do our jobs, we have to deal with the realities of the prison." Officer Bowers responded, "Is it the same way with the gang leaders in here?"

"Now you're catching on, kid. It's like the inmates say—you have to give a man respect if you want respect from him," answered Stones.

Officer Bowers went home that night and thought through what Officer Stones had said to him. He concluded that prison stability might depend not only on the power of inmates but also on how officers use their own power among inmates. Later that night a statement Stones had made to him three months earlier rang through his head: Remember, Bowers, inmates run the joint.

Case Study Questions

1. What types of power do you believe would be the most effective in gaining control of Nantucket Prison?

2. Do you think Stones is effective as a corrections officer in his interaction with prisoners? If so, why? If not, why not?

3. What are some problems with negotiating with prisoners to maintain control of a prison? Will negotiating give corrections officers increased legitimacy among prisoners? Is that good or bad for the prison? Why or why not?

For Discussion

1. Of the types of power described in this chapter, which do you think is the most relevant to a specific agency of the criminal justice system? Are the types of power exhaustive, or can you think of others besides the French and Raven typology presented here? Describe the strengths and weaknesses of this typology in criminal justice organizations.

2. What do you believe is the role of power in criminal justice administration? Is power important to agencies of criminal justice? What kind of power? Is it critical to have power as a criminal justice manager, and, if so, should this power be internally or externally based? Finally, describe instances where criminal justice administrators have abused their power, and offer suggestions about how we can control these individuals.

3. Distinguish between power and authority. Do you believe the foundation of criminal justice organizations is power or authority? Why? Give examples in everyday criminal justice life that reflect the differences among these concepts.

4. Discuss the role of politics in criminal justice organizations. Is politics critical to these organizations, and, if so, how should it be controlled? Is it true, as Long said years ago, that "politics is the lifeblood of administration" (1949:257) in public agencies like criminal justice organizations? Comment on the relevance of power to criminal justice administration and the survival of criminal justice organizations.

5. Is political behavior too pervasive within criminal justice organizations? Do legislatures, public interests, and private interests have too much influence on the organizations of criminal justice? If so, what would you recommend to alter such a situation? Provide some suggestions.

For Further Reading

Culbert, S. A., and McDonough, J. J. *Radical Management: Power Politics and the Pursuit of Trust.* New York: Free Press, 1985.

Kotter, J. P. *Power and Influence.* New York: Free Press, 1985.

Lehr, D. and O'Neill, G. *Black Mass: The True Story of an Unholy Alliance Between the FBI and the Irish Mob.* New York: HarperCollins, 2001.

Mintzberg, H. *Power In and Around Organizations.* Englewood Cliffs, NJ: Prentice-Hall, 1983.

Pfeffer, J. *Power in Organizations.* Marshfield, MA: Pitman, 1981.

Srivastva, S. (Ed.) *Executive Power: How Executives Influence People and Organizations.* San Francisco: Jossey-Bass, 1986.

CHAPTER

11

ORGANIZATIONAL
CONFLICT

Once the conflict began, the spiteful and invidious nature of the interpersonal and intergroup behaviors created an organizational paranoia that was very contagious and difficult to treat. What makes this case even more serious is that it is not atypical in its dynamics when compared to other cases of conflict in correctional institutions. However, there is very little information about how to deal with such conflict. Until more is known about this kind of organizational problem in human service organizations, a great deal of public employee time, energy, and commitment, in addition to taxpayers' dollars, will continue to be wasted on inefficient and ineffective programs.

(Duffee, 1986:270)

Conflict is frequently, but not always, negatively valued by organization members. To the extent that conflict is valued negatively, minor conflicts generate pressures toward resolution without altering the relationship; and major conflicts generate pressures to alter the form of the relationship or to dissolve it altogether. If inducements for participation are sufficiently high, there is the possibility of chronic conflict in the context of a stable relationship.

(Pondy, 1985:389)

Managing conflict is my job. When something goes wrong, the thunderbolt from the Governor's office goes through my office to the regional office and onto the district office. From there it proceeds to the supervisor and finally the heat is felt by the lowly worker. He/she has to deal with the conflict that ensues. If we do not work together to deal with the conflict beginning with the upper levels of the department, the employee at the bottom of the organization is going to feel manipulated and frustrated. My primary concern is that conflict among employees and between employees and offenders and employees and the community does not get out of hand. Managing this conflict is one of the most important things I do as director of the Department of Corrections.

(Director James Gomez, California Department of Corrections, January 1996, speaking to employees at a graduation ceremony of the Leadership Institute)

The dynamic quality of a fragmented criminal justice system promotes a balance of power between antagonistic interests as it encourages adaptation and change. As societal attitudes and values fluctuate, the system can make corresponding changes. Unification would limit the ability of components to adjust their outputs to specific individual cases, to changes that occur over time and to overreactions and mistakes by other components. Furthermore, the balance which (sic) results from the exertion of influence on components by other components would be limited.

(Wright, 1999).

This chapter addresses a subject that many academics, practitioners, and policy makers interested in criminal justice find perplexing—the process of conflict in criminal justice organizations. We have all worked in organizations and have experienced conflict, whether it is disagreement with the boss about our work assignment or about the overall direction of the organization. Conflict is endemic to all organizations, including those in the criminal justice system. This chapter examines conflict in criminal justice organizations by exploring several topics.

First, we define conflict in organizations and examine the stages in a conflict episode. We describe what conflict in criminal justice organizations means and, more important, the process of conflict. We should then be able to understand why conflict exists in criminal justice organizations and the complex dynamics associated with the conflict process.

Second, we explore the types of conflict behaviors exhibited by people in organizations. In this section of the chapter, our discussion focuses on existing knowledge from the literature on organizational behavior about the process of conflict in organizations and applies these ideas to the operations of criminal justice organizations.

Third, we examine the topic of conflict management, suggesting various interventions and exploring the dimensions of conflict outcome. We suggest also that a proper analysis of conflict and its resolution must consider how conflict reaches well beyond the borders of individual criminal justice organizations.

Finally, the chapter concludes with a discussion of the role of conflict in criminal justice organizations and how conflict management can enhance the effectiveness of these organizations.

Conflict Defined

Like other topics this book has explored, the idea of conflict is one that is intuitively understood yet technically difficult to assess or measure. For this reason, researchers interested in conflict in organizations often employ a number of different conceptualizations. Conflict is defined as a dynamic process in which two or more individuals in an organization interact in such a way as to produce "conflict episodes" that may or may not lead to hostile behaviors (Pondy, 1985:383). Pondy, for example, suggests four ways in which conflict can be understood in organizations. First, researchers often explore the antecedent conditions of conflict, such as resource scarcity, policy differences, and disagreements concerning preferred outcomes for the organization. When, for example, a treatment specialist does not agree with an immediate correctional supervisor on inmate supervision, the disagreement may be a precursor to conflict between subordinate and supervisor. This is the classic goal conflict that occurs within correctional institutions. In this example, the treatment specialist may believe that the primary goal of the institution should be the treatment of offenders, whereas the correctional supervisor may hold that security concerns of the institution override treatment programming.

Second, conflict in organizations can be understood as producing affective states in workers, such as stress, hostility, or anxiety. In our example, a corrections officer who is upset by what she perceives as an incorrect policy choice by the immediate supervisor may experience a great deal of stress as a consequence and ultimately become dysfunctional to the organization. Much of the research on stress in criminal justice organizations may reflect the worker's inability to deal effectively with a conflict situation in the workplace. The examination of stress among criminal justice employees may thus require an exploration of the conflict process in those organizations. For this reason, perhaps, criminal justice organizations have introduced conflict management seminars for their employees.

Third, conflict can be viewed from the individual employee's cognitive states. Once again, in our corrections officer example, the officer may or may not be aware of the conflict she has with the supervisor. Researchers interested in conflict processes in organizations have examined employees' awareness of conflict in their organizations and the degree to which it influences their behavior. We may, for example, survey corrections officers and ask them whether they perceive conflict situations in their work and how they deal with these situations. Corrections officers are, in fact, good at adapting to or accommodating the conflict inherent in their roles. As Lipsky (1988) suggests, much of what street-level bureaucrats, such as police officers and corrections officers, accomplish they do through a series of accommodations (Stojkovic, 1990). Similar findings have been found among criminal justice administrators (Stojkovic, 1995). We would add that these accommodations may be in reaction to the conflict situations they face.

Fourth, conflict in organizations has been examined by exploring the conflict behavior itself, whether it is passive resistance or outright confrontational or aggressive behavior. Many researchers interested in correctional institutions can understand this form of conflict research because of the voluminous material on the nature of disturbances or riots in correctional institutions. Much of the research has examined the etiology of these riots (Barak-Glantz, 1985; DiIulio, 1987; Useem & Kimball, 1989).

Types of Conflict

We can identify four types of conflict in organizations, each of which requires a different adjustment mechanism. They are personal conflict, group conflict, intraorganizational conflict, and interorganizational conflict. (See Chapter 8 for a discussion of goal conflict.)

Personal Conflict

Personal conflict exists within the individual and usually is some form of goal conflict or cognitive conflict. Typically, this form of conflict results from failed expectations. For example, a young police officer who holds certain ideals about the police profession may find that many of them are not consistent with the reality of the police role or the police organization. He may feel a great deal of personal conflict because he cannot reconcile his own expectations with those of his superiors. In short, he may feel what Festinger (1957) refers to as "cognitive dissonance."

To deal with this conflict, the young police officer may change his expectations to bring them in line with the organization's expectations, or he may seek to understand the conflict and thereby reduce its impact on him. Whatever his decision, it will affect his future behavior. In the extreme case, the officer may decide to leave the organization because he cannot resolve his personal conflict. For this reason, conflict-management programs, which we discuss later in the chapter, are critical to criminal justice organizations.

Group Conflict

Group conflict occurs in organizations when individual members disagree on some point of common interest. The resolution of the conflict is essential to the survival of the group and may even enhance the effectiveness of the group in the long run. Take, for example, a group of police officers who work in a patrol unit. A conflict arises because of a disagreement over ticket writing. The department has formal expectations about the number of tickets the group is supposed to issue, but the officers have their own norms, which are different. Conflict occurs because some officers in the group believe that the expectations of their superiors override the group's informally derived expectations. The ensuing conflict can improve the coordination and communication processes of the group by forcing them to be cohesive and coordinated in determining an acceptable level of ticket writing. Obviously, if the conflict escalates too far, possibly because proper conflict resolution techniques are not employed, then the group may disintegrate. Group conflict can also be healthy and productive if it is properly handled by the immediate supervisor. In our example, the sergeant can use certain techniques to benefit the group in the long term.

Another form of group conflict is *intergroup conflict,* in which groups within an organization compete for valuable and limited resources. If we look at police organizations and examine the multiple groups within them, we can see why intergroup conflict exists. Many police departments are composed of functional units—patrol, detective, vice, juvenile, and traffic—each with its own objectives and tasks. Given differing tasks and finite resources, it is common for conflict situations to arise. If, for example, the detective unit is favored by the chief and given the most resources, conflict is likely to ensue. The other units may perceive the chief's favoritism toward the detective unit as an unfair advantage and request increased allocations for their own units. In this example, the chief may resolve the conflict by providing good reasons for giving more resources to the detective unit than to the other units. However, if the other units believe that the explanation is inadequate, the conflict may escalate.

When the conflict among the competing units does escalate, the police chief can use the competition among the groups as a mechanism to engender improved performance. Thus, intergroup conflict may be healthy for the organization. An example of this type of administrative use of competition was documented by Arthur Schlesinger (1958) in his analysis of the presidency of Franklin Delano Roosevelt. Roosevelt was able to use the conflict generated by competing governmental units to control information about the workings of the federal bureaucracy while simultaneously generating improved levels of performance among subordinates. This method of conflict management may be effective, but if particular units continually fail in the process, they may become demoralized and assume a defeatist attitude that will be detrimental to the organization in the long term. If it escalates too far, intergroup conflict can be counterproductive. In our example, the competition among the different police units must be monitored to ensure that it remains effective and beneficial.

Intraorganizational Conflict

While group conflict deals with the relationships within and between groups in organizations, *intraorganizational* conflict is generated by the structural makeup of an organization—that is, by formal authority in the organization and how it is delegated. There are four major types of intraorganizational conflict: vertical conflict, horizontal conflict, line-staff conflict, and role conflict (Hellriegel, Slocum, & Woodman, 1995).

Vertical Conflict. *Vertical conflict* exists between workers at different levels in an organizational hierarchy. Within a department of corrections, for example, corrections officers sit below sergeants, sergeants sit below lieutenants, and so forth—a paramilitary model that makes vertical conflict an inevitable event as superiors try to control the behavior of officers. The relationship between corrections officers and prisoners is so tenuous that conflict usually ensues whenever superiors try to tell officers how to relate to inmates. This perceived encroachment by supervisors on officers' jobs is the antecedent condition for conflict. In fact, a body of knowledge about corrections work supports the vertical nature of conflict in correctional institutions, not only between supervisor and subordinate but also between inmate and officer (see Lombardo, 1981; Crouch & Marquart, 1989; Johnson, 2002). Whatever the location, it would be fair to say that vertical conflict is ubiquitous within correctional institutions. Similar research findings support widespread vertical conflict in police organizations (Angell, 1971:19–29; Mastrofski, 1991).

Horizontal Conflict. *Horizontal conflict* is exhibited by units that are at the same hierarchical level in an organization. Our previous example of conflict among the various units in a police department can also be understood as an example of horizontal conflict. If the multiple police units are of equal rank, then the conflict is horizontal. If, however, they are not at the same hierarchical level in the organization, the conflict is vertical.

Horizontal conflict is most evident when there is too much concern for task accomplishments within one unit. If the juvenile unit, for example, seeks increased resources for its investigation of gang-related activities and the arrests of gang members, granting the request may work against the larger purpose of the unit and the department—to maintain order in society. This overemphasis on gang-related activity may produce conflict with other units because they perceive the activities of the juvenile unit to be counter to their own goals—for example, the public relations unit or the crime prevention unit may be trying to establish positive ties with gang members—or because they feel the activity wastes finite departmental resources.

Line-Staff Conflict. *Line-staff conflict* is readily apparent in public organizations, where staff personnel are used to augment and supplement the work of line managers. Criminal justice agencies also have support personnel who work with line managers to accomplish the objectives of the organization. Such people as legal advisors in police organizations or treatment and medical personnel in correctional institutions are good examples. The line-staff distinction in correctional institutions is a noteworthy one because it has generated much conflict between traditional security

Say "Yes" to Conflict Within Your Organization

When I was asked to write my thoughts on "conflict" within a criminal justice setting, my immediate thought, as chairperson of the Parole Commission, was that I don't write about conflict, I cause it. From my perspective, organizational conflict is a normal process that helps promote change within the organization. Conflict and conflict management help tone the organization, requiring it to be responsive to the dynamic, ever-changing world we live in.

Even though conflict is inherent in any organizational system, it appears to emanate both from the role of the chairperson and the need for the chairperson to serve as a lightning rod for conflict in the criminal justice system. Areas where conflict exists with a new chairperson include:

- The Parole Commission staff: New ideas, new approaches, goals to streamline the overall process as well as be responsive to overcrowding and the needs of victims and victim's families have all resulted in conflict, planning, and change.

- The media: The Parole Commission is an easy target; the expectation is that the commission should not have released any offender who exhibits further criminal behavior. It is clearly the responsibility of the Parole Commission to give release authorization, but predicting human behavior many years into the future is not possible.

- The general public: Polls seem to indicate that the public in general requires only one thing from the Parole Commission: that is, do not release anyone. With spiraling costs and an opportunity to discuss alternatives in focus groups, however, the public will often view options within the criminal justice system.

- Probation and parole staff and intensive sanctions staff: These staffs expect more from incarceration than is possible, given the limited resources of treatment programs, particularly the resource of incarceration "time."

- The institution staff: This staff has had to change its understanding and expectations on how role assignments should be performed, given the overcrowding within the correctional institutions.

- Victims and their families: One would expect that conflict with the Parole Commission would relate only to "time," but victims and victim's families, like any group, can be placed on a continuum in terms of their expectations of the criminal justice system and their need for punishment. The primary conflict with victims and victim's families has been attempting to make the system understandable, accessible, and open to feedback.

- Inmates: Here conflict has been as varied as one would probably expect from 8,500 inmates. It may be a required program, length of time, classification level, or an individual parole decision.

- Judges, district attorneys, public defenders: A combination of both role ambiguity and role conflict exists with these groups, and conflict management must be focused on education, communication, and a more collaborative effort toward agreed-upon goals.

- Advocacy groups: Advocacy groups such as Families of Murdered Children, Victims of Violent Offenses, and Mothers Against Drunk Driving challenge the role of the Parole Commission but serve an important role in changing the system through a planned and deliberate conflict approach.

- Community and institution treatment programs: One of the primary areas of concern among treatment providers appeared to be their desire to have a "better clientele." It is as if the Parole Commission was keeping good and responsive inmates hidden and sending them only the most difficult clients.

All the areas and groups mentioned have helped mold my behavior and actions to be an effective chairperson. I hope that I have molded the behaviors of these groups in turn by my interaction and persistent communication to encourage mutual understanding of our roles, expectations, and objectives.

JOHN HUSZ, SUPERINTENDENT
Milwaukee Secure Detention Facility
Former Chairperson
Wisconsin Parole Commission

personnel and those whose goals are treatment and physical care. Like correctional institutions, police organizations have much conflict between line personnel and staff. The most notable causes of these conflicts are the line personnel's perception that staff workers are trying to assume authority over basic line functions, the inability of the two groups to communicate effectively, the claim that staff people take the credit for successful programs yet are quick to point the finger of blame at line personnel when something goes wrong, and the claim that line personnel do not believe that staff people see the "big picture" of a specific program (Swanson, Territo, & Taylor, 1993).

Role Conflict. *Role conflict* is probably the most common in criminal justice organizations. Role conflict occurs when an individual is not able to comprehend or accomplish assigned tasks. The source of the conflict may be faulty communication between subordinate and supervisor, disagreement between the subordinate and the supervisor about the tasks required, conflicting expectations from differing supervisors, or differing expectations among the groups the subordinate belongs to as to the role of the subordinate. Regardless of its causes, role conflict as a form of intraorganizational conflict has been documented extensively in the criminal justice literature. (See Philliber's [1987] review of the literature on role conflict among corrections officers.)

Role conflict and role ambiguity are not the same. *Role ambiguity* occurs when a subordinate perceives that information about the required tasks of the job is unclear and inconsistent, whereas role conflict occurs when a subordinate perceives incompatible expectations about how the tasks should be performed. In other words, role ambiguity denotes inconsistencies in the knowledge needed to complete a job, and role conflict denotes inconsistencies about what is expected of the subordinate. It would be fair to say that criminal justice employees frequently experience both role conflict and role ambiguity in their jobs.

Finally, we must comment on the effects of role conflict in criminal justice organizations. Research has suggested that role conflict in both correctional institutions and police departments is not only widespread, but may also lead to many other problems experienced by both these organizations, including high turnover, absenteeism, and low morale. (See Alpert and Dunham [1997] for a good review of these problems in police organizations.) In particular, role conflict can be traced to stress found in police organizations. We know, for example, that people can react in a number of ways to role conflict, including being aggressive toward superiors, attempting to reduce conflict by communicating effectively with superiors, and withdrawing from the organization. Withdrawal is a reaction that is seen too often in criminal justice organizations. Thus, future research needs to provide concrete suggestions about how role conflict can be reduced.

Interorganizational Conflict

Interorganizational conflict occurs when different organizational units share a common purpose but disagree about how that purpose will be achieved. This type of conflict arises when a separate organizational unit (such as one component of the criminal justice system) perceives its goals and objectives to be in conflict with those of other units. Take, for example, the jail and its links to other components of the criminal justice system. The jail has as its central task the control of two offender populations: pretrial detainees (people awaiting trial because they could not make bail and those who have committed serious crimes and are being preventively detained) and those who have already been convicted of a crime and are serving a sentence.

Although these are the two primary groups housed within the jail and its central purpose is to maintain a safe and secure environment for them, the jail is also used by prosecutors, police, and probation and parole personnel for other purposes. Prosecutors use the jail to coerce recalcitrant inmates to plea bargain. The threat of staying in jail encourages the defendant to "cop a plea" and relieves the pressures of the prosecutor's overcrowded caseload. The jail thus serves the organizational interests of prosecutors because it ensures a smoothly operating system of plea-bargaining and caseload reduction, and it serves similar interests of both the police and probation and parole personnel. The police use jail as a repository for the "rabble" (Irwin, 1986) who are found on the streets of our major cities and as an inducement for defendants to confess to a crime or to serve as witnesses against other suspects (Rottman & Kimberly, 1975). Probation and parole officers use jail as a convenient place for offenders who are suspected of committing either a technical violation or a new crime. In many large urban jails, a sizable number of people are awaiting revocation hearings, and jail in this case gives probation and parole personnel control over their clients. In short, jail serves all these components of the criminal justice system and helps them all meet their goals (Kerle, 1998).

But while the jail can be critical for the accomplishment of these goals, it can equally be a place of interorganizational conflict. We can examine, for example, the links between jails and other correctional agencies. Commonly, jails house offenders who cannot be placed in state prisons or detention settings because they are overcrowded. Data from the U.S. Bureau of Justice Statistics (2001) indicate that many local jails are holding inmates for federal, state, and local authorities. An estimated 10 percent of all jail inmates are prisoners held for state or federal authorities. This situation creates much conflict between the jail and correctional institutions. Typically, the conflict is resolved through a feedback process between the jail and other correctional institutions. In effect, jails have communicated directly to correctional institutions that they will not or cannot receive more state prisoners into their facilities. In many cases, this interorganizational conflict can be resolved only by the jail's refusing to take inmates from other jurisdictions until the overcrowding problem is resolved.

As another example, jail overcrowding can be caused by the refusal of judges to implement rational bail guidelines for those suspected of a crime. Many jails are overcrowded with individuals who could be bailed out and pose no threat to the community. The question becomes: Why won't judges institute rational bail guidelines if overcrowding is a problem in the jail? The answer lies in the fact that the jail is not of primary importance to them. What is important is that some type of punishment be given to people who have violated the laws. A little jail time reminds the suspect that the court is serious about the crime committed. Judges may feel even more strongly about using the jail in this way when the person has been before the courts in the past and behavior has not changed. In this example, the judge may have goals that differ from those of the sheriff who runs the jail, and the disagreement about the relative importance of each goal leads to interorganizational conflict in the system. This same type of interorganizational conflict can be seen in correctional institutions with respect to the delivery of services, such as education and medical attention (see Duffee, 1986: 274–276), specifically when the provision of these services is the responsibility of another state bureaucracy, such as a state department of public health or education.

Clearly, interorganizational conflict is common in criminal justice. The resolution of such conflict depends on the ability of separate organizational units to coordinate their efforts and increase their level of communication to ensure long-term preservation of their links. The resolution of interorganizational conflicts, both among the components of the criminal justice system and between those organizations and other state bureaucracies, may be the single most important issue facing administrators of the criminal justice system today.

Stages of a Conflict Episode

Although this typology helps us define and categorize conflict in criminal justice organizations, Pondy (1985:382) believes that it does not add to our understanding of the process of conflict. To understand the conflict process, he suggests that research must consider conflict episodes. More importantly, Pondy (1985) emphasizes that not all conflict situations lead to overt aggression or hostility. In other words, the conflict situation may never come to fruition. In fact, the purpose of conflict management programs in organizations is to prevent the escalation of events that lead to actual aggressive or hostile behavior by employees. In addition, however, not all conflicts are resolved with conflict management techniques; some, for example, may disappear because one of the parties does not perceive the situation as a conflict situation. It is critical, therefore, to identify the various stages of a conflict episode, as Pondy (1985:383–386) suggests.

The five stages of a conflict episode are presented in Figure 11-1. The stages are latent conflict, perceived conflict, felt conflict, manifest conflict, and conflict aftermath. These stages are affected by both environmental and organizational factors, as Figure 11-1 shows. Consistent with the idea that a conflict episode is dynamic, we can see that the entire episode evolves from the aftermath of a preceding conflict episode. In this way, all conflict episodes are interrelated and have a degree of continuity. Conflict in organizations must thus be understood beyond the immediate situation.

Latent Conflict. This stage of the conflict occurs when the conditions that are the underlying sources of the conflict are present. According to Pondy (1985:383), *latent conflict* is typically rooted in competition for scarce resources, drives for autonomy, or divergence of subunit goals. Each one of these roots can be seen in the organizations of criminal justice. In the typical police department, scarcity of resources produces fierce levels of competition among the various subunits when, for example, the juvenile unit demands increased resources to combat gang activity or the vice unit seeks additional officers to arrest drug dealers. Drives for autonomy can also create conflict in police organizations. When immediate supervisors attempt to control the behavior of officers and the officers, as a group, seek autonomy or control over their work environments, conflict is inevitable. Finally, divergence of subunit goals occurs "when two parties who must cooperate on some joint activity are unable to reach a

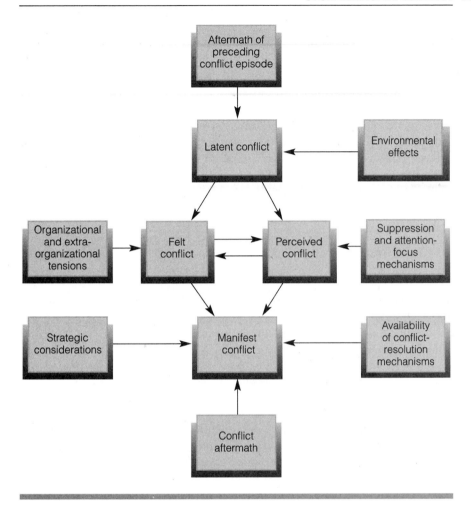

FIGURE 11-1   The Dynamics of a Conflict Episode (From L. R. Pondy, "Organizational Conflict: Concepts and Models," *Administrative Science Quarterly, 12,* 1967. Adapted by permission of *Administrative Science Quarterly.*)

consensus on concerted action" (Pondy, 1985 : 383). Patrol officers, for example, who must work together and cannot agree on how to complete their tasks will have much latent conflict.

All three components of latent conflict are present in prison settings. Scarcity of resources is evidenced by limited space, overcrowding, and minimal attention to such areas as treatment programs. Subunits in the prison organization—such as treatment personnel and security personnel—compete for these limited resources, each believing that its goals are most critical to the prison. And we see drives for autonomy in correctional institutions among both corrections staff and prisoners. Corrections staff seek additional input into how institutions are run, while prisoner groups demand control over their lives and prison conditions.

Perceived Conflict.   The stage of the conflict episode known as *perceived conflict* occurs when at least one of the two parties recognizes that a conflict situation exists. When they do, they may seek to escalate the conflict episode or choose to deflect it. A police officer, for example, may have a perceived conflict with her partner; she can decide to suppress the conflict because she doesn't believe it to be a major issue, or she can decide that the issue is important to her. The officer may decide to suppress the perceived conflict between herself and her partner over who is going to drive the squad car, yet she may want to push the perceived conflict to the next stage over the issue of handling recalcitrant suspects. The important point is that once we consciously recognize the conflict between ourselves and another individual, we have control over whether the conflict episode will proceed into the next stage.

Felt Conflict.   *Felt conflict* occurs when a party personalizes the conflict situation. For example, Officer A may be aware of a conflict between herself and her partner, but she doesn't allow the conflict to upset her. However, Officer B may be so upset by a perceived conflict that it now affects his relationship with his partner. Once personalized, the conflict not only is felt by the individuals concerned but may also become dysfunctional for the organization. This stage of the conflict episode is critical to organizations; proper handling of the conflict situation in this stage is extremely important to the long-term stability of any organization, including those in the criminal justice system.

Manifest Conflict.   After the conflict situation has been perceived and felt by a party, it may move into *manifest conflict*. This stage of the conflict episode is characterized by overt or covert behavior to bring out the conflict. In prisons, for example, manifest conflict may be expressed in riots or disturbances. These types of overt situations are rare, however, even for prisons. More often than not, manifest conflict takes the covert form of deliberate blockage by one party of the other party's goals.

Going back to our police officer example, if Officer B knowingly frustrates his partner in such a way that she cannot attain her goals, then manifest conflict is surely present. At this point tension between the two may be the greatest. More important, at this juncture managers must step into the conflict situation to diffuse it before it becomes dysfunctional to the organization. As a result, it is critical that immediate supervisors be able to recognize manifest conflict among their subordinates. Supervisors must also recognize that they may be the source of manifest conflict in the organization. In fact, it is all too common in criminal justice for frontline supervisors to be perceived as facilitators of manifest conflicts instead of diffusers. Even worse, often the conflicts in criminal justice organizations are not among employees but between the employees and their supervisors or administrators. In all these cases, the superior must take care not to escalate the manifest conflict but facilitate its resolution.

Conflict Aftermath.   At this point in the conflict episode, if the antecedent conditions (competition for scarce resources, drives for autonomy, and divergent subunit goals) are dealt with in a satisfactory manner, the conflict will dissolve. Such a resolution is the hope of those who are interested in keeping organizational conflict to a minimum and want to learn from the conflict episode. If, however, the antecedent conditions are not addressed but are only suppressed for the short term, then the conflict will continue to surface like a wound that has not been properly attended to. If the conflict continues, we enter the stage of *conflict aftermath*. The danger of this stage of the conflict episode is that it may become serious or, worse yet, so weaken the relationship between the two actors that it can never be fully repaired. In this way, conflict episodes become part of a dynamic process. We can see how the conflict aftermath occurs in the components of the criminal justice system. In prisons where the antecedent conditions of conflict (as described previously) are never resolved, for example, the conflict is allowed to fester until another disturbance occurs.

Conflict Behaviors

Awareness of conflict behaviors helps us understand the role that conflict plays in criminal justice organizations. Moreover, it enables us to develop and implement effective conflict management programs in these organizations.

Conflict behaviors can be understood by examining a model proposed by Thomas (1985). The model has two dimensions, each representing an individual's intention in a conflict situation. The two dimensions are cooperativeness, attempting to satisfy the other party's concerns, and assertiveness, attempting to satisfy one's own concerns. Different combinations of these two dimensions, according to Thomas, can create five conflict behaviors, as shown in Figure 11-2. Each one of these behaviors reflects an individual's attempt to deal with a conflict situation.

Competing behavior (assertive, uncooperative) occurs when one person is willing to place his or her own concerns above the concerns of the other person. Typically, force and even violence occur in this conflict situation. In addition, competing behavior seeks the resolution of the conflict in a fashion that maximizes the person's own interests.

Accommodating behavior (unassertive, cooperative) satisfies the concerns of the other individual rather than one's own concerns in a conflict situation. This behavior may be rare in organizations because it is difficult to understand why one would neglect one's own interests and maximize another's, yet we all know this does happen in everyday life.

Avoiding behavior (unassertive, uncooperative) neglects both the person's own concerns and the concerns of the other person. People who exhibit avoiding behavior want a minimal amount of friction in their interactions and do everything in their power to make sure no problems occur between themselves and others.

Collaborating behavior (assertive, cooperative) attempts to satisfy the demands and concerns of both parties in a conflict situation; it is a type of conflict behavior that few possess yet many desire.

Finally, *compromising behavior* (intermediate in both assertiveness and cooperativeness) seeks the middle ground. People who exhibit this type of conflict behavior realize that they cannot always get what they want and further recognize that conflict resolution demands some give and take by both sides. Sacrifice, in other words, is part of this type of conflict behavior.

Individually, no conflict style is bad or good. Whether a conflict behavior is appropriate depends on the context and situation. Accordingly, Thomas (1985: 399)

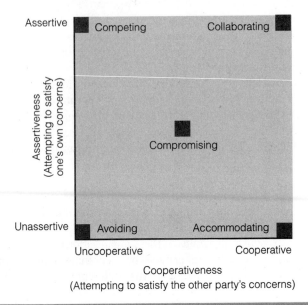

FIGURE 11-2 A Two-Dimensional Model of Conflict Behavior (From T. Ruble and T. K. Thomas, "Support for a Two-Dimensional Model of Conflict Behavior," *Organizational Behavior and Human Performance,* 1976, *16,* 145. Copyright © 1976 by Academic Press. Adapted by permission of the author.)

suggests that in some situations specific conflict behaviors are better than others. For example, it has been said that conflict management is at the heart of running a modern police department. How chiefs respond to various conflict situations is critical to perceptions about their effectiveness as leaders. When chiefs believe that their way of doing things is correct, it may be appropriate for them to take a stand and compete on the issue. When an emergency arises and a quick response is needed, the competing form of conflict behavior may also be the most appropriate, though we do not want to say it is always the best choice.

As another example, a citizen group that demands a different form of patrolling in its neighborhood has an understanding of and perspective on the allocation of police officers within the community. The group may also have some knowledge of how and when police resources can be used to combat crime in its neighborhood. This type of information may be valuable to the chief in a number of ways, from creating positive relationships with the community to getting important feedback from residents on how police resources can be distributed in the community. If the police chief's intention is to gain ideas about crime control from the community, then the collaborating form of conflict behavior may be most appropriate.

If, however, the chief believes that this issue of community input into police operations is trivial or unimportant to the department, he or she may perceive that avoiding the conflict is the appropriate response. If the chief's perception is incorrect, however, this type of conflict behavior may prove to be deleterious to the department. For this reason, selecting the correct conflict behavior for the situation is critical to organizations today and to criminal justice organizations in particular.

This example describes a conflict situation between a police chief and a group outside the police organization. Conflict situations, however, can also occur within organizations, and it is equally important for criminal justice organization administrators to select the correct conflict behavior in such situations.

Conflict Management

Thomas (1985:405–411) identifies two ways of dealing with conflict situations: process interventions and structural interventions. *Process interventions* attempt to "become directly involved in the ongoing sequence of events" (Thomas, 1985:405) that result in the conflict. *Structural interventions* attempt to alter the conditions in an organization that influence the direction of conflict episodes. Each intervention aims for conflict resolution. Using both allows us to deal with conflict in criminal justice organizations. Although these interventions are designed for intraorganizational conflict, they can also be partially applied to interorganizational conflicts.

Process Interventions

Process interventions fall into two categories. First, *consciousness-raising interventions* attempt to change the "internal experiences of the parties" that shape their behaviors. This type of intervention requires that the manager or supervisor intervene indirectly in the conflict, suggesting how the competing parties can reconceptualize their perceptions and thus remove the conditions that created the conflict. Second, *interaction management* occurs when a supervisor intervenes directly in the conflict situation between two subordinates, suggesting how the two parties can change their behaviors to resolve this conflict and avoid future conflicts. Both types of process interventions thus require active participation by supervisors for the conflict to be reduced. Next we review some of the organizational conditions that can be altered by process interventions from administrators and managers. Our examination of these conditions includes criminal justice examples.

Personal Characteristics. Conflict episodes in organizations are a result of multiple factors, including the personalities of those involved in the conflict. Our personalities affect how we deal with conflict. As Thomas (1985:406) puts it, individuals in organizations have "repertoires" in dealing with conflict that are rooted in their personalities, and these repertoires can be difficult to deal with. Sometimes an individual's position in an organization cannot be altered even though that person may have a poor conflict repertoire. More often than not, other employees try to adapt to this type of personality in hopes of minimizing conflict. For example, if a police sergeant has a competitive repertoire, we often tell subordinates that they are going to have to live with this person and learn to accept the situation. Obviously, if the situation becomes nonproductive, then actions must be taken by those supervisors above the sergeant to deal with the conflict. In this example, interaction management has been a tool used by police managers to deal with personality differences among subordinates. Usually the police manager attempts to get the conflicting parties to focus on job responsibilities and how those cannot be hindered by personality differences.

Informal Rules.   All organizations have written and unwritten rules about employee behavior. These rules are critical to the operation of the organization. For example, when there is a conflict between officers, going to the sergeant or the lieutenant may not be approved by the informal code among officers. Dealing with conflict episodes in police organizations, therefore, may require an understanding of the role the informal code plays in such situations. The informal code may accept reasonable attempts by police administrators to resolve the conflict. Though such activities as serving as an arbitrator or "referee" between two disputants may prove helpful, the police administrator always must be aware that such an interaction management strategy could be limited by the informal code and should, therefore, proceed cautiously.

Constituent Pressure.   All organizations experience pressure and competition among groups, known as *constitutent pressure,* that typically force cohesiveness within the groups. Examining a correctional organization highlights this concept. The treatment-versus-custody debate that has raged for years is a good example of how groups become cohesive when they feel threatened. Prison administrators have been unable to deal with the conflict that ensues from constituent pressures, but they could do so by using process intervention—as in getting both groups to realize the benefits to the organization of resolving their conflicts. In this example, the prison administrator could show how the dual functions of treatment and custody serve the purpose of maintaining prison order and also help each group accomplish its goals. In this way, the administrator is trying to raise the consciousness of members in both groups.

Conflict of Interest.   According to Thomas (1985:407), the precursor of *conflict of interest* exists in organizations when the concerns of two parties in an organization are incompatible. Such conflict is escalated when both parties are competing for limited resources. In prisons, for example, we know that limited funds are available for all programs, particularly treatment programs. Satisfying custodial concerns invariably leads to a reduction in resources for those groups in the prison who are interested in treatment. Unless there is some "organizational slack," as Thomas (1985: 407) states, it will be difficult for the prison organization to meet the objectives of both groups, thereby increasing the likelihood of conflict. This conflict episode in prison organizations has existed for many years, and unless further resources are granted these organizations, it is unlikely to diminish. If nothing else, this situation has forced prisons to define the objectives and purposes of their organizations, given their limited funds and resources. Moreover, it may not be apparent how process interventions resolve conflicts resulting from conflicts of interest. Actually, interactive management can resolve the conflict between treatment workers and custody personnel by clearly stating the central purpose of the prison. Once parties recognize that, for example, custody concerns are supposed to override treatment goals, the conflict could be resolved. Treatment employees may recognize that the demands, and therefore more resources, should be given to the custody function.

Thomas (1985:408) says that the degree of competition among conflicting interests in an organization is determined by the stakes involved (the degree to which the issue at conflict is important) and the interdependence among the competing parties (the relative connection between the groups when competing for high stakes). For example, the corrections officer staff may compete with the treatment staff for scarce resources in the prison independently (*parallel striving*) or seek to block the possibility of the treatment group's achieving its goals (*mutual interference*). Thomas (1985:409) suggests that parallel striving may increase the efforts of groups to work toward organizational goals, whereas mutual interference disrupts each group's attempt to accomplish organizational goals.

Power and Status. Power and status play an important part in the conflicts that occur in organizations and also affect their level of intensity. Obviously, because of the power differential between them, a police officer does not seek to enter into conflictual relationships with an immediate supervisor. In fact, avoidance as a conflict behavior is common in situations where great power differentials exist between the parties. Moreover, some organizational units have greater status and levels of power than others. As a result, departments have to be conscious of their relative power and status before making requests of other departments. Although treatment personnel in prisons, for example, do not have much power, they may believe they have higher status than guards, both in prison and society. This belief may be part of the reason for the high level of conflict between treatment staff and custodial staff, though we would not want to reduce the explanation of all conflict between the two groups to status differentials. Another possible process intervention is the prison administration's making both treatment personnel and custodial workers aware of their relative importance to the prison. Indeed, proper prison administration involves educating workers in what role they play to achieve organizational goals. This awareness in both groups may lead to the reduction of conflict between them.

Organizational Policy. An *organizational policy* is often created to minimize a conflict. However, if rules are nothing but the result of "political struggles" (Thomas, 1985: 410), we would expect that rules and organizational policies are only a short-term response. Opinions among groups in police departments on what type of enforcement action should be taken may vary considerably; therefore, we may make a policy that states when and how an arrest will be made. This policy, however, will not resolve the issue but will only take it temporarily out of the forefront of organizational business. We would, therefore, expect that once the issue arises again, another rule will be created to deal with the situation and appease the competing parties. Making a new policy that attempts to eliminate conflict between two parties in an organization can be perceived as a process intervention.

Structural Interventions

While process interventions are concerned with conflict episodes, *structural interventions* are designed to reduce conflict by examining and altering preexisting conditions of the organization that promote conflict. These conditions are ongoing and part of the structure within the manager's system. Thomas (1985:410–411) describes two types of structural interventions that can be employed: selection and training interventions and contextual-modification interventions.

Selection and Training Interventions. *Selection interventions* use screening procedures to choose the people best for the organization and the job. Both police organizations and corrections departments attempt to select the most favorable candidates for positions within their organizations. They hope that they have chosen the people who can perform the tasks of the job and whom they can work with. In addition, they attempt to train people to work in the way they believe is most conducive to accomplishing organizational objectives. Administrators hope that through such interventions they can minimize conflict and increase the effectiveness of the organization.

Contextual-Modification Interventions. *Contextual-modification interventions* attempt to change the context within which parties interact. Such changes typically require forceful management and leadership in the policy development process. For example, conflict of interest in correctional organizations between treatment staff and custodial groups can be reduced, in part, by reducing competition for scarce resources between the groups. If a manager can acquire increased resources for both groups, there is no longer any reason for competition. Through this contextual modification, the manager has increased the likelihood that each group will be able to meet its own needs while fulfilling the needs of the organization. Yet accomplishing this modification is easier said than done. In fact, contextual modifications in criminal justice organizations require great awareness of interorganizational conflict, a topic we examined previously in the chapter.

Limits to Conflict Management

Although conflicts requiring contextual modification may be resolved, other conflicts are more intractable because managers have even less control over their resolution. For example, conflicts escalate in correctional settings when there is limited space for housing prisoner populations. Overcrowding produces conflict between and among inmates and staff, but corrections administrators do not have the resources to add space. A possible solution to the conflict is to build additional prisons, yet this may be a short-term solution because further resources are not going to be available when prison space again becomes limited.

Instead, a satisfactory solution to the problem may require attention to nonincarcerative mechanisms for dealing with offenders. Given the reality of limited resources in prison settings, the conflict may require solutions that reach well beyond the boundaries of the organization to both the interorganizational and the societal level. Many organizational conflicts in criminal justice are thus not satisfactorily addressed because it is beyond the scope of these organizations to resolve the latent conditions that perpetuate these conflicts.

Administrators must accept that sometimes they will not be able to handle a conflict situation; sometimes they will fail in their attempts to deal with conflicts both internal and external to the organization. This failure, however, does not relegate them to doing nothing. The reasonable position is to learn from mistakes and go forward to resolve similar conflicts in the future with the knowledge gained from our past experiences.

Is Conflict Management Possible
in Criminal Justice Administration?

According to Thomas (1985:412–415), successful conflict management deals with all three dimensions of conflict outcomes. The first is *goal attainment* by conflicting parties. In the conflict between treatment staff and custodial personnel, goals must be attained by either one group or the other or both. In an optimal sense, both parties should gain something from the conflict. Although desirable, such an outcome is highly improbable in this case; Thomas even states that one would not want to grant every party equal weight in the conflict. Custodial functions, for example, may be more important to the prison organization than treatment programs, or vice versa. If the conflict does resolve anything, it may be the priority of one function over the other. For this reason, effective criminal justice administration requires communication of the priorities in an organization. Once subordinates understand these priorities, the number of conflicts in the organization may decrease. This same line of reasoning can be extended to conflict at the interorganizational level. Clear communication among the components in the criminal justice system will reduce the likelihood of long-term conflict among them. If an administrator perceives that the parties in conflict are of equal value, however, then the optimal strategy is some type of compromise so that each believes that it received a portion of what it sought in the conflict.

Second, administrators in the criminal justice system must be aware of the *consequences* of a conflict episode for the people involved. If, for example, treatment staff perceive that they have been treated unfairly by the administration of the institution in resolving a conflict, this perception may adversely affect their productivity and outlook toward the job. Such long-term effects on performance can also be the result of interorganizational conflict. Because the parts of the system are so interdependent, it is crucial that administrators understand the importance of maintaining stable relationships with each other, as this chapter's case study demonstrates. These relationships may be the most pivotal aspect of effective criminal justice administration today. Here, collaboration seems to be the best possible method for dealing with conflict. The collaboration strategy enables conflicting parties to see that their concerns are being recognized even though they may not get what they want.

Third, conflict management in the criminal justice system must be *economical of time and effort*. A tremendous amount of effort is put into dealing with conflicts both within criminal justice organizations and outside their boundaries. Energy used to deal with conflicts could be used for constructive activities within the organization. Good criminal justice administrators understand, therefore, the importance of efficient conflict management in their organizations.

This point leads us to the question: Is conflict management possible in criminal justice organizations? We think that it is not only possible but essential. The key lies in improving communication both within and among the components of the system. At present, communication is fragmented at both levels. For conflict management to work, this problem of poor communication is going to have to be resolved. Improving communication will require some structural changes, including more specific lines of communication in the organization. At the interorganizational level, this would mean raising the consciousness (process intervention) of criminal justice administrators to help them see that improved communication is essential to their effectiveness.

The Role of Conflict in Organizations

A number of views have been advanced over the years about the role that conflict plays in organizations. Our position is that conflict in criminal justice organizations can be both beneficial and harmful. Much of the conflict that occurs is good in the sense that it promotes change in those organizations; conflict makes the system responsive to the demands of a changing environment (Wright, 1999). Assume, for example, that a police organization is viewed as non-responsive to demands from the community for changes in the way police services are delivered. In this situation, conflict may arise not only between community groups and those who run the department but also between department administrators and the officers. If the department does become responsive to the community, rank-and-file officers may feel that the department is trying to appease the community groups to their detriment. Conflict in this situation may be good because it forces the department to rethink its relationship with both the community and its own officers, a task that can be beneficial to the organization's operations and delivery of services. The ultimate goal of conflict management in the system of criminal justice should be an increase in organizational effectiveness.

Conflict can also be harmful. If, in the previous example, conflict between the officers and the department over the role of the community escalates to the point that the functioning of police units is jeopardized, then conflict has become detrimental to the long-term operation of the department. Management has failed to control the escalation of conflict, and, as a result, the effectiveness of the organization may be diminished.

Conflict in criminal justice organizations is, however, a normal process, and eliminating it is not only unrealistic but also counterproductive to their long-term health. In short, conflict serves a useful function. Although long-term and deeply entrenched conflict is of no value to any organization, conflict enables an organization to grow and adapt successfully to its environment. Because conflict in criminal justice organizations seems inevitable given the fact of frequently incompatible goals, managers have to learn how to live with, adapt to, and cope with it. Conflict management programs need to be developed to train managers and administrators how to do so effectively.

Summary

This chapter discussed the concept of conflict and applied it to the criminal justice system. There are stages in the conflict process and various ways of understanding conflict behaviors. Conflict is endemic to criminal justice organizations, and it is an intricate process. Conflict must be viewed beyond the boundaries of the organization as an interorganizational phenomenon. Administrators of criminal justice systems today constantly deal with conflicts that arise among them as system actors. System interactions produce conflicts among the components, and it is the responsibility of administrators to deal with such conflicts.

Effective criminal justice administration demands the proper management of conflict. We believe that conflict management cannot be discussed without talking about increased interaction and communication among the components of the criminal justice system. Although improved communication has been recommended for years, the criminal justice system is increasingly called on to be efficient in its delivery of services. This goal is possible only if the issue of conflict is addressed directly by those who manage and administer the system.

Case Study

Drug Enforcement: Business as Usual

Madison County has over 1 million residents and thirty police departments. One department—the Milledgeville Police Department—is by far the largest in the county. The other twenty-nine police departments are fairly small and represent communities with populations of ten thousand to fifty thousand. The Milledgeville Police Department has over 1,500 sworn police officers and jurisdictional authority over close to two-thirds of the county, a population of over 600,000 residents.

The most pressing law enforcement problem in Milledgeville is the presence of new "designer" drugs and other illegal narcotics being sold at the schools and all night party establishments known as "Raves." For the smaller departments in Madison County, drugs had not been a problem until recent years when a number of young persons were arrested for delivering large quantities of crystal meta-amphetamine to the high schools. The drugs had caused the death of three students in three communities.

Having received a 1-million dollar federal grant for drug enforcement efforts, the thirty jurisdictions within the county decided to establish a multi-jurisdictional task force to improve and coordinate law enforcement efforts directed toward drugs in the community. The money would be used for a pilot project to develop new interagency strategies to improve drug enforcement in the county. Since the Milledgeville Police Department viewed the drug problem as being worse in their city when compared to the other cities, the police chief—Chief David Bascom—believed his department should receive the largest share of the federal dollars coming from the grant. Yet he also believed that the primary purpose of the grant was to improve the coordination of law enforcement practices among the differing police departments and to develop a unified strategy among them. This is where the conflict began. Chief Bascom agreed to convene a meeting of the county's police chiefs to see how best they would spend the money.

Chief Hayes from the Shadow Point Police Department viewed the drug problem as a broader issue that reached well beyond Milledgeville. He advocated that the monies be split equally among the thirty police departments in the county to allow them each to address drug enforcement in their own way. He viewed the federal dollars as a way for him to subsidize overtime for his officers working in the high school. Other chiefs wanted the monies to be concentrated in smaller cities within the county where something good could be accomplished. They viewed the larger cities within the county as awash with drugs and thought no amount of money was going to get them ahead of the problem. Chief Bascom held the view that drug problems in the county were primarily restricted to certain areas of Milledgeville and that there was a direct connection between Milledgeville and other cities in the county regarding drug dealing. His city was the main source, with local gangs distributing the drugs to the smaller communities within the county.

To this assertion there was no agreement among the police chiefs. Chief Beckman, from a mid-size community in the county, expressed the following sentiment, "We don't know if Milledgeville is the source of these drugs. My problem is that kids with a basic knowledge of chemistry are making this stuff in their garages. They are not traveling to Milledgeville to make these drugs. Marijuana, cocaine, and heroin may be a problem in Milledgeville but not in my community. I have other problems." To this claim another police chief responded, "Maybe we should talk about what is the drug problem and what we can reasonably pursue as a drug enforcement strategy in the county." This view, however, was lost on most of the chiefs.

The discussion became more contentious when it was learned that many of the current drug enforcement efforts in the county were conflicted and lacked any communication and coordination among the various police agencies. Chief Arthur, from the smallest community in the county, angrily described how one of his officers was almost killed by a Milledgeville officer during a drug buy gone bad when the Milledgeville officer saw a weapon on the buyer. Chief Arthur stated, "We need better intelligence and coordination on who is doing what out there. We have no way of knowing who the good guys and bad guys are. We were lucky my guy wasn't killed."

After much discussion and contentiousness, Chief Bascom saw his efforts to get the police departments in the county together on a unified drug enforcement strategy heading for failure. Not only was the money a paltry sum, but there was no agreement among the chiefs on how the money would be spent. Most importantly, very few departments even wanted to discuss how they would coordinate their efforts and who would have leadership responsibility and command authority. Most departments wanted their officers to report to their own supervisors, not a centralized authority to be determined later once the operations began. They could not agree on a memorandum of understanding on whom had authority to do what and under what conditions and who was responsible if something went wrong. To Chief Bascom the discussions were depressing.

He saw the meeting spiraling out of control, so he asked in a firm voice, "What do you want to do with the money? We agreed to accept this money as a pilot project to see if we can increase our communication and coordination to improve drug enforcement in the county. What do I tell the feds?" Chief Jones who was quiet through most of the discussion answered, "Tell them we do law enforcement differently in the county and that we feel the money would be better spent by allowing each department to take its equal share to do its own thing concerning drug enforcement." Chief Bascom responded, "If we say that, then we will lose the money. The grant was not designed to subsidize business as usual, but to create innovative ways to improve drug enforcement among the communities within the county." Chief Jones responded cynically, "Tell them they can have their money back. We will never be able to agree on what our purposes are and who will get what, so it's not worth the hassle. I say business as usual."

Case Study Questions
1. What type of conflict is described in the case study?
2. What would you suggest to improve the communication and coordination among police agencies concerning drug enforcement efforts?
3. How does a "business as usual" strategy work against a criminal justice organization? Who should take the lead in trying to deal with interorganizational conflict among criminal justice agencies?

For Discussion

1. Describe a potential conflict situation in a criminal justice setting. Suggest possible ways this conflict could be resolved. Also, describe what you believe the role of a criminal justice administrator should be in such a situation, and why. Is there a specific conflict behavior that would be useful to deal with this conflict situation, and what is it?

2. Choose a conflict situation in one of the components of the criminal justice system and describe its various stages. Identify the stage you think the conflict could be managed in and the supervisor's role in the management process. Moreover, are there conflict situations beyond the control of the immediate supervisor? If so, mention a few, and discuss why they can not be dealt with effectively by management personnel in that component of the criminal justice system.

3. Interorganizational conflict is common in the criminal justice system. Suggest methods that administrators can employ to decrease this conflict. Is interorganizational conflict in the criminal justice system inevitable?

4. Invite the local police chief to class to discuss the conflicts that arise in his or her department. Ask the chief to describe the methods employed to decrease conflict. Finally, ask about the department's position on the role of conflict management programs in policing. Do you think such programs are useful in reducing conflict?

For Further Reading

Alpert, G., and Dunham, R. *Policing Urban America,* 3rd ed. Prospect Heights, IL: Waveland, 1997.

Duffee, D. *Correctional Management: Change and Control in Correctional Organizations.* Prospect Heights, IL: Waveland, 1986.

Pondy, L. R. "Organizational Conflict: Concepts and Models." *Administrative Science Quarterly,* 1967, 12, 296–320.

Thomas, K. W. "Conflict and Conflict Management." In *Handbook of Industrial and Organizational Psychology,* edited by M. D. Dunnette, pp. 889–935. Chicago: Rand McNally, 1976.

Tosi, H. L., and Hamner, W. C. (Eds.) *Organizational Behavior and Management,* 4th ed. Cincinnati, OH: Grid, 1985.

PART FOUR

PROCESSES
IN CRIMINAL
JUSTICE
ORGANIZATIONS

Organizations pursue goals and accomplish tasks. As we will
see, these are complicated issues, but they are the issues that set
organizations apart from individuals and groups. Managers must
be concerned with how their organizations carry out those tasks
and how well they perform. These are important concerns in
criminal justice, where goals are often unclear and conflicting
and where few unambiguous measures of accomplishment exist.
In Part Four, our focus extends beyond the individual and group
to the ways that organizations pursue their goals and accomplish
their tasks. We first consider decision making within organizations, then turn to the difficult process of determining the effectiveness of organizations. The final two chapters examine the
process of change in criminal justice organizations and the role
of research in these organizations.

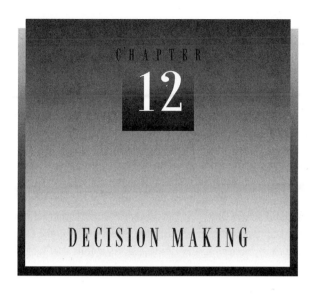

CHAPTER

12

DECISION MAKING

The task of "deciding" pervades the entire administrative organization quite as much as the task of "doing"—indeed, it is integrally tied up with the latter.

(Simon, 1957:1)

The U.S. Sentencing Commission guidelines have failed. No policy initiative can succeed if its legitimacy is denied by the people who must implement it; evidence from a variety of sources demonstrates that most judges and defense counsels and many prosecutors resent and resist the guidelines. No policy initiative can be said to succeed if it does not achieve its primary stated goals; the Commission constantly reiterates that its goals are achievement of "uniformity" and reduction of "unwarranted disparities" in federal sentencing. A variety of sources demonstrate the absence of credible evidence that disparities have declined. Most notably, the U.S. General Accounting Office (GAO), reviewing the Commission's claims that its guidelines have lessened disparities, concluded that it is "impossible to determine how effective the sentencing guidelines have been in reducing overall sentencing disparity."

(Tonry, cited in Stojkovic, Klofas, & Kalinich, 1999)

I relish cases where a deal has been worked out. All the pressure is off. No one is on my back. They are really no problem.

(Probation officer discussing sentencing recommendations in plea-bargained cases, quoted in Rosecrance, 1985:542)

We always write in our reports, "Just what force was necessary?" What if you don't take enough force? Well, how in the hell do you know how much force is necessary? I say take all you got in case you need it.

(Corrections officer, quoted in Roszell,1986)

A decision is a judgment, a choice between alternatives. Every day corrections managers make critical decisions that affect the safety and well-being of the community. In corrections, there are two types of decisions: case management decisions and organizational decisions. What decisions one makes depends upon the position one holds in the hierarchy. The higher the manager is in the organization, the more likely it is that he or she will be concerned primarily with organizational decisions.

(Houston, 1999)

Decision making is one of the most important concerns for managers in all organizations. Managers make decisions with long-term consequences by reviewing and altering their agency's mission, establishing long-term goals as a result of formal planning, or changing the agency's philosophy and operations. For example, the shift from traditional to community policing is, in effect, a decision to alter the agency's purpose, structure, and activities of its police officers. Managers also make decisions on budget allocation, policies, and operating procedures that constrain the decision making of its subordinates. Having made the higher order decision outlined above, managers also oversee the decisions of their subordinates. Subordinates regularly decide what policies and procedures apply to a particular situation and often ignore policies and procedures when making operational decisions. Hindsight provides us with examples of good and bad decision making at all levels of an organization. Part of the continued success of Johnson & Johnson has been attributed to the decision to keep Tylenol on the market under its original name despite the publicity about deaths from product tampering with cyanide in the early 1980s. However, the decision to change the formula for Coca-Cola in 1985 met with such resistance that the company had to bring "Classic Coke" back on the market. The space shuttle disaster in 1985 resulted in the death of seven astronauts and set back military and civilian space programs in the United States by three years. That explosion was at least partially attributable to a faulty decision process in which well-known problems with the booster rocket seals did not lead to redesign efforts, and the fateful launch went forward despite engineers' warnings about the potential effect of the cold weather on the seals' ability to hold.

In criminal justice, decision making is no less important. Severe prison and jail overcrowding has been blamed on decisions that were based on faulty population projections. In 1984, the police decision to drop an incendiary bomb on the roof of a house to evict a cult in Philadelphia ultimately resulted in the burning of some sixty homes and created a costly political firestorm. In the late 1970s, the U.S. government's decision to spray the herbicide paraquat on Mexican marijuana led to reduced supplies of the drug but also created concerns about the possible health effects of tainted supplies. This concern ultimately stimulated domestic production of the illegal crop (Brecher, 1986).

Decision making in criminal justice extends well beyond the policy formulation process with its parallels in the business world. In criminal justice, countless decisions are made about the clients of the system. From the reporting of a crime to the police through the final discharge of an offender, each step in the criminal process is marked by a decision made by workers in the criminal justice system. Figure 12-1 is a partial list of such decisions. Lipsky (1980) indicates that these decisions, often made by frontline staff, are more important than executive decisions in determining organizational policy. In fact, some scholars have argued that the conglomeration of different criminal justice agencies with different jurisdictions can only be understood as a system by recognizing that the disparate organizations are linked by the decisions made about offenders (Newman, 1986).

In this chapter we examine the process of decision making in criminal justice. We turn first to issues of theory and the growing recognition of the limits of rationality. Next, the focus is on two issues in criminal justice decision making that appear to represent extremes in our assumptions about rationality. First, we investigate discretion in decision making, a topic often criticized by those seeking rational processes. Second, we study prediction, a topic often assumed to be linked to high degrees of rationality. These two issues have engendered more discussion in criminal justice than other decision making topics. Finally, we consider the ways in which managers can influence the decision-making process in criminal justice in an effort to increase rationality.

1. Has a crime occurred in the eyes of a victim or a bystander?
2. Should a crime be reported to the police?
3. Should police be dispatched to the scene?
4. Should police regard the event as a criminal offense?
5. Should investigators be called in?
6. Should an arrest be made?
7. Should search warrants be issued?
8. Should arrest warrants be issued?
9. Should a police officer fire at a suspect?
10. Should an alleged offender be detained in jail?
11. Should a citation be issued?
12. Should bail be set and at what amount?
13. Should release-on-recognizance be allowed?
14. Should an alleged offender be prosecuted?
15. Should an alleged offender enter a diversion program?
16. With what priority should prosecution be undertaken?
17. Is an alleged offender competent to stand trial?
18. Should motions be granted?
19. Is an alleged offender guilty?
20. Is an alleged offender not guilty due to insanity?
21. Should an offender be incarcerated or allowed to remain in the community?
22. How long should the sentence be?
23. Should there be special conditions to the sentence?
24. What level of security does an offender need?
25. When and how should the levels of security change?
26. Should an incarcerated offender be transferred?
27. Should disciplinary reports be written?
28. Is an offender guilty of disciplinary infractions?
29. What are appropriate sanctions for disciplinary violations?
30. To what program should an offender be assigned?
31. Should an offender be transferred or committed to a mental hospital?
32. Should an incarcerated offender be paroled?
33. Should parole or community release be revoked?
34. Should an offender be discharged?

FIGURE 12-1   A Partial List of Decisions Made About Criminal Cases

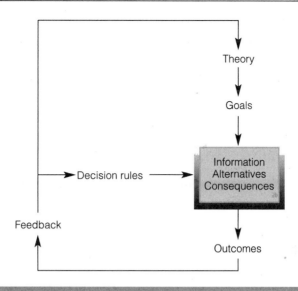

FIGURE 12-2 Elements of a Decision

What Is a Decision?

The decisions you made when you opened your closet this morning and the parole board's decision not to parole mass murderer Richard Speck may seem to have little in common. Your choice of garb and Speck's continued incarceration, however, both resulted from processes that share some basic elements. Those elements are shown in Figure 12-2.

In general, some *theory* or broad framework guides most decisions. As you examine your wardrobe, your selection of what to wear may simply be based on your beliefs about what looks good on you, but complex decisions may involve sophisticated theories. In his study of parole board decision making, for example, Hawkins (1983) found that broad support of *classicalism* or *positivism* frames board members' decisions. That is, some members of the parole board place great importance on whether an offender has been punished for a suitable time, whereas others are concerned with evidence of rehabilitation or change in the offender's outlook. Wilson's (1968) styles of policing may also be seen as broad frameworks within which police officers make decisions to arrest or not arrest. Officers in departments characterized by the *watchman style*, with its primary focus on maintenance of order, may be reluctant to arrest if less drastic means will control a disturbance. Officers in *legalistic* departments, however, may invoke their power to arrest based solely on whether a statute has been violated.

Goals in the decision-making process are specific to each decision, and they refer to what a decision maker would like to achieve. In a decision to prosecute a particular case, the prosecuting attorney's goal may be to gain a conviction; in the decision to dispatch a police car to a burglary scene or to schedule an appointment, a dispatcher's goal may be the efficient use of personnel. Goals may not always be so obvious, however. In his study of probation officers' sentencing recommendations, Rosecrance (1985) concluded that "ball park recommendations" serve the goal of maintaining credibility with the judge and may have little to do with particular cases.

Decision makers also need three kinds of information. First, they must be aware of alternatives, or choices. If there are no alternatives, there is no decision to make. Second, they must also be aware of the possible consequences of the alternatives. If consequences do not differ or if there are no expectations regarding consequences, an alternative can be selected only at random. Third, some information is needed about the subject of the decision in order to guide the selection among the alternatives. A judge's sentencing decision can illustrate the importance of information. Evidence of a convicted offender's crime and criminal history provides a basis for selection among the sentencing alternatives as provided by statute. All of this information is considered in light of the expected consequences of each possible sentence. Among these consequences may be included danger to the public if an offender remains in the community, the possible brutalizing effects of a prison term on a youthful offender, and public dissatisfaction if a substantial penalty is not imposed.

The availability of the information, however, does not necessarily produce a decision. That information must be processed. Processing occurs through the *decision rules*, which govern how the elements of the decision are combined. In criminal justice, many decisions rely on essentially *clinical* decision rules, which are based on education, training, and experience. Arrest decisions, sentencing decisions, and classification decisions usually rely on the clinical judgments of individuals. At the other extreme are *quantitative* decision rules, involving the assignment of numerical weights to pieces of information. Those weights are added to produce a sum, which dictates the decision. Scales based on these principles have been developed for use in prosecution, bail, sentencing, and parole decisions.

The processing of information according to decision rules produces *outcomes*. People are arrested, sentenced, transferred between prisons, or paroled. Policies are implemented, changed, or dismantled. The outcome is the result of the decision. In many (but not all) cases, the decision process is not completed with the outcome. Many types of decisions are repeated again and again. Police officers soon face new decisions about whether or not to arrest, and judges continue to sentence convicted offenders. In a *cybernetic,* or *self-correcting, decision model,* the outcome of prior decisions provides feedback to influence future decisions. Cybernetic decision processes are based on mechanical models similar to the thermostat in a house. When the heat is turned on, the temperature rises until the preset temperature high is reached; then the thermostat turns off the heat until the preset low temperature is reached, at which point the heat comes on again. Criminal justice feedback is not nearly so simple, but the same principles apply. Police officers' arrest practices are influenced by prosecutors' decisions to pursue prosecution or dismiss charges. Parole board decisions are influenced by information about the failure of some parolees.

Feedback may affect future decisions through its influence on theory, decision rules, information, or all three. For example, corrections decision making has been greatly affected by feedback from research in the mid-1970s that suggested that treatment programs had little effect (see Cullen & Gilbert, 1982). Theoretical frameworks supportive of treatment were replaced by the principle of just deserts—that is, punishment proportionate to the crime committed—and decision goals focused on equity in sentencing and time served. In parole, for example, information about participation in prison programs became less important than it had been, and some parole boards all but abandoned clinical decision rules and adopted numerical scales to assist in decision making.

Feedback about police intervention in spousal abuse cases has also influenced arrest decisions. Increasingly, police departments are encouraging or requiring arrest in domestic disputes, especially if there is some sign of physical violence (Morash, 1986). In the past, police and prosecutorial decisions were greatly influenced by feedback showing that many women did not pursue prosecution of husbands or boyfriends in domestic violence cases. Police officers were encouraged to negotiate settlements at the scene and counsel the participants or make referrals to social service agencies. Feedback with a different content was generated by several well-publicized cases of continued abuse and even homicide and by research studies showing that arrest is most likely to prevent further violence (Sherman & Berk, 1984). That feedback has altered the decision-making process in favor of arrest over mediation. Yet even this finding is not uniform, because some research has also shown pro-arrest policies to be ineffectual in deterring future violence among offenders (Sherman, 1992).

Decision-Making Theory: From Rationality to the Garbage Can

At first glance, the diagram of decisions in Figure 12-2 appears to be a model of perfect rationality. The goals of a specific decision are identified and needed information is processed according to agreed-upon decision rules and is considered within some theoretical framework. The diagram also suggests directions for improving the decision-making process. Increasing consistency in theory, increasing agreement on goals and decision rules, and improving quality of information will produce increasingly rational decisions. In criminal justice, as in other fields, rationality in decision making may be assumed to be a requirement for effectiveness and efficiency. As Gottfredson (1975) points out, however, although we may strive for rational decisions, achieving rationality is unlikely and probably impossible.

At one time, scholars of decision making believed the process could best be understood as a rational one that could produce optimal results or "correct" answers for given situations (Murray, 1986). This view assumed, for example, that an obviously correct answer existed to the question of whether a given suspect should be arrested or paroled. It was assumed that a specific policy on the deployment of patrol cars or the choice of a site on which to build a prison could be objectively regarded as the best solution to the problem.

In an influential book, March and Simon (1958) first questioned the rationality of the decision-making process. They pointed out that decisions were made on the basis of *bounded rationality,* partly because decision makers are incapable of collecting and handling the kinds of information needed for completely rational decisions:

1. Rationality requires a complete knowledge and anticipation of the consequences that follow each choice. In fact, knowledge of consequences is always fragmentary.

2. Since these consequences lie in the future, imagination must supply the lack of experienced feeling in attaching value to them. But values can only be imperfectly anticipated.

3. Rationality requires a choice among all possible alternative behaviors. In actual behavior, only very few of these possible alternatives come to mind.

Perrow (1981:2) outlines the thesis of bounded rationality:

> We cannot process large amounts of information but only limited bits, and those slowly. We tend to distort the information as we process it. We cannot gather information very well even if we could process it: we do not always know what is relevant information, inasmuch as we do not understand how things work. Above all, we cannot even be sure of what we want the information for because we cannot be sure what our preferences are. We have trouble discovering what we want. We also have contradictory preferences, or contradictory goals, and are unable to fulfill all of them at once. As a consequence, we do not look for the optimal solutions: we have to settle for "satisfycing," taking the first acceptable solution that comes along.

A good example of satisfycing students can readily understand is the decision process they followed to select a university to attend. A rational decision would have required that the prospective college student have an accurate view of their career goals and precisely what university offered the major and/or classes they would need to take to direct them toward their careers. Also, students would need a good grasp of the various reputations universities have in general and would have with prospective employers. Students also have to factor in all costs (tuition, living expenses, cost relating to living various distances from home, and so on). This approach is followed partially by some students. But most prospective college students do not have clear career goals to guide their decision-making process. More importantly, it is impossible for prospective students to have all of the information suggested on all of the colleges and universities across the country, or even their home state. Most likely, the student's choice of what university or college to attend is a process of "satisfycing." That is, students get available information from high school counselors, blend that information with what they hear from their friends and family, consider a cost range that is roughly affordable, and select a number of colleges and universities to consider. For some students, they chose to attend a local community college because of the cost and convenience. Making decisions as suggested is not bad. The point is that deciding on what university or college to attend is not purely rational, but can be sensible.

Working under conditions of bounded rationality is common to all organizations, and, therefore, is the nature of decision making within the criminal justice system. Many decisions, especially those regarding offenders, are characterized by volumes of information about their history and background. It is important to recognize that the information is selectively collected and interpreted and that decision processes are influenced by the organizations of the criminal justice system.

Satisfycing, or the attainment of acceptable rather than optimal results, is also a useful concept in criminal justice. Sound management decisions can be made, however, with limited, incomplete information. For example, in New York City, detectives will not investigate burglaries in which less than $10,000 in property is taken. This policy is clearly not optimal, but it is regarded as a minimally acceptable compromise between investigation goals and the need to use human-power efficiently. In the courtroom, the extent to which home detention is used as a response to jail crowding may reflect satisfycing between concerns for punishment and concerns about overcrowding.

An extension of the concept of bounded rationality also merits our attention. Cohen, March, and Olsen (1972) use the analogy of the garbage can to describe one model of decision making. Decision makers handle problems of ambiguity by developing sets of *performance programs,* or standardized methods of responding to problems. Organizations thus possess a repertoire of responses, or a garbage can full of ready-made answers in search of problems. The link to bounded rationality, however, is the idea that the garbage can must also contain the problems. That is, a decision maker will not think a situation needs action until that situation is defined in terms of solutions available (see Pinfield, 1986). When necessary, organization members modify their perceptions of problems to justify their actions (Staw & Ross, 1978). Hall (1987) suggests that individuals also possess garbage cans of solutions and problems. Movie comic crime fighter Detective Frank Drebbin (played by actor Leslie Nielsen), for example, has a standard response to "scum-sucking leeches" in his garbage can. Only after a citizen is defined in those terms does Detective Drebbin resort to his limited repertoire of violence. Westley (1970), in fact, found a similar preprogrammed response in his classic study of the police. He reported that a major justification for the use of violence was that a suspect was considered guilty.

Although the garbage can analogy may not help us understand all decisions in criminal justice (Mohr, 1976), some research suggests the usefulness of the model. Sudnow's (1965) examination of the public defender's office describes a process by which public defenders' decisions about defense strategies are the results of defining clients by using existing categories rather than individually considering the merits of each case. Public defenders have set practices of encouraging defendants to plead guilty as soon as possible if their cases have the hallmarks of a typical offense, or, as Sudnow calls it, a "normal crime." A young male arrested for burglary who has a prior record for burglary, for example, is encouraged to plead guilty even if he insists on his innocence. Atypical defendants get the benefit of a close examination of the strengths and weaknesses of their case. But typical defendants who resist pressures to plead guilty early may find themselves defined as recalcitrant. As the garbage can model would suggest, the existing solution for such cases involves proceeding to trial with a public defender who assumes the defendant is guilty. The trial then takes on the characteristics of a ritualized conspiracy against the defendant.

In a study of police investigations, Waegel (1981) argues that research strategies that focus on the decision-making processes of individual investigators have severe limitations. It is fruitful, rather, to study the existing shared categorizations of cases. In other words, he supports studying the garbage can of solutions to which police investigations (the problems) will be applied. Much of police investigation, then, involves "mapping the features of a particular case onto a more general and commonly recognized type of case" (1981:265). The most basic categories into which investigations are placed are routine versus non-routine cases.

Characteristics of the victim, offense, and suspects figure into the categorization of cases, and these characteristics trigger different levels of investigation. In some cases the distinction between routine and non-routine is obvious, while in others the detective forces a fit. In either case, assumptions about the nature of the incident and the parties involved guide case handling. The ability to type cases quickly is important in investigations. Waegel points out that the necessity to report on the status of cases influences whether or not a case is regarded as routine. Cases can be open, closed, or—if leads have been unproductive—suspended. We can observe the other side of this process of applying problems to existing solutions in case skimming. A steady stream of arrests is produced by working on only those cases that appear potentially solvable from information in the original patrol officer's report and summarily suspending the remainder of the cases.

The garbage can analogy has its appeal as a means of understanding some decision making in criminal justice. We need to be careful, however, not to let the cuteness of the imagery muck up our analysis. Solutions and problems in the can are not collected in some random fashion, after all. The approach to problems as well as the problems themselves represent the interests and history of the organization and its members. Thus little in the way of entirely new material is likely to enter into the decision-making process (Hall, 1982:181).

Thus, stability and even routinization of decision making are products of bounded rationality. In this organizational perspective, the boundaries determine the context of decision making, and those boundaries are the product of organizational processes, such as limiting the kinds of information available or viewed as relevant, establishing procedures, and requiring reports, as well as less obtrusive controls (see Perrow, 1986:128).

Another important contribution of the concept of bounded rationality is recognition of the cognitive limitations of individual decision makers. Not only must decision makers deal with multiple goals and possibly conflicting theories, and not only are they controlled by organizational practices, but they can also effectively handle only small quantities of information. Research has demonstrated, for example, that people can recall only seven or eight bits of information without developing some process or shorthand method for recalling the data (Burnham, 1975). This finding suggests that studying the ways people process information is important to understanding their decisions. In the following sections we examine the influence of culture on decision making, the role of politics in decision making, characteristics of the decision makers, and finally the characteristics of the information used in decisions.

Organizational Culture and Decision Making

Satisficing and garbage can decision making are both processes bound by organizational culture. Defining problems and recognizing acceptable and workable solutions —whether it is assigning parking, prescribing procedures, or developing long-term strategic planning—are framed within the context of an organization's culture. For our purposes here, organizational culture is defined as ready-made answers to problems (Simon & March, 1958) or a set of basic assumptions and beliefs shared by organizational members that are taken for granted (Schein, 1997). Hence the prevalence in agencies of such common proverbial wisdom as, "We have always done it that way," "It worked in the past," "If it ain't broke, don't fix it," and the like. Assumptions and beliefs are learned responses to problems that are valued enough to pass on to new members through both the formal and informal socialization processes. Specifically, assumptions about who makes decisions and at what level of the organization and what information is utilized in decision making are not necessarily based upon rational thought or reflection on mission or goals. Rather, the "decisions on who make decisions, when and how" are based upon past practices, routines, and assumptions about who is best suited to make decisions and what information is considered reliable. For example, in traditional hierarchical agencies, decision making is, in theory, centralized as the classical assumption in that wisdom and the "big picture" are to be found at the organization's apex. If experience is highly valued, information from the organization's memory bank, usually anecdotal in nature, is readily accepted. In this case, statistics would be compiled for external consumption—often wrongly referred to as accountability—and may even be used to expose a problem. But the problem exposed would show the organization was not meeting public expectations (for example, arrest rates were down, inmate assault rates up, and so on).

A problem is defined as such based upon deeply rooted values and mores. For example, a deeply rooted value in corrections is that inmates must be subject to staff control. Inmate autonomy in this framework is viewed as a problem, and inmate participation in governance, a solution proposed by some prison reformers (Murton, 1976), as anathema—in part because it is contrary to these basic values. Sparrow (1999) suggests that moving from traditional policing to community policing will require a major shift in the organizational culture of police agencies. The shift would impact the framework for decision making because information that would drive decisions, long and short term, would derive from community members' problems, needs, and satisfaction with police services rather than from traditional statistics such as crime, arrest and conviction rates, and response time. In addition, decisions would be made in coordination with community members rather than at the chief's desk.

In a classic article, Rosecrance (1999) challenges the "myth" of individualized decisions on criminal sentences and questions the value of the information accumulated on criminal defendants in Presentence Investigation Reports (PSI) for sentencing decisions. Rosecrance sees the presentence investigation instead as more ceremonial than instructive. Criminal sentencing is likely to be based upon an accumulation of past practices framed within a heuristic assessment that classifies identified groups of offenders as either deserving of incarceration or more lenient dispositions. Court work groups, in effect, predetermine criminal sentences, and most of the rituals that surround sentencing serve to legitimize ready-made solutions. Walker (1994) further explains this process by using the analogy of thermodynamics in organizations, which describes a social process wherein courtroom work groups—judges, prosecuting and defense attorneys, probation officers—blunt, evade, and circumvent any proposed changes in existing philosophies, principles, or operations. In effect, equilibrium is set and protected by a deeply entrenched courtroom culture with long-standing beliefs, values, assumptions, and legitimizing rituals.

The entrenched beliefs, values, assumptions, and legitimizing rituals frame and perpetuate the decision-making process. To the extent that decisions on criminal sentencing are bound by culture, the PSI will serve to provide information crucial to fitting the decision to incarcerate or release an offender to the community within accepted but implicit, culturally determined informal guidelines. For this reason recommendations written by probation officers as members of the culture generally correlate with sentencing decisions. Hence, the cultural context within which decisions are made is crucial to an understanding of decision-making processes among criminal justice practitioners. This implicit decision-making process can be explained more directly. Over time, the court work group reaches a consensus on offenders who clearly deserve probation or lenient sentences and, at the other end of the continuum, offenders who deserve imprisonment or tougher criminal sentencing. Placing offenders somewhere along this sentencing continuum will be based upon facts, such as the offender's criminal history, circumstances of the crime, and so on. The important point is that an unwritten consensus or agreement evolves over time on what facts and circumstances dictate the sentence criminal offenders will receive.

Politics and Decision Making

The political scientist Norton Long once noted that power is the lifeblood of politics. Possessing power becomes important, therefore, to decision making, but understanding that power also influences decision making is critical as well. No effective criminal justice administrator or manager underestimates the power and influence of politics, both internal and external, on decision making. *Internal politics* are the processes by which interested parties within the organization express their concern and seek implementation and acceptance of their ideas and practices. Bolman and Deal (1997) suggest that political behaviors within organizations are not all bad, but that for politics to be constructive, leaders and managers must understand the importance of agenda setting, working and forming coalitions, and bargaining and negotiating. With these ideas as decision rules, administrators can focus their energies on directing political influence toward productive ends.

External politics consist of the influence that outside parties exert on the organization's definition of mission, the appropriate types of operations the organization exhibits, and the directions it takes. Outside groups constantly put pressure on organizations to move in directions that are favorable to their interests. These pressures serve as constraints for decision makers as well as increase the ambiguity about which decisions are relevant, which should receive priority, and when they should be made. A confluence of external interests shapes the ways in which decisions will be made, and administrators are often left with too many demands, too few resources, and too little time to make effective decisions. Nowhere is this truer than in the sphere of decision making within public organizations, especially criminal justice organizations.

Internal Politics and Decision Making

The role of internal politics on decision making cannot be understated. Criminal justice organizations are made up of multiple and conflicting individuals and groups. The interests presented by various individuals and groups form internal political behaviors that seek to advance particular interests and concerns along identifiable dimensions. Police departments, for example, are fraught with internal politics along the dimensions of race, age, gender, years of experience, and education, to mention only a few issues. These dimensions also interact to produce a more complex picture of internal politics. Young, highly educated, inexperienced police officers have very different interests than more seasoned, older, less educated police officers. The internal struggles that ensue sometimes can be vicious and produce a tremendous toll on officers, their supervisors, police administrators, and even the public at large. Coalescing these multiple interests into a unified group working toward identifiable objectives and goals is a major challenge for police administrators (Fyfe, Greene, Walsh, Wilson, & McLaren, 1997). Decision making within a context of diverse interests among employees becomes a problematic activity, particularly for supervisors and administrators who are expected to be sensitive to these interests, and in some cases (such as sexual harassment) are mandated by law. Also the compartmentalization of organizations into, for example, treatment and custody components of corrections systems and specialized units in police organizations create competition for resources and influence over significant policy decisions.

External Politics and Decision Making

External politics influence decision making in ways that become difficult for administrators to address. Concern for external interests even becomes a central activity among criminal justice administrators. Departments of corrections, for example, were under tremendous pressures since the early 1990s to respond to perceptions of ever-growing crime problems. Proponents of incarceration strategies have suggested that sending more offenders to prison has a direct effect on crime rates (Mitchell, 1997), even though evidence is scant to suggest that an increase in incarceration will have an effect on crime rates. For corrections administrators, however, the pressure to accept more offenders has been unprecedented, and correctional leadership and management have become extremely difficult as a consequence. Succumbing to the demands of these external groups, most notably legislators and governors, departments of corrections have been receiving record numbers of offenders, with an annual average growth rate of 9 percent per year since 1980 (U.S. Bureau of Justice Statistics, 2000).

The most direct effect of these pressures has been on decision making among corrections officials. The dramatic increase in governmental budgets for corrections has also awakened legislator interest in their now large and visible investment, and a tendency for legislators to micromanage the system has become apparent. Currently, legislation to ban recreational activity in prisons is taking hold across the states. Legislators in Ohio and Michigan have also prescribed the addition of gun towers to prisons following escapes and disturbances and have added officer positions to prisons beyond departmental requests. Behind such legislation are correctional officer union lobbyists who attempt to influence administrative policy through pressure on legislators.

The most pronounced effect has been the degree to which politics influences the practices of departments of corrections. Top correctional officials have seen a greater degree of invasiveness in their decision making, as political concerns of external groups have taken precedence over the operational concerns of administrators and managers in running their facilities. Correctional administrators, however, have been unable to marshal enough external political support to get politics out of the decision-making process and to develop appropriate political technologies to help them do this (Baro, 1994). One director of a large correctional department resigned largely over what he viewed to be an overly aggressive court system, coupled with a meddling legislator and an entirely political governor who sought to micromanage his department. With politicians making unrealistic demands on correctional officials, such as the abolition of parole, no good time, and "three strikes and you're out" initiatives, correctional administrators are left asking what exactly they do administer and under what conditions. For many corrections officials, external politics has had an adverse effect on their decision-making capabilities. Short of keeping politics entirely out of corrections—an unrealistic goal—administrators need the ability to function in the political arena so that desirable outcomes for corrections are possible.

Flanagan and colleagues (1996) report that based on their survey of 648 correctional administrators across the country, many support activities and routines that assist prisoners in their treatment and development. Yet the current political environment, which emphasizes a get-tough posture, precludes them from publicly advocating for such amenities, even if these activities actually improve their capabilities to manage correctional institutions. The surveyed correctional administrators suggested that prisons would be more efficient and effective places if external politics could be kept to a minimum, but that outcome is highly unlikely. Similar concerns have been expressed by police chiefs (Gardner, 1997), parole commissioners (Husz, 1996), and community-based corrections officials (Dickey, 1996).

Characteristics of Decision Makers

Although organizational and political factors are important in understanding the notion of bounded rationality, some research in criminal justice has focused on the decision makers themselves. In studying parole decision making, Wilkins (1975b) uncovered fundamental differences in the way people process information. He first asked decision makers to make interim decisions after reviewing only limited items of information. Some of the decision makers, however, found it impossible to make decisions based on the limited information, even when they were told that they could indicate a low level of confidence in the decision. These decision makers would not consider making a decision without information they regarded as "sufficient." From this line of research, Wilkins described four types of decision makers. This typology is relevant to a large number of criminal justice decisions, which are characterized by uncertainty and a relatively large amount of available information. These decisions may concern intensity of investigation, sentences, or classification or transfer of prisoners.

Decision makers described by Wilkins as *sequentialists* use their experience to determine what items of information are most important. Then they consider items in a sequential fashion, one at a time, based on their view of each item's importance. These decision makers are able to make interim decisions, and each additional item of information adds to or lowers their level of confidence in the decision. Wilkins compares this decision-making process with the logic of the statistical procedure known as *stepwise regression,* in which the most important information is considered first, followed by information that contributes less and less to the end result.

A second type identified by Wilkins is the *ah yes! decision maker.* Instead of employing a sequential search strategy, they collect large amounts of information and search for patterns in that information. Only after they find a pattern they are familiar with do these decision makers exclaim, "Ah, yes, this is the typical such-and-such!" Then they make a decision. If the data do not fit precisely into existing patterns, ah yes! decision-makers reinterpret the data to fit those patterns.

Although the most pronounced distinctions are between people who process information sequentially and those who do not, Wilkins also identifies two additional types of decision makers. The *simplifier* reduces complex problems to their simplest form. On a parole board, the simplifier asks questions like, "Anything negative known about this man?" or "What are the problems with this case?" Finally, Wilkins describes the *ratifiers,* whose information search strategy is to wait for comments by someone else and then associate themselves with that person's viewpoint. These decision makers may review the case file to agree with comments from a caseworker, probation officer, or warden, or they may look to another member of the parole board for direction.

In his observation study of parole board decision making, Hawkins (1983) also considered the boundaries of rationality. Rather than focusing on types of decision makers, however, he discusses processes by which "a structure is imposed on the knowledge available in any case." Hawkins indicates that decision makers often use a few master categories in deciding what is relevant. For example, a parole board member may regard the facts of an offense and the criminal record as central. All board members may not agree, however; some, for example, may find a person's record during incarceration the most important piece of information. Decision makers in criminal justice also often make certain assumptions about the people involved. When a convict's story varies from the official record, for example, conflicts are often resolved in favor of the record. This decision is made not by clarifying the fact but by viewing the convict with suspicion because of his or her status. Finally, Hawkins indicates that decision makers often structure their data by resorting to precedent. They categorize cases in ways that allow the cases to be "handled in the usual way." For both Wilkins and Hawkins, significantly, the categories used and the structure given to information are *not* evident in the content of the information; they are imposed by the decision maker.

Characteristics of Information

Although decision makers must find some way to structure information to use it in decisions, some characteristics of the information itself contribute to that process. Clearly the most important characteristic is accuracy. The point that improved decisions can be made with accurate information may seem simple, but accuracy of information is a major problem in criminal justice for several reasons. First, case files and other collections of information used by decision makers are compiled from numerous agencies and officials along the way. They often contain incomplete or incorrect information that may be repeated and given inappropriate weight by decision makers as an offender moves from the police through the courts and to corrections. The information will also resurface if a person is rearrested.

Bail Decision Making

Bail decisions require jurisdictions to balance potentially conflicting goals of release on the least restrictive means necessary and public safety. At times, the decision makers must also be risk takers. Decisions should be made taking into consideration what a tolerable rate of pretrial failure might be for a given jurisdiction, what is successful pretrial release and how that is measured, how are the available resources used in release decisions, and how is the use of jail space decided and justified. To balance these concerns, and adhere to constitutional and legislative guidelines regarding release and detention, appropriate information on community ties, prior criminal history, record of court appearances, and compliance with previous court-imposed release should be available to bail decision makers.

Pretrial release agencies can improve bail decision making by providing complete, accurate and neutral information to the court, identifying those for whom alternatives to pretrial incarceration are appropriate, and monitoring released defendants to reduce the likelihood of failure to appear or pretrial rearrest.

In Milwaukee County, the pretrial program operated by the Wisconsin Correctional Service (WCS) provides these services by conducting objective risk assessments on defendants prior to an initial appearance and bail hearing; by conducting interviews with defendants to determine community ties; and by providing supervision and case management to defendants who are released but who need to comply with specific conditions placed on them by the court.

To complete the risk assessment, pretrial staff requires access to county jail and criminal court records on each defendant prior to the initial court appearance. In Milwaukee County, the jail information system, C/CJIS, provides arrest and booking information, including all charges and statute numbers. C/CJIS also indicates if the defendant has holds from additional jurisdictions or from the Division of Corrections for a probation or parole violation. This information is recorded on a Bail Guidelines worksheet. The Bail Guidelines worksheet assigns points to charge severity, previous failure to appear, pending cases, age at arrest, and defendant's access to telephone. After the points are tallied, probability of failure to appear and charge severity are plotted on a grid or matrix. Each cell of the grid indicates release without conditions, release with minimum conditions, or release with maximum conditions.

The pretrial interview is structured to provide background information that will help the bail evaluation caseworker make appropriate recommendations for release conditions to the Intake Court. Theoretically, a defendant with a grid score indicating release without special conditions would not be subject to a pretrial interview since there would be a presumption of release on recognizance for this defendant. However, the program has developed standards for overriding the bail guideline and allowing an interview to take place. Special attention is given to defendants who present symptoms or a history of severe and persistent mental illness or substance abuse. Unusual behavior described in a criminal complaint may be cause for an override. Often the District Attorney reviewing the arrest and making a charge decision will request a complete assessment on a person scoring in the least severe and least risk category. With this information the District Attorney may choose to defer prosecution with special conditions relating to treatment involvement or compliance with conditions relating to other circumstances. WCS staff will also accommodate requests received from family members expressing concern.

Supervised Pretrial Services are provided as an alternative to pretrial detention for eligible defendants. Defendants are released on the condition that they comply with special conditions stipulated by the court and monitored by the Pretrial Service Agency. Supervised Pretrial Release (SPR) acts as an important alternative to detention by allowing for the safe release of higher-risk defendants who may otherwise not be eligible for less restrictive options.

In most jurisdictions where Supervised Pretrial Services are provided, levels of supervision are established. In Milwaukee County, SPR conditions fall into three categories: (1) contact conditions that require defendants to report by telephone or in person to the pretrial service staff on a regularly scheduled basis; (2) problem-oriented conditions that may affect pretrial release behavior, such as substance abuse or mental health treatment, involvement in educational or job training, and counseling or involvement in other social services programming; and (3) conditions that restrict movements or associations.

Eventually some defendants will fail to comply with some or all of the release conditions. The credibility of the Supervised Pretrial Services program will depend on the effectiveness of its monitoring efforts and the responsiveness to compliance failures and violations of conditions. For this reason, programs should have set responses to condition violations and should work closely with the judiciary to develop appropriate responses to violations. In Milwaukee, the sanctions most recommended by the Pretrial Services for condition violations are remedial in nature, such as requiring enrollment in treatment or social service programming and are designed to correct the defendant's behavior as a means of reducing the risk of failure to appear or of rearrest.

MARILYN WALCZAK
Former Program Administrator
Wisconsin Correctional Service

BOWNE SAYNER
Former Assistant Executive Director
Wisconsin Correctional Service

Second, much of the information needed in criminal justice decisions is collected from people who have an interest in the outcomes or the process. Victims want arrests to be made, and convicts want to be paroled. McCleary (1977) has shown that parole officers' records are compiled for purposes that may include threatening a parolee or justifying revocation. Probation officers also write presentence investigations to court the favor of judges (Rosecrance, 1985). This interest in decision outcomes does not necessarily mean that reports are fabrications or that information is intentionally skewed, but it may mean that the data subtly reflect the range of the collector's purposes.

A third problem of accuracy in criminal justice information lies in the need for decision makers to use summary information about people. Because criminal histories, personality assessments, and records of adjustment are often presented in summary fashion, distortions are difficult to avoid. Remington, Newman, Kimball, Melli, and Goldstein (1969:697) found these examples in presentence investigations:

> He is a nice looking, clean cut, all-American appearing young man. Beneath this, however, he is as cold as ice. He is an expert manipulator, playing one person against another, with an amazing ability to say just what he thinks you want to hear. He is a loser plain and simple. He is sexually inadequate, vocationally inadequate and mentally inadequate. He has failed in everything—schools, jobs, military service, with his family, and with his wife. He has even failed as a crook. There is absolutely no reason to think that he can make it on probation and probably prison won't help him much. The only thing I can recommend is incarceration for as long as possible and then hope for the best.

Because legislation and case law now allow disclosure of presentence investigation reports to most defendants, such generalizations would be rare today. Most probation officers are trained to write less opinionated and more factual reports.

But factual reports do not necessarily eliminate the problem of using summary information. The quest for accuracy is partly responsible for the proliferation of standardized information collection devices that assign numerical weights to factual data. The addition of the weights creates a score that summarizes the information. Such devices are frequently used in bail, sentencing, and parole decisions. The devices appear to report information with high degrees of accuracy. Assigning a score of 0 if a person is employed or a 1 if unemployed certainly has the appearance of being more accurate than describing an offender as "vocationally inadequate." But the devices can also distort the information. For example, if the offender is a seasonal worker, is she to be classified as employed or unemployed? Should criminal histories be based on charges made at the time of arrest or at conviction, when plea bargains may have been struck? Often lengthy and complex instructions are needed to address these and similar problems. In addition, a basic question of accuracy is raised by the fact that the information presented in narrative sentences or numerical scores is often gathered from the offender himself.

Another characteristic of information is the order in which it is presented. Research indicates that because many decision makers use sequential methods to search for and analyze information, the first pieces of information are likely to be more influential than later pieces. This *order effect* (Burnham, 1975) is important in criminal justice because often the first information used by decision makers is the facts of a crime or an offender's prior record. This order contributes to cautious decision making.

Because of the order effect, new information—that is, information introduced after a tentative decision has been reached—does not have the same influence as if it were introduced earlier. Decision makers using sequential strategies become invested in their decisions and tend to devalue new information. Wilkins (1975b) found that decision makers often continue to ask for items of information long after a tentative decision has been made. In his experience, however, additional items never changed the decision.

Information about the availability of alternatives can also influence decisions. In criminal justice, many decisions are perceived as resulting in one of only two possible solutions. These dichotomous outcome choices include such things as to arrest or not arrest, to prosecute or not prosecute, to parole or not parole. Dichotomies like these often support *minimax strategies* by decision makers. These are strategies designed to minimize the maximum loss that could result from a given decision outcome, and they produce very conservative or low-risk decisions. A police officer, for example, may arrest a juvenile vandal if the only alternative is doing nothing, and a parole board may deny parole if outright release is the only other option. However, the introduction of alternatives, such as diversion programs, prerelease options, or even shortening a convict's parole review date, may alter decision outcomes in a less conservative direction.

It is important to appreciate the boundaries of rationality in decision making. We have examined the origins of those boundaries and have discussed how they function in organizational processes, the cognitive limitations of decision makers, and the nature of information itself. In the next sections we examine two important topics in criminal justice decision making—discretion and prediction—and focus on the limits of rationality in these areas.

Discretion

In a significant collection of works on the subject, Atkins and Pogrebin (1981) define discretion as applying to "a situation in which an official has latitude to make authoritative choices not necessarily specified within the source of authority which governs his decision making." Lipsky (1980) points out that latitude in decision making by frontline staff is one of the defining characteristics of human service organizations. In criminal justice organizations staff have broad discretionary powers to invoke the criminal process or to send a suspect or offender on to the next stage. For police, the power is to arrest or not to arrest. Prosecutors exercise broad discretion in the charging decision, and judges have wide latitude in managing the judicial process and in sentencing. In corrections, probation officers, prison staff, and parole officials exercise discretion over program placement, penalties for rule infractions, and release.

Critics of discretionary decision making argue that it often amounts to a total lack of control, "decision making unfettered by constraints of law or policy" (Gottfredson & Gottfredson, 1980:350). A classic statement of this position is provided by Goldstein (1960), who studied police discretion. Goldstein argues that police have a legal mandate to pursue full enforcement of the law. To his regret, however, circumstances, such as limitations of time and money as well as ambiguities in the definitions of laws, make full enforcement unrealistic. In being forced to adopt selective enforcement practices, the police make decisions that determine the level of law enforcement throughout the criminal process, but no clear guidelines constrain those decisions. Goldstein points out that the decision not to arrest is one that often escapes public scrutiny but one that controls the gate to the entire criminal justice system. Low-visibility decisions, such as police bargains not to seek charges in exchange for information or not to arrest if an assault victim will not sign a complaint, therefore, undermine "a major criminal law objective of imposing upon all persons officially recognized minimum standards of human behavior" (1960:38).

In corrections, the American Friends Service Committee (1971) takes an extreme position on discretion in their classic critique of the rehabilitation model. They argue that the discretion inherent in indeterminate sentences and requirements for program participation often serve illegitimate custodial rather than legitimate treatment aims. They feel that discretion permits prison administrators to use release or denial of parole as a carrot-and-stick control mechanism. Discretion even supports such practices as using offender attitudes or characteristics, for example, hair length or race, as a basis for criminal justice intervention from arrest through parole.

Critics of discretion in criminal justice, then, have argued that the latitude given frontline staff has led to uncontrolled decision making, which results in illegitimate and even corrupt practices. They see a solution to these problems in imposing increased control on decision makers. Thus, the American Friends Service Committee strongly supports determinate sentencing, and Goldstein (1984:80) states that "the . . . ultimate answer is that the police should not be delegated discretion not to invoke the criminal process." His first recommendation is that legislatures should write statutes to reduce or eliminate ambiguity and to make police decisions visible and thus subject to review. These reforms, it would seem, are designed to increase the rationality of decision making by severely restricting or eliminating discretion. Under this view, then, wide discretion is inconsistent with a rational model of organizational decision making.

A somewhat different perspective on discretion is also present in the literature. In their seminal work on bounded rationality, March and Simon (1958) suggested there is room for discretion in their theory. When a general goal in decision making is specified but means remain unspecified, they say, the decision maker is left with supplying the means-ends connection. The choice of means-ends connection, however, is not completely unconstrained. Discretion can then involve, for example, following guidelines that can be triggered only after additional information is obtained, as when a police officer must decide whether violence has occurred in a domestic dispute before deciding whether an arrest is to be made. Discretion may also involve deciding on a course of action based on expectations about others' decisions, as when police officers decide not to arrest in minor cases because they believe the cases will not be prosecuted. Or discretion may involve drawing on memory or experience, as when a police officer does not make an arrest because similar arrests in the past have not led to prosecutions.

This view of discretion, then, is based on the idea that the goals of decisions are often general and complex and that discretionary decisions are not completely unregulated. Three significant implications follow from this perspective. First, discretion can be viewed as necessary and useful. Second, the boundaries or regulations of discretionary decisions can be studied and understood. And third, because they can be understood, these regulations can be influenced without eliminating discretion.

The belief that discretion is necessary is now common in criminal justice. An accepted argument is put forth by Lipsky (1980), who suggests that discretion in the human services is needed because of the complexity of the task. In policing, for example, whether an assault and battery has occurred can be a complex question requiring police discretion. As in all decisions, some order must be imposed on the information available. Questions about the amount of force needed, the level of injury, and the relationship between the parties are complex. This complexity means that discretion is useful. Newman (1981), for example, argues that the discretionary process of plea bargaining can promote fairness by addressing the variability and complexity of offenses. Gottfredson, Hoffman, Sigler, and Wilkins (1975) argue that parole board discretion fulfills the same purposes.

A bounded rationality model of discretion also provides direction for the study and reform of decision making. Implicit in the work on sentencing and parole guidelines by Wilkins, Gottfredson, and Kress (Kress, 1980) is the view that such decisions are not completely uncontrolled or lacking in rationality. When they studied sentence disparity in courts, these authors found that the vast majority of these discretionary decisions could be explained by a small set of information items. An example of these items and the scale used to summarize them is presented in Figure 12-3. Items providing information about a defendant, such as prior criminal record, and items about the crime, such as degree of violence or injury to the victim, accounted for 85 percent of sentencing decisions. The remaining 15 percent of sentences could not be explained by the small list of items and would need to be studied as individual cases.

The recognition that discretionary decisions can be highly predictable also suggests methods of affecting those decisions. Wilkins and Gottfredson and Kress all describe a method of *structuring* judicial discretion without greatly restricting or eliminating it. Sentence averages or narrow intervals based on sentences that have already been handed down by judges can be constructed for all the combinations of offense and offender scores. The resulting guidelines reflect sentencing policy in the court because they are based on sentences actually given out. Sample guidelines are presented in Figure 12-4. Judges are given the guidelines and are told that they can issue sentences outside the guidelines (while remaining inside statutory limitations) but must provide explicit written reasons for the deviation. The guidelines are then updated at regular intervals so that they continue to reflect current court policy.

By structuring rather than eliminating discretion, this process recognizes that sentencing is a complex process in which judicial discretion is useful and beneficial. Instead of viewing discretionary decisions as unconstrained by law or policy, this approach is based on identifying and building on implicit constraints. The patterns of previous decisions reveal those constraints, and studying those patterns provides a productive method for influencing discretion while still noting its importance. The bounded rationality perspective can thus provide a useful method for addressing problems of discretion.

Offender _____ Docket number _____

Judge _____ Date _____

Offense(s) convicted of: _____

_____

_____

Crime score

A. Injury
   0 = No injury
   1 = Injury
   2 = Death _____ +

B. Weapon
   0 = No weapon
   1 = Weapon possessed
   2 = Weapon present and used _____ +

C. Drugs
   0 = No sale of drugs
   1 = Sale of drugs _____ =

Crime
score

Offender score

A. Current legal status
   0 = Not on probation/parole, escape
   1 = On probation/parole, escape _____ +

B. Prior adult misdemeanor convictions
   0 = No convictions
   1 = One conviction
   2 = Two or more convictions _____ +

C. Prior adult felony convictions
   0 = No convictions
   1 = One conviction
   2 = Two or more convictions _____ +

D. Prior adult probation/parole revocations
   0 = None
   1 = One or more revocations _____ +

E. Prior adult incarcerations (over 60 days)
   0 = None
   1 = One incarceration
   2 = Two or more incarcerations _____ =

Offender
score

Guideline sentence _____

Actual sentence _____

Reasons (if actual sentence does not fall within guideline range):

FIGURE 12-3 Sample Sentencing Guidelines Worksheet (From J. Kress, *Prescriptions for Justice.* Cambridge, MA: Ballinger © 1980, 311.)

FIGURE 12-4   Sample Felony-Sentencing Grid (Kress, 1980: 313)

Prediction

Although some authors have considered discretionary decision making as nearly devoid of rationality from an organizational perspective, the opposite assumptions seem common in discussions of *prediction*. Although recent advances have involved mathematical models, whether decisions are made by highly trained experts employing clinical methods or by statisticians applying complex formulas, the prediction of human behavior is generally thought of as a highly rational scientific process. Even when non-experts make predictive decisions, their lack of expertise is generally not viewed as detracting from the rationality of the process. In this section we examine the extent to which such assumptions of rationality are justified.

Many decisions in criminal justice involve the prediction of future behavior. After reviewing studies of decision making in the field, Gottfredson and Gottfredson (1980:334) describe prediction as "omnipresent" in the criminal justice system. Bail decisions, sentencing decisions, and parole decisions obviously involve predictions, but so do many other decisions made by workers in the criminal justice process. Classification into risk categories for probation involves prediction. Prediction figures into sentencing recommendations by probation officers, into corrections caseworkers' reviews of inmates for transfer, and into assistant prosecutors' determinations of charges and priorities for prosecution. Even police officers' decisions to arrest, issue a citation, or use a diversion program involve predictions.

In considering the usefulness of a pure rationality theory of these decisions, let us first consider the methods used in prediction. Two broad categories exist: clinical methods and statistical methods. *Clinical methods* involve assessments that focus on such factors as personality variables, situational variables, and the interaction of these variables. They may or may not involve the use of standardized tests, such as personality assessments, and they may or may not involve personal interviews. In death penalty cases in Texas, for example, psychiatrists make predictions about the likelihood of future violence by relying on hypothetical descriptions of the criminal record and character of convicted murderers. The heart of clinical methods, then, is the use of expertise in selecting and interpreting data from a variety of sources.

By contrast, *statistical methods* of prediction specify precisely what information is to be used and how it is to be interpreted. These methods use mathematical formulas that incorporate information about individuals to produce probability estimates of behavior. To make these estimates, information on the individual whose behavior is being predicted is compared with information on a large sample of individuals whose behavior in similar situations is known. For example, the information items that were originally found to be the best predictors of whether a convicted offender would continue to offend at a high rate and, therefore, should receive a long prison sentence (Greenwood, 1982 : 50) are the following: was convicted before for the same type of offense; was incarcerated more than 50 percent of the preceding two years; was convicted before age sixteen; served time in a state juvenile facility; used drugs in the preceding two years; used drugs as a juvenile; was employed less than 50 percent of the preceding two years. The scale produced with these items was used in support of a policy of selective incapacitation.

Statistical prediction methods were first used in criminal justice in 1928, when Burgess produced expected rates of failures on parole by developing a scale that assigned a point for each characteristic of an individual that was correlated with parole failure in a large sample of previously released offenders. The higher the total score, the more likely a person was to fail on parole, and, therefore, the stronger the argument for denying parole. Since then, sophisticated methods have been developed that use multivariate models to account for the differences in the importance of some predictor items and the interaction effects of the items. The prediction instruments used with this method resemble the instrument in Figure 12-3, but all the variables are selected for their strength in predicting some specific behavior, such as parole failure or failure on pretrial release.

Currently, much of the literature in criminal justice reveals a preference for statistical methods of prediction. An authoritative volume on the subject of prediction and classification in criminal justice does not even mention clinical prediction methods (Gottfredson & Tonry, 1987). Clinical approaches to classification are mentioned only as a stage in the development of more sophisticated models in Brennan (1987). Much of the pessimism surrounding clinical prediction may be related to questions of accuracy (which we will take up later in this section) and to the negative publicity surrounding some cases. A national newsmagazine, for example, dubbed Dr. James Grigson "Doctor Death" after his pronouncement, in the death penalty hearing of Thomas Barefoot, that he was 100 percent certain in his prediction of future dangerousness. In an *amicus curiae* brief to the Supreme Court in the Barefoot case, the American Psychiatric Association (1982) maintained that such predictions cannot be made with accuracy and that psychiatrists should not be permitted to testify in death penalty proceedings about predictions of future dangerousness. The court, however, viewed prediction as integral to criminal justice and ultimately rejected the APA's position.

The case in support of statistical methods as well as the criticisms of clinical methods can, however, be overstated. The American Psychiatric Association rejected only long-term clinical predictions and even questioned statistical predictions in these cases. There is support for short-term clinical predictions, especially when informed by statistical data and attention to unique conditions in an individual's environment (Monahan, 1981). It is equally true, however, that incompetent clinical assessments have their parallels in sloppy statistical procedures, which may involve improper sampling or unreliable measurement.

These points notwithstanding, clinical predictions may be unavoidable. Adequate databases for statistical methods do not exist for many decisions made in criminal justice. There may be few data on the characteristics of those who succeed in a diversion program or on those who fail to adjust in one particular medium security prison. Even where statistical data do exist, clinical processes remain relevant. A juvenile vandal's motives will continue to be relevant to a prosecutor deciding on charges, and racist attitudes and the tensions they produce will be relevant to prison placement. On this subject, Monahan (1981) presents a sensible argument that statistical data may be most useful within a context of clinical decision making.

It follows, then, that examining the assumptions about rationality that underlie both clinical and statistical predictions can be productive. Toward that end, we examine several factors important to all predictions of behavior. First, all decisions based on prediction involve a *criterion,* such as dangerousness, repeat offending, failure on parole, failure on pretrial release. Defining the criterion variable, however, can be difficult. Monahan (1981) discusses the difficulties in defining dangerousness. What specific behaviors entail dangerousness? Must they be overt acts? Must they cause injury? At first, these questions may seem relevant only to clinical predictions, in which no objective measurement of the criterion is made.

With statistical methods, however, equally difficult problems arise. Should predictions about future criminality be made based on official arrest records or on self-report studies of offenders? These two criteria may produce different results (Farrington, 1987). Likewise, success on parole may involve anything from upstanding citizenship to drug-addicted fringe lifestyles in which arrest is avoided. Failures may range from a repetition of major violations to revocation for technical violations (Glaser, 1969).

Clearly, viewing prediction as a purely rational process requires an unambiguous criterion variable. In clinical prediction, the failure to define the criterion in unambiguous terms is a problem, whereas with statistical methods the need for precise measurements may mask the ambiguities.

Predictor variables are the variables used to predict the criterion. In clinical prediction, they may differ from case to case but can include, for example, assessments of stability and subjective views of adjustment. With statistical methods, the predictors are the same for all cases and may include variables like age at first arrest and number of juvenile convictions. With either method, appreciating the limits of rationality remains relevant. It is impossible to know all the variables that may be pertinent, and information may arguably be different for different cases. Another difficulty is that often only the variables available in an official record make it into statistical processes.

Perhaps the most difficult problem in prediction relates to the *base rate* of the criterion variable. The base rate is the proportion of individuals in a population who exhibit the criterion. For example, the base rate for parole failure is the percentage of all paroled inmates who fail. For predictions to be useful, then, they must improve on the base rate. If, for example, 20 percent of all parolees fail on parole, then parolees released based on predictions must fail at a rate below 20 percent for the predictions to be useful. If prediction produced failures of more than 20 percent, the parole board would be better off simply releasing everyone because that would produce a failure rate of only 20 percent. Of course, no parole board would abdicate responsibility in this way, but the point illustrates the importance of understanding the base rate.

Base rates are problematical in criminal justice predictions for two reasons. First, the base rate is frequently unknown by decision makers. This is particularly true in clinical predictions, where studies to determine base rates may not have been undertaken. Not knowing the base rate may lead to dramatic over predictions of such things as parole or pretrial release failures. Base rates, however, also present problems in statistical predictions. For example, because the base rates for parole failure have generally been based only on the behavior of people released by parole boards, the rate for all potential releases is not known. The rates as well as the predictors have not been calculated on a representative sample of parole-eligible inmates.

Second, base rates are often low—that is, much of the behavior we seek to predict is rare. For example, in his development of statistical predictions in bail decision-making, Goldkamp (1985) found that only 12 percent of pretrial releasees failed to appear in court. For the predictions to be useful, then, they must improve on a 12 percent failure rate. The rub is that for statistical reasons, as base rates get farther and farther from a proportional distribution of 50/50 in a population, it becomes increasingly difficult to predict. Behavior that is statistically rare, such as violent crime, dangerousness, or parole failure, is very difficult to predict.

An additional issue is relevant to our discussion of the rationality of prediction: the consequences of predictions and our view of their accuracy. A parole board would certainly be well regarded if only 10 percent of its parolees were rearrested. Although at first glance the board's predictions seem highly accurate, a closer examination is required. Figure 12-5 reveals that there are, in fact, four possible consequences to the parole decision as well as other predictions. Those predicted to succeed will be released and will either succeed or fail. Those predicted to fail, however, will continue to be incarcerated and could succeed or fail but are not given the chance.

In our example, the 10 percent of parolees who fail are known as *false negatives:* the prediction that they would not fail was incorrect. By considering only these, however, it is clear that a parole board that releases few inmates will always be regarded as more accurate than a parole board willing to take more risks. To complete the assessment of accuracy, then, we must also consider the *false positives,* or the percentage of inmates whom the board predicts would fail and who would, in fact, actually not fail if they were released. In the example in Figure 12-5, we see that 60 percent of those predicted to fail would actually succeed. Of course, there is a problem with this rate. If the board predicts that inmates will fail, the board won't let them out. In reality, the false positive rate is rarely known.

Only if our parole board is willing to release the inmates whom they expect to fail can we completely evaluate the success of the predictions. Although such releases rightly do not occur, in some instances courts have required the release of offenders who had been predicted to be violent based on clinical prediction methods. Subsequent studies of these offenders have found that approximately 60 percent of them did not engage in violence (see Monahan, 1981). Overall, these studies have prompted the conclusion that clinical predictions of violence are incorrect in approximately two

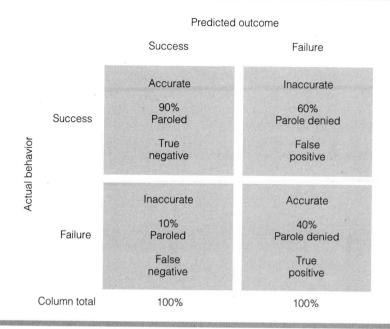

Predicted outcome

FIGURE 12-5   Hypothetical Outcomes from Parole Predictions

out of three cases. Studies of statistical predictions use statistical procedures to estimate false positive rates. These studies have revealed only slightly better results than
the other studies, generally with false positive rates of around 40 percent to 50 percent.

The issue of false positives raises two questions relevant to the rationality of prediction. First, as we already mentioned, the false positive rate is rarely known in
terms of actual predictions. Decision makers, then, often do not have information
critical to the prediction process. Second, the tolerance of different rates of false positives is a policy determination that has nothing to do with scientific methods. Even
with some idea of its rate of false positives, a parole board must decide how many offenders it is willing to keep in prison in order to prevent criminal offenses. The lower
the acceptable percentage of false positives (that is, those denied parole who would
not fail), the higher will be the percentage of false negatives (that is, released offenders who commit crimes); and the more we are concerned with reducing the number
of false negatives, the higher will be the rate of false positives. It may be appropriate,
for example, for the board to release only extremely low-risk candidates while still
knowing that 60 percent (but not knowing which 60 percent) of those they reject for
parole would not commit offenses. Whether decision makers should accept false positive rates of 60 percent or higher is a policy question distinct from the prediction
process itself.

All of this analysis suggests that even under the best circumstances claims about
the rationality of prediction can be overstated. In considering the highly technical aspects of prediction, we should not overlook the conceptual problems connected with
specifying the criterion, identifying appropriate predictors, appreciating the base rate,

and determining the tolerable ratios of false positives and false negatives. Understanding these aspects of prediction can be productive in guiding decision studies and improving prediction. In the final section of this chapter we consider the ways in which managers can influence and improve the decision-making process in criminal justice.

Improving Criminal Justice Decisions

Early in this chapter we noted that improvement in criminal justice decision making means making rational decisions. Although completely rational decision making may be an unattainable goal, the process can be moved in the direction of being more rational than it now is from an organizational perspective. The question remains, however: What is rational from an organizational perspective? From a theoretical viewpoint, this is a complex question, but the matter may be simplified by identifying recurrent themes in the literature on criminal justice decision making. These themes can guide the improvement of decision making.

One important theme in criminal justice decision making is equity. *Equity* in criminal justice processing means that similar offenders in similar circumstances are treated in similar ways. It does not mean that all offenders are treated alike, but it does mean that differences in treatment should be based on some meaningful distinctions among the offenders. Legal and ethical arguments support the goal of equity in decision making.

A second theme is *accuracy*. It is obvious that we should strive to see that persons not guilty of crimes are not arrested and that those released on parole do not commit additional crimes. It is equally important to strive to see that guilty persons are subject to arrest and that those denied parole based on prediction would, in fact, fail.

Equity and accuracy, however, provide only limited direction for decision makers. Sentencing guidelines, for example, may iron out inequities across judges, but the guidelines themselves say little about the purpose of sentencing an offender to prison. A third theme, then, is *consistency with theory*. Many theories exist about such issues as the purpose of police intervention, prosecution, or the punishment and treatment of offenders. Decision makers should strive to articulate the theories that underlie their decisions and to make future decisions consistent with those theories. We must appreciate, however, that the theories may be inconsistent with concerns for equity and accuracy. Deterrence theory, for example, may require the arrest and prosecution as well as long sentences for only a few people accused of crimes such as tax evasion or failure to register for the draft (see Morris, 1982).

A fourth theme of decision making in criminal justice is *consistency with resources*. While we strive for consistency with theory, we must also consider pragmatic interests. The decision to arrest or issue a citation should be influenced by the availability of jail space (see Hall, Henry, Perlstein, & Smith, 1985). Prosecutors need to be sensitive to court backlog, and even if there is a disproportionately high number of maximum security prison cells, classification officers must find ways to distinguish between those who will and will not fill those spaces. Although long-term planning can change available resources, decision makers must also confront short-term necessities.

Finally, a fifth theme in the literature of criminal justice is that *decisions should contribute to future decisions*. Both the process and the outcome should help to improve decision making in the future. This theme implies a cybernetic approach to improving decisions, which recognizes that all future decisions are affected by previous decisions. Decision making should be guided by continuing assessments of equity, accuracy, and consistency with theory and resources. In this way improving decision making becomes an ongoing, evolutionary process (Gottfredson & Gottfredson, 1980).

The five general themes we have just discussed also provide us with specific ideas for influencing the decision-making process. Those ideas involve the development of decision-making policies, concern with the people who make decisions, and concern with the information used in decision making.

When similar decisions are made time and time again, as many criminal justice decisions are, organizations need to formulate explicit policies about them. Those policies must address the theories underlying the decisions and the goals of particular decisions as well as the types of information to be used and the decision rules for processing information. Without such policies, no guides exist for examining the consequences of decision making and no basis exists for systematically studying and increasing the effectiveness of decisions. Policy makers, however, should appreciate the complexity of criminal justice decisions and the potential uniqueness of individual cases. Decision policies should provide for flexibility. The use of sentencing guidelines illustrates one approach to flexibility. The guidelines allow judges to go outside the expected sentence range but require a written explanation of the reasons for the deviation.

In improving decision making, attention must also be paid to the decision makers themselves. Decision processes should be structured to de-emphasize personality variables and subjective confidence levels. When possible, group, rather than individual, decisions should be encouraged. Groups tend to be more willing to take risks than individuals. Group decisions, then, lessen the conservative influences of minimax criteria. Group discussion about what information is considered relevant and how information is processed also encourages consistency in both the process and outcome of decisions.

Decision makers should also be encouraged to frame their decisions as probability estimates (Burnham, 1975), for two reasons. First, the accuracy of those estimates can then be checked against actual behavior; and second, policy can dictate the outcome of decisions when probability estimates are made explicit. For example, parole board policy should dictate whether an offender should be released when that individual is regarded as having a 60 percent chance of succeeding. In addition, decision makers should be trained and retrained by examining both the process and results of previous decisions.

Attention should also be paid to the information used in decision making. Efforts should be made to ensure that the information used is reliable and valid. For example, information on the seriousness of the offense, the length of criminal history, or adjustment to incarceration should be recorded and measured consistently by all decision makers. And decision makers should be encouraged to use information that research has demonstrated is relevant to the results of the decision.

Along with reliability and validity, format is important. Information should be presented to decision makers in sequential as well as summary form to accommodate the variety of search processes among decision makers. Efforts should also be made to avoid the influences of order effects and to assure adequate consideration of new information. Information on alternatives must also be adequate for decision making. When possible, dichotomous outcomes should be avoided because they increase the likelihood that minimax strategies would be invoked. Intermediate steps—such as citation as an alternative to arrest or release and revised parole, or classification dates as an alternative to denial— should be encouraged.

Finally, to make the improvement of decision making an evolutionary process, decision makers should have feedback about decisions they have made in the past. This information is most useful when presented in the form of correct-answer feedback (Burnham, 1975). Correct-answer feedback not only tells decision makers whether past decisions were correct but also provides information about why some decisions were correct while others were not. For example, correct-answer feedback to a parole board would report the percentage of parolees who failed and also provide information about the characteristics of offenders who are most likely to fail. This feedback, then, can influence the information that decision makers regard as relevant, how the information is combined, and even the theories underlying the decision process. With modern computing and statistical capabilities, even decision makers in small organizations and agencies should have access to correct-answer feedback.

Summary

In few fields are the study and improvement of decision making as important as in criminal justice, where the decisions made create a system out of disparate agencies and define the organizational policies of those agencies. Decision making pervades the roles of managers and frontline staff members in criminal justice. In this chapter we considered the theory and process of decision making and examined ways to improve the decisions made in criminal justice.

Improvement in decision making means rational decisions. But that goal must be considered within the context of the limits of rationality in the decision-making process. We argue that an explicit understanding of the cultural and political constraints on decision making is vital to approaching a more rational decision making process. Attempting to impose rational decision-making procedures and techniques on an organization without considering implicit and hidden constaints is doomed to failure. Organizations, individual decision makers, and information itself constrain decision making and assure that a purely rational model of decisions is not possible under the conditions of ambiguity that exist in criminal justice. Decision makers impose order where goals may conflict and large amounts of information are available. An extension of the theoretical perspective suggests that some decision making can best be understood as a process of defining problems in terms of the solutions that already exist.

Recognition of the limits of rationality can help us understand and improve the decision-making process. Although discretion has sometimes been characterized as unguided by organizational policy, viewing discretionary decisions from the perspective of bounded rationality provides direction for change while still preserving the desirable qualities of discretion. The bounded rationality perspective also suggests that neither clinical nor statistical prediction should be regarded as an entirely rational process.

The limits of rationality are not inflexible, however. Those limits can be pushed back by managers seeking increasingly rational decisions. In the literature of criminal justice, several themes are consistent with the pursuit of increased rationality. The goal of rational decisions suggests attention to equity, accuracy, consistency with theory and resources, and the development of self-correcting processes.

In the next chapter we continue to focus on the question of rationality in criminal justice organizations by examining the complex question of organizational effectiveness in a field where goals are complex and often conflicting.

Case Study

Rational Sentencing:
Whose Rationality?

Mary had worked as a probation officer for a little over a year. She had a degree in criminology and criminal justice and was excited about working in probation. After a few weeks of un-programmed on-the-job training, she was pleased that much of her university coursework had given her some basis for the procedural aspect of the work. Mary especially felt that her college instructor, an ex-probation officer, had given her a fairly good grasp of the presentence investigation process (PSI). As a result, she was assigned her own PSI work more quickly than most novices. However, a novice she was, and she hadn't been given many complex or perplexing cases.

Her last PSI assignment had been a bit more complex than most. She had been assigned a PSI on a sex offender, specifically statutory rape. A 22-year-old male had a month-long sexual relationship with a 16-year-old girl. When her parents discovered the relationship, they filed charges over the objections of the girl. The defendant had an earlier arrest for disorderly conduct as a result of a fight in a local tavern and a number of speeding tickets; he had worked steadily but had moved from job to job as an auto mechanic. He also admitted to being a recovering drug and alcohol addict. Mary verified his attendance in recovery treatment, and tests showed that he was drug and alcohol free. The girl apparently had a difficult relationship with her parents, had dropped out of school, and was a drug and alcohol abuser. She convinced Mary during the PSI process that she was attempting to recover from her addictions and the defendant was the only significant person in her life who was supporting her attempt to recover. The girl also admitted to being sexually active and did not view her relationship with a 22-year-old male as anyone's business.

Mary collected a great deal of additional information and considered her recommendation. She was in favor of granting the defendant probation on the condition he avoid contact with the 16-year-old. Mary also applied a statistical risk prediction model, which helped her conclude the defendant would not be a likely candidate for recidivism. She recommended probation with the condition the defendant would not have any contact with the girl until she turned 18 and presented her recommendation to her supervisor Brian.

Immediately Brian said, "Mary, I don't like your recommendation. We don't like to put sex offenders on probation."

"This is technically a sex offense," Mary answered, "but I don't see any evidence of the defendant digressing and getting involved with young girls as a pattern. I think he and the girl's mutual neuroses met, which resulted in their relationship. I think it had more to do with the similar needs and personality disorder they both share."

"Cool," said Brian. "What if he meets a 14-year-old who's a loser like him?"

"Look, Brian, I did a risk prediction on him, and I really don't believe there is much of a chance of this repeating itself," Mary answered. "If he keeps his interest in the victim, she will be an adult in about eighteen months and the case is closed."

Brian closed the file and looked at her. "Mary, let me be honest with you. A month before you got here, we took a chance and put a child molester on probation. We did that because his parents had a team of lawyers and psychologists testify that he would be OK, and I suspect there were some social links between the prosecutor, the judge, and the family of the creep. The family of the victim seemed charitable and felt the scumbag would benefit from psychiatric guidance. They didn't want to harm this asshole's life, the humiliation of being arrested was enough punishment—you know all the arguments. Well, the judge went against our unwritten policy and put him on probation. Guess what? He stocked his glove compartment back up with candy and was cruising the local elementary school a month after he was on probation. He snatched some kid into his car and fortunately was caught. Unfortunately, the press got hold of the whole thing, and we took the heat."

"But it's not rational to compare that case with this one," Mary protested. "It's apples and oranges."

"Sure, at its essence. But symbolically it's a sex offense, and the press and all of the holier-than-thou groups are waiting for us to put a sex offender on probation. Believe me, the judge will not put this guy back on the street. Consider him a burnt offering to the public for our last mistake."

"That's ugly," Mary declared. "I can't let this guy go to prison to satisfy some base political and vindictive needs of the public. The judge is supposed to have the courage to dispense justice, not satisfy the rabble."

"Easy, Mary, that won't solve anything," Brian smiled. "Work out a compromise. Why don't you recommend jail time followed by some form of computer monitoring with probation?"

"Well, this disappoints me. But I guess you're saying if I recommend probation, he is going to prison."

Brian stood up. The meeting was over. "That's right. You're catching on now."

Case Study Questions

1. What role should political concerns have in decision making? In the case study, should rational guidelines have more importance in the decision than potential political concerns?

2. What cultural aspects of the organization's decision making did Mary learn through this experience? In addition, what limitations are present within "rational" models of decision making when they are implemented within an organization's culture?

3. In this case study could cultural and political concerns be made part of the formal decision making processes? Can these cultural and political concerns be kept out of decision making? Can prediction models address these concerns?

For Discussion

1. Consider a probation officer contemplating a decision to seek revocation of a client's probation. What theories might underlie such a decision? What are the goals? What kinds of information should the officer seek? What kinds of feedback might the probation officer want in order to influence later decisions?

2. A police officer witnesses two people arguing and shoving each other on the street and must decide what to do about it. What do you think is the range of things that the officer can do? How well does a rational model of decision making explain the choices an officer has? How well do other models, including the garbage can model, explain the officer's position?

3. Of the types of decision makers described in this chapter, which best describes your own approach? If you were a judge making a sentencing decision, what items of information would you want? How many items would you collect? If you could collect only four items, what would they be? Could you make a sentencing decision based on those items? How confident would you be of the decision?

4. Design a process for determining, on a case-by-case basis, which juveniles should be diverted from court processing. Is this a predictive decision? What is being predicted? How should the decision process be structured? Who should make the decisions? What kinds of information should be used? How should it be presented? How would you evaluate the decisions?

For Further Reading

Atkins, B., and Pogrebin, M. *The Invisible Justice System: Discretion and the Law.* Cincinnati, OH: Anderson, 1981.

Gottfredson, D. M., and Tonry, M. (Eds.). *Prediction and Classification: Criminal Justice Decision Making.* Chicago: University of Chicago Press, 1987.

Gottfredson, M. R., and Gottfredson, D. M. *Decisionmaking in Criminal Justice: Toward a Rational Exercise of Discretion.* Cambridge, MA: Ballinger, 1980.

Murray, M. *Decisions: A Comparative Critique.* Marshfield, MA: Pitman, 1986.

Schein, E. H. *Organizational Culture and Leadership,* 2nd ed. San Francisco: Jossey-Bass, 1997.

CHAPTER

13

ORGANIZATIONAL EFFECTIVENESS

If the original report doesn't call it a [Uniform Crime Reports burglary], the insurance company won't pay off, but a lot of victims don't know that. When they find out, they want to change the report. That's not possible, of course. Once the report's filed, it's all over. So what they do is call the crime in again. We'll dispatch an officer, and in most cases a new complaint report comes in here.

(City police clerk quoted in McCleary, Nienstedt, & Erven, 1982:364)

There is no future in making collars! I used to be active, but it got me nothing. So now I work off the books [without paying taxes]. That way I keep the money, not the government. I leave the collars to the hotshots that still believe they will get promoted.

(Police officer quoted in Walsh, 1986:282)

The reason the county gets so many child-abuse cases is because the district attorney has encouraged reporting by doctors and other professionals. Who says we recommended those dispositions? It is the judge who has the responsibility of imposing the sentence. The reason child molesters avoid jail in this county is judges refuse to send these people to jail.

(Prosecutors explaining their prosecution and sentence records, "Offenders Escape Through Cracks," 1987:2)

I do believe, we all do—from the director to the warden to the boss in the cell-block—that prisons can be run well. Prisons don't have to be unsafe, unclean, uneducational. Good programs and good safety go together with good management.

(Texas prison major quoted in DiIulio, 1987:146)

One of the difficulties involved in the measurements that have been done . . . is that they are aggregated measures which do not take into account political, cultural, social realities. . . . Unless and until measurement is based on . . . some sense of community boundaries . . . whether it's political or moral boundaries within that group of people who live there and interact—it doesn't make any sense because you're collapsing apples and oranges, horses, mules, and so on.

(Peter Manning, professor of criminal justice, commenting on measurements of police effectiveness at a National Institute of Justice workshop, 1996)

Revision of performance measurement systems to reflect the diverse responsibilities of an ever-broadening police role is something many executives still need to accomplish . . .regardless of whether they have any interest in changing their organization's current approach to policing. Changes in policing philosophies only make more apparent the need for management to acknowledge and support activities that effective officers have conducted but that have gone officially unrecognized.

(Oettmeier & Wycoff, 1998)

For many people, the very concept of organization implies purpose, and the question of how well purposes are met is central to understanding organizations. *Organizational effectiveness* is thus a central theme in both the pragmatically oriented literature on management and the theoretically oriented literature of organizational behavior. For many managers, determining effectiveness involves identifying the criteria with which to assess effectiveness, measuring these criteria, and weighing the various outcomes. Implicit in these steps, however, are important theoretical questions such as: Effectiveness for whom? How are outcomes to be measured? What is a good outcome? Such inescapable questions illustrate the complexity of the concept of organizational effectiveness.

That complexity is evident in many discussions of organizations (see Peters & Waterman, 1982). For example, Tayloristic managers might cringe at a policy that 3M Company finds central to its effectiveness. At 3M, some employees are expected to steal company time and material for their own creative enterprises in the hopes that this theft will produce marketable innovations. (Those sticky Post-It notes illustrate the potential for success in this approach.) Managers at Ford also grappled with definitions of organizational effectiveness when, in the late 1970s, they allegedly used a cost-benefit analysis to decide not to recall Pintos, even though they knew the faulty gas tank design was linked to fires and the subsequent deaths of some of their customers (Cullen, Maakestad, & Cavender, 1987).

In criminal justice, the question of effectiveness is equally complicated. For example, what criteria for effectiveness should drive prison policies on overcrowding? In the mid-1980s, the Illinois Department of Corrections granted massive numbers of good-time deductions, thus permitting the early release of thousands of prisoners, before the courts intervened to stop the policy. Although the department argued that the policy was necessary for the effective management of the prison population, prosecutors argued that it violated correction's fundamental purpose of protecting the public from convicted criminals (Austin, 1986).

The Florida Department of Corrections faced a similar situation when it retroactively rescinded good time credits for prisoners, thereby delaying the release of some offenders and reincarcerating others when it was found that they were let out too soon. Some offenders went to court, and the Supreme Court ruled that such a policy of rescinding good time credits was in violation of the Constitution's ex post facto clause prohibiting, in effect, retroactive punishment. The result was the release of hundreds of felons, some of whom were serious offenders. Arguing from a public protection perspective, some politicians advocated that a constitutional amendment be passed to prevent the provision of good time credits to prisoners on the basis of advancing public protection as the primary purpose of criminal sentencing (CNN, 1997).

The complexity of the effectiveness issue is also seen in then federal prosecutor Rudolph Giuliani's support of a three-year prison sentence in the largest case of insider stock trading. In late 1987, after an investigation lasting nearly two years, Ivan Boesky was convicted of illegally making hundreds of millions of dollars by trading stocks based on insider information not available to the public. Giuliani defended the sentence, which made Boesky eligible for parole after one year, by pointing out that Boesky had cooperated with the investigation and had provided information useful in several other cases. He argued that cooperation is necessary in such complex cases and that a stiffer sentence may have sent the wrong message to other stock traders considering cooperating with the prosecution.

In this chapter we examine the questions posed by these examples. We begin by defining effectiveness and noting the political consequences of this definition. We then focus on theories of organizational effectiveness, paying special attention to the limitations of the models used frequently in organizational assessments. After examining a variety of methods for assessing effectiveness, the chapter ends with a discussion of key issues to consider in determining the effectiveness of criminal justice organizations.

What Is Organizational Effectiveness?

In the literature on organizations the term *effectiveness* has been used in many ways. Most commonly, effectiveness refers to the degree of congruence between organizational goals and some observed outcome. This definition, however, masks many complicated concerns. For example, some have argued that organizational survival is the best indicator of effectiveness (Hannan & Freeman, 1977). Others have focused on adaptability to the environment rather than simply on survival. Most scholars focusing on organizational goals have also argued that effectiveness is a multidimensional concept and have advocated the use of multiple measures to assess it. In the literature on organizations, then, effectiveness remains a largely ambiguous and ill-defined concept. Some scholars have even questioned the value of the concept in the scientific study of organizations (Pfeffer, 1977b). Few scholars, however, would doubt the value of the concept for management.

Cameron (1981) identifies three reasons why the concept of organizational effectiveness remains muddled. First, there are important differences in the way scholars have conceptualized organizations. Some have suggested that organizations are best viewed as rational entities pursuing goals. In this view, a police department may be viewed as attempting to control all crime. An organization, however, might also be viewed as responding to strategic constituencies. In this view, police managers may be most concerned with their impact on property crime in a business district. Or police organizations may be viewed as primarily meeting the needs of their members through pay schedules or shift and holiday assignments. A second but related reason for the confusion surrounding the concept of effectiveness is the complexity of organizations. To the extent that organizations pursue goals, those goals are often complex, multiple, and conflicting. This complexity prohibits the identification of specific indicators of effectiveness that can be applied across organizations. Third, the confusion has been enhanced by the fact that researchers have often used different, non-overlapping criteria, thus limiting the accumulation of empirical evidence about organizational effectiveness.

Scholarly discussions of effectiveness do make one thing clear. Effectiveness is not a single phenomenon. Organizations can be effective or ineffective in a number of different ways, and these ways may be relatively independent of one another. There is, however, little agreement on the specific criteria that should be considered in examining organizational effectiveness. In a review of the research, Campbell (1977) identified thirty different criteria that have been proposed seriously as indices of organizational effectiveness. The list includes productivity, efficiency, employee absenteeism, turnover, goal consensus, conflict, participation in decision making, stability, and communications. In criminal justice it is easy to imagine as long a list of idiosyncratic measures: crime rates, arrest rates, conviction rates, sentences, victim satisfaction, incapacitation, recidivism, humaneness, attention to legal rights, worker satisfaction, increasing budgets. Obviously, such measures may often be independent or even conflicting.

In light of ambiguities about a general definition of organizational effectiveness, perhaps the best approach is to address first the question of why we try to assess the effectiveness of organizations. Scholars give many answers to that question. They may be interested in accounting for the growth or decline of organizations; they may wish to investigate interactions between organizations and their environments; or they may seek to understand the antecedents of effectiveness.

For managers, however, the answer is straightforward. Beliefs about effectiveness influence how organizations are managed. Notions of effectiveness undergird many management decisions, and effectiveness studies can have direct and tangible consequences for organizations and their members.

In criminal justice organizations, those consequences may be felt in a variety of areas, including budget, personnel, and even mission. Treatment programs may be dismantled if they do not lower recidivism rates. Civilian staff may replace sworn officers in traffic control and other assignments when cost effectiveness is considered (Harring, 1982). Managers or their subordinates may be fired in the face of indicators of ineffectiveness. Prison wardens may resign following disturbances or escapes; police chiefs may be forced out by dissatisfied officers (Mastrofski, 1996). Managers may even redefine their goals in response to effectiveness studies. In the mid-1970s, treatment came to be regarded as ineffective and departments of corrections redefined their mission by emphasizing incapacitation and punishment. Prompted by the same research, probation agencies took on responsibilities for victim services, pretrial supervision, and increased surveillance of offenders (Petersilia & Turner, 1993). Some have suggested the relevance of a crime control approach to making probation and parole more effective (Petersilia, 2000).

Concern with effectiveness, in short, can often lead to the redistribution of resources within and across organizations. In a completely rational model of organizations, changes in budget, personnel, or mission may appear to be logical consequences of efforts to assess and improve effectiveness. As we pointed out in Chapter 12, however, rationality has its limits within organizations. Conflicting goals, inadequate information, and the need to "satisfyce" rather than optimize limit organizational rationality. Under these circumstances, effectiveness can be viewed as subject to the same bounded rationality as decision making. Effectiveness, therefore, might best be understood as a normative, value-laden concept used to distribute resources between and within organizations.

For many criminal justice organizations, conflicting goals and inadequate information are no small concerns. Take, for example, the microscope that many prisons find themselves under. During the 1990s many states saw massive expansion and growth in the number of prisons they managed. Prison expansion became the norm for many states trying to get control of a bourgeoning prison population, yet at the same time both critics and supporters were raising questions about the effectiveness of such efforts. Some states, California, for example, passed laws that required the department of corrections to take aggressive steps in its treatment of drug offenders. Under pressure from multiple interests, the rational pursuit of public safety through imprisonment was questioned by some. And efforts to redirect the effectiveness question toward what was actually being done to assist offenders and away from simply warehousing them became important. Societal protection is still important, but treatment expectations became normative as well. Prison effectiveness was being assessed on how prisons fit into the larger picture of changing criminal behavior. Similar concerns have been raised by those who question police strategies on how they fit into the larger question of societal protection and community well-being (see Oettmeier & Wycoff, 1998).

Effectiveness studies, like all evaluation research, take place within a political context. According to Weiss (1972), this context intrudes in three ways. First, the organizations, programs, or offices are the creatures of political decisions. They have been proposed, created, funded, and staffed through political processes. Second, the results of effectiveness studies feed into the political processes that sustain or change the organization. Third, the studies are political themselves because they involve implicit statements about the legitimacy of goals and interests within the organization (Lovell, 1994).

Appreciation of the complexity of organizations and the political context of evaluation highlights one important question that undergirds all discussions of organizational effectiveness: effectiveness for whom? Regardless of the theory of effectiveness under consideration and regardless of how data may be gathered and analyzed, this question remains relevant.

Many studies of effectiveness adopt the perspective of the organization's dominant coalition by reflecting the interests of those in power. As Hall (1982:286) notes, effectiveness "lies in the eye and mind of the beholder, with the important qualification that some beholders are more powerful than others." Police managers, for example, may argue that arrest rates are the best indicator of effectiveness. Corrections managers may regard low levels of inmate violence and few escapes as indicators of effectiveness. Other constituencies, however, may have alternative views. Internal constituencies led by union stewards may base an assessment of effectiveness on working conditions. This was the case in 1979 in the largest prison guard strike in history. New York corrections officers had to be replaced by the National Guard when they walked off the job to protest a perceived lack of control over inmates and their low status within the organization (Jacobs & Zimmer, 1983). Similar views have been expressed by the California Correctional Peace Officers Union about the safety and welfare of their members, who work in a highly volatile and tense environment where overcrowding and inmate violence have escalated and the Department of Corrections has been unable to convince the public that additional monies should be set aside to build more prisons (Gomez, 1996).

One of the most significant cases in the history of prisoner litigation also illustrates the importance of the question of effectiveness-for-whom and the importance of power in determining whose view prevails. Prior to the case of *Ruiz v. Estelle* (1980), the Texas Department of Corrections (TDC) was widely regarded as highly effective based on its low costs, low incidence of reported violence, and the general cleanliness of its institutions. A combination of internal and external constituents, however, saw the matter differently. Inmates, prison reform lawyers, and the federal court came to regard the TDC as grossly ineffective. As one lawyer noted, "While corrections in Texas may be cheap in some senses, the system exacts intolerable costs to the human rights of the citizens in its custody and its unlawful practices must be remedied" (quoted in Martin & Ekland-Olson, 1987). These differing views figured prominently in the longest and most expensive prisoners' rights trial to date, a case that, after long and bitter battles, led to the near-total reorganization of the TDC. The case was finally resolved when the presiding judge, William Wayne Justice, threatened to impose fines up to $24 million a month against the Department of Corrections for contempt and failure to comply with court orders. The case was settled between the judge and the TDC after progress had been made to rectify the unconstitutional conditions within Texas prisons.

The importance of the question of perspective is also demonstrated in a study of the use of telephones to arrange bail for pretrial inmates. Here another powerful external constituency was involved. An experiment in the Tombs, a detention prison in lower Manhattan, proved that many inmates could raise bail money simply by being given access to telephones. The social scientists conducting the study felt that increased availability of telephones not only would benefit inmates but also would increase organizational effectiveness by reducing crowding and saving large sums of money on pretrial detention. Implementation of increased access to telephones was resisted, however, when prosecutors intervened. This external constituency opposed the policy because it was seen as weakening their position in plea bargaining. Because detained arrestees are more likely than released arrestees to plead guilty, the prosecutors attempted to block increased access to telephones (Lenihan, 1977).

These examples illustrate varying perspectives on organizational effectiveness. Dominant coalitions, powerful internal constituencies, and powerful external constituencies may all have different ideas as to what makes for an effective organization. Because those perspectives may lead to different distributions of resources in organizations, it is critical to understand whose perspective underlies any discussion of the effectiveness of an organization. Oftentimes discussions on organizational effectiveness within criminal justice organizations frame the debate on how measures of organizational activity are limited and provide no new insights on how effectiveness can be addressed. Where there has been improvement in examining organizational effectiveness within criminal justice organizations, it has been led by the police field.

Sparrow (1999) discusses how issues of police effectiveness can be examined by posing different questions concerning police operations. Take, for example, the question of police efficiency. Sparrow suggests that the traditional police department responds to this question by examining detection and arrest rates as the measures of police performance. Sparrow offers an alternative view by framing the question differently. Under a community-policing model, this question would be answered by examining the degree to which the community is free from crime and disorder. Effectiveness, therefore, is dependent on the perspective offered and what questions of interest are advanced. For some, arrest rates reflect some measure of activity among police; for others unless this activity is tied to larger concerns, such as the absence or presence of public disorder, it has limited utility when discussing organizational effectiveness (Oettmeier & Wycoff, 1998).

Police organizations are not the only criminal justice entities where these questions are being asked. Changing the nature of questions and answers concerning organizational effectiveness can be found in probation and parole organizations, prison systems, and court operations as well.

Writers and researchers during the 1990s began to raise questions on how organizational effectiveness can be assessed differently. The emphasis has been on changing the way in which we understand and gauge performance measures and organizational effectiveness within criminal justice organizations (see U.S. Bureau of Justice Statistics, 1993). A particular emphasis has been on distinguishing organizational outputs (for example, arrests) from organizational outcomes (for example, crime reduction), with the goal of improving employee performance evaluation and organizational effectiveness.

Theories of Organizational Effectiveness

Hannan and Freeman (1977) point out that some theoretical perspective must underlie any discussion of effectiveness. Even the question of whether an organization is regarded as succeeding or failing will depend on theory. In this section we review the major theoretical perspectives on the assessment of organizational effectiveness.

The Goal Model

The goal model is the most common theoretical perspective on effectiveness, and, as Hall (1982:278) suggests, it is both simple and complex. In its simplest form, the goal model defines *effectiveness* as the degree to which an organization realizes its goals (Etzioni, 1964:8). The model posits that organizations can be understood as rational entities. In using this perspective, evaluators assume that an organization's goals can be identified, that organizations are motivated to meet those goals, and that progress toward them can be measured. Evaluating companies by their profits is, perhaps, the most obvious example of this approach. In criminal justice, such measures of effectiveness as arrest rates, conviction rates, and recidivism all reflect the goal model.

There are some difficulties with this model. As we noted in Chapter 12, research has revealed the limitations of the rational model of organizations. Many commentators have also noted the difficulties involved in defining an organization's goals (Simon, 1964; Etzioni, 1960); most organizations have multiple and, frequently, conflicting goals. Even manufacturing firms must balance quantity with quality goals and concern for short-term profits with long-term considerations. The situation is still more complicated in criminal justice. Police departments are charged with controlling crime but must also ensure due process. They also generate revenue through enforcement practices, reduce fear of crime, maintain order, and satisfy their employees, as well as pursue many other goals. Identification of some primary goal or goals is clearly a difficult task and one that again raises the question of effectiveness-for-whom.

Nevertheless, all public organizations have numerous goals (Hannan & Freeman, 1977:111). In his study of street-level bureaucracies, Lipsky (1980) considered the impact of these goals on effectiveness. He argues that one of the characteristics of public organizations is that their conflicting goals reflect conflicts absorbed by the organization from society at large. For example, the public generally supports services for welfare recipients, but the same public argues for reductions in welfare rolls and cutbacks in services. The public also wants to see offenders rehabilitated but at the same time wants prison to be, at least, uncomfortable. One implication of Lipsky's argument is that public organizations are designed to be ineffective when effectiveness is ascertained by a broad-based goal model.

A second problem with the goal approach also relates to the question of what goals should be considered but poses that question differently. Perrow (1961) distinguishes between official goals and operative goals. *Official goals* are generally for public consumption and can be found in annual reports and broad policy statements. Such goals as "to serve and to protect," however, provide little guidance for what goes on in an organization on a daily basis. *Operative goals* are generally derived from official goals but tell us exactly what the organization is trying to do.

The difference between official and operative goals is illustrated in Sykes's study of Trenton Prison. He argues that because we know little of the technology needed to "treat" offenders and because punishment must be tempered with humaneness, prison cannot accomplish either official goal. Instead, the regimen of incarceration reveals an operative goal of simply retaining custody through benign means. The Texas prison system confronted the same dilemma that Sykes describes but apparently resolved it in a different fashion. While neither treatment nor punishment was actively pursued, the TDC did follow a strict and sometimes brutal regimen directed at maintaining order (see DiIulio, 1987). Considering only official goals invokes unrealistic standards and ignores goals that are actually being pursued. Considering only operative goals, however, makes it impossible to compare effectiveness across organizations.

A third problem with focusing on organizational goals relates to the consequences of measuring goal attainment. On one hand, this approach means that behavior that is not viewed as relating to goals is not measured and, therefore, is not viewed as contributing to effectiveness. Police officers' compassion toward victims of crime or a judge's exhortations to an impressionable juvenile go unrecognized if effectiveness is measured by arrest statistics or cases processed. On the other hand, the effectiveness criteria selected may go farther and actually alter desirable behavior that is not recognized in the measurement process. While studying an employment agency, Blau (1964) observed that the choice of evaluation criteria had a dramatic effect on behavior within the organization. When the agency was evaluated on its job placement rate, employment counselors shifted their focus from clients who were difficult to place to clients who were the most likely to find work and who may even have been successful without the agency. Measuring goal attainment, then, not only leaves some activity within an organization unrecognized but may narrow activity so that only those goals whose attainment is measured are met.

A final concern about the goal model of effectiveness deals with the relationship between goal attainment and consequences for the organization. In public organizations this relationship is not at all straightforward. Lipsky (1980:35), for example, suggests that the demand for services in street-level bureaucracies will always increase to meet (or exceed) supply. He illustrates the point with the example of a health care clinic forced to move out of a poor neighborhood in an effort to control the demand for services. The more successful the clinic was at providing services, the greater was the demand. The evidently bottomless demand necessitated either cutbacks in the quality of services or making services difficult to obtain by increasing transportation problems for clients. The attainment of goals thus led to drastic changes for the organization. Similarly, Wilson (1989) argues that the question of effectiveness is always a sensitive issue for public bureaucracies, since much of what they do cannot be understood from a purely "market perspective."

Whereas goal attainment may have negative consequences for some organizations, failure may not only not have negative consequences, it may, in fact, have some positive consequences. For example, it is difficult to envision cutbacks in the police because crime rates increase! Likewise, when Martinson (1974) and others declared correctional treatment a failure in the mid-1970s, prison populations and resources for prisons began to soar. When some goals are considered, then, prisons may look ineffective, but the consequences may be positive for the organization.

The goal model, then, is a complex framework in which to consider organizational effectiveness. Despite its limitations, however, the assessment of effectiveness continues to be largely a process of identifying goals, measuring them, and comparing the results against some standard. The reader, however, should be aware of the problems and limitations of this perspective.

Some Alternatives to the Goal Model

The goal model is a broad and complex means of examining organizational effectiveness. In response to problems with this goal approach, several other models have been developed that view effectiveness differently. One of these, the *internal process* model, is consistent with human relations perspectives in organizational analysis (see Likert, 1967; Perrow, 1986). It argues that effective organizations are those in which there is little internal strain, where information flows easily both horizontally and vertically, and where internal functioning is smooth and characterized by trust and benevolence toward individuals (Cameron, 1981). To the extent that this model is concerned with morale within an organization, it may be seen as simply focusing on a limited set of goals. Such a narrow focus, however, is not without its benefits, especially in fields like criminal justice, when agreement on other goals may be difficult to reach.

Another perspective has been described as the counterparadigm to the goal model (see Hall, 1982:286). *Participant-satisfaction,* or *strategic-constituency, models* are not concerned with questions of morale as the names may suggest. Instead, they view effective organizations as serving the interests of key constituencies (see Hall, 1982; Cameron, 1981), which may include resource providers, suppliers, users of an organization's products, or even clients in social service agencies. Effective organizations are able to maintain the contributions of these constituencies. For example, this model might highlight the importance of good relations between the police and the prosecutor's office or might explain why public defenders often maintain good relationships with their supposed adversaries in the courtroom. The model may also explain why some organizations fail. The Willowbrook School on Staten Island, a school for the retarded, was closed in the late 1970s after failing to satisfy parents' groups and the courts (Rothman & Rothman, 1984). An investigative reporter had sneaked into the school and revealed deplorable conditions on the local television station. Eventually a parents' group was organized, and it successfully fought the institution.

Another view of organizational effectiveness incorporates many of the elements in the approaches already discussed. Steers (1977) describes this *process approach.* Under this model, effectiveness is described as a process rather than an end state, as might be the case under the goal model. The process approach consists of three related components: goal optimization, a systems perspective, and an emphasis on behavior within organizations. *Goal optimization* refers to the need to balance goals and thus to optimize multiple goals rather than fully achieve a particular one. A *systems view* incorporates concerns for changes in an organization's environment. And the *behavioral emphasis* suggests attention to the possible contributions of individual employees to organizational effectiveness. Under this model, then, the effective organization is one in which goals are responsive to the environment, optimization of multiple goals is pursued, and employees all contribute to meeting those goals. Bolman and Deal (1997) refer to the value of such a perspective as providing multiple views, or "frames," from which the question of organizational effectiveness can be addressed.

One last important theory of organizational effectiveness is a substantial deviation from the others. Yuchtman and Seashore (1967) developed the *system resource model* from an empirical investigation of the effectiveness of seventy-five independent insurance agencies. In this model, organizations are not assumed to possess goals, nor is goal accomplishment a relevant consideration. Instead, an organization is effective to the extent that it can obtain needed resources from its environment. As Seashore and Yuchtman note, the effectiveness of an organization can be defined as the "ability to exploit its environment in the acquisition of scarce and valued resources to sustain its functioning" (1967:893). Thus, whereas the goal model emphasizes output, the system resource model is concerned with inputs.

This difference in orientation can produce useful insights in areas where the goal model may lead to confusion. For example, under the goal model, the failure of probation agencies to rehabilitate clients may be regarded as ineffectiveness. The system resource model, however, would lead to the conclusion that these same agencies have been highly effective because they were able to change their mission and attract resources for custodiary oriented surveillance programs such as intensive supervision or electronic home monitoring. Likewise, if running safe and humane prisons was a goal of the Louisiana Corrections Department, then a 1975 court decision ordering sweeping reforms indicates that the organization was ineffective. However, then Corrections Secretary C. Paul Phelps has said that "the court order was the best thing that ever happened to corrections in [the] state" (cited in Rideau & Sinclair, 1982). Such a proclamation is understandable from a system resource perspective because the court order gave the department considerable political power and financial resources to make needed improvements. Similar conclusions have been generated by those involved in local corrections and the management of jail facilities (Artison, 1996).

Methods of Assessing Effectiveness

Reviewing a variety of theoretical perspectives on effectiveness is useful because it not only points out the limitations of the goal model but also provides alternative ways of considering organizations. In examining studies of effectiveness, however, it is clear that the goal model dominates efforts to assess organizations. Studies based on this model involve the identification and measurement of some goal or goals. Most frequently this type of study has used a method referred to as *variable analysis.* Sophisticated studies of this type try to examine causal links in the attainment of some goal. For example, they may examine the contribution of training or supervision style to job satisfaction. Before discussing some of the pragmatic uses of this design, it is important to note that other types of effectiveness studies are possible.

Perrow (1977) describes two alternatives to variable analysis. In *gross-malfunctioning analysis,* the target of inquiry is failed or failing organizations. The analysis may examine the reasons behind a commercial bankruptcy, the disappearance of a social service program, a police department reorganization, or a major prison riot. Perrow describes gross-malfunctioning analysis as reflecting a "primordial" concern with effectiveness because it deals with basic questions of outcome. He argues that the subtleties of complex goals or goal displacement become irrelevant when organizations fail dramatically. Gross mismanagement, Perrow suggests, is easy to spot, and understanding it is a useful guide to improving organizations.

One example of gross-malfunctioning analysis can be seen in the report of the National Advisory Commission on Civil Disorders (1968), also known as the Kerner Commission. The group was formed to investigate the causes of the urban riots that occurred in 1967 in major cities across the country, including Los Angeles, Newark, Detroit, and New York. The commission found that African Americans in each of the cities complained of police misconduct—harassment, brutality, and even the improper use of deadly force. Although many causes of the riots were cited in the report, these practices, along with aggressive patrol practices in urban ghettos, were seen as major contributing factors to the unrest. Law-and-order candidates for the presidency rejected its conclusions (Cronin, Cronin, & Milakovich, 1981:66), but the Kerner Commission maintained that at the height of the civil rights movement, police organizations continued to rely on enforcement strategies reflecting policies of racism and neglect. Similar findings have been offered by subsequent commissions examining the role the police played in urban disturbances (Christopher Commission, 1991; *Fire and Police Commission Report,* Milwaukee, Wisconsin, 1991).

The history of Texas prisons also illustrates the potential benefits of gross-malfunctioning analysis. Texas prisons, too, failed to adapt to a changing environment. Prisoner litigation cost millions of dollars, was associated with increased violence and instability, and ultimately led to the reorganization of the prison system. Martin and Ekland-Olson's (1987) history of the litigation makes it clear that the policies of harassing inmate litigants and their lawyers and of ignoring or violating court orders exacerbated problems for the prison system. Additionally, Baro (1994) argues that much of the poor performance of the Texas Department of Corrections can be tied to the inadequate development of "political technologies" to cope with changing environmental conditions, notably the growing influence of the courts in the day-to-day operations of the Texas prisons.

Perrow's (1977) second alternative to variable analysis is called *revelatory analysis*. While variable analysis seeks to answer the question of how well some goal is being met, revelatory analysis asks who is getting what from an organization. In other words, revelatory analysis directly addresses the question of effectiveness-for-whom by investigating how organizations are used by groups inside and outside organizations. Prisons, then, may be effective by virtue of the employment opportunities they provide in rural areas. This fact explains why many rural communities have actively sought to attract these institutions, which seem relatively ineffective by a simple variable analysis. Likewise, Perrow suggests that organizations can be effective at meeting the individual needs of employees. A police department, for example, may be regarded as effective by some because it offers a work schedule of four ten-hour days per week, which allows officers to maintain second jobs or engage in their favorite hobbies. In a variable analysis, employee morale may be seen as significant because of its assumed effect on goals such as productivity. In a revelatory analysis, however, morale may be regarded as significant in and of itself.

Variable Analysis in Criminal Justice

In the assessment of organizational effectiveness, *variable analysis* refers to research designs that attempt to measure the attainment of some goal. Measurement of some outcome variable is often accompanied by investigation of the relationship between that outcome and independent variables. These studies, then, not only lead to general statements about effectiveness based on goal attainment but also provide information on what may contribute to effectiveness and thus on how effectiveness may be enhanced. For example, studies using crime rates as measures of police effectiveness may examine the relationship between that dependent variable and independent variables such as police expenditures, numbers of personnel, or intensity of investigation (Wycoff, 1982).

Variable analysis is the most common approach to studying effectiveness in criminal justice. In this section we examine five issues critical to these assessments and reveal the complexity of this approach.

What Domain of Activity Is the Target of the Assessment?

This question recognizes that organizations have multiple goals and that an assessment of effectiveness may not deal with all of them. As with all organizations, we could assess the effectiveness of criminal justice organizations in providing a safe and comfortable working environment for workers or managers, or we could assess their effectiveness at garnering or spending budgetary resources. There are also many activities unique to criminal justice organizations. For example, Wycoff (1982) focuses on the effects of crime control activity by the police. Vanagunas (1982), however, argues that only a small amount of police activity deals with crime-related events and that, for the "consumer" of police services, problems unrelated to crime are more frequent and more important than criminal problems. He suggests using a human service model in the evaluation of the police, which would include evaluating conflict reduction efforts and emergency services. Mastrofski and Wadman (1991) argue that a distinction must be made between *performance appraisal* and *performance measurement*. The former refers to the processes central to the evaluation of an individual's performance, while the latter refers to the relationship between performance and actual goal accomplishment. The latter determination is often difficult for criminal justice administrators to make. Again, the central issue is what goal(s) is/are being assessed in the evaluation process.

Oettmeier and Wycoff (1998) propose a three-dimensional model to performance measurement within police organizations under a community-policing model. This model suggests that the community-policing model can evaluate along individual, group, and organizational dimensions to ascertain how well the community-policing model is achieving its objectives and goals. In addition, Oettmeier and Wycoff employ the imagery of a cube to describe how these three dimensions can also be addressed by examining the incidents, patterns, and problems in the community and how the department responds through activities, programs, or strategies. Taken together, the model offers 27 different cubes that reflect the goals and responses of the department when operating under a community-policing model.

Such questions about the activity or activities being assessed are central. Assessments of courts may focus on efficiency in the processing of cases or equity in the dispensation of sentences (see Goodstein & Hepburn, 1985; Hardy, 1983). Likewise, corrections programs have often been assessed on their ability to change offender behavior through rehabilitation, but some observers have suggested focusing on fairness (Fogel & Hudson, 1981). And, most recently, attention has turned to deterrence (Phillips, McCleary, & Dinitz, 1983), incapacitation (Greenwood, 1982), and crime control (Petersilia, 1995). The National Institute of Justice released a cost-benefit study that analyzed the financial savings brought about by crime reductions due to imprisonment (Zedlewski, 1987), even though many have questioned the primary assumptions associated with the findings (Zimring & Hawkins, 1995).

The selection of the *domain of activity* is a significant step in the evaluation of effectiveness. That selection bears directly on many of the issues we have discussed— most notably, the question of effectiveness-for-whom, the fact that goals often conflict, and the tendency for effectiveness criteria to influence behavior within organizations.

What Do the Variables Mean?

After some domain of activity is selected, the next important consideration is validity, or finding variables that actually provide measures of effectiveness in the selected domain of activity. The problem is not a simple one. For example, recidivism rates have often been used as a measure of the effectiveness of rehabilitation programs. In fact, Martinson's (1974) famous critique of correctional treatment was based on the programs' failure to reduce recidivism rates. As he summarized his findings: "With few and isolated exceptions, the rehabilitative efforts that have been reported so far have had no appreciable effect on recidivism" (1974:49). That summary influenced the move away from a rehabilitation model and toward a just deserts, or punishment, model.

Organizational Effectiveness and Jails

There are undoubtedly a number of ways to attempt to measure organizational effectiveness in a county jail or municipal facility. "Effectiveness" is perhaps an elusive concept, which may encompass a number of definitions.

In a jail or detention setting, one way of approaching the issue of organizational effectiveness is by looking at the perceived mission of the organization and then assessing the extent to which there seems to be a commitment to fulfilling that mission throughout the various levels of employees in the agency. The "mission" of a correctional/detention facility is basically the management's philosophy and broad general goals for the operation.

Not every jail has the same perceived "mission." But whatever the mission, one of the hallmarks of an effective jail/detention operation is the extent to which all members of the organization have a common understanding of their mission and work together, in as unified a way as possible, to accomplish its various elements. In very general terms, some of the key ways this happens include the following steps:

1. Development by management of a clearly articulated, written mission statement. Such a statement should set forth, briefly and succinctly, the basic philosophy and key goals of the organization. It should be realistic and achievable, not just a nice-sounding but unrealistic piece of fluff. Ideally, the statement should reflect the ideas and input not just of the agency's chief executive officer but also of key managers, supervisors, and even line staff members.

   Once a mission statement has been developed, it should be promulgated to all employees as well as to relevant persons and agencies in the community. Additionally, an effort should be made to ensure that all employees actually understand the mission statement—whether through training or by some other mechanism. Doing so helps ensure that the mission statement is actually taken seriously by those to whom it applies.

2. Development of written policies and procedures based on essential elements of the written mission statement. An organization can really only be effective if all staff members have clear and consistent knowledge and understanding of their job task expectations. In a jail/detention agency, the standard formal method for ensuring such knowledge and understanding is development of written policies and procedures on all significant aspects of the jail/detention operation. In developing policies, it is important to seek maximum "buy-in" and support from all staff members, particularly first-line supervisors. One way to do this is to involve as many staff members as possible in development of the policies.

   The agency's mission statement should be the first component of the policy manual, and that mission should drive the contents of the policies. That is, the contents of policies and procedures should reflect and incorporate the philosophy and goals of the agency and should serve as the mechanism for realization of the mission.

3. Implement the mission statement and policies, and train staff members on the contents of the policies. Once policies and procedures have been developed, there must

be some sort of mechanism for implementing them—that is, distributing copies to all relevant staff members—and for training staff members in the contents of the policies and procedures. The goal is to ensure that all staff members truly know and understand the policies and procedures so that they will follow them properly. There are certainly options for training, including traditional classroom training, roll-call training, computerized training, and the like.

4. Supervision of staff members to ensure compliance with policies. Even when management has done an effective job of developing and implementing policies and procedures and training staff on the contents of those policies, there must be good, ongoing supervision of staff members to ensure compliance with those policies. This is usually the role of first-line supervisors, such as sergeants. Supervisors have a very important role in ensuring that line staff members understand and follow the agency's mission and policies and procedures. Unless supervisors themselves actively support the mission and policies and then attempt to ensure that line staff members also do so, it is much less likely that the organization will be effective.

    Good supervision should not only involve such usual "negative reinforcement" procedures as reprimands, counseling, and discipline, but also—and perhaps more important—"positive reinforcement" techniques, praising employees for doing the right thing, such as following agency policies appropriately. Positive motivation of employees is a management/supervision approach that can be quite effective and should be used more often as a means of promoting effectiveness.

5. Ongoing review of the agency's mission and policies, and revision as necessary. The philosophy and operation of a jail/detention organization is never static. Ideas change, new ideas and approaches develop, and, of course, there are always revisions in laws and other operational standards. Thus, one of the keystones of an effective organization is that management proactively plans for review of the agency's mission and of the written policies and procedures, to determine whether or not these remain current and, if not, if any revisions are necessary. Such reviews should occur both as necessary and at routine intervals, such as annually.

If and when it has been determined that revisions or updates to the mission statement and/or policies and procedures are necessary, then, of course, such revisions should be made, and all staff members made aware of the changes.

An organization that does not routinely review and update its mission and its policies will become stagnant and cannot remain effective.

MARTIN DRAPKIN, COORDINATOR
Wisconsin Jail Officer Training Program
Wisconsin Department of Justice
Bureau of Training and Standards

In fact, however, there is every reason to question the use of recidivism as a satisfactory measure of rehabilitation. As Maltz (1984) points out, without paying attention to how programs are expected to affect recidivism, it is impossible to tell just what recidivism rates measure. They may also be measuring the effects of punitiveness and, therefore, special deterrence rather than rehabilitation. In other words, "it may not be possible to disentangle the effects of the carrot (rehabilitation) from those of the stick (special deterrence)" (Maltz, 1984:11).

The situation is equally complex with other measures of criminal justice effectiveness. For example, Chicago police and prosecutors were criticized for failing to successfully prosecute a large number of people arrested for drug offenses. It was later reported that the primary motive for the drug possession arrests was to get gang members off the streets for brief periods of time. The police were using the charges in much the way they had once used charges of public intoxication. It was argued, therefore, that successful prosecution was not an appropriate criterion for effectiveness because failure to prosecute did not mean what the critics suggested ("The Court Retorts," 1987). (Whether arrests should be used in this way raises a completely different question about effectiveness criteria.)

Reported crime, arrest rate, and clearance rate are the most frequently employed outcome measures in assessments of the police. Problems with the validity of these measures, however, have been well documented (see Wycoff, 1982). In one series of case studies, McCleary, Nienstedt, and Erven (1994) demonstrated that official crime statistics may sometimes be the result of organizational behavior that has little to do with effectiveness. In one of the cases, the authors explained a major drop in Uniform Crime Reports (UCR) burglary rates in one city by a significant change in investigation and recording procedures. The city changed procedures to require investigation of burglaries before they were recorded by the UCR clerks rather than have investigations follow the official recording. With the change in procedures, many events that would have been recorded as burglaries based on the initial patrol officers' reports were not viewed as meeting UCR definitions by the investigating detectives.

In a second case study, a "crime wave" coincided with the retirement of a police chief of long tenure. The study argues that the chief had "wished" crime rates down by rewarding district commanders who produced low UCR rates. That "wish" was then passed down through the ranks. With the chief's retirement, the hierarchical authority patterns within the department disintegrated, and crime rates rose.

Finally, McCleary, Nienstedt, and Erven found another unsuspected source of a crime wave. In one city, the task of directly supervising police dispatchers was removed from shift sergeants. Without the experience and protection of the sergeants, dispatchers began to send police officers to respond to many calls that otherwise would have been handled informally. Department statisticians experienced the increased dispatching of officers as a crime wave.

One final example illustrates the political issues inherent in defining effectiveness criteria. Morash and Greene (1986) report two studies that came to radically different conclusions about the effectiveness of female police officers. The curious thing is that both studies were done by the same consulting firm in the same city (Philadelphia) in the same year. In the first study, criteria for effectiveness were developed by using sophisticated techniques to find consensus among police administrators. In that study, resolving problems without arrests was an indicator of effectiveness, and female officers were found to be as effective as their male counterparts. Later, as a response to court proceedings and the city administration's concern with violent confrontations, a second study was conducted in which the decision to arrest was viewed as an indicator of effectiveness. By this criterion, women were not found to be as effective as male officers. The studies illustrate that not only do organizational factors influence outcomes but also that the way those outcomes are viewed is the result of value judgments and political decisions.

How Are the Variables Measured?

The problems just discussed relate to how effectiveness criteria are conceptualized and understood. Another aspect of the problem involves the measurement of the variables. The question is not necessarily one of inaccurate measurements. Although computational errors do occur, the significant problem is the choices made among measures that may all be mathematically correct. Some measures may be more suitable than others to the specific effectiveness problem being addressed. For example, in calculating crime rates in an urban area, considering only the number of crimes per 100,000 residents ignores the fact that many potential victims (and offenders) commute into the city every day.

The literature on measuring recidivism provides many illustrations of the importance of knowing how outcome variables are measured. While there are many examples of inappropriate models and formulas used in recidivism research, even mathematically correct equations may produce widely different results. Recidivism can be defined as the proportion of some specified group of offenders who fail, according to some criteria, within some specified time. At a minimum, then, measuring recidivism for some group of offenders requires identification of a failure criterion and a follow-up period. Failure may involve anything from rearrest to a return to prison with a new sentence, and the follow-up period may be anything from a few months to many years. *Recidivism* rates can thus vary greatly according to the failure criterion and the length of the follow-up period. The easier it is to fail and the longer the follow-up, the higher will be the recidivism rate. To illustrate the point, Hoffman and Stone-Meierhoefer (1980) computed recidivism rates on a sample of released prison inmates using various failure criteria and follow-up periods. When return to prison was the criterion for failure and a one-year follow-up was used, the recidivism rate was 8.7 percent. When arrest was used as the failure criterion with a six-year follow-up, the same sample produced a recidivism rate of 60.4 percent.

An inquiry into effectiveness by Wilkins (1976) also demonstrates the complexity of using recidivism measures. The Maryland Institute for Defective Delinquents at Patuxent, a well-known treatment facility, reported a recidivism rate of 7 percent using rearrest with a one-year follow-up. This rate was well below the 65 percent reported by similar facilities. When Wilkins examined the data, he found that the institute had used a unique way of figuring recidivism. The treatment program involved a period of institutionalization followed by three years of outpatient supervision and services. The institute counted an offender as a recidivist only if the juvenile was not returned to the institution during the three-year outpatient phase and was later arrested. Those who were returned to the institute during their period of outpatient services were not counted among the recidivists. Wilkins showed that the likelihood of anyone from any program failing after three years was about 7 percent and that Patuxent did no better than other institutions when the three- year outpatient period was included in the analysis.

Petersilia and Turner (1993) also found very high rates of failure among offenders on intensive probation and parole due to the nature of the interaction between offender and agent. Increased surveillance and supervision of offenders led to an increase in "technical violations," which caused many offenders to be sent back to jail or prison. The authors suggest that different ways of assessing intensive probation and parole supervision be developed in addition to the traditional measure of recidivism. The research underscores two important points about the measurement of variables. Those conducting studies of effectiveness need to be aware of the implications of selecting different ways of measuring outcomes, and the reader of reports on effectiveness must understand precisely how the outcome variables were measured.

Alternatives to Outcome Measures

Until now, our discussion has focused primarily on outcome variables as indicators of effectiveness. Crime rates, arrest rates, convictions, and recidivism are all measures of the outcome of organizational activity in criminal justice. There are, however, many limitations to such variables. They are complicated and expensive to measure. They can often be assessed only long after some activity has taken place. And many factors outside the organization may influence them. It is easy to see, for example, that police can have only a limited impact on crime rates and that many factors other than prison may contribute to an ex-offender's return to crime.

In response to the problems of outcome measures, many managers and researchers have turned to measures of process or structure as indicators of effectiveness (Scott, 1977). *Process measures* are measures of the activities assumed to cause effectiveness within organizations. For example, assessments of probation and parole agencies have incorporated variables such as the length of time probation/parole officers spend in supervision of each case or the length of time they spend in face-to-face contact with parolees. Judges might examine the length of time a case takes to go from indictment to final disposition, and police managers often examine numbers of traffic stops made by officers. The advantage of these measures is that they are easy to collect and are likely to be easier than outcome measures to influence directly. A disadvantage lies in the fact that they may not be as highly related to outcome measures as is often assumed.

Structure measures are still further removed from outcomes. These variables measure organizational features or participant characteristics that are presumed to have an impact on effectiveness. Courts have used the ratio of corrections officers to inmates as a measure of inmate safety in prison. Likewise, the level of training among staff has been used in assessing the effectiveness of many criminal justice agencies. One way of viewing these measures is to regard them as measures of organizational inputs that serve as surrogate measures for outputs.

Using Multiple Measures of Effectiveness

There has been considerable criticism of evaluation efforts that use single measures as indicators of effectiveness (see Chen & Rossi, 1980). Whether structure, process, or outcome variables are used, single measures have often been regarded as too simplistic and often uninformative. Single-variable measures assess achievement of only one goal and are, therefore, based on a lack of appreciation of the complexity of multiple goals within organizations. Furthermore, single-measurement analyses inevitably conclude that a goal either has been reached or has not been reached. A program is thus regarded as a success or as a failure. Such a conclusion provides a static, one-shot view of effectiveness and little information on how an organization might change or improve.

Multigoal/multimeasure designs give a more comprehensive view of organizational effectiveness than single measures do. These designs utilize a variety of measures to assess achievement of multiple goals. In doing so, they permit examination of the effectiveness of different domains of organizational activity and examination of the relationship between achievement of various goals. These models can also view effectiveness as an ongoing activity and thus provide information about how an organization can improve.

Blomberg (1983) provides an example of the multigoal/multimeasure approach in assessing the effectiveness of juvenile diversion programs. These programs have often been evaluated from a single-goal perspective. They have often been regarded as failing because the goal of diverting nonserious offenders from the criminal justice system has been displaced as the diversion programs became an add-on intervention rather than an alternative. In other words, through net widening, diversion programs have sometimes come to serve clients who would not even have been arrested if the diversion program did not exist. Where evaluations have focused on rearrest data, these single-outcome measures have also not shown these programs to be effective.

Blomberg is critical of the simplicity of such evaluations. As an alternative, he suggests a multigoal/multimeasure approach that incorporates at least three broad measurements. First, measures of structure identify the types of youth served by the diversion programs, including such variables as age, ethnicity, social status, and offense history. Second, measures of services provided by the programs can distinguish between various types and intensities of programs. Finally, outcome measures such as rearrest data should be included. Taken together, these variables recognize that different types of programs may serve different types of youth. The evaluation, therefore, addresses the question of what-works-for-whom and thus provides information for program improvement.

Another model multigoal/multimeasure evaluation is an assessment of the juvenile corrections system in Massachusetts (Coates, Miller, & Ohlin, 1978). Researchers from the Harvard Center for Criminal Justice carried out the evaluation of the community-based system that replaced juvenile institutions after they were closed by Jerome Miller, the commissioner of youth services in the early 1970s. The study incorporated a variety of structure, process, and outcome variables.

The assessment began with a theoretical model of community-based corrections as running along a continuum from institutionalization to normalization. Variables such as the types of relationships between staff and inmates and the types and extent of links to the community were used to distinguish between facilities that were more like institutions and facilities that were more open and approximated normal life. The researchers found that some of the programs had social climates and links to the community that nearly duplicated those of institutions. Most often, these programs focused on changing offenders' values rather than reintegrating them into the community. This structural dimension was then examined to see how it related to process and outcome variables.

The process variables were decisions made to place youths in the various types of programs. The researchers found that youths with more extensive records were more likely to be placed in the less open programs. Thus many youths did not benefit from the new treatment programs, and those most needing the innovative programs were least likely to get them.

The study also incorporated a variety of outcome measures. Cost and recidivism outcomes were examined, as were a variety of attitudes in the short and long term. Attitudes were examined at release from the program and again at six months after release. The evaluation revealed that the open, or normalized, programs had the most positive effects but that these modest program effects diminished when the youths returned to their homes.

The complex design of the Massachusetts evaluation permitted conclusions that went far beyond commenting on the success or failure of the community-based programs. The study showed that most youth offenders could be handled in the community-based system. Another finding was that "community based" was an inadequate description and masked a wide range of programs. Another finding was that the more open programs were more likely to be successful. The evaluation also produced significant recommendations for program improvement, which ranged from increasing links to the community to strengthening advocacy work and follow-up in the community.

These five issues illustrate the complexity of variable analysis in the assessment of organizational effectiveness. At first glance, these issues may appear to deal with narrow technical problems. Careful consideration, however, reveals that they get to the heart of understanding organizational effectiveness under the goal model. Attention to these issues will require that decisions be made about what goals are relevant to effective organizations, how attainment of those goals can be assessed appropriately, and what benefits their assessment can have for members of the organization.

Attention to the issues will also suggest that the assessment of effectiveness can be an ongoing activity that provides information for the continuing change and improvement of organizations. Skogan (1996) suggests that any evaluation of a program must have a basic understanding of the "logic model of the program." This logic model has four specific components: *intervention* (level of effort involved), *context* (surroundings and circumstances where the intervention is being placed), *mechanism* (how the program is to affect the outcome), and, finally, *outcomes* (anticipated outcomes of the program). By following this logic model, it is possible to make more definitive statements concerning program effectiveness. Other researchers have noted how assessments of program effectiveness have become critical for criminal justice administration, no longer simply a luxury, but a requirement. (See Fyfe, Greene, Walsh, Wilson, & McLaren [1997] for a discussion of program effectiveness as it relates to police performance issues.)

Summary

In this chapter we have considered what effectiveness may mean and how it might be assessed in criminal justice. These are complex questions in any field and are particularly difficult in criminal justice, where goals are many and often conflicting. For managers, however, some answers to these questions are necessary. Beliefs about how effective an organization is and how it may increase its effectiveness, whether these beliefs are the result of complicated empirical studies or are uninformed by data, influence how resources are distributed and what goes on in the organization.

Given the implications of effectiveness evaluations and the complexity of goals in criminal justice, the importance of the question of effectiveness-for-whom must be recognized. Offenders, frontline staff, managers, and those outside criminal justice may have different ideas of what makes for an effective criminal justice organization. The perspective of those in power within organizations often underlies effectiveness studies, but other constituencies, including organized employees and the courts, can also be influential.

Although there are a variety of theoretical perspectives on organizational effectiveness, the goal model is the one most often adopted by managers. Variable analyses based on this model, however, illustrate how complex the model is. Key conceptual questions must be addressed. Decisions must be made about what goals to measure and how to measure them and about the use of process and structure measures as surrogates for outcomes. One approach to the complex conceptual issues of variable analysis is the use of a multigoal/multimeasure approach. This approach recognizes the complexity of programs and organizations and allows managers to look beyond simple measures of success or failure.

With the proper design, the study of organizational effectiveness need not be a static assessment of how well an organization meets a goal or goals. It can be an ongoing process that produces empirically based recommendations for continued improvement. In the following chapter we deal directly with the improvement of criminal justice through the process of organizational change.

Case Study

A Probation Officer's View of Effectiveness

Only a week on the job and the new chief probation officer calls a meeting of our whole department with an agenda item ominously titled "plans for a comprehensive evaluation." That's where all the trouble began in the first place. A "comprehensive evaluation" is what led to the resignation of the previous chief.

Of course, that evaluation wasn't done in the department. Six months ago, the local newspaper ran a special series on the probation department. For three Sundays in a row they raked us over the coals. In Part I, they showed that over 60 percent of our felony probationers were rearrested within a year. Part II claimed that all we officers do is sit around the office and drink coffee. In Part III, the social service agencies in town chimed in by saying we don't provide any rehabilitation services.

That's not what did the chief in, though. No, we did him in. His reaction to the newspaper stories was to jump all over us. We had to do even more paperwork to show how busy we were. He made us work long hours on cases that were no threat to anyone. He made me spend a week tracking down a shoplifter who missed one appointment. It turned out the guy was in the hospital for a hernia operation. My wife almost put me in the hospital when I had to miss my son's birthday party to prove the shoplifter shouldn't have his probation revoked.

Yeah, things got pretty nasty around here. So, after a few guys quit and caseloads went up, we started talking union. Now we're part of an organization of county workers all across the country. With our first set of grievances, the boss's ulcer acted up, and pretty soon we were facing this new guy from the outside. Just what we all need, another "comprehensive evaluation."

Later, at the meeting . . .

Allen Jones, chief probation officer: Okay, now to the next agenda item, plans for a comprehensive evaluation.

Gus Murdock, union steward: Wait a minute. There's no point in doing an evaluation. As long as caseloads are over 100, we know what your numbers will show.

Jones: Gus, I don't want to do an evaluation to show how bad we are or even how good we are. I think that if we can start to collect some information and see how things relate to each other, we can start working in a direction that we all find beneficial.

Jon Seltzer, probation officer: Well, right off, I'm leery of using those same recidivism rates again. Felony probationers are always going to have a high failure rate. At the very least, we have to look at what is also happening with our misdemeanants and other less serious offenders and at differences within those groups.

Murdock: Let's get back to caseloads. Nothing is gonna change if we don't get the numbers down.

Jones: Okay, Gus, but we can't get the numbers down until we fill our three vacancies. And even then I'm not sure we can expect smaller caseloads to reduce recidivism. The size of the caseload doesn't tell us anything about what probation officers are actually doing with their cases.

Murdock: Well, what are you suggesting?

Jones: First, we need to see how much time the officers are spending with clients. I mean, how much can you spend if you're carrying 100 people on a caseload? And how much time is spent on paperwork?

Murdock: Maybe that information can give us some baseline data and show how we can increase the time spent with clients without taking it out of the officers' hides.

Seltzer: Yeah, but there's more to it than how much time you spend with them. We should also keep track of where the time is spent. I mean, it may make a difference if you spend it with them in the office havin' coffee or out in the field.

Murdock: You're right. But what you *do* with the time may also be important. For example, some of you are good at hard-nosed surveillance—keeping them honest.

Now maybe that works with some clients. But right now I'm working on getting my cases hooked up with some of these social service agencies. Maybe that will work for some of them, too.

Jones: Okay, now we're getting somewhere. We need to look at what the officers do, how that relates to the success or failure of all different kinds of clients, and how it can be improved. And we need to do this sort of thing at least once a year so we can build on the results.

Murdock: And you're gonna do all of this without increasing our workload?

Jones: No false promises, but together we can keep any additional work to a minimum. And one last thing. I think we need to include a good survey of job satisfaction. The bottom line is that we need to make this a good place to work. Now on to the next agenda item. How are we going to train the new officers, and how do we evaluate the training? It's probably all baloney, but let's give this evaluation a chance. It may get us back to what probation is supposed to be all about. We'll see.

Case Study Questions

1. Whose interests were served in the newspaper's evaluation of this department, and whose will be served by the proposed evaluation?

2. What theory or theories of effectiveness are represented in the proposed new evaluation format?

3. What process and outcome measures are included in the evaluation? What domain of activity do these cover? Is the meaning of the variables clear?

For Discussion

1. Local jails are complex organizations with multiple goals. Consider how you might assess the effectiveness of your own local jail. What internal and external constituencies exist? How might their views of effectiveness differ from that of the jail administration?

2. Describe the goals of your local police department. How do official and operative goals compare? What variables would you suggest using to measure achievement of those goals? Is the meaning of the variables clear?

3. Consider the effectiveness of a probation agency using a variety of theoretical perspectives. Would you reach similar conclusions using a goal, strategic constituency, and system resource model of effectiveness? Under what circumstances might the theories lead to different conclusions about the agency's effectiveness?

4. Develop a plan for a multigoal/multimeasure evaluation of a victim witness assistance program administered through the prosecutor's office. What kinds of structure, process, and outcome variables would you be interested in? How would you use the evaluation procedure to provide information for the ongoing assessment and improvement of the program?

For Further Reading

Bolman, L. G., and Deal, T. *Reframing Organizations: Artistry, Choice, and Leadership,* 2nd ed. San Francisco: Jossey-Bass, 1997.

Flemming, R. B. *Punishment Before Trial: An Organizational Perspective of Felony Bail Processes.* New York: Longman, 1982.

Fyfe, J., Greene, J., Walsh, W., Wilson, O., and McLaren, R. *Police Administration,* 5th ed. New York: McGraw-Hill, 1997.

Martin, S. J., and Eckland-Olson, S. *Texas Prisons: The Walls Came Tumbling Down.* Austin, TX: Texas Monthly Press, 1987.

Oettmeier, T. N. and Wycoff, M. A. *Personnel Performance Evaluations in the Community Policing Context.* Washington, DC: United States Department of Justice, 1998.

CHAPTER

14

CHANGE
AND INNOVATION

Many of the criminal justice system's difficulties stem from its reluctance to change old ways, or, to put the same proposition in reverse, its reluctance to try new ones. The increasing volume of crime in America establishes conclusively that many of the old ways are not good enough. Innovation and experimentation in all parts of the criminal justice system are clearly imperative. They are imperative with respect both to entire agencies and to specific procedures. Court systems need reorganization and case-docketing methods need improvement; police-community-relations programs are needed and so are ways of relieving detectives from the duty of typing their own reports; community-based correctional programs must be organized, and the pay of prison guards must be raised. Recruitment and training, organization and management, research and development all require reexamination and reform.

(President's Commission on Law Enforcement and the Administration of Justice, 1967:141)

All the frantic activity in criminal and juvenile justice reform has resulted in an unchanged system or an extension of its reach. Reform movements have widened, strengthened, or created different nets of social control as organizational dynamics resist, distort, and frustrate the reform's original purpose. Reformers have ignored the surrounding political, social, economic, and ideological context in which their reforms occur. Future efforts at change . . . must include detailed analyses of the larger political structure and its connections with the social control apparatus if more substantive results are to be realized.

(Austin & Krisberg, 1981, cited in Doleschal, 1982:137)

Change is inevitable, progress is not.

(Unknown)

Because the "Violence Against Women Act" was part of an omnibus bill, it is not possible to assess the direct impact of the O.J. Simpson case on its ultimate passage. One can postulate, however, that after the O.J. Simpson allegations, it would have been difficult for most Members of Congress to oppose the legislation. The Simpson case appears to have provided the basis for Congressional consensus. The consensus was that domestic violence is a crime with national dimensions, and, therefore, the federal government had a responsibility to address the problem.

(Stolz, 1999, cited in Cole, Gertz, & Bunger, 2002:101)

This chapter focuses on organizational change within the criminal justice system and its organizations. Organizational change and its attendant concepts and theories cover minor procedural changes within an agency as well as sweeping reforms that change the philosophy and operations of an entire system. At one extreme, changes can take place in an agency because of internal decisions; at the other, major system-wide change is typically the result of reform movements that emanate from cohesive groups in society at large.

Historically, such organizational change takes place within the context of general social changes that create, or are created by, new perspectives, ideas, or paradigms. For example, the criminal justice workforce is rapidly becoming more diverse with the inclusion of minorities and women. This change, which itself will impact the system, has its roots in the earlier civil rights movement that, in turn, produced legislation ensuring minorities and women an equal right to employment opportunities, which again led to affirmative action requirements and programs.

Rothman (1980) argues that the prison reforms that took place at the beginning of the last century were the natural consequence of the Progressive era of 1890–1920, during which all social institutions were being questioned and changed. Perceived need for reform and change in the criminal justice system, however, preceded the Progressive era; attempts to bring reform to the criminal justice system began at least as early as the mid-1800s, when prison reform was pursued in New York and Pennsylvania. In essence, our present parole system, which is now being challenged and has been eliminated in some states, was developed in the late 1800s to emulate the "successful" system of penology developed by Sir Walter Crofton in Ireland (Barnes & Teeters, 1959). In 1870, penologists from across the United States met in Cincinnati at the National Congress of Penitentiary and Reformatory Discipline. The goal of this congress's dedicated members was to reform and reorganize the existing American penal system. In 1931, the National Commission on Law Observance and Enforcement published the fourteen-volume Wickersham Commission Report, which provided recommendations to improve our criminal justice systems' ability to manage crime and delinquency.

The President's Commission of 1967, quoted at the beginning of this chapter, was followed in 1973 by massive volumes from the National Advisory Commission on Criminal Justice Standards and Goals on recommendations to improve police, courts, corrections, and the juvenile justice system. The commission was provided with $1.75 million through the Law Enforcement Assistance Administration (LEAA), which had been created in the 1960s to respond to increasing crime, civil and racial disturbances, and looting during riots. The unrest, both civil and political, shed doubt on the ability of criminal justice institutions to impose law and order, rehabilitate and control offenders, and in general impose social control in a just and efficient manner. Because change and innovation were seen as desperately needed throughout the system, millions of dollars in grants were provided to state and local criminal justice agencies through LEAA to assist them in making their operations effective and efficient and in the hope that the standards and goals promulgated by the National Advisory Commission would be implemented.

Today, the effectiveness and practices of the criminal justice system are continually being challenged by society or the political and legal system. Passage of the Violence Against Women Act in 1994 and anti-drug legislation during the 1980s not only created a more direct federal response to crime, it also led to significant changes across the components of the criminal justice system. Police agencies are being restructured through the implementation of foot patrol units or team policing. The practice of indeterminate sentencing and parole has been challenged by both liberal and conservative members of the public (Cullen & Gilbert, 1982; Tonry, 1999), and traditional judicial sentencing practices are being challenged. In short, the perceived need for reform within the criminal justice system is an ever-present constant, and both substantive and symbolic changes have been made over time to meet that need. In the long term, real change as well as the pressure for change has been a part of the criminal justice system and will continue to be so in the future.

Change as manifested in simple agency alterations or in major reforms may be purposive or crescive (Warren, 1977). *Crescive change* is inadvertent or unplanned, independent of an organization's control, and may come about in spite of organizational efforts at self-direction. Crescive change can result from environmental influences on an organization or from internal organizational conflict (see Chapters 3 and 11 on organizational environments and conflict). *Purposive change* results from conscious, deliberate, and planned efforts by organizational members, typically managers. It may be a response to changing environmental conditions or pressures, to internal conflict, or to organizational members' perceived needs to change or improve aspects of their system. Crescive and purposive change are obviously not mutually exclusive processes. Purposive change represents an "intervention into a flow of events that will in any case result in change. . . . Consequently, the decision is not whether or not there will be change, but rather what one's part will be in shaping or channeling inexorable change" (Warren, 1977:10).

It is beyond the scope of this chapter to consider every possible change within an organization. We will be concerned here primarily with purposive, or planned, change as it applies to the agencies of the criminal justice system. Change can take place at every level of an organization and in every nook and cranny. An organization may change its mission and social function or may continuously change procedures. Throughout, we discuss organizational change as a general phenomenon rather than its innumerable specific applications in every facet of a criminal justice agency or system. As we have seen in moving from the 20th century into the 21st century, there have been many changes within criminal justice organizations. All of these changes have altered, to some degree, how criminal justice agencies are responding to crime. Why change occurs is, therefore, a critical question for the administration and management of criminal justice organizations.

Why Change Occurs

As we have said, change can emanate from inside or outside an agency's environment. To the extent that members are aware of environmental changes or internal conflict that may affect the agency's operations or outputs, the agency may enter into deliberate or planned change efforts. Before executives actively make some form of change effort, however, they must first perceive a need for change, that "something is broke and needs to be fixed." When an agency is performing improperly or below capacity, it is suffering a *performance gap* that may be recognized by agency executives, personnel, clients, or other constituencies (Downs, 1967). "Whenever an official detects some performance gap between what he is doing and what he believes he ought to be doing, he is motivated to search for alternative actions satisfactory to him" (1967:191). Therefore, a change effort will usually be initiated in an agency only after officials perceive a performance gap or are convinced that a performance gap exists.

A performance gap may be produced by any of four major events: employee turnover, internal structural or technical changes, external or environmental changes, and repercussions of an agency's performance (Downs, 1967). Any of these events taken separately or collectively can cause disequilibrium in an agency (Chin, 1966). Turnover of personnel will lead to differences in the collective behaviors of organizational members, regardless of official agency goals. New employees may have different goals, values, or work ethics from older employees. They may also view the mission of the agency differently. Newly appointed executives may cast the agency in a new role and ascertain that existing policies do not match that role. For example, younger corrections officers are less concerned with inmate use of marijuana than older officers are (Kalinich, 1984); the change in prison composition from traditional inmates to street gangs has also affected operations (Irwin, 1980). New organizational members with different values and ethics are, therefore, primary forces for internal change (Steers, 1977) as well as conflict.

Advanced communications and recording technology supplied by computer systems have created a clear performance gap in the criminal justice system. Although computer technology provides the potential for increased efficiency in communication and record keeping, most criminal justice practitioners must be trained to work with this advanced technology before it can be useful to criminal justice agencies. In addition, computer crimes are on the increase and criminal justice agencies must learn new techniques to prevent this new kind of white-collar crime as well as to solve computer crimes and prosecute the sophisticated computer fraud criminal. Chapter 3 is rich in examples of how the environment creates organizational change. Organizational change can be understood as a bridge that links an organization with its environment. The use of bridging strategies "presumes the presence of decision makers who survey the situation, confront alternatives as well as constraints, and select a course of action" (Scott, 1987:200). In other words, organizations modify their internal workings to adapt to external environmental pressures and constraints. Hence, the adaptation process is a form of purposive change in response to a perceived performance gap. Expansion of the use of community mental health services in county jails, for example, is a response to the increase in the number of mentally ill jail inmates (Swank & Winer, 1976) and to contemporary standards of care for inmates imposed on corrections systems (Embert, 1986).

Unexpected and unintended consequences following a routine agency performance may create repercussions that make a performance gap evident. Such routine activities often have the potential to upset the agency's dynamic equilibrium (Downs, 1967; Chin, 1966). For example, the discovery of police corruption will upset the balance and stability of a police agency. Also, prisons may be replete with brutality and corruption or may be managed by inmate gangs, but this corruption or lack of control by the prison staff may not be apparent until it becomes manifest in a riot or inmate disturbance. Prosecutors and judges may be viewed as entering into "liberal" plea bargaining or giving convicted offenders "lenient" sentences if the public suddenly becomes concerned with crime (LaFave, 1970).

If agency directors perceive a performance gap in their organization, they must first determine whether the gap is a short-term, or situational, phenomenon or if the gap is a long-term problem relating to some fundamental aspect of the agency (Spiro,

1958; Kalinich, Stojkovic, & Klofas, 1988). If the performance gap is viewed as a short-term phenomenon, agency executives may choose to ignore it. If it cannot be ignored, they may enter into "sales," or persuasive, tactics to convince their critics that no problem exists (Downs, 1967). If such persuasion is not effective, the agency executives may placate critics by making limited changes in the bureau's "window dressing" (Wilensky, 1967) or symbol structure (Kalinich, Lorinskas, & Banas, 1985). Organizations that passively adapt to pressures for change will typically take this as a first step without analyzing the scope of the problems they are facing. They will routinely seek the least diverse and least costly change that will most readily satisfy, or at least not disrupt, its members or external constituents (Downs, 1967; Sharkansky, 1972). As discussed in Chapter 3, criminal justice agencies are skilled at altering symbols and window dressing to placate pressure groups. If, however, the agency executives themselves perceive the performance gap as a fundamental organizational problem, they may attempt to bring about substantial change.

The Process of Organizational Change

The optimal approach to creating substantial change in an agency is to enter into a deliberate and rational process of planned change. A behavioral view suggests, however, that most organizational change is not purely rational or deliberate. Planned change requires that decision makers come to rational decisions. To do so, they must possess all pertinent information and must not be constrained by time or other resource limitations in the planning and decision-making process. However, decision makers at best operate under conditions of *bounded rationality* (March & Simon, 1958), in which they have limited knowledge and a finite amount of time and resources to dedicate to the decision-making process. An extension of the concept of bounded rationality is the *garbage can theory,* which suggests that organizational change is typically less than a deliberate, rational process (see Chapter 12 on decision making).

The garbage can theory posits a model of organizations in which problems become receptacles for people to toss in solutions that interest them. Thus, agency decision makers have favorite solutions stored away that are searching for problems (Perrow, 1986). The "can" becomes an opportunity for agency members or decision makers to pull out their pet solution, which may include their own agenda—a restructuring of agency priorities, a reallocation of resources, an improvement in their own status within the agency, or implementation of a favorite program. As competition among organizational members and decision makers over which solution to select proceeds, the original problem may get lost or take on a new form or a life of its own (Cohen, March, & Olsen, 1972; Rainey, 1997). As a consequence of competition among agency decision makers, unintended outcomes no one considered at the beginning of the process may be created. Solutions that lead to unintended outcomes can be "fatal remedies," which we discuss later in this chapter, when the outcomes are harmful to the agency's mission (Sieber, 1981). For example, diversion programs created to limit the flow of offenders into the criminal justice and juvenile system have broadened rather than reduced the system's net and thus increased the intake of offenders (Decker, 1985; Doleschal, 1982). To avoid serious organizational change resulting from garbage can choices that lead organizations to select fatal remedies to close their performance gaps, agencies ideally should enter into the process of planned change.

Planned organizational change consists of "a set of activities designed to change individuals, groups, and organization structure and process" (Goodman & Kruke, 1982). Planned change requires innovation and accepts problems as opportunities to pursue real improvement in an agency's performance. Conversely, planned change is not a passive adaptation to environmental pressures or a minimal attempt to reduce organizational tensions (Warren, 1977). Examples of passive change in response to tensions abound in criminal justice. The cliché that criminal justice administrators are reactive rather than proactive suggests that a passive, adaptive approach to change may dominate the criminal justice system. Units to improve police-community relations sprang up after the civil disturbances of the late 1960s in a weak attempt to give police agencies the appearance of being sensitive to minority needs (Radelet, 1986). These units were typically funded poorly and were not much more than a token attempt to respond to a fundamental problem (Block & Specht, 1973). Corrections is famous for changing labels: from guards to corrections officers, convicts to prisoners to inmates and, in some states, to residents. Such minimal attempts to meet pressures for change with the least costly approach are habitual for organizations in general (Sharkansky, 1972).

Planned change requires first overcoming organizational decision-making routines, such as garbage can solutions, seeking knee-jerk quick fixes, confusing symptoms with problems, overzealously protecting boundaries, and using least-cost solutions and methods to placate external pressures. Planned change also requires a view to the future rather than merely adapting to immediate pressures and problems. Leadership and vision are required to overcome these bad organizational habits that quietly subvert planned change.

Planned change, therefore, begins with leadership and a vision about what an agency should be doing in the present and future as well as its structural and cultural basis. Leaders establish direction and develop a vision of the future. They align people and influence the creation of teams and coalitions that accept or acquire a shared vision and provide people with an understanding of the path or strategies to achieve a vision. Leaders also are motivators who inspire and energize people to overcome obstacles and resistance to change. To the extent that obstacles to achieving a vision are found in the organization's structure, habits, or routines, leaders are antithetical to managers, whose role is to protect the existing structure, routines and practices. In short, leaders create change (Kotter, 1990; Stojkovic & Farkas, 2003).

Vision is the process of looking to the future for challenges that will impact an organization and looking inward for a better way of meeting the organization's mission (Nanus, 1992). Implicit in this statement is the need to identify present and future changes, which requires looking to the future using demographic projections—a technical chore—and understanding subtle current trends that may, for example, influence the future. Consider the corrections officers who predicted many of the future demands and changes that would be imposed upon correction in the near future (see Chapter 3); they had a vision but were not in a leadership position to make the changes necessary to meet the new set of challenges. Identifying present and future changes also requires a judgment on the degree to which the organization or system can influence the future. Simply informing the political leaders about the predictions may have sensitized legislators to the need for change. Looking internally, the visionary leader constantly seeks ways of changing the formal and informal structures and the culture of his or her system to improve the product or service quality.

W. Edwards Deming, renowned for developing total quality management (TQM) and credited with turning Japanese industry into the world's leading competitor, argues that American leaders in industry and government need to make a commitment to quality and to think of success as a long-term effort as opposed to quarterly profits, number of arrests, court backlogs, or today's problems. Challenging the existing operating principles, organizational philosophy, values, excessive reliance on accountability, and judgments by numbers and other sacred cows of American management, Deming's primary advice is to make a commitment to quality (Deming, 1986). Deming is a model for visionary leaders who wish to create both change and sensitive systems responsive to change. Meaningful change begins with visionary leaders who use the techniques and tools for planning, but are not subverted by the formal planning process, which in turn is routinely held hostage by tradition, structure, culture, and organizational politics.

Planned change requires an ongoing and substantive commitment to the long-run health of an organization. It demands routine and continuous examination of the agency's operations as well as the expectations and demands of its clients and constituents to discover existing and potential problems that will create performance gaps. These problems must be comprehensively examined and identified as substantive or mission problems, fundamental or policy-related problems, procedural problems, or circumstantial problems. After problems are understood with some clarity, then solutions can be developed and ultimately implemented. In other words, planned change requires an ongoing examination and continuous restructuring of goals, policies, procedures, practices, and behaviors. An occasional discovery of a performance gap or single look at a problem is insufficient; doing this creates a ridged system of decision making in which traditional and familiar problems recur and are met with traditional and familiar solutions. (For example, the timeworn solution for the treatment-custody conflict in corrections is an old friend—"training.") Moreover, the traditional decision-making routine views symptoms as problems, and any analysis is stunted. The basis of successful analysis for decision making, and hence for planning, is a "continuous cycle of formulating the problem, selecting objectives, designing alternatives, collecting data, building models, weighing costs against performance, testing for sensitivity, questioning assumptions and data, re-examining the objectives . . . and so on, until satisfaction is achieved or time or money forces a cutoff" (Quade, 1977:157).

From our general discussion of planned change so far, it becomes clear that deliberate and extensive effort is required in the process. Typically, organizational members expend their energies pursuing established goals, performing internal maintenance activities, adapting to environmental pressures (Selznick, 1949), and protecting agency routines. Planned change requires a break from these routines. To become free of this habitual momentum, organizations often create a permanent core of executives whose role is the implementation of planned change through a formalized planning process.

Planning in Criminal Justice

Planning can be thought of as the systematic application of the concept of planned change. Planning has been defined as "any deliberate effort to increase the proportion of goals attained by increasing awareness and understanding of the factors involved" (Dahl, 1959 : 340). More simply, planning is a process that precedes decision making, that gives explicit consideration to the future, and that seeks coordination among sets of interrelated decisions or actions (Hudzik & Cordner, 1983). Planning ideally allows the achievement of ends and the making of rational choices among alternative programs (Davidoff & Reiner, 1962).

The planning process is the first step in developing and implementing planned change. It is a process of "lining up the ducks" by identifying the immediate and future needs of an agency and the goals that must be met, then devising a systematic way in which to meet these needs and goals. In short, the tasks of planners are identifying agency goals and problems, forecasting, and generating and testing alternatives (Hudzik & Cordner, 1983). Each of these tasks deserves additional discussion.

Identifying an agency's goals may sound simplistic, even unnecessary. In planning and decision making, however, the basic purposes of the agency for rational planning must be reviewed consistently to gain a clear understanding of mission or goals as well as the values implicit in the agency's purpose. Often, the agency mission may be ignored in favor of day-to-day routines or lost in agency folklore about its social role. Hence, frequent reviews of an organization's purpose can remind administrators of the basic mission and goals, facilitate the promulgation of policies and procedures that are congruent with the agency's basic purpose, and assist in long-term planning.

Reviewing the basic mission is also important in viewing an agency's goals in the light of changing environmental demands and constraints. The mission of jails, for example, has changed dramatically over the years. Traditionally, the major purpose of prisons and jails was security or to prevent inmates from escaping or rioting. This was seen as contributing to the public safety mission of the criminal justice system. The health, safety, and welfare of inmates were a low-level concern. Although security remains an important function, the health, safety, and welfare of inmates is now equal to the security objective. Hence, planning for correctional institutions that does not consider the health and welfare of inmates will be, at best, inadequate. Correctional institutions house a growing number of mentally ill inmates, inmates who are HIV positive, inmates with drug addictions, and a growing number of homeless citizens. Professionals in the field report that homeless or poor parolees often violate their parole to return to prison for refuge or needed medical or dental treatment. Corrections systems need to face these realities to understand and redraft their real mission, goals, and objectives before entering into any major planning efforts.

Police agencies often focus on crime fighting as their major or even sole mission and ignore the vast service aspect of policing (Adams, 1971; Mastrofski, 1996).

Planning that is based on crime-fighting folklore and that excludes crime prevention and the vast array of services provided by police agencies will obviously miss the police system's broader mission. Thus, examining agency goals in the planning process may force agencies to adjust their missions and goals in light of contemporary social demands and expectations rather than simply in conformity with traditional values or agency folklore.

The identification of problems is crucial to planning and to avoiding the garbage can approach to management. Planners and managers who perceive a performance gap need to analyze the root causes of the gap or problem. This process involves looking through a layer of possibilities to extract the probable basic causal factors. For example, we often hear that low morale in a given police agency is causing a low level of productivity. However, morale and productivity are not necessarily causally related (Perrow, 1986), although that is often the commonsense conclusion. More important to locate and examine are the basic organizational problems that create both low productivity and low morale. It may be discovered, as often happens, that low levels of productivity and morale both relate to employees' lack of certainty about their role (March & Simon, 1958), which may relate to the agency's failure to identify its goals with clarity. A lack of clarity about the organization's mission and goals will make it difficult for the agency to promulgate policies and procedures and provide training that relates to current constraints on and expectations of its operational personnel. For example, police officers are often publicly criticized for their behaviors, and jail personnel are made responsible for inmate deaths through civil litigation. If, however, they are not being guided by clear policies, procedures, and training in areas in which they are subject to criticism and legal action, they will react with extreme uncertainty toward their work.

Forecasting is obviously an important aspect of planning, especially long-term planning. Assumptions about the future are implicit in any decision. However, it is often assumed that the future will replicate the present. Forecasting requires planners and decision makers to project into the future to understand prospective problems and to estimate the impact decisions will have on the agency or its constituents. Predicting crime rates is a common procedure and can be utilized in assessing the future needs of criminal justice agencies. In retrospect, the overcrowding in prisons could have been predicted, and, in fact, some people within the formal political structure did predict overcrowding and attempted to expand the prison system. Again, the impact of de-institutionalizing the mentally ill has led to an increased number of mentally ill individuals in the nation's prisons and jails, where they are not provided with adequate treatment (Petrich, 1976). Systematic and formal forecasting of the impact of de-institutionalization might have led to a secondary set of decisions and plans to improve the abilities of correctional institutions to treat mentally ill inmates.

Generating and selecting appropriate alternative solutions to problems is another crucial step in planning. Planners must construct a series of possible alternative solutions for the problems that have been identified. These solutions must take into account present and future constraints. Typically, the generation of alternatives begins with past strategies or ideas that seem to fit within the agency's philosophy, structure, knowledge–technology core, or resource limitations. If alternatives generated within these limitations are not deemed satisfactory, more creative or innovative alternatives then need to be found (Hudzik & Cordner, 1983). As overcrowding continues to plague prisons and jails, alternative solutions are being sought. Efforts are being made to control the influx of offenders into institutions by creating sentencing guidelines for judges (Kratcoski & Walker, 1978), using appearance tickets in lieu of arrests for certain offenses, and creating special bail-bond programs for indigent offenders (Harris, 1984). These alternatives, which all fall well within the present structure and general philosophy of the criminal justice system, have been promulgated since the 1930s (Barnes & Teeters, 1959).

In spite of these efforts, the problem of overcrowding continues. Hence, alternatives to incarceration are being sought. New forms of community corrections place incarcerated offenders in work-release programs, weekend or day parole, or community centers prior to their eventual release from confinement. Other innovative alternatives have been utilized to address overcrowding, including emergency release (parole consideration for inmates ninety days away from their minimum sentence date); early release of sentenced, nonviolent jail inmates; and court orders that require jails to refuse arrestees in certain crime categories when those jails are overcrowded. Home confinement in lieu of a jail or prison sentence has also been utilized in conjunction with computer-monitored anklets or bracelets (Schmidt, 1989). These alternatives can be considered innovative to the extent they are not traditional processes in the criminal justice system. But such innovative approaches often prove to be politically unpopular. In fact, the governor of Michigan discontinued the use of emergency release in 1986 in reaction to public criticism. Others, however, have emphasized how framing community correctional alternatives as enhancing public safety and crime control efforts as a useful strategy deflect public criticism (Petersilia, 2000).

It is important to point out that the application of these alternatives to institutional overcrowding is not necessarily the result of any long-term planning or planned change. Rather, these alternatives were created in reaction to a desperate state of affairs and, in many respects, exemplify the garbage can approach to change. Legitimate planning would have considered the possibility of overcrowding before the fact, and alternatives would have been implemented in time to meet the crisis. Forecasting overcrowding, understanding the reasons overcrowding would occur, and creating alternatives to deal with overcrowding would have been a good example of rational planning. Had the innovative alternatives been implemented, planned change would have occurred.

Planning in general, as we have described it here, is at best difficult and bound by constraints. Purely rational planning may be especially difficult for criminal justice agencies. *Rational planning* requires that an agency's goals are congruent rather than contradictory, are clear and known to agency members or decision makers, and that means-ends relationships are understood (Hudzik & Cordner, 1983). However, goals for criminal justice agencies are often vague and conflicting. Means-ends relationships and methods to achieve agency goals are often unknown or uncertain. Rehabilitation of criminal offenders, for example, can take on several meanings and is but one of many goals of corrections. To the extent that rehabilitation requires a degree of freedom for inmates from prison routines, it may come squarely into conflict with security concerns of the custodial staff. Further, reliable means of achieving some form of long-term behavioral change in offenders do not exist. In fact, empirical evidence to date suggests that most rehabilitation programs have not had any long-term effect on offenders' post-release behavior (Lipton, Martinson, & Wilkes, 1975).

At best, therefore, planning for rehabilitation programs is a disjointed, incremental process in which programs may be developed and then tested for acceptability, effectiveness, and unintended consequences (Lindblom, 1959). The value of planning for criminal justice agencies should not be minimized. The planning process has the potential of clarifying goals or at least prioritizing agency objectives. Further, means-ends relationships can be developed through agency research-and-development efforts. It is theorized, for example, that prison classification programs can identify inmates who are amenable to particular types of rehabilitation programs (Austin, 1983). Hence, rehabilitation goals and means can be offender specific and designed to take into account the constraints and conflicting goals of the prison system.

However, changing an institution's classification system and developing an array of treatment programs that can coexist with security needs will take a great deal of organizational skill and energy beyond the formal planning process. Planning is the initial and perhaps simplest step in organizational change. The creation of desired planned change throughout an agency may require its members to replace old values, habits, relationships, and routines with a new repertoire of behaviors. New ways of thinking about goals or performing tasks, therefore, will typically meet with resistance. Understanding and overcoming resistance and obstacles to change are, perhaps, the most important and difficult aspects of planned change.

Resistance to Change

Planning is the technical aspect of planned change. Implementing change is the human and more difficult aspect of planned change. The human side requires that agency members change their work behaviors and possibly their values, depending on the breadth or depth of the prescribed change. Change may also require restructuring of routines, and particular characteristics of innovations, such as cost, may create obstacles for their implementation. Hence, a natural resistance to change exists in almost all organizations. External obstacles to change abound and often are difficult to identify in planning. Recall our opening quote: "Reformers have ignored the surrounding political, social and ideological context in which reforms occur." Obstacles and sources of resistance to change must be identified and eliminated or controlled if planned change is to be successful. If obstacles to change are beyond the control of an agency or its planners, plans may have to be tailored within those constraints. In this section, we discuss the major sources of resistance to change. Table 14-1 provides a summary of individual and organizational sources.

Personal Sources

As Table 14-1 shows, agency employees may resist change for any number of personal reasons. Corrections officers, for example, may resist the use of due process for inmate discipline because it may necessitate a loss of their power and discretion. Cor-

TABLE 14-1

Personal and Organizational Sources of Resistance to Change

PERSONAL SOURCES	ORGANIZATIONAL SOURCES
1. Misunderstanding of purpose, mechanics, or consequesnces of change	1. Reward system
2. Failure to see need for change	2. Interdepartmental rivalry or conflict, leading to an unwillingness to cooperate
3. Fear of unknown	
4. Fear of loss of status, security, power, etc.	3. Sunk costs in past decisions and actions
5. Lack of identification or involvement with change	4. Fear that change will upset current balance of power between groups and departments
6. Habit	5. Prevailing organizational climate
7. Vested interests in status quo	6. Poor choice of method of introducing change
8. Group norms and role prescriptions	
9. Threat to existing social relationships	7. Past history of unsuccessful change attempts and their consequences
10. Conflicting personal and organizational objectives	8. Structural rigidity

Source: Steers, R. M., *Organizational Effectiveness: A Behavioral View*, p. 167. Copyright 1977 Goodyear Publishing Company, Inc. Reprinted by permission of the author.

rections officers may also perceive that this loss of power could lead to a dramatic change in their relationships with inmates. From a broad perspective, changing guard-inmate relationships may interfere with the norms of the corrections officers' subculture (Lombardo, 1985). In some cases, the fear of loss of control over the inmate population has led to an actual loss of control, perhaps as a self-fulfilling prophecy.

In the police area, effecting better police community relations through programming or training officers to interact in new ways with civilians has been resisted by police officers who see the world as divided into "us and them" and regard community relations as an appeasement program that weakens police authority (Skolnick & Bayley, 1986). Personal resistance is especially apparent in areas where community policing or foot patrol is being implemented. Community policing officers who walk the beat are viewed by other officers as "social workers" and are "not real cops" (Trojanowicz & Carter, 1988). Many traditional police officers and administrators view the role of the community police officer as being in conflict with their traditional role. They also believe that community policing will bring loss of power because it requires police to associate and identify with civilians who have traditionally been viewed as the recipients of coercive control by law enforcement personnel (Skolnick & Bayley, 1986; Mastrofski, 1996). Police officers given a foot patrol assignment must also leave the comfort and security provided by the well-armed patrol car and its communication system.

For courts, the establishment of sentencing guidelines also has the potential of taking discretion and power away from judges, prosecutors, and probation officers, all of whom have a vested interest in criminal sentencing (Tonry, 1999). Utilizing court administrators to manage court procedures and case flow has been accepted in principle. However, court administrators deal with judicial personalities and egos that resist administrative control, which is the substance of such programs. Prosecutors may resist the creation of community corrections programs or liberalized bail bond systems, seeing these programs as contrary to their role of protecting the community from criminal offenders. In good conscience, prosecuting attorneys have often expressed the fear that reducing confinement in favor of community programs would cause an increase in crime and delay case processing because offenders on liberalized bail bond programs are likely to fail to appear for their court hearings. This fear of liberalized bond systems, however, has not proven realistic (Vetter & Territo, 1984).

Organizational Sources

An agency's traditional practices, values, structure, or leadership can influence the success or failure of its attempts to implement change. A case study of a local jail illustrates resistance to change as a consequence of organizational climate and sunk costs in past decisions and routines. A consent decree promulgated by a federal district court ordered a local jail to modify the existing facility and provide contact visitations and other services to inmates (Schafer, 1986). Immediately following the consent decree, a steering committee comprised of local jail and criminal justice officials was formed to plan the change and provide guidance for its implementation. In spite of the decree and the show of good faith signaled by the formation of a steering committee, county governmental officials and the sheriff actively dragged their feet on compliance. Much of the system's energy was focused instead on attempting to circumvent and renegotiate the consent decree. Jail administrators along with the local political leaders created a negative climate within the jail and community that greatly slowed the process of change, which did not begin until five years after the original court order (Schafer, 1986).

An inappropriate reward–punishment system may hamper desirable change. Since the 1970s, attempts have been made to upgrade the quality of corrections officers in local jails. In many jurisdictions, however, corrections officers receive a lower wage than road patrol officers within the same agency, which motivates corrections officers to strive for a transfer to the road patrol. In addition, corrections officers' who perform well in jails are typically rewarded by being transferred to road patrol, leaving the less talented or motivated personnel to continue as corrections officers. There are, of course, other advantages to working in a police department rather than in a correctional facility. However, the reward system described here clearly retards the best efforts of jail administrators to upgrade their staff (Kerle, 1998).

Organizations with rigid structures are typically those with well-established traditions, belief systems, routines, and practices, as well as little history of change. Large, powerful organizations that are capable of influencing their environments will also typically place more effort into resisting change than into conforming to pressures for change (Scott, 1987).

Organizations that readily facilitate change also have several characteristics in common. Besides having a history of change, Burnes and Stalker (1961) and

Hage and Aiken (1970) found that change-ready organizations share the following characteristics:

1. High complexity in terms of professional training of organizational members
2. High decentralization of power
3. Low formalization
4. Low stratification in differential distribution of rewards
5. Low emphasis on volume (as opposed to quality) of production
6. Low emphasis on efficiency in cost of production or service
7. High level of job satisfaction among organizational members

While these characteristics may be antithetical to change resisters, many are also antithetical to criminal justice agencies, which tend to be centralized and highly formalized. Job satisfaction, especially among corrections officers, tends to be low (Toch & Klofas, 1982). Police agencies and often courts tend to emphasize volume, with police agencies often resorting to arrest rates as a benchmark for success and courts placing emphasis on efficient case flow (Grau, 1980).

Organizational change requires, in essence, altering the organization's routines. Routines develop in all organizations that survive for an extended period of time, and they provide certainty and purpose to organizational members. Of equal importance, routines are the skills that govern all aspects of organizations, from formal record keeping and daily work practices to the ongoing truce between management and subordinates. It is management's job to maintain routines (Nelson & Winter, 1982). To the extent that routines are altered, the basic skills of an organization, the guideposts for its members' behavior, are being challenged, and management's role in maintaining routines must be set aside. An organization, and its members, will face uncertainty with the elimination of well-established routines and therefore will resist their elimination.

Routines within the criminal justice system and its agencies are abundant, are typically well established, and emanate from a variety of sources, some of which are beyond the control of administrators and staff. The criminal justice system has a rich tradition of established routines (Atkins & Pogrebin, 1981), many of which relate to important values in society in general. A proposed change for the criminal justice system—one, for example, that limits police authority—could also be viewed as a threat to law and order, an important belief of the general public and the law enforcement community. Hence, such a change can be readily resisted.

More specifically, many criminal justice routines are imposed by statute and case law, and subroutines are created within the organization to establish conformity—or the appearance of conformity—to prevailing laws. The court system performs extensive rituals that are considered significant in protecting the rights of defendants. For example, defendants appear in a formal courtroom for sentencing. At a criminal sentencing hearing, the defense attorney pleads for leniency, and the prosecuting attorney may counter by requesting the court to impose a harsh sentence to "protect the public." This process is honored and acted out even though sentencing decisions are typically decided well in advance of the formal hearing. The formal hearing is symbolic of the court's duty to protect the rights of the offender. The suggestion that the formal sentencing hearing be dispensed with in cases where a clear decision has been made to place an offender on probation—a suggestion that would save the court time and expense—has not been well received (Robin, 1975). The routine has historical ritualistic value and is difficult to set aside.

In addition, large police agencies and correctional systems are organized along bureaucratic lines and are often considered to be paramilitary organizations. They have a clear chain of command and a hierarchy of authority supported with formal rules and regulations. The rigid formality of such agencies requires and creates a set of routines, often seen as a statement of organizational purpose, that are difficult to eliminate or alter; hence, agencies are resistant to change. The extent to which change will be resisted is thus, in part, a function of the rigidity or flexibility of an organization and its members.

Resistance to change is also a function of the magnitude and depth of the change being proposed. A proposed change that focuses on a single aspect of the behavior of a few agency members or on a limited number of procedures that are not frequently used will be met with much less resistance than change in fundamental aspects of an organization. Fundamental change often requires a shift in agency ideologies, a major shift in operations and programming, and a dramatic shift in the role of the line or service delivery personnel (Duffee, 1986). Fundamental change, therefore, encounters a great deal more resistance than attempts to create circumstantial or procedural change. It is easier to create special units within a police agency to focus on police-community relations or crime prevention than to change the policies and procedures of the entire agency. The practices, behaviors, and attitudes of most agency members do not have to be altered if special functions are assigned to a few members included in the specialized units. Similarly, it is easier to use short-term measures to alleviate overcrowding, such as emergency release procedures (described previously), than to build new correctional facilities or expand the use of community corrections. A change as fundamental as creating community corrections centers may run into resistance from the public as well as being merely difficult from an organizational perspective.

Organizations whose members are unionized face another potentially powerful constraint on change. Management-labor contracts often call for specific behavior on the part of both management and labor. These agreements reinforce particular routines and make them unalterable for the duration of the contract. Police unions have had a significant impact on policy decisions in many jurisdictions and have eroded the power and discretion of police administrators to make changes (Swanson, Territo, & Taylor, 1997). Corrections officers' unions have also been on the increase across the nation, and they will ultimately have a powerful impact on corrections policies historically reserved for management. When unions and administrators share the same objectives, the union can be a powerful ally in planning and implementing change. If they are not in accord, unions can become a major obstacle to the implementation of planned change. We must consider, however, that unions ideally represent the interests and views of the rank and file. If the critical mass of the rank and file is opposed to it, a planned change is unlikely to be implemented, regardless of whether or not they belong to a union.

Finally, we must briefly touch on forces in the environment that thwart an organization's attempt at innovation. Successful innovation within an organization is dependent, in part, on the positive association between external pressures for change and internally perceived need for change (Griener, 1967). In other words, when an agency's constituents and members both perceive a performance gap, the momentum for change will be strengthened by congruent pressures. Public support is, therefore, important to effect planned change. Conversely, public opposition to change or support for the status quo will hinder major change or change visible to the public. Attempts to establish corrections centers in communities, for example, have typically been vociferously challenged by community members (Smykla, 1981). Innovation in police agencies often faces criticism from community members who have a preference for traditional police operations (Skolnick & Bayley, 1986).

Characteristics of Innovations

Previously in this chapter, we suggested that the nature of innovation itself would affect resistance to change. For example, we stated that fundamental change would require greater effort than altering the procedures of a system because resistance to a fundamental change would be greater than resistance to a circumstantial change. In this section, we discuss the characteristics of innovations that affect resistance to change (see Zaltman, Duncan, & Holbeck, 1973).

The first set of characteristics relates to the social and economic cost and cost effectiveness of innovation and change. Innovations with a higher price tag will be implemented with greater reluctance. An innovation that creates a high return on the initial investment or will improve an agency's efficiency will be more attractive than one that does not. For example, the initial cost of implementing substantive and comprehensive rehabilitation programs throughout a corrections system may be extremely high. If, however, recidivism could be cut drastically by such programs, the long-term savings to corrections and the criminal justice system may pay off the initial investment. The establishment of comprehensive rehabilitation programs would also be attractive if they had the potential of making inmate management efficient.

The extent to which organizational change creates risk or uncertainty will also affect the likelihood of innovation. In this regard, less complex innovations that are compatible with the existing organizational structure will pose less risk and uncertainty to an agency than incompatible, complex ones. Also, change that is reversible creates less apprehension and has less potential for causing risk and uncertainty. Moving from well-established, traditional indeterminate sentencing and parole to determinate sentencing will be difficult to reverse (Cullen & Gilbert, 1982). Hence, most states have resisted such a sweeping change.

Plans for innovations that emanate within organizations and are timely have a better opportunity for acceptance than externally imposed or poorly timed innovations because internal innovations have greater credibility. Timeliness suggests that innovative ideas are put forward to meet a need at a moment when consensus about the problem and its source exists among organizational members. Timely ideas have a stronger chance of survival in an organization than ideas that must be sold to or forced on agency members. The concept of house arrest or home confinement coupled with the use of electronic monitoring techniques of offenders is timely. First, overcrowding has created a desperate situation. Second, monitored home confinement may be more acceptable than traditional forms of community corrections from the public's point of view as it is more punitive, restrictive, and secure.

Finally, the larger the mass of people involved in the change process, the more implementation will be impeded. If innovation is likely to affect the general public or external groups, more individuals will be involved in the process of change than if these groups are not affected. Moving from traditional policing and institutional corrections to community policing and community corrections will ultimately involve community members, who will also be part of the decision-making and innovation process.

So far, we have discussed obstacles to organizational change on the individual and organizational level. We have also examined some of the characteristics of innovations themselves that may slow or prevent their implementation. In the next section we provide an overview of some of the general prescriptions for overcoming resistance to change in organizations.

Overcoming Resistance to Change

As we have seen, resistance to change seems to be a natural characteristic of most organizations and their members. Efforts to create change within an organization require overcoming its natural resistance to assuming a new or modified mission, creating and implementing new goals and procedures, and ultimately altering the arrangement of its activities (Katz & Kahn, 1978). As we have suggested, recognizing the need for change and planning for change are the first steps in the change process. However, a chief of police or a director of a corrections system cannot simply decree change by issuing a memo or a direct order through the chain of command. Because a degree of alienation exists between administrators and line staff in criminal justice agencies (McCleary, 1978; Toch, Grant, & Galvin, 1975; Stojkovic & Farkas, 2003), it is likely that decrees from administrators to subordinates may increase resistance to change rather than lead to the implementation of innovations. Change ultimately requires a set of strategies for unfreezing, changing, and refreezing the behavior of an organization's members to overcome resistance to change (Lewin, 1948).

The responsibility for overcoming resistance to change within an agency typically falls on change agents—usually management (Bennis, 1966). The extent to which managers have a commitment to change and are capable of overcoming change-resistant staff is an important determinant of successful implementation of planned change (Bennis, 1966; Zaltman, Duncan, & Holbeck, 1973; Skolnick & Bayley, 1986; Sparrow, 1999). Strategies for change can be aimed at individuals in an agency, the agency's structure and system, or the organizational climate (the interpersonal style of relationships)—or at combinations of these targets (Huse, 1975; Steers, 1977). Table 14-2 provides a crisp summary of techniques that can be applied to change individual members, organizational structures, or the organizational climate.

TABLE 14-2

Comparison of Three General Approaches for Initiating Organizational Changes

APPROACHES FOR INITIATING CHANGE	TYPICAL INTERVENTION TECHNIQUES	INTENDED IMMEDIATE OUTCOMES	ASSUMPTIONS ABOUT THE MAJOR CAUSES OF BEHAVIOR IN ORGANIZATIONS
Individuals	Education, training, socialization, attitude change	Improvements in skill levels, attitudes, and motivation of people	Behavior in organizations is largely determined by the characteristics of the people who compose the organization
Organizational structure and systems	Modification of actual organizational practices, procedures, and policies that affect what people do at work	Creation of conditions to elicit and reward member behaviors that facilitate organizational goal achievement	Behavior in organizations is largely determined by the characteristics of the organizational situation in which people work
Organizational climate and interpersonal style	Experiential techniques aimed at increasing members' awareness of the social determinants of their behavior and helping them learn new ways of reacting to and relating to each other within the organizational context	Creation of systemwide climate that is characterized by high interpersonal trust and openness; reduction of dysfunctional consequences of excessive social conflict and competitiveness	Behavior in organizations is largely determined by the emotional and social processes that characterize the relations among organization members

Source: Porter, L. W., Lawler, E. E., III, and Hackman, J. R., *Behavior in Organizations*, p. 440. Copyright 1975 by McGraw-Hill Book Co. Reprinted by permission.

Individual Change Strategies

The assumption underlying this approach is that individuals or groups of individuals within an agency must modify their attitudes, skills, and behaviors. For example, corrections officers had to relearn certain aspects of their work to implement the due process model of corrections; officers who were accustomed to almost complete discretion in disciplining inmates had to adapt to a process that allowed inmates their "day in court" (*Wolff v. McDonnell,* 1974). Consequently, shifting corrections officers into the new disciplinary process required some resocialization because they no longer had total discretion in disciplining inmates. It also required a new set of skills for officers, who were now required to prepare their cases thoroughly, write a complete report, and testify in a formal hearing. Ideally, corrections officers should have been provided with a clear explanation of their new role, training programs to provide new knowledge, skills commensurate with the new task, and programs to help them accept the liberal approach to inmate management (Duffee, 1986). The extent to which corrections officers were provided with these supplements is not clear. If the due process procedures were implemented by decree, which is within traditional practices for paramilitary systems, the hearing procedures predictably met with strong resistance by corrections officers.

Structural and Systems Change Strategies

Realizing improved methods may require a rearrangement of an organization's policies, procedures, and reward–punishment system. In other words, to achieve desired change, modifying the basic structure of the organization in a major way, as opposed to simply altering the work behaviors of the members, may be needed. Before workers' behaviors can change, basic structural aspects of the system that constrain their behaviors must be changed. For example, a major performance gap exists in jails. Typical jail operations are not geared to provide the range of care and services that jail inmates are presently entitled to (see Kalinich & Klofas, 1986). It has been argued that physical structure is a major constraint that limits jail corrections officers from sufficient contact with inmates to provide adequate supervision and management (Nelson, 1986). Therefore, new jail facilities constructed across the nation, known as "new-generation jails," allow corrections officers to readily observe all inmates for whom they are responsible. In addition, policies and procedures congruent with the contemporary mission of jails must be introduced in the new facilities as well as in traditional facilities. Corrections officers are required to take an active role, interacting with inmates and identifying problems before they take on crisis proportions, rather than a passive role of intervening in crises with coercive force (Zupan, 1991).

Similarly, moving from traditional to community policing, controlling sentencing disparity with sentencing guidelines, and expanding the methods and availability of community corrections all require restructuring various aspects of the respective systems. In all the examples, old routines must be set aside in favor of new routines, and old roles of many of the key actors for new ones. Because change in routines and roles often curtail the authority and discretion of the actors, they may require some philosophical reorientation. Providing organizational members with training and making structural changes may not, therefore, be sufficient strategies in themselves to bring about desired change. The core of an organization—its culture, behavioral regularities, rituals, norms, dominant values, and climate—may have to be modified to facilitate the adoption of new routines and member role behaviors required to complete the change process (Schein, 1985; Steers, 1977; Schein, 1997).

Organizational Climate Change Strategies

As Table 14-2 shows, the assumption behind attacking organizational climate to initiate change is that the behaviors in an organization are largely a product of the organization's culture (Schein, 1997). An organization's routines and its members' work behaviors are constrained by the collective value structure and the emotional and social interaction among its members. An organizational climate also has the following dimensions (Steers, 1977: 102):

1. Task structure: the degree to which the methods used to accomplish tasks are spelled out by an organization

2. Reward–punishment relationship: the degree to which the granting of additional rewards, such as promotions and salary increases, is based on performance and merit instead of other considerations like seniority, favoritism, and so forth

3. Decision centralization: the extent to which important decisions are reserved for top management

4. Achievement emphasis: members' desire to do a good job and contribute to the performance objectives of the organization

5. Training and development emphasis: the degree to which an organization tries to support the performance of individuals through appropriate training and development experiences

6. Security versus risk: the degree to which pressures in an organization lead to feelings of insecurity and anxiety in its members

7. Openness versus defensiveness: the degree to which people try to cover their mistakes and look good rather than communicate freely and cooperate

8. Status and morale: the general feeling among individuals that the organization is a good place in which to work

9. Recognition and feedback: the degree to which employees know what their supervisors and management think of their work and the degree to which management supports employees

10. General organizational competence and flexibility: the degree to which an organization knows its goals and pursues them in a flexible and innovative manner. Includes the extent to which it anticipates problems, develops new methods, and develops new skills in members before problems become crises.

The task at hand, therefore, is to create a climate within an organization that facilitates change in its culture and simultaneously affects traditional agency practices and habits to allow changes in the values, attitudes, and personal interactions of its members. For example, if organizational members tend to be defensive and insecure, they will be reluctant to venture into new roles, even if they are dictated by management. Returning to our example of new-generation jails, corrections officers are being asked to interact with inmates rather than simply keep them locked up. This change poses a new set of risks for corrections officers. If they feel they will be "burned" by the bosses if they make mistakes, they will attempt to delegate many of their responsibilities back up to their supervisors. In effect, they will cling to their old roles and routines.

In addition, if communication is poor or decision making is centralized, it will be difficult to gain the active participation of organizational members in the change process (Duffee, 1986). If corrections officers are not involved in the transition from a traditional jail to a new-generation jail, they are not likely to have complete knowledge of the change process or to identify with the purpose of the new system. Conversely, management will have, at best, a contaminated feedback loop from the line staff and will not be able to assess accurately the efficacy of the transition. With a contaminated feedback loop, even incremental change will not be successful (Lindblom, 1959).

Creating an organizational climate that is conducive to cooperative change can be an overwhelming task, especially if the change is prompted by extreme conflict within an agency. However, any change within an agency that goes beyond the alteration of simple procedures or consensual change will probably face impediments from the environmental and cultural dimensions of the system. Therefore, steps for dealing with an agency's climate should be considered in the early phases of planned change. In the next section we will examine a series of human relations techniques and training programs for improving an agency's climate that have been utilized with some frequency. The approaches fall loosely into the category of organizational development.

Organizational Development

Organizational development (OD) focuses on the environmental influences of an organization. The process attempts to alter simultaneously a system's values, routines, and structures in an attempt to create an atmosphere in which obstacles to change can be identified and minimized (French, 1969). Traditionally, OD programs have been the responsibility of a single change agent, an individual whose sole role is to promote change within a system. The *change agent* may come from within an agency—usually from management—or may be a consultant from outside the agency. These are some of the objectives of OD programs (French, 1969:24):

1. To increase the level of trust and support among organizational members
2. To increase the incidence of confronting problems rather than ignoring them
3. To create an environment where authority is based on expertise as well as title
4. To increase the level of personal satisfaction among organizational members
5. To increase open communication within the organization

These objectives are congruent with the dimensions of organizational climate shown in Table 14-2. This makes sense because OD focuses on organizational practices and social-political systems because each affects the system's environment, and vice versa. As a field of social and management science, OD relies on a multidisciplinary approach and draws heavily on psychology, sociology, and anthropology as well as on information from motivation, personality, and learning theory and on research on group dynamics, leadership, power, and organizational behavior (Hellriegel, Slocum, & Woodman, 1995). The techniques used in OD are based, in part, upon Theory Y assumptions that individuals are responsible and can be motivated most readily when they are given responsibility (see Chapter 5 on motivation). Hence the techniques are aimed at getting organizational members' active contribution in identifying agency problems and developing solutions rather than leaving that task to a few of the management elite.

OD techniques and programs include survey feedback, a pencil-and-paper method of gathering information from agency members, and team building, which allows agency members to form groups that do not conform to traditional social or authority-oriented patterns. Team building, therefore, creates fresh subsets of interpersonal communications among agency members and overcomes traditional barriers to communication.

Training, such as sensitivity training, that focuses on agency members' values, perceptions of agency problems, and commitments to agency goals is a common OD technique. Training of this nature facilitates information gathering, open communication, and examination of personal objectives within the framework of role objectives and organizational objectives. Such techniques and programs attempt to get organizational members actively involved in the change process while providing them with an opportunity for open dialogue across ranks to improve communication, examine problems and solutions, and identify impediments to change.

We can discuss the application of OD techniques to criminal justice agencies best in a critical manner. In effect, OD requires active participation of organizational members in the process of management, and especially change. Criminal justice agencies, however, are typically bureaucratic, paramilitary organizations in which communications flow predominantly downward. Upward communication, while theoretically possible, is severely limited (see Chapter 4 on communication). Lateral communication is contrary to organizational structure and practices. The preponderance of traditional routines precludes the quality and quantity of member participation in organizational decision-making that is requisite to the practice of OD. The management style of corrections administrators, for example, is often autocratic and, therefore, does not allow for corrections officers' participation in change (Duffee, 1986). Thus, utilizing change agents—outside consultants or internal specialists— on an *ad hoc* basis when change seems to be inevitable will have limited value. The outcome of *ad hoc* attempts at change within rigid systems that do not routinely facilitate open communication and participation among members will be changes in written policies and procedures that will be passively resisted by the line staff. While planned change is the optimal approach to meeting public demands in an effective way, in criminal justice agencies these plans often produce unintended consequences or fatal remedies. Simply put, the whole notion of planned change is based on a series of attitudes and practices of organizational administrators and managers that run contrary to the traditional attitudes and practices of criminal justice administrators. This concept is discussed briefly in the next section.

A Police Chief's Experience in Creating New Policies and Procedures

In 1984, I was the new chief of police of a medium-size city in the Midwest. The department had operated with some degree of success over the years, based upon an accumulation of past practices that were handed down from veteran members to new recruits. The informal manner in which the department had been run led me to believe good management would be my main concern. It was my view that the department needed to change many of its past practices and become more formal than in the past.

I began my management efforts by doing an informal administrative audit of the department. I found that there were very few written formal policies or procedures. The past practice of developing policies and procedures was based upon memos written by the chief, who had written about fifteen memos over a ten-year period. The memos were then circulated to the troops, who were to read, sign, and return the memos to the chief. Their signatures served to indicate that they were knowledgeable about the directions given in the memo and responsible for carrying out the orders implicit in the chief's memos. The signed memos were then thrown into a folder and placed into a file drawer where they remained, unless needed for disciplinary purposes.

To further my informal administrative audit, I asked the officers how they viewed the departmental policies and procedures. The consistent comment from them was, "What policies and procedures?" Policy, at least formal policy, was not a concern for anyone in the department. From my point of view, however, a modern police department could not operate without written policies and procedures. I took it upon myself to create and formalize policies and procedures for the department. I spent about three months collecting policies and procedures from other departments to use as a grid as I wrote the first official policy and procedure manual for our department. I assumed that by creating formal policies and procedures I was bringing the department out of the Dark Ages and giving the officers badly needed direction. This was especially crucial in light of the high rate of litigation against police agencies, much of which is based upon inadequate or inappropriate policies and procedures. After three months of work, I called a mandatory staff meeting of all law enforcement personnel to present them the newly written policies and procedures.

I was pumped. I put a ton of work into the project and made some significant operational changes that I thought would be of great benefit to the department and the officers. Through the development of the policies and procedures, I had updated and changed many of the departmental past practices that I thought were antiquated. I assumed I was preparing a basis for our police operations that the officers would appreciate. With high hopes for praise or at least recognition for my hard work, I passed out the new policy and procedure manuals and waited. I guess I wasn't waiting for applause, but at least some recognition or discussion—even some disagreement would have been nice! But what I received was silence and indifference. I asked for questions, and there were none. After a grueling and disappointing fifteen minutes, during which most of those in attendance spent most of their time looking around or at their feet, I dismissed the meeting. The troops put their manuals in their lockers and went about their business. I doubt if they ever bothered to look at my creation, even for amusement. Needless to say, they went about their business following well-established past practices. Any resemblance between what I had written and what the troops were doing was purely coincidental.

I learned a number of things as a result of this disappointing experience. First, it was apparent that the leader cannot make changes by decree. Simply writing policies and procedures will make little impact except that it took a great deal of my time. Change requires that people do their jobs differently, and written memos or policies do not guarantee that work routines will change. I also learned that people who are expected to change need to be involved in the change process. In reflecting upon my disastrous first meeting, it was clear that the troops had absolutely no ownership over the new policies. I was "pumped" because the new policies were my creation. The troops were bored because they had been handed a manual. For them to be as excited as I was about the change, they needed to be involved to the same extent I was in the development of the new departmental policies.

My first task was to get all the officers actively involved in the creation of our new policies and procedures. I also thought it would help bring them together if they were involved in developing policies for the entire department rather than their own subcomponent or task. I created committees across ranks to discuss issues and problems and recommend departmental policies and procedures to me. I then wrote new policies based upon the committees' verbal input. After committing the input to writing, I circulated the recommended policies and procedures to all personnel for their input. When I had reviewed everyone's input, I wrote the new policies and procedures in their final form.

The results were generally positive. Some of the officers minimized their involvement, but many took an active part in the development of our new policies and procedures and even shared my excitement. Most of the officers took pride of ownership over what they saw as their work. Those that didn't like the final product at least knew the new policies and procedures.

The lessons I learned are simple and worth repeating. Change cannot be done by decree. The people who will ultimately be affected by change must be part of the planning and change process. Written policies and procedures alone will gather dust unless the people who are expected to follow the policies and procedures are familiar with them, understand them, and believe they are relevant to the work. I also learned how little I would have known about my own department and how it really operated if I had simply ordered my troops to follow the new policies and procedures I had written.

TERRY FISK

Director, Grand Valley State University
Regional Police Academy

Unintended Consequences of Change

The final outcomes of a change effort may be different from those desired by change agents or planners. At times, change may be harmful either because the outcomes are unintended or the remedies are "fatal." Fatal remedies are the result of the natural regressive effects of social engineering (Sieber, 1981). Earlier scholars, including Weber, Marx, and Engels, have written about regressive effects. More recently, sociologists have studied the fatal remedies of governmental programs (Banfield, 1974). However, the prescriptive literature on organizational change does not address this phenomenon. In brief, Sieber (1981) advises that social interventions fail because policy makers and planners fall into regressive traps for several reasons. (We will cover only a few of Sieber's principles here.) First, the multiplicity and priority of goals of target groups may not be understood thoroughly, if they are understood at all. It may be of little value, for example, to provide minimum-wage jobs for teenagers who make large sums of money selling drugs. Interventions may be exploited by undesirable groups. It was unfortunately common for federal grants provided for improvement of inner cities during the War on Poverty to end up in the pockets of fraudulent contractors. In addition, goals may be displaced by the bureaucratic emphasis on process rather than outcome. For example, when the Drug Enforcement Administration (DEA), whose mission is to protect the public from health-threatening drugs, sprayed paraquat, a toxic herbicide, on marijuana crops in Mexico in an attempt to eliminate a major supply source, the poisoned crop harmed consumers.

During the 1970s, reformers led the way to decriminalize a number of victimless crimes. When two states abolished public drunkenness laws, arrests for public drunkenness were eliminated and public inebriates were taken off the streets at a high rate by law enforcement officers under the rubric of "protective custody." Gallup, New Mexico, with a population of 18,000, checked drunken persons into its jail for protective custody 26,000 times (Doleschal, 1982:141). The protective custody cases were held in a large drunk tank, void of mattresses and basic amenities. The drunk tank was considered exempt from jail standards because protective custody did not rise to the level of criminal arrest. (See Doleschal, 1982, for an excellent review of criminal justice reforms that not only failed but exacerbated the problem they were intended to solve.)

Program evaluation needs may also pervert the desired ends because agencies may evaluate program outcomes that are readily measurable or show favorable results rather than the program's original goals (Hoos, 1983). Providing a program for one group or creating a change may provoke opposing groups into action to thwart interventions and create their own. In California during the early 1970s, for example, liberal groups unhappy with what they considered the unfair, indeterminate sentencing system fought for the establishment of determinate sentences. Liberals viewed this change as a just and humane system and a benefit to offenders and inmates. The inmates' union joined the liberal factions. Once the issue was made public, conservative law-and-order groups also joined the reform movement in favor of the determinate sentencing system. This coalition of groups felt the existing system was excessively lenient and did not provide sufficiently long sentences for inmates. The conservative element of the coalition became more influential than the liberals, and determinate sentences were established. However, the sentence structure implemented provided longer sentences for inmates than the indeterminate system it replaced, contrary to the liberals' original intent (Travis, Latessa, & Vito, 1985; Holt, 2000).

Other fatal criminal justice remedies are widespread. The evidence suggests that diversion programs actually widen the criminal justice net instead of diverting offenders (Decker, 1985; Doleschal, 1982). In addition, decriminalization of victimless crimes seems to increase arrest for related misdemeanors; and community corrections programs that survive become, in effect, small prisons within the community (Doleschal, 1982). Doleschal argues: "The highly disturbing findings of evaluations show that well-intentioned humanitarian reforms designed to lessen criminal justice penalties either do not achieve their objectives or actually produce consequences opposite [to] those intended" (1982:133).

We have just skimmed the surface of the concept of unintended consequences and fatal remedies. Often they are inevitable, simply because the principles of rational planning do not allow us to deal with unknown and unpredictable phenomena. We frequently fall into the trap of promoting regressive intervention strategies because of our myopic vision. The intended outcomes of "sting" operations, for example, are to reduce crime by enticing thieves into the operation and make quick and solid arrests. However, the "street" vision of police officers allows them to predict the unintended consequences: increases in theft and the crime rate during the tenure of the sting operation. Such anecdotal predictions are often verified in studies of sting operations (Langworthy, 1989). However, policy level innovators are compelled to overlook such contingencies. Why? The answer lies in traditional management practices, styles, and philosophies that promote and protect the formal structure of the organization, along with its values, operating principles, and assumptions. The successful change agent needs to be free of traditional organizational paradigms to possess the vision to look for future contingencies. The visionary leader needs to have an understanding of the cultural forces within his or her own organization that limit vision (Stojkovic & Farkas, 2003).

Implications for Criminal Justice Managers

Managers seek stability, order, and certainty. Planning and budgeting are completed within a context for stability and control. Managers and administrators police the organization's boundaries to keep out disruptive influences and provide the organization with stability. They also enter into calculated exchange relationships with the agency's tasks environment to acquire resources and support (see Chapter 3). By virtue of their tasks, their view is narrow, and planning serves to solve problems that threaten stability. Change requires leadership and vision (see Chapter 7) that creates new paradigms—the set of rules and assumptions that guide us in inputting and processing information and leads us to conclusions, decisions, or understanding. The rules and assumptions of an organization are typically ingrained in both the formal and informal structures, routines, and culture and often go unchallenged. Developing new paradigms requires recognizing and setting aside the assumptions that dominate the organization.

Sparrow (1999) offers an excellent description of the paradigm shift required to move from a traditional police agency to community policing. Table 14-3 provides a succinct summary of the profoundly different assumptions about purpose, process, and relationship with the community that are implied in traditional and community policing, respectively (Sparrow, 1999).

The new set of assumptions required to move to a community policing system necessarily affect the organization's structural, human resource, political, and symbolic frames (Bolman & Deal, 1997; also see Chapter 2). This implies that leaders who would be change agents must have an understanding of the four organizational frames and the ability to create strategies to impact each frame. It is doubtful that any one individual will have such a complete knowledge of an organization. However, individuals throughout an organization have knowledge in the various pieces of the puzzle and should be recruited to participate in the leadership and change role. In this regard, long-term planning will be nothing more than a high-tech exercise, lacking any holistic understanding of the organization.

The importance of leadership and a holistic approach is demonstrated by Skolnick and Bayley (1986), who identify four factors crucial to change and innovation in police agencies attempting to become crime-prevention oriented. First, they cite "the chief's abiding, energetic commitment to the values and implications of a crime-prevention-oriented police department" (1986:220). They argue that the chief must be more than an advocate of new programs; he or she must infuse the entire organization with a sense of purpose that supports the logic of new programs or innovations. Second, the chief must promote the values and programs he or she is advocating by motivating and even manipulating departmental personnel into accepting those values. A series of tactics used to motivate or manipulate personnel was identified (Skolnick & Bayley, 1986:222–223):

1. Influencing younger members, then promoting them to positions of influence
2. Urging retirement of older officers and replacing them with new officers who can be successfully indoctrinated
3. Identifying and enlisting older officers who will buy into new ideas
4. Training middle managers through the chief's office to ensure proper indoctrination
5. Sending trained middle managers into the field in leadership positions to indoctrinate other members of the organization
6. Applying the coercive power of the chief's office to punish those fighting change

Third, once a program is established, conscious efforts must be maintained to keep it in place and protect its integrity, since the natural tendency for a police agency is to fall back on old routines. Fourth, "innovation is unlikely to happen without public support" (Skolnick & Bayley, 1986:223; see also Chapter 4). Public support is needed at least to obtain resources for new programs, and it may come in the demand for better services from a criminal justice agency. A critical public can be an opportunity for a change-oriented executive, because creating new programs to deliver services to a critical public can garner public support. However, criminal justice agencies

TABLE 14-3

Traditional Versus Community Policing: Questions and Answers

	TRADITIONAL	COMMUNITY POLICING
Who are the police?	A government agency principally responsible for law enforcement.	Police are the public, and the public are the police: the police officers are those who are paid to give full-time attention to the duties of every citizen.
What is the relationship of the police force to other public service departments?	Priorities often conflict.	The police are one department among many responsible for improving the quality of life.
What is the role of the police?	Focusing on solving crimes.	A broader problem-solving approach.
How is police efficiency measured?	By detection and arrest rates.	By the absence of crime and disorder.
What are the highest priorities?	Crimes that are high value (e.g. bank robberies) and those involving violence.	Whatever problems disturb the community most.
What, specifically, do police deal with?	Incidents.	Citizens' problems and concerns.
What determines the effectiveness of police?	Response times.	Public cooperation.
What view do police take of service calls?	Deal with them only if there is no real police work to do.	Vital function and great opportunity.
What is police professionalism?	Swift effective response to serious crime.	Keeping close to the community.
What kind of intelligence is most important?	Crime intelligence (study of particular crimes or series of crimes).	Criminal intelligence (information about the activities of individuals or groups).
What is the essential nature of police accountability?	Highly centralized; governed by rules, regulations, and policy directives; accountable to the law.	Emphasis on local accountability to community needs.
What is the role of headquarters?	To provide the necessary rules and policy directives.	To preach organizational values.

continued on next page

TABLE 14-3, *continued*

Traditional Versus Community Policing: Questions and Answers

	TRADITIONAL	COMMUNITY POLICING
What is the role of the press liaison department?	To keep the "heat" off operational officers so they can get on with the job.	To coordinate an essential channel of communication with the community.
How do the police regard prosecutions?	As an important goal.	As one tool among many.

Source: Malcom K. Sparrow, *Perspectives on Policing.* Monograph 9, National Institute of Justice, and the Program in Criminal Justice Policy and Management, John F. Kennedy School of Government, Harvard University, November 1988.

have traditionally been insular and often subjected to criticism over spurious, highly visible incidents. The public may also be suspicious of new programs developed by criminal justice agencies. Nonetheless, public support is crucial and can be obtained only when leadership possesses "an abiding, energetic commitment" to change.

Leaders need to develop a high level of sophistication about the organization's political and task environments alike to be successful change agents. Potential stakeholders, allies, threats, and opportunities must be recognized. Criminal justice officials, for example, see the media as a threat and rarely attempt to cultivate support through the media. Also, criminal justice administrators typically have limited abilities to influence the political system and rarely have lobby groups to support them. In addition, high-ranking criminal justice administrators are appointed by and work at the will of governors, mayors, and other political bodies. They are not in a position on their own to speak publicly or freely without fear of reprisals. What is needed is the development of coalitions with citizen groups and individuals who can influence the political system. For example, unions, which are usually viewed as a threat, can be utilized as a powerful political arm of an organization.

Administrators may attempt to create change to improve the organizational climate or to increase productivity. Decisions to improve the quality of services require leaders to be responsive to changing demands from their constituencies, as well as internal assessments of quality. Ideally, changing conditions, constraints, or demands should be anticipated, and changes made within the agency should be congruent with environmental shifts. If the ideal is not achieved, performance gaps should be recognized and steps taken to close them—which is easier to say than to do. As we have discussed, many of the obstacles to change lie within the traditional folklore, routines, and structure of criminal justice agencies themselves. The rank and file becomes infected with their agencies' past, perhaps making them less likely to find change desirable than their bosses, who may develop some degree of environmental sensitivity as a function of their position.

Purposive rather than crescive change in an organization requires a commitment to responsiveness and innovation, at least at the administrative level. Proactive responsiveness requires systematic methods of gathering input from constituents, the work environment, and agency members as well as useful methods of evaluating service delivery and programs. Purposive change also requires that organizational members identify with the goals of the agency and be committed to personal as well as organizational success. This again requires that agency members have an opportunity to participate actively in decisions at every level and, therefore, commit themselves to change. To the extent criminal justice agencies are paramilitary bureaucracies or are managed from the top down, agency members will be discouraged from any form of participation in planned change. The "view from the street" will never be integrated into planning. Change will not come about through decrees from the top. Updated policy and procedure manuals may do no more than gather dust. Requiring staff to "read and sign" new memoranda will not change their work-related behavior. Ideally, staff must be involved at all levels of the change process. Staff involvement will allow planners to tap staff expertise and improve the likelihood that staff will accept change. Finally, organizational members must have a fairly clear sense of their new role and possess the knowledge, skills, and tools to carry out the new tasks involved.

In sum, planned change in criminal justice depends on agency administrators' alertness to the need for change and innovation, readiness to set aside traditional management styles, and ability to create a climate within their agencies that fosters communication and criticism from the ranks. Finally, they must be willing to expend the resources required to implement change. In general, criminal justice managers who would themselves be change agents must free themselves and their personnel from firmly rooted organizational values that contain major obstacles to change.

Summary

In this chapter we have examined the origins of change and the process of organizational change. In addition, we have discussed at length the obstacles and sources of resistance to innovation and change along with prescribed approaches to overcoming resistance to change. We have emphasized the value of planned change and planning.

However, the chapter paints a pessimistic picture of the ability of criminal justice agencies to successfully implement or even consciously enter into a process of planned change. The traditions of the criminal justice system, coupled with its often vague and always conflicting and multiple goals, work against true planning and creative innovation. We have, however, provided sufficient conceptual knowledge and information for students and practitioners who view planned change as a worthy and important venture.

Out of necessity, we have repeated many of the concepts presented throughout this book in this chapter. Planned change and innovation of any magnitude in the criminal justice system and its organizations will invariably involve environmental concerns, communication, leadership, decision making, job design and enrichment, personnel motivation, and power, as well as all the other topics we have covered. Whether we want it to be or not, the criminal justice system is dynamic, not static. An agency's ability to manage change is manifest in good management and committed leadership. Good management and leadership is based in part on a sound cognitive, if not intuitive, grasp of theories of organizational behavior and administrative theory as they apply to criminal justice agencies.

Case Study

A Radical Approach

A new police chief who wanted to move from traditional to community policing had just been appointed for the City of North Star, with a population of about 100,000. His appointment came on the heels of the election of a new sheriff who ran on a "reinventing local government" campaign. The budgets for law enforcement and corrections were shrinking at local, county, and state levels, but the problems left to law enforcement, the courts, and corrections were on the rise. The crime rate had turned upward, especially for juvenile crimes. A number of juvenile gangs were evolving, a phenomenon new to the relatively stable community. The local jail was at capacity and attempts to develop community corrections programs were not popular with local judges. Probation and parole caseloads for adults and juveniles were growing and were difficult to manage, which was a key reason prosecutors and judges were reluctant to expand the use of community corrections. The economic base of the community was shrinking, bringing in its wake a growing number of street people, vagrants and beggars, who were becoming more aggressive and intimidating citizens in the commercial districts and shopping malls. There also was concern that summer tourism would be harmed by the growing number of vagrants.

The new police chief and sheriff met to discuss the problems. Both were progressive and believed in cooperation and were not fearful of even radical innovation. They concluded that their budgets would gradually decrease during the next decade but that demand for services would, however, increase. Meanwhile public satisfaction with services from the criminal justice system, already eroded, would continue to slip. They also recognized that the public had been whipped into a get-tough anti-crime mood by political leaders in response to growing community problems. They agreed in principle on a radical approach, reasoning that their jurisdictions should first be merged at the operational level so they could combine resources. Further, they believed that the county should be divided into a number of areas in which law enforcement officers, adult and juvenile probation officers, and parole officers could work together in teams. The teams would share responsibilities for crime prevention, including gang intervention, community policing, and community corrections. It would be an ambitious task, but they believed that the coordinated and concerted efforts of all of the criminal justice agencies resources working at the community level would rationally allocate the eroding resource base and provide effective and visible prevention, enforcement, and corrections programs to the community.

Case Study Questions

1. How should this plan be packaged and sold to the political leaders and the public? How should the plan be sold to the corrections agencies and judges? Identify other groups or agencies that will have a stake in realigning the system.

2. What opportunities exist that would lend support for their plan?

3. Identify the threats to this plan from the external environment and the political environment.

4. How will the roles of law enforcement officers and the corrections staff be modified? Identify the personal and organizational obstacles that will impede the role change. How will the formal side of the agencies have to be structured to facilitate the goals of the proposed plan?

For Discussion

1. To what extent does an agency's reliance on its folklore to enhance its self-image impede planned change? Police agencies, for example, may see themselves as fighting a war on crime, or corrections administrators may see the primary role of their institutions as rehabilitation.

2. A growing number of line-level criminal justice practitioners have college degrees. Will the advanced education of these practitioners create greater or less resistance to change from within criminal justice organizations?

3. What must a corrections administrator consider in deciding whether to police the agency's boundaries or succumb to pressures for change?

4. Define a criminal justice agency problem that you are familiar with and understand in some depth. Discuss why the problem exists, develop alternative solutions, decide which solution is the most feasible, and, finally, consider what negative or unintended consequences might result from implementing your selected alternative solution.

5. To what extent does the classic paramilitary structure of police and corrections organizations create a climate that is not conducive to change?

For Further Reading

Duffee, D. *Correctional Management: Change and Control in Correctional Organizations.* Prospect Heights, IL: Waveland, 1986.

Hudzik, J., and Cordner, G. *Planning in Criminal Justice Organizations and Systems.* New York: Macmillan, 1983.

Nanus, B. *Visionary Leadership.* San Francisco: Jossey-Bass, 1992.

Sieber, S. *Fatal Remedies: The Ironies of Social Intervention.* New York: Plenum, 1981.

Skolnick, J. H., and Bayley, D. H. *The New Blue Line: Police Innovation in Six American Cities.* New York: Free Press, 1986.

Stojkovic, S. and Farkas, M. A. *Correctional Leadership: A Cultural Perspective.* Belmont, CA: Wadsworth Press, 2003.

CHAPTER

15

RESEARCH IN CRIMINAL
JUSTICE ORGANIZATIONS

Unanimous agreement exists that the justice system ought to be efficient, effective and fair. Less accord, however, exists about how best to secure these essential qualities or how to measure whether they have been achieved. . . . Unlike marks on a ruler, criminal justice measures are not neutral standards but are factors that enter into the process being analyzed—identifying relative degrees of improvement in fairness in sentencing, for example, would still indicate that the sentencing process was giving weight to information not legally relevant.

(*Greenfeld, 1993:v*)

Based on an extensive review of available data, the Team came to the conclusion that jail expansion is not an appropriate response to the current jail overcrowding problem. The Team believes that the long-term solution to jail overcrowding in Monroe County is changing how the criminal justice system does business by utilizing the tools of Total Quality Management.

(*Monroe County Jail Utilization System Team, 1994:2*)

Bill Polito—Tough on Crime—No alternative sentences—no electronic monitoring, no early release.

(*Television ad for judicial election campaign in Monroe County, New York, 1996*)

• • • [T]he field of corrections desperately is in need of evaluation and research that will allow for a better targeting of available resources. As funding of prisons and prison systems becomes strained, prison administrators are constantly being called on to justify existing programs and continually are searching for programs that can stand the test of cost-benefit analysis.

(*Frank Wood, correctional administrator, as cited by Riveland, 1999*)

To today's students of management in criminal justice, the 1967 President's Commission on Law Enforcement and the Administration of Justice may seem to deserve little more than an historical footnote. But the commission's contributions to contemporary criminal justice have been far greater than such a brief mention would suggest. And its projections for the field in the year 2000 were even grander. Emphasizing that criminal justice was best thought of as a system rather than disconnected agencies and organizations, the commission envisioned a system governed by a process of rational planning. Although the commission found little empirical research to guide its recommendations at the time, research was to play a central role in the future. In the commission's vision, empirical research "would provide a powerful force for change in the field of criminal justice" (President's Commission, 1967).

Historically, research has also had many other champions who might have been expected to influence the management of criminal justice. From Frederick Taylor, who sought statistical definitions of a good day's work, through Kurt Lewin, whose "action research model" was driven by the dictum, "Research that produces nothing but books will not suffice" (1947:203), generations of management models in business and industry have regarded the collection and analysis of data as critical. In today's widespread "quality" movement in industry, research plays a central role in the management process.

In this chapter we will examine the role of research in criminal justice organizations. We begin by considering the impact of social science research of the kind envisioned thirty years ago by the President's Commission. We will then look more closely at the nature of research in the organizational context, considering such varied types as basic, applied, evaluation, and action research.

"Knowledge for What?"

In a classic work published in 1939, Robert Lynd asked the question "Knowledge for what?" in considering the role of social sciences in American culture. The debate over the appropriate relationship between social science research and public policy continues today (see Postman, 1992).

One distinction relevant to that debate can be made between basic and applied research. *Basic research* seeks to understand fundamental issues of process and structure in ways that may not immediately be useful to practitioners. In education, for example, basic research has examined such issues as the process of learning or the developmental stages that children pass through (see Miller, 1986). In criminal justice, basic research examines the causes of crime, the nature of social control, and the social structure of correctional institutions. The primary purpose of *applied research,* in contrast, is to develop knowledge that is directly useful to practitioners. In education, that has included testing the effectiveness of various educational methods or programs and gathering other data that can be of use to decision makers.

The debate over the relative value of basic and applied research in the social sciences centers on several issues. Some authors have argued that basic research is more important than applied research because it influences practitioners' fundamental understanding and views of reality and, therefore, influences practice in the long term; they also point out that there is little evidence suggesting that applied research has significantly influenced practice. Others contend that basic research produces axioms that are too general to be useful and are sometimes even trivial. Proponents of applied research argue that methodologically sound studies, particularly studies that evaluate current practices, can have a significant impact. Still others argue that a respect for both applied and basic research is the best way to advance useful knowledge (Miller, 1986).

Some researchers and managers have also envisioned a different relationship between research and practice. While they insist that useful research should not compromise methodological soundness, they also note the importance of a team approach. Managers and, ultimately, frontline workers must appreciate the value of research, and social scientists must be able to respond to the needs of practitioners. They argue that working together emphasizes both process and product and is most likely to produce useful knowledge.

For many researchers, criminal justice is an applied field in which studies should be designed in a way to influence practice. There are certainly many examples of sound and significant applied research in this field, and some of the work has involved strong partnerships between researchers and practitioners. For example, scholars such as James Fyfe and Lawrence Sherman have conducted research that has been influential in policing; Todd Clear has completed valuable research in probation and parole supervision; and Hans Toch and James Jacobs have done important research in the field of corrections.

Despite these examples, however, it is widely acknowledged that the practice of criminal justice has not been directly affected by social science research to the degree the President's Commission predicted. And this problem is not limited to criminal justice. In reviews of the utilization of research findings in public policy, the general conclusion has been that academic research has had relatively little influence on policy decisions (see Lester, 1993), at least in the short run. On the other hand, the evidence is not universally negative. In fact, Weiss (1987) reported that although only a small percentage of specific recommendations of research are followed, a much larger percentage are used to influence how policy makers think about issues.

One thing is clear: although practitioners often report that greater exposure to social science research would be helpful and researchers report an interest in producing studies that will be used in policy discussions, the link between these interests has often not been successful. In fact, an entire field of study, known as dissemination and utilization of knowledge (Havelock, 1979), has developed to help understand and improve this process. These interests are also being reflected more directly in criminal justice. The National Institute of Justice (NIJ), the agency that funds that majority of government-supported research on crime and criminal justice, has begun emphasizing the importance of partnerships between academics and criminal justice agencies.

Criminal Justice Organizations and Knowledge Utilization

One example of efforts to understand knowledge utilization is provided by Rick Lovell (1988), who examined the use of research in a state corrections department. When Lovell interviewed top administrators, including research staff, to see how research information was used in the agency, he found little "instrumental" use of research data—that is, studies seldom directly influenced decision making. Symbolic use, or the use of research findings as justification of budgets, for example, was a more common practice. More common, although still fairly infrequent, were claims of *conceptual* use of research. In those cases, managers claimed to have been informed or enlightened by research but cited no specific use of findings in decision making.

Lovell also found that certain characteristics of the organization and its management influenced how information was used. The absence of any coordination of research utilization efforts combined with the functional division of the organization to limit use of research information. Subunits were left to solve problems on their own, with no expectation that research would be a necessary part of that process. Furthermore, management was seen as crisis oriented and the solution of immediate problems was seen as precluding the examination and use of research information. Research was perceived as a luxury the organization didn't have time for.

Other studies have also shown that organizational structure and management influence the use of research in organizations. A study of social work practice in schools (Chavkin, 1986), for example, found that formalization and centralization affected the likelihood that some research findings would influence practice. Specifically, the authors examined the implementation of research-based recommendations that social workers change their activities from traditional casework management to organizational and community change activities. The more that social workers' tasks were governed by formal rules and the more decision-making power was centralized in the head of the organization, the less likely were research findings to be implemented. In schools with fewer rules and less central control, social workers were better able to utilize research findings to change their activities.

In his corrections study, Lovell also described another reason that research findings may not influence practice in some organizations. Police departments, courts, and corrections agencies all exist in highly political environments. At the upper levels of organization management in those environments, many questions of policy are strongly tied to questions of value and preference. No matter how defensible a practice may be on research grounds, no one can afford to be seen as insensitive to community standards—whether that means being seen as soft on crime or as excessive in the use of force or other forms of social control. Facts may play a secondary role when decisions are driven by such political considerations.

The Researcher and Knowledge Utilization

There is also another side to understanding the utilization of research in public policy. While we have considered organizational impediments to the use of research, researchers can also contribute to problems in the research-practice relationship.

One reason researchers and practitioners may see the world differently is that, in fact, they see different worlds. Many practitioners may never be exposed to available research at all. Lovell, for example, found that although corrections managers had access to research in journals, magazines, and other publications, that information was not coordinated or organized in any systematic and accessible way. The most important source of information for managers appeared to be the word of trusted colleagues or staff members.

Meanwhile, the common method of dissemination of the results of social science research in criminal justice and other fields is still through the specialized journal literature of the field. There, in the language of their disciplines and in the conventions of scientific research, academics communicate, largely with one another. The writing style and narrow dissemination of academic research have been identified as major reasons that some administrators report that research findings are of little use in their decision-making process (Light & Newman, 1992). Decision makers in organizations may have little time or ability to digest research findings directly but may instead rely on people with whom they have direct relationships.

Recent years have seen significant efforts to improve the dissemination of research findings and, in the process, to improve the relationship between researchers and practitioners. A program for police executives held regular sessions at Harvard University, for example, in which practitioners and researchers gathered regularly over several years to review research and practice in the area of community policing. The National Institute of Corrections has successfully used academics and practitioners in providing technical assistance for prisons and jails. The National Council on Crime and Delinquency (NCCD) has also formed effective relationships between researchers and practitioners as states have struggled to find ways to project prison population growth and address crowding.

These examples go beyond simply addressing problems of dissemination and reveal a second common problem: that of mutual understanding. Academic researchers and practitioners may have different views on the value of data. Expertise in methodology and statistics gives researchers confidence that conclusions based on the analysis of data are technically sound and rational; the better the methodology, the greater confidence they have in their conclusions. For practitioners, however, additional expectations may need to be met.

Practitioners must be convinced first of all that research findings are relevant to the problems they face. National studies or research done in other jurisdictions may seem too distant to them, despite the soundness of the methods. Furthermore, since even the best studies must acknowledge their limitations, policy makers may be hesitant to accept their conclusions. Practitioners may be far less comfortable than academics with notions of probability, confidence levels, and statistical significance. Thus, academics need to do a better job communicating the meaning and value of such ideas.

Another factor enters into the sometimes different views of practitioners and researchers: practitioners and researchers may emphasize different aspects of data. Researchers are trained to value what is typical or average; mean, median, and mode—measures of central tendency—are their bread and butter. When the strength of relationships is considered, the unusual case may be seen as an outlier and may sometimes even be excluded from correlation or regression studies, but it is always denigrated for its atypical character.

For the practitioner, however, it is the outlier rather than the typical case that often demands attention. Researchers may be surprised to find administrators who are sometimes wildly inaccurate in their estimates of some data. Parole board members may overestimate recidivism; some police, prosecutors, and judges may know little of crime rates or actual time spent in prison for average inmates. But they will all know the details of the extreme outliers. Those are the unusual but sensational cases that shape public sentiment. Their recidivism ends furlough programs, closes halfway houses, or leads to defeat in bids for reelection. In the language of the statistician, central tendency may be the focus of researchers, but variance will always be a concern for the practitioner.

Researchers must come to appreciate that the outlier is more than a statistical anomaly in the real world. And practitioners must appreciate that the unusual case cannot be allowed to obscure our understanding of the ordinary. Like technical issues of probability and significance, these issues also may best be addressed through closer working relationships.

The Nature of Social Science Research and Knowledge Utilization

A still more basic problem has been raised by some academics who question whether social science research has reached a level of sophistication sufficient to merit influencing public policy. Elliot (1990) responded to a call for greater influence (see Petersilia, 1993) by sounding a note of caution. He argued that criminologists should be more hesitant to offer advice to policy makers. Although experimental design research of the highest quality has become more common, Elliot notes that such studies are still few in number and that little data in criminal justice have been collected over a long enough period of time to ensure confident conclusions.

One example of research that Elliot suggests should temper academics' enthusiasm for influencing policy is the studies of police response to domestic violence. The Minneapolis domestic violence experiment (see Sherman & Cohn, 1989) was a well-designed and well-executed study in which responses to domestic violence calls were randomly assigned to responses of arrest and nonarrest with counseling, respectively. The research demonstrated that arresting suspects of domestic violence could reduce recidivism, as measured in repeated police calls to the same address. Those conclusions were regarded as support for a movement reflected in state statutes and departmental policy calling for mandatory arrest when there was evidence of any injury or physical confrontation in domestic violence calls.

Although mandatory arrest policies have been widely adopted, even the authors of the research later cautioned policy makers about moving too quickly to implement policy based on their findings. In the meantime, other research failed to replicate the Minneapolis findings. Replication, or retesting experiments in different settings and at different times to see if the same or similar results are found, should be a standard research procedure. In this case, the Minneapolis findings were not only not replicated in other cities, there was some support for the opposite conclusion. Some evidence, for example, suggested that social class makes a difference; arrests in middle- and upper-class cases could be successful, but in lower- and working-class families arrests could actually increase the chances of future violence in the home.

The Minneapolis example raises important questions about the relationship between research and public policy. Should the initial findings have been released and promoted before they had been subjected to the replication test? If not, at what point and how do we judge the readiness of research to influence policy? How many replications are sufficient? One answer, of course, is that as long as the research design is sound and appropriate limitations are discussed, the release and use of research is appropriate. The fact that future research may alter findings is simply part of the process of scientific exploration.

The experience with the Minneapolis research, however, suggests that even that answer may be insufficient. One reason the original research may have been so influential was that it supported policies that were already favored for other reasons. Many victims' advocates and feminists had supported policies of arrest because these policies were seen as fair and just. It is reasonable to wonder how widely implemented the research would have been if its original findings did not support arrest decisions. A hint may lie in the fact that the revised findings have not reversed the course of public policy.

The domestic violence studies raise one additional issue about the relationship between research and policy. The original finding—that arrest worked—was regarded as an unambiguous conclusion for policy makers to act on. But as the replication attempts showed, research does not always yield such tidy findings. What, for example, could be the policy implications of findings that arrests may reduce violence in middle-class households but increase it in others? Wouldn't a policy that overtly treated people differently based on their social class conflict with other values? While the effectiveness of certain policies may be a comfortable subject for researchers to address, other problems are not solved by increasing methodological rigor.

Domestic violence research and policy provide one illustration of the potential complexity of the research–practice relationship. While it may seem straightforward to many that objective analysis of data should guide public policy, the situation is much less clear when we examine specific issues. That lack of clarity suggests that research can be, and perhaps should be, only one of a variety of factors considered in policy making and in the decisions of practitioners. Research, then, can contribute to policy but is not likely to be the only, or even the primary, basis for it.

This conclusion does not suggest an inferior role for research in the public policy or administrative process. Quite the opposite is true. A major consequence of taking research seriously is that doing so opens up the policy process for critical examination. Data take policy out of the realm of simple preferences or untested assumptions. A commitment to research is a commitment to defending policy choices as rational. Research may not be the only rational influence in decision making, but taking it seriously means that other influences should be subjected to the same scrutiny as the research findings.

These are issues that are typically not covered in undergraduate or graduate research courses. Instead, researchers' training may lead them to expect that quality research will drive rational policy choices: that research will have an authoritative role. They may expect their work to direct, rather than simply, influence decision making. These misunderstandings of the policy-making process can sometimes be at the heart of researchers' complaints that even their best efforts are not directly used by policy makers. Similar misunderstandings may also lead researchers to underestimate the long-term and indirect effects of their work.

Data and the Utilization of Knowledge

We have examined the potential for barriers to applying knowledge in the context of organizations, researchers, and the research process. Another obstacle may arise from the nature of the data themselves.

When the 1967 President's Commission made its recommendations, the Uniform Crime Reports provided the only major source of information on crime, and there was skepticism about the accuracy of those reports. Since then, the UCR have improved, and an incident-based reporting system is being implemented that will provide even more valuable data. Other sources of data have also been developed, including the National Crime Victims Survey and surveys of jail and prison inmates.

Crime Analysis and Patrol Allocation

Within the Milwaukee Police Department, the Crime Analysis Section (CAS) is assigned to the Patrol Bureau and provides research services to the Special Operations Bureau (SOB), Criminal Investigation Bureau (CIB), and department administration. Some data products are provided on a regular (weekly or monthly) basis, while others are provided as needed. A few of the contributions made by the CAS to the crime fighting efforts of the MPD include providing crime pattern maps to district and bureau commanders and presenting the maps at weekly command staff meetings; mapping addresses of persons released on parole, probation, and intensive sanctions; and providing data for personnel staffing distribution and budgeting.

At the weekly command staff meetings the CAS presents computerized city maps displayed on screen with four-week comparisons of robberies, burglaries, auto thefts, and various quality-of-life issues. This display, in addition to the same maps provided in hard copy, allows all in the room to view crime patterns as they emerge. Senior commanders then query the district and bureau commanders about what is or was being done about particular crime patterns. For instance, have any arrests been made, have any directed patrol missions (DPMs) been formed, and are they aware of any similarities? Because these maps are updated each week, the commanders can expect to have their areas of crime patterns revisited. This regular revisitation allows commanders to evaluate the effectiveness of their efforts. Ineffective efforts are cause for reevaluation and redirection of assets.

The Milwaukee Police Department has always been interested in where persons released by the Wisconsin Department of Corrections have come to reside within the city of Milwaukee. Until the inception of the CAS, the individual release reports were filed in a cabinet to be reviewed by any detective or patrol officer who had the fortitude to wade through the mound of papers. The acquisition of desktop databases has allowed the CAS to store data on persons released on parole, probation, and intensive sanctions (PPIS) electronically for easy retrieval. The information received from the DOC is minimal, including name, approved address, date of birth, and offenses for which they had been convicted. CAS personnel search department data files to obtain the identification number (if arrested in the city) and full physical description. The new data is added to the database, from which maps are created to display the address of the parolee at the time of release.

These maps by themselves are of minimal use. When used in conjunction with maps of offenses, however, they can be telling. For instance, persons convicted of sexual assault have been found to have a high incidence of recidivism. If, in mapping sexual assaults, the CAS or investigative personnel find a pattern or series developing, they can take the maps of assaults and overlay them (electronically or with acetates) with the maps of persons convicted of sexual assault and released to the community. If a parolee shows up in the neighborhood experiencing a pattern or series of assaults, that parolee immediately becomes a suspect in need of further investigation. The same is true of burglary and robbery parolees.

In addition to maps, printed tables are created from the database listing name, address, date of birth, description and such, and are sent out to the various districts and bureaus. District commanders have used these tables to assign police officers to check these persons for wants and warrants. Many have been found to have outstanding warrants and are visited by the officers; subsequent arrests of these people have cleared additional offenses.

In an effort to ensure equitable distribution of police personnel among the various work shifts, the CAS is tasked with collecting data on the number of calls-for-service based on call priority and day and hour the calls were dispatched. These data are then graphed for evaluation by command administrative staff, who compare the number of calls with the number of assigned police personnel. These personnel can then be redistributed among the shifts as necessary to meet the needs of the community and the department. To date, these reviews have been done annually.

The command administration of the Milwaukee police department also uses CAS research to evaluate the need for additional police personnel. Besides calls-for-service, the number of offenses reported and arrests made are tallied by the CAS. From these numbers and those of previous years as well as census forecasts, mathematical projections can be made estimating future numbers of crimes to be reported and arrests to be made. These projections allow command administrative staff to determine whether or not additional police personnel may be needed in the future, with enough lead time to budget monies, recruiting, and training time to have these new personnel on staff as the increased need arrives.

The CAS has experienced an increasing number of requests for its services over the last several years. As a result, additional personnel have been assigned and new computers have been requested to meet this increased demand. Ever-improving knowledge of what is actually happening within the city, obtained in a timely manner, has allowed district and bureau commanders to target problem areas with increased patrols and community-oriented policing programs.

CONRAD W. ZVARA
Milwaukee Police Department

While these data may be useful for some research purposes, such as describing national trends, they are often much less useful for management purposes. Surveys that use national sampling frames and scientific methods do not often permit comparisons at the local level. Even the Uniform Crime Reports, which record all reported crime, may be of limited use. The aggregation or combination of data at the national, statewide, and even city level will mask great differences within the jurisdiction. Furthermore, crime and other rates depend on population estimates for their accuracy, and such estimates are less accurate for local levels. The irony is that while there is some reason for confidence in some of the measures used in criminal justice research, those measures are the least reliable at the local level, and that is where data can be the most influential in the decision-making and management processes.

Developing useful and reliable data has been a particular concern in the area of drug policy. There, too, national surveys of drug use can be informative but provide little data to direct drug treatment or intervention at the local level. Reuter (1993) has described the problems with estimates of the prevalence of drug use as well as measures of expenditures on drugs. These measures should be important for drug policy but remain little used because the estimates often suffer from a perceived lack of credibility (in the case of self-reported drug use) and because the politics of drug policy has not placed a premium on the use of data. Reuter also points out that although prevalence estimates are cheapest and easiest at the national level, local estimates remain the most useful. The high cost of accurate local-level data, however, may mean that they are little used in the policy process.

It is critical, then, that data be valid and reliable if they are to be part of the decision-making or policy-making process. But validity and reliability must be considered in the context of the decisions being made. And since most criminal justice services are provided at the local level, that is the level at which we need accurate data. That is also why, as we shall discuss later, some researchers have placed a high priority on involving consumers of research in the development of the measures and methods they use.

In-House Research

In-house research, not to be contrasted with out-house research, refers to the development of the capacity within organizations to address their own data and research needs. This capacity is often provided through separate units or research offices within the organizations. Frederick Taylor's development of a managerial class trained in time and motion studies was an early example of a manager's interest in increasing the research capacity of his organization. Now research offices report directly to the highest executives in most large companies and many public organizations.

In policing, crime analysis units track crime trends and evaluate policy choices. In courts, sophisticated management information systems have been developed to track cases and control backlogs. In corrections, in-house research units monitor objective classification systems, track population movement and disciplinary procedures, and, in some cases, regularly measure the social climate of institutions.

There is great potential for in-house research efforts to overcome some of the problems discussed here. In-house research units can establish credibility and gain the support of managers to overcome organizational resistance to research. They can also integrate researchers into the fabric of organizations, thus overcoming the limitations associated with outside researchers and the research process. The potential strength of in-house research is found in the potential for close partnerships between managers and researchers. That is the relationship described by Toch and Grant (1982) in their review of in-house research at General Motors under manager Howard Carlson. Under Carlson, the role of researchers was to help solve problems as they affected the line organizations. That meant that researchers could not be isolated in their offices in front of their computers but instead had to work with frontline staff in defining problems appropriately, collecting and analyzing the necessary data, and helping staff respond to results of analyses.

The "quality" movement in industry today emphasizes the importance of in-house research. Although he disliked the term, W. Edwards Deming has been seen as the founder of *total quality management* (TQM). He taught statistically based quality control measures in Japanese industries before leading the quality movement in this country in the 1980s and early 1990s. Deming's vision of management, however, went well beyond statistics and technical methods. He emphasized the need for organizations to develop the capacity for problem solving (Deming, 1986).

Because knowledge is a key component of that capacity, total quality management has emphasized the knowledge-building process. The heart of that process has been reliance on data-based analysis and teamwork that brings managers, workers, and researchers together to define and solve problems. Total quality management with an emphasis on customer orientation, research, and participation has been a significant movement in major companies, including AT&T, Kodak, and many others.

As with many innovations that take hold in the private sector, public organizations have also begun to utilize TQM principles. While there is room for debate about the precise definition of customer and the fit between TQM in the private and public sector may not be perfect, TQM has had some success in criminal justice management. In Monroe County, New York, the county executive hired a TQM manager out of retirement from a major company to apply the TQM principles to local government. As in many counties, there was strong political pressure to build an addition to the jail. The TQM consultant, along with the director of public safety, assembled a team of managers and staff from across the criminal justice system. The judges, police chiefs, prosecutors, and defense attorneys oversaw the collection and analysis of data on the jail population. They discovered that the jail was filled with people detained for minor offenses, almost all of whom would be released from jail in a short time anyway. (They even found that misdemeanor suspects were staying in jail longer than their felony suspect counterparts!) In their report (Monroe County, 1994), the team noted, "This data clearly shows that a system processing problem exists in Monroe County. . . . Based on an extensive review of the available data, the Team came to the conclusion that jail expansion was not an appropriate response to the current jail overcrowding problem."

The most interesting point of this experience is that many members of the team had worked together for years in an ineffectual effort to coordinate efforts in the local criminal justice system. The TQM requirement—that the team respond to the data—seemed to make an important difference. The Team now faces new challenges, however. The resignation of the county executive and a subsequent election have once again put jail expansion on the agenda. And the new executive is less enamored of TQM methods or of research in general.

If those TQM efforts hold and the process of considering data continues over time, it will be a model of rational planning. There are also other examples of successful in-house research efforts. For many years into the 1980s, innovative and important research was done through the research division of the California Youth Authority. The research office of the New York State Department of Mental Hygiene conducted important studies of mental illness and crime. Today, however, these studies are perhaps best seen as examples of successful efforts by dedicated and creative researchers and research-oriented managers and not necessarily of institutionalized practices.

Significant criticism has also been directed against in-house research efforts. Sometimes those critics have highlighted the tendency of in-house research to amount to little more than counting and accounting procedures. Police department research units may be consumed by the process of counting reported crimes or recording the characteristics of persons arrested. In corrections, what passes for research may simply be tracking prisoners throughout the prisons and logging levels of education or mental health histories. In many agencies, a primary function of research may be to justify program budgets.

One study provides insight into the circumstances under which in-house research may have little impact on management in criminal justice organizations. Lovell and Kalinich (1992) examined the role and potential for in-house research in a large nonprofit organization that provided a variety of criminal justice services, including diversion and treatment programs. Researchers, administrators, and program managers all indicated that there was minimal use of research despite the existence of a separate research office staffed by competent researchers.

A variety of factors contributed to the lack of use of research in this organization. Chief among them was the ambiguous role of the research department despite its high level of activity. Top administrators had failed to clarify the research role to program managers, who often saw potential conflict between research findings and their own expertise. For their part, the researchers tended to claim credibility based on technical expertise rather than on position and influence in the organization.

Clearly, problems in the research–practice relationship can persist when the research function is moved in-house. But there are also lessons to be taken from the experience of others. Administrative support for the research function is critical. If top administrators do not have a clear role for their research office, managers underneath them may view research as irrelevant or perhaps even as conflicting with their own expertise. Researchers must also strive for fuller integration into the organization; they must actively seek an integral role in the main functions of the organization. To stand aside, aloof but ready to offer expertise to the trenches, is a position that dooms researchers to limited influence. And part of the researchers' efforts must include more effective communication in all phases of the research process, from the development of research problems through the design and implementation of studies and the reporting and interpretation of results.

Knowledge as Truth

Up to this point in the discussion, we have been operating under certain assumptions about the value and meaning of data. It is now time to make those assumptions explicit and to consider other ways of understanding this subject.

In the world of research, data are often thought of simply as recorded observations. In other words, they are seen as neutral facts. Rational conclusions are to be drawn from dispassionate analysis of those facts. Under these assumptions, research contributes to what has been called rational-empirical strategies for change as described by the organizational theorists Robert Chin and Kenneth Benne (1969). Under these strategies, policies are followed because they are correct or, at least, represent the best or most rational choice, given the available data. The world of evaluation research is often presented in this fashion; objective data are gathered to determine if a program works or not.

Of course, a model of rational planning is based on the assumption that planners are rational. But data may not be the only rational influence on decision makers. They are also influenced by a myriad of other considerations, from budgetary to political. And even data based rationality is no simple idea. As Chapter 13 on effectiveness has shown, the question of whether something works is complicated. Works for whom? By whose criteria? To what degree? And what will happen if it is seen to work or not work? These are only a few of the questions that spring easily to mind. In answering them, it is easy to see that data are not always and may never be wholly neutral. Underneath all information lie the beliefs and assumptions of those who collect and analyze it. The claim of fact or truth, then, is not a neutral claim but rather is a claim to a kind of power, the power of knowledge. This can include the power to define the situation and to say what is and is not important. In some cases, it is expert power, as we discussed in Chapter 10, which examined power in organizations.

Knowledge as Power

The power of knowledge may contribute to rational processes within organizations, processes that can promote or resist change based on empirical evidence. But that power may also be used in change strategies that Chin and Benne (1969) have described as power–coercive strategies. Under these strategies, research is a source of coercive power. An example can be found in the housing testing programs that take place in cities around the country. Field researchers follow up on advertisements for rental housing or work with realtors; white and minority couples present similar records of employment and assets and are trained to standardize their approaches with landlords or realtors. Evidence of differential treatment based on the race of the couples is then used to make legal cases against landlords and realtors. Another example involved identifying and changing biased treatment of restaurant customers around the United Nations building in New York (Selltiz, 1955). When couples were treated differently based on their race, legal action wasn't necessary. Showing the data to owners and managers with the threat of continued "study" of their discrimination was sufficient to change practices.

Consumer advocate Ralph Nader has also effectively used research to influence organizations. Nader began his career with a review of automobile accident data published in *Unsafe at Any Speed* (1965). That research contributed to General Motor's decision to take the Corvair out of production. Since then, the consumer movement has often made use of research by people unaffiliated with the organizations they seek to influence.

In criminal justice, outside groups have also used research to provoke change. The movement to stiffen penalties against drunken driving, for example, was led by court-watch efforts that recorded and publicized judges' sentencing practices. An important part of the strategy of the grassroots organization Mothers Against Drunk Driving (MADD) was to pressure judges and politicians by revealing the facts about how drunk drivers were being treated by the criminal justice system (see Jacobs, 1989).

Concern over the use of knowledge in this way may be what causes some managers to resist research. In some cases, fear of knowledge from outside sources can reach a level of organizational paranoia that breeds distrust and isolation from others (Havelock, 1979). It may lead managers to resist evaluation studies for fear that results will be interpreted in a thumbs-up or thumbs-down manner. When evaluation is done in that way, the research may be interpreted as determining that a program is a failure instead of simply suggesting approaches to program change and improvement. Fearing the power–coercive use of data by others, managers may be particularly concerned about research conducted by people who are not directly affiliated with their organization.

Managers themselves can use data in a power–coercive manner, however. It is not uncommon for researchers to be approached to do evaluations because managers are under pressure to show how well their program works. In one recent example, program managers sought an evaluation of a transitional housing program for welfare mothers in an effort to attract funding. The staff had initially selected people to participate in the program and had then selected those they regarded as "graduates" from all those who had been through the program. An "independent" researcher was asked to follow up on the graduates. Not surprisingly, the researcher offered the conclusion that the program was successful in helping women get off welfare services. Of course, a research design with two layers of nonrandom selection and no control groups does not justify such conclusions. Whether based on naiveté or deliberate manipulation, such evaluations are not likely to be helpful in the long run.

Knowledge as Understanding

For many years, U.S. agricultural researchers worked with West African farmers to increase crop yields. But often their research bore little fruit.

Many recommendations, such as delaying spring planting to first plow and fertilize the fields of this semiarid savanna area, were not acted upon. It was not, however, until the researchers collaborated more closely with farmers that they realized their mistake. Farmers did not plow and fertilize their fields because fertilizer prices were relatively high compared to the costs of using more land. It was more economical to get low yields from large plots than to increase production on small plots. As a result of the research, farmers and researchers turned their attention to building an agricultural infrastructure that could produce cheaper fertilizer.

In the preceding example, knowledge of ways to increase crop production provided neither compelling insight nor the power to bring about change. Indeed, the problems faced by the farmers were not even what the researchers had presumed they were. Instead, it was only through the collaborative efforts of farmers and researchers that advancements could be made.

Chin and Benne describe a category of change strategies that they call *normative-reeducative strategies*. These strategies emphasize that understanding is a transactional process in which information is taken in, interpreted, and acted upon according to the consumer's values and experiences. The impetus for change comes not from the expert's analysis but rather from collaboration and experienced-based learning.

To describe normative-reeducative strategies that are based in the collection and analysis of data, Kurt Lewin coined the term *action research*. He developed the model in studies focused on changing consumer behavior during shortages of meat and other commodities during World War II (see Lewin, 1948). Lewin stressed the need for strengthening the relationships among research, training, and action. And he emphasized the need for collaborative relationships in organizations in which managers, workers, and researchers came together to understand the need for change, to develop the knowledge base necessary to bring about change, and to monitor the process of change. For Lewin, action research was never to be less scientific than other research efforts, but it was to engage many new participants in the process of formulating the research problem and in identifying and interpreting data that would be seen as valid and potent. In fact, the action research model data could serve the very powerful function of testing and sometimes disconfirming the biases and prejudices of the participants.

In one famous example, the manager of a pajama factory employed a student of Lewin's to deal with middle managers' concerns about the productivity of older female workers. The managers designed a study to investigate how much the company was losing as a result of the limited productivity of this workforce (Marrow & French, 1945). They developed the measures of effectiveness and were closely questioned so as not to leave out any important issues. The involvement and commitment of these managers to the research made the findings—that the older female workers were among the most productive—all the more powerful in influencing their hiring and supervision decisions.

In discovering the productivity levels of the female workers and disconfirming their own biases, the pajama factory managers demonstrated a key role for data in Lewin's action research model. Change, Lewin argued, comes about when the status quo cannot hold, when forces supporting change outweigh those resisting it. The power of self-generated knowledge is the power to unfreeze the status quo. Involvement in research has the potential to unfreeze managers by disconfirming their expectations and undermining their prejudices. Here research does not simply chronicle the need for change or record its consequences. Instead, action research is itself a strategy for bringing about change.

A variety of methods have been developed to support collaborative research efforts. One approach is to incorporate data feedback to those involved in the process of change. In the preceding example, managers received feedback about older workers' performance. Wilkins (see Kress, 1980) has also used data feedback to influence judges' sentencing decisions. Under his approach, sentencing guidelines are based on average sentences handed out for specific offenses. Judges can then consider whether any particular case warrants sanctions more or less severe than the average.

Data feedback methods have also been supplemented by the use of employee and client surveys. Survey feedback methods pioneered in the 1950s by Floyd Mann (1950) and his associates have been used widely in the private sector. The procedure includes the systematic collection of data from organization members on a wide range of topics, including supervisory styles, communication patterns, and worker satisfaction. In some cases, standardized surveys developed and tested in other settings have been used to measure organizational climate, management style, and other variables, with the results fed back to members of the organization. The Federal Bureau of Prisons now routinely measures the social climate of its institutions using such survey methods.

The use of standardized measures may enhance the validity and reliability of the data, but there is also value in having members of the organization develop the instruments to measure what they regard as important and, in some cases, carry out the research themselves. Such participation in research has been advocated by Chris Argyris (1957), who sees "organic research" as a way of drawing on the expertise of people, increasing their competence, and avoiding the dependency or resistance that may result from noninvolvement.

Involvement in research can enhance the meaningfulness and sense of ownership of the data. In one example, jail officers developed a survey of inmate program preferences during the planning and construction of a new jail. The officers, who shared responsibility for program planning for the facility, presumed inmates would rank recreational programming as most important and would have little interest in education or vocational training. In fact, their interests were just the opposite. The officers, surprised to learn of the inmates' priorities, eventually invited inmates to participate in planning educational programming for the facility.

In a classic example of participatory research in criminal justice, Toch and Grant (1975) involved police officers in studying the use of force. Police administrators in the agency recognized that some officers had high rates of reported complaints from citizens and high rates of reported uses of force. Toch and Grant recruited the officers with the worst records for a research project on the use of force. The officers tape-recorded and analyzed their interactions with citizens; their goal was to identify the dynamics of incidents that produced undesirable exchanges. As the officers' own interactions with citizens changed in response to their new knowledge, they went on to train others in managing police–citizen encounters. The study continues to serve as a model of problem solving that uses the expertise of frontline staff to address important problems in policing (Skolnick & Fyfe, 1993).

These examples illustrate the potential contributions of research to a process of organizational change. They take research beyond the collection and analysis of data that is separate and apart from the participants. These efforts emphasize a process of self-study in which not only facts but how they are understood and how they motivate action are important. Self-study makes it possible for participants to supplement their intuition and unsystematic knowledge based on experience with externally gathered facts. As Toch and Grant have described: "The process translates staff hunches into research questions and defines arenas for experimentation: it also leads to expanded personal horizons, learning and growth" (1982 : 166).

Knowledge and the Future of Criminal Justice Administration

The purpose of this book has been to provide an examination of the major dimensions that affect and influence criminal justice administration. Whether we are discussing the workings of police departments, correctional agencies, prosecutors' offices, or court systems, there is much benefit in analyzing them as organizations. Through an organizational analysis, criminal justice agencies are better understood, and it is possible to create useful prescriptions for criminal justice administrators.

We stated in the preface that we had three themes we sought to address in this edition of the book. First and foremost, we wanted to focus on what we know about criminal justice organizations from the perspective of many disciplines: political science, sociology, psychology, and, in addition, the burgeoning research conducted by those academically trained in criminal justice. Second, we wanted a systemic focus when viewing criminal justice administration. Very few texts even discuss the interrelatedness and interdependence found among criminal justice organizations. We have sought to discuss these issues in the context of various organizational and administrative dimensions. Whether the topic is decision making, conflict, structure, or job design, to mention a few, we were interested in issues and research across the components of the criminal justice system, that is, police, prosecution, courts, and corrections. Finally, we sought an understanding of criminal justice administration through the integration of theory, research, and practice. We felt through proper integration of these elements, our understanding of criminal justice administration would be more complete.

We conclude the book by discussing how these three themes are predicated on knowledge, information, and the systematic collection, analysis, and application of data to improve criminal justice administration. The 21st century is upon us. The expectations for criminal justice administrators are much higher in this new century than in the past, largely due to limited resources, increased visibility, and constant review by groups with conflicting interests and thoughts on how criminal justice organizations are to be administered. With the availability of more sophisticated technologies, criminal justice administration stands at the precipice of a new world. This new world reflects a guarded optimism on how criminal justice organizations will be led and managed by administrators incorporating these newer technologies.

As this text is being written the United States has experienced a direct terrorist attack on its own soil, the magnitude of which is unprecedented in the history of the country. Criminal justice administrators have been asked to respond with newer and more sophisticated strategies to combat crime and criminals, including terrorists. The foundation for these 21st-century crime strategies will be how well we integrate knowledge, data, and information into the conceptualization of the crime problem, a response to it, and a redirection, if needed, of our efforts predicated on data-informed decision making. Yet, decision making is not the only issue amenable to this process. The entire operation of criminal justice organizations and the actions of their administrators will rely more on quality data, information, and knowledge. We have discussed many of these issues in the context of the organizational topics and dimensions presented in this book.

For the criminal justice administrator, informed intuition and experience will not be enough. Complex systems of data collection, data analysis, and strategic assessment will become the norm for administrative actions and behaviors. Knowledge, data, and information will become critical and essential for effective criminal justice administration. Whether criminal justice administrators are addressing issues of structure, conflict, strategies to motivate employees, organizational effectiveness, the environment, or any other topic the chapters have addressed in this book, knowledge, information, and data will be the foundation upon which future criminal justice administration will be understood and assessed.

What does the 21st century hold for criminal justice administration? We believe that across the components of the criminal justice system a greater emphasis will be placed on the creation of appropriate knowledge, data, and information to address crime. There will be expectations by public groups, private concerns, and the government itself that criminal justice administrators do things in a different way. Criminal justice administration has evolved as society as evolved. The Internet, integrated data systems and files, more invasive surveillance technologies, and ways to train and supervise employees electronically will become the mainstream of criminal justice operations. With these changes will come the possibility of greater review of the operations of their criminal justice systems by communities. Concerns about accountability will become more pronounced, and criminal justice administrators will have to justify their requests for increased dollars and personnel to combat crime. With this increased accountability will come more concern for how criminal justice administrators are recruited, selected, and retained. At the core of these activities will be the search for knowledge, data, and information. Unlike his/her predecessors in the 20th century, the 21st-century criminal justice administrator will have more expectations placed upon him/her, resources will be tighter, and questions of effectiveness and efficiency will be recurrent. How these new criminal justice administrators respond to these concerns will be the essence of criminal justice administration into the future.

Summary

In this chapter we have examined the potential contributions of science to the practice of criminal justice. We began by considering the hypothesis that the collection and analysis of data would contribute to an increasingly rational approach to management in criminal justice. In fact, interest in the advancement of research was one of the most important directions established by the President's Commission on Law Enforcement and the Administration of Justice in 1967. Although progress has been made, the hopes of that commission have yet to be realized. In fact, debate continues over whether social science research has reached a level of sophistication that justifies its greater influence.

Despite disagreements on the value of basic and applied research, a variety of factors can be identified that may affect the way research can influence practice in the field of criminal justice. Managers can send strong messages in support of or against research by the priority they give it in their organizations and by the way they encourage experimentation. Researchers themselves can become more aware of the concerns of consumers of their work and must make the tools of science more understandable and accessible; they must demonstrate the relevance of their data. Researchers and their advocates must also accept that while they may be influential contributors, they will not be the sole influence on management and policy making. These are among the key issues when organizations develop their own research capacity in house.

It is possible, however, to miss the forest for the trees. While the technical issues will always be important, it is also critical to consider the meaning of data within the context of management and change in organizations. For some, research may stand for facts and the truth. Others may see such views as claims of power: the power of the knowledgeable. And, participatory research and self-study may give meaning and ownership to data. In these strategies may lie the greatest potential for research to affect the criminal justice system. Finally, we concluded with the importance of criminal justice knowledge, data, and information to the future of criminal justice administration. Challenging days lie ahead for criminal justice administrators. How well they address these challenges will be dependent, to a large degree, on how they acquire knowledge, process information, and analyze data and how these processes alter the ways in which criminal justice administrators do business in the 21st century.

Case Study

Police Technology and Research, Patrol Allocation, and Politics

Captain Jill Roberts was a ten-year veteran with the Willows Police Department. She had risen from the ranks, beginning with a patrol assignment, a brief stint with narcotics and vice, three years as a police sergeant, and two years as a lieutenant, before getting promoted to the rank of captain. Captain Roberts was a stickler for detail, often showing up at roll calls unannounced. Her reputation among the rank-and-file officers was that she was fair and earned her promotions and that she was particularly sensitive to the needs of ordinary street cops. She was viewed by her subordinates as a "cop's cop," something she was proud of and attempted to portray as part of her management style. Her overriding interest, however, was to improve the department's decision-making capabilities by modernizing its equipment and the way it handled information.

To that end, she petitioned the police chief for some time to develop a comprehensive plan on the allocation of police resources, specifically patrol allocation decisions. She wanted the department to purchase more advanced equipment and computer technology for making these decisions. She was most interested in how the quantity and quality of information could be improved within the department. By improving the department's capabilities to process information, she felt officers could be more responsive to the community's needs as well as their own practical require-ments. Captain Roberts had heard about new computer hardware and software be-ing used in big city police departments for analyzing crime data. She was particularly fascinated by how other departments had instituted research bureaus and incorpo-rated modern technologies in their provision of police services. With the chief's ap-proval, she began to work on a plan to do the same for the Willows police department.

Both the Chicago Police Department and the New York City police department had upgraded their computer capabilities, enabling them to have automatic data en-try and retrieval on criminal activities in the various police districts across their re-spective cities. What interested Captain Roberts was that the data on where crime was located, peak times of crime commission, and police response could be fed back to precinct captains in the form of graphs and tables. Captain Roberts liked the idea that this information could then be used to restructure the allocation of police re-sources: the more crime-prone sections of the city would get more resources to ad-dress specific crime problems. In addition, the computer software allowed the pre-cincts to measure their crime levels and types of police responses across all police districts and make appropriate comparisons. Summaries could be created that dis-played variations by season, month, and even week.

This enhanced computer technology offered unlimited opportunities to police departments to improve the efficiency of patrol allocations. Remembering her days as a criminal justice student at a local university, Captain Roberts recalled how her pro-fessors tried to get students to view the importance of information collection and re-search in making practical decisions in criminal justice organizations. She recalled one professor who harped on the fact that there was really no singular system of crim-inal justice, that communities varied in crime and criminal justice responses, and ef-fective strategies of crime control had to be generated at the local level. Hence, effec-tive crime control efforts begin with an analysis of the problem and an appreciation of research methodology. At the time, student Roberts had no way of understanding the relevance of these ideas, but today Captain Roberts could see how such ideas are invaluable to police departments.

By combining modern technology with the findings of other communities, Cap-tain Roberts could develop a systematic plan to evaluate the needs of the City of Wil-lows, borrowing strategies from other communities where useful, but also employ-ing the computer technology to organize crime data in a useful and constructive way. This would mean that she would have to make a pitch to the chief about the impor-tance of reviewing current research, the relevance of computer technology to the de-partment, and potential hurdles or obstacles to these ideas. In short, Captain Roberts needed a research plan.

She approached the police chief with her ideas and a tentative plan of action. The chief disseminated a rough draft of her plan to all command staff and precinct cap-tains for discussion at the next staff meeting. Expecting some initial resistance, Cap-tain Roberts began the presentation of her plan by noting the benefits to the depart-ment as a whole and the precincts individually. After a brief presentation, she took questions from the other police captains. On the whole, the four other precinct cap-tains spoke against her plan.

One captain whose district had the lowest crime rates responded that he did not like the idea of his precinct being compared to other districts on prevalence of crime and police response. He was worried that the information would be used against him and his officers. In addition, the idea of shifting police resources based on crime statistics was particularly disturbing to all four precinct captains. One captain noted that if more resources were put into his district, the district with the highest crime rate, and crime did not go down, how would that be interpreted by the chief? Another captain noted that the coordination of effort would be difficult. He suggested that his officers, sergeants, and lieutenants would be overworked under such a plan, something that the police union would possibly have a grievance against. And another captain spoke of possible negative reactions among officers, who could be suspicious of how the information would be used against them. He further suggested that this would bring the union down on the department.

Other concerns expressed included the following: How will the information be used by the chief and police administrators as well as by the mayor and other politicians? Will the technology be used to ensure greater accountability among police supervisors, such as lieutenants and sergeants, as well as patrol officers? What about the allocation of police resources? What if a local politician gets wind of the plan and views it as a negative—that his district might lose some police presence because it was a low crime district? How easily will police supervisors and officers seek to manipulate the data?

Captain Roberts responded to the captains by saying that messages out of city hall are to improve the delivery of police services and to document efforts. This technology, along with a systematic research plan to evaluate police performance, could be a big positive for the department. She talked about how patrol allocation decisions could be more rationally based and empirically informed, thus providing the department ammunition in the annual budget wars with the mayor, the common council, and the city manager. By employing this technology and operationalizing a research plan to evaluate police allocation decisions, the department would be putting its best foot forward and could rationally defend its budgetary requests, something that most city government departments are not able to do. Moreover, the department could be regarded as a bright spot in the police profession by disseminating the research plan and the associated technology like the Chicago and New York City police departments are doing. Information could be published in both practical-oriented police magazines as well as scholarly journals published by academics. The city would look good, and so would the Willows Police Department.

Chief Frank Begun listened intently to both Captain Roberts' ideas and the criticisms of the plan by precinct captains. Chief Begun was a seasoned politician who had been with the department for the past twenty years, the last five years as police chief. He had seen politicians come and go, progressive ideas such as this one squashed for political reasons, and the political landscape change with the interests of differing mayors, business concerns, and vocal community groups. Chief Begun's primary concern was how was this plan going to make him look good while minimizing any political costs and stabilizing the internal politics of the department as expressed by the police union, the officers, and their supervisors. To him, the plan had too many uncertainties.

The chief was also concerned about the financial costs of the technology, the time it would take to become functional, and the training time and costs for both officers and supervisors. Captain Roberts responded that it would be a protracted process, taking probably three to five years to fully operationalize, yet they could shorten that time by learning from the mistakes committed by other departments who had developed similar plans. Chief Begun could not be convinced, however. He asked her how she suggested the department might deal with the "politics" of her plan.

By this Chief Begun meant who would lose and who would gain under such a plan. More specifically, how would this idea be viewed by the mayor's office? Would the mayor see this as an attempt by the police department to steal some of his political thunder, and if so, how would the department respond? What about politicians who were afraid of a potential loss of police presence in their districts, a criticism offered by one of the other captains? Most important, could this plan actually open the department up to more criticism, not only by angry politicians but also by other community groups who wanted to see the department become more responsive to their pet projects and concerns? Captain Roberts replied that she did not have any specific answers to the Chief's questions.

Chief Begun went on to say that her lack of specificity about how these political consequences were going to be addressed troubled him and that he would not even consider the plan further until she thought out these issues more thoroughly. He proposed that she reconsider her plan in light of his concerns as well as the criticisms offered by the other precinct captains. She would be given an opportunity to reintroduce the plan at the next staff meeting with answers to these criticisms and questions. Captain Roberts responded that she looked forward to working on the plan further. Upon leaving the meeting, she overheard one captain say to another: "Technology and research, what's it good for?" His seasoned colleague responded, "Absolutely nothing, as far as politics is concerned." Captain Roberts hoped to prove them wrong.

Case Study Questions

1. What practical advice would you give Captain Roberts about the political problems of her proposed plan? Can they be addressed realistically? Identify the major political actors whose interests would be affected by Captain Roberts' plan.

2. How would internal politics within the Willows Police Department work against Captain Roberts' plan? How would you handle such considerations? Would these considerations be different dependent upon the affected group, such as police officers versus police supervisors?

3. Should concerns about efficiency be the most important goal in police organizations? What competing goals are working against Captain Roberts' plan? How could Captain Roberts' plan be more of a hindrance rather than a benefit to the Willows Police Department?

For Discussion

1. How do you think research has influenced the criminal justice system since the President's Commission in 1967? What examples can you give of research findings that have had a direct or indirect bearing on practice in the field?

2. Critique the major sources of data about crime in the United States. What are their strengths and weaknesses? How should they be used in research, and how should that research influence management and policy? What cautions would you suggest?

3. How has research been used in your own experience studying criminal justice? In your education, has research generally been viewed as offering facts and truth? Have you seen examples in political campaigns or other circumstances where research has been used as a source of coercive power? Have any of your assignments reflected a participatory or self-study approach? If not, what would such assignments look like?

4. Follow your local paper or talk with criminal justice officials in your community to identify a problem area facing criminal justice. Now design a research project to address it. In fact, design three: one reflecting a rational–empirical approach, one based on power–coercive uses of data, and one based on normative-reeducative self-study methods. Which strategy do you think would be most effective, and why?

For Further Reading

Deming, W. Edwards. *Out of the Crisis*. Cambridge, MA: M.I.T. Press, 1986.

Toch, H., and Grant, J. D. *Reforming Human Services: Change Through Participation*. Beverly Hills, CA: Sage, 1982.

U.S. Bureau of Justice Statistics. *Performance Measures for the Criminal Justice System*. Washington, DC: U.S. Government Printing Office, 1993.

REFERENCES

Adams, T. F. *Police Patrol: Tactics and Techniques.* Englewood Cliffs, NJ: Prentice-Hall, 1971.

Allison, G. T. *Essence of Decision.* Boston: Little, Brown, 1969.

Alpert, G. P., and Dunham, R. *Policing Urban America.* Prospect Heights, IL: Waveland, 1988.

Alpert, G. P., and Dunham, R. *Policing Urban America,* 3rd ed. Prospect Heights, IL: Waveland, 1997.

American Friends Service Committee. *Struggle for Justice.* New York: Hill and Wang, 1971.

American Psychiatric Association. *Brief amicus curiae in the Case of* Barefoot v. Estelle. Washington, DC: American Psychiatric Association, 1982.

Angell, J. E. "Towards an Alternative to Classical Police Organizational Arrangements." *Criminology,* 1971, *19,* 19–29.

Archambeault, W. G., and Archambeault, B. J. *Correctional Supervisory Management: Principles of Organization, Policy and Law.* Englewood Cliffs, NJ: Prentice-Hall, 1982.

Archambeault, W. G., and Wierman, C. L. "Critically Assessing the Utility of Police Bureaucracies in the 1980's: Implications of Management Theory Z." *Journal of Police Science and Administration,* 1983, *11*(4), 420–429.

Argyris, C. *Personality and Organization.* New York: Harper & Row, 1957.

Argyris, C. *Interpersonal Competence and Organizational Effectiveness.* Homewood, IL: Dorsey Press, 1962.

Artison, R. Personal communication, September 1996.

Atkins, B., and Pogrebin, M. *The Invisible Justice System: Discretion and the Law.* Cincinnati, OH: Anderson, 1981.

Austin, J. "Assessing the New Generation of Prison Classification Models." *Crime and Delinquency,* 1983, *29,* 523.

Austin, J. "Using Early Release to Relieve Prison Crowding: A Dilemma for Public Policy." *Crime and Delinquency,* 1986, *32,* 404–502.

Austin, J., and Krisberg, B. "Wider, Stronger and Different Nets: The Dialectics of Criminal Justice Reform." *Journal of Research in Crime and Delinquency,* 1981, *18*(1): 165–169.

Auten, J. H. "Police Management in Illinois." *Journal of Police Science and Administration,* 1985, *13*(4), 325–337.

Bacharach, S. B., and Lawler, E. E. *Power and Politics in Organizations.* San Francisco: Jossey-Bass, 1980.

Baker. T. J. "Designing the Job to Motivate." *FBI Law Enforcement Bulletin,* 1976, *45*(11), 3–7.

Banfield. E. *The Unheavenly City*. Boston: Little, Brown, 1974.

Barak-Glantz, I. L. "The Anatomy of Another Prison Riot." In *Prison Violence in America,* edited by M. Braswell, S. Dillingham, and R. Montgomery, Jr., pp. 47–72. Cincinnati, OH: Anderson, 1985.

Barefoot v. *Estelle.* 103 S. Ct. 3383 (1983).

Barnard, C. *The Functions of the Executive.* Cambridge, MA: Harvard University Press, 1938.

Barnes, H., and Teeters, N. *New Horizons in Criminology.* Englewood Cliffs, NJ: Prentice-Hall, 1959.

Baro, A. "The Loss of Local Control over Prison Administration," *Justice Quarterly,* 1988, 5(3) 127–143.

Baro, A. "The Loss of Local Control over Prison Administration." In *The Administration and Management of Criminal Justice Organizations: A Book of Readings,* 2nd ed., edited by S. Stojkovic, J. Klofas, and D. Kalinich. Prospect Heights, IL: Waveland, 1994, 79–93.

Baron, R., and Greenberg, J. *Behavior in Organizations: Understanding and Managing the Human Side of Work.* Boston: Allyn and Bacon, 1990.

Bass, B. M. (Ed.). *Stodgill's Handbook of Leadership.* New York: Free Press, 1981.

Baugher, D. *Measuring Effectiveness.* San Francisco: Jossey-Bass, 1951.

Bayley, D. *Police for the Future.* New York: Oxford Univeristy Press, 1994.

Beeman, D. R. and Starkey, T. W. "The Use and Abuse of Corporate Politics." *Business Horizons,* 1987, March-April, 1–15.

Belknap, J. "The Economics-Crime Link." *Criminal Justice Abstracts,* 1989, 21(1): 140–157.

Bennett, B. "Motivation Hang-Ups of the Police Mystique." *Police Human Relations,* 1981, 1, 136–146.

Bennett, R. R. "Becoming Blue: A Longitudinal Study of Police Recruit Occupational Socialization." *Journal of Police Science and Administration,* 1984, 12, 47–58.

Bennis, W. "Leadership in Administrative Behavior." In *The Planning of Change,* edited by W. Bennis, K. Benne, and R. Chin, pp. 62–79. New York: Holt, Rinehart & Winston, 1966.

Benton, W., and Silberstein, J. "State Prison Expansion: An Explanatory Model." *Journal of Criminal Justice,* 1983, 11, 121–128.

Bierstedt, R. "An Analysis of Social Power." *American Sociological Review,* 1950, 15(6), 730–738.

Bittner, E. *The Functions of the Police in Modern Society: A Review of Background Factors, Current Practices, and Possible Role Models.* Chevy Chase, MD: National Institute of Mental Health, 1970.

Blake, R. R., and Mouton, J. S. *The Managerial Grid.* Houston: Gulf, 1964.

Blanchard, K. H., and Hersey, P. *Management of Organizational Behavior.* Englewood Cliffs, NJ: Prentice-Hall, 1977.

Blau, P. *The Dynamics of Bureaucracy.* Boston: Little, Brown, 1955.

Blau, P. *Exchange and Power in Social Life.* New York: John Wiley, 1964.

Block v. *Rutherford.* USSC, 104 S.C. 3227 (1984).

Block, P. B., and Specht, D. *Neighborhood Team Policing.* Washington, DC: U.S. Government Printing Office, 1973.

Blomberg, T. "Diversion's Disparate Results and Unresolved Questions: An Integrative Evaluation Perspective." *Journal of Research in Crime and Delinquency,* 1983, *20,* 24–38.

Blumberg, A. "The Practice of Law as a Confidence Game." *Law and Society Review,* 1967, *1,* 15–39.

Bolman, L., and Deal, T. *Reframing Organizations: Artistry, Choice, and Leadership,* 2nd ed. San Francisco: Jossey-Bass, 1997.

Book, C., Terrance, A., Atkin, C., Bettinghaus, E., Donohue, W., Farace, R., Greenberg, B., Helper, H., Milkovich, M., Miller, G., Ralph, D., and Smith, T. *Human Communication: Principles, Context, and Skills.* New York: St. Martin's Press, 1980.

Booth, W., and Harwick, C. "Physical Ability Testing for Police Officers in the 80's." *The Police Chief,* January 1984, 39–41.

Bopp, W. J. "Organizational Democracy in Law Enforcement." In *Administration of Justice System: An Introduction,* edited by D. T. Shanahan, pp. 84–102. Boston: Holbrook Press, 1977.

Bratton, W. "New York Crime Rate Down Forty-Five Percent." *New York Times,* February 12, 1996.

Brecher, E. M. "Drug Laws and Drug Law Enforcement: A Review Based on 111 Years of Experience." *Drugs and Society,* 1986, *1,* 1–28.

Brennan, T. "Classification: An Overview of Selected Methodological Issues." In *Prediction and Classification: Criminal Justice Decision Making,* edited by D. M. Gottfredson and M. Tonry, pp. 201–248. Chicago: University of Chicago Press. 1987.

Brief, A. P., Munro, J., and Aldag, R. J. "Correctional Employees' Reactions to Job Characteristics: A Data Based Argument for Job Enlargement." *Journal of Criminal Justice,* 1976, *4,* 223–230.

Brinkerhoff G., and White L. *Sociology.* Minneapolis: West, 1991.

Britton, D. "Perceptions of the Work Environment Among Correctional Officers: Do Race and Sex Matter?" *Criminology,* 1997, *35,* 1, 85–106.

Brown, D. C. *Civilian Review of Complaints Against the Police: A Survey of the United States Literature.* Research and Planning Paper 19. London: Home Office, 1983.

Brown, W. J. "Operation Citizen Participation: A Report on Public Perceptions of Police Service Delivery." *Journal of Police Science and Administration,* 1983, *1*(2), 129–135.

Bureau of Justice Statistics. "Prisoners, 1992." Washington, DC: U.S. Department of Justice, 1993.

Bureau of Justice Statistics. "Correctional Populations in the United States." Washington, DC: U.S. Department of Justice, 2000.

Bureau of Justice Statistics. "Sourcebook of Criminal Justice Statistics, 2000." Washington, DC: U.S. Department of Justice, 2000.

Bureau of Justice Statistics. "Prisoners in 2000." Washington, DC: U.S. Department of Justice, 2001.

Burgess, E. W. "Factors Determining Success or Failure on Parole." In *The Workings of the Indeterminate Sentence Law and the Parole System in Illinois,* edited by A. Bruce, E. W. Burgess, and A. J. Harno. Springfield, IL: Illinois State Board of Parole, 1928, 47–60.

Burnes, T., and Stalker, G. *The Management of Innovation.* London: Tavistock, 1961.

Burnham, W. R. "Modern Decision Theory and Corrections." In *Decision-Making in the Criminal Justice System: Review and Essays,* edited by D. M. Gottfredson, pp. 93–103. Rockville, MD: National Institute of Mental Health, 1975.

Buzawa, E. S. "Determining Patrol Officer Job Satisfaction." *Criminology,* 1984, *22,* 61–81.

Byham, W. C. and Thornton, G. C. *Assessment Centers and Managerial Performance.* New York: Academic Press, 1982.

California Department of Corrections. "Crime in California." Sacramento, CA: California Department of Corrections, 1994a.

California Department of Corrections. *Leadership Training Institute Curriculum.* Sacramento, CA: California Department of Corrections, 1994b.

Cameron, K. "The Enigma of Organizational Effectiveness." In *Measuring Effectiveness,* edited by D. Baugher. San Francisco: Jossey-Bass, 1981.

Camp, C. G. and Camp, G. M. "The Corrections Yearbook 2000: Adult Corrections." Middletown, CT: Criminal Justice Institute, Inc., 200.

Campbell, J. "On the Nature of Organizational Effectiveness." In *New Perspectives on Organizational Effectiveness,* edited by P. S. Goodman and J. S. Pennings, pp. 13–55. San Francisco: Jossey-Bass, 1977.

Capowich, G. "Police Communication Systems and Boundary Spanning: An Exploratory Case Study of Information Distortion." Paper presented at the Academy of Criminal Justice Series, 1998.

Carlisle, H. M. *Management: Concepts and Situations.* Chicago: SRA, 1976.

Carp, R., and Wheeler, R. "Sink or Swim: The Socialization of a Federal District Judge." *Journal of Public Law,* 1972, *21,* 359–393.

Carroll, L. Hacks, *Blacks and Cons: Race Relations in a Maximum Security Prison.* Lexington, MA: Lexington Books, 1974.

Carroll, S. J., and Tosi, H. L. *Management by Objectives: Applications and Research.* New York: Macmillan, 1973.

Carter, D., Sapp, A., and Stephens, D. *The State of Police Education: Policy Directions for the 21st Century.* Washington, DC: Police Executive Research Forum, 1989.

Carter, R. M., and Wilkins, L. T. "Caseloads: Some Conceptual Models." In *Probation, Parole and Community Corrections,* edited by R. M. Carter and L. T. Wilkins, pp. 211–232. New York: John Wiley, 1976.

Center for Assessment of the Juvenile Justice System. *Youthful Gangs and Appropriate Police Response,* 1982.

Center for the Study of Mass Communications Research. *Media Crime Prevention Campaign.* Denver: University of Denver, 1982.

Chapper, J. "Oral Argument and Expediting Appeals: A Compatible Combination." *Journal of Law Reform,* 1983, *16*(3), 517–526.

Charles, M. T. *Policing the Streets.* Springfleld, IL: Charles C. Thomas, 1986.

Chavkin, N. F. "The Practice-Research Relationship: An Organizational Link." *Social Service Review,* 1986, *60,* 241–250.

Cheek, F., and Miller, M. *Prisoners of Life: A Study of Occupational Stress Among State Corrections Officers.* Washington, DC: American Federation of State, County, and Municipal Employees, 1982.

Cheek, F., and Miller, M. "The Experience of Stress for Corrections Officers." *Journal of Criminal Justice,* 1983, *11,* 105–120.

Chen, H., and Rossi. P. "The Multi-Goal, Theory Driven Approach to Evaluation: A Model Linking Basic and Applied Social Science." *Social Forces,* 1980, *59,* 106–120.

Cherniss, C. *Staff Burnout: Job Stress in the Human Services.* Beverly Hills, CA: Sage, 1980.

Chin, R. "The Utility of System Models and Developmental Models for Practitioners." In *The Planning of Change,* edited by W. Bennis, K. Benne, and R. Chin, pp. 297–313. New York: Holt, Rinehart & Winston, 1966.

Chin, R., and Benne, K. D. General Strategies for Effecting Changes in Human Systems. In *The Planning of Change,* edited by W. Bennis, K. D. Benne, and R. Chin, pp. 32–56. New York: Holt, Rinehart & Winston, 1969.

Christopher Commission Report. *Report of the Independent Commission on the Los Angeles Police Department: Summary.* Los Angeles, CA: City of Los Angeles, 1991.

Chubb, J., and Moe, T. *Politics, Markets, and America's Schools.* Washington, DC: Brookings Institution, 1990.

Clear, T. "Ophelia the CCW: May 11, 2010." In *Crime and Justice in the Year 2010,* edited by J. Klofas and S. Stojkovic. Belmont, CA: Wadsworth, 1995.

Clear, T., and Cole, G. *American Corrections,* 3rd ed. Belmont, CA: Wadsworth, 1994.

Clear, T. R., and O'Leary, V. *Controlling the Offender In the Community.* Lexington, MA: Lexington Books, 1983.

Clynch, E. J., and Neubauer, D. W. "Trial Courts as Organizations: A Critique and Synthesis." *Law and Policy Quarterly,* 1981, *3,* 69–94.

Clynch, E. J., and Neubauer, D. "Trial Courts as Organizations: A Critique and Synthesis." In *The Administration and Management of Criminal Justice Organizations: A Book of Readings,* 3rd ed., edited by S. Stojkovic, J. Klofas, and D. Kalinich, Prospect Heights, IL: Waveland, 1999, 69–88.

CNN. "Florida Releases Prisoners." News report, March 1997.

Coates, R., Miller, A., and Ohlin, L. *Diversity in a Youth Correctional System.* Cambridge, MA: Ballinger, 1978.

Cohen, M. D., March, J. G., and Olsen, J. P. "A Garbage Can Model of Organizational Choice." *Administrative Science Quarterly,* 1972, *17,* 1–25.

Cole, G. *The American System of Criminal Justice.* Pacific Grove, CA: Brooks/Cole, 1983.

Cole, G. (Ed.). *Criminal Justice: Law and Politics.* 8th ed. Pacific Grove, CA: Brooks/Cole, 2002.

Cole, G., Hanson, R., and Silbert, J. "Mediation: Is It an Effective Alternative to Adjudication in Resolving Prisoner Complaints?" *Judicature,* 1982, *5*(10), 481–489.

Conley, J. *The 1967 President's Crime Commission Report: Its Impact 25 Years Later.* Cincinnati, OH: Anderson, 1994.

Conover, T. *Newjack: Guarding Sing Sing.* New York, NY: Random House, 2000.

Conser, J. A. "Motivational Theory Applied to Law Enforcement Agencies." *Journal of Police Science and Administration,* 1979, *7*(3), 285–291.

Cordner, G. W. "Review of Work Motivation Theory and Research for the Police Manager." *Journal of Police Science and Administration,* 1978, *6*(3), 286–292.

Cordner, G. W., and Hudzik, J. *Planning in Criminal Justice Organizations.* New York: Macmillan, 1983.

"The Court Retorts...." *Chicago Tribune,* August 10, 1987, p. 2.

Craig, M. "Improving Jury Deliberations: A Reconsideration of Lesser Included Offense Instructions." *Journal of Law Reform,* 1983, *16*(3), 561–584.

Cronin, T., Cronin, T. Z., and Milakovich, M. *U.S. v. Crime in the Streets.* Bloomington, IN: Indiana University Press, 1981.

Crank, J. and Langworthy, R. "An Institutional Perspective on Policing." *The Journal of Criminal Law and Criminology,* Vol. 83, pp. 338–363, 1992.

Crouch, B., and Marquart, J. *An Appeal to Justice: Litigated Reform of Texas Prisons.* Austin, TX: University of Texas Press, 1989.

Crouch, B., and Marquart, J. "On Becoming a Prison Guard." In *The Administration and Management of Criminal Justice Organizations: A Book of Readings,* 3rd ed., edited by S. Stojkovic, J. Klofas, and D. Kalinich. Prospect Heights, IL: Waveland, 1999, 266–296.

Crozier, M. *The Bureaucratic Phenomenon.* Chicago: University of Chicago Press, 1964.

Culbert, S. A., and McDonough, J. J. *Radical Management: Power Politics and the Pursuit of Trust.* New York: Free Press, 1985.

Cullen, F. T., and Gilbert, K. *Reaffirming Rehabilitation.* Cincinnati, OH: Anderson, 1982.

Cullen, F. T., Maakestad, W. J., and Cavender, G. *Corporate Crime Under Attack. The Ford Pinto Case and Beyond.* Cincinnati, OH: Anderson, 1987.

Cushman, D., and Whiting, G. "An Approach to Communications Theory: Toward Consensus on Rules." *Journal of Communications,* 1972, *22,* 217–238.

Dahl, R. "The Concept of Power." *Behavioral Science,* 1957, *2*(3), 201–215.

Dahl, R. "The Politics of Planning." *International Social Science Journal,* 1959, *11,* 340–353.

Dalton, M. *Men Who Manage.* New York: John Wiley, 1959.

Danzinger, S., and Weinstein, M. "Employment Location and Wage Rates of Poverty-Area Residents." *Journal of Urban Economics,* 1976, *44,* 425–448.

Davidoff, P., and Reiner, T. "A Choice Theory of Planning." *Journal of the American Institute of Planners,* 1962, *30,* 258–274.

Decker, S. "A Systematic Analysis of Diversion: Net Widening and Beyond." *Journal of Criminal Justice,* 1985, *3*(8), 207–216.

Deming, W. Edwards. *Out of the Crisis.* Cambridge, MA: M.I.T. Press, 1986.

Denhardt, R. *Theories of Public Organization.* Monterey, CA: Brooks/Cole, 1984.

Dershowitz, A. *The Best Defense.* New York: Random House, 1983.

Dickey, W. *From the Bottom Up: Probation Supervision in a Wisconsin Community.* Madison, WI: University of Wisconsin Law School, 1988.

Dickey, W. *Governor's Task Force on Sentencing and Corrections: Final Report.* Madison, WI: State of Wisconsin, 1996.

Dickinson, G. "Change in Communications Policies." *Corrections Today,* 1984, *46*(1), 58–60.

DiIulio, J. *Governing Prisons: A Comparative Study of Correctional Management.* New York: Free Press, 1987.

DiIulio, J. *No Escape: The Future of American Corrections.* Glenview, IL: Basic Books/ Harper-Collins, 1991.

Doering. C. D. *A Report on the Development of Penological Treatment at Norfolk Prison Colony in Massachusetts.* New York: Bureau of Social Hygiene, 1940.

Doleschal, G. "The Dangers of Criminal Justice Reform." *Criminal Justice Abstracts,* 1982, 133–152.

Downs, A. *Inside Bureaucracy.* Boston: Little, Brown, 1967.

Dubin, R. "Power, Function, and Organization." *Pacific Sociological Review,* 1963, 6(1), 16–24.

DuBrin, A. *Fundamentals of Organizational Behavior.* New York: Pergamon Press, 1978.

Duffee, D. *Correctional Management: Change and Control in Correctional Organizations.* Englewood Cliffs, NJ: Prentice-Hall, 1980.

Duffee, D. "The Interaction of Organization and Political Constraints on Community Prerelease Programs." In *The Politics of Crime and Justice,* edited by E. Fairchild and V. Webb, pp. 99–119. Beverly Hills, CA: Sage, 1985.

Duffee, D. *Correctional Management: Change and Control in Correctional Organizations.* Prospect Heights, IL: Waveland, 1986.

Duffee, D., and O'Leary, V. "Formulating Correctional Goals: The Interaction of Environment, Belief, and Organizational Structure." In *Correctional Management,* edited by D. Duffee. Englewood Cliffs, NJ: Prentice-Hall, 1980, 36–56.

Duncan, R. B. "The Characteristics of Organizational Environments and Perceived Environmental Uncertainty." *Administrative Science Quarterly,* 1972, *17,* 313–327.

Dupree, Max. *Leadership Is an Art.* New York: Brill. 1989.

Eck, J., and Spelman, W. "Who Ya Gonna Call: The Police as Problem-Busters." In *The Administration and Management of Criminal Justice Organizations: A Book of Readings,* 3rd ed., edited by S. Stojkovic, J. Klofas, and D. Kalinich. Prospect Heights: IL: Waveland, 1999, 97–113.

Eisenstein, J. *Politics and the Legal Process.* New York: Harper & Row, 1973.

Eisenstein, J., Flemming, R., and Nardulli, P. *The Contours of Justice: Communities and Their Courts.* Boston: Little, Brown, 1988.

Elliot, D. "On Policy Relevance and the Future of Criminology: A Response to Joan Petersilia's 1990 ASC Presidential Address." Unpublished manuscript, 1990.

Ellsworth, R. B., and Ellsworth, J. J. "The Psychiatric Aide: Therapeutic Agent or Lost Potential?" *Journal of Psychiatric Nursing and Mental Health Services,* 1970, *8,* 7–13.

Embert, P. "Correctional Law and Jails." In *Sneaking Inmates Down the Alley: Problems and Prospects in Jail Management,* edited by D. Kalinich and J. Klofas. Springfield, IL: Charles C. Thomas, 1986, 63–84.

Emerson, R. E. "Power-Dependence Relations." *American Sociological Review,* 1962, 27(1), 31–40.

Emmery, F., and Emmery, M. "Participative Design: Work and Community Life." In *Democracy at Work,* edited by F. Emmery and E. Thorsund, pp.147–170. Leiden, The Netherlands: Martinus Nijhoff, 1974.

Emmery, F., and Trist, E. L. "The Causal Texture of Organizational Environments." *Human Relations,* 1965, *18,* 21–32.

Ermer, V. B. "Recruitment of Female Police Officers in New York City." *Journal of Criminal Justice,* 1978, *6,* 233–246.

Etzioni, A. "New Direction in the Study of Organizations and Society." *Social Research,* 1960, *27,* 223–228.

Etzioni, A. *A Comparative Analysis of Complex Organizations.* New York: Free Press, 1961.

Etzioni, A. *Modern Organizations.* Englewood Cliffs, NJ: Prentice-Hall, 1964.

Fairchild, E. "Interest Groups in the Criminal Justice Process." *Journal of Criminal Justice,* 1981, *9,* 181–194.

Fairchild, E., and Webb, V. (Eds.). *The Politics of Crime and Justice.* Beverly Hills, CA: Sage, 1985.

Farace, R., Monge, P., and Russell, H. *Communicating and Organizing.* New York: Random House, 1977.

Faris, R. *Social Disorganization.* New York: Ronald Press, 1948.

Farrington, D. P. "Predicting Individual Crime Rates." In *Prediction and Classification: Criminal Justice Decision Making,* edited by D. M. Gottfredson and M. Tonry, pp. 52–102. Chicago: University of Chicago Press, 1987.

Feeley, M. *The Process Is the Punishment.* New York: Russell Sage Foundation, 1979.

Festinger, L. *A Theory of Cognitive Dissonance.* Evanston, IL: Row, Peterson, 1957.

Fiedler, F. A. *A Theory of Leadership Effectiveness.* New York: McGraw-Hill, 1967.

Fielding, N. G., and Fielding, J. L. "A Study of Resignation During British Police Training." *Journal of Police Science and Administration,* 1987, *15,* 24–36.

Fire and Police Commission. *A Report to Mayor John O. Norquist and the Board of Fire and Police Commissioners.* Milwaukee, WI: Mayor's Commission on Police-Community Relations, October 1991.

Fischer, F., and Sirianni, C. *Critical Studies In Organization and Bureaucracy.* Philadelphia: Temple University Press, 1984.

Flanagan, T., Johnson, W., and Bennett, K. "Job Satisfaction Among Correctional Executives: A Contemporary Portrait of Wardens of State Prisons for Adults." *The Prison Journal,* 1996, *76,* 4, 385–397.

Flemming, R. B. *Punishment Before Trial: An Organizational Perspective of Felony Bail Processes.* New York: Longman, 1982.

Fogel, D., and Hudson, J. *Justice as Fairness.* Cincinnati, OH: Anderson, 1981.

Frankel, M. E. *Criminal Sentences: Law Without Order.* New York: Hill and Wang, 1973.

Frazier, C., and Block, W. "Effects of Court Officers on Sentencing Severity." *Criminology,* 1982, *20,* 257–272.

French, J. R. P., and Raven, B. "The Bases of Social Power." In *Group Dynamics,* 3rd ed., edited by D. Cartwright and A. Zander, pp. 259–269. New York: Harper & Row, 1968.

French, W. L. "Organizational Development: Objectives, Assumptions and Strategies." *California Management Review,* 1969, *12*(2), 23–35.

French, W. L. "The Emergence and Early History of Organizational Development with Reference to Influences upon and Interactions Among Some of the Key Actors." In *Contemporary Organization Development: Current Thinking and Applications,* edited by D. Warrick, pp. 12–27. Glenview, IL: Scott, Foresman, 1985.

Frey, W. "Central City White Flight: Racial and Non-Racial Causes." *American Sociological Review,* 1979, *44,* 435–448.

Fyfe, J. "Good Policing." In *The Administration and Management of Criminal Justice Organizations: A Book of Readings,* 3rd ed., edited by S. Stojkovic, J. Klofas, and D. Kalinich, Prospect Heights, IL: Waveland, 1999, 113–133.

Fyfe, J. Personal communication on effective supervision strategies within police organizations, 1996.

Fyfe, J. Greene, J., Walsh, W., Wilson, O., and McLaren R. *Police Administration,* 5th ed. New York: McGraw-Hill, 1997.

Gaines, L., Southerland, M., and Angell, J. *Police Administration.* New York: McGraw-Hill, 1991.

Gaines, L. K., Tubergen, N. V., and Paiva, M. A. "Police Officer Perceptions of Promotion as a Source of Motivation." *Journal of Criminal Justice.* 1984, *12*(3), 265–274.

Galbraith, J. *Designing Complex Organizations.* Reading, MA: Addison-Wesley, 1973.

Galliher, J. "Explanations of Police Behavior: A Critical Review and Analysis." In *The Ambivalent Force,* edited by A. Blumberg and E. Niederhoffer. New York: Holt, Rinehart & Winston, 1985, 62–93.

Gandz, J., and Murray, V. "The Experience of Workplace Politics." *Academy of Management Journal,* 1980, *23,* 237–251.

Gardner, T. Statements made at crime trends workshop, Madison, WI, March 1997.

Geller, W. A. (Ed.). *Police Leadership in America: Crisis and Opportunity.* Chicago: American Bar Association, 1985.

Ghorpade, J., and Atchison, T. J. "The Concept of Job Analysis: A Review and Some Suggestions." *Public Personnel Management,* 1980, *9,* 134–144.

Glaser, D. *Effectiveness of a Prison and Parole System.* Indianapolis: Bobbs-Merrill, 1969.

Glauser, M., and Tullar, W. "Communicator Style of Police Officers and Citizen Satisfaction with Officer/Citizen Telephone Conversations." *Journal of Police Science and Administration,* 1985, *13*(1), 70–77.

Goffman, E. *Asylums.* Garden City, NY: Doubleday, 1961.

Goldfarb, R. *Jails: The Ultimate Ghetto.* Garden City, NY: Anchor Press/Doubleday, 1975.

Goldkamp, J. S. *Policy Guidelines for Bail: An Experiment In Court Reform.* Philadelphia: Temple University Press, 1985.

Goldstein, H. "Police Discretion Not to Invoke the Criminal Process." *Yale Law Journal,* 1960, *69,* 33–42.

Goldstein, H. "Police Discretion Not to Invoke the Criminal Process: Low-Visibility Decisions in the Administration of Justice." In *Criminal Justice: Law and Politics,* 8th ed., edited by G. F. Cole, 109–126. Belmont, CA: Wadsworth, 2002

Goldstein, H. *Problem-Oriented Policing.* New York: McGraw-Hill, 1990.

Gomez, J. Presentation to the first class of graduates of the California Department of Corrections Leadership Institute, Chico, CA, February 1995.

Gomez, J. Presentation to the third class of graduates of the California Department of Corrections Leadership Institute, Chico, CA, January 1996.

Goodman, P. S., and Kurke, L. B. "Studies of Change in Organizations: A Status Report." In *Changes in Organizations: New Perspectives on Theory, Research, and Practice,* pp. 280–315. San Francisco: Jossey-Bass, 1982.

Goodstein, L., and Hepburn. J. *Determinate Sentencing and Imprisonment: A Failure of Reform.* Cincinnati, OH: Anderson, 1985.

Gottfredson, D. M. *Decision-Making in the Criminal Justice System: Review and Essays.* Rockville, MD: National Institute of Mental Health, 1975.

Gottfredson, D. M., Hoffman. P. B., Sigler, M. H., and Wilkins, L. T. "Making Parole Policy Explicit." *Crime and Delinquency,* 1975, *21,* 7–17.

Gottfredson, D. M., and Tonry, M. (Eds.). *Prediction and Classification: Criminal Justice Decision Making.* Chicago: University of Chicago Press, 1987.

Gottfredson, M. R., and Gottfredson, D. M. *Decisionmaking in Criminal Justice: Toward a Rational Exercise of Discretion.* Cambridge, MA: Ballinger, 1980.

Grau, C. W. "Limits of Planned Change in Courts." In *Misdemeanor Courts—Policy Concerns and Research Perspectives,* edited by J. J. Alfini, pp. 271–300. Racine, WI: Johnson Foundation, 1980.

Grau, J. "Technology and Criminal Justice," in Muraskin, R. and Brooks, A. (Eds.) *Vision for Change,* pp. 231–247. New York, NY: Prentice Hall, 1999.

Greene, J., Bynum, T., and Cordner, G. "Planning and the Play of Power: Resource Acquisition Among Criminal Justice Agencies." *Journal of Criminal Justice,* 1986, *14,* 529–544.

Greenfeld, L. A. Foreword to *Performance Measures for the Criminal Justice System.* Washington, DC: U.S. Department of Justice, 1993.

Greenwood, P. *Selective Incapacitation.* Santa Monica, CA: Rand, 1982.

Griener, L. "Antecedents of Planned Change." *Journal of Applied Behavioral Sciences,* 1967, *21,* 51–86.

Griffin, G. R., Dunbar, R. L. M., and McGill, M. E. "Factors Associated with Job Satisfaction Among Police Personnel." *Journal of Police Science and Administration,* 1978, *6*(1), 77–85.

Grubb, N. "The Flight to the Suburbs of Population Employment." *Journal of Urban Economics,* 1982, *11,* 348–367.

Gulick, L. H. "Notes on the Theory of Organization," in *Papers on the Science of Administration,* edited by L. H. Gulick and L. Urwick, pp. 3–13. New York: The Institute of Public Administration, 1937.

Guy, E., Platt, J., and Zwerling, S. "Mental Health Status of Prisoners in an Urban Jail." *Criminal Justice and Behavior,* 1985, *12,* 29–53.

Guyot, D. "Political Interference Versus Political Accountability in Municipal Policing." In *The Politics of Crime and Justice,* edited by E. Fairchild and V. Webb, pp. 120–143. Beverly Hills, CA: Sage, 1985.

Gyllenhammer, P. "Changing Work Organization at Volvo." In *Perspectives on Job Enrichment,* edited by W. Soujaren, pp. 77–99. Atlanta: School of Business Administration, Georgia State University, 1975.

Hackman, J. R., and Oldham, G. R. *Work Redesign.* Reading, MA: Addison-Wesley, 1987.

Hagan, J. *Victims Before the Law: The Organizational Domination of Criminal Law.* Toronto: Butterworth, 1983.

Hage, J., and Aiken, M. *Social Change in Complex Organizations.* New York: Random House, 1970.

Hage, J., and Dewar, R. "Elite Values Versus Organizational Structure in Predicting Innovation." *Administrative Science Quarterly,* 1973, *18*(3), 279–290.

Hagedorn, J. *Forsaking Our Children: Bureaucracy and Reform in the Child Welfare System.* Chicago, IL: Lake View Press, 1995.

Hahn, H. "A Profile of Urban Police." In *The Police Community,* edited by J. Goldsmith and S. Goldsmith. Pacific Palisades, CA: Palisades Publishers, 1974, 109–129.

Hall, A., Henry, D. A., Perlstein, J. J., and Smith, W. F. *Alleviating Jail Crowding: A Systems Perspective.* Washington, DC: U.S. Government Printing Office, 1985.

Hall, R. H. *Organizations: Structure and Process,* 4th ed. Englewood Cliffs, NJ: Prentice-Hall, 1987.

Halperin, M. "Shaping the Flow of Information." In *Bureaucratic Power in National Politics,* 3rd ed., edited by F. Rourke, pp. 102–115. Boston: Little, Brown, 1978.

Hannan, M. T., and Freeman, J. "Obstacles to Comparative Studies." In *New Perspectives on Organizational Effectiveness,* edited by P. S. Goodman and J. M. Pennings, pp. 106–131. San Francisco: Jossey-Bass, 1977.

Hannan, M. T., and Freeman, J. "Structural Inertia and Organizational Change." *American Sociological Review,* 1984, *49,* 929–964.

Hardy, K. "Equity in Court Dispositions." In *Evaluating Performance of Criminal Justice Agencies,* edited by G. P. Whitaker and C. D. Phillips, pp. 151–173. Beverly Hills, CA: Sage. 1983.

Harring, S. "Taylorization of Police Work. " *Insurgent Sociologist,* 1982, *4,* 25–32.

Harris, P. W., and Hartland, G. R. "Developing and Implementing Alternatives to Incarceration—A Problem of Planned Change in Criminal Justice." *University of Illinois Law Review,* 1984, *2,* 319–364.

Harris, R. N. *The Police Academy: An Inside View.* New York: John Wiley, 1973.

Hatry, H. P., and Greiner, J. M. *How Police Departments Better Apply Management-by-Objectives and Quality Circle Programs.* Washington, DC: National Institute of Justice, U.S. Department of Justice, 1984.

Havelock, R. G. *Planning for Innovation.* Ann Arbor, MI: Institute for Social Research, 1979.

Hawkins, K. "Assessing Evil." *British Journal of Criminology,* 1983, *23,* 101–127.

Hayslip, D. *Can Correction Officers Be Motivated?* Paper presented at the annual meeting of the Academy of Criminal Justice Sciences, Louisville, KY, 1982.

Hellriegel, D., and Slocum. J. W. *Organizational Behavior.* St. Paul, MN: West, 1979.

Hellriegel, D., Slocum, J. W., and Woodman, R. W. *Organizational Behavior,* 7th ed. Minneapolis, MN: West, 1995.

Henderson, M., and Hollin, C. "A Critical Review of Social Skills Training with Young Offenders." *Criminal Justice and Behavior,* 1983, *10*(3), 316–341.

Henry, N. *Public Administration and Public Affairs.* Englewood Cliffs, NJ: Prentice-Hall, 1975.

Hepburn, J. R. "The Exercise of Power in Coercive Organizations: A Study of Prison Guards." *Criminology,* 1985, *23*(1), 145–164.

Hernandez, A. P. "Motivation and Municipal Police Departments—Models and an Empirical Analysis." *Journal of Police Science and Administration,* 1982, *10*(3), 284–288.

Hershey, P. and Blanchard, K. *Management of Organizational Behavior.* Englewood Cliffs, NJ: Prentice-Hall, 1977.

Herzberg, F. *Work and the Nature of Man.* New York: World, 1966.

Herzberg, F. "Participation Is Not a Motivator." *Industry Week,* 1978, *198,* 39–44.

Herzberg, F., Mausner, B., and Snyderman, B. B. *The Motivation to Work.* New York: Wiley, 1959.

Hiam, A. *Motivating & Rewarding Employees: New and Better Ways to Inspire Your People.* Holbrook, NJ: Adams Media Corporation, 1999.

Hicksen, D., Hinings, C., Lee, C., Schenck, R., and Pennings, J. "A Strategic Contingencies Theory of Intraorganizational Power." In *Readings in Organizational Behavior and Human Performance,* edited by W. J. Scott and L. L. Cummings, pp. 63–96. Homewood, IL: Richard D. Irwin, 1973.

Hinings, C. R., Pugh, D. S., Hicksen, D. J., and Turner, C. "An Approach to the Study of Bureaucracy." *Sociology,* 1967, *1*(1), 61–72.

Hoffman, P., and Stone-Meierhoefer, B. "Reporting Recidivism Rates: The Criterion and Follow-Up Issues." *Journal of Criminal Justice,* 1980, *8,* 53–60.

Holt, N. "Parole in the Future," in Petersilia, J. (ed.) *Community Corrections: Probation, Parole, and Intermediate Sanctions,* pp. 14–30, New York, NY: Oxford University Press, 1998.

Hoos, I. R. *Systems Analysis in Public Policy.* Los Angeles: University of California Press, 1983.

Houghland, J. G., and Wood, J. R. "Control in Organizations and Commitment of Members." *Social Forces,* 1980, *59*(1), 85–105.

Houghland, J. G., Shepard, J. M., and Wood, J. R. "Discrepancies in Perceived Organizational Control: Their Decrease and Importance in Local Churches." *The Sociological Quarterly,* 1979, *20*(1), 63–76.

House, R. J. *Power In Organizations: A Social Psychological Perspective.* Unpublished manuscript, University of Toronto, 1984.

House, R. J., and Mitchell, T. R. "Path-Goal Theory of Leadership." In *Organizational Behavior and Management,* 4th ed., edited by H. L. Tosi and W. C. Hamner, pp. 491–500. Cincinnati, OH: Grid, 1985.

Houston, J. *Correctional Management: Functions, Skills, and Systems,* 2nd ed. Chicago: Nelson-Hall, 1999.

Hudzik, J., and Cordner, G. *Planning in Criminal Justice Organizations and Systems.* New York: Macmillan, 1983.

Huse, E. *Organizational Development and Change.* Minneapolis, MN: West, 1975.

Husz, J. Personal communication, December 1996.

Iannone, N. *Police Supervision.* New York: McGraw-Hill, 1994.

Ideus, K. *Staffing and Personnel Management—A Humanistic Look.* Rockville, MD: National Institute of Justice, 1978.

Inbau, F., Reid, J., and Buckley, J. *Criminal Interrogation and Confessions.* Baltimore: Williams, Lippincott, & Wilkins, 1986.

International Association of Chiefs of Police. *Police Supervision.* Dubuque, IA: Kendall/Hunt, 1985.

Irwin, J., and Austin, J. *It's About Time: America's Imprisonment Binge,* 2nd ed. Belmont, CA: Wadsworth, 1997.

Irwin, J. *Prisons in Turmoil.* Boston: Little, Brown, 1980.

Irwin, J. *The Jail: Managing the Underclass in American Society.* Berkeley, CA: University of California Press, 1986.

Irwin, J., and Austin, J. *It's About Time: America's Imprisonment Binge.* 3rd Edition, Belmont, CA: Wadsworth Publishing Company, 2002.

Jacks, I. "Positive Interaction: Everyday Principles of Correctional Rehabilitation." In *Psychological Approaches to Crime and Its Correction: Theory, Research, Practice,* edited by I. Jacks, pp. 424–443. Chicago: Nelson-Hall, 1984.

Jacobs, D. "Dependency and Vulnerability: An Exchange Approach to the Control of Organizations." *Administrative Science Quarterly,* 1974, *19,* 45–59.

Jacobs, J. *Drunk Driving: An American Dilemma.* Chicago: University of Chicago Press, 1989.

Jacobs, J. B. *Stateville: The Penitentiary In Mass Society.* Chicago: University of Chicago Press, 1977.

Jacobs, J. B. *The Unionization of the Guards.* Proceedings of the Thirteenth Interagency Workshop, Sam Houston State University. Huntsville, TX, 1978.

Jacobs, J. B. (Ed.). *New Perspectives on Prisons and Imprisonment.* Ithaca, NY: Cornell University Press, 1983a.

Jacobs, J. B. "The Prisoners' Rights Movement and Its Impacts." In *New Perspectives on Prisons and Imprisonment,* edited by J. B. Jacobs, pp. 33–60. Ithaca, NY: Cornell University Press, 1983b.

Jacobs, J. B., and Grear, M. P. "Drop Outs and Rejects: An Analysis of the Prison Guard's Revolving Door." *Criminal Justice Review.* 1977, 2, 57–70.

Jacobs, J. B., and Retsky, H. C. "Prison Guard." *Urban Life,* 1975, *4,* 5–29.

Jacobs, J. B., and Zimmer. L. "Collective Bargaining and Labor Unrest." In *New Perspectives on Prisons and Imprisonment,* edited by J. B. Jacobs, pp. 142–159. Ithaca. NY: Cornell University Press, 1983.

James, B. "Computer Assisted Instruction." *American Jails,* 1996, *9*(6): 27–31.

Johnson, R. "Informal Helping Networks in Prison: The Shape of Grass Roots Correctional Intervention." *Journal of Criminal Justice,* 1977, 7, 53–70.

Johnson, R. *Hard Time: Understanding and Reforming the Prison,* 2nd ed. Belmont, CA: Wadsworth, 1996.

Johnson, R. *Hard Time: Understanding and Reforming the Prison.* 3rd Edition, Belmont, CA: Wadsworth Publishing Company, 2002.

Joint Commission on Correctional Manpower and Training. *A Time to Act.* Washington, DC: U.S. Government Printing Office, 1969.

Josephson, E., and Josephson, M. *Man Alone: Alienation in Modern Society.* New York: Laurel, 1975.

Julian, J. "Compliance Patterns and Communication Blocks in Complex Organizations." *American Sociological Review,* 1966, *31*(3), 382–389.

Jurik, N. C., and Winn, R. "Describing Correctional-Security Dropouts and Rejects: An Individual or Organizational Profile?" *Criminal Justice and Behavior,* 1987, *14*(1), 5–25.

Kagehiro, D., and Werner, C. "Divergent Perceptions of Jail Inmates and Correctional Officers: The 'Blame the Other–Expect to Be Blamed' Effect." *Journal of Applied Social Psychology,* 1981, *11*(6), 507–528.

Kalinich, D. *Power, Stability, and Contraband: The Inmate Economy.* Prospect Heights, IL: Waveland, 1984.

Kalinich, D. "Criminal Justice Education: Coming in in the Middle of the Movie." In *The Future of Criminal Justice Education*, edited by R. Muraskins. Brookville, NY: Long Island University Criminal Justice Institute, 1987.

Kalinich, D., and Banas, D. "Systems Maintenance and Legitimization: An Historical Illustration of the Impact of National Task Forces and Committees on Corrections." *Journal of Criminal Justice*, 1984, *12,* 61–71.

Kalinich, D., and Klofas, J. (Eds.) *Sneaking Inmates Down the Alley: Problems and Prospects of Jail Management.* Springfleld, IL: Charles C. Thomas, 1986.

Kalinich, D., Lorinskas, L., and Banas, D. "Symbolism and Rhetoric: The Guardians of the Status Quo in the Criminal Justice System." *Criminal Justice Review,* 1985, *10,* 41–46.

Kalinich, D., and Stojkovic, S. "Contraband: The Basis for Legitimate Power in a Prison Social System." *Criminal Justice and Behavior,* 1985, *12,* 435–451.

Kalinich, D., Stojkovic, S., and Klofas. J. "Toward a Political-Community Theory of Prison Organization." *Journal of Criminal Justice,* 1988, *16*(3), 217–230.

Karger, H. "Burnout as Alienation." *Social Service Review,* 1981, *55,* 270–283.

Katz, D., and Kahn, R. L. *The Social Psychology of Organizations,* 2nd ed. New York: John Wiley, 1978.

Katzev, R., and Wishart, S. "The Impact of Judicial Commentary Concerning Eyewitness Identifications on Jury Decision Making." *The Journal of Criminal Law and Criminology,* 1985, *76*(3), 733–745.

Kaufman, H. "Organization Theory and Political Theory." *The American Political Science Review,* 1964, *58*(1), 5–14.

Kaufman. H. "Administrative Decentralization and Political Power." *Public Administration Review,* 1969, *29,* 3–15.

Kelling, G. "Order Maintenance, the Quality of Urban Life, and Police: A Line of Argument." In *Police Leadership in America.* Chicago: American Bar Foundation, 1985, 296–308.

Kelling, G. L. *Police and Communities: The Quiet Revolution.* Washington, DC: National Institute of Justice, 1988.

Kelly, J. E. *Scientific Management, Job Redesign and Work Performance.* New York: Academic Press, 1982.

Kerle, K. E. *American Jails: Looking to the Future.* Boston, MA: Butterworth-Heinemann, 1998.

Klockars, C. "The Rhetoric of Community Policing." In *Community Policing: Rhetoric or Reality,* edited by J. Greene and S. Mastrofski. New York: Praeger, 1991, 19–36.

Klofas, J., Smith, S., and Meister, E. "Harnessing Human Resources in Local Jails: Toward a New Generation of Planners." In *Sneaking Inmates Down the Alley,* edited by D. Kalinich and J. Klofas, pp. 193–208. Springfleld, IL: Charles C. Thomas, 1986.

Klofas, J., and Toch, H. "The Guard Subculture Myth." *Journal of Research in Crime and Delinquency,* 1982, *19,* 169–175.

Knapp Commission. *Report on Police Corruption.* New York: George Braziller, 1972.

Kohfeld, C. W. "Rational Cops, Rational Robbers, and Information." *Journal of Criminal Justice,* 1983, *11*(5), 459–466.

Kolonski, H., and Mendelsohn, R. *The Politics of Local Justice.* Boston: Little, Brown, 1970.

Kopelman, R. "Job Redesign and Productivity: A Review of the Evidence." *National Productivity Review,* 1985, *4*(3): 237–255.

Kotter, J. *A Force for Change.* New York: Macmillan, 1990.

Kotter, J. P. *Power and Influence.* New York: Free Press, 1985.

Kouzes, J., and Posner, B. *The Leadership Challenge: How to Keep Getting Extraordinary Things Done in Organizations.* San Francisco: Jossey-Bass, 1997.

Kratcoski, P. C., and Walker, D. B. *Criminal Justice in America.* Glenview, IL: Scott, Foresman, 1978.

Kreman, B. "Search for a Better Way of Work: Lordstown, Ohio." In *Humanizing the Workplace,* edited by R. P. Fairchild, pp. 17–41. Buffalo, NY: Prometheus, 1973.

Kreps, G. *Organizational Communication,* 2nd ed. White Plains, NY: Longman, 1990.

Kress, J. *Prescriptions for Justice: The Theory and Practice of Sentencing Guidelines.* Cambridge, MA: Ballinger, 1980.

Kuykendall, J. "Police Managerial Styles—A Grid Analysis." *American Journal of Police,* 1985, *4*(1), 38–70.

Kuykendall, J., and Unsinger, P. C. "The Leadership Styles of Police Managers." *Journal of Criminal Justice,* 1982, *10*(4), 311–322.

LaFave, W. L. "The Prosecutor's Discretion in the United States." *American Journal of Comparative Law,* 1970, *18,* 532–548.

Langworthy, R. *The Structure of Police Organizations.* New York: Praeger, 1986.

Langworthy, R. "Do Stings Control Crime? An Evaluation of a Police Fencing Operation," *Justice Quarterly,* 1989, *6*(1): 27–45.

Lasky, G. L., Gordon, B. C., and Srebalus, D. J. "Occupational Stressors Among Federal Correctional Officers Working in Different Security Levels." *Criminal Justice and Behavior,* 1986, *13,* 317–327.

Lauffer, A. *Understanding Your Social Agency,* 2nd ed. Beverly Hills, CA: Sage, 1984.

Law Enforcement Management and Administrative Statistics (LEMAS). "Local Police Departments." Washington, DC: U.S. Department of Justice, 1999.

Lawler, E. J. (Ed.) *Advances in Group Processes.* Greenwich, Conn: Jai, 1986.

Lawrence, P. R., and Lorsch, J. W. "Differentiation and Integration in Complex Organizations." *Administrative Science Quarterly,* 1967, *12*(1), 1–47.

Lawrence, P R., and Lorsch, J. *Developing Organizations: Diagnosis and Action.* Reading, MA: Addison-Wesley, 1969.

Lawrence, P. "Professionals or Civil Servants? An Examination of the Probation Officer's Role." *Federal Probation,* 1984, *43,* 3–13.

Lee, J. H., and Visano, L. H. "Official Deviance in the Legal System." In *Law and Deviance,* edited by H. L. Ross, pp. 215–250. Beverly Hills, CA: Sage, 1981.

Lehr, D. and O'Neill, G. *Black Mass: The True Story of an Unholy Alliance Between the F.B.I. and the Irish Mob.* New York, NY: Harper-Collins, 2001.

Leiberg, G. "Computers Then and Now." *American Jails,* 1996, *9*(6): 23–27.

Lenihan, K. J. "Telephones and Raising Bail: Some Lessons in Evaluation Research." *Evaluation Quarterly,* 1977, *1,* 569–586.

Lester, J. The Utilization of Policy Analysis by State Officials. *Knowledge: Creation Diffusion, Utilization,* 1993, *14,* 267–290.

Levinson R., and Gerard, R. "Functional Units: A Different Correctional Approach." *Federal Probation,* 1973, *37,* 8–16.

Lewin, K. "Group Decision and Social Change." In *Readings in Social Psychology,* edited by E. E. Maccoby, T. M. Newcomb, and E. L. Hartley, pp. 197–211. New York: Holt, Rinehart & Winston, 1947.

Lewin, K. "Action Research and Minority Problems." In *Resolving Social Conflicts: Selected Papers in Group Dynamics,* edited by K. Lewin, pp. 5–100. New York: Harper & Row, 1948.

Liebentritt, D. *The Making of a Prison Guard.* Unpublished manuscript, Center for Studies in Criminal Justice, University of Chicago Law School, 1974.

Light, S., and Newman, T. "Awareness and Use of Social Science Research Among Executive and Administrative Staff Members of State Correctional Agencies." *Justice Quarterly,* 1992, *9,* 299–319.

Likert, R. *New Patterns of Management.* New York: McGraw-Hill, 1961.

Likert, R. *The Human Organization.* New York: McGraw-Hill, 1967.

Lindblom, C. "The Science of Muddling Through." *Public Administration Review,* 1959, *19,* 79–88.

Lindquist, C. A., and Whitehead, J. T. "Guards Released from Prison: A Natural Experiment in Job Enlargement." *Journal of Criminal Justice,* 1986, *14,* 283–294.

Lipsky, M. *Street-Level Bureaucracy.* New York: Russell Sage Foundation, 1980.

Lipsky, M. "Toward a Theory of Street-Level Bureaucracy." In *Criminal Justice: Law and Politics,* 5th ed., edited by G. F. Cole, pp. 24–41. Belmont, CA: Wadsworth, 2002.

Lipton, D., Martinson, R., and Wilkes, J. *The Effectiveness of Correctional Treatment: A Survey of Treatment Evaluation Studies.* New York: Praeger, 1975.

Lodahl, J., and Gordon. G. "Funding the Sciences in University Departments." *Educational Record,* 1973, *54,* 74–82.

Lombardo, L. X. *Guards Imprisoned: Correctional Officers at Work.* New York: Elsevier, 1981.

Lombardo, L. X. "Group Dynamics and the Prison Guard Subculture: Is the Subculture an Impediment to Helping Inmates?" *International Journal of Offender Therapy and Comparative Criminolog,* 1985, *29,* 79–90.

Long, N. "Power and Administration." *Public Administration Review,* 1949, *9,* 257–264.

Long, S. "Early Integration into Groups: A Group to Join and Group to Create," *Human Relations,* 1984, *37,* 311–332.

Longenecker, C. O., Gioia, D. A., and Sims, H. P., Jr. "Behind the Mask: The Politics of Employee Appraisal." *Executive,* 1987, *1*(3), 183–194.

Lord, R. G. "Functional Leadership Behavior: Measurement and Relation to Social Power and Leadership Perceptions." *Administrative Science Quarterly,* 1977, *22*(1), 114–133.

Lovell, R. "Research Utilization in Complex Organizations: A Case Study in Corrections." *Justice Quarterly,* 1988, *5,* 258–280.

Lovell, R. "Research Utilization in Complex Organizations: A Case Study in Corrections." In *The Administration and Management of Criminal Justice Organizations: A Book of Readings,*

3rd ed., edited by S. Stojkovic, J. Klofas, and D. Kalinich. Prospect Heights, IL: Waveland, 1999, 457–477.

Lovell, R., and Kalinich, D. "The Unimportance of In-House Research in a Professional Criminal Justice Organization." *Criminal Justice Review,* 1992, *17,* 77–93.

Lovell, R., and Stojkovic, S. "Myths, Symbols, and Policymaking in Corrections." *Criminal Justice Review,* 1987, *2* (3), 225–239..

Luke, J. S. *Catalytic Leadership: Strategies for an Interconnected World.* San Francisco, CA: Jossey-Bass Publishers, 1998.

Lynch, R. G. *The Police Manager: Police Leadership Skills,* 3rd ed. New York: Random House, 1986.

Lynd, R. *Knowledge for What?* Princeton, NJ: Princeton University Press, 1939.

Maltz, M. *Recidivism.* New York: Academic Press, 1984.

Mann, F. "Putting Human Relations Research Findings to Work." *Michigan Business Review,* 1950, *2,* 16–20.

Manning, P. "Measuring What Matters, Part One: Measures of Crime, Fear, and Disorder." Washington, DC: U.S. Department of Justice, 1996.

Manning, P. *Police Work: The Social Organzation of Police.* Prospect Heights, IL: Waveland Press, Inc., 1997.

Manning, P. K. *Organizational Communications.* New York: Aldine de Gruyter, 1992.

Manning, P. K., and Redlinger, L. J. "Invitational Edges of Corruption: Some Consequences of Narcotics Law Enforcement." In *Drugs and Politics,* edited by P. Rock, pp. 279–310. New Brunswick, NJ: Transaction Books, 1977.

Manning, P. K., and Van Maanen, J. *Policing: A View from the Streets.* Santa Monica, CA: Goodyear, 1978.

March, J. G. "The Business Firm as a Political Coalition." *Journal of Politics,* 1962, *24,* 662–678.

March, J. G., and Simon, H. A. *Organizations.* New York: Wiley, 1958.

Marquart, J. W. "Doing Research in Prison: The Strengths and Weaknesses of Full Participation as a Guard." *Justice Quarterly,* 1986a, *3,* 15–32.

Marquart, J. W. "Prison Guards and the Use of Physical Coercion as a Mechanism of Prisoner Control." *Criminology,* 1986b, 24(2), 347–366.

Marsden, P. V. "Introducing Influence Processes into a System of Collective Decisions." *American Journal of Sociology,* 1981, *86,* 1203–1235.

Martin, S. J., and Ekland-Olson, S. *Texas Prisons: The Walls Came Tumbling Down.* Austin: Texas Monthly Press, 1987.

Martinson, R. "What Works? Questions and Answers About Prison Reform." *Public Interest,* 1974, *35,* 22–54.

Maslach, C. "Burned-Out." *Human Behavior,* 1976, *5,* 16–22.

Maslach, C., and Jackson, S. "Burned-Out Cops and Their Families." *Psychology Today,* 1979, *12,* 59–62.

Maslach, C., and Jackson, S. "The Measurement of Experienced Burnout." *Journal of Occupational Behavior,* 1981, *2,* 99–113.

Maslow, A. H. *Motivation and Personality.* New York: Praeger, 1986.

Maslow, A. H. "A Theory of Motivation." *Psychological Review,* 1943, *50,* 370–396.

Mastrofski, S. "Community Policing as Reform: A Cautionary Tale." In *Community Policing: Rhetoric or Reality,* edited by J. Greene and S. Mastrofski. New York: Praeger, 1991, 314–342.

Mastrofski, S. "Measuring What Matters, Part One: Measures of Crime, Fear, and Disorder." Washington, DC: U.S. Department of Justice, 1996.

Mastrofski, S., and Wadman, R. "Personnel and Agency Performance Measurement." In *Local Government Police Management,* 3rd ed., edited by W. Geller. Washington, DC: International City Management Association, 1991.

Mayo, E. *The Human Problems of Industrial Civilization.* Boston: Harvard Business School, 1946.

Mays, G., and Taggart, W. "Court Clerks, Court Administrators, and Judges: Conflict in Managing the Courts." *Journal of Criminal Justice,* 1986, *14,* 14–22.

Mays, G. L., and Gray, T. (Eds.). *Privatization and The Provision of Correctional Services.* Cincinnati, OH: Anderson Publishing Company, 1996.

McCleary, R. "Correctional Administration and Political Change." In *Prison Within Society,* edited by Lawrence Hazelrigg, pp. 113–154. New York: Doubleday, 1968.

McCleary, R. "How Parole Officers Use Records." *Social Problems,* 1977, *24,* 576–589.

McCleary, R. *Dangerous Men.* Beverly Hills, CA: Sage, 1978.

McCleary, R. "How Structural Variables Constrain the Parole Officer's Use of Discretionary Power." *Social Problems,* 1985, *32,* 141–152.

McCleary, R., Nienstedt, B. C., and Erven, J. M. "Uniform Crime Reports as Organizational Outcomes: Three Time Series Experiments." *Social Problems,* 1982, *29,* 361–372.

McCleary R., Nienstedt, B., and Erven, J. M."Uniform Crime Reports as Organizational Outcomes: Three Time Series Experiments." In *The Administration and Management of Criminal Justice Organizations: A Book of Readings,* 3rd ed., edited by S. Stojkovic, J. Klofas, and D. Kalinich. Prospect Heights, IL: Waveland, 1999, 292–306.

McClelland, D. A. "Toward a New Theory of Motive Acquisition." *American Psychologist,* 1965, *20,* 321–323.

McGregor, D. M. "The Human Side of Enterprise." In *Classics of Organizational Behavior,* edited by W. E. Natemeyer, pp. 12–18. Oak Park, IL: Moore, 1978.

McShane, M., and Krause, W. *Community Corrections.* New York: Macmillan, 1993.

Meisner, S. "Economic Distribution and Societal Homicide Rates: Further Evidence of the Cost of Inequality." *American Sociological Review,* 1989, *54*(4): 579–611.

Melancon, D. "Quality Circles: The Shape of Things to Come?" *Police Chief,* 1984, *51*(11), 54–55.

Melone, A. "Criminal Code Reform and Interest Group Politics of the American Bar Association." In *The Politics of Crime and Justice,* edited by E. Fairchild and V. Webb, pp. 37–56. Beverly Hills, CA: Sage, 1985.

Menke, B. A., Zupan, L. L., and Lovrich, N. P. *A Comparison of Work-Related Attitudes Between New Generation Correction Officers and Other Public Employees.* Paper presented at the annual meeting of the Academy of Criminal Justice Sciences, Orlando, FL, 1986.

Meyer, J., and Rowan, B. "Institutionalized Organizations: Formal Structures as Myths and Ceremony." *American Journal of Sociology,* 1978, *83,* 340–363.

Meyers, S., and Simms, M. (Eds.) *The Economics of Race and Crime.* New Brunswick, NJ: Transaction Books, 1989.

Michels, R. *Political Parties*. New York: Free Press, 1949.

Miller, L. "The Application of Research to Practice." *American Behavioral Scientist*, 1986, *30*, 70–80.

Mintzberg, H. *Power In and Around Organizations*. Englewood Cliffs, NJ: Prentice-Hall, 1983.

Missonellie, J., and D'Angelo, J. *Television and Law Enforcement*. Springfield, IL: Charles C. Thomas, 1984.

Mitchell, G. Statements made during a debate on prison expansion, Milwaukee, WI: The Institute for Wisconsin's Future, January 1997.

Mohr, L. B. "Organizations, Decisions, and Courts." *Law and Society*, 1976, *10*, 621–642.

Monahan, J. *Predicting Violent Behavior: An Assessment of Clinical Techniques*. Beverly Hills, CA: Sage, 1981.

Monroe County, New York. *Jail Utilization System Team: Proposal for a Comprehensive Community-Based Corrections Program*. 1994.

Moran, T. K., and Lindner, C. "Probation and the Hi-Technology Revolution: Is a Reconceptualization of the Traditional Probation Officer Role Model Inevitable?" *Criminal Justice Review*, 1985, *10*, 25–32.

Morash, M. "Wife Battering." *Criminal Justice Abstracts*, 1986, *18*, 252–271.

Morash, M., and Greene, J. "Evaluating Women on Patrol." *Evaluation Review*, 1986, *10*, 230–255.

More, H. W., Jr. *Criminal Justice Management: Text and Readings*. St. Paul, MN: West, 1977.

Morgenbesser, L. "Psychological Screening Mandated for New York Correctional Officer Applicants." *Corrections Today*, 1984, *46*, 28–29.

Morris, N. *Madness and the Criminal Law*. Chicago: University of Chicago Press, 1982.

Morse, J. J. "A Contingency Look at Job Design." *California Management Review*, 1973, *16*, 67–75.

Muir, W. *Police: Streetcorner Politicians*. Chicago: University of Chicago Press, 1977.

Murphy, P. V. "The Prospective Chief's Negotiation of Authority with the Mayor." In *Police Leadership In America: Crisis and Opportunity*, edited by W. A. Geller, pp. 30–41. Chicago: American Bar Association, 1985.

Murray, M. *Decisions: A Comparative Critique*. Marshfield, MA: Pitman, 1986.

Murton, T. *The Dilemma of Prison Reform*. New York: Holt, Rinehart & Winston, 1976.

Nader, R. *Unsafe at Any Speed: The Designed-in Dangers of the American Automobile*. New York: Grossman, 1965.

Nanus, B. *Visionary Leadership*. San Francisco: Jossey-Bass, 1992.

National Advisory Commission on Civil Disorders. *Report of the National Advisory Commission on Civil Disorders*. New York: Dutton, 1968.

National Advisory Commission on Criminal Justice Standards and Goals. *Corrections*. Washington, DC: U.S. Government Printing Office, 1973a.

National Advisory Commission on Criminal Justice Standards and Goals. *Police*. Washington, DC: U.S. Government Printing Office, 1973b.

National Institute of Justice (NIJ). "Civil Rights and Criminal Justice: Employment Discrimination Overview." *Research in Brief*. Washington, DC: U.S. Department of Justice, 1995.

National Jail Coalition. *Covering the Jail.* Washington, DC: 1984.

Nelson, R. "Changing Concepts in Jail Design." In *Sneaking Inmates Down the Alley: Problems and Prospects in Jail Management,* edited by D. Kalinich and J. Klofas, pp. 167–180. Springfield, IL: Charles C. Thomas, 1986.

Nelson, R., and Winter, S. *An Evolutionary Theory of Economic Change.* Boston: Belknap Press, 1982.

Neubauer, D. *American Courts and the Criminal Justice System.* Belmont, CA: Brooks/Cole, 1983.

Newman, D. "Plea Bargaining." In *Order Under Law,* edited by R. Culbertson and M. Tezak, pp. 166–179. Prospect Heights, IL: Waveland, 1981.

Newman, D. *Introduction to Criminal Justice.* New York: Random House, 1986.

Niederhoffer, A. *Behind the Shield: The Police in Urban Society.* New York: Doubleday. 1969.

Nokes, P. "Purpose and Efficiency in Human Social Institutions." *Human Relations,* 1960, *13,* 141–155.

Nuchia, S. M. "First Amendment Freedom of Speech and the Police Officer's Criticism of Departmental Policy and His Superiors." *Journal of Police Science and Administration,* 1983, *11*(4), 395–401.

Oettmeier, T. N., and Wycoff, M. A. *Personnel Performance Evaluations in the Community Policing Context.* Washington, DC: U.S. Department of Justice, 1998.

O'Keefe, G., and Mendelsohn, H. *Taking a Bite Out of Crime: The Impact of a Mass Media Crime Prevention Campaign.* Washington, DC: U.S. Government Printing Office, 1984.

O'Reilly, C. A., and Pondy, L. R. "Organizational Communications." In *Organizational Behavior,* edited by S. Kerr, pp. 138–162. Cincinnati, OH: Grid, 1979.

O'Reilly, C. A., and Roberts, K. H., "Information Filtering and Organizations: Three Experiments." *Organizational Behavior and Human Performance,* 1974, *11*(2), 253–265.

Olsen, M. *The Logic of Collective Action: Public Goods and the Theory of Groups.* Cambridge, MA: Harvard University Press, 1973.

Osborn, R., and Hunt, J. "Environmental and Organizational Effectiveness." *Administrative Science Quarterly,* 1974, *19,* 231–246.

Ouchi, W. *Theory Z: How American Business Can Meet the Japanese Challenge.* Reading, MA: Addison-Wesley, 1981.

Pandarus, P. "One's Own Primer of Academic Politics." *American Scholar,* 1973, *42,* 569–592.

Parker, D. *Crime by Computer.* New York: Scribner's, 1976.

Parsons, T., *Structure and Process in Modern Societies.* New York: Free Press, 1960.

Perrow, C. "The Analysis of Goals in Complex Organizations." *American Sociological Review,* 1961, *26,* 194–208.

Perrow, C. "Departmental Power and Perspective in Industrial Firms." In *Power in Organizations,* edited by M. Zald, pp. 59–89. Nashville: Vanderbilt University Press, 1970.

Perrow, C. "Three Types of Effectiveness Studies." In *New Perspectives on Organizational Effectiveness,* edited by P. S. Goodman and J. M. Pennings, pp. 96–105. San Francisco: Jossey-Bass, 1977.

Perrow, C. "Disintegrating Social Sciences." *New York University Educational Quarterly,* Winter 1981, 2–9.

Perrow, C. *Complex Organizations: A Critical Essay,* 3rd ed. New York: Random House, 1986.

Peters, T. *Thriving on Chaos: Handbook for a Management Revolution.* New York: Harper & Row, 1987.

Peters, T. *Thriving on Chaos: Handbook for a Management Revolution.* New York, NY: Harper and Row, 3rd Edition, 1994.

Peters, T., and Waterman, R. *In Search of Excellence: Lessons from American's Best-Run Companies.* New York: Harper & Row, 1982.

Petersilia, J. "Defending the Practical Value of Criminological Research." *Journal of Research in Crime and Delinquency,* 1993, *30,* 497–505.

Petersilia, J. "A Crime Control Rationale for Reinvesting in Community Corrections." *The Prison Journal,* Vol. 75, No. 4, pp. 497–505, 1995.

Petersilia, J. "A Crime Control Rationale for Reinvesting in Community Corrections." *The Prison Journal,* 1995, 75, *4,* 479–498.

Petersilia, J. *Community Corrections: Probation, Parole, and Intermediate Sanctions.* New York, NY: Oxford University Press, 1998.

Petersilia, J., and Turner, S. "Intensive Probation and Parole." *Crime and Justice,* 1993, *17,* 281–335.

Petrich, J. "Psychiatric Treatment in Jail: An Experiment in Health-Care Delivery." *Hospital and Community Psychiatry,* 1976, 413–415.

Pettigrew, A. M. *The Politics of Organizational Decision-Making.* London: Tavistock, 1973.

Pfeffer, J. "Power and Resource Allocation in Organizations." In *New Directions in Organizational Behavior,* edited by B. Staw and G. R. Salancik, pp. 235–265. Chicago: St. Clair Press, 1977a.

Pfeffer, J. "Usefulness of the Concept." In *New Perspectives on Organizational Effectiveness,* edited by P. S. Goodman and J. M. Pennings, pp. 132–145. San Francisco: Jossey-Bass, 1977b.

Pfeffer, J. "The Micropolitics of Organizations." In *Environments and Organizations,* edited by M. W. Meyer, pp. 29–50. San Francisco: Jossey-Bass, 1978.

Pfeffer, J. *Power in Organizations.* Marshfield, MA: Pitman, 1981.

Pfeffer, J., and Salancik, G. R. "Organizational Decision-Making as a Political Process: The Case of a University Budget." *Administrative Science Quarterly,* 1974, *19*(2), 135–151.

Philliber, S. "Thy Brother's Keeper: A Review of the Literature on Correctional Officers." *Justice Quarterly,* 1987, *4*(1), 9–38.

Phillips, C. D., McCleary, B. W., and Dinitz, S. "The Special Deterrent Effect of Incarceration." In *Evaluating Peformance of Criminal Justice Agencies,* edited by G. P. Whitaker and C. D. Phillips, pp. 237–264. Beverly Hills, CA: Sage, 1983.

Phillips, R. L., and McConnell, C. R. *The Effective Corrections Manager: Maximizing Staff Performance in Demanding Times.* Gaithersburg, MD: Aspen Publications, 1996.

Pindur, W., and Lipiec, S. "Creating Positive Police-Prosecutor Relations." *Journal of Police Science and Administration,* 1982, *10*(1), 28–33.

Pinfield, L. T. "A Field Evaluation of Perspectives on Organizational Decision Making." *Administrative Science Quarterly,* 1986, *31,* 365–388.

Podsakoff, P. M., and Schriesheim, C. A. "Field Studies of French and Raven's Bases of Power: Reanalysis, Critique, and Suggestions for Future Research." *Psychological Bulletin,* 1985, *97*(3), 387–411.

Pogrebin, M. R., and Poole, E. D., "The Sexualized Work Environment: A Look at Women Jail Officers." *The Prison Journal,* 77:41–57.

Pondy, L. R. "Organizational Conflict: Concepts and Models." In *Organizational Behavior and Management,* 4th ed., edited by H. L. Tosi and W. C. Hamner, pp. 381–391. Cincinnati, OH: Grid, 1985.

Poole E. D., and Regoli, R. M. "Role Stress, Custody Orientation and Disciplinary Actions: A Study of Prison Guards." *Criminology,* 1980, *18,* 215–226.

Porter, L. W. *Organizations as Political Animals.* Presidential address to the Division of Industrial Organizational Psychology, 84th annual meeting of the American Psychological Association, Washington, DC, 1976.

Porter, L. W., Allen, R. W., and Angle, H. L. "The Politics of Upward Influence in Organizations." *Organizational Behavior,* 1981, *3,* 109–149.

Porter, L. W., Lawler, E. E.,III, and Hackman, J. H. *Behavior in Organizations.* New York: McGraw-Hill, 1975.

Postman, Neil. *Technopoly: The Surrender of Culture to Technology.* New York: Knopf, 1992.

Powers, R. *Secrecy and Power: The Life of J. Edgar Hoover.* New York: Free Press, 1987.

President's Commission on Law Enforcement and Criminal Justice. *The Challenge of Crime in a Free Society.* Washington, DC: U.S. Government Printing Office, 1967.

President's Commission on Law Enforcement and the Administration of Justice. *Task Force Reports: Summary and Conclusions.* Washington, DC: U.S. Government Printing Office, 1967a.

President's Commission on Law Enforcement and the Administration of Justice. *Task Force Report: Corrections.* Washington, DC: U.S. Government Printing Office, 1967b.

Price, B. "A Study of Leadership Strength of Female Police Executives." *Journal of Police Science and Administration,* 1974, *2,* 219–226.

Pritchard, R., and Karasick, B. "The Effects of Organizational Climate on Managerial Job Performance." *Organizational Behavior and Human Performance,* 1973, *9,* 128–147.

Quade, E. "Systems Analysis Techniques for Public Policy Problems." In *Perspectives on Public Bureaucracy,* edited by F. Kramer, pp. 151–174. Cambridge, MA: Winthrop, 1977.

Quinney, R. *Critique of the Legal Order.* Boston: Little, Brown, 1974.

Radelet, L. *The Police and the Community,* 4th ed. New York: Macmillan, 1986.

Rainey, H. "Public Agencies and Private Firms: Incentive Structures, Goals, and Individual Roles." *Administration and Society,* 1983, *15,* 207–242.

Rainey, H. *Understanding and Managing Public Organizations.* San Francisco: Jossey-Bass, 1997.

Rainey, H. G. *Understanding and Managing Public Organizations.* 2nd Edition. San Francisco, CA: Jossey-Bass Publishers, 1997.

Reddin, T. "Are You Oriented to Hold Them?" *Police Chief,* 1966, 33, 12–20.

Reid, S. *Crime and Criminology.* New York: Holt, Rinehart & Winston, 1982.

Reiss, A. J. "Career Orientations, Job Satisfaction and the Assessment of Law Enforcement Problems by Police Officers." In *Studies in Crime and Law Enforcement, by the President's Commission on Law Enforcement and the Administration of Justice.* Washington, DC: U.S. Government Printing Office, 1967.

Reiss, A. J. *The Police and the Public.* New Haven, CT: Yale University Press, 1971.

Remington, F., Newman, D., Kimball, E., Melli, M., and Goldstein, H. *Criminal Justice Administration*. Indianapolis, IN: Bobbs-Merrill, 1969.

Reuss-Ianni, E. *Two Cultures of Policing: Street Cops and Management Cops*. New Brunswick, NJ: Transaction Books, 1984.

Reuter, P. "Prevalence Estimation and Policy Formulation." *The Journal of Drug Issues*, 1993, *23*, 167–184.

Ricker, L. "Anatomy of Jail Automation—Case Study: Marion County Department of Corrections." *American Jails*, 1996, *9*(6): 9–19.

Rideau, W., and Sinclair, B. *Inside Angola*. New Orleans: Louisiana Department of Corrections, 1982.

Roberg, R. R. *Police Management and Organizational Behavior: A Contingency Approach*. St. Paul, MN: West, 1979.

Robin, G. D. "Judicial Resistance to Sentencing Allowability." *Crime and Delinquency*, 1975, *21*, 201–212.

Roethlisberger, F. J., and Dickson, W. J. *Management and the Worker*. Cambridge, MA: Harvard University Press, 1939.

Rokeach, M., Miller, G., and Snyder, J. A. "The Value Gap Between the Police and the Policed." *Journal of Social Issues*, 1971, *27*, 155–171.

Rosch, J. "Crime as an Issue in American Politics." In *The Politics of Crime and Justice*, edited by E. Fairchild and V. Webb, pp. 19–34. Beverly Hills, CA: Sage, 1985.

Rosecrance, J. "The Probation Officer's Search for Credibility: Ball Park Recommendations." *Crime and Delinquency*, 1985, *31*, 539–554.

Rosecrance, J. "Probation Supervision: Mission Impossible." *Federal Probation*, 1986, *60*(1), 25–31.

Rosecrance, J. "Getting Rid of the Prima Donnas: The Bureaucratization of a Probation Department." In *The Administration and Management of Criminal Justice Organizations: A Book of Readings*, 3rd ed., edited by S. Stojkovic, J. Klofas, and D. Kalinich. Prospect Heights, IL: Waveland, 1999a, 175–187.

Rosecrance, J. "Maintaining the Myth of Individualized Justice: Probation Presentence Reports." In *The Administration and Management of Criminal Justice Organizations: A Book of Readings*, 2nd ed., edited by S. Stojkovic, J. Klofas, and D. Kalinich. Prospect Heights, IL: Waveland, 1999b, 355–374.

Roszell, S. *Other Prisoners*. Chicago: John Howard Association, 1986.

Rothman, D. J. *Conscience and Convenience*. Boston: Little, Brown, 1980.

Rothman, D. J., and Rothman, S. M. *The Willowbrook Wars*. New York: Harper & Row, 1984.

Rottman, D. B., and Kimberly, J. R. "The Social Context of Jails." *Sociology and Social Research*, 1975, *59*, 344–361.

Rourke, F. *Bureaucracy, Politics, and Public Policy*, 2nd ed. Boston: Little, Brown, 1976.

Rourke, F. *Bureaucratic Power in National Politics*, 4th ed. Boston: Little, Brown, 1986.

Ruble, T., and Thomas, T. K. "Support for a Two-Dimensional Model of Conflict Behavior." *Organizational Behavior and Human Performance*, 16, 145. New York: Academic Press, 1976.

Ruiz v. Estelle, 503 F. Supp. 1265 (1980).

Ryan, E. *A Multidimensional Analysis of Conflict in the Criminal Justice System.* Jonesboro, TN: Pilgrimage, 1981.

Saari, D. J. *American Court Management: Theories and Practices.* Westport, CT: Quorum Books, 1982.

Salancik, G. R., and Pfeffer, J. "Who Gets Power—and How They Hold on to It: A Strategic Contingency Model of Power." *Organizational Dynamics* (American Management Association), Winter 1977, 5, 3–21.

Sarrata, B., and Jeppensen, J. C. "Job Design and Staff Satisfaction in Human Service Settings." *Journal of Community Psychology,* 1977, 5, 229–236.

Schafer, N. "Jails and Judicial Review: Special Problems for Local Facilities." In *Sneaking Inmates Down the Alley: Problems and Prospects in Jail Management,* edited by D. Kalinich and J. Klofas, pp. 127–146. Springfield, IL: Charles C. Thomas, 1986.

Schattschnieder, E. *Two Million Americans in Search of Government.* New York: Holt, Rinehart & Winston, 1969.

Schay, B. "Effects of Performance-Contingent Pay on Employee Attitudes." *Public Personnel Management,* 1988, 17, 237–250.

Schein, E. H. *The Psychological Contract: Organizational Psychology,* 2nd ed. Englewood Cliffs, NJ: Prentice-Hall, 1970.

Schein, E. H. "The Individual, the Organization and the Career: A Conceptual Scheme." *Journal of Applied Behavioral Science.* 1971, 7, 401–426.

Schein, E. H. *Organizational Culture and Leadership,* 2nd ed. San Francisco: Jossey-Bass, 1997.

Schlesinger, A. M., Jr. "Roosevelt as Chief Administrator." In *The Coming of the New Deal.* Boston: Houghton Mifflin, 1958.

Schmalleger, F. *Criminal Justice Today: An Introductory Text for the 21st Century.* 5th Edition. Upper Saddle River, NJ: Prentice-Hall Publishers, 1997.

Schmidt, A. K. "Electronic Monitoring of Offenders Increases." *National Institute of Justice Reports,* 1989, 2(12), 2–5.

Schulhofer, S. "No Job Too Small: Justice Without Bargaining in the Lower Criminal Courts." *American Bar Foundation Research Journal,* 1985, Summer, 519–598.

Scott, E. *Police Referral in Metropolitan Areas: A Summary Report.* Washington, DC: U.S. National Institute of Justice, 1981.

Scott, R. *Organizations: Rational, Natural, and Open Systems.* Englewood Cliffs, NJ: Prentice-Hall, 1987.

Scott, W. R. "Effectiveness of Organizational Effectiveness Studies." In *New Perspectives on Organizational Effectiveness,* edited by P. S. Goodman and J. M. Pennings, pp. 63–95. San Francisco: Jossey-Bass, 1977.

SEARCH Group, Inc. "State Law and the Confidentiality of Juvenile Records." *Security and Privacy,* 1982, 5(2), 1–12.

Selke, W., and Bartoszek, M. "Police and Media Relations: The Seed of Conflict." *Criminal Justice Review,* 1984, 9(2), 25–30.

Sellin, T. "Historical Glimpses of Training for Prison Service." *Journal of the American Institute of Criminal Law and Criminology,* 1934, 3–27.

Selltiz, C. "The Use of Survey Methods in a Citizens' Campaign Against Discrimination." *Human Organization*, 1955, *14*, 19–25.

Selznick, P. *TVA and the Grass Roots*. Berkeley, CA: University of California Press, 1949.

Selznick, P. *Leadership in Administration*. New York: Harper & Row, 1957.

Shanahan, D. *Patrol Administration: Management by Objectives*, 2nd ed. Boston: Allyn and Bacon, 1985.

Sharkansky, I. *Public Administration: Policy Making in Governmental Agencies*. Chicago: Markham, 1972.

Sharp, E. B. "Street-Level Discretion in Policing: Attitudes and Behaviors in the Deprofessionalization Syndrome." *Law and Policy Quarterly*, 1982, *4*, 167–189.

Sheppard, H. L., and Herrick, N. Q. *Where Have All the Robots Gone?* New York: Free Press, 1972.

Sherman, L. *Policing Domestic Violence*. New York: Free Press, 1992.

Sherman, L., and Cohn, E. G. "The Impact of Research on Legal Policy: The Minneapolis Domestic Violence Experiment." *Law and Society Review*, 1989, *23*, 117–144.

Sherman, L. W. "Becoming Bent: Moral Career Concepts of Corrupt Policemen." In *Police Corruption: A Sociological Perspective*, edited by L. Sherman, pp. 191–208. New York: Doubleday, 1974.

Sherman, L. W. "Middle Management and Police Democratization: A Reply to John E. Angell." *Criminology*, 1975, *12*(4), 363–377.

Sherman, L. W., and Berk, R. "The Specific Deterrent Effects of Arrest in Domestic Assault." *American Sociological Review*, 1984, *49*, 261–272.

Sherman, L. W., Milton, C. H., and Kelly, T. V. *Team Policing: Seven Case Studies*. Washington, DC: Police Foundation, 1973.

Sherman, M., and Hawkins, G. *Imprisonment in America: Closing the Future*. Chicago: University of Chicago Press, 1981.

Shichor, D. "Crime Patterns and Socioeconomic Development: A Cross-National Analysis." *Criminal Justice Review*, 1990, *15*(1): 64–78.

Sieber, S. *Fatal Remedies: The Ironies of Social Intervention*. New York: Plenum Press, 1981.

Siedman, H. *Politics, Position and Power*. New York: Oxford University Press, 1970.

Simon, H. "On the Concept of Organizational Goals." *Administrative Science Quarterly*, 1964, *9*, 1–22.

Simpson, R. L., and Simpson, I. H. "The Psychiatric Attendant: Development of an Occupational Self-Image in a Low Status Occupation." *American Sociological Review*, 1959, *24*, 389–392.

Skogan, W. "Measuring What Matters, Part One: Measures of Crime, Fear, and Disorder." Washington, DC: U.S. Department of Justice, 1996.

Skolnick, J. H. *Justice Without Trial: Law Enforcement in a Democratic Society*. New York: Wiley, 1966.

Skolnick, J. H., and Bayley, D. H. *The New Blue Line: Police Innovation in Six American Cities*. New York: Free Press, 1986.

Skolnick, J. H., and Fyfe, J. *Above the Law: Police and Excessive Use of Force*. New York: Free Press, 1993.

Skolnick, J. H., and McCoy, C. "Police Accountability and the Media." *American Bar Foundation Research Journal,* 1984, *3,* 521–557.

Smykla, J. D. *Community Based Corrections: Principles and Practices.* New York: Macmillan, 1981.

Snyder, R., and Morris, J. "Organizational Communications and Performance." *Journal of Applied Psychology,* 1984, *69*(3), 461–465.

Sparrow, M. K. *Implementing Community Policing.* Washington, DC: National Institute of Justice, 1988.

Sparrow, M. K. "Perspectives on Policing." Monograph no. 9, National Institute of Justice and the Program in Criminal Justice Policy and Management, John F. Kennedy School of Government, Harvard University, November, 1994.

Sparrow, M. K. "Implementing Community Policing," in Stojkovic, S., Kalinich, D., and Klofas, J. (eds.). *The Administration and Management of Criminal Justice Organizations: A Book of Readings.* 3rd Edition. Prospect Heights, IL: Waveland Press, Inc., 1999.

Special Task Force to the Secretary of Health, Education, and Welfare. *Work in America.* Cambridge, MA: M.I.T. Press, 1973.

Spiro, H. "Comparative Politics: A Comprehensive Approach." *American Political Science Review,* 1958, *56*(3), 577–595.

Srivastva, V. (Ed.). *Executive Power: How Executives Influence People and Organizations.* San Francisco: Jossey-Bass, 1986.

Stastny, C., and Tyrnauer, G. *Who Rules the Joint: The Changing Political Culture of Maximum-Security Prisons in America.* Lexington, MA: Heath, 1982.

Staw, B. M., and Ross, J. "Commitment to a Policy Decision: A Multi-Theoretical Perspective." *Administrative Science Quarterly,* 1978, *23,* 40–64.

Steadman, H., Monahan, J., Duffee, B., Hartstone, E., and Robbins, P. "The Impact of the State Mental Hospital Deinstitutionalization on United States Prison Populations, 1968–1978." *The Journal of Criminal Law and Criminology,* 1984, *75,* 474–490.

Steers, R. M. *Organizational Effectiveness: A Behavioral View.* Santa Monica, CA: Goodyear, 1977.

Stoddard, E. R. "Blue Coat Crime." In *Thinking About Police: Contemporary Readings,* edited by C. B. Klockars. New York: McGraw-Hill, 1983.

Stohr, M., Lovrich, N., Menke, B., and Zupan, L. "Staff Management in Correctional Institutions: Comparing DiIulio's 'Control Model' and 'Employee Investment Model' Outcomes in Five Jails." *Justice Quarterly,* 1994, *11,* 3, 471–498.

Stojkovic, S. "Social Bases of Power and Control Mechanisms Among Prisoners in a Prison Organization." *Justice Quarterly,* 1984, *1*(4), 511–528.

Stojkovic, S. "Social Bases of Power and Control Mechanisms Among Correctional Administrators in a Prison Organization." *Journal of Criminal Justice,* 1986, *14,* 157–166.

Stojkovic, S. "An Examination of Compliance Structures in a Prison Organization: A Study of the Types of Correctional Officer Power." Unpublished manuscript, University of Wisconsin, Milwaukee, 1987.

Stojkovic, S. "Accounts of Prison Work: Corrections Officers' Portrayals of Their Work World." In *Perspectives on Social Problems,* edited by G. Miller and J. Holstein. Greenwich, CT: Jai Press, 1990.

Stojkovic, S. Conversation with police chiefs at training workshop on future crime trends, Wisconsin Rapids, WI, October 1995.

Stojkovic, S. Comments presented at the California Department of Corrections Leadership Institute, Chico, CA, January 1997.

Stojkovic, S. and Farkas, M. A. *Correctional Leadership: A Cultural Perspective.* Belmont, CA: Wadsworth Publishing Company, 2003.

Stojkovic, S., Kalinich, D., and Klofas, J. *The Administration and Management of Criminal Justice Organizations: A Book of Readings,* 3rd ed. Prospect Heights, IL: Waveland, 1999.

Stojkovic, S., and Lovell, R. *Corrections: An Introduction,* 2nd ed., Cincinnati, OH: Anderson, 1997.

Stoller, H. E. "Need for Achievement in Work Output Among Policemen." Unpublished doctoral dissertation, Illinois Institute of Technology, 1977.

Stolz, B. "Congress and Criminal Justice Policy Making: The Impact of Interest Groups and Symbolic Politics." *Journal of Criminal Justice,* 1985, *13,* 307–320.

Stolz, B. A. "Congress, Symbolic Politics and the Evolution of the 1994 'Violence Against Women Act'." *Criminal Justice Policy Review,* Vol. 10, No. 3, pp. 401–428, 1999.

Stone, C., and Stoker, R. *Deprofessionalization and Dissatisfaction in Urban Service* Agencies. Paper presented at the 37th annual meeting of the Midwest Political Science Association, Chicago, 1979.

Studt, E. *Surveillance and Service in Parole.* Washington, DC: U.S. Department of Justice, 1978.

Styskal, R. A. "Power and Commitment in Organizations: A Test of the Participation Thesis." *Social Forces,* 1980, *57*(4), 925–943.

Sudnow, D. "Normal Crimes: Sociological Features of the Penal Code in a Public Defender Office." *Social Problems,* 1965, *12,* 255–276.

Sutherland, E., and Cressey, R. *Criminology.* Philadelphia: Lippincott, 1978.

Swank, G. E., and Winer, D. "Occurrence of Psychiatric Disorders in County Jail Populations." *American Journal of Psychiatry,* 1976, *133*(11), 1331–1337.

Swanson, C. R., and Territo, L. "Police Leadership and Interpersonal Communication Styles." In *Managing Police Work: Issues and Analysis,* edited by J. R. Greene, pp. 123–139. Beverly Hills, CA: Sage. 1982.

Swanson, C. R., Territo, L., and Taylor, R. W. *Police Administration: Structures, Processes, and Behavior.* 4th ed. New York: Macmillan, 1997.

Sykes, G. *The Society of Captives.* Princeton, NJ: Princeton University Press, 1958.

Sykes, G., and Messinger, S. L. "The Inmate Social System." In *Theoretical Studies in Social Organization of the Prison,* edited by R. A. Cloward, D. R. Cressey, G. H. Grosser, R. McCleary, L. E. Ohlin, G. Sykes, and S. Messinger. New York: Social Science Research Council, 1960, 1–34.

Tannenbaum, A. S. "Control in Organizations: Individual Adjustment and Organizational Performance. " *Administrative Science Quarterly,* 1962, *7*(2), 236–257.

Taylor, F. W. *Two Papers on Scientific Management.* London: Routledge & Kegan Paul, 1919.

Taylor, F. W. *Scientific Management.* New York: Harper & Row, 1947.

Terkel, S. *Working.* New York: Random House, 1974.

Territo, L., Swanson, J. R., and Chamelin, N. "The Police Selection Process." In *Policing Society,* edited by W. C. Terry, pp. 187–196. New York: John Wiley, 1985.

Terry, W. C. "Police Stress as an Administrative Problem: Some Conceptual and Theoretical Difficulties." *Journal of Police Science and Administration,* 1983, *11,* 156–164.

Terry, W. C. *Policing Society.* New York: Wiley, 1985.

Thomas, K. W. "Organizational Conflict." In *Organizational Behavior and Management,* 4th ed., edited by H. L. Tosi and W. C. Hamner, pp. 392–416. Cincinnati, OH: Grid, 1985.

Thompson, J. *Organizations in Action.* New York: McGraw-Hill, 1967.

Thompson, J., Svirdoff, M., and McElroy, J. *Unemployment and Crime: A Review of Theories and Research.* Washington, DC: U.S. Department of Justice, 1981.

Thorston, S. "Cultural Conflict and Crime," *Social Science Research Council,* 1938, 63–70.

Tifft, L. L. "Control Systems, Social Bases of Power and Power Exercise in Police Organizations." In *Policing: A View from the Street,* edited by P. K. Manning and J. Van Maanen, pp. 90–104. Santa Monica, CA: Goodyear, 1978.

Toch, H. "Is a 'Correction Officer' Always a 'Screw'?" *Criminal Justice Review,* 1978, *3,* 19–35.

Toch, H., and Grant, J. D. *Reforming Human Services: Change Through Participation.* Beverly Hills, CA: Sage, 1982.

Toch, H., Grant, J. D., and Galvin, R. *Agents of Change: A Study of Police Reform.* Cambridge, MA: Schenkman, 1975.

Toch, H., and Klofas, J. "Alienation and Desire for Job Enrichment Among Correction Officers." *Federal Probation,* 1982, *46,* 322–327.

Tonry, M. "The Failure of the U.S. Sentencing Commission's Guidelines." In *The Administration and Management of Criminal Justice Organizations: A Book of Readings,* 3rd ed., edited by S. Stojkovic, J. Klofas, and D. Kalinich. Prospect Heights, IL: Waveland, 1999, 307–323.

Tosi, H. L., Rizzo, J. R., and Carroll, S. J. *Managing Organizational Behavior.* Marshfield, MA: Pitman, 1986.

Travis, L., Latessa, E., and Vito, G. "Agenda Building in Criminal Justice: The Case of Determinant Sentencing." *American Journal of Criminal Justice,* 1985, *10*(1), 1–21.

Trenholm, S., and Jensen, A. *Interpersonal Communication,* 2nd ed. Belmont, CA: Wadsworth, 1992.

Trojanowicz, R. *An Evaluation of the Neighborhood Foot Patrol Program in Flint, Michigan.* East Lansing, MI: National Neighborhood Foot Patrol Center, 1983.

Trojanowicz, R., and Banas, D. *Perceptions of Safety: A Comparison of Foot Patrol Versus Motor Patrol Officers.* East Lansing, MI: National Neighborhood Foot Patrol Center, 1985.

Trojanowicz, R., and Bucqueroux, B. *Community Policing: A Contemporary Perspective.* Cincinnati, OH: Anderson, 1990.

Trojanowicz, R., and Carter, D. *The Philosophy and Role of Community Policing.* East Lansing, MI: National Neighborhood Foot Patrol Center, 1988.

Trojanowicz, R., Steele, M., and Trojanowicz, S. *Community Policing: A Taxpayer's Perspective.* East Lansing, MI: National Neighborhood Foot Patrol Center, 1986.

Tullar, W. L., and Glauser, M. J. "Communicator Style of Police Officer and Citizen Satisfaction with Officer/Citizen Telephone Conversations." *Journal of Police Science and Administration,* 1985, *13*(1), 70–72.

Tully, H., Winter, J., Wilson, T., and Scanlon, T. "Correctional Institution Impact and Host Community Resistance." *Canadian Journal of Criminology,* 1982, *24*(2), 133–139.

Tylor, E. *Primitive Culture: Research into the Development of Mythology, Philosophy, Religion, Arts, and Customs,* vol. 1. London: John Murray, 1958.

United States Department of Justice. "Enforcing the ADA: Looking Back on a Decade of Progress. A Special Tenth Anniversary Status Report from the Department of Justice." Washington, DC: U.S. Department of Justice, July 2000.

U.S. Bureau of Justice Statistics. *Prisoners in 1987.* Washington, DC: U.S. Department of Justice, 1988.

U.S. Bureau of Justice Statistics, *Prisoners in 1994.* Washington DC: U.S. Department of Justice, 1995.

Useem, B. and Kimball, P. *States of Siege: U.S. Prison Riots 1971–1986.* New York: Oxford University Press, 1989.

Van Buren, W. "Computer-Based Training." *American Jails,* 1996, *9*(6): 20–23.

Van Maanen, J. "Observations on the Making of a Policeman." *Human Organization,* 1973, *4,* 407–418.

Van Maanen, J. "Police Socialization: A Longitudinal Examination of Job Attitudes in an Urban Police Department." *Administrative Science Quarterly,* 1975, *20,* 266–278.

Van Maanen, J. "People Processing: Strategies of Organizational Socialization." In *Managing Organizations,* edited by D. A. Nadler, M. L. Tushman, and N. G. Hatvany, pp. 144–157. Boston: Little, Brown, 1982.

Van Maanen, J. "Learning the Ropes." In *Policing Society,* edited by W. C. Terry. New York: Wiley, 1985, 68–88.

Van Zelst, R. "Sociometrically Selected Work Teams Increase Production." *Personal Psychology,* 1952, *5,* 175–185.

Vanagunas, S., "Planning for the Delivery of Urban Police Services." In *Managing Police Work: Issues and Analysis,* edited by J. Greene, pp. 203–216. Beverly Hills, CA: Sage, 1982.

Vetter, H., and Territo, L. *Crime and Justice in America: A Human Perspective.* St. Paul, MN: West, 1984.

Waegel, W. B. "Case Routinization in Investigative Police Work." *Social Problems,* 1981, *28,* 263–275.

Wahler, C., and Gendreau, P. "Assessing Correctional Officers." *Federal Probation,* 1985, *49,* 70–74.

Waldron, R. J. *The Criminal Justice System.* Boston: Houghton Mifflin, 1984.

Walker, S. *Sense and Nonsense About Crime: A Policy Guide.* Pacific Grove, CA: Brooks/Cole, 1985.

Walker, S. *Sense and Nonsense About Crime and Drugs,* 3rd ed. Belmont, CA: Wadsworth, 1994.

Walmsley, G., and Zald, M. *The Political Economy of Public Organizations.* Lexington, MA: Heath, 1973.

Walsh, W. F. "Patrol Officer Arrest Rates: A Study of the Social Organization of Police Work." *Justice Quarterly,* 1986, *3,* 271–290.

Waltman, J. "Nonverbal Communications in Interrogation: Some Applications." *Journal of Police Science and Administration,* 1983, *11*(2), 166–169.

Walton, M. *The Deming Management Method.* New York: Perigee, 1986.

Warren, D. I. "Power, Visibility, and Conformity in Formal Organizations." *American Sociological Review,* 1968, *33*(6), 951–970.

Warren, E. "The Economic Approach to Crime." In *Criminal Justice Studies,* edited by G. Misner, pp. 172–180. St. Louis: C. V. Mosby, 1981.

Warren, R. *Social Change and Human Purpose: Toward Understanding and Action.* Chicago: Rand McNally, 1977.

Weber, M. *The Theory of Social and Economic Organization.* New York: Free Press, 1947.

Weick, K. *The Social Psychology of Organizing,* 2nd ed. Reading, MA: Addison-Wesley, 1979.

Weimann, G. "Sex Differences in Dealing with Bureaucracy." *Sex Roles,* 1985, *12,* 777–790.

Weiner, J., and Johnson, R. "Organization and Environment: The Case of Correctional Personnel Training Programs." *Journal of Criminal Justice,* 1981, *9,* 441–450.

Weiss, C. "The Circuitry of Enlightenment: Diffusion of Social Science Research to Policy Makers." *Knowledge: Creation, Diffusion Utilitization,* 1987, *8,* 274–281.

Weiss, C. H. "Evaluation Research in the Political Context." In *Handbook of Evaluation Research,* edited by E. L. Struening and M. Guttentag, pp. 13–26. Beverly Hills, CA: Sage, 1972.

Welch, M. *Corrections: A Radical Approach.* Upper Saddle River, NJ: Prentice-Hall Publishers, 1996.

Westley, W. *Violence and the Police: A Sociological Study of Law, Custom and Morality.* Cambridge, MA: M.I.T. Press, 1970.

Whisenand, P., and Ferguson, F. *The Managing of Police Organizations,* 4th ed. Englewood Cliffs, NJ: Prentice-Hall, 1996.

Whitehead, J. T. "Job Burnout in Probation and Parole: Its Extent and Intervention Implications." *Criminal Justice and Behavior,* 1985, *12,* 91–110.

Whitehead, J. T., and Lindquist, C. A. "Correctional Officer Job Burnout: A Path Model." *Journal of Research in Crime and Delinquency,* 1986, *23,* 23–42.

Wildavsky, A. *The Politics of the Budgetary Process.* Boston: Little, Brown, 1974.

Wilensky, H. *Organizational Intelligence.* New York: Basic Books, 1967.

Wilkins, L. T. "Information Overload: Peace or War with the Computer." In *Parole: Legal Issues/Decision-Making/Research,* edited by W. E. Amos and C. L. Newman, pp. 141–157. New York: Federal Legal Publications, 1975a.

Wilkins, L. T. "A Typology of Decision-Makers?" In *Parole: Legal Issues/DecisionMaking/Research,* edited by W. E. Amos and C. L. Newman, pp. 159-168. New York: Federal Legal Publications, 1975b.

Wilkins, L. T. "Treatment of Offenders at Patuxent." *Rutgers Law Review,* 1976, *29,* 45–60.

Willett, T. C. "The 'Fish Screw' in the Canadian Penitentiary Service." *Queen's Law Journal,* 1977, *3,* 424–449.

Williamson, O. E. "The Economics of Organizations: The Transactions-Cost Approach." *American Journal of Sociology,* 1981, *87,* 548–577.

Wilson, J. Q. *Bureaucracy: What Government Agencies Do and Why They Do It.* Glenview, IL: Basic Books, 1989.

Wilson, J. Q. *Varieties of Police Behavior.* Cambridge, MA: Harvard University Press, 1968.

Witham, D. C. "Management Control Through Motivation." *FBI Law Enforcement Bulletin,* 1980, *49*(2), 6–11.

Wolff v. *McDonnell.* 94 S. Ct. 2963 (1974).

Wood, F. Comments made in "Prison Management Trends, 1975–2025," by Riverland C. in Tonry, M. and Petersilia, J. (eds.). *Prisons*. Chicago: University of Chicago Press, 1999.

Wright, K. "The Desirability of Goal Conflict Within the Criminal Justice System." *Journal of Criminal Justice*, 1981, *9*, 209–218.

Wright, K. *Effective Prison Leadership*. Binghamton, NY: William Neil, 1994.

Wycoff, M. A. "Evaluating the Crime-Effectiveness of Municipal Police." In *Managing Police Work: Issues and Analysis*, edited by J. Greene, pp. 15–36. Beverly Hills, CA: Sage, 1982.

Yeager, M. "Unemployment and Imprisonment." *Journal of Criminal Law and Criminology*, 1979, *75*, 586–593.

Yuchtman, E., and Seashore, S. "A System-Resource Approach to Organizational Effectiveness." *American Sociological Review*, 1967, *32*, 891–903.

Yukl, G. *Leadership in Organizations*. 7th Edition. Englewood Cliffs, NJ: Prentice-Hall Publishers, 2002.

Yukl, G. A. *Leadership in Organizations*. Englewood Cliffs, NJ: Prentice-Hall, 1981.

Zaltman, G., Duncan, R., and Holbeck, J. *Innovations and Organizations*. New York: Wiley, 1973.

Zander, A. "Resistance to Change: Its Analysis and Prevention." *Advanced Management*, 1950, *15–16*, 9–11.

Zedlewski, E. W. "Making Confinement Decisions." Washington, DC: *National Institute of Justice*, 1987.

Zimring, F., and Hawkins, G. *Incapacitation: Penal Confinement and the Restraint of Crime*. New York: Oxford University Press, 1995.

Zupan, L. *Jails: Reform and the New Generation Philosophy*. Cincinnati, OH: Anderson, 1991.